ESSAYS IN HONOR OF JERRY HAUSMAN

ADVANCES IN ECONOMETRICS

Series Editors: Juan Carlos Escanciano,
Thomas B. Fomby, R. Carter Hill,
Eric Hillebrand, and Ivan Jeliazkov

Recent Volumes:

Volume 20B: Econometric Analysis of Financial and Economic Time Series – Edited by Dek Terrell and Thomas B. Fomby

Volume 21: Modelling and Evaluating Treatment Effects in Econometrics – Edited by Daniel L. Millimet, Jeffrey A. Smith and Edward Vytlacil

Volume 22: Econometrics and Risk Management – Edited by Jean-Pierre Fouque, Thomas B. Fomby and Knut Solna

Volume 23: Bayesian Econometrics – Edited by Siddhartha Chib, Gary Koop, Bill Griffiths and Dek Terrell

Volume 24: Measurement Error: Consequences, Applications and Solutions – Edited by Jane Binner, David Edgerton and Thomas Elger

Volume 25: Nonparametric Econometric Methods – Edited by Qi Li and Jeffrey S. Racine

Volume 26: Maximum Simulated Likelihood Methods and Applications – Edited by William Greene and R. Carter Hill

Volume 27A: Missing Data Methods: Cross-Sectional Methods and Applications – Edited by David M. Drukker

Volume 27B: Missing Data Methods: Time-Series Methods and Applications – Edited by David M. Drukker

Volume 28: DSGE Models in Macroeconomics: Estimation, Evaluation, and New Developments – Edited by Nathan Balke, Fabio Canova, Fabio Milani and Mark A. Wynne

ADVANCES IN ECONOMETRICS VOLUME 29

ESSAYS IN HONOR OF JERRY HAUSMAN

EDITED BY

BADI H. BALTAGI

Syracuse University, Syracuse, NY

R. CARTER HILL

Louisiana State University, Baton Rouge, LA

WHITNEY K. NEWEY

Massachusetts Institute of Technology (MIT), Cambridge, MA

HALBERT L. WHITE

University of California, San Diego, CA

MAPLE GROVE / MAY 2013

Emerald

United Kingdom – North America – Japan
India – Malaysia – China

Emerald Group Publishing Limited
Howard House, Wagon Lane, Bingley BD16 1WA, UK

First edition 2012

British Library Cataloguing in Publication Data
A catalogue record for this book is available from the British Library

ISBN: 978-1-78190-307-0
ISSN: 0731-9053 (Series)

CONTENTS

PART III: SPECIFICATION TESTING

LIST OF CONTRIBUTORS

Lee C. Adkins	Department of Economics, Oklahoma State University, Stillwater, OK, USA
Shahram Amini	Department of Finance, Virginia Polytechnic Institute and State University, Blacksburg, VA, USA
Badi H. Baltagi	Department of Economics and Center for Policy Research, Syracuse University, Syracuse, NY, USA
Anil K. Bera	Department of Economics, University of Illinois at Urbana-Champaign, Urbana-Champaign, IL, USA
Hild Marte Bjørnsen	Norwegian Agricultural Economics Institute, Oslo, Norway
Francesco Bravo	Department of Economics, University of York, York, UK
Georges Bresson	ERMES (CNRS), Université Paris II/SORBONNE Universités, Paris, Cedex, France
Cristina M. Caminita	LSU Libraries, Louisiana State University, Baton Rouge, LA, USA
Randall C. Campbell	Department of Finance and Economics, Mississippi State University, Mississippi State, MS, USA
John C. Chao	Department of Economics, University of Maryland, College Park, MD, USA
Angela Cheptea	INRA-UMR SMART (Agrocampus-Ouest), Rennes, France

Viera Chmelarova	Department of Economics and International Business, Sam Houston State University, Huntsville, TX, USA
Catherine Dehon	Université libre de Bruxelles, ECARES and iCite, SBS-EM, Brussels, Belgium
Michael S. Delgado	Department of Agricultural Economics, Purdue University, West Lafayette, IN, USA
Peter H. Egger	Swiss Federal Institute of Technology Zürich, Zürich, Switzerland
Juan Carlos Escanciano	Department of Economics, Indiana University, Bloomington, IN, USA
Thomas B. Fomby	Department of Economics, Southern Methodist University, Dallas, TX, USA
Marco Gallegati	Department of Economics and Social Sciences, Faculty of Economics "G. Fuà", Polytechnic University of Marche, Ancona, Italy
Marjorie Gassner	Universite libre de Bruxelles, ECARES and iCite, SBS-EM, Brussels, Belgium
Nicky Grant	Faculty of Economics, University of Cambridge, UK
Matthew Harding	Department of Economics, Stanford University, Stanford, CA, USA
Jerry A. Hausman	Department of Economics, MIT, Cambridge, MA, USA
Daniel J. Henderson	Department of Economics, Finance and Legal Studies, University of Alabama, Tuscaloosa, AL, USA
R. Carter Hill	Department of Economics, Louisiana State University, Baton Rouge, LA, USA

Eric Hillebrand	Center for Research in Econometric Analysis of Time Series (CREATES), Department of Economics and Business, Aarhus University, Aarhus C, Denmark
Ivan Jeliazkov	Department of Economics, University of California, Irvine, CA, USA
George G. Judge	The Graduate School and Giannini Foundation, University of California, Berkeley, CA, USA
Yu-Hsien Kao	Department of Economics, University of Illinois at Urbana-Champaign, Urbana-Champaign, IL, USA
Michaela Kesina	Swiss Federal Institute of Technology Zürich, Zürich, Switzerland
Carlos Lamarche	Department of Economics, University of Kentucky, Lexington, KY, USA
Iuliana Matei	University of Paris 1 Pantheon-Sorbonne and CNRS, CES University of Paris 1, BD De L'Hopital, Paris, Cedex, France
Ashok K. Mishra	Department of Agricultural Economics and Agribusiness, Louisiana State University, Baton Rouge, LA, USA
Ron C. Mittelhammer	Economic Sciences and Statistics, School of Economic Sciences, Washington State University, Pullman, WA, USA
Michael D. S. Morris	Spears School of Business, Oklahoma State University, Tulsa, OK, USA
Whitney K. Newey	Department of Economics, MIT, Cambridge, MA, USA
Taisuke Otsu	Cowles Foundation and Department of Economics, Yale University, New Haven, CT, USA
Christopher F. Parmeter	Department of Economics, University of Miami, Miami, FL, USA

James B. Ramsey	Department of Economics, New York University, New York, NY, USA
Monalisa Sen	Department of Economics, University of Illinois at Urbana-Champaign, Urbana-Champaign, IL, USA
Liangjun Su	School of Economics, Singapore Management University, Singapore
Norman R. Swanson	Department of Economics, Rutgers University, New Brunswick, NJ, USA
Vincenzo Verardi	University of Namur (CRED) and Université libre de Bruxelles, ECARES and iCite, Brussels, Belgium
Halbert L. White	Department of Economics, University of California, San Diego, CA, USA
Tiemen Woutersen	Department of Economics, Eller College of Management, University of Arizona, Tuscon, AZ, USA
Hector O. Zapata	Department of Agricultural Economics and Agribusiness, Louisiana State University, LSU AgCenter, Baton Rouge, LA, USA

THE GENESIS OF THE HAUSMAN SPECIFICATION TEST

Jerry A. Hausman, MIT
September 3, 2012

I would like to thank Carter Hill and other people at LSU who helped organize a very enjoyable conference on the Hausman Specification Test in February 2012. Many of the chapters in this volume were given at the conference. I was pleased to be around many friends at the conference, and I found the chapters very interesting. I especially appreciate the chapter by Professor Hector Zapata and Ms. Cristina Camanita, which considered the diffusion of my econometrics ideas. In particular, I did not know that these techniques were widely used in other disciplines. I found their approach very innovative and very interesting.

I am often asked by students where the idea of the Hausman Specification Test came from. I remember being asked by an MIT colleague one afternoon the following question: I did ordinary least squares and generalized least squares and the parameter estimates differ by a lot. What should I think about the results? I thought about the question for the afternoon and then took the subway home – in those days assistant professor took the subway which cost 10 cents (!) off-peak. Since I got off at the last stop, I could think about a problem without missing my stop. Those day preceded iPods and iPhones so I had no distractions. The subway and subsequent ride took about 35 minutes. As I walked home from the trolley, I figured out the answer.

Halbert White was my teaching assistant at the time – one of many terrific TAs over the years including Ben Bernanke, Whitney Newey, and too many other to mention. I discussed the result the next day with Halbert and we decided there was a result that might be useful. Zvi Griliches and Tom Rothenberg were especially helpful in suggesting revisions to the original 1978 *Econometrica* paper.

I have always liked the idea of comparing the two estimates of a given unknown parameter vector. As econometricians we often have economic knowledge regarding the approximate values of the coefficients, so a comparison need not only be based on the results of a statistic and its *p*-value, but rather we can bring economic knowledge to bear on the problem. Many alternative test formulations, e.g., efficient score tests, look at residuals and miss out on the opportunity to bring economic knowledge to work. Another offspring of the 1978 paper and the subsequent Hausman–Taylor (1981) *Econometrica* paper is that random effects models are often not a good idea because the random effects are correlated with the right-hand-side variables. Bill Taylor and I derived a technique which allows for this problem but still permits estimation of variables that do not change over time. As econometricians we know that exchangeability conditional on the right-hand-side variables often is unlikely to be correct and should always be tested if feasible. An estimation technique which overcomes this problem has been used often in applied research.

Above I noted that Halbert White and Zvi Griliches were both very helpful in the development of the specification test. I end on a sad note that Halbert White died shortly after the conference and Zvi Griliches died 12 years earlier, both from cancer. Halbert and Zvi were good friends in both academic and non-academic areas. I often talk about them when teaching graduate students and think of them when working on new econometric problems.

I thank Carter Hill again for an interesting conference and this volume of chapters which consider new approaches to specifications tests and their applications.

INTRODUCTION

We are pleased to introduce *Advances in Econometrics Volume 29: Essays in Honor of Jerry Hausman*. This volume contains research papers on the theory and practice of econometrics that are linked to, or related to, or inspired by the work of Jerry Hausman. We have divided the contributions into three sections: Estimation, Panel Data and Specification Testing. A visit to Professor Hausman's web page (http://economics.mit.edu/faculty/hausman) will show that he has published extensively in these three areas. His remarkable influence is outlined in "The Diffusion of Hausman's Econometric Ideas" by Zapata and Caminita. Their paper is presented first, before the sections, as it examines way the diffusion of Jerry Hausman's econometric ideas using citation counts, citing authors, and source journals of his most referenced citers.

Some of the papers included here were presented at a research conference held February 17–19, 2012, on the campus of Louisiana State University. The conference was sponsored by the Department of Economics at Louisiana State University, as well as LSU's Division of Economic Development, the Department of Agricultural Economics and Agribusiness, and the LSU Real Estate Research Center. The purpose of the conference was to bring together the authors of the papers for discussion, debate, and feedback.

We note with sadness that Halbert White passed away in March 2012. Halbert was a co-editor of this volume and co-author of one of the contributions. Halbert's work was the subject of *Advances in Econometrics Volume 17: Maximum Likelihood Estimation of Misspecified Models: Twenty Years Later* (2003).

Badi H. Baltagi
R. Carter Hill
Whitney K. Newey
Halbert L. White

THE DIFFUSION OF HAUSMAN'S ECONOMETRIC IDEAS

Hector O. Zapata and Cristina M. Caminita

ABSTRACT

This paper examines the diffusion of Jerry Hausman's econometric ideas using citation counts, citing authors, and source journals of his most referenced citers. Bibliographic information and citation counts of references to econometrics papers were retrieved from Thomson Reuters Web of Science and analyzed to determine the various ways in which Hausman's ideas have spread in econometrics and related disciplines. Econometric growth analysis (Gompertz and logistic functions) is used to measure the diffusion of his contributions. This analysis reveals that the diffusion of Hausman's ideas has been pervasive over time and disciplines. For example, his seminal 1978 paper continues to be strongly cited along exponential growth with total cites mainly in econometrics and other fields such as administrative management, human resources, and psychology. Some of the more recent papers have a growth pattern that resembles that of the 1978 paper. This leads us to conclude that Hausman's econometric contributions will continue to diffuse in years to come. It was also found that five journals have published the bulk of the top cited papers that list Hausman as a reference, namely, Econometrica, Journal of Econometrics, Review of Economic Studies, Academy of Management Journal, *and the* Journal of Economic Literature. *"Specification tests in econometrics" is Hausman's*

Essays in Honor of Jerry Hausman
Advances in Econometrics, Volume 29, 1–29

ISSN: 0731-9053/doi:10.1108/S0731-9053(2012)0000029006

dominant contribution in this citation analysis. We found no previous research on the econometric modeling of citation counts as done in this paper. Thus, we expect to stimulate methodological improvements in future work.

Keywords: Econometrics; specification tests; citation analysis; scholarly communication; scientometrics

JEL classification: B31; C50

INTRODUCTION

Jerry Hausman has contributed some of the most influential ideas in the advancement of econometrics. Prominent among his writings is his seminal paper "Specifications Tests in Econometrics" (Hausman, 1978), which has been cited in over 300 journals and by more than 1,000 authors of various nationalities and languages. Any quantitative analysis of Hausman's contributions is likely to be incomplete and an underestimate of his full intellectual impact, and while a debate exists on how to best quantify a scientist's research contributions, citation analysis seems a reasonable bibliometric research method to use in studying this aspect of his scholarship. Citations are also useful indicators of the utility that a scientist's published research generates for the scientific community and researchers cast their votes on the value of published articles via this metric. One unique feature of citations to Hausman's papers is that they concentrate in a few fields, namely, economics, social sciences, finance, and business, and these categories have good coverage in databases often used in citation analyses in economics (e.g., Baltagi, 2007; Chang, Mcaleer, & Oxley, 2011a; Chang, Mcaleer, & Oxley, 2011b; Kim, Morse, & Zingales, 2006).

The main purpose of this paper is to provide a historical account of the diffusion of Hausman's econometric ideas by using time series citation measures of his papers retrieved from the Web of Science databases. By limiting the scope of this task to a manageable set of highly cited papers, we accomplish the following objectives: first, we provide a chronological citation account of the diffusion of Hausman's major contributions to econometrics; second, we identify the research impact of Hausman's ideas within econometrics and related disciplines; third, we study the multi-generational (co-citation) impact and evolution of econometric research that can be traced through cited references to Hausman's papers; and fourth, we introduce a citation growth analysis of the most influential papers by using the 1978 paper as an illustration of a typical growth pattern.

The remainder of the paper is organized as follows. Section two provides a brief description of citation analysis research methods and a review of recent citation studies in economics. Section three describes the Web of Science data used in our paper. The fourth section assesses the diffusion of Hausman's econometric ideas by conducting a citation analysis of a set of highly cited papers, mapping the distribution of references to Hausman's papers in a historiograph, and visualizing the network of Hausman's top citers. Section five conducts a growth curve analysis of some of Hausman's highly cited papers. The last section contains a summary of the findings and conclusions.

CITATION ANALYSIS METRICS

De Bellis (2009) defines bibliometrics as the study of the counts of books, articles, publications, and citations, regardless of disciplinary bounds (p. 3). Studies of scholarship of science based on the quantitative research methods of bibliometrics are known as scientometrics. The primary bibliometric research method is citation analysis. In his influential *Science* article "Citation Indexes for Science," Garfield (1955) explains that by creating an index of citation linkages among papers and then analyzing them through citation counts, journal title counts, author co-citation counts, and so on, the results of the analysis can provide researchers with important information not only about the significance of a particular work or the evolution of a particular discipline but also about their own works and the diffusion of their ideas.

Although scientometrics and its research methods have long been the study of librarians and information scientists, researchers within other fields have employed citation analyses to evaluate the productivity of research teams, academic departments, and individual scholars. Diamond (2000) describes the approaches to scientometrics used by economists and identifies George Stigler as the most prominent economist to advocate the use of scientometrics for the measurement of academic productivity. In a number of recent articles, economists have studied the research and communication behavior of their peers. Kim et al. (2006) presented a citation analysis study to list the most highly cited papers in economics published since 1970. Baltagi (2007) ranked individuals and academic institutions in econometric theory and in economics over a period of 17 years. Chang et al. (2011a) have studied economists' scholarly productivity using various research assessment measures (RAM) of Thomson Reuters Web of Science. They generated a number of tables listing the 25 most highly cited papers in high impact econometrics journals. They also listed the 100 most highly cited econometrics articles in leading econometrics journals and were able to identify seven Nobel Laureates among the authors of these papers. Chang et al. (2011b) also studied RAM to determine what makes a great journal in economics. We follow similar procedures in this paper to study Hausman's econometric articles.

DATA

The Econometrics subsection of Hausman's current curriculum vitae (CV) hosted on his MIT webpage[1] was used as a bibliographic reference to search for papers in the Web of Science databases.[2] Of the 67 articles listed in the econometrics sections of his CV, 36 were found in the Web of Science.[3] Since Web of Science indexes papers published in journals ranked in Journal Citation Reports, Hausman's book chapters, conference papers, and papers published in foreign language journals were not found and were not included in our dataset. The bibliographic information, cited references, citation counts, languages, and countries were exported into text and Excel files for Hausman's 36 papers and the most highly cited papers published by his citers. An arbitrary citation count threshold of 200 was used to identify the most highly cited papers written by Hausman's citers. Only papers with a citation count of 200 or more in Web of Science were identified. The result was a dataset of 157 papers that included Hausman's 36 econometrics papers and the 121 top cited papers published by his citers. The text file was analyzed in HistCite™,[4] an algorithmic historiography software package developed by Eugene Garfield to analyze and visualize the linkages among scientific papers.

THE DIFFUSION OF HAUSMAN'S IDEAS

Among Hausman's econometrics papers, "Specification Tests in Econometrics," published in *Econometrica* in 1978, is perhaps the most familiar to researchers. The influence of this paper in the literature is pervasive and it has been cited about 3,000 times within Web of Science. Hausman's ideas and those related to his collaborative research have diffused to a set of 157 highly cited papers published in 45 journals. The appendix lists these papers ranked by citation count. Table 1 shows the distribution of papers across journal titles. For example, *Econometrica* and the *Journal of Econometrics* have published 55 of the 157 papers (35.03%). Over one-third of the papers

Table 1. The Diffusion of Hausman's Ideas Across Journal Titles.

Journal Title	No. of Articles
Econometrica	33
Journal of Econometrics	22
American Economic Review	8
Strategic Management Journal	7
Journal of Political Economy	6
Rand Journal of Economics	6
Review of Economics and Statistics	6
Journal of Economic Literature	5
Journal of Financial Economics	5
Administrative Science Quarterly	4
Economics Letters	3
Academy of Management Journal	3
Journal of Marketing Research	3
Review of Economic Studies	3
American Journal of Political Science	2
American Journal of Sociology	2
Annals of Economic and Social Measurement	2
International Economic Review	2
Journal of Business & Economic Statistics	2
Journal of Human Resources	2
Journal of Monetary Economics	2
Journal of the American Statistical Association	2
Quarterly Journal of Economics	2
Review of Financial Studies	2
Annual Review of Psychology	1

Note: Other journals with one paper cited include *Annual Review of Sociology; Econometric Theory; Economic Inquiry; Economic Journal; Financial Management; Journal of Applied Econometrics; Journal of Consumer Research; Journal of Economic Dynamics & Control; Journal of Economic Perspectives; Journal of Environmental Economics and Management; Journal of Finance; Journal of International Economics; Management Science; Medical Care; MIS Quarterly; Organization Science; Psychological Bulletin; Psychometrika; Sociological Methods & Research; World Development.*

have been published in these two dominantly theoretical econometrics journals. The remaining 101 papers in the dataset were published in journals covering a variety of disciplines. These journal titles include *Strategic Management Journal*, *Administrative Science Quarterly*, *Annual Review of Psychology*, *Annual Review of Sociology*, *MIS Quarterly*, *Medical Care*, *Organization Science*, and *Psychological Bulletin*.

Fig. 1 shows the top cited authors in the dataset by the number of cites they have received. Halbert White, one of Hausman's former students, is the most

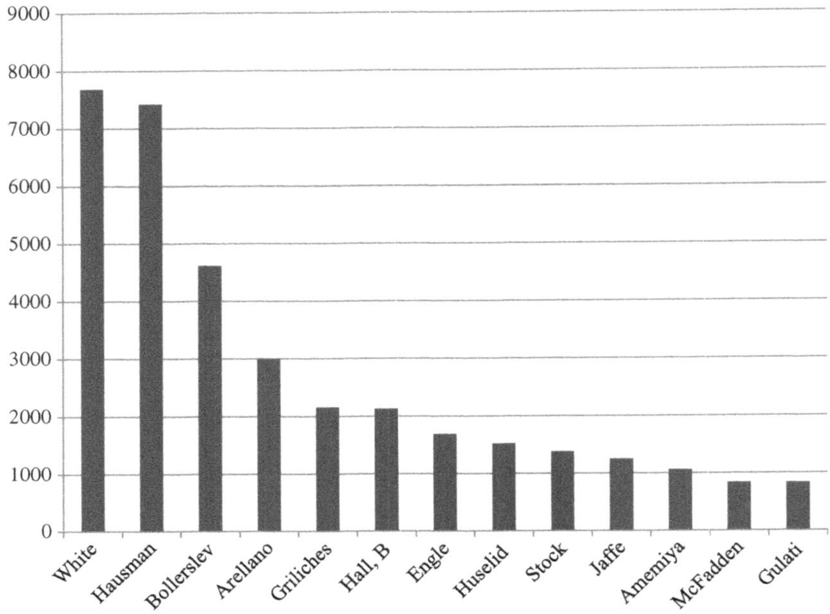

Fig. 1. Top Authors Citing Hausman.

cited author in the dataset. Self-citations are also noted in Fig. 1. In his discussion of an author's image makers, bibliometrician and information scientist Howard White (2001) explains that an author being his own top image maker (citer) is not uncommon. It seems natural that as ideas evolve, knowledge that expands those ideas would require citing the original and related works. However, in Hausman's case, White is his top image maker, receiving 7,689 cites for two papers published in *Econometrica* in the early 1980s. Other highly cited authors include Bollerslev, whose five papers included in the dataset received 4,621 cites; Arellano, whose two coauthored papers received 3,002 cites; and Griliches, whose three papers have received 2,162 cites.

Fig. 2 shows the 10 most cited papers in the dataset. The highest ranked is White's (1980) "A Heteroskedasticity-Consistent Covariance-Matrix Estimator and a Direct Test for Heteroskedasticity." White (1980) presented an estimator that is consistent even when the disturbances of the linear regression model are heteroskedastic. The test's flexibility and easy implementation generated wide applicability in applied econometrics. White suggested using Hausman's test (1978) as a practical way to test model

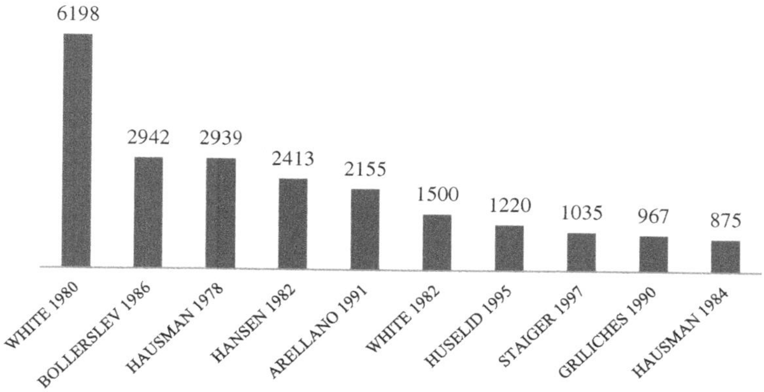

Fig. 2. Top 10 Papers Citing Hausman by Total Times Cited.

specification in cases when the investigator was unsure about the model when rejection occurred. He also pointed out that the Hausman test was sensitive to model misspecification but not heteroskedasticity. When the null of no misspecification is not rejected by a Hausman test, White's test identifies heteroskedasticity when rejection occurs. Although references to White's (1980) heteroskedasticity test paper are not direct links to Hausman's 1978 paper, it can be argued that White contributed to an expansion of the use of Hausman's specification test in various disciplines.

To identify the influence and dissemination of Hausman's ideas through White's scholarship, a closer examination of the articles that cite White (1980) is needed to determine the percentage of those papers that also cited Hausman's papers. When we began to investigate Hausman's influence in econometrics and discovered that White (1980) had a greater number of citations than Hausman (1978), we hypothesized that White's 1980 paper may be a gateway for researchers to Hausman's work in econometrics. We completed an initial citation analysis in Web of Science to identify the top 50 highest cited papers that list White (1980) in their cited references. We then analyzed this set of 50 papers to identify those that also listed Hausman in their cited references. Thirteen (26%) of these 50 papers cite both White (1980) and at least one of Hausman's papers. Thus, total co-citations for White and Hausman are potentially high given that 6,198 papers retrieved in Web of Science list White (1980) as a cited reference. White and McCain (1998) show that identifying sets of authors frequently cited together within a body of research can map scholarship trends and the people who contribute to them, as well as showing that scholarly literatures change in intelligible ways over time (p. 327). Identifying clusters of Hausman's co-cited authors, such as White, can show concentrated areas of scholarship within a field, and in turn show how his work is applied in conjunction with the work of his peers or of authors outside of his specialization.

Six of the top 10 papers citing Hausman were published in *Econometrica* between 1978 and 1997. One paper each was published in the *Journal of Econometrics*, *Review of Economic Studies*, *Academy of Management Journal*, and the *Journal of Economic Literature*. The publication dates of the top cited papers are important to note when using citation counts as evidence of influence or diffusiveness. In Hausman's case, the older the paper, the higher the chances of its being cited as a reference, but some relatively younger papers are following a growth pattern that resembles their predecessors. More current papers have less of an opportunity to be referenced. This citing behavior is evident even among Hausman's most current econometric papers, with his papers published in 2000–2011 receiving 80 cites or fewer since their publication. The most current of Hausman's articles, co-authored with Lewis, Menzel, and Newey in 2011, had only received one cite at the time of this study.

Journal Impact Visualization

HistCite™ can be used to generate historiographs tracing the citing history of a group of papers. Garfield, Pudovkin, and Istomin (2003) explain that the historiography of scholarly topics is important not only to show linkages between citers and citees and to map the knowledge creation and referencing in a particular field but also to show how a field's information has diffused to other fields and to determine when paradigm shifts have occurred. The historiograph created with the top 25 cited papers in the dataset provides a rudimentary citation genealogy of Hausman's ideas.

Fig. 3 shows the HistCite™ generated historiograph of the links among these top papers. Dates of publication are listed along the left-hand side of the historiograph. Each square node represents a paper, and the number within each node corresponds to the paper's publication date in chronological order. For example, Berndt, Hall, Hall, and Hausman (1974) is the second oldest by publication date of the 157 papers in the dataset. Therefore, its node is labeled with the number "2" and is in line with the 1974 year along the left side of the historiograph. The legend at the bottom of the historiograph also shows the correspondence of node labels with the date of publication. Nodes are linked by cited references, and these links are represented by connecting lines.

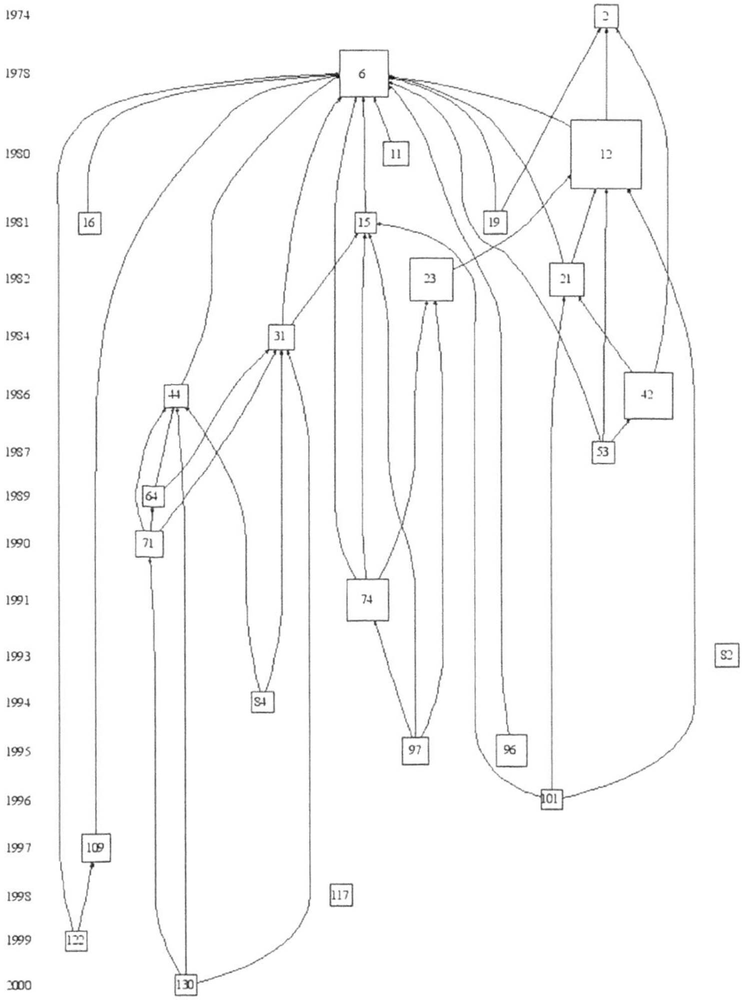

Legend:

2 Berndt et al. (1974)
6 Hausman (1978)
11 Bentler (1980)
12 White (1980)
15 Hauman & Taylor (1981)
16 Nickell (1981)
19 Amemiya (1981)
21 White (1982)
23 Hansen (1982)
31 Hausman (1984)
42 Bollerslev (1986)
44 Jaffe (1986)
53 French (1987)
64 Jaffe (1989)
71 Griliches (1990)
74 Arellano (1991)
82 Albert(1993)
84 Henderson (1994)
96 Huselid (1995)
97 Arellano (1995)
101 Yermack (1996)
109 Staiger (1997)
117 Beck (1998)
122 Frankel (1999)
130 Ahuja (2000)

Fig. 3. Historiograph of Hausman's Econometric Ideas.

HistCite™ shows links backward in time, and so all of the arrows point toward cited references. For example, node 130, Ahuja's (2000a) *Administrative Science Quarterly* paper, is the most recently published of the top 25 papers by citation count. It lists nodes 71, 44, and 31 in its cited references and is represented as linking back to these nodes in the historiograph. Node 31 is Hausman, Hall, and Griliches' (1984) *Econometrica* paper; node 44 is Jaffe's (1986) *American Economic Review* paper; and node 71 is Griliches' (1990) *Journal of Economic Literature* paper. If we continue to trace the cited references backward, we see that Jaffe and Hausman et al. cite Hausman's specification test paper published in 1978.

A relevant pattern to note is the diffusion of Hausman's ideas across journals over time. Nodes 6, 12, 15, 16, 21, and 23, which are chronologically placed in the 1978–1989 section of the historiograph, are all papers published in *Econometrica*. According to Kim et al. (2006), the most highly cited papers in econometrics during the 1970s and 1980s were published in *Econometrica*, *The Journal of Political Economy*, and *American Economic Review*. Eleven of the 25 papers within the historiograph's dataset were published in either *Econometrica* or the *American Economic Review* and span the years 1978–1989. Kim et al. (2006) also note that in the early 1970s, 77% of the most highly cited papers within their dataset were theoretical[5] in content. The pattern of a large concentration of methodological papers published in the 1970s and 1980s, which are then used to inform the methodologies of empirical papers in the 1990–2000 decade, is observable in the cited references visualized in the historiograph.

As we link the papers forward in time, we see that Hausman's papers are cited in journals in various disciplines, particularly among management and administrative science journals. Of the 11 papers published from 1990 to 2000, 3 papers were published in *Strategic Management Journal*, *Academy of Management Journal*, and *Administrative Science Quarterly*, respectively. Huselid (1995) uses Hausman's test "to evaluate the ordinary-least-squares (OLS) regression assumption that the High Performance Work Practices scales are exogenous in profitability models" (p. 666). Ahuja (2000a) cites Hausman et al.'s (1984) models developed from the Poisson distribution to design his model specification (p. 436). Henderson and Cockburn (1994) use Hausman et al.'s (1984) paper to estimate patterns of maximum likelihood in their hypotheses regarding firm effects in pharmaceutical research (p. 68). Hausman's ideas also contributed to political science during this time period. Beck, Katz, and Tucker (1998) studied binary time-series-cross-section (BTSCS) data with a dependent variable using examples and applications from international relations (p. 1260). Beck et al. (1998) cited

Han and Hausman's (1990) *Journal of Applied Econometrics* paper to support their argument that BTSCS data is grouped duration data (p. 1266).

Citation Network Visualization

The historiograph shows a chronological relationship among the top 25 papers in the dataset. A chronological genealogy of citations is one part of the story of the diffusion of Hausman's econometrics ideas. An analogical visualization and cross tabulation of the relationships among these papers can show the co-citation relationships and concentrations of references to particular sets of papers. To create the citation network visualization, we used Pajek. Pajek is a program for Windows developed by Batagelj and Mrvar (2004) to analyze and visualize large networks. To map the spatial relationships between Hausman and his citers, the historiograph generated from HistCite™ was exported as a Pajek.net file. This document was then imported into Pajek for network visualization. The resulting visualization is a circular arrangement of each of the 25 papers and line-and-arrow connections between papers (Fig. 4).

This visualized network shows a basic pattern of co-citation among Hausman and the other authors of the top 25 cited papers. Table 2 shows the cross tabulation of instances of co-citation among the 25 papers in the set and the institutional affiliations of authors. The authors with whom Hausman is most frequently cited are Hausman himself, with four instances of co-citation; Jaffe, with four instances of co-citation; White, with four instances of co-citation; Hansen, with two instances of co-citation; Staige and Stock, with one instance of co-citation; and Arellano and Bond, with one instance of co-citation. According to White and McCain (1998), author co-citation analysis can be used to visualize a field through a representative slice of its literature, and can identify influential authors and their intellectual relationships from the citation record.

The citation growth stages of a paper over time and the subfields and specializations that develop within a field can also be identified through author co-citation analysis. For example, in this limited dataset of 25 papers, Jaffe has been co-cited with Hausman four times. Both of Jaffe's papers were published in the late 1980s in *American Economic Review*. Both apply econometric theory, the first in "Technological Opportunity and Spillovers of Research-and-Development" (1986), and the second in "Real Effects of Academic Research" (1989).

Hausman's papers in the dataset include his coauthored 1984 paper with Hall and Griliches on the patent R and D relationship. Henderson and

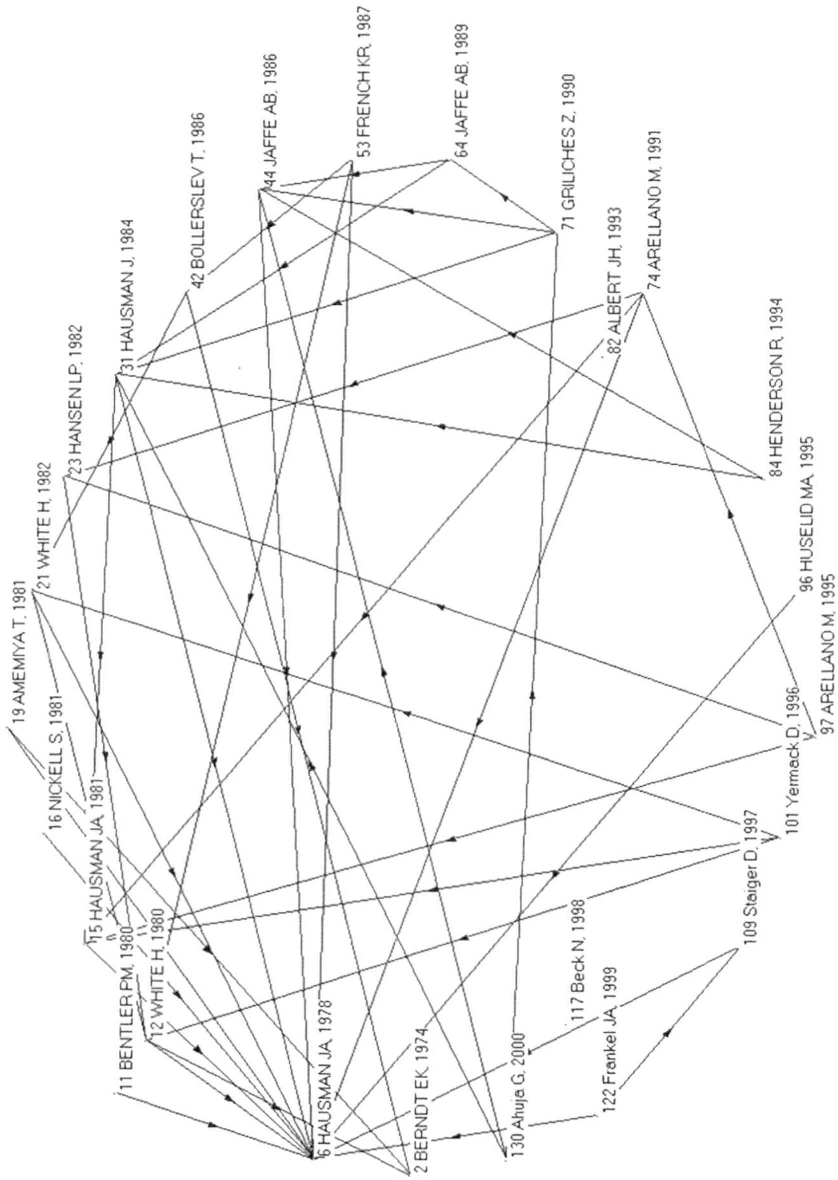

Fig. 4. Hausman's Citation Network Visualization of Top 25 Papers.

Table 2. Hausman's Most Frequently Co-Cited Authors and Their Institutional Affiliations.

Co-Cited Author	No. of Co-Citation Instances	Institutional Affiliation
Hausman[a]	4	MIT 1972 – present Harvard University 1982–1987 Oxford University – visiting professor, dates unspecified on CV
Jaffe[b]	4	Harvard University 1985–1994 *Education* S. M. MIT 1978 S. B. MIT 1976
White[c]	4	*Education* PhD MIT 1976
Hansen[d]	2	Harvard University 1986 MIT 1983
Arellano[e] and Bond[f]	1	*Arellano* University of Oxford 1985–1989 *Bond* Nuffield College, Oxford 1990–present
Staiger[g] and Stock[h]	1	*Staiger* Harvard University 1992–1998 *Education* PhD MIT 1990 *Stock* Harvard University 1983–present

[a]Retrieved from http://economics.mit.edu/faculty/hausman/cv.
[b]Retrieved from http://www.brandeis.edu/das/jaffe/docs/jaffe-cv.pdf.
[c]Retrieved from http://weber.ucsd.edu/~hwhite/CV%20HW%2012-22-09.pdf.
[d]Retrieved from http://home.uchicago.edu/~lhansen/.
[e]Retrieved from http://www.cemfi.es/~arellano/macv.pdf.
[f]Retrieved from http://www.ifs.org.uk/staff/cvsteve.pdf.
[g]Retrieved from http://www.dartmouth.edu/~dstaiger/Papers/CVDS.pdf.
[h]Retrieved from http://www.economics.harvard.edu/faculty/stock/cv/Stock_cv_June_12.pdf.

Cockburn's paper on "Exploring Firm Effects in Pharmaceutical Research" cites Hausman et al.'s 1984 paper and Jaffe's 1986 paper. Connecting Hausman et al. (1984) and Jaffe (1986) through co-citation analysis can show the disciplines in which their work has been used to study technology and growth, in this case within the study of pharmaceutical research. Clearly, a more complete co-citation analysis of Hausman's work would identify the extent of the diffusion of Hausman's ideas far beyond theoretical and applied econometrics.

GROWTH IN CITATIONS[6]

Hausman (1978) pointed out that one of the most important areas for research in econometrics was specification testing. The proliferation (growth) of model specification tests in the econometrics literature provides strong support for this argument. The high number of citations for the 1978 paper is one example of this and other important ideas introduced by Hausman. We focus on the 1978 paper in this section because its citation growth pattern is representative of a growth pattern associated with the most highly cited papers. Also, Hausman (1978) is a visible convergence point for cited references in both the historiograph and the network visualization and serves as the most influential and diffusive of Hausman's papers by citation count alone. As will become obvious in this section, many of these papers have experienced exponential growth, but some have begun to taper off relative to the 1978 paper that continues to receive high citations.

Hausman (1978) introduced a general form of specification tests based on a comparison of two estimators of the parameter vector of the null model that, when the null model is true, an asymptotically efficient estimator must have zero covariance with its difference from a consistent but asymptotically inefficient estimator. The introduction of this extended framework for a large class of alternative hypotheses found fast applicability in advancing theoretical and applied work in econometrics. A first search on Web of Science of Hausman (1978) resulted in 2,929 total citations with about 85 citations per year. Fig. 5 clearly illustrates the exponential growth in citations. Naturally, the minimum citation count was in 1979, but it is very remarkable that over a 33-year period, the highest number of cited references Hausman (1978) received were in 2011. The bulk of the references (over 92%) are from journal articles, followed by proceeding papers (about 6%); the remaining references fall into reviews, notes, editorial materials, letters, and book reviews. Most of the cited references to the 1978 paper, based on Web of Science journal title subject categories, are classified as pertaining to economics (61%); social sciences mathematical methods (13%); business finance (10%); business (7%); and other subjects such as management, mathematics interdisciplinary applications, statistics probability, health policy services, environmental studies, agricultural economics policy, planning and development, industrial relations labor, public environmental occupational health, and other smaller number of citations to sociology, political science, operations research management sciences, urban studies, international relations, environmental sciences, public administration, education educational research, geography, demography, and social sciences biomedical. Thus, over 90% of the cited references to the 1978

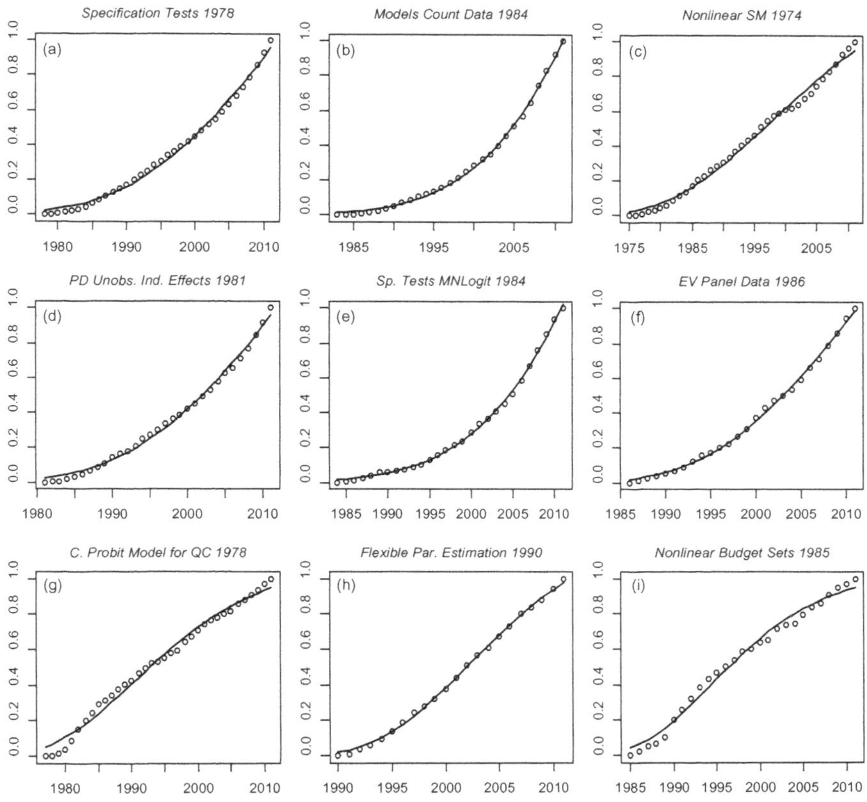

Fig. 5. Hausman's Articles with Over 100 Cites Ranked from Highest (Top Left) to Lowest (Bottom Right), 1974–2011.

paper fall into the first four Web of Science journal title subject categories: economics, social sciences mathematical methods, business finance, and business and management.

Journals Citing Hausman (1978)

About 314 journal titles have published papers that list Hausman (1978) as a cited reference. The top citing journals include the *Journal of Econometrics* (3.8%), *Applied Economics* (3.6%), *Review of Economics and Statistics* (2.5%), *Economics Letters* (2.0%), *Econometrica* (1.5%), *American Journal of Agricultural Economics* (1.3%), *American Economic Review* (1.2%), *Health Economics* (1.2%), and *Journal of Applied Econometrics* (1.2%). The remaining journals had 0.97% or less of the total citations, and to list a few selected journals they include the *Southern Economic Journal*, *International Economic Review*, *World Development*, *Journal of Business Economic Statistics*, *Oxford Bulletin of Economics and Statistics*, *Economic Journal*, *Land Economics*, *Journal of Labor Economics*, *Weltwirtschaftliches Archiv/Review of World Economics*, *European Economic Review*, *Agricultural Economics*, *Economica*, *Journal of Futures Markets*, *Journal of the American Statistical Association*, *Journal of Marketing*, *Kyklos*, *Manchester School*, *Scottish Journal of Political Economy*, *Statistics in Medicine*, *Food Policy*, *Japan and the World Economy*, *Australian Journal of Management*, *Panoeconomicus*, *American Statistician*, *British Journal of Management*, *Investigaciones Economicas*, *Multivariate Behavioral Research*, *Scientometrics*, *Statistica Sinica*, *World Politics*, and *Youth Society*.

Top Institutions Citing Hausman (1978)

The top five institutions by percentage of citations[7] are MIT (2.3%), Harvard University (2.1%), the National Bureau of Economic Research (2.1%), and University of North Carolina (1.9%). Other institutions in the top 10 tier include Duke University, Yale University, University of California-Berkeley, University of Pennsylvania, and University of Chicago.

Countries and Languages Citing Hausman (1978)

Hausman (1978) has had a global impact in the econometric literature. Based on Web of Science analysis by countries and territories, the bulk of citations were from the United States (61%), followed by England (9.8%), Canada (6.3%), Spain (3.4%), and Germany (3.2%). There was a long list of countries that cited the 1978 paper with less than 3% citations. Naturally, most of the citations have been in English (95.5%), followed by French (0.3%), German (0.3%), Spanish (0.2%), and other languages. As Baltagi (2007) shows, the top 10 countries publishing in econometrics for the period 1989–2005 are the United States, the United Kingdom, Canada, the Netherlands, Australia, France, Spain, Germany, Italy, and Japan. The geographical citations of Hausman's (1978) paper extracted from Web of Science correlate with Baltagi's (2007) findings.

Gompertz Growth Curves

Fig. 5 shows the Gompertz growth curves[8] for citation proportions (total citations by year over total cumulative citations). The rate of growth in citations of the 1978 paper continues to accelerate (highest citations were in 2011), suggesting that model specification tests are a prominent area of research in econometrics, a merit to Hausman's visionary contribution. Given the mix of related disciplines conducting econometric model-based research, it seems natural that the use of Hausman's specification test will be a strong driver of future citations.

The growth rate of Hausman's (1978) paper in Fig. 5 is representative of the growth rate in other top cited papers with over 100 cites per paper. The Gompertz curves appear to be a reasonable representation of citation proportions. Except for the bottom left and right curves, the growth in citations are increasing at an increasing rate, and this diffusion pattern is steeper for Hausman (1978); Hausman, Hall, and Griliches (1984); Hausman and McFadden (1984); Griliches and Hausman (1986); Hausman, Abrevaya, and Scott-Morton (1998); and Hausman and Ruud (1987). The papers on "conditional probit models" and "nonlinear budget sets" seem to have exhausted their citation growth.

SUMMARY AND CONCLUSIONS

Model specification tests in econometrics and Hausman appear to be synonymous. While his seminal 1978 paper dominates the citation record, this paper is only one of the 36 econometrics papers indexed by Web of Science. Of Hausman's top seven most cited econometrics papers within our dataset, each receiving more than 300 cites, five were published in *Econometrica*, one in the *Journal of Econometrics*, and the other in *Annals of Economic and Social Measurement*. All the seven papers were published between 1974 and 1986. Overall, *Econometrica* and the *Journal of Econometrics* published over one-third of the 36 papers included in our dataset.

Three of Hausman's ideas that have been consistently cited in the literature are "Specification Tests in Econometrics" (1978), "Econometric Models for Count Data with an Application to the Patents R and D Relationship" (1984) coauthored with Hall and Griliches, and "Estimation and Inference in Nonlinear Structured Models" (1974) coauthored with Berndt, B. Hall, and R. Hall, best known as BHHH.[9] Five journals have published the bulk of the top cited papers that list Hausman as a reference: *Econometrica*, *Journal of*

Econometrics, *Review of Economic Studies*, *Academy of Management Journal*, and the *Journal of Economic Literature*. A historiograph was generated to trace the citing history of the top 25 highly cited papers and to map the diffusion of Hausman's econometric ideas across time, much as a genealogy maps the history and diffusion of families across time. Suffice it to say that Hausman's impact on econometrics has been profound and its multidisciplinary spread has been pervasive. Likewise, the diffusion of his ideas has been geographically global and has been published in multiple languages, with English as the dominant language.

Gompertz growth curves of citations were estimated to illustrate patterns of growth in Hausman's top nine cited papers. Five of the top seven most cited papers are characterized by exponential growth that started early in Hausman's career and continue to be highly cited today. The findings in this research, based on WoS databases, provide unequivocal evidence that the diffusion of Hausman's econometric ideas has contributed to advances in econometrics, and compelling reasons exist to believe that the diffusion of his ideas will continue in years to come.

NOTES

1. Hausman's CV retrieved from http://economics.mit.edu/faculty/hausman/cv
2. Every citation database, from Web of Science to Google Scholar, has limitations that affect the total number of citation counts listed for authors. Web of Science by design covers only the top-ranked journals in various subject areas. Google Scholar covers the entire web, and citation count data found in Google Scholar is much larger and is found in a greater number of sources than Web of Science covers. For a review of the strengths and weaknesses of the citation databases available on the market, see Neuhaus, C., & Daniel, H.-D. (2008). Data sources for performing citation analysis: An overview. *Journal of Documentation*, *64*(2), 193–210. doi: 10.1108/00220410810858010.
3. Retrieved from Web of Science February 3, 2012.
4. Retrieved from http://thomsonreuters.com/products_services/science/science_products/a-z/histcite/.
5. Baltagi (2007, p. 956) list of journals that publish general econometrics papers included *Econometrica and the American Economic Review*.
6. We thank Anil Bera for suggesting a comparison to a logistic growth curve.
7. Institutions do not necessarily correspond to the institutional affiliations of citing authors.
8. Logistic growth curves were also estimated but not reported, since they were identical to the Gompertz curves shown in Fig. 5. Of course, the results presented here are an initial econometric investigation that may lead to fruitful future research. One shortcoming of the methods used here is that the measurements on the dependent variable may vary from one citation database to another (e.g., Google

Scholar generates a citation count that differs from that of Web of Science), and future models should account for such measurement differences.

9. BHHH appears to be an econometric dictionary word. Searching for BHHH in Google Scholar generates an extensive list of articles that use it as if it were a common word. At least one highly cited article that emerges in such a search discusses BHHH without citing Berndt et al. (1974). This suggests another implicit (unaccounted for) citation to Hausman's contributions.

ACKNOWLEDGMENTS

We thank two referees for their helpful comments that improved the content and exposition of this paper. Special thanks to Jerry Hausman for his interest in our work and for sharing his thoughts and a bit of the history of his ideas. We also thank the organizers, sponsors, and participants of the 11th Advances in Econometrics conference.

REFERENCES

Batagelj, V., & Mrvar, A. (2004). Pajek – Analysis and visualization of large networks. In M. Jünger & P. Mutzel (Eds.), *Graph drawing software* (pp. 77–103). Berlin, Heidelberg: Springer Berlin Heidelberg.

Baltagi, B. H. (2007). Worldwide econometrics rankings: 1989–2005. *Econometric Theory, 23*, 952–1012. doi: 10.1017/S026646660707051X

De Bellis, N. (2009). *Bibliometrics and citation analysis: From the science citation index to cybermetrics*. Lanham, MD: Scarecrow Press.

Diamond, A. (2000). The complementarity of scientometrics and economics. In B. Cronin & H. B. Atkins (Eds.), *The web of knowledge: A festschrift in honor of Eugene Garfield* (pp. 321–336). Metford, NJ: Information Today, Inc.

Chang, C., Mcaleer, M., & Oxley, L. (2011a). Great expectatrics: Great papers, great journals, great econometrics. *Econometric Reviews, 30*, 583–619.

Chang, C., Mcaleer, M., & Oxley, L. (2011b). What makes a great journal great in economics? The Singer not the song. *Journal of Economic Surveys, 25*, 326–361.

Garfield, E. (1955). Citation indexes for science. *Science, New Series, 122*(3159), 108–111.

Garfield, E., Pudovkin, A., & Istomin, V. (2003). Why do we need algorithmic historiography? *Journal of the American Society for Information Science and Technology, 54*, 400–412.

Huselid, M. A. (1995). The Impact of Human Resource Management Practices on Turnover, Productivity, and Corporate Financial Performance. *The Academy of Management Journal, 38*(3), 635–672. doi:10.2307/256741

Kim, E. H., Morse, A., & Zingales, L. (2006). What has mattered to economics since 1970. *Journal of Economic Perspectives, 20*(4), 189–202. doi: 10.1257/jep.20.4.189.

White, H. D. (2001). Authors as citers over time. *Journal of the American Society for Information Science & Technology, 52*(2), 87–108.

White, H. D., & McCain, K. W. (1998). Visualizing a discipline: An author co-citation analysis of information science, 1972–1995. *Journal of the American Society for Information Science, 49*(4), 327–355.

APPENDIX: PAPERS RANKED BY CITATION COUNT (CITATION COUNTS ARE BOLDED IN PARENTHESES)

1. **(6198)** White, H. (1980). A Heteroskedasticity-Consistent Covariance Matrix Estimator and a Direct Test for Heteroskedasticity. *Econometrica*.
2. **(2942)** Bollerslev, T. (1986). Generalized Autoregressive Conditional Heteroskedasticity. *Journal of Econometrics*.
3. **(2939)** Hausman, J. (1978). Specification Tests in Econometrics. *Econometrica*.
4. **(2413)** Hansen, L. (1982). Large Sample Properties of Generalized-Method of Moments Estimators. *Econometrica*.
5. **(2155)** Arellano, M., & Bond, S. (1991). Some Tests of Specification for Panel Data: Monte Carlo Evidence and an Application to Employment Equations. *Review of Economic Studies*.
6. **(1500)** White, H. (1982). Maximum-Likelihood Estimation of Mis-specified Models. *Econometrica*.
7. **(1220)** Huselid, M. (1995). The Impact of Human Resource Management Practices on Turnover, Productivity, and Corporate Financial Performance. *Academy of Management Journal*.
8. **(1035)** Staiger, D., & Stock, J. (1997). Instrumental Variables Regression with Weak Instruments. *Econometrica*.
9. **(967)** Griliches, Z. (1990). Patent Statistics as Economic Indicators – A Survey. *Journal of Economic Literature*.
10. **(875)** Hausman, J., Hall, B. H., & Griliches, Z. (1984). Econometric-Models for Count Data with an Application to the Patents R and D Relationship. *Econometrica*.
11. **(847)** Arellano, M., & Bover, O. (1995). Another Look at the Instrumental Variable Estimation of Error-Components Models. *Journal of Econometrics*.
12. **(749)** Bentler, P. (1980). Multivariate Analysis with Latent Variables: Causal Modeling. *Annual Review of Psychology*.
13. **(735)** Berndt, E., Hall, B., Hall, R., & Hausman, J. (1974). Estimation and Inference in Nonlinear Structural Models. *Annals of Economic and Social Measurement*.
14. **(725)** Albert, J., & Chib, S. (1993). Bayesian-Analysis of Binary and Polychotomous Response Data. *Journal of the American Statistical Association*.

15. **(719)** Amemiya, T. (1981). Qualitative Response Models – A Survey. *Journal of Economic Literature.*
16. **(676)** Jaffe, A. (1986). Technological Opportunity and Spillovers of Research-and-Development: Evidence from Firms Patents, Profits, and Market Value. *American Economic Review.*
17. **(665)** Nickell, S. (1981). Biases in Dynamic-Models with Fixed Effects. *Econometrica.*
18. **(628)** Beck, N., Katz, J., & Tucker, R. (1998). Taking Time Seriously: Time-Series-Cross-Section Analysis with a Binary Dependent Variable. *American Journal of Political Science.*
19. **(611)** French, K., Schwert, G., & Stambaugh, R. (1987). Expected Stock Returns and Volatility. *Journal of Financial Economics.*
20. **(597)** Henderson, R., & Cockburn, I. (1996). Scale, Scope, and Spillovers: The Determinants of Research Productivity in Drug Discovery. *Rand Journal of Economics.*
21. **(588)** Frankel, J., & Romer, D. (1999). Does Trade Cause Growth? *American Economic Review.*
22. **(584)** Jaffe, A. (1989). Real Effects of Academic Research. *American Economic Review.*
23. **(572)** Ahuja, G. (2000a). Collaboration Networks, Structural Holes, and Innovation: A Longitudinal Study. *Administrative Science Quarterly.*
24. **(569)** Hausman, J, & Taylor, W. (1981). Panel Data and Unobservable Individual Effects. *Econometrica.*
25. **(552)** Yermack, D. (1996). Higher Market Valuation of Companies with a Small Board of Directors. *Journal of Financial Economics.*
26. **(525)** Boulding, W., Kalra, A., Staelin, R., & Zeithaml, V. (1993). A Dynamic Process Model of Service Quality-From Expectations to Behavioral Intentions. *Journal of Marketing Research.*
27. **(518)** Robinson, P. (1988). Root-N-Consistent Semiparametric Regression. *Econometrica.*
28. **(501)** Zucker, L., Darby, M., & Brewer, M. (1998). Intellectual Human Capital and the Birth of US Biotechnology Enterprises. *American Economic Review.*
29. **(500)** Bollerslev, T. (1987). A Conditionally Heteroskedastic Time-Series Model for Speculative Prices and Rates of Return. *Review of Economics and Statistics.*
30. **(496)** Engle, R., Lilien, D., & Robins, R. (1987). Estimating Time-Varying Risk Premia in the Term Structure-The Arch-M Model. *Econometrica.*

31. **(476)** Engle, R., & Kroner, K. (1995). Multivariate Simultaneous Generalized Arch. *Econometric Theory*.
32. **(474)** Mcdonald, J. F., & Moffitt, R. A. (1980). The Uses of Tobit Analysis. *Review of Economics and Statistics*.
33. **(468)** Hausman, J., & Mcfadden, D. (1984). Specification Tests for the Multinomial Logit Model. *Econometrica*.
34. **(466)** Bollerslev, T. (1990). Modeling the Coherence in Short-Run Nominal Exchange-Rates-A Multivariate Generalized Arch Model. *Review of Economics and Statistics*.
35. **(460)** Bollerslev, T., Engle, R., & Wooldridge, J. (1988). A Capital-Asset Pricing Model with Time-Varying Covariances. *Journal of Political Economy*.
36. **(425)** Gulati, R., & Gargiulo, M. (1999). Where Do Interorganizational Networks Come From? *American Journal of Sociology*.
37. **(421)** Lee, L. (1983). Generalized Econometric-Models With Selectivity. *Econometrica*.
38. **(407)** Gulati, R., & Singh, H. (1998). The Architecture of Cooperation: Managing Coordination Costs and Appropriation Concerns in Strategic Alliances. *Administrative Science Quarterly*.
39. **(404)** Levine, R., Loayza, N., & Beck, T. (2000). Financial Intermediation and Growth: Causality and Causes. *Journal of Monetary Economics*.
40. **(391)** Lancaster, T. (1979). Econometric Methods for the Duration of Unemployment. *Econometrica*.
41. **(384)** Baum, J., Calabrese, T., & Silverman, B. (2000). Don't Go It Alone: Alliance Network Composition and Startups' Performance in Canadian Biotechnology. *Strategic Management Journal*.
42. **(381)** Petersen, M. (2009). Estimating Standard Errors in Finance Panel Data Sets: Comparing Approaches. *Review of Financial Studies*.
43. **(379)** Selden, T. M., & Song, D. Q. (1994). Environmental Quality and Development: Is There a Kuznets Curve for Air-Pollution Emissions? *Journal of Environmental Economics and Management*.
44. **(376)** Kamakura, W. & Russell, G. (1989). A Probabilistic Choice Model for Market-Segmentation and Elasticity Structure. *Journal of Marketing Research*.
45. **(375)** Gardner, W., Mulvey, E., & Shaw, E. (1995). Regression-Analyses of Counts and Rates-Poisson, Overdispersed Poisson, and Negative Binomial Models. *Psychological Bulletin*.
46. **(374)** Huber, J., Payne, J., & Puto, C. (1982). Adding Asymmetrically Dominated Alternatives-Violations of Regularity and the Similarity Hypothesis. *Journal of Consumer Research*.

47. **(369)** Mcfadden, D. (1989). A Method of Simulated Moments for Estimation of Discrete Response Models without Numerical-Integration. *Econometrica.*
48. **(352)** Berry, S. (1994). Estimating Discrete-Choice Models of Product Differentiation. *Rand Journal of Economics.*
49. **(346)** Amemiya, T. (1984). Tobit Models – A Survey. *Journal of Econometrics.*
50. **(339)** Stock, J., Wright, J., & Yogo, M. (2002). A Survey of Weak Instruments and Weak Identification in Generalized Method of Moments. *Journal of Business & Economic Statistics.*
51. **(338)** Winship, C., & Radbill, L. (1994). Sampling Weights and Regression-Analysis. *Sociological Methods & Research.*
52. **(329)** Townsend, R. M. (1994). Risk and Insurance in Village India. *Econometrica.*
53. **(327)** Himmelberg, C., Hubbard, R., & Palia, D. (1999). Understanding the Determinants of Managerial Ownership and the Link between Ownership and Performance. *Journal of Financial Economics.*
54. **(323)** Powell, J. (1984). Least Absolute Deviations Estimation for the Censored Regression-Model. *Journal of Econometrics.*
55. **(322)** Coe, D., Helpman, E., & Hoffmaister, A. (1997). North-South R&D Spillovers. *Economic Journal.*
56. **(320)** Griliches, Z., & Hausman, J. (1986). Errors in Variables in Panel Data. *Journal of Econometrics.*
57. **(315)** Beck, T., Levine, R., & Loayza, N. (2000). Finance and the Sources of Growth. *Journal of Financial Economics.*
58. **(312)** Angrist, J., & Krueger, A. (1991). Does Compulsory School Attendance Affect Schooling and Earnings. *Quarterly Journal of Economics.*
59. **(312)** Hall, B., & Ziedonis, R. (2001). The Patent Paradox Revisited: An Empirical Study of Patenting in the US Semiconductor Industry, 1979–1995. *Rand Journal of Economics.*
60. **(310)** Huselid, M., Jackson, S., & Schuler, R. (1997). Technical and Strategic Human Resource Management Effectiveness as Determinants of Firm Performance. *Academy of Management Journal.*
61. **(309)** Hubbard, R. (1998). Capital-Market Imperfections and Investment. *Journal of Economic Literature.*
62. **(307)** Dubin, J., & Mcfadden, D. (1984). An Econometric-Analysis of Residential Electric Appliance Holdings and Consumption. *Econometrica.*

63. **(305)** Rivers, D., & Vuong, Q. (1988). Limited Information Estimators and Exogeneity Tests for Simultaneous Probit Models. *Journal of Econometrics*.
64. **(299)** Hausman, J., & Wise, D. (1978). Conditional Probit Model for Qualitative Choice-Discrete Decisions Recognizing Interdependence and Heterogeneous Preferences. *Econometrica*.
65. **(296)** Rosenkopf, L., & Nerkar, A. (2001). Beyond Local Search: Boundary-Spanning, Exploration, and Impact in the Optical Disk Industry. *Strategic Management Journal*.
66. **(295)** Bernheim, B., Shleifer, A., & Summers, L. (1985). The Strategic Bequest Motive. *Journal of Political Economy*.
67. **(295)** Battese, G., & Coelli, T. (1988). Prediction of Firm-Level Technical Efficiencies with a Generalized Frontier Production Function and Panel Data. *Journal of Econometrics*.
68. **(286)** Stuart, T. (2000). Interorganizational Alliances and the Performance of Firms: A Study of Growth and Innovation Rates in a High-Technology Industry. *Strategic Management Journal*.
69. **(285)** Mroz, T. A. (1987). The Sensitivity of an Empirical-Model of Married Women's Hours of Work to Economic and Statistical Assumptions. *Econometrica*.
70. **(281)** Clogg, C., Petkova, E., & Haritou, A. (1995). Statistical-Methods for Comparing Regression-Coefficients between Models. *American Journal of Sociology*.
71. **(278)** King, A., & Lenox, M. (2000). Industry Self-Regulation without Sanctions: The Chemical Industry's Responsible Care Program. *Academy of Management Journal*.
72. **(276)** Mullahy, J. (1986). Specification and Testing of Some Modified Count Data Models. *Journal of Econometrics*.
73. **(275)** Darr, E., Argote, L., & Epple, D. (1995). The Acquisition, Transfer, and Depreciation of Knowledge in Service Organizations: Productivity in Franchises. *Management Science*.
74. **(266)** Swait, J., & Louviere, J. (1993). The Role of the Scale Parameter in the Estimation and Comparison of Multinomial Logit-Models. *Journal of Marketing Research*.
75. **(266)** Engle, R., & Russell, J. (1998). Autoregressive Conditional Duration: A New Model for Irregularly Spaced Transaction Data. *Econometrica*.
76. **(265)** Becker, G., Grossman, M., & Murphy, K. (1994). An Empirical-Analysis of Cigarette Addiction. *American Economic Review*.

77. **(265)** Shaw, J., Johnson, J., & Coons, S. (2005). US Valuation of the Eq-5d Health States-Development and Testing of the D1 Valuation Model. *Medical Care*.
78. **(264)** Henderson, R., & Cockburn, I. (1994). Measuring Competence-Exploring Firm Effects in Pharmaceutical Research. *Strategic Management Journal*.
79. **(263)** Gray, S. (1996). Modeling the Conditional Distribution of Interest Rates as a Regime-Switching Process. *Journal of Financial Economics*.
80. **(259)** Muthen, B., Kaplan, D., & Hollis, M. (1987). On Structural Equation Modeling with Data that Are Not Missing Completely at Random. *Psychometrika*.
81. **(259)** Ahuja, G. (2000b). The Duality of Collaboration: Inducements and Opportunities in the Formation of Interfirm Linkages. *Strategic Management Journal*.
82. **(256)** Cornwell, C., Schmidt, P., & Sickles, R. (1990). Production Frontiers with Cross-Sectional and Time-Series Variation in Efficiency Levels. *Journal of Econometrics*.
83. **(254)** Caves, D., Christensen, L., & Tretheway, M. (1984). Economies of Density Versus Economies of Scale: Why Trunk and Local-Service Airline Costs Differ? *Rand Journal of Economics*.
84. **(253)** Baillie, R., & Bollerslev, T. (1989). The Message in Daily Exchange Rates: A Conditional-Variance Tale. *Journal of Business & Economic Statistics*.
85. **(253)** Owen-Smith, J., & Powell, W. (2004). Knowledge Networks as Channels and Conduits: The Effects of Spillovers in the Boston Biotechnology Community. *Organization Science*.
86. **(251)** Cooley, T., & Leroy, S. (1985). Atheoretical Macroeconometrics: A Critique. *Journal of Monetary Economics*.
87. **(247)** Heckman, J., & Macurdy, T. (1980). A Life-Cycle Model of Female Labor Supply. *Review of Economic Studies*.
88. **(246)** Abowd, J., Kramarz, F., & Margolis, D. (1999). High Wage Workers and High Wage Firms. *Econometrica*.
89. **(244)** Hermalin, B., & Weisbach, M. (1991). The Effects of Board Composition and Direct Incentives on Firm Performance. *Financial Management*.
90. **(240)** Winship, C., & Mare, R. (1992). Models for Sample Selection Bias. *Annual Review of Sociology*.
91. **(240)** Sorensen, J., & Stuart, T. (2000). Aging, Obsolescence, and Organizational Innovation. *Administrative Science Quarterly*.

92. **(240)** Ahuja, G., & Lampert, C. (2001). Entrepreneurship in the Large Corporation: A Longitudinal Study of How Established Firms Create Breakthrough Inventions. *Strategic Management Journal.*
93. **(239)** Danziger, S., Haveman, R., & Plotnick, R. (1981). How Income Transfer Programs Affect Work, Savings, and the Income Distribution: A Critical Review. *Journal of Economic Literature.*
94. **(238)** Ait-Sahalia, Y. (1996). Testing Continuous-Time Models of the Spot Interest Rate. *Review of Financial Studies.*
95. **(237)** Evans, W, Oates, W., & Schwab, R. (1992). Measuring Peer Group Effects: A Study of Teenage Behavior. *Journal of Political Economy.*
96. **(235)** Cox, D. (1987). Motives for Private Income Transfers. *Journal of Political Economy.*
97. **(235)** Head, K., Ries, J., & Swenson, D. (1995). Agglomeration Benefits and Location Choice-Evidence from Japanese Manufacturing Investments in the United States. *Journal of International Economics.*
98. **(233)** Hsieh, D. (1991). Chaos and Nonlinear Dynamics: Application to Financial Markets. *Journal of Finance.*
99. **(232)** Lazear, E. (1990). Job Security Provisions and Employment. *Quarterly Journal of Economics.*
100. **(232)** Bauer, P. (1990). Recent Developments in the Econometric Estimation of Frontiers. *Journal of Econometrics.*
101. **(232)** Poole, K., & Rosenthal, H. (1991). Patterns of Congressional Voting. *American Journal of Political Science.*
102. **(232)** Zakoian, J. (1994). Threshold Heteroskedastic Models. *Journal of Economic Dynamics & Control.*
103. **(230)** Frenkel, J. (1981). Flexible Exchange Rates, Prices, and the Role of News: Lessons from the 1970s. *Journal of Political Economy.*
104. **(230)** Stern, D. (2004). The Rise and Fall of the Environmental Kuznets Curve. *World Development.*
105. **(228)** Zucker, L., Darby, M., & Armstrong, J. (1998). Geographically Localized Knowledge: Spillovers or Markets? *Economic Inquiry.*
106. **(226)** Butler, J., & Moffitt, R. (1982). A Computationally Efficient Quadrature Procedure for the One-Factor Multinomial Probit Model. *Econometrica.*
107. **(225)** Hermalin, B., & Weisbach, M. (1988). The Determinants of Board Composition. *Rand Journal of Economics.*
108. **(223)** Ashenfelter, O., & Krueger, A. (1994). Estimates of the Economic Return to Schooling from a New Sample of Twins. *American Economic Review.*

109. **(217)** Ahuja, G., & Katila, R. (2001). Technological Acquisitions and the Innovation Performance of Acquiring Firms: A Longitudinal Study. *Strategic Management Journal.*
110. **(216)** Willis, R., & Rosen, S. (1979). Education and Self-Selection. *Journal of Political Economy.*
111. **(216)** Hall, B. H., Jaffe, A., & Trajtenberg, M. (2005). Market Value and Patent Citations. *Rand Journal of Economics.*
112. **(215)** Fitzgerald, J., Gottschalk, P., & Moffitt, R. (1998). An Analysis of Sample Attrition in Panel Data: The Michigan Panel Study of Income Dynamic. *Journal of Human Resources.*
113. **(215)** Nevo, A. (2001). Measuring Market Power in the Ready-To-Eat Cereal Industry. *Econometrica.*
114. **(214)** Kogut, B., & Chang, S. J. (1991). Technological Capabilities and Japanese Foreign Direct Investment in the United States. *Review of Economics and Statistics.*
115. **(214)** Stuart, T. (1998). Network Positions and Propensities to Collaborate: An Investigation of Strategic Alliance Formation in a High-Technology Industry. *Administrative Science Quarterly.*
116. **(213)** Altonji, J., & Shakotko, R. (1987). Do Wages Rise With Job Seniority. *Review of Economic Studies.*
117. **(212)** Hitt, L, & Brynjolfsson, E. (1996). Productivity, Business Profitability, and Consumer Surplus: Three Different Measures of Information Technology Value. *MIS Quarterly.*
118. **(211)** Kormendi, R. (1983). Government Debt, Government Spending, and Private Sector Behavior. *American Economic Review.*
119. **(211)** Card, D. (2001). Estimating the Return to Schooling: Progress on Some Persistent Econometric Problems. *Econometrica.*
120. **(211)** Keller, W. (2004). International Technology Diffusion. *Journal of Economic Literature.*
121. **(209)** Vandeven, W., & Vanpraag, B. (1981). The Demand for Deductibles in Private Health Insurance: A Probit Model with Sample Selection. *Journal of Econometrics.*
122. **(208)** Pritchett, L., & Summers, L. (1996). Wealthier Is Healthier. *Journal of Human Resources.*
123. **(207)** Banks, J., Blundell, R., & Lewbel, A. (1997). Quadratic Engel Curves and Consumer Demand. *Review of Economics and Statistics.*
124. **(205)** Carlton, D. (1983). The Location and Employment Choices of New Firms: An Econometric Model with Discrete and Continuous Endogenous Variables. *Review of Economics and Statistics.*

125. **(205)** Cameron, A., & Trivedi, P. (1990). Regression-Based Tests for Overdispersion in the Poisson Model. *Journal of Econometrics*.
126. **(204)** Mizon, G., & Richard, J. (1986). The Encompassing Principle and Its Application to Testing Nonnested Hypotheses. *Econometrica*.
127. **(202)** Newey, W. (1985). Generalized Method of Moments Specification Testing. *Journal of Econometrics*.
128. **(202)** Newey, W., & West, K. (1987). Hypothesis Testing with Efficient Method of Moments Estimation. *International Economic Review*.
129. **(195)** Han, A., & Hausman, J. (1990). Flexible Parametric Estimation of Duration and Competing Risk Models. *Journal of Applied Econometrics*.
130. **(122)** Hausman, J. (1985). The Econometrics of Nonlinear Budget Sets. *Econometrica*.
131. **(110)** Hausman, J., & Wise, D. (1979). Attrition Bias in Experimental and Panel Data: The Gary Income Maintenance Experiment. *Econometrica*.
132. **(86)** Hausman, J, Abrevaya, J., & Scott-Morton, F. (1998). Misclassification of the Dependent Variable in a Discrete-Response Setting. *Journal of Econometrics*.
133. **(82)** Hausman, J., & Ruud, P. (1987). Specifying and Testing Econometric-Models for Rank-Ordered Data. *Journal of Econometrics*.
134. **(81)** Hausman, J., & Wise, D. (1977). Social Experimentation, Truncated Distributions, and Efficient Estimation. *Econometrica*.
135. **(77)** Hahn, J., & Hausman, J. (2002). A New Specification Test for the Validity of Instrumental Variables. *Econometrica*.
136. **(63)** Hausman, J., Newey, W., & Powell, J. (1995). Nonlinear Errors-in-Variables Estimation of Some Engel Curves. *Journal of Econometrics*.
137. **(58)** Hausman, J. (1975). Instrumental Variable Approach to Full Information Estimators for Linear and Certain Nonlinear Econometric Models. *Econometrica*.
138. **(52)** Hausman, J, & Newey, W. (1995). Nonparametric Estimation of Exact Consumers Surplus and Deadweight Loss. *Econometrica*.
139. **(43)** Hausman, J., Newey, W., Ichimura, H., & Powell, J. (1991). Identification and Estimation of Polynomial Errors-in-Variables Models. *Journal of Econometrics*.
140. **(42)** Hausman, J. (2001). Mismeasured Variables in Econometric Analysis: Problems from the Right and Problems from the Left. *Journal of Economic Perspectives*.
141. **(41)** Hahn, J. Y., & Hausman, J. (2003). Weak Instruments: Diagnosis and Cures in Empirical Econometrics. *American Economic Review*.

142. **(34)** Hausman, J. (1979). Econometrics of Labor Supply on Convex Budget Sets. *Economics Letters.*
143. **(24)** Hahn, J. Y., & Hausman, J. (2002). Notes on Bias in Estimators for Simultaneous Equation Models. *Economics Letters.*
144. **(24)** Hausman, J., Newey, W., & Taylor, W. (1987). Efficient Estimation and Identification of Simultaneous Equation Models with Covariance Restrictions. *Econometrica.*
145. **(17)** Hausman, J., & Taylor, W. (1983). Identification in Linear Simultaneous Equations Models with Covariance Restrictions: An Instrumental Variables Interpretation. *Econometrica.*
146. **(13)** Hausman, J., & Watson, M. (1985). Errors in Variables and Seasonal Adjustment Procedures. *Journal of the American Statistical Association.*
147. **(12)** Hausman, J. (1974). Full Information Instrumental Variables Estimation of Simultaneous Equations Systems. *Annals of Economic and Social Measurement.*
148. **(11)** Hausman, J., Stock, J., & Yogo, M. (2005). Asymptotic Properties of the Hahn-Hausman Test for Weak Instruments. *Economics Letters.*
149. **(7)** Harding, M., & Hausman, J. (2007). Using a Laplace Approximation to Estimate the Random Coefficients Logit Model by Nonlinear Least Squares. *International Economic Review.*
150. **(7)** Hahn, J., Hausman, J., & Kuersteiner, G. (2007). Long Difference Instrumental Variables Estimation for Dynamic Panel Models with Fixed Effects. *Journal of Econometrics.*
151. **(5)** Hausman, J. (2003). Commentary-Triangular Structural Model Specification and Estimation with Application to Causality. *Journal of Econometrics.*
152. **(4)** Burda, M., Harding, M., & Hausman, J. (2008). A Bayesian Mixed Logit-Probit Model for Multinomial Choice. *Journal of Econometrics.*
153. **(4)** Hausman, J., & Pesaran, H. (1983). The J-Test as a Hausman Specification Test. *Economics Letters.*
154. **(3)** Hausman, J., & Kuersteiner, G. (2008). Difference in Difference Meets Generalized Least Squares: Higher Order Properties of Hypotheses Tests. *Journal of Econometrics.*
155. **(2)** Hausman, J. (2001). Microeconometrics. *Journal of Econometrics,* 100(1), 33–35.
156. **(1)** Abrevaya, J., Hausman, J. A., & Khan, S. (2010). Testing for Causal Effects in a Generalized Regression Model with Endogenous Regressors. *Econometrica.*
157. **(1)** Hausman, J., Lewis, R., Menzel, K., & Newey, W. (2011). Properties of the Cue Estimator and a Modification with Moments. *Journal of Econometrics.*

PART I
ESTIMATION

COMBINING TWO CONSISTENT ESTIMATORS

John C. Chao, Jerry A. Hausman, Whitney K. Newey, Norman R. Swanson and Tiemen Woutersen

ABSTRACT

This chapter shows how a weighted average of a forward and reverse Jackknife IV estimator (JIVE) yields estimators that are robust against heteroscedasticity and many instruments. These estimators, called HFUL (Heteroscedasticity robust Fuller) and HLIM (Heteroskedasticity robust limited information maximum likelihood (LIML)) were introduced by Hausman, Newey, Woutersen, Chao, and Swanson (2012), but without derivation. Combining consistent estimators is a theme that is associated with Jerry Hausman and, therefore, we present this derivation in this volume. Additionally, and in order to further understand and interpret HFUL and HLIM in the context of jackknife type variance ratio estimators, we show that a new variant of HLIM, under specific grouped data settings with dummy instruments, simplifies to the Bekker and van der Ploeg (2005) MM (method of moments) estimator.

Essays in Honor of Jerry Hausman
Advances in Econometrics, Volume 29, 33–53

ISSN: 0731-9053/doi:10.1108/S0731-9053(2012)0000029007

Keywords: Endogeneity; instrumental variables; jackknife estimation; many moments; Hausman (1978) test

JEL classification: C13; C31

INTRODUCTION

One idea that is associated with Jerry Hausman is the idea of combining two estimators. For example, Hausman (1978) takes the difference between an efficient estimator and a robust estimator and derives the now famous Hausman test.[1] Another example is Hahn and Hausman (2002), who examine the difference between a forward and reverse Two Stage Least Squares (TSLS) estimator. This chapter shows how a weighted average of a forward and reverse Jackknife IV estimator (JIVE) yields estimators that are robust against heteroscedasticity and many instruments. These estimators, called HFUL and HLIM were introduced by Hausman, Newey, Woutersen, Chao, and Swanson (2012), but without derivation. Combining consistent estimators is a theme that is associated with Jerry Hausman and, therefore, we present this derivation in this volume.[2]

Jackknife IV estimators were proposed by Phillips and Hale (1977), Blomquist and Dahlberg (1999), Angrist, Imbens, and Krueger (1999), and Ackerberg and Deveraux (2009). In their paper " The Case Against JIVE," Davidson and MacKinnon (2006) show that JIVE performs poorly compared to LIML, due to the large dispersion of the JIVE. However, Chao, Swanson, Hausman, Newey, and Woutersen (2012) show that Jackknife IV (JIV) is consistent in a heteroscedastic and many instruments framework (unlike LIML). The HLIM and HFUL estimators discussed in this chapter have less dispersion than the JIV estimator.

In addition, another result of this chapter is that we show how modifying the numerator of the HLIM objective function yields a new estimator. In particular, we replace the numerator of the HLIM objective function with the objective function of so-called JIV1 estimator of Angrist et al. (1999) when forming our new estimator. In the special case that all instruments are dummy variables, this new estimator is the estimator proposed by Bekker and van der Ploeg (2005: BP). In closing, our recommendation is to use heteroskedasticity robust estimators. In this context, HFUL is particularly attractive because it is robust to many weak instruments and heteroskedasticity. In addition to these properties, it also has finite sample moments. Monte Carlo results supporting these findings are reported in Hausman et al. (2012).

In the remainder of this chapter we provide a setup (in section "The Model and Previous Estimators"), interpret HFUL as a combination estimator (in section "Combining Forward and Reverse JIVE"), and compare HFUL with other variance ratio type estimators, such as the MM estimator of BP (2005) in setion "Comparing Variants of HLIM and HFUL with the MM Estimator of Bekker and van der Ploeg."

DERIVING A HETEROSCEDASTICITY ROBUST ESTIMATOR

The Model and Previous Estimators

The model that we consider is given by

$$\underset{n\times 1}{y} = \underset{n\times G}{X}\,\underset{G\times 1}{\delta_0} + \underset{n\times 1}{\varepsilon}$$

$$X = \Upsilon + U$$

where n is the number of observations, G the number of right-hand side variables, Υ is a matrix of observations on the reduced form, and U is the matrix of reduced form disturbances. For our asymptotic approximations, the elements of Υ will be (implicitly) allowed to depend on n, although we suppress dependence of Υ on n for notational convenience. Estimation of δ_0 will be based on an $n \times K$ matrix, Z, of instrumental variable observations. We will assume that $Z_1,\ldots,Z_n$ are nonrandom and that observations (ε_i, U_i) are independent across i and have mean zero, where the Z_i denote the ith row (observation) of Z, ε_i is the ith element of ε, and U_i is the transpose of the ith row of U.

This model allows for Υ to be a linear combination of Z, that is, $\Upsilon = Z\pi$ for some $K \times G$ matrix π. Furthermore, columns of X may be exogenous, with the corresponding column of U being zero. The model also allows for Z to approximate the reduced form. For example, let X_i and Υ_i denote the ith row (observation) for X and Υ, respectively. We could have $\Upsilon_i = f_0(w_i)$ be an unknown function of a vector w_i of underlying instruments and $Z_i = (p_{1K}(w_i),\ldots,p_{KK}(w_i))'$ for approximating functions $p_{kK}(w)$, such as power series or splines, where $k = 1,\ldots,K$. In this case linear combinations of Z_i may approximate the unknown reduced form, for example, as in Donald and Newey (2001).

To describe previous estimators, let $P = Z(Z'Z)^{-1}Z'$. The LIML estimator $\tilde{\delta}^*$ is given by

$$\tilde{\delta}^* = \arg\min_{\delta} \hat{Q}^*(\delta), \hat{Q}^*(\delta) = \frac{(y-X\delta)'P(y-X\delta)}{(y-X\delta)'(y-X\delta)}$$

The Fuller (1977) estimator (FULL) is obtained as

$$\breve{\delta}^* = (X'PX - \breve{\alpha}^* X'X)^{-1}(X'Py - \breve{\alpha}^* X'y)$$

for $\breve{\alpha}^* = [\tilde{\alpha}^* - (1-\tilde{\alpha}^*)C/n]/[1-(1-\tilde{\alpha}^*)C/n]$ and $\tilde{\alpha}^* = \hat{Q}(\tilde{\delta}^*)$, for C a positive constant. Under homoscedasticity, FULL has moments of all orders, is approximately mean unbiased for $C=1$, and is second order admissible for $C \geq 4$ under standard large sample asymptotics.[3] Both LIML and FULL are members of a class of estimators of the form

$$\hat{\delta}^* = (X'PX - \hat{\alpha}^* X'X)^{-1}(X'Py - \hat{\alpha}^* X'y)$$

For example, LIML has this form for $\hat{\alpha}^* = \tilde{\alpha}^*$, FULL for $\hat{\alpha}^* = \breve{\alpha}^*$, and 2SLS for $\hat{\alpha}^* = 0$.

We use Fisher consistency to characterize the problem with heteroskedasticity and many instruments. Fisher consistency means that the derivative of the objective function at the truth converges to zero when normalized correctly. This condition is necessary for consistency. For expository purposes, consider first 2SLS, having objective function $(y-X\delta)'P(y-X\delta)$. The derivative of this objective function, times $-1/2n$, is equal to $X'P\varepsilon/n$. Like means, quadratic forms converge to their expectations under appropriate conditions. By virtue of independence and $E[\varepsilon_i] = 0$ we have

$$E[X_i P_{ij} \varepsilon_j] = E[X_i] P_{ij} E[\varepsilon_j] = 0, i \neq j$$

where P_{ij} is the ij^{th} element of the projection matrix P. Thus,

$$\begin{aligned}\frac{1}{n}X'P\varepsilon &= \frac{1}{n}E[X'P\varepsilon] + o_p(1) = \frac{1}{n}\sum_{i,j=1}^{n} E[X_i P_{ij}\varepsilon_j] + o_p(1) \\ &= \frac{1}{n}\sum_{i=1}^{n} E[X_i P_{ii}\varepsilon_i] + o_p(1) = \frac{1}{n}\sum_{i=1}^{n} E[U_i\varepsilon_i]P_{ii} + o_p(1)\end{aligned}$$

so the Fisher consistency condition is $\sum_{i=1}^{n} E[U_i \varepsilon_i] P_{ii}/n \to 0$. Because of many instruments,

$$P_{ii} \nrightarrow 0$$

and hence 2SLS is not consistent, even under homoscedasticity, where $E[U_i\varepsilon_i]$ is constant over i. (Refer to Bekker, 1994, for further details.)

For LIML, with objective function $\hat{Q}^*(\delta)$ given above, we have

$$(-\varepsilon'\varepsilon/2n)\partial\hat{Q}^*(\delta_0)/\partial\delta = \frac{1}{n}\left(X - \frac{X'\varepsilon}{\varepsilon'\varepsilon}\varepsilon\right)' P\varepsilon = \frac{1}{n}(X - \varepsilon\hat{\gamma}')'P\varepsilon, \hat{\gamma} = X'\varepsilon/\varepsilon'\varepsilon$$

Let $\sigma_i^2 = E[\varepsilon_i^2], \gamma_i = E[X_i\varepsilon_i]/\sigma_i^2 = E[U_i\varepsilon_i]/\sigma_i^2$, and $\gamma^{(n)} = \sum_i E[X_i\varepsilon_i]/\sum_i \sigma_i^2 = \sum_i \sigma_i^2\gamma_i/\sum_i\sigma_i^2$. By standard arguments $X'\varepsilon/\varepsilon'\varepsilon - \gamma^{(n)} \xrightarrow{p} 0$ and $\varepsilon'P\varepsilon/n$ is bounded in probability. Thus, similar to 2SLS,

$$\begin{aligned}\frac{1}{n}(X - \varepsilon\hat{\gamma}')'P\varepsilon &= \frac{1}{n}(X - \varepsilon\gamma^{(n)'})'P\varepsilon + o_p(1) = \frac{1}{n}E[(X - \varepsilon\gamma^{(n)})'P\varepsilon] + o_p(1)\\ &= \sum_{i=1}^{n} E[(X_i - \gamma^{(n)}\varepsilon_i)P_{ii}\varepsilon_i]/n + o_p(1) = \sum_{i=1}^{n}(\gamma_i - \gamma^{(n)})P_{ii}\sigma_i^2/n + o_p(1)\end{aligned}$$

It follows that, for LIML, the Fisher consistency condition is

$$\frac{1}{n}\sum_{i=1}^{n}(\gamma_i - \gamma^{(n)})P_{ii}\sigma_i^2 \to 0.$$

There are two interesting cases where this condition holds.

(A) γ_i does not vary with i : In this case, $\gamma_i = \gamma^{(n)}$ so that the term on the left is identically zero. Thus, homoscedasticity in the coefficient $\gamma_i = E[X_i\varepsilon_i]/E[\varepsilon_i^2]$ of the regression of X_i on ε_i leads to Fisher consistency of LIML.

(B) P_{ii} does not vary with i : In this case $\sum_i(\gamma_i - \gamma^{(n)})P_{ii}\sigma_i^2 = P_{11}\sum_i(\gamma_i - \gamma^{(n)})\sigma_i^2 = 0$. When the instruments are dummy variables, sometimes referred to as grouping instruments, this condition is satisfied if all of the columns of Z have the same number of ones, i.e. the group sizes are equal. Bekker and van der Ploeg (2005) showed that this condition gives consistency of LIML for grouping instruments.[4]

In the general heteroscedastic case where γ_i and $P_{ii}\sigma_i^2$ are correlated across i, the Fisher consistency condition will not be satisfied and so LIML will not be consistent. Furthermore, due to weak instruments the bias may be large even when $\sum_i(\gamma_i - \gamma^{(n)})P_{ii}\sigma_i^2/n$ is small. Analogous arguments can also be used to show that, with heteroskedasticity, FULL and LIML are inconsistent under many instruments. BP (2005) and Hausman et al. (2012) point out that LIML can be inconsistent with heteroskedasticity but this appears to be the first characterization of Fisher consistency of LIML.

The lack of consistency of these estimators under many instruments and heteroskedasticity can be attributed to the presence of the $i=j$ terms in the double sums in their first order conditions. One way to make the estimators robust to heteroskedasticity is to remove these terms. A version, $\bar{\delta}$, of 2SLS without the $i=j$ terms solves the normal equations

$$0 = X'P(y-X\bar{\delta}) - \sum_{i=1}^{n} P_{ii}X_i(y_i - X'_i\bar{\delta}) = \sum_{i\neq j} X_i P_{ij}(y_j - X'_j\bar{\delta})$$

Solving for $\bar{\delta}$ gives

$$\bar{\delta} = \left(\sum_{i\neq j} X_i P_{ij} X'_j\right)^{-1} \sum_{i\neq j} X_i P_{ij} y_j = \left(X'PX - \sum_{i=1}^{n} P_{ii}X_i X'_i\right)^{-1}\left(X'Py - \sum_{i=1}^{n} P_{ii}X_i y_i\right)$$

This is the second JIV estimator (JIV2) of Angrist et al. (1999). Because the normal equations remove the $i=j$ terms, this estimator is Fisher consistent. It was pointed out by Ackerberg and Deveraux (2009) and Chao et al. (2012) that it is consistent under many weak instruments and heteroskedasticity.

Under homoscedasticity and many weak instruments this estimator turns out to not be efficient. Also, Davidson and MacKinnon (2005) argue that it has inferior small sample properties under homoscedasticity, when compared with LIML. Using the weighted average of forward and reverse JIVE overcomes these problems.

Combining Forward and Reverse JIVE

The heteroskedasticity robust LIML estimator (HLIM) is obtained by dropping $i=j$ terms from the numerator of the LIML objective function,

$$\tilde{\delta} = \arg\min_{\delta} \hat{Q}(\delta), \hat{Q}(\delta) = \frac{\sum_{i\neq j}(y_i - X'_i\delta)P_{ij}(y_j - X'_j\delta)}{(y-X\delta)'(y-X\delta)}$$

Similar to JIV, $\tilde{\delta}$ will be consistent under heteroskedasticity because the $i=j$ terms have been removed from the normal equations. Here we will show consistency, asymptotic normality, and consistency of an asymptotic variance estimator.

As is the case with LIML, this estimator is invariant to normalization. Let $\bar{X} = [y, X]$. Then $\tilde{d} = (1, -\tilde{\delta}')'$ solves

$$\min_{d:d_1=1} \frac{d'\left(\sum_{i\neq j} \bar{X}_i P_{ij} \bar{X}'_j\right)d}{d'\bar{X}'\bar{X}d}$$

Another normalization, such as imposing that another d is equal to 1 would produce the same estimator, up to the normalization.

Also, computation of this estimator is straightforward. Similarly to LIML, $\tilde{\alpha} = \hat{Q}(\tilde{\delta})$ is the smallest eigenvalue of $(\bar{X}'\bar{X})^{-1}\sum_{i\neq j}\bar{X}_i P_{ij}\bar{X}'_j$. Also, first order conditions for $\tilde{\delta}$ are

$$0 = \sum_{i\neq j} X_i P_{ij}(y_j - X'_j\tilde{\delta}) - \tilde{\alpha}\sum_i X_i(y_i - X'_i\tilde{\delta})$$

Solving gives

$$\tilde{\delta} = \left(\sum_{i\neq j} X_i P_{ij} X'_j - \tilde{\alpha}X'X\right)^{-1}\left(\sum_{i\neq j} X_i P_{ij} y_j - \tilde{\alpha}X'y\right)$$

This HLIM estimator has a similar form to LIML except that the $i = j$ terms have been deleted from the double sums.

It is interesting to note that LIML and HLIM coincide when P_{ii} is constant. In that case,

$$\hat{Q}^*(\delta) = \hat{Q}(\delta) + \frac{\sum_i (y_i - X'_i\delta)P_{ii}(y_i - X'_i\delta)}{(y - X\delta)'(y - X\delta)} = \hat{Q}(\delta) + P_{11}$$

so that the LIML objective function equals the HLIM objective function plus a constant. This explains why constant P_{ii} will lead to LIML being consistent under heteroskedasticity.

By replacing $\tilde{\alpha}$ with some other value $\hat{\alpha}$ we can form a k-class version of a jackknife estimator, having the form

$$\hat{\delta} = \left(\sum_{i\neq j} X_i P_{ij} X'_j - \hat{\alpha}X'X\right)^{-1}\left(\sum_{i\neq j} X_i P_{ij} y_j - \hat{\alpha}X'y\right)$$

The JIV2 estimator of Angrist et al. (1999) is obtained by setting $\hat{\alpha} = 0$. Now, as shown in Hausman et al. (2012), under homoscedasticity and many weak instruments, HLIM is more efficient than JIV2. Moreover, we conjecture that HLIM is more efficient than any other estimator in this class, under homoscedasticity and many weak instruments. A heteroskedasticity consistent version of FULL is obtained by replacing $\tilde{\alpha}$ with $\hat{\alpha} = [\tilde{\alpha} - (1-\tilde{\alpha})C/n]/[1-(1-\tilde{\alpha})C/n]$, where C is a positive constant. The small sample properties of this estimator are unknown, but we expect its performance relative to HLIM to be similar to that of FULL relative to LIML. As pointed out by Hahn, Hausman and Kuersteiner (2004), FULL has much smaller dispersion than LIML with weak instruments, so we expect the same for HFUL. Monte Carlo results given in Hausman, Hausman and Kuersteiner (2012) confirm these properties.

An asymptotic variance estimator is useful for constructing large sample confidence intervals and tests. To describe it, let $\hat{\varepsilon}_i = y_i - X'_i\hat{\delta}$, $\hat{\gamma} = X'\hat{\varepsilon}/\hat{\varepsilon}'\hat{\varepsilon}$, $\hat{X} = X - \hat{\varepsilon}\hat{\gamma}'$

$$\hat{H} = \sum_{i \neq j} X_i P_{ij} X'_j - \hat{\alpha} X'X, \hat{\Sigma} = \sum_{i,j=1}^{n} \sum_{k \notin \{i,j\}} \hat{X}_i P_{ik} \hat{\varepsilon}_k^2 P_{kj} \hat{X}'_j + \sum_{i \neq j} P_{ij}^2 \hat{X}_i \hat{\varepsilon}_i \hat{\varepsilon}_j \hat{X}'_j$$

The variance estimator is

$$\hat{V} = \hat{H}^{-1} \hat{\Sigma} \hat{H}^{-1}$$

We can interpret the HLIM estimator $\tilde{\delta}$ as a combination of forward and reverse jackknife IV (JIV) estimators. For simplicity, we give this interpretation in the scalar δ case. Let $\tilde{\varepsilon}_i = y_i - X'_i\tilde{\delta}$ and $\tilde{\gamma} = \sum_i X_i \tilde{\varepsilon}_i / \sum_i \tilde{\varepsilon}_i^2$. First-order conditions for $\tilde{\delta}$ are

$$0 = -\frac{\partial \hat{Q}(\tilde{\delta})}{\partial \delta} \sum_i \tilde{\varepsilon}_i^2 / 2 = \sum_{i \neq j} (X_i - \tilde{\gamma}\tilde{\varepsilon}_i) P_{ij} (y_j - X'_j \tilde{\delta}) = \sum_{i \neq j} [(1 + \tilde{\gamma}\tilde{\delta}) X_i - \tilde{\gamma} y_i] P_{ij} (y_j - X'_j \tilde{\delta})$$

The forward JIV estimator $\bar{\delta}$ is

$$\bar{\delta} = \left(\sum_{i \neq j} X_i P_{ij} X_j \right)^{-1} \sum_{i \neq j} X_i P_{ij} y_j$$

The reverse JIV is obtained as follows. Dividing the structural equation by δ_0 gives

$$X_i = y_i / \delta_0 - \varepsilon_i / \delta_0$$

Applying JIV to this equation to estimate $1/\delta_0$ and then inverting gives the reverse JIV

$$\bar{\delta}^r = \left(\sum_{i\neq j} y_i P_{ij} X_j\right)^{-1} \sum_{i\neq j} y_i P_{ij} y_j$$

Collecting terms in the first-order conditions for HLIM gives

$$\begin{aligned} 0 &= (1+\tilde{\gamma}\tilde{\delta})\sum_{i\neq j} X_i P_{ij}(y_j - X'_j\tilde{\delta}) - \tilde{\gamma}\sum_{i\neq j} y_i P_{ij}(y_j - X_j\tilde{\delta}) \\ &= (1+\tilde{\gamma}\tilde{\delta})\sum_{i\neq j} X_i P_{ij} X_j(\bar{\delta} - \tilde{\delta}) - \tilde{\gamma}\sum_{i\neq j} y_i P_{ij} X_j(\bar{\delta}^r - \tilde{\delta}) \end{aligned}$$

Dividing through by $\sum_{i\neq j} X_i P_{ij} X_j$ gives

$$0 = (1+\tilde{\gamma}\tilde{\delta})(\bar{\delta} - \tilde{\delta}) - \tilde{\gamma}\tilde{\delta}(\bar{\delta}^r - \tilde{\delta}) \tag{1}$$

Now, let δ_0 be the true value of δ, and define

$$\gamma^* = \sum_{i=1}^{n} E[X_i\varepsilon_i] / \sum_i E[\varepsilon_i^2]$$

Note that as $n \to \infty$, $\tilde{\delta} \xrightarrow{p} \delta_0$ and $\tilde{\gamma} - \gamma^* \xrightarrow{p} 0$; and, hence, expression (1) implies that

$$o_p(1) = (1+\gamma^*\delta_0)(\bar{\delta} - \tilde{\delta}) - \gamma^*\delta_0(\bar{\delta}^r - \tilde{\delta})$$

Rewriting the above equation, we obtain

$$\tilde{\delta} = (1+\gamma^*\delta_0)\bar{\delta} - \gamma^*\delta_0\bar{\delta}^r + o_p(1) \tag{2}$$

which shows that, at least for n large, $\tilde{\delta}$ can be written as a linear combination of forward and reverse JIV estimators. Moreover, if we were to assume error homoskedasticity, then it can be shown that under many weak instrument asymptotics that for $\delta_0 \neq 0$,

$$Var(\bar{\delta}^r) - Var(\bar{\delta}) = 2\frac{\sigma_{\varepsilon\varepsilon}^2}{\delta_0^2}\left(1 + 2\frac{\sigma_{X\varepsilon}}{\sigma_{\varepsilon\varepsilon}}\delta_0\right) = \frac{\sigma_{\varepsilon\varepsilon}^2}{\delta_0^2}\left(\frac{1}{2} + \gamma^*\delta_0\right)$$

where $Var(\bar{\delta})$ and $Var(\bar{\delta}^r)$ denote the variances of the (many-weak-instrument) limiting distribution of $\bar{\delta}$ and of $\bar{\delta}^r$, respectively, and where, to simplify notations, we have let $\sigma_{\varepsilon\varepsilon} = E[\varepsilon_i^2]$ and $\sigma_{X\varepsilon} = E[X_i\varepsilon_i]$. It follows that $\bar{\delta}^r$ and $\bar{\delta}$ are equally efficient, i.e., $Var(\bar{\delta}^r) = Var(\bar{\delta})$, if and only if

$$\gamma^*\delta_0 + \frac{1}{2} = 0$$

Now, define $\theta = \gamma^{*}\delta_0 + (1/2)$, and we can rewrite Eq. (1) as

$$\tilde{\delta} = \left(\theta + \frac{1}{2}\right)\bar{\delta} - \left(\theta - \frac{1}{2}\right)\bar{\delta}^{r} + o_p(1) \tag{3}$$

Note that expression (3) shows that $\tilde{\delta}$ puts equal weight of 1/2 on both $\bar{\delta}$ and $\bar{\delta}^{r}$ when they are equally efficient but puts more weight on $\bar{\delta}$ when $\theta > 0$ (i.e., when the forward JIV is more efficient) and put more weight on $\bar{\delta}^{r}$ when $\theta < 0$ (i.e., when the reverse JIV is more efficient). This result is analogous to that of Hahn and Hausman (2002) where under homoscedasticity LIML is shown to be an optimal combination of forward and reverse bias corrected two stage least squares estimators.

Finally, if we replace $\tilde{\gamma}$ in Eq. (1) above by some other estimator $\bar{\gamma}$ and the $\tilde{\gamma}\bar{\delta}$ coefficient following the minus sign by $\bar{\gamma}\tilde{\delta}$ we obtain a linearized version of this equation that can be solved for $\hat{\delta}$ to obtain

$$\dot{\delta} = \frac{\bar{\delta}}{1 - \bar{\gamma}(\bar{\delta} - \bar{\delta}_r)}$$

This estimator will be asymptotically equivalent to the HLIM and the HFUL estimator.

Comparing Variants of HLIM and HFUL with the MM Estimator of Bekker and van der Ploeg

BP (2005) considered estimators that are consistent with dummy instruments and group heteroskedasticity. A particular interesting estimator which BP (2005) propose is referred to as the MM estimator. It turns out that this MM estimator is a special case of a type of jackknifed LIML estimator, where the numerator quadratic form corresponds to the objective function of JIV1 instead of that of JIV2 (as in HLIM). More specifically, consider an estimator which minimizes the following modified variance ratio

$$\begin{aligned} Q_{JLIM}(\delta) &= \frac{(y - X\delta)'(P - D_P)(I_n - D_P)^{-1}(y - X\delta)}{(y - X\delta)' M D_P (I_n - D_P)^{-1}(y - X\delta)} \\ &= \frac{Q_{JIV1}(\delta)}{(y - X\delta)' M D_P (I_n - D_P)^{-1}(y - X\delta)} \end{aligned} \tag{4}$$

where $M = I_n - P$ and $D_P = diag(P_{11}, \ldots, P_{nn})$. Note that the numerator of (4) is simply the objective function of JIV1, since minimizing $Q_{JIV1}(\delta)$ with respect to δ leads to the estimator

$$\hat{\delta}_{JIV1} = (X'(P-D_P)(I_n-D_P)^{-1}X)^{-1}X'(P-D_P)(I_n-D_P)^{-1}y$$
$$= \left(\sum_{i\neq j} X_i P_{ij}(1-P_{jj})^{-1}X'_j\right)^{-1} \sum_{i\neq j} X_i P_{ij}(1-P_{jj})^{-1}y_j$$

which is the jackknife IV estimator originally proposed by Phillips and Hale (1977). See Chao et al. (2012) for further discussion.

It is also possible to rewrite the objective function (4) in an alternative form which will be more convenient for the purpose of establishing a correspondence with the results of BP (2005). To proceed, note first that, by elementary algebraic manipulations, it is easy to show that

$$(P-D_P)(I_n-D_P)^{-1} = P-MD_P(I_n-D_P)^{-1}$$

Hence, we can rewrite Eq. (4) as

$$\begin{aligned} Q_{JLIM}(\delta) &= \frac{(y-X\delta)'[P-MD_P(I_n-D_P)^{-1}](y-X\delta)}{(y-X\delta)'MD_P(I_n-D_P)^{-1}(y-X\delta)} \\ &= \frac{(y-X\delta)'P(y-X\delta)}{(y-X\delta)'MD_P(I_n-D_P)^{-1}(y-X\delta)} - 1 \\ &= Q^*_{JLIM}(\delta) - 1 \end{aligned}$$

so that the estimator which minimizes $Q_{JLIM}(\delta)$ is clearly the same as the one which minimizes

$$Q^*_{JLIM}(\delta) = \frac{(y-X\delta)'P(y-X\delta)}{(y-X\delta)'MD_P(I_n-D_P)^{-1}(y-X\delta)} \tag{5}$$

To show that the estimator obtained from Eq.(5) specializes to the MM estimator of BP (2005) with dummy-variable instruments and across-group heteroskedasticity, consider the grouped data IV regression model studied in their paper, which takes the form

$$y_{ij} = x'_{ij}\delta + \varepsilon_{ij}$$

$$x_{ij} = \pi_j + v_{ij}$$

for $i = 1, \ldots, n_j$ and $j = 1, \ldots, m$. Stacking first the observations within each group, we obtain (for $j = 1, \ldots, m$)

$$y_j = \begin{pmatrix} y_{1j} \\ y_{2j} \\ \vdots \\ y_{n_j,j} \end{pmatrix}, X_j = \begin{pmatrix} x'_{1j} \\ x'_{2j} \\ \vdots \\ x'_{n_j,j} \end{pmatrix}, \varepsilon_j = \begin{pmatrix} \varepsilon_{1j} \\ \varepsilon_{2j} \\ \vdots \\ \varepsilon_{n_j,j} \end{pmatrix}, V_j = \begin{pmatrix} v'_{1j} \\ v'_{2j} \\ \vdots \\ v'_{n_j,j} \end{pmatrix}$$

and also let

$$Z_j = \iota_{n_j} e'_{j,m}$$

where $\iota_{n_j} = (1, 1, \ldots, 1)'$ is an $(n_j \times 1)$ vector of ones and $e_{j,m}$ is the jth column of a $m \times m$ identity matrix. Using these notations, it is easily seen that the IV model studied in BP (2005) can be written in our notations as

$$y = X\delta + \varepsilon \tag{6}$$

$$X = Z\Pi + V \tag{7}$$

where $y = (y'_1, y'_2, \ldots, y'_m)'$, $X = (X'_1, X'_2, \ldots, X'_m)'$, $Z = (Z'_1, Z'_2, \ldots, Z'_m)'$, $\Pi = (\pi_1, \pi_2, \ldots, \pi_m)'$, $\varepsilon = (\varepsilon'_1, \varepsilon'_2, \ldots, \varepsilon'_m)'$, and $V = (V'_1, V'_2, \ldots, V'_m)'$ with the components of these vectors and matrices being as defined above. Moreover, with dummy-variable instruments as considered in BP (2005), we have

$$\begin{aligned} P &= Z(Z'Z)^{-1}Z' \\ &= \begin{pmatrix} n_1^{-1}\iota_{n_1}\iota'_{n1} & 0 & \cdots & 0 \\ 0 & n_2^{-1}\iota_{n_2}\iota'_{n2} & \ddots & \vdots \\ \vdots & \ddots & \ddots & 0 \\ 0 & \cdots & 0 & n_m^{-1}\iota_{n_m}\iota'_{nm} \end{pmatrix} = \begin{pmatrix} P_1 & 0 & \cdots & 0 \\ 0 & P_2 & \ddots & \vdots \\ \vdots & \ddots & \ddots & 0 \\ 0 & \cdots & 0 & P_m \end{pmatrix} \end{aligned}$$

$$D_P = \begin{pmatrix} n_1^{-1} I_{n_1} & 0 & \cdots & 0 \\ 0 & n_2^{-1} I_{n_2} & \ddots & \vdots \\ \vdots & \ddots & \ddots & 0 \\ 0 & \cdots & 0 & n_m^{-1} I_{n_m} \end{pmatrix}$$

and

$$M = I_n - P = \begin{pmatrix} M_1 & 0 & \cdots & 0 \\ 0 & M_2 & \ddots & \vdots \\ \vdots & \ddots & \ddots & 0 \\ 0 & \cdots & 0 & M_m \end{pmatrix}$$

where $n = \sum_{j=1}^{m} n_j$. Hence, in this setting, (5) specializes to the MM objective function given in equation (13) of BP (2005). Namely,

$$\begin{aligned} Q^*_{JLIM}(\delta) &= \frac{(y - X\delta)' P (y - X\delta)}{(y - X\delta)' M D_P (I_n - D_P)^{-1} (y - X\delta)} \\ &= \frac{\sum_{j=1}^{m} (y_j - X_j\delta)' P_j (y_j - X_j\delta)}{\sum_{j=1}^{m} (y_j - X_j\delta)' [n_j^{-1}/(1 - n_j^{-1})] M_j (y_j - X_j\delta)} \\ &= \frac{\sum_{j=1}^{m} (y_j - X_j\delta)' P_j (y_j - X_j\delta)}{\sum_{j=1}^{m} (y_j - X_j\delta)' (n_j - 1)^{-1} M_j (y_j - X_j\delta)} \\ &= \frac{n \sum_{j=1}^{m} \delta'_{\Delta} w_j \bar{Y}_j \bar{Y}'_j \delta_{\Delta}}{\sum_{j=1}^{m} \delta'_{\Delta} S_j \delta_{\Delta}} \\ &= n Q_{MM}(\delta) \end{aligned} \tag{8}$$

where $\delta_{\Delta} = (1, -\delta')'$, $w_j = n_j / \sum_{j=1}^{m} n_j = n_j / n$

$$\bar{Y}_j = \tfrac{1}{n_j} \sum_{i=1}^{n_j} (y_{ij}, x'_{ij})'$$

$$S_j = \tfrac{1}{n_j - 1} \sum_{i=1}^{n_j} \left(\begin{pmatrix} y_{ij} \\ x_{ij} \end{pmatrix} - \bar{Y}_j \right) \left(\begin{pmatrix} y_{ij} \\ x_{ij} \end{pmatrix} - \bar{Y}_j \right)'$$

as defined in their paper. Note a slight difference in our notations and that of BP (2005) in that we set

$$M_j = I_{n_j} - P_j = I_{n_j} - n_j^{-1} \iota_{n_j} \iota'_{n_j}$$

here, whereas

$$M_j = w_j \bar{Y}_j \bar{Y}'_j$$

in the notations of BP (2005).

Now, given that the numerator of Eq. (4) corresponds to the objective function of JIV1, we can show, following arguments similar to that used for proving Theorems 1 and 2 of Hausman et al. (2012), that the estimator which minimizes $Q_{JLIM}(\delta)$ is consistent and asymptotically normal under many instrument and many weak instrument asymptotics. Indeed, in the special case with dummy instruments and across-group heteroskedasticity, BP (2005) have already shown that the MM estimator is consistent and asymptotically normal under group-asymptotics which takes $m \to \infty$ holding each n_j fixed, for $j = 1, \ldots m$. However, it should be noted that the MM estimator will not in general be consistent under group asymptotics in the presence of more general instruments which are not group indicators. To analyze more fully situations where the MM estimator may or may not be consistent, we consider the following slight generalization of the setup studied in BP (2005). Namely, consider

$$y_{ij} = x'_{ij}\delta + \varepsilon_{ij}$$

$$\underset{G\times 1}{x_{ij}} = \underset{1\times 1}{z_{ij}} \; \underset{G\times 1}{\pi_j} + \underset{G\times 1}{v_{ij}}$$

for $j = 1, \ldots, m$ and $i = 1, \ldots, n_j$, so that we allow for instruments which are possibly not group indicators. Now, from the previous discussion, it is apparent that the MM estimator can be equivalently obtained by minimizing the alternative objective function

$$Q^*_{MM}(\delta) = \frac{\sum_{j=1}^{m} (y_j - X_j\delta)'[P_j - (n_j - 1)^{-1} M_j](y_j - X_j\delta)}{\sum_{j=1}^{m} (y_j - X_j\delta)'(n_j - 1)^{-1} M_j (y_j - X_j\delta)}$$

where $P_j = z_{\cdot j}(z'_{\cdot j} z_{\cdot j})^{-1} z'_{move\cdot j}$ with $z_{\cdot j} = \left(z_{1j}, z_{2j}, .., z_{n_j j}\right)'$ and $M_j = I_{n_j} - P_j$. All other notations are as defined previously. Now, in large samples, this objective function will be close to

$$\bar{Q}_{MM}(\delta) = \frac{\sum_{j=1}^{m} E\{(y_j - X_j\delta)'[P_j - (n_j-1)^{-1}M_j](y_j - X_j\delta)\}}{\sum_{j=1}^{m} E\{(y_j - X_j\delta)'(n_j-1)^{-1}M_j(y_j - X_j\delta)\}}$$

To gain some insight into conditions under which the limiting objective function $\bar{Q}_{MM}(\delta)$ may be minimized at $\delta = \delta_0$, we define $P_{j,ii}$ to be the ith diagonal element of P_j and let

$$\sigma^2(i,j) = E[\varepsilon_{ij}^2], \vartheta(i,j) = E[x_{ij}\varepsilon_{ij}], \varpi(i,j) = \tfrac{1}{n_j-1}(1 - P_{j,ii})$$

$$W(i,j) = \tfrac{P_{j,ii} - \varpi(i,j)}{\varpi(i,j)}, \pi(i,j) = \tfrac{\varpi(i,j)}{m}$$

Note that, by straightforward calculations, we obtain

$$\begin{aligned}
&\frac{\partial}{\partial\delta}\bar{Q}_{MM}(\delta)\Big|_{\delta=\delta_0} \\
&= \frac{-2\sum_{j=1}^{m} E(X'_j[P_j - (n_j-1)^{-1}M_j]\varepsilon_j)}{\sum_{j=1}^{m}(n_j-1)^{-1}E(\varepsilon'_jM_j\varepsilon_j)} \\
&\quad + 2\frac{\sum_{j=1}^{m} E(\varepsilon'_j[P_j - (n_j-1)^{-1}M_j]\varepsilon_j)}{\left[\sum_{j=1}^{m}(n_j - 1^{-1})E(\varepsilon'_jM_j\varepsilon_j)\right]^2}\sum_{j=1}^{m}\left(\frac{1}{n_j-1}\right)E(X'_jM_j\varepsilon_j) \\
&= \frac{-2}{\sum_{j=1}^{m}\sum_{i=1}^{n_j}\sigma^2(i,j)\pi(i,j)}\left\{\sum_{j=1}^{m}\sum_{i=1}^{n_j}W(i,j)\left(\vartheta(i,j) - \sigma^2(i,j)\frac{\sum_{j=1}^{m}\sum_{i=1}^{n_j}\vartheta(i,j)\pi(i,j)}{\sum_{j=1}^{m}\sum_{i=1}^{n_j}\sigma^2(i,j)\pi(i,j)}\right)\pi(i,j)\right\} \\
&= -2(\hat{E}[\sigma^2(i,j)])^{-1}\hat{E}\left[W(i,j)\left\{\vartheta(i,j) - \frac{\hat{E}[\vartheta(i,j)]}{\hat{E}[\sigma^2(i,j)]}\sigma^2(i,j)\right\}\right] \\
&= -2(\hat{E}[\sigma^2(i,j)])^{-1}\hat{E}[W(i,j)\psi(i,j)]
\end{aligned} \tag{9}$$

where, in the expressions above, we have taken

$$\hat{E}[\vartheta(i,j)] = \sum_{j=1}^{m}\sum_{i=1}^{n_j}\vartheta(i,j)\pi(i,j), \quad \hat{E}[\sigma^2(i,j)] = \sum_{j=1}^{m}\sum_{i=1}^{n_j}\sigma^2(i,j)\pi(i,j)$$

$$\psi(i,j) = \vartheta(i,j) - \tfrac{\hat{E}[\vartheta(i,j)]}{\hat{E}[\sigma^2(i,j)]}\sigma^2(i,j), \quad \hat{E}[W(i,j)\psi(i,j)] = \sum_{j=1}^{m}\sum_{i=1}^{n_j}W(i,j)\psi(i,j)\pi(i,j)$$

Now, we can interpret $W(i,j)$, $\sigma^2(i,j)$, and $\psi(i,j)$ as functions of the discrete random variables (indices) i and j, which have joint probability mass distribution (pmf) given by $\pi(i,j)$. Moreover, interpret

$$\pi(j) = \sum_{i=1}^{n_j} \pi(i,j) = \sum_{i=1}^{n_j} \frac{\varpi(i,j)}{m} = \frac{1}{m}\sum_{i=1}^{n_j} \frac{1}{n_j-1}(1-P_{j,ii}) = \frac{1}{m}$$

as the marginal pmf of j and define

$$\pi(i|\ j) = \frac{\pi(i,j)}{\pi(j)} = \varpi(i.j)$$

to be the conditional pmf of i given j. Furthermore, observe that

$$\hat{E}[W(i,j)|j] = \sum_{i=1}^{n_j} W(i,j)\pi(i|j) = \sum_{i=1}^{n_j}[P_{j,ii}-(n_j-1)^{-1}(1-P_{j,ii})] = 0$$
$$\hat{E}[W(i,j)] = \hat{E}[\hat{E}[W(i,j)|j]] = 0 \text{ (by law of iterated expectations)}$$

so that, in particular,

$$\hat{E}[W(i,j)\psi(i,j)] = \widehat{Cov}(W(i,j),\ \psi(i,j)) + \hat{E}[W(i,j)]\hat{E}[\psi(i,j)] = \widehat{Cov}(W(i,j), \psi(i,j))$$

Hence, we can rewrite Eq. (9) as

$$\frac{\partial}{\partial\delta}\bar{Q}_{MM}(\delta)\bigg|_{\delta=\delta_0} = -2(\hat{E}[\sigma^2(i,j)])^{-1}\widehat{Cov}(W(i,j), \psi(i,j)) \tag{10}$$

from which it follows that $\delta = \delta_0$ is a critical point of $\bar{Q}_{MM}(\delta)$ if and only if

$$\widehat{Cov}(W(i,j), \psi(i,j)) = 0$$

since

$$\widehat{E}[\sigma^2(i,j)] = \sum_{j=1}^{m}\sum_{i=1}^{n_j} \sigma^2(i,j)\pi(i,j) \leq C\sum_{j=1}^{m}\sum_{i=1}^{n_j} \pi(i,j) = C<\infty$$

holds under a condition that the second moments of $\{\varepsilon_{ij}\}$ are uniformly bounded.

Next, consider the situation where error variance is homoskedastic within-group, but there may be heteroskedasticity across groups, i.e., for each $j, \sigma^2(i,j) = \sigma^2(j)$ and $\vartheta(i,j) = \vartheta(j)$ so that $\psi(i,j) = \psi(j)$. Here, by the law of iterated expectations

$$\widehat{Cov}(W(i,j), \psi(i,j)) = \hat{E}[W(i,j)\psi(j)] = \hat{E}_j\left[\psi(j)\hat{E}[W(i,j)|j]\right] = 0$$

so that $\delta = \delta_0$ is a critical point of $\bar{Q}_{MM}(\delta)$ in this case. This suggests that, in the absence of within-group heteroskedasticity, the MM estimator will be consistent even in situations where the available instruments are not group indicators. On the other hand, suppose that instruments are group indicators as assumed in BP (2005); then, $P_{j,ii} = 1/n_j$ for $i = 1, ..., n_j$; and it follows that

$$W(i,j) = P_{j,ii} - (n_j - 1)^{-1}(1 - P_{j,ii}) = \frac{1}{n_j} - \frac{1}{n_j - 1}\left(1 - \frac{1}{n_j}\right) = 0$$

for $i = 1, .., n_j$ and for each j, so that, trivially,

$$\widehat{Cov}(W(i,j), \psi(i,j)) = 0$$

Note that this is true even with within-group heteroskedasticity. Finally, given the possibility of within-group heteroskedasticity and instruments which are not group indicators; we obtain in general

$$\begin{aligned}
&\widehat{Cov}(W(i,j), \psi(i,j)) \\
&\quad = \hat{E}[W(i,j)\psi(i,j)] \\
&\quad = \sum_{j=1}^{m}\sum_{i=1}^{n_j}\left(\frac{P_{j,ii} - \varpi(i,j)}{\varpi(i,j)}\right)\psi(i,j)\pi(i,j) \\
&\quad = \frac{1}{m}\sum_{j=1}^{m}\sum_{i=1}^{n_j}[P_{j,ii} - (n_j - 1)^{-1}(1 - P_{j,ii})]\ \psi(i,j) \\
&\quad = \frac{1}{m}\sum_{j=1}^{m}\left(\frac{n_j}{n_j - 1}\right)\sum_{i=1}^{n_j}\left\{P_{j,ii} - \left(\frac{1}{n_j}\right)\right\}\psi(i,j) \neq 0
\end{aligned}$$

Hence, $\delta = \delta_0$ may not be a critical point of $\bar{Q}_{MM}(\delta)$ in more general settings; and it can be shown that, unlike HLIM, the MM estimator will not be consistent when both non-dummy instruments and within-group heteroskedasticity are present, although a generalization of the MM estimator obtained by minimizing Eq. (4) will be.

It is also of interest to compare the asymptotic distribution of the MM estimator to that of HLIM in the setting studied by BP (2005), i.e., in the setting with across-group heteroskedasticity (but within-group homoscedasticity) and dummy-variable instruments. Under group asymptotics, it can be shown, following the same argument as that used to prove Theorem 2 of Hausman et al. (2012), that

$$V_{MM}^{-1/2}(\hat{\delta}_{MM}-\delta_0) \xrightarrow{d} N(0, I_G), \text{ as } m \to \infty$$

where

$$V_{MM} = H_{MM}^{-1}(\bar{\Omega}_{MM} + \Psi_{MM})H_{MM}^{-1} \tag{11}$$

and where

$$H_{MM} = \frac{1}{m}\sum_{j=1}^{m} n_j \pi_j \pi_j', \quad \bar{\Omega}_{MM} = \frac{1}{m}\sum_{j=1}^{m} n_j \sigma_j^2 \pi_j \pi_j'$$

$$\Psi_{MM} = \frac{1}{m}\sum_{j=1}^{m} \sum_{1\le i\ne k\le n_j} \left(\frac{1}{n_j-1}\right)^2 \{E[\varepsilon_{ij}^2]E[\bar{V}_{kj}\bar{V}'_{kj}] + E[\bar{V}_{ij}\varepsilon_{ij}]E[\varepsilon_{kj}\bar{V}'_{kj}]\}$$

$$= \frac{1}{m}\sum_{j=1}^{m}\left(\frac{n_j}{n_j-1}\right)\Xi_{MM,j}$$

Here, $\bar{V}_{ij} = v_{ij}-(\bar{\sigma}_{21}/\bar{\sigma}^2)\varepsilon_{ij}$, with $\bar{\sigma}_{21} = m^{-1}\sum_{j=1}^{m} E[v_{ij}\varepsilon_{ij}]$ and $\bar{\sigma}^2 = m^{-1}\sum_{j=1}^{m} E[\varepsilon_{ij}^2]$. Also, $\Xi_{MM,j} = E[\varepsilon_{ij}^2]E[\bar{V}_{kj}\bar{V}'_{kj}] + E[\bar{V}_{ij}\varepsilon_{ij}]E[\varepsilon_{kj}\bar{V}'_{kj}]$, where the dependence of $\Xi_{MM,j}$ on the index j only is due to the fact that we have within-group homoscedasticity. On the other hand, for HLIM, we obtain

$$V_{HLIM}^{-1/2}(\hat{\delta}_{HLIM}-\delta_0) \xrightarrow{d} N(0,I_G), \text{ as } m \to \infty$$

where

$$V_{HLIM} = H_{HLIM}^{-1}(\bar{\Omega}_{HLIM} + \Psi_{HLIM})H_{HLIM}^{-1} \tag{12}$$

and where

$$H_{HLIM} = \frac{1}{m}\sum_{j=1}^{m}(n_j-1)\pi_j\pi'_j, \bar{\Omega}_{HLIM} = \frac{1}{m}\sum_{j=1}^{m}\frac{(n_j-1)^2}{n_j}\sigma_j^2\pi_j\pi'_j$$

$$\Psi_{HLIM} = \frac{1}{m}\sum_{j=1}^{m}\sum_{1\le i\ne k\le n_j}\left(\frac{1}{n_j}\right)^2\{E[\varepsilon_{ij}^2]E[\tilde{V}_{kj}\tilde{V}'_{kj}] + E[\tilde{V}_{ij}\varepsilon_{ij}]E[\varepsilon_{kj}\tilde{V}'_{kj}]\}$$

$$= \frac{1}{m}\sum_{j=1}^{m}\left(\frac{n_j-1}{n_j}\right)\Xi_{HLIM,j}$$

with $\tilde{V}_{ij} = v_{ij}-(\bar{\bar{\sigma}}_{21}/\bar{\bar{\sigma}}^2)\varepsilon_{ij}$, $\bar{\bar{\sigma}}_{21} = \left(\sum_{j=1}^{m} n_j\right)^{-1}\sum_{j=1}^{m} n_j E[v_{ij}\varepsilon_{ij}]$ and

$\bar{\bar{\sigma}}^2 = \left(\sum_{j=1}^{m} n_j\right)^{-1}\sum_{j=1}^{m} n_j E[\varepsilon_{ij}^2]$;

and $\Xi_{HLIM,j} = E[\varepsilon_{ij}^2]E[\tilde{V}_{kj}\tilde{V}'_{kj}] + E[\tilde{V}_{ij}\varepsilon_{ij}]E[\varepsilon_{kj}\tilde{V}'_{kj}]$

Comparing Eq. (11) with Eq. (12) for the case where $n_j = n_*$ for all j, i.e., for the case where the size of the sample is the same for all groups; we see that

$$\bar{\bar{\sigma}}_{21} = \left(\sum_{j=1}^{m} n_j\right)^{-1} \sum_{j=1}^{m} n_j E[v_{ij}\varepsilon_{j,i}] = \frac{1}{mn_*}\sum_{j=1}^{m} n_*\sigma_{21,j} = \frac{1}{m}\sum_{j=1}^{m}\sigma_{21,j} = \bar{\sigma}_{21}$$

$$\bar{\bar{\sigma}}^2 = \left(\sum_{j=1}^{m} n_j\right)^{-1} \sum_{j=1}^{m} n_j E[\varepsilon_{j,i}^2] = \frac{1}{mn_*}\sum_{j=1}^{m} n_*\sigma_j^2 = \frac{1}{m}\sum_{j=1}^{m}\sigma_j^2 = \bar{\sigma}_{21}$$

so that

$$\tilde{V}_{ij} = v_{ij} - (\bar{\bar{\sigma}}_{21}/\bar{\bar{\sigma}}^2)\varepsilon_{ij} = v_{ij} - (\bar{\sigma}_{21}/\bar{\sigma}^2)\varepsilon_{ij} = \bar{V}_{ij}$$

and, thus,

$$\begin{aligned}
\Xi_{MM,j} &= E[\varepsilon_{ij}^2]E[\bar{V}_{kj}\bar{V}'_{kj}] + E[\bar{V}_{ij}\varepsilon_{ij}]E[\varepsilon_{kj}\bar{V}'_{kj}] \\
&= E[\varepsilon_{ij}^2]E[\tilde{V}_{kj}\tilde{V}'_{kj}] + E[\tilde{V}_{ij}\varepsilon_{ij}]E[\varepsilon_{kj}\tilde{V}'_{kj}] \\
&= \Xi_{HLIM,j} \\
&= \Xi_j \ (say)
\end{aligned}$$

for $j = 1, ..., m$ and $i, k = 1, ..., n_j$. It follows that in this case

$$\begin{aligned}
&V_{MM} \\
&\quad = H_{MM}^{-1}(\bar{\Omega}_{MM} + \Psi_{MM})H_{MM}^{-1} \\
&\quad = \left(\frac{1}{m}\sum_{j=1}^{m} n_*\pi_j\pi'_j\right)^{-1}\left[\frac{1}{m}\sum_{j=1}^{m} n_*\sigma_j^2\pi_j\pi'_j + \frac{1}{m}\sum_{j=1}^{m}\left(\frac{n_*}{n_*-1}\right)\Xi_j\right]\left(\frac{1}{m}\sum_{j=1}^{m} n_*\pi_j\pi'_j\right)^{-1} \\
&= \left(\frac{1}{m}\sum_{j=1}^{m}\pi_j\pi'_j\right)^{-1}\left[\frac{1}{mn_*}\sum_{j=1}^{m}\sigma_j^2\pi_j\pi'_j + \frac{1}{mn_*}\sum_{j=1}^{m}\left(\frac{1}{n_*-1}\right)\Xi_j\right]\left(\frac{1}{m}\sum_{j=1}^{m}\pi_j\pi'_j\right)^{-1} \\
&= \left(\frac{1}{m}\sum_{j=1}^{m}(n_*-1)\pi_j\pi'_j\right)^{-1}\left[\frac{1}{m}\sum_{j=1}^{m}\frac{(n_*-1)^2}{n_*}\sigma_j^2\pi_j\pi'_j + \frac{1}{m}\sum_{j=1}^{m}\left(\frac{n_*-1}{n_*}\right)\Xi_J\right] \\
&\quad \times \left(\frac{1}{m}\sum_{j=1}^{m}(n_*-1)\pi_j\pi'_j\right)^{-1} \\
&= H_{HLIM}^{-1}(\bar{\Omega}_{HLIM} + \Psi_{HLIM})H_{HLIM}^{-1} = V_{HLIM}
\end{aligned}$$

Hence, in the special case where the number of observations are the same in each group, the asymptotic covariance matrix of the MM estimator is equivalent to that of HLIM. However, in the more general case where n_j varies with j, the covariance matrices are not equal, but it does not appear that there is a uniform ranking of the two estimators in terms of asymptotic efficiency since the relative "size" of the covariance matrices in this case will depend on the values of the underlying parameters. This is analogous to the result obtained in Chao et al. (2012), where JIV1 and JIV2 are not found to dominate each other in terms of asymptotic efficiency under many-instrument and many-weak-instrument asymptotics.

ACKNOWLEDGEMENT

We all are indebted to Jerry for his advice, insights, wisdom, and wit. We thank Kei Hirano and James Fisher for helpful comments and discussions. Thanks are also owed to the editor, Carter Hill, as well as three anonymous referees for many useful comments on an earlier version of the chapter.

NOTES

1. Hausman (1978) had received close to 9000 citations at the time of the writing of this chapter (according to google scholar).
2. More specifically, we present a derivation for HLIM. However, similar arguments and interpretations can also be made in the case of HFUL.
3. See Fuller (1977) for more detailed discussion.
4. Note that P_{ii} does not converge to 0 under many instruments because the trace of $P = \sum_i P_{ii} = k$. This means that if k and n are approximately of the same order of magnitude, say under a reasonably balanced design (say, $k/n \to C$, for C a constant) then P_{ii} does not go to zero, as it is approximately of order k/n (assuming a reasonably balanced design).

REFERENCES

Ackerberg, D. A., & Deveraux, P. (2009). Improved JIVE estimators for overidentified models with and without heteroskedasticity. *Review of Economics and Statistics*, *91*, 351–362.

Angrist, J. D., Imbens, G. W., & Krueger, A. (1999). Jackknife instrumental variables estimation. *Journal of Applied Econometrics*, *14*, 57–67.

Bekker, P. A. (1994). Alternative approximations to the distributions of instrumental variable estimators. *Econometrica*, *62*, 657–681.

Bekker, P. A., & van der Ploeg, J. (2005). Instrumental variable estimation based on grouped data. *Statistica Neerlandica*, *59*, 506–508.
Blomquist, S., & Dahlberg, M. (1999). Small sample properties of LIML and jackknife IV estimators: Experiments with weak instruments. *Journal of Applied Econometrics*, *14*, 69–88.
Chao, J. C., Swanson, N. R., Hausman, J. A., Newey, W. K., & Woutersen, T. (2012). Asymptotic distribution of JIVE in a heteroskedastic IV regression with many instruments. *Econometric Theory*, *28*, 42–86.
Donald, S. G., & Newey, W. K. (2001). Choosing the number of instruments. *Econometrica*, *69*, 1161–1191.
Davidson, R., & MacKinnon, J. G. (2006). The case against JIVE. *Journal of Applied Econometrics*, *21*, 827–833(With discussion and reply.).
Fuller, W. A. (1977). Some properties of a modification of the limited information estimator. *Econometrica*, *45*, 939–954.
Hahn, J., & Hausman, J. A. (2002). A new specification test for the validity of instrumental variables. *Econometrica*, *70*, 163–189.
Hahn, J., Hausman, J. A., & Kuersteiner, G. (2004). Estimation with weak instruments: Accuracy of higher order bias and MSE approximations. *Econometrics Journal*, *7*, 272–306.
Hausman, J. A. (1978). Specification tests in econometrics. *Econometrica*, *46*, 1251–1571.
Hausman, J. A., Newey, W. K., Woutersen, T., Chao, J., & Swanson, N. R. (2012). IV estimation with heteroskedasticity and many instruments. *Quantitative Economics*, *3*, 211–255.
Phillips, G. D. A., & Hale, C. (1977). The bias of instrumental variable estimators of simultaneous equation systems. *International Economic Review*, *18*, 219–228.

A MINIMUM MEAN SQUARED ERROR SEMIPARAMETRIC COMBINING ESTIMATOR

George G. Judge and Ron C. Mittelhammer

ABSTRACT

In the context of competing theoretical economic–econometric models and corresponding estimators, we demonstrate a semiparametric combining estimator that, under quadratic loss, has superior risk performance. The method eliminates the need for pretesting to decide between members of the relevant family of econometric models and demonstrates, under quadratic loss, the nonoptimality of the conventional pretest estimator. First-order asymptotic properties of the combined estimator are demonstrated. A sampling study is used to illustrate finite sample performance over a range of econometric model sampling designs that includes performance relative to a Hausman-type model selection pretest estimator. An important empirical problem from the causal effects literature is analyzed to indicate the applicability and econometric implications of the methodology. This combining estimation and inference framework can be extended to a range of models and corresponding estimators. The combining estimator is novel in that it provides directly minimum quadratic loss solutions.

Essays in Honor of Jerry Hausman
Advances in Econometrics, Volume 29, 55–85

ISSN: 0731-9053/doi:10.1108/S0731-9053(2012)0000029008

Keywords: Estimator combination; Stein-like shrinkage; semiparametric estimation and inference; quadratic loss; indirect noisy observations; disequilibrium economic processes

JEL classifications: C13; C14; C36

INTRODUCTION

In information recovery in economics, the indirect noisy sample outcome data are known and the corresponding economic–econometric models are conceptual in nature and unknown. As a result, the observed outcomes of economic behavioral processes are statistical in nature, and the parameters of the econometric model, structural or otherwise, are unobserved and indeed are unobservable. The observed dynamic, noisy indirect economic data come from economic processes that are usually hidden in nature and seldom if ever are in equilibrium. To deal with the out-of-equilibrium possibility of two or more distinct models and the role of time in the information recovery process, we consider a competing family of plausible econometric models–estimation rules. To cope with the statistical complexity involved in dealing with the uncertainty of choices that result, in this paper we investigate the econometric implications of forming an affine combination of competing members of a family of semiparametric estimators, under quadratic loss. In particular, by semiparametric, we mean that no particular parametric family of distributions will be implied by the underlying model specifications. Alternative members of the family of economic models lead to alternative econometric models and estimation rules that have alternative estimation and inference implications. The overall goal is to define natural adaptive semiparametric estimation and inference methods that have superior risk-quadratic loss performance, and that are free of subjective modeling–estimator choices and tuning parameters.

Given a family of econometric models and estimators, to introduce the combination estimator idea, we consider a two-member family for expository purposes, where the combination of the two estimators L and S is defined by the affine combination:

$$\beta(\alpha) = \alpha\beta_S + (1 - \alpha)\beta_L. \tag{1}$$

The objective is to identify a weighted combination of the two estimators with minimum expected quadratic risk. The mean square error (MSE) of this combination is defined by

$$\begin{aligned}\mathrm{MSE}(\beta(\alpha)) &= E\left(\|\alpha(\beta_S - \beta) + (1-\alpha)(\beta_L - \beta)\|^2\right)\\ &= \alpha^2\mathrm{MSE}(\beta_S) + (1-\alpha)^2\mathrm{MSE}(\beta_L)\\ &\quad +2\alpha(1-\alpha)E[(\beta_S - \beta)'(\beta_L - \beta)].\end{aligned} \tag{2}$$

The estimation problem is one of solving the first-order necessary condition for the value of α that minimizes the MSE of the affine combination of the two estimators.

We emphasize that the combining estimation method we propose is general in nature in terms of members of the family of competing estimators. So long as appropriate estimates of the MSE terms and inner cross product $E[(\boldsymbol{\beta}_s-\boldsymbol{\beta})'(\boldsymbol{\beta}_L-\boldsymbol{\beta})]$ in Eq. (2) can be defined, an estimate of the α that minimizes the MSE of the estimator combination can be devised, and the estimation approach can be implemented. However, in order to explicitly define, develop, and demonstrate the reach of the combination semiparametric estimation method, we consider two competing economic–econometric models–estimators that are very familiar to econometricians. One alternative, the single equation linear statistical model and least squares (LS) estimator, has, relative to a simultaneous equations competitor, low variability and may be biased. The other alternative, the overidentified simultaneous equations econometric model and the two-stage least squares (2SLS) estimator, is consistent but may be highly variable and inefficient. Since 1940, the endogenous nature of economic data processes and consistent simultaneous equation estimators have dominated the competing linear model and its possibility of LS bias. Recognizing the econometric model–estimator uncertainty underlying the nature of the indirect noisy observations and the corresponding moments linked to the behavioral system, we demonstrate an estimator that is an affine combination of the 2SLS and classical linear model (LS) estimators that may be superior to either estimator under expected quadratic loss. Using this familiar special case suggests how the general approach may be applied to other competing econometric model–estimator families.

A BIT OF HISTORY

Combining estimators is not a new idea, although widespread empirical application of estimator combinations does not yet appear to have occurred, perhaps owing to both the variety and the restricted applicability of many of the approaches presented to date. One early thread of literature, whose origin can be traced back to Kahn (1968), and which is summarized in Arnholt and Hebert (2001), concerns the estimation of scalar parameters via linear combinations of two estimators of the parameter when certain characteristics of the distribution of the estimators are assumed known. Such assumptions include various combinations of unbiasedness and/or independence of the estimators, as well as knowing (1) the coefficient of variation of the estimators, or (2) the ratio of the variance of the estimator divided by the square of the parameter being estimated is not a function of the parameter, or (3) the ratio of the variances of the estimators are known. Under various combinations of these specialized assumptions, linear combination estimators that either minimize variance (for the case of combining unbiased estimators) or minimize MSE are defined.

More general vector estimation results, in the case where multivariate normality prevails, were initiated by James and Stein (1961), who combined the k-variate maximum likelihood (ML) estimator with a k-dimensional fixed null vector and demonstrated quadratic risk-dominating Stein rule estimators, such as $\delta^S(\mathbf{y}) = (1 - \alpha/||\hat{\boldsymbol{\beta}}||^2)\hat{\boldsymbol{\beta}}$, when $0<a<2(k-2)$. Stein revealed that neither ML nor unbiased estimation has low risk under conditions normally found in practice. Efron and Morris (1973a, 1973b) presented an alternative empirical Bayes approach to Stein estimation. Stigler (1990) provided another derivation based on a Galton prospective. A very general class of estimators, that improves quadratic risk-wise on $\hat{\boldsymbol{\beta}}$, follows from Judge and Bock (1978) and Stein (1981, 1955). For the general multivariate normal case, the class of pseudo-Bayes–Stein rules having risk less than that of $\hat{\boldsymbol{\beta}}$ is very large (see, e.g., Judge & Bock, 1978). Making use of Stein-like estimators, Sclove, Morris, and Radhakrishnan (1972) and Judge and Bock (1978) demonstrated the nonoptimality of preliminary test estimators that result from a hypothesis testing basis for dealing with model uncertainty. Green and Strawderman (1991) consider a parametric statistical model setting where $\hat{\boldsymbol{\beta}}$ and $\tilde{\boldsymbol{\beta}}$ are independent k-dimensional normally distributed data-based estimators with known covariance matrices $\sigma^2\mathbf{I}_K$ and $\tau^2\mathbf{I}_K$, and demonstrate that the best linear combination of the independent random vector estimators, under quadratic loss, yields the risk-dominating estimator:

$$\delta^{GS}(\hat{\boldsymbol{\beta}}, \tilde{\boldsymbol{\beta}}) = (1 - (k-2)\sigma^2/||\hat{\boldsymbol{\beta}} - \tilde{\boldsymbol{\beta}}||^2)(\hat{\boldsymbol{\beta}} - \tilde{\boldsymbol{\beta}}) + \tilde{\boldsymbol{\beta}} \tag{3}$$

Given this conceptual base, Kim and White (2001) provided an expression for the asymptotic risk and bias of the Green–Strawderman Stein-type estimators, which also applies to cases of correlated estimators. Beran (2010) indicates that Stein's ideas are fundamental for studies of modern regularization estimators that rely on multiple shrinkage, whether implicitly or overtly. Judge and Mittelhammer (2012) demonstrate that Stein's ideas are contained in a convex combination of entropy-likelihood functional.

Focusing on combinations of purely semiparametric models in a vector estimation context, Judge and Mittelhammer (2004) demonstrated a minimum quadratic loss (MQL) semiparametric basis for combining two variants of the linear model estimation problem under quadratic loss. Judge and Mittelhammer (2007) introduced a method for combining semiparametric estimators that was based on an alternative information theoretic metric utilizing empirical likelihood principles that led to element-wise convex combinations of regression-type estimators and that exhibited attractive MSE performance relative to traditional estimator competitors. In the current paper, we continue the investigation of combinations of dependent, and possibly biased, and/or inconsistent vector estimators of parameters in semiparametric models, and seek a combined estimator that is superior in MSE to either component estimator or to a pretest estimator that chooses between the two estimators.

A FAMILY OF ECONOMETRIC MODELS–ESTIMATORS AND THE COMBINING ESTIMATOR IDEA

The Database and the Estimator Family

Suppose the observed data are the result of a sampling process of the form

$$y_i = \mathbf{X}_{i.}\mathbf{B} + \varepsilon_i \tag{4}$$

where i is the indexes observations, y_i is the dependent variable, $\mathbf{X}_{i.}$ is a $1 \times k$ vector of covariates, ε_i is an unobservable error with $E[\varepsilon_i]=0$, and $\mathbf{B}$ is a $k \times 1$ vector of unknown parameters. In addition, consider a $1 \times m$ vector of instrumental variables (IVs), $\mathbf{Z}_{i\cdot}$, that are independent of ε_i. We assume that the data-sampling process consists of independent observations[1] on sample outcomes $[\mathbf{X}_{i\cdot}, \mathbf{Z}_{i\cdot}, \varepsilon_i]$, for $i=1, \ldots, n$.

In this context, under a variety of mild regularity conditions, the LS estimator

$$\mathbf{B}_{\mathrm{LS}} = (\mathbf{X}'\mathbf{X})^{-1}\mathbf{X}'\mathbf{y} = \mathbf{B} + (\mathbf{X}'\mathbf{X})^{-1}\mathbf{X}'\boldsymbol{\varepsilon} \tag{5}$$

is unbiased and consistent for **B**, when **X** and $\boldsymbol{\varepsilon}$ are uncorrelated. However, when one or more of the $\mathbf{X}'_{j}s$ are correlated with $\boldsymbol{\varepsilon}$, the LS estimator is biased and inconsistent. To cope with this situation, it is traditional to make use of an $n \times k$ matrix of IVs, which are correlated with **X** but independent of the noise $\boldsymbol{\varepsilon}$, to define the sample moments or IV estimator:

$$\mathbf{B}_{\mathrm{IV}} = (\mathbf{Z}'\mathbf{X})^{-1}\mathbf{Z}'\mathbf{y} \tag{6}$$

If there are more IVs **Z** than covariates **X,** so that $m>k$, the 2SLS or generalized method of moments may be used to define a consistent estimator of **B**. In this case, the resulting IV estimator is generalized to

$$\mathbf{B}_{\mathrm{2SLS}} = (\mathbf{X}'\mathbf{P}_{\mathbf{Z}}\mathbf{X})^{-1}\mathbf{X}'\mathbf{P}_{\mathbf{Z}}\mathbf{y} \tag{7}$$

where $\mathbf{P}_{\mathbf{Z}} = \mathbf{Z}(\mathbf{Z}'\mathbf{Z})^{-1}\mathbf{Z}'$. This collapses to the initial IV estimator (6), when the number of instruments is equal to the number of covariates in the matrix **X**. Under appropriate regularity conditions on the data-sampling process, the estimators (6) and/or (7) are consistent, asymptotically normal, and efficient estimators of **B**. We refer to the estimator in Eq. (7) as the 2SLS estimator, realizing that one could interchangeably refer to it as a generalized method of moments estimator.

An Affine Combination of 2SLS and LS

In this section, we focus on the idea of defining an affine combination of the 2SLS and LS estimators that, in the case where some regressors are not orthogonal to the noise term, is superior, under quadratic loss, to either estimator separately. The 2SLS estimator is consistent, but tends to have larger variances than the LS estimator, which is inconsistent, but less variable. An analytical finite sample MSE comparison is difficult, and in fact generally intractable without knowledge of the sampling distribution underlying the data. However, operating semiparametrically, it is possible to seek MSE improvements based on asymptotic moments, which under general conditions can be viewed as estimates or approximations to their finite sample counterparts when there is sufficient overidentification so that at least the first two moments of the estimator exists.[2]

The estimator defined via a combination of 2SLS and LS is given by

$$\mathbf{B}(\alpha) = \alpha\mathbf{B}_{2SLS} + (1-\alpha)\mathbf{B}_{\mathrm{LS}} \tag{8}$$

The MSE of this affine combination is defined by

$$\begin{aligned}\mathrm{MSE}(\mathbf{B}(\alpha)) &= \mathrm{E}\left(||\alpha(\mathbf{B}_{2\mathrm{SLS}}-\mathbf{B}) + (1-\alpha)(\mathbf{B}_{\mathrm{LS}}-\mathbf{B})||^2\right)\\ &= \alpha^2\mathrm{MSE}(\mathbf{B}_{2\mathrm{SLS}}) + (1-\alpha)^2\mathrm{MSE}(\mathbf{B}_{\mathrm{LS}})\\ &\quad + 2\alpha(1-\alpha)\mathrm{E}[(\mathbf{B}_{2\mathrm{SLS}}-\mathbf{B})'(\mathbf{B}_{\mathrm{LS}}-\mathbf{B})]\end{aligned} \tag{9}$$

The estimation problem is then one of choosing the value of α so as to minimize the MSE of the combination of the two estimators. When proceeding semiparametrically, defining the finite sample expectations involved in the evaluation of the MSE in Eq. (9) is generally intractable. However, it is possible to define large sample approximations to all of the components of the MSE calculation, and thereby derive an approximation to the optimal affine combination of the LS and 2SLS estimators. We pursue the details of such an approach in the next section.

Optimal Affine Combination of LS and 2SLS: Asymptotics

The 2SLS estimator used in the combination has, under a variety of regularity conditions, an asymptotic normal distribution, $\mathbf{B}_{2\mathrm{SLS}} \overset{a}{\sim} N(\mathbf{B}, \mathrm{Cov}(\mathbf{B}_{2\mathrm{SLS}}))$. Under iid sampling, the covariance matrix of the asymptotic distribution takes the standard well-known form

$$\mathrm{Cov}(\mathbf{B}_{2\mathrm{SLS}}) = \sigma^2((\mathbf{X}'\mathbf{Z})(\mathbf{Z}'\mathbf{Z})^{-1}(\mathbf{Z}'\mathbf{X}))^{-1} \tag{10}$$

(see appendix for a demonstration of this result, as well as asymptotic results for the more general case where sampling is *not* identical across observations). The covariance matrix can be estimated by using

$$\hat{\sigma}^2 = (n-k)^{-1}(\mathbf{y}-\mathbf{X}\mathbf{B}_{2\mathrm{SLS}})'(\mathbf{y}-\mathbf{X}\mathbf{B}_{2\mathrm{SLS}}) \tag{11}$$

in place of σ^2 in Eq. (10), leading to the estimator $\hat{\mathrm{Cov}}(\mathbf{B}_{2\mathrm{SLS}})$. For purposes of representing an asymptotic approximated MSE, one can treat the $\mathbf{B}_{2\mathrm{SLS}}$ estimator as (asymptotically) unbiased. Thus, the MSE of the estimator is the covariance matrix given by Eq. (10), which is estimated based on Eq. (11).

Given that one or more regressors are not orthogonal to the noise term, the LS estimator is not consistent, and for purposes of representing an asymptotic approximated MSE, is (asymptotically) biased. In order to estimate the bias, covariance matrix, and the MSE for the LS estimator, let $\hat{\mathbf{e}} = \mathbf{y} - \mathbf{X}\mathbf{B}_{2\mathrm{SLS}}$

represent the consistent estimator of the noise vector outcomes, based on the $\mathbf{B}_{2SLS}$ estimator. The LS estimator can be represented as

$$\mathbf{B}_{LS} = \mathbf{B} + (\mathbf{X}'\mathbf{X})^{-1}\mathbf{X}'\boldsymbol{\varepsilon} \tag{12}$$

and the finite sample bias in the LS estimator is represented by $\mathbf{Bias}(\mathbf{B}_{LS}) = \mathrm{E}(\gamma_n) = \mathrm{E}[(\mathbf{X}'\mathbf{X})^{-1}\mathbf{X}'\boldsymbol{\varepsilon}]$, where $\gamma_n = (\mathbf{X}'\mathbf{X})^{-1}\mathbf{X}'\boldsymbol{\varepsilon}$. Given that $n^{-1}\mathbf{X}'\boldsymbol{\varepsilon} \xrightarrow{p} \boldsymbol{\xi}$ and $n^{-1}\mathbf{X}'\mathbf{X} \xrightarrow{p} \mathbf{Q}_{XX}$ for positive definite symmetric $\mathbf{Q}_{XX}$, it follows from Slutsky's theorems that

$$\gamma_n = (n^{-1}\mathbf{X}'\mathbf{X})^{-1}n^{-1}\mathbf{X}'\boldsymbol{\varepsilon} \xrightarrow{p} \mathbf{Q}_{XX}^{-1}\boldsymbol{\xi} \tag{13}$$

The value of $\gamma \equiv \mathrm{plim}(\gamma_n) = \mathbf{Q}_{XX}^{-1}\boldsymbol{\xi}$, which we assume is finite, can be estimated consistently under various general regularity conditions using the following estimator (see appendix)

$$\hat{\gamma}_n = (\mathbf{X}'\mathbf{X})^{-1}\mathbf{X}'\hat{\mathbf{e}} \tag{14}$$

Assuming $\lim_{n\to\infty}\mathrm{E}(\gamma_n) = \lim_{n\to\infty}\mathrm{E}[(\mathbf{X}'\mathbf{X})^{-1}\mathbf{X}'\boldsymbol{\varepsilon}] = \mathbf{Q}_{XX}^{-1}\boldsymbol{\xi}$, which will be the case if the random sequence $\{\gamma_n\}$ is uniformly integrable,[3] $\hat{\gamma}_n$ will consistently estimate the finite sample $\mathbf{Bias}(\mathbf{B}_{LS})$, that is, $(\hat{\gamma}_n - \mathrm{E}(\gamma_n)) \xrightarrow{p} \mathbf{0}$. One can also argue that the asymptotic bias, in the sense of the mean of the asymptotic distribution of the LS estimator, is being consistently estimated by $\hat{\gamma}_n$. This follows from the fact that under various regularity conditions (see appendix),

$$\mathbf{B}_{LS} \overset{a}{\sim} N(\mathbf{B} + (n^{-1}\mathbf{X}'\mathbf{X})^{-1}\xi_n, n^{-1}Q_{XX}^{-1}\textstyle\sum_{X'e}^{*}\mathbf{Q}_{XX}^{-1}) \tag{15}$$

where $\xi_n = E(n^{-1}\mathbf{X}'\varepsilon)$ and $\Sigma_{\mathbf{X}'\varepsilon}^{*} = \lim_{n\to\infty}(\mathrm{Cov}(n^{-1/2}\mathbf{X}'\boldsymbol{\varepsilon}))$. Thus, $(\hat{\gamma}_n - (n^{-1}\mathbf{X}'\mathbf{X})^{-1}\xi_n) \xrightarrow{p} \mathbf{0}$, assuming uniform integrability whereby $\lim_{n\to\infty}\xi_n = \boldsymbol{\xi}$.

Regarding an estimate of the asymptotic covariance matrix of the LS estimator in Eq. (15), we seek a consistent estimator of $\Xi = \mathbf{Q}_{XX}^{-1}\sum_{X'\varepsilon}^{*}\mathbf{Q}_{XX}^{-1}$. Note via Slutsky's theorems that

$$(n^{-1}\mathbf{X}'\mathbf{X}^{-1}\mathrm{Cov}\left(\mathbf{n}^{-1/2}\sum_{\mathrm{i}=1}^{\mathbf{n}}\mathbf{e}_{\mathrm{i}}\mathbf{X}_{\mathrm{i.}}'\right)(\mathbf{n}^{-1}\mathbf{X}'\mathbf{X})^{-1} \xrightarrow{\mathbf{p}} \Xi \tag{16}$$

Thus, consistent estimation of Ξ depends on establishing a consistent estimator for the middle covariance matrix term in Eq. (16). Given the independence of $[\mathbf{X}_{i\cdot}\varepsilon_i]$, for $i = 1, \ldots, n$, a consistent estimate of the covariance matrix can be provided by

$$\hat{\mathrm{Cov}}(n^{-1/2}\mathbf{X}'\boldsymbol{\varepsilon}) = n^{-1}\sum_{i=1}^{n}\left(\mathbf{X}'_{i.}\hat{e}_i - n^{-1}\sum_{i=1}^{n}\mathbf{X}'_{i.}\hat{e}_i\right)\left(\mathbf{X}'_{i.}\hat{e}_i - n^{-1}\sum_{i=1}^{n}\mathbf{X}'_{i.}\hat{e}_i\right)' \tag{17}$$

if the random variables $\mathbf{X}_i'.\varepsilon_i$, $i = 1, \ldots, n$ are identically distributed or have a common mean (see appendix). Finally, a consistent estimator of the LS asymptotic covariance matrix in Eq. (15) is given by

$$\begin{aligned}\hat{\mathrm{Cov}}(\mathbf{B}_{\mathrm{LS}}) = (\mathbf{X}'\mathbf{X})^{-1}\Bigg[\sum_{i=1}^{n}&\left(\mathbf{X}'_{i.}\hat{e}_i - n^{-1}\sum_{i=1}^{n}\mathbf{X}'_{i.}\hat{e}_i\right)\\ &\times\left(\mathbf{X}'_{i.}\hat{e}_i - n^{-1}\sum_{i=1}^{n}\mathbf{X}'_{i.}\hat{e}_i\right)'\Bigg](\mathbf{X}'\mathbf{X})^{-1}\end{aligned} \tag{18}$$

The one expression that is still needed for defining the MSE of the combination in Eq. (8) is the expectation of the cross-product term, $\sum_{\times} = E(\mathbf{B}_{2\mathrm{SLS}} - \mathbf{B})(\mathbf{B}_{\mathrm{LS}} - \mathbf{B})'$. The expectation of this outer product term can, if the data-sampling process is iid, be approximated by

$$\begin{aligned}\hat{\sum}_{\times} &= ((\mathbf{X}'\mathbf{Z})(\mathbf{Z}'\mathbf{Z})^{-1}(\mathbf{Z}'\mathbf{X}))^{-1}(\mathbf{X}'\mathbf{Z})(\mathbf{Z}'\mathbf{Z})^{-1}\\ &\times\left[\sum_{i=1}^{n}\left(\hat{e}_i\mathbf{Z}'_{i.} - n^{-1}\sum_{i=1}^{n}\mathbf{Z}'_{i.}\hat{e}_i\right)\left(\hat{e}_i\mathbf{X}'_{i.} - n^{-1}\sum_{i=1}^{n}\mathbf{X}'_{i.}\hat{e}_i\right)'\right](\mathbf{X}'\mathbf{X})^{-1}\end{aligned} \tag{19}$$

(see appendix). Note, since the instruments are uncorrelated with the noise term, the term $n^{-1}\sum_{i=1}^{n}\mathbf{Z}'_{i.}\hat{e}_i$ converges to zero, as the sample size increases. Thus, Eq. (19) may be estimated with the bracketed term replaced by $\sum_{i=1}^{n}\hat{e}_i^2\mathbf{Z}'_{i.}\mathbf{X}_{i.}$ (see appendix). Whether there is an appreciable difference in MSE performance from calculating the MSE optimal estimator in one way or the other is an open empirical question.

Given Eqs. (9)–(19), the value of the MSE of the estimator combination in Eq. (8) can be approximated for any given value of α, and an optimal α may be derived along the lines of Judge and Mittelhammer (2004), or fundamentally by solving the first-order conditions for minimizing MSE. For known values of the MSE components, the optimal choice for α is

$$\alpha_{\mathrm{o}} = 1 - \frac{\mathrm{tr}(\mathrm{Cov}(\mathbf{B}_{2\mathrm{SLS}})) - \mathrm{tr}\left(\sum_{\times}\right)}{\mathrm{E}(\gamma_n)'\mathrm{E}(\gamma_n) + \mathrm{tr}(\mathrm{Cov}(\mathbf{B}_{\mathrm{LS}})) + \mathrm{tr}(\mathrm{Cov}(\mathbf{B}_{2\mathrm{SLS}})) - 2\mathrm{tr}\left(\sum_{\times}\right)} \tag{20}$$

and the minimum MSE combined estimator is the one depicted by Eq. (8), with Eq. (20) substituted for the value of α, that is, $\mathbf{B}(\alpha_{\mathrm{o}})$. Regarding motivation for the "correction term" $\mathrm{tr}(\mathrm{Cov}(\mathbf{B}_{2SLS})) - \mathrm{tr}(\sum_{\times})$ in the numerator of the ratio in Eq. (20), note first that the weight moves toward 1, and the MQL estimator toward the 2SLS estimator: the less variable is the 2SLS estimator, that is, as the diagonal elements of its covariance matrix $\mathrm{Cov}(\mathbf{B}_{2SLS})$ decline. In addition, if $\mathrm{tr}(\Sigma_{\times})$ is notable and positive, so that the biases of the LS and 2SLS estimators tend to move in the same direction and are appreciable, then the opportunity to offset LS bias with reduced 2SLS bias is muted, and more weight on the LS estimator is warranted.

Based on the MSE component estimators developed above, a consistent estimator of the optimal α_o can be defined by substituting the various vector and matrix components of Eq. (20). An estimated minimum MSE combined estimator is defined by Eq. (8), with the estimated value of α_o inserted as $\mathbf{B}(\hat{\alpha}_o)$. An alternative consistent estimator of the denominator term in Eq. (20) may be calculated simply as $(\mathbf{B}_{2SLS}-\mathbf{B}_{LS})'(\mathbf{B}_{2SLS}-\mathbf{B}_{LS})$ (see appendix). An estimate of Eq. (20) may be expressed as

$$\hat{\alpha}_o = 1 - \frac{\mathrm{tr}(\hat{\mathrm{Cov}}(\mathbf{B}_{2SLS})) - \mathrm{tr}\left(\hat{\sum}_{\times}\right)}{(\mathbf{B}_{2SLS} - \mathbf{B}_{LS})'(\mathbf{B}_{2SLS} - \mathbf{B}_{LS})} \tag{21}$$

Using Eq. (21), the estimated optimal estimator may be expressed in a "Stein-like" form as

$$\mathbf{B}(\hat{\alpha}_o) = \mathbf{B}_{2SLS} - \frac{\hat{\tau}_o}{||\mathbf{B}_{2SLS} - \mathbf{B}_{LS}||^2}(\mathbf{B}_{2SLS} - \mathbf{B}_{LS}) \tag{22}$$

where $\hat{\tau}_o \equiv \mathrm{tr}(\hat{\mathrm{Cov}}(\mathbf{B}_{2SLS})) - \mathrm{tr}(\hat{\Sigma}_{\times})$. We refer to the optimally combined estimator, as the "*minimum quadratic loss*" (MQL) estimator, and denote it as $\mathbf{B}_{MQL}$. Note that the MQL estimator $\mathbf{B}(\hat{\alpha}_o)$ is akin "adaptive methods" of estimation in statistics, whereby the weights applied to each of the estimators is a function of a "selector statistic" (see Hogg, 2006, who defines a general adaptive estimator in the form of a weighted combination of component estimators).

Asymptotics of $\boldsymbol{B}_{MQL}$

Given the definition of the estimated MQL estimator, we next consider its asymptotic properties. The estimator can be represented as

$$\hat{\mathbf{B}}_{MQL} = \hat{\alpha}_o \mathbf{B}_{2SLS} + (1 - \hat{\alpha}_o)\mathbf{B}_{LS} \tag{23}$$

Given that $\hat{\alpha}_o - \alpha_0 \xrightarrow{p} 0$ and $\alpha_o \rightarrow 1$, because $\mathrm{tr}(\mathrm{Cov}(\mathbf{B}_{2SLS}))$ and $\mathrm{tr}(\Sigma_{\times})$ converge to zero as the sample size increases without bound, $\hat{\mathbf{B}}_{QML}$ inherits the consistency property of $\mathbf{B}_{2SLS}$, so that $\hat{\mathbf{B}}_{MQL} \xrightarrow{p} \mathbf{B}$.

Building on the consistency result, note that

$$n^{1/2}(\hat{\mathbf{B}}_{MQL} - \mathbf{B}) = \hat{\alpha}_o n^{1/2}(\mathbf{B}_{2SLS} - \mathbf{B}) + (1 - \hat{\alpha}_o)n^{1/2}(\mathbf{B}_{LS} - \mathbf{B}) \tag{24}$$

and since $\hat{\alpha}_o - \alpha_0 \xrightarrow{p} 0$, Slutsky's theorems lead to $n^{1/2}(\hat{\mathbf{B}}_{MQL} - \mathbf{B})$ having the same limiting distribution as $\alpha_o n^{1/2}(\mathbf{B}_{2SLS} - \mathbf{B}) + (1 - \alpha_o)n^{1/2}(\mathbf{B}_{LS} - \mathbf{B})$, the (optimal) affine combination of the centered and scaled 2SLS and LS estimators. We demonstrate in the appendix that

$$\begin{bmatrix} n^{1/2}(\mathbf{B}_{2SLS} - \mathbf{B}) \\ n^{1/2}\left(\mathbf{B}_{LS} - \mathbf{B} - (n^{-1}\mathbf{X}'\mathbf{X})^{-1}\xi_n\right) \end{bmatrix} \xrightarrow{d} N\left(\begin{bmatrix} 0 \\ 0 \end{bmatrix}, \begin{bmatrix} \sigma^2(\mathbf{Q}_{XZ}\mathbf{Q}_{ZZ}^{-1}\mathbf{Q}_{ZX})^{-1} & \Psi_{2SLS,LS} \\ \psi'_{2SLS,LS} & \mathbf{Q}_{XX}^{-1}\sum^{*}_{\mathbf{X}'\varepsilon}\mathbf{Q}_{XX}^{-1} \end{bmatrix}\right) \tag{25}$$

where $\boldsymbol{\Psi}_{2SLS,LS}$ is the matrix of covariances between elements of $\mathbf{B}_{2SLS}$ and $\mathbf{B}_{LS}$. It follows that

$$\begin{aligned} n^{1/2}(\hat{\mathbf{B}}_{MQL} - \mathbf{B}) &\xrightarrow{d} N(\mathbf{0}, \alpha_o^2\sigma^2(\mathbf{Q}_{XZ}\mathbf{Q}_{ZZ}^{-1}\mathbf{Q}_{ZX})^{-1} \\ &+ (1 - \alpha_o)^2\mathbf{Q}_{XX}^{-1}\Sigma^{*}_{\mathbf{X}'\varepsilon}\mathbf{Q}_{XX}^{-1} + \alpha_o(1 - \alpha_o)(\Psi_{2SLS,LS} + \Psi'_{2SLS,LS})) \end{aligned} \tag{26}$$

For large sample sizes, by definition of α_o, the estimated minimum MSE estimator, $\hat{\mathbf{B}}_{MQL}$, will be quadratic risk superior to either the 2SLS or LS estimators based on large sample approximations to the moments. For inference purposes, the limiting distribution can be estimated by replacing α_o and ε with their consistently estimated counterparts, and estimating the limit matrices with appropriate moments based on observed $\mathbf{X}$ and $\mathbf{Z}$. Note that when the sample size is allowed to increase to *infinity*, it follows from the limiting result $\alpha_o \rightarrow 1$ that the distributional characteristics of the $\hat{\mathbf{B}}_{MQL}$ will ultimately coincide with $\mathbf{B}_{2SLS}$.

SAMPLING EXPERIMENTS

In this section, we use sampling experiments to illustrate some of the characteristics of the finite sample behavior of the combination estimator approach, when applied to an overidentified econometric model. We compare the optimal affine combination of LS–2SLS estimators to the 2SLS estimator that would be typically used by applied econometricians in this data-sampling context. In addition, we consider using a pretest estimator to choose between the 2SLS and the LS estimator, based on Hausman's (1978) test for endogeneity, and compare the performance of the combined estimator to the pretest estimator. The combined estimator was defined using Eq. (20) with all unknown vector and matrix components replaced by their respective component estimators, as developed above.

Design of the Sampling Experiment

The model contains three IVs, in addition to one endogenous and one exogenous regressor, that are used as a basis for estimating the model's unknown parameters. Specifically, the model is given by

$$Y_i = X_{1i}B_1 + X_{2i}B_2 + \varepsilon_i, \quad i = 1, \ldots, n \tag{27}$$

$$\begin{bmatrix} \varepsilon \\ X_1 \\ X_2 \\ Z_1 \\ Z_2 \\ Z_3 \end{bmatrix} \sim iid\ N\left([0], \begin{bmatrix} 1 & \rho_{\varepsilon,X_1} & 0 & 0 & 0 & 0 \\ \rho_{\varepsilon,X_1} & 1 & \rho_{X_1,X_2} & \rho_{X_1,Z_i} & \rho_{X_1,Z_i} & \rho_{X_1,Z_i} \\ 0 & \rho_{X_1,X_2} & 1 & \rho_{X_2,Z_i} & \rho_{X_2,Z_i} & \rho_{X_2,Z_i} \\ 0 & \rho_{X_1,Z_i} & \rho_{X_2,Z_i} & 1 & \rho_{Z_i,Z_j} & \rho_{Z_i,Z_j} \\ 0 & \rho_{X_1,Z_i} & \rho_{X_2,Z_i} & \rho_{Z_i,Z_j} & 1 & \rho_{Z_i,Z_j} \\ 0 & \rho_{X_1,Z_i} & \rho_{X_2,Z_i} & \rho_{Z_i,Z_j} & \rho_{Z_i,Z_j} & 1 \end{bmatrix} \right), \tag{28}$$

and $\mathbf{B} = [1\ \ 2]'$. In this sampling design, the regressor X_1 is correlated with the noise term, while the regressor X_2 is not. We examine two degrees of nonorthogonality between X_1 and ε, one moderate ($\rho_{\varepsilon,X_1} = 0.5$) and one relatively strong ($\rho_{\varepsilon,X_1} = 0.75$). We also examine two degrees of correlation between the regressor variables given by $\rho_{X_1,X_2} = 0.25$ and 0.5, the latter portraying a notable amount of multicollinearity that often occurs with economic data. The IVs (Z_1, Z_2, Z_3) are specified to be each moderately correlated ($\rho_{X_1,Z_i} = .25$) with the endogenous regressor X_1, and with each other ($\rho_{Z_i,Z_j} = 0.25$).

The model is estimated using sample sizes of $n = 25$, 50, 100, 200, and 500, and employs $m = 100{,}000$ repeated samples to calculate MSE measures of fit defined by $\widehat{\mathrm{MSE}}(B_j) = m^{-1}\sum_{i=1}^{m}(\hat{B}_{ji} - B_j)^2$, for $j = 1, 2$. We report the trace of the MSE matrix in Table 1.

Table 1. Mean Squared Error Results for 100,000 Replications.

$\rho_{\varepsilon,X_1}, \rho_{X_1,X_2}$	n	F-test of IV Strength	$\mathbf{B}_{\text{LS}}$	$\mathbf{B}_{\text{2SLS}}$	$\mathbf{B}_{\text{MQL}}$	$\mathbf{B}_{\text{pretest}}$
	25	2.027	0.3746	0.6813	0.3468	0.3738
	50	2.699	0.3350	0.3649	0.2276	0.3290
0.5, 0.25	100	4.215	0.3187	0.1691	0.1423	0.2816
	200	7.325	0.3104	0.0764	0.0806	0.1652
	500	16.687	0.3051	0.0292	0.0318	0.0336
	25	1.620	0.6381	1.2383	0.6308	0.6373
	50	1.936	0.5928	0.8632	0.4675	0.5881
0.5, 0.5	100	2.729	0.5743	0.4658	0.3164	0.5463
	200	4.378	0.5647	0.2191	0.1901	0.4254
	500	9.372	0.5587	0.0760	0.0813	0.1187
	25	2.027	0.7195	0.6594	0.5066	0.7071
	50	2.700	0.6979	0.3587	0.3023	0.5937
0.75, 0.25	100	4.216	0.6894	0.1685	0.1471	0.2823
	200	7.323	0.6843	0.0765	0.0701	0.0764
	500	16.699	0.6814	0.0292	0.0284	0.0292
	25	1.620	1.2808	1.2207	1.0189	1.2697
	50	1.936	1.2645	0.8116	0.7167	1.1655
0.75, 0.5	100	2.732	1.2569	0.4668	0.3875	0.7769
	200	4.376	1.2531	0.2167	0.1693	0.2566
	500	9.380	1.2510	0.0759	0.0681	0.0743

Note: n denotes sample size, ρ_{ε,X_1} denotes correlation between the residual and the endogenous regressor, and ρ_{X_1,X_2} denotes correlation between the endogenous and exogenous regressors. The F-test is the average F-statistic value for testing the significance of the instruments (Z) in a regression of the residuals of the projection of X_1 onto X_2, regressed on the residuals of the projection of Z onto X_2 (see Stock, Wright, & Yugo, 2002, p. 521). The observed MSEs are presented in the final four columns.

Regarding the strength of the instruments implied by the sampling design, we calculated the F-test presented in Stock, Wright, and Yugo (2002) for this purpose. In particular, X_1 and Z were each projected onto the included exogenous regressor X_2, a regression of $X_1's$ residuals on Z's residuals was performed, and the F-test of the significance of Z's residuals was conducted. The average value of the F-test for each of the sampling scenarios is reported ahead in Table 1. Based on the guidelines presented in Stock et al. (their Section 4.1), all scenarios would be considered "weak instrument" scenarios, except for the case where $n = 500$, and the case where $\rho_{X_1,X_2} = 0.25$ and $n = 200$, which could arguably be considered only marginally weak.

Pretest Estimator Implementation

The Hausman pretest estimator implemented in this section is the original and familiar "contrast version" of the test based on the usual chi-square statistic:

$$H_v = (\mathbf{B}_{2SLS} - \mathbf{B}_{LS})'[\mathrm{Cov}(\mathbf{B}_{2SLS}) - \mathrm{Cov}(\mathbf{B}_{LS})]^{+}(\mathbf{B}_{2SLS} - \mathbf{B}_{LS}) \sim \text{chi-square}(v) \tag{29}$$

where "+" denotes a generalized inverse of the covariance matrix difference, and the degrees of freedom, v, is equal to the number of potentially endogenous variables in the model specification. Based on the data-sampling process described above, $v=1$ in the current application. The Hausman pretest estimator is defined as

$$\mathbf{B}_{\text{pretest}} = \begin{Bmatrix} \mathbf{B}_{LS} \\ \mathbf{B}_{2SLS} \end{Bmatrix} \text{ if } H_v \begin{Bmatrix} < \\ \geq \end{Bmatrix} \chi^2(1-\alpha, v) \tag{30}$$

where, $\chi^2(1-\alpha,v)$ is the $(1-\alpha)$th percentile of the chi-square distribution with v degrees of freedom. See Chmelarova and Hill (2010) for further discussion and some variations on the implementation of the Hausman test, and Sen and Saleh (1987) on pretest and shrinkage in linear models.

A difficulty in implementing the pretest estimator is the issue of the level of type-I error to choose in applying the Hausman (1978) test. In the current application, we choose the typical value of $\alpha=0.5$ that practitioners might use in testing the hypothesis of endogeneity. The sampling results ahead indicate that the pretest estimator can be beaten in risk (Sen & Saleh, 1987) and is consistent with Potscher and Leeb (2005), who demonstrated the poor risk properties of consistent pretest estimators.

Sampling Performance Comparisons

The MSE results of the sampling experiments are presented in Table 1, and the graphical representations of the MSE of $\mathbf{B}_{MQL}$, compared to the MSEs of $\mathbf{B}_{2SLS}$, $\mathbf{B}_{LS}$, and $\mathbf{B}_{\text{pretest}}$, are presented in Figs. 1–4. These sampling comparisons illustrate how the combination estimator adapts to the sampling behaviors of the component estimators and produces superior quadratic risk performance.

First of all, the inconsistency of the $\mathbf{B}_{LS}$ estimator and the consistency of the $\mathbf{B}_{2SLS}$, $\mathbf{B}_{\text{pretest}}$, and $\mathbf{B}_{QML}$ estimators are both evident from the MSE

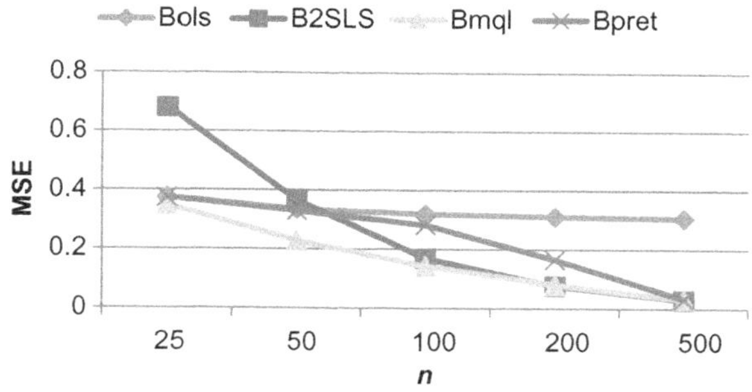

Fig. 1. MSE Comparisons: $\rho_{X_1,\varepsilon} = 0.5$ and $\rho_{X_1,X_2} = 0.25$.

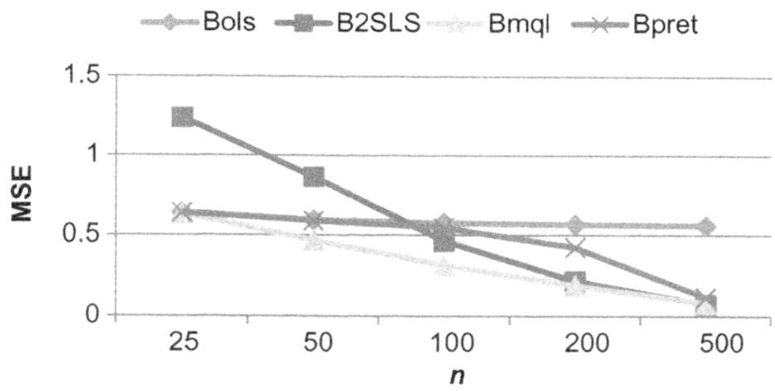

Fig. 2. MSE Comparisons: $\rho_{X_1,\varepsilon} = 0.5$ and $\rho_{X_1,X_2} = 0.5$.

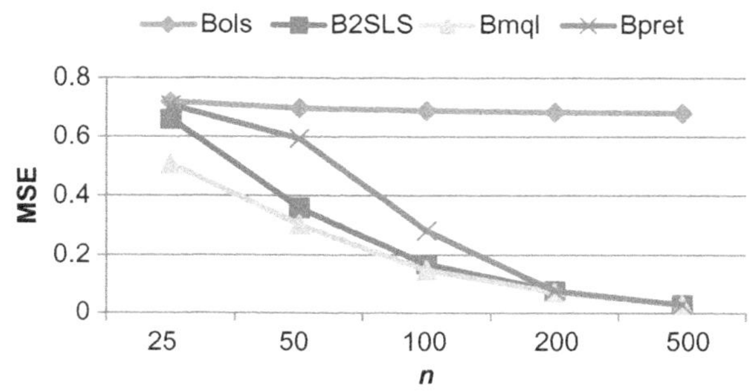

Fig. 3. MSE Comparisons: $\rho_{X_1,\varepsilon} = 0.75$ and $\rho_{X_1,X_2} = 0.25$.

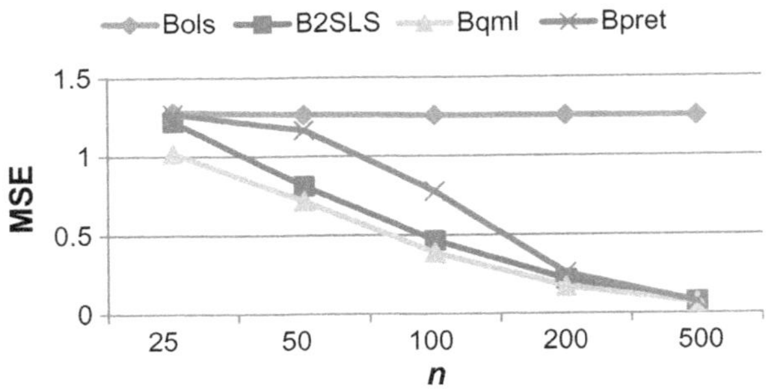

Fig. 4. MSE Comparisons: $\rho_{X_1,\varepsilon} = 0.75$ and $\rho_{X_1,X_2} = 0.5$.

graphs. For all of the latter three estimators, the MSE is minimal when the sample size assumes its largest value of $n = 500$.

When endogeneity is moderate, $\mathbf{B}_{\text{QML}}$ is very substantially MSE superior to $\mathbf{B}_{\text{2SLS}}$, for the smaller sample sizes. It is not until the sample size is 200 and larger that the 2SLS estimator closes the MSE gap, at which point the performance of the two estimators is similar. The 2SLS estimator is particularly sensitive to the increased collinearity between the RHS variables for the smaller sample sizes, whereas the combination estimator exhibits more stability. The combination estimator is also superior to both the LS and pretest estimators. For the LS estimator, the superiority increases as the sample size increases. For the pretest estimator, the superiority is most substantial for the intermediate sample sizes and dissipates at the sample size extremes.

In the case where endogeneity is more pronounced, the combination estimator, $\mathbf{B}_{\text{QML}}$, continues to exhibit MSE superiority over the alternative estimators. Superiority is less substantial relative to the $\mathbf{B}_{\text{2SLS}}$ estimator, although, as before, the MSE gap does not dissipate until the sample size is 200 or greater. The superiority of the combination estimator over the LS estimator is even more substantial than for the lower degree of endogeneity, and the gap widens considerably as the sample size increases. The superiority of the combination estimator over the pretest estimator is again substantial for the intermediate sample sizes, although the superiority dissipates quickly, being significantly diminished when $n = 200$ as opposed to $n = 500$.

The decomposition of the MSE levels into bias and variance components differs across the alternative estimators (see Figs. 5 and 6). The $\mathbf{B}_{\text{QML}}$ estimator has a tendency to be somewhat more biased but substantially less

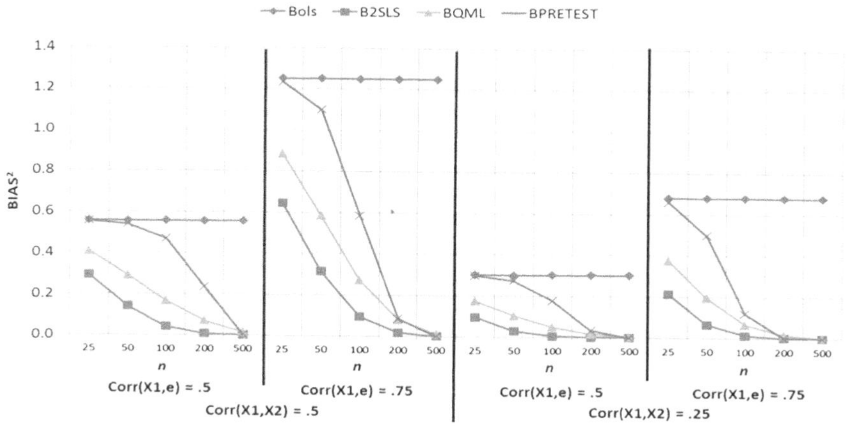

Fig. 5. Squared Bias Component of MSE for $n = 25$, 50, 100, 250, and 500.

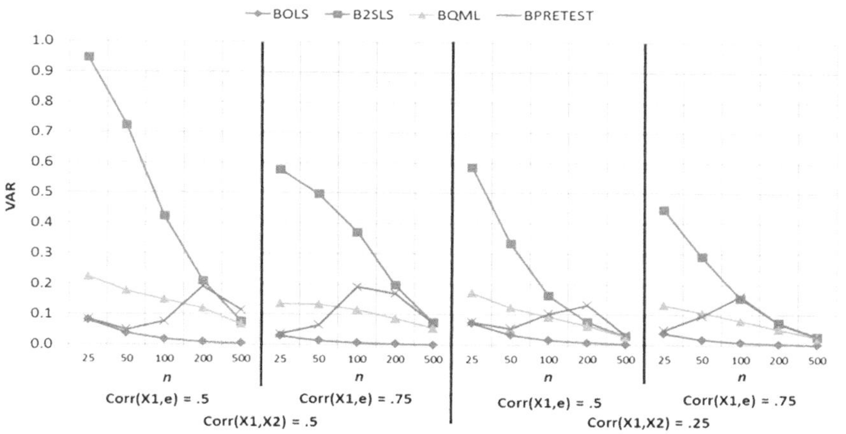

Fig. 6. Variance Component of MSE for $n = 25$, 50, 100, 250, and 500.

variable than the $\mathbf{B}_{2SLS}$ estimator. In the case where regressor correlation is the higher value of 0.50, the variance gap between the two estimators is very large for the smaller sample sizes and does not dissipate until the largest sample size of $n = 500$ is reached. In a relative sense, the bias gap is more moderate between the estimators, and it becomes quite modest when a sample size of $n = 200$ is reached.

In the case of low correlation between the regressors, the bias gap is small, when the sample size reaches $n = 100$. The $\mathbf{B}_{LS}$ estimator has uniformly smallest variance, but also has uniformly highest bias. The $\mathbf{B}_{pretest}$ estimator has low variances at the extremes of the sample sizes, with notably larger variances for the intermediate sample sizes. The pretest estimator's variance is smaller than either 2SLS or the QML estimator, for the smallest sample sizes. The pretest estimator continues to dominate the 2SLS estimator, but is inferior to the QML estimator for the intermediate sample sizes, and then variances become nearly equal at the largest sample size of 500. The pretest estimator exhibits substantially more bias than either $\mathbf{B}_{QML}$ or $\mathbf{B}_{2SLS}$ for the smaller sample sizes and the bias gap dissipates when the sample size is 200 or larger. In the case of a high regressor correlation and low level of endogeneity, a substantial bias persists until the largest sample size of 500 is reached.

The effect of a higher level of endogeneity is to accentuate the superiority of the $\mathbf{B}_{QML}$ estimator over the $\mathbf{B}_{LS}$ and pretest estimators, and diminish the level of superiority of the $\mathbf{B}_{QML}$ estimator over the $\mathbf{B}_{2SLS}$ estimator. In terms of the MSE decomposition into bias and variance components, a high level of endogeneity diminished the variance gap between the $\mathbf{B}_{2SLS}$ estimator and the other estimators, while at the same time increasing the bias gap between the $\mathbf{B}_{2SLS}$ and the alternative estimators.

Overall, the sampling results illustrate that the combining approach provides a method of adapting naturally to varying amounts of sample information and alternative data-sampling processes, while achieving the goal of minimizing the expectation of quadratic loss. The simulations also illustrate the variance versus bias behavior of the estimators. The sampling results indicate that the $\mathbf{B}_{QML}$ estimator can provide a shield against poor sampling performance of the 2SLS or LS methods, while also providing protection from unfortunate choices of either method driven by the outcome of a pretest decision.

AN EMPIRICAL APPLICATION OF THE ESTIMATOR COMBINATION METHODOLOGY

In this section, we illustrate the empirical application of the combining estimation methodology by examining an IV model that has been previously discussed in the literature. The example we analyze is that of Angrist and Krueger (1991, 2001), a data set that has recently been revisited by Imbens and Rosenbaum (2005) and Hansen, McDonald, and Newey (HDN) (2010). In this counterfactual model-data set, the quarter of birth is used as IVs to estimate the returns to schooling. The data are based on an extract from the 1980 US census consisting of $n = 329{,}509$ observations on men who were born between 1930 and 1939. Variables in the data set include the natural log of weekly wages, the year of birth (1930–1939), quarter of birth (1–4), place of birth (1980 census state codes), and education level (highest grade completed, ranging from 0 to 20).

Following HDN (2010), the simultaneous equation specification of the model uses the log of wages as the dependent variable, with explanatory variables consisting of education level, 50 state indicator variables, and 9 birth-year indicators. The coefficient of primary interest is the education level parameter, which measures the returns to years of schooling. Indicator variables for the quarter of birth were chosen as IVs in the estimation of the structural equation because of their role as exogenous explanatory variables in the determination of education level in the model estimated by HDN.

We start by estimating the parameters of the structural equation, and the standard errors of the estimates, by LS and 2SLS, and these results are reported in Table 2. We next provide an estimate of $\mathbf{B}_{MQL}$, and its covariance matrix, based on the weight represented by Eq. (20).[4] The results relating to the schooling coefficient are presented in Table 2, as well as the value of the combining coefficient $\hat{\alpha}_o$. We also present the outcome of the Hausman test for choosing between LS and 2SLS estimator, if pretest estimation were to be pursued.

The MSE-minimizing combined estimator recognizes the differing sampling behavior of the two estimators and applies roughly three-quarters weight (0.7668) to the 2SLS estimator and one-quarter weight to the LS estimator. The resulting $\mathbf{B}_{MQL}$ estimate measures the value of more education, while also reflecting the effect of quarter of birth on how much education individuals received. By using a minimum MSE estimation objective and recognizing the uncertain nature of the returns to schooling model, the average impact of the treatment estimated by the combined

Table 2. Results for the Returns to Schooling Model.

Estimator	$\mathbf{B}_{LS}$	$\mathbf{B}_{2SLS}$	$\mathbf{B}_{MQL}$
Treatment effect	0.0673	0.1077	0.0983
Standard error	0.0004	0.0195	0.0150
$\hat{\alpha}_o$	0.7668		
Hausman $\chi^2(1)$	4.2775		
(*p-value*)	(0.0386)		

estimate $\mathbf{B}_{MQL}$ is nearly a full percentage point less than implied by the impact suggested by the single-model 2SLS estimate.

In addition to being a minimum MSE estimate of the returns to schooling, in terms of inference, the estimated precision of $\mathbf{B}_{MQL}$ is also greater than that of $\mathbf{B}_{2SLS}$. If one performs the Hausman test, the results suggest that the $\mathbf{B}_{2SLS}$ estimator should be chosen at the 0.05 level of significance. The nonoptimality, under quadratic loss, of applying traditional testing–pretest methods, as it is related to model–estimator choice, was discussed earlier.

In summary, the two traditional estimation methodologies provide different estimation and inference results concerning the average treatment effect. The combination estimator recognizes the possible uncertain out-of-equilibrium nature of the data-model process and provides, in the case of overidentified experimental economic models, a minimum MSE alternative for the single model 2SLS-IV estimator often employed in estimating treatment effects.

SUMMARY AND IMPLICATIONS

We recognize in this paper that the observed data underlying economic behavioral processes and systems are statistical in nature, and that these data come from processes that are seldom in equilibrium. This means that a data set may have several possible histories, competing econometric models and estimators. To recognize and deal with this statistical complexity, we consider, in a quadratic loss context, a range of alternative econometric models and corresponding data-dependent estimators as possibilities for describing the indirect noisy effects outcome data. To provide a familiar econometric model family base, we focus on a structural econometric model and a combining estimator approach, driven by expected quadratic risk, of the LS and 2SLS estimators. The method is general in approach and has estimation and inference implications over a range of possible econometric information recovery contexts.

In sampling experiments used to illustrate and characterize sampling performance, the combined estimator performed well in both a finite and asymptotic sampling context, and over a range of sampling processes. In terms of estimation, the risk superiority of the combined estimator relative to the LS and pretest estimators is evident. For smaller sample sizes of 100 or less, the combined estimator also displayed superiority relative to the 2SLS estimator, although for larger sample sizes, the performance of both estimators was quite similar. We underscore that the combining estimator was notably superior to 2SLS in cases of weak instruments, but performance of the two estimators was similar when the instruments were stronger. Thus, the combination estimator provided enhanced precision in situations where 2SLS would be expected not to perform especially well, but it did not degrade performance when 2SLS was also expected to perform reasonably well.

In terms of inference, the small sample pretesting risk results indicate the nonoptimality of model and estimator pretesting under quadratic (squared error) loss. In spite of the long known negative statistical implications of pretesting, we note its use continues unabated in applied econometrics. In contrast, the combination estimator provides an easily implementable alternative that, unlike the pretest estimator, is defined by a well-defined optimal estimation loss objective.

We have developed the semiparametric MQL combining formulation in a particular two-estimator context. In fact, whenever there is heterogeneity in terms of estimator sampling behavior, there is the potential of achieving a minimum expected loss estimator by examining a combined version. Two examples are Judge and Mittelhammer (2004) and Mittelhammer and Judge (2005). Extensions to combining the semiparametric formulations of LS and GMM are straightforward. It would have been interesting over a half of century ago to use the combination formulation to assess the 2SLS and Wold (1954 causal chain) estimators, with the data and econometric models of that day.

The combination concept is very general and provides the possibility for improving the performance of a range of semiparametric estimators. The key to implementation, if one is using a moment-based loss function, is that measures for calculating the loss can be derived for use as a basis for forming the optimal combination. The combination estimation method developed in this paper may be applied as long as moments of the limiting distributions can be established, and estimates of them can be calculated to form the optimal combination of estimators.

NOTES

1. This allows for a more parsimonious development of the combining concepts and estimators in this paper. The methodology can be extended to accommodate dependence in various forms by resorting to more general and intricate central limit theory and convergence results, such as those found in the work of White (1984).

2. While we concentrate on the overidentified case, it is still possible to proceed by basing the loss function on moments of the limiting distributions of the estimators when finite moments are unavailable.

3. This also relies on the finiteness of $\mathbf{Q}_{XX}^{-1}\xi$. It is tacitly assumed that all indicated expectations exist.

4. Differences in the estimates from using the alternative combining weight given by Eq. (21) were effectively imperceptible.

5. More generally, one could proceed with $E(\varepsilon\varepsilon'|\mathbf{Z}) = \Omega$if sampling was independent, but not identical, recognizing possible heteroskedasticity in the noise term.

ACKNOWLEDGMENT

We acknowledge the helpful comments of J. Angrist, R. Beran, M. Grendar, J. Hausman, R.C. Hill, J. Lee, and S. Song.

REFERENCES

Angrist, J., & Krueger, A. (1991). Does compulsory school attendance affect schooling and earning? *Quarterly Journal of Economics*, *106*, 979–1014.

Angrist, J., & Krueger, A. (2001). Instrumental variables and the search for identification: From supply and demand to natural experiments. *Journal of Economic Perspectives*, *15*, 69–85.

Arnholt, A. T., & Hebert, J. L. (2001). *Optimal combinations of pairs of estimators*. Retrieved from http://interstat.statjournals.net/YEAR/2001/articles/0103002.pdf.

Beran, R. (2010). The unbearable transparency of stein estimation. A festschrift in honor of Jana Jureckova. *IMS Collection*, *7*, 25–54.

Chmelarova, V., & Hill, C. (2010). The Hausman pretest estimator. *Economic Letters*, *108*, 96–99.

Efron, B., & Morris, C. (1973a). Stein's estimation rule and its competitors—An empirical Bayes approach. *Journal of the American Statistical Association*, *68*, 117–130.

Efron, B., & Morris, C. (1973b). Combining possibly related estimation problems. *Journal of Royal Statistical Society, Series B*, *35*, 379–421.

Green, E. J., & Strawderman, W. E. (1991). James-Stein-type estimator for combining unbiased and possibly biased estimators. *Journal of the American Statistical Association*, *86*, 1001–1006.

Hansen, C., McDonald, J., & Newey, W. (2010). Instrumental variables estimation with flexible distributions. *Journal of Business and Economic Statistics*, *28*, 13–25.

Hausman, J. (1978). Specification tests in econometrics. *Econometrica*, *46*, 1251–1271.

Hogg, R. V. (2006). Adaptive methods. In *Encyclopedia of statistical sciences* (pp. 1–5). New York: Wiley.

Imbens, G. W., & Rosenbaum, P. R. (2005). Robust, accurate confidence intervals with a weak instrument: Quarter of birth and education. *Journal of Royal Statistical Society, Series A*, *168*, 109–126.

James, W., & Stein, C. (1961). Estimation with quadratic loss. In *Proceedings of the fourth Berkeley symposium on mathematical statistics and probability* (Vol. 1, pp. 361–380). Berkeley, CA: University of California Press.

Judge, G. G., & Bock, M. E. (1978). *The statistical implications of pre-test and stein-rule estimators in econometrics*. Amsterdam, The Netherlands: North-Holland.

Judge, G., & Mittelhammer, R. (2004). A semiparametric basis for combining estimation problems under quadratic loss. *Journal of the American Statistical Association, 99*, 479–487.

Judge, G., & Mittelhammer, R. (2007). Estimation and inference in the case of competing sets of estimating equations. *Journal of Econometrics, 138*, 513–531.

Judge, G., & Mittelhammer, R. (2012). *An information theoretic approach to econometrics*. New York: Cambridge University Press.

Kahn, R. A. (1968). A note on estimating the mean of a normal distribution with known coefficient of variation. *Journal of the American Statistical Association, 63*, 1039–1041.

Kim, T. H., & White, H. (2001). James-Stein type estimators in large samples with application to the least absolute deviation estimator. *Journal of the American Statistical Association, 96*, 697–705.

Mittelhammer, R., & Judge, G. (2005). Combining estimators to improve structural model estimation under quadratic loss. *Journal of Econometrics, 128*, 1–30.

Potscher, B., & Leeb, H. (2005). *Can one estimate the unconditional distribution of post-model selection estimators*? Munich Personal RePEc Archive.

Sclove, S. L., Morris, C., & Radhakrishnan, R. (1972). Non optimality of preliminary test estimators for the multinormal mean. *Annals of Mathematical Statistics, 43*, 1481–1490.

Sen, P., & Saleh, A. (1987). On preliminary tests and shrinkage estimation in linear models. *Annals of Statistics, 15*, 1580–1592.

Serfling, R. J. (1980). *Approximation theorems of mathematical statistics*. New York: Wiley.

Staiger, D., & Stock, J. H. (1997). Instrumental variables regression with weak instruments. *Econometrica, 65*, 557–586.

Stein, C. (1981). Estimation of the parameters of a multivariate normal distribution. *Annals of Statistics, 9*, 1135–1151.

Stein, C. (1955). Inadmissibility of the usual estimator for the mean of a multivariate distribution. In *Proceedings of the third Berkeley symposium on mathematical statistics and probability* (Vol. 1, pp. 197–206), Berkeley, CA: University of California Press.

Stigler, S. (1990). A Galton prospective on shrinkage estimators. *Statistical Science, 5*, 147–155.

Stock, J. H., & Wright, J. H. (2000). GMM with weak identification. *Econometrica, 5*, 1055–1096.

Stock, J. H., Wright, J. H., & Yugo, M. (2002). A Survey of weak instruments and weak identification in generalized method of moments. *Journal of Business and Economic Statistics, 20*, 518–529.

White, H. (1984). *Asymptotic theory for econometricians* (228p). Orlando, FL: Academic Press.

Wold, H. (1954). Causality in econometrics. *Econometrica, 22*, 162–167.

APPENDIX: ASYMPTOTICS OF MSE COMPONENT ESTIMATORS

As in Staiger and Stock (1997) and Stock and Wright (2000), instead of making more primitive assumptions on the errors and exogenous variables, we instead state so-called high-level moment conditions that they must satisfy, which permits application of the results to both time series and cross-section contexts where the primitive conditions generally differ. However, we emphasize that in our results here, conditions are assumed that maintain root-n consistency and asymptotic normality of all of the estimators under consideration.

Asymptotic Distribution of $\mathbf{B}_{2SLS}$

The normal asymptotic distribution of the 2SLS estimator can be established under a variety of primitive conditions that enable various central limit theorems (CLTs) and convergence results to be applied. We motivate the distribution here assuming that the data-sampling process supports some standard convergence assumptions and an appropriate CLT that justifies the limiting distribution assumption stated below under independent sampling. We also note results in the special case of iid sampling.

Assume that

(1) $[\mathbf{X}_{i\cdot}, \mathbf{Z}_{i\cdot}, \varepsilon_i]$, for $i=1, \ldots, n$, are independent, as are $\mathbf{Z}$ and ε,

(2) $n^{-1}\mathbf{Z}'\mathbf{X} \xrightarrow{p} \mathbf{Q}_{ZX}$ with $\mathbf{Q}_{ZX}$ having full column rank,

(3) $n^{-1}\mathbf{Z}'\mathbf{Z} \xrightarrow{p} \mathbf{Q}_{ZZ}$ for p.d. symmetric $\mathbf{Q}_{ZZ}$,

(4) $\sum_{\mathbf{Z}'\varepsilon}^{-1/2}(n^{-1/2}\mathbf{Z}'\boldsymbol{\varepsilon}) \xrightarrow{d} N(\mathbf{0}, \mathbf{I})$, and $\lim_{n\to\infty}(\sum_{\mathbf{Z}'\varepsilon} \equiv \text{Cov}(n^{-1/2}\mathbf{Z}'\boldsymbol{\varepsilon})) = \sum_{\mathbf{Z}'\varepsilon}^{*}$, a p.d. symmetric matrix, and

(5) the sequence $\{n^{-1}\mathbf{Z}'\mathbf{Z}\}$ is uniformly integrable, and expectations of the sequence elements exist for all n.

Then

$$n^{1/2}(\mathbf{B}_{2SLS} - \mathbf{B}) \xrightarrow{d} N(\mathbf{0}, (\mathbf{Q}_{XZ}\mathbf{Q}_{ZZ}^{-1}\mathbf{Q}_{ZX})^{-1}\mathbf{Q}_{XZ}\mathbf{Q}_{ZZ}^{-1} \sum\nolimits_{\mathbf{Z}'\varepsilon}^{*}\mathbf{Q}_{ZZ}^{-1}\mathbf{Q}_{ZX}(\mathbf{Q}_{XZ}\mathbf{Q}_{ZZ}^{-1}\mathbf{Q}_{ZX})^{-1}) \quad \text{(A.1)}$$

and if sampling is iid, the limiting distribution specializes to

$$n^{1/2}(\mathbf{B}_{2SLS} - \mathbf{B}) \xrightarrow{d} N\left(\mathbf{0},\ \sigma^2\left(\mathbf{Q}_{XZ}\mathbf{Q}_{ZZ}^{-1}\mathbf{Q}_{ZX}\right)^{-1}\right) \tag{A.2}$$

where $\mathbf{Q}_{XZ} = \mathbf{Q}'_{XZ}$, so that the asymptotic distribution of the estimator can be written as

$$\mathbf{B}_{2SLS} \overset{a}{\sim} N\left(\mathbf{B},\ \sigma^2\left((\mathbf{X}'\mathbf{Z})(\mathbf{Z}'\mathbf{Z})^{-1}(\mathbf{Z}'\mathbf{X})\right)^{-1}\right) \tag{A.3}$$

Proof. Under conditions 1–3 above, it follows from Slutsky's theorems that

$$n^{1/2}(\mathbf{B}_{2SLS} - \mathbf{B}) \xrightarrow{d} \left(\mathbf{Q}_{XZ}\mathbf{Q}_{ZZ}^{-1}\mathbf{Q}_{ZX}\right)^{-1}\mathbf{Q}_{XZ}\mathbf{Q}_{ZZ}^{-1}\left(n^{-1/2}\mathbf{Z}'\varepsilon\right) \tag{A.4}$$

Invoking condition 4 in the context of Eq. (A.4) then leads to the validity of Eq. (A.1). If sampling is iid, then applying iterated expectations,

$$\sum\nolimits_{Z'\varepsilon} \equiv E((n^{-1}\mathbf{Z}'\varepsilon\varepsilon'\mathbf{Z})) = E(n^{-1}\mathbf{Z}'E(\varepsilon\varepsilon'|\mathbf{Z})\mathbf{Z}) = \sigma^2 E(n^{-1}\mathbf{Z}'\mathbf{Z}) \tag{A.5}$$

because $E(\varepsilon\varepsilon'|\mathbf{Z}) = \sigma^2\mathbf{I}$ under iid sampling.[5] Condition 5 in conjunction with condition 3 then implies $\lim_{n\to\infty} E(n^{-1}\mathbf{Z}'\mathbf{Z}) = \mathbf{Q}_{ZZ}$, so that $\sum_{Z'\varepsilon} \to \sum^*_{Z'\varepsilon} = \sigma^2\mathbf{Q}_{ZZ}$. Substituting this result into Eq. (A.1) validates Eq. (A.2), which in turn motivates the validity of Eq. (A.3).

Consistency of $\hat{\gamma}_n = (\mathbf{X}'\mathbf{X})^{-1}\mathbf{X}'\hat{\mathbf{e}}$ *for* $\gamma = \mathbf{Q}_{XX}^{-1}\xi$

Assume that

(1) $n^{-1}\mathbf{Z}'\mathbf{X} \xrightarrow{p} \mathbf{Q}_{ZX}$ with $\mathbf{Q}_{ZX}$ having full column rank,

(2) $n^{-1}\mathbf{Z}'\mathbf{Z} \xrightarrow{p} \mathbf{Q}_{ZZ}$ for p.d. symmetric $\mathbf{Q}_{ZZ}$,

(3) $n^{-1}\mathbf{X}'\mathbf{X} \xrightarrow{p} \mathbf{Q}_{XX}$ for positive definite symmetric $\mathbf{Q}_{XX}$,

(4) $n^{-1}\mathbf{Z}'\varepsilon \xrightarrow{p} \mathbf{0}$, and

(5) $n^{-1}\mathbf{X}'\varepsilon \xrightarrow{p} \xi$.

Then $(\hat{\gamma}_n - \gamma) \xrightarrow{p} \mathbf{0}$.

Proof. Note that the estimator $\hat{\gamma}_n$ can be expressed as

$$(n^{-1}\mathbf{X}'\mathbf{X})^{-1}n^{-1}\mathbf{X}'\hat{\mathbf{e}} = (n^{-1}\mathbf{X}'\mathbf{X})^{-1}n^{-1}\mathbf{X}'(\mathbf{Y} - \mathbf{X}(\mathbf{X}'\mathbf{Z}(\mathbf{Z}'\mathbf{Z})^{-1}\mathbf{Z}'\mathbf{X})^{-1}$$
$$\mathbf{X}'\mathbf{Z}(\mathbf{Z}'\mathbf{Z})^{-1}\mathbf{Z}'\mathbf{Y})$$
$$= (n^{-1}\mathbf{X}'\mathbf{X})^{-1}n^{-1}\mathbf{X}'\boldsymbol{\varepsilon} - (n^{-1}\mathbf{X}'\mathbf{Z}(n^{-1}\mathbf{Z}'\mathbf{Z})^{-1}n^{-1}\mathbf{Z}'\mathbf{X})^{-1}n^{-1}$$
$$\mathbf{X}'\mathbf{Z}(n^{-1}\mathbf{Z}'\mathbf{Z})^{-1}n^{-1}\mathbf{Z}'\boldsymbol{\varepsilon}$$

It follows from conditions 1–5 and Slutsky's theorems that

$$\text{plim}((\mathbf{X}'\mathbf{X})^{-1}\mathbf{X}'\hat{\mathbf{e}}) = \mathbf{Q}_{XX}^{-1}\xi - ((\mathbf{Q}'_{ZX}\mathbf{Q}_{ZZ}^{-1}\mathbf{Q}_{ZX})^{-1}\mathbf{Q}'_{ZX}\mathbf{Q}_{ZZ}^{-1}$$
$$\text{plim}(n^{-1}\mathbf{Z}'\boldsymbol{\varepsilon})) = \mathbf{Q}_{XX}^{-1}\xi$$

since $\text{plim}(n^{-1}\mathbf{Z}'\boldsymbol{\varepsilon}) = \mathbf{0}$.

Asymptotic Distribution of $\boldsymbol{B}_{LS}$

Assume that

(1) $[\mathbf{X}_{i\cdot},\varepsilon_i]$, for $i = 1, \ldots, n$, are independent,

(2) $n^{-1}\mathbf{X}'\mathbf{X} \xrightarrow{\text{p}} \mathbf{Q}_{XX}$ for positive definite symmetric $\mathbf{Q}_{XX}$,

(3) $E(n^{-1}\mathbf{X}'\boldsymbol{\varepsilon}) = \xi_n$ exists $\forall n$,

(4) $\sum_{\mathbf{X}'\varepsilon}^{-1/2}(n^{-1/2}\mathbf{X}'\boldsymbol{\varepsilon} - n^{1/2}\xi_n) \xrightarrow{\text{d}} N(\mathbf{0}, \mathbf{I})$, and $\lim_{n\to\infty}(\sum_{\mathbf{X}'\varepsilon} \equiv \text{Cov}(n^{-1/2}\mathbf{X}'\boldsymbol{\varepsilon}))$ $= \sum_{\mathbf{X}'\varepsilon}^{*}$, a p.d. symmetric matrix.

Then

$$n^{1/2}(\mathbf{B}_{\text{LS}} - \mathbf{B} - (n^{-1}\mathbf{X}'\mathbf{X})^{-1}\xi_n) \xrightarrow{\text{d}} N(\mathbf{0}, \mathbf{Q}_{XX}^{-1}\textstyle\sum_{\mathbf{X}'\varepsilon}^{*}\mathbf{Q}_{XX}^{-1}) \tag{A.6}$$

and

$$\mathbf{B}_{\text{LS}} \overset{a}{\sim} N(\mathbf{B} + (n^{-1}\mathbf{X}'\mathbf{X})^{-1}\xi_n,\ n^{-1}\mathbf{Q}_{XX}^{-1}\textstyle\sum_{\mathbf{X}'\varepsilon}^{*}\mathbf{Q}_{XX}^{-1}) \tag{A.7}$$

Proof. First note that

$$n^{1/2}(\mathbf{B}_{\text{LS}} - \mathbf{B} - (n^{-1}\mathbf{X}'\mathbf{X})^{-1}\xi_n) = (n^{-1}\mathbf{X}'\mathbf{X})^{-1}(n^{-1/2}\mathbf{X}'\boldsymbol{\varepsilon} - n^{1/2}\xi_n) \tag{A.8}$$

which, by condition 2 and Slutsky's theorems, has the same limiting distribution as $\mathbf{Q}_{XX}^{-1}(n^{-1/2}\mathbf{X}'\boldsymbol{\varepsilon} - n^{1/2}\xi_n)$. Now note by condition 4 and the continuity of the inverse square root operator that $\sum_{\mathbf{X}'\varepsilon}^{-1/2} \rightarrow \sum_{\mathbf{X}'\varepsilon}^{*-1/2}$, so that $\sum_{\mathbf{X}'\varepsilon}^{-1/2}(n^{-1/2}\mathbf{X}'\boldsymbol{\varepsilon} - n^{1/2}\boldsymbol{\xi}_n)$ and $\sum_{\mathbf{X}'\varepsilon}^{*-1/2}(n^{-1/2}\mathbf{X}'\boldsymbol{\varepsilon} - n^{1/2}\boldsymbol{\xi}_n)$ share the same limiting distribution. It follows that

$$\begin{aligned}\mathbf{Q}_{XX}^{-1}(n^{-1/2}\mathbf{X}'\boldsymbol{\varepsilon} - n^{1/2}\boldsymbol{\xi}_n) &= \mathbf{Q}_{XX}^{-1}\sum\nolimits_{\mathbf{X}'\varepsilon}^{*1/2}\sum\nolimits_{\mathbf{X}'\varepsilon}^{*-1/2}(n^{-1/2}\mathbf{X}'\boldsymbol{\varepsilon} - n^{1/2}\boldsymbol{\xi}_n) \\ &\xrightarrow{d} N(\mathbf{0}, \mathbf{Q}_{XX}^{-1}\sum\nolimits_{\mathbf{X}'\varepsilon}^{*}\mathbf{Q}_{XX}^{-1})\end{aligned} \tag{A.9}$$

which validates Eq. (A.6). Then Eq. (A.7) follows immediately from Eq. (A.6) via a linear combination of normally distributed random variables.

Consistent Estimation of Cov($n^{-1}\mathbf{X}'\boldsymbol{\varepsilon}$)

Assume the conditions stated in Eq. (A.3). The covariance matrix is by definition

$$\begin{aligned}\mathrm{Cov}(n^{-1/2}\mathbf{X}'\boldsymbol{\varepsilon}) &= n^{-1}\mathrm{E}\left[(\mathbf{X}'\boldsymbol{\varepsilon} - E(\mathbf{X}'\boldsymbol{\varepsilon}))(\mathbf{X}'\boldsymbol{\varepsilon} - E(\mathbf{X}'\boldsymbol{\varepsilon}))'\right] \\ &= n^{-1}E\left[\left(\sum_{i=1}^{n}\mathbf{X}'_{i.}\varepsilon_i - E\sum_{i=1}^{n}\mathbf{X}'_{i.}\varepsilon_i\right)\left(\sum_{i=1}^{n}\mathbf{X}'_{i.}\varepsilon_i - E\sum_{i=1}^{n}\mathbf{X}'_{i.}\varepsilon_i\right)'\right] \\ &= n^{-1}E\left[\left(\sum_{i=1}^{n}(\mathbf{X}'_{i.}\varepsilon_i - E(\mathbf{X}'_{i.}\varepsilon_i))\right)\left(\sum_{i=1}^{n}(\mathbf{X}'_{i.}\varepsilon_i - E(\mathbf{X}'_{i.}\varepsilon_i))\right)'\right]\end{aligned} \tag{A.10}$$

By the independence of $\varepsilon_i\mathbf{X}'_{i\cdot}$, $i = 1, \ldots, n$, the expectations of the cross-product terms in the expansion of the last RHS term in Eq. (A.10) are zero valued, as

$$E[(\varepsilon_i\mathbf{X}'_{i.} - E(\mathbf{X}'_{i.}\varepsilon_i))(\varepsilon_j\mathbf{X}'_{j.} - E(\mathbf{X}'_{j.}\varepsilon_j))] = \mathbf{0} \quad \text{for} \quad i \neq j \tag{A.11}$$

It follows that the definition of the covariance matrix simplifies to

$$\begin{aligned}\mathrm{Cov}(n^{-1/2}\mathbf{X}'\boldsymbol{\varepsilon}) &= n^{-1}E\left[\left(\sum_{i=1}^{n}(\mathbf{X}'_{i.}\varepsilon_i - E(\mathbf{X}'_{i.}\varepsilon_i))(\mathbf{X}'_{i.}\varepsilon_i - E(\mathbf{X}'_{i.}\varepsilon_i))'\right)\right] \\ &= n^{-1}E\left(\sum_{i=1}^{n}\varepsilon_i^2\mathbf{X}'_{i.}\mathbf{X}_{i.}\right) - n^{-1}\sum_{i=1}^{n}E(\mathbf{X}'_{i.}\varepsilon_i)E(\mathbf{X}'_{i.}\varepsilon_i)'\end{aligned} \tag{A.12}$$

If the noise terms were observable, and $[\mathbf{X}_{i\cdot},\varepsilon_i]$, for $i = 1, \ldots, n$, were iid, or else $\mathbf{X}'_{i\cdot}\varepsilon_i$ for $i = 1, \ldots, n$ had common means, a consistent estimator of the covariance matrix is defined by

$$n^{-1}\left(\sum_{i=1}^{n}\varepsilon_i^2\mathbf{X}_{i.}'\mathbf{X}_{i.}\right)-n^{-1}\sum_{i=1}^{n}\left(n^{-1}\sum_{i=1}^{n}\mathbf{X}_{i.}'\varepsilon_i\right)\left(n^{-1}\sum_{i=1}^{n}\mathbf{X}_{i.}'\varepsilon_i\right)' \tag{A.13}$$

and consistency is maintained by replacing the noise terms by the consistent estimator $\hat{\mathbf{e}}$, as

$$\begin{aligned}\hat{\mathrm{Cov}}(n^{-1/2}\mathbf{X}'\varepsilon)&=n^{-1}\left(\sum_{i=1}^{n}\hat{e}_i^2\mathbf{X}_{i.}'\mathbf{X}_{i.}\right)-n^{-1}\sum_{i=1}^{n}\left(n^{-1}\sum_{i=1}^{n}\mathbf{X}_{i.}'\hat{e}_i\right)\left(n^{-1}\sum_{i=1}^{n}\mathbf{X}_{i.}'\hat{e}_i\right)'\\&=n^{-1}\sum_{i=1}^{n}\left(\mathbf{X}_{i.}'\hat{e}_i-n^{-1}\sum_{i=1}^{n}\mathbf{X}_{i.}'\hat{e}_i\right)\left(\mathbf{X}_{i.}'\hat{e}_i-n^{-1}\sum_{i=1}^{n}\mathbf{X}_{i.}'\hat{e}_i\right)'\end{aligned} \tag{A.14}$$

following the approach of White (1984, pp. 134–136).

Consistent Estimation of $\Sigma_\times = \mathrm{E}(\boldsymbol{B}_{2SLS}-\boldsymbol{B})(\boldsymbol{B}_{LS}-\boldsymbol{B})'$

The approach to defining a consistent estimator of $\Sigma_\times$ is essentially analogous to the approach used in Eq. (A.14) above. Assume the conditions in both Eqs. (A.1) and (A.3). The expectation of this outer product term can be written as

$$\begin{aligned}\sum\nolimits_\times \equiv\ & E[((n^{-1}\mathbf{X}'\mathbf{Z})(n^{-1}\mathbf{Z}'\mathbf{Z})^{-1}(n^{-1}\mathbf{Z}'\mathbf{X}))^{-1}\\&\times(n^{-1}\mathbf{X}'\mathbf{Z})(n^{-1}\mathbf{Z}'\mathbf{Z})^{-1}(n^{-1}\mathbf{Z}'\varepsilon)(n^{-1}\varepsilon'\mathbf{X})(n^{-1}\mathbf{X}'\mathbf{X})^{-1}]\end{aligned} \tag{A.15}$$

As $n\to\infty$, it is evident that the outer bracketed random matrix converges to the zero matrix, since all parenthetical terms converge in probability to finite matrix or vector limits, including $n^{-1}\mathbf{Z}'\varepsilon \xrightarrow{p} \mathbf{0}$ and $n^{-1}\mathbf{X}'\varepsilon \xrightarrow{p} \xi$, so that $(n^{-1}\mathbf{Z}'\varepsilon)(n^{-1}\varepsilon'\mathbf{X}) \xrightarrow{p} \mathbf{0}$. Assuming uniform integrability of the random matrix sequence, it follows that $\lim_{n\to\infty}\sum_\times = \mathbf{0}$, and so one approach to estimating the term, at least asymptotically, would be to set it to its limiting zero value.

Alternatively, to account for its convergence path, consider estimating a scaled version of the matrix, $n\Sigma_\times$, which is defined as equal to Eq. (A.15) with the term $(n^{-1}\mathbf{Z}'\varepsilon)(n^{-1}\varepsilon'\mathbf{X})$ now replaced with $(n^{-1}\mathbf{Z}'\varepsilon\varepsilon'\mathbf{X})$. Similar in approach to Eq. (A.15) above based on Slutsky's theorems, note that consistent estimation of $n\Sigma_\times$ depends on consistently estimating $(n^{-1}\mathbf{Z}'\varepsilon\varepsilon'\mathbf{X})$, since all other matrix terms comprising $n\Sigma_\times$ converge to finite matrix limits. Similar in form to Eq. (A.10),

$$E(n^{-1}\mathbf{Z}'\boldsymbol{\varepsilon}\boldsymbol{\varepsilon}'\mathbf{X}) = n^{-1}E\left[\left(\sum_{i=1}^{n}\mathbf{Z}_{i.}'\boldsymbol{\varepsilon}_i\right)\left(\sum_{i=1}^{n}\mathbf{X}_{i.}'\boldsymbol{\varepsilon}_i\right)'\right]$$
$$= n^{-1}E\left[\left(\sum_{i=1}^{n}(\varepsilon_i^2\mathbf{Z}_{i.}'\mathbf{X}_{i.})\right)\right] \tag{A.16}$$

where the last term follows because $E(\mathbf{Z}_{i.}'\varepsilon_i\varepsilon_j\mathbf{X}_{j.}) = \mathbf{0}$ for $i \neq j$ by independence and the fact that $E(\mathbf{Z}_{i.}'\varepsilon_i) = \mathbf{0}$. Again following the approach of White (1984, pp. 134–136), if the noise terms were observable, a consistent estimator for Eq. (A.16) would be given by $n^{-1}\sum_{i=1}^{n}(\varepsilon_i^2\mathbf{Z}_{i.}'\mathbf{X}_{i.})$, and consistency is maintained by replacing the noise terms by the consistent estimator $\hat{\mathbf{e}}$, yielding

$$\hat{\sum}_x = ((\mathbf{X}'\mathbf{Z})(\mathbf{Z}'\mathbf{Z})^{-1}(\mathbf{Z}'\mathbf{X}))^{-1}(\mathbf{X}'\mathbf{Z})(\mathbf{Z}'\mathbf{Z})^{-1}\left(\sum_{i=1}^{n}\hat{e}_i^2\mathbf{Z}_{i.}'\mathbf{X}_{i.}\right)(\mathbf{X}'\mathbf{X})^{-1} \tag{A.17}$$

Given that $E(n^{-1}\sum_{i=1}^{n}\mathbf{Z}_{i.}'\varepsilon_i) = \mathbf{0}$, the value of $E[(\sum_{i=1}^{n}\mathbf{Z}_{i.}'\varepsilon_i)(\sum_{i=1}^{n}\mathbf{X}_{i.}'\varepsilon_i)']$ is actually the covariance between the two parenthetical random vectors, so that an asymptotically equivalent estimator for $\hat{\sum}_x$ can be defined with $\sum_{i=1}^{n}(\hat{e}_i\mathbf{Z}_{i.}' - n^{-1}\sum_{i=1}^{n}\mathbf{Z}_{i.}'\hat{e}_i)(\hat{e}_i\mathbf{X}_{i.}' - n^{-1}\sum_{i=1}^{n}\mathbf{X}_{i.}'\hat{e}_i)'$ replacing $\sum_{i=1}^{n}\hat{e}_i^2\mathbf{Z}_{i.}'\mathbf{X}_{i.}$ in Eq. (A.17).

Alternative Estimator for

$$\mathrm{E}(\boldsymbol{\gamma}_n)'\mathrm{E}(\boldsymbol{\gamma}_n) + tr(Cov(\mathbf{B}_{LS})) + tr(Cov(\mathbf{B}_{2SLS})) - 2\,tr(\textstyle\sum_{\times})$$

Note that

$$E(\mathbf{B}_{\mathrm{2SLS}} - \mathbf{B}_{\mathrm{LS}})'(\mathbf{B}_{\mathrm{2SLS}} - \mathbf{B}_{\mathrm{LS}}) = E||(\mathbf{B}_{\mathrm{2SLS}} - \mathbf{B}) - (\mathbf{B}_{\mathrm{LS}} - \mathbf{B})||^2$$
$$= E||\mathbf{B}_{\mathrm{LS}} - \mathbf{B}||^2 + E||\mathbf{B}_{\mathrm{2SLS}} - \mathbf{B}||^2 - 2E((\mathbf{B}_{\mathrm{2SLS}} - \mathbf{B})'(\mathbf{B}_{\mathrm{LS}} - \mathbf{B}))$$
$$= ||\mathrm{Bias}(\mathbf{B}_{\mathrm{LS}})||^2 + \mathrm{tr}(\mathrm{Cov}(\mathbf{B}_{\mathrm{LS}})) + \mathrm{tr}(\mathrm{Cov}(\mathbf{B}_{\mathrm{2SLS}})) - 2E((\mathbf{B}_{\mathrm{2SLS}} - \mathbf{B})'(\mathbf{B}_{\mathrm{LS}} - \mathbf{B})) + ||\mathrm{Bias}(\mathbf{B}_{\mathrm{2SLS}})||^2$$
$$= E(\boldsymbol{\gamma}_n)'E(\boldsymbol{\gamma}_n) + \mathrm{tr}(\mathrm{Cov}(\mathbf{B}_{\mathrm{LS}})) + \mathrm{tr}(\mathrm{Cov}(\mathbf{B}_{\mathrm{2SLS}})) - 2E(\textstyle\sum_{\times}) + ||\mathrm{Bias}(\mathbf{B}_{\mathrm{2SLS}})||^2 \tag{A.18}$$

Thus, apart from the trailing bias term relating to the 2SLS estimator, the random scalar $(\mathbf{B}_{2SLS}-\mathbf{B}_{LS})'(\mathbf{B}_{2SLS}-\mathbf{B}_{LS})$ is an unbiased estimator of the denominator of Eq. (20). Being that the 2SLS estimator is asymptotically unbiased and consistent for $\mathbf{B}$, one can proceed by ignoring the asymptotically irrelevant bias term and treating $(\mathbf{B}_{2SLS}-\mathbf{B}_{LS})'(\mathbf{B}_{2SLS}-\mathbf{B}_{LS})$ as a consistent approximation to the denominator in Eq. (20).

Multivariate Normal Limiting Distribution of

$$\begin{bmatrix} n^{1/2}(\mathbf{B}_{2SLS} - \mathbf{B}) \\ n^{1/2}(\mathbf{B}_{LS} - \mathbf{B} - (n^{-1}\mathbf{X}'\mathbf{X})^{-1}\xi_n) \end{bmatrix}$$

Assume the conditions in Eqs. (A.1), (A.3), and (A.5). Then under an appropriate multivariate CLT,

$$\begin{bmatrix} n^{1/2}(\mathbf{B}_{2SLS} - \mathbf{B}) \\ n^{1/2}(\mathbf{B}_{LS} - \mathbf{B} - (n^{-1}\mathbf{X}'\mathbf{X})^{-1}\xi_n) \end{bmatrix} \xrightarrow{d} N\left(\begin{bmatrix} 0 \\ 0 \end{bmatrix}, \begin{bmatrix} \sigma^2(\mathbf{Q}_{XZ}\mathbf{Q}_{ZZ}^{-1}\mathbf{Q}_{ZX})^{-1} & \psi_{2SLS,LS} \\ \psi'_{2SLS,LS} & \mathbf{Q}_{XX}^{-1}\sum^{*}_{\mathbf{X}'\varepsilon}\mathbf{Q}_{XX}^{-1} \end{bmatrix}\right) \tag{A.19}$$

where $\Psi_{2SLS,LS} = \lim_{n\to\infty}(n\sum_{\times})$, where $\Sigma_{\times}$ is defined in Eq. (A.15).

Proof. The marginal normal limiting distributions have already been established in sections "Asymptotic Distribution of $\mathbf{B}_{2SLS}$" and "Asymptotic Distribution of $\mathbf{B}_{LS}$." Now consider the full concatenated random vector on the LHS of Eq. (A.19). Note that

$$\begin{aligned} &\begin{bmatrix} n^{1/2}(\mathbf{B}_{2SLS} - \mathbf{B}) \\ n^{1/2}(\mathbf{B}_{LS} - \mathbf{B} - (n^{-1}\mathbf{X}'\mathbf{X})^{-1}\xi_n) \end{bmatrix} \\ &= \begin{bmatrix} (n^{-1}\mathbf{X}'\mathbf{Z}(n^{-1}\mathbf{Z}'\mathbf{Z})^{-1}n^{-1}\mathbf{Z}'\mathbf{X})^{-1}n^{-1}\mathbf{X}'\mathbf{Z}(n^{-1}\mathbf{Z}'\mathbf{Z})^{-1}n^{-1/2}\mathbf{Z}'\varepsilon \\ (n^{-1}\mathbf{X}'\mathbf{X})^{-1}(n^{-1/2}\mathbf{X}'\varepsilon - n^{1/2}\xi_n) \end{bmatrix} \\ &\xrightarrow{d} \begin{bmatrix} (\mathbf{Q}_{XZ}\mathbf{Q}_{ZZ}^{-1}\mathbf{Q}_{ZX})^{-1}\mathbf{Q}_{XZ}\mathbf{Q}_{ZZ}^{-1}n^{-1/2}\mathbf{Z}'\varepsilon \\ \mathbf{Q}_{XX}^{-1}(n^{-1/2}\mathbf{X}'\varepsilon - n^{1/2}\xi_n) \end{bmatrix} \end{aligned} \tag{A.20}$$

Thus, whether the limiting distribution is multivariate normal depends entirely on the limiting distribution of

$$\begin{bmatrix} n^{-1/2}\mathbf{Z}'\boldsymbol{\varepsilon} \\ n^{-1/2}\mathbf{X}'\boldsymbol{\varepsilon} - n^{1/2}\boldsymbol{\xi}_n \end{bmatrix} = \begin{bmatrix} n^{-1/2}\sum_{i=1}^{n}\mathbf{Z}'_{i.}\varepsilon_i \\ n^{-1/2}\sum_{i=1}^{n}(\mathbf{X}'_{i.}\varepsilon_i - E(\mathbf{X}'_{i.}\varepsilon_i)) \end{bmatrix} \tag{A.21}$$

which is the sum of n independent zero mean $(m+k) \times 1$ random vectors. Such sums of independent random variables can be assumed to converge to multivariate normal distributions under a variety of CLTs (e.g., White, 1984, section V.2, or Serfling, 1980, section 1.9).

The two covariance matrices on the block diagonal of the distribution in Eq. (A.19) have already been demonstrated in sections "Asymptotic Distribution of $\mathbf{B}_{2SLS}$" and "Asymptotic Distribution of $\mathbf{B}_{LS}$." The off-diagonal block of covariance entries follows directly from the results provided in section "Consistent Estimation of $\Sigma_{\times} = E(\mathbf{B}_{2SLS}-\mathbf{B})(\mathbf{B}_{LS}-\mathbf{B})'$" and Eq. (A.17).

AN EXPOSITORY NOTE ON THE EXISTENCE OF MOMENTS OF FULLER AND HFUL ESTIMATORS

John C. Chao, Jerry A. Hausman, Whitney K. Newey, Norman R. Swanson and Tiemen Woutersen

ABSTRACT

In a recent paper, Hausman, Newey, Woutersen, Chao, and Swanson (2012) propose a new estimator, HFUL (Heteroscedasticity robust Fuller), for the linear model with endogeneity. This estimator is consistent and asymptotically normally distributed in the many instruments and many weak instruments asymptotics. Moreover, this estimator has moments, just like the estimator by Fuller (1977). The purpose of this note is to discuss at greater length the existence of moments result given in Hausman et al. (2012). In particular, we intend to answer the following questions: Why does LIML *not have moments? Why does the Fuller modification lead to estimators with moments? Is normality required for the Fuller estimator to have moments? Why do we need a condition such as Hausman et al. (2012), Assumption 9? Why do we have the adjustment formula?*

Essays in Honor of Jerry Hausman
Advances in Econometrics, Volume 29, 87–106

ISSN: 0731-9053/doi:10.1108/S0731-9053(2012)0000029009

Keywords: Endogeneity; instrumental variables; jackknife estimation; many moments; existence of moments

JEL classification: C13; C31

INTRODUCTION

The linear model with endogeneity is one of the most popular models in economics and there exist several estimators for this model. The Two Stage Least Squares estimator is inconsistent if there are many moments (see Bekker, 1994; Kunitomo, 1980). Another estimator, the LIML (Limited Information Maximum Likelihood) estimator does not have moments. As a result, simulation shows that the latter estimator suffers from high dispersion in finite sample, see, e.g. Hahn, Hausman, and Kuersteiner (2004). These authors suggested the Fuller (1977) estimator as a solution to this problem for LIML. However, the Fuller estimator is inconsistent under many-instrument asymptotics if there is heteroskedasticity in the data. In a recent paper, Hausman Newey, Woutersen, Chao, and Swanson (2012) propose a new estimator, HFUL (Heteroscedasticity robust Fuller), for the linear model with endogeneity. In that paper, we show that HFUL is consistent and asymptotically normally distributed in the many instruments and many weak instruments asymptotics, even in the presence of heteroscedasticity. Moreover, we also show that HFUL has moments, just like the estimator proposed by Fuller (1977). The purpose of this note is to expound the existence of moments results given in Hausman et al. (2012). Thus, in this note, we intend to answer the following questions:

Q1: Why does *LIML* not have moments?
Q2: Why does the Fuller modification lead to estimators with moments?
Q3: Is normality required for the Fuller estimator to have moments?
Q4: Why do we need a condition such as Hausman et al. (2012), Assumption 9?
Q5: Why do we have the adjustment formula $\hat{\alpha} = [\tilde{\alpha} - (1-\tilde{\alpha})C/n][1-(1-\tilde{\alpha})C/n]^{-1}$ in *HFUL*, and what are the effects of C on the asymptotic properties of *HFUL*?

To keep our discussion as intuitive as possible, we adopt the simplest possible setup: a Gaussian, exactly identified IV regression with one endogenous regressor, orthonormal instrument, and a canonical error structure, that is

$$y = x\delta_0 + \varepsilon \tag{1}$$

$$x = z\pi_0 + v \tag{2}$$

where $z'z/n = 1$. The reduced form representation y is easily seen as

$$y = z\phi_0 + \zeta$$

where $\phi_0 = \pi_0\delta_0$ and $\zeta = \varepsilon + v\delta_0$. To keep notation simple, we also assume that the IV regression is in what has been called the canonical form, so that

$$\begin{pmatrix} \zeta_i \\ v_i \end{pmatrix} \sim i.i.d.N(0, I_2) \tag{3}$$

where ζ_i and v_i are the ith element of the random vectors $\zeta = (\zeta_1, \ldots, \zeta_n)'$ and $v = (v_1, \ldots, v_n)'$, respectively. With this simple, stripped-down setup, we can present the essential ideas behind our results while avoiding some of the technical difficulties and tedious calculations associated with having non-normality, heteroskedasticity, and many and/or weak instruments.

In this simple setting, it is easily seen that the OLS estimators of the reduced form parameters ϕ and π have the following joint normal distribution

$$\begin{pmatrix} \hat{\phi}_n \\ \hat{\pi}_n \end{pmatrix} = \begin{pmatrix} z'y/n \\ z'x/n \end{pmatrix} \sim N\left(\begin{pmatrix} \phi_0 \\ \pi_0 \end{pmatrix}, n^{-1}I_2\right) \tag{4}$$

Note that $\hat{\phi}_n$ and $\hat{\pi}_n$ are independent in this case.

Given the simplicity of the setup here, the existence and non-existence of moment results given below are not new but are presented here so as to illustrate some of the issues involved. In fact, Fuller (1977) has already established the existence of moments of his estimator for a IV regression model under homoskedastic, Gaussian error assumptions and a fixed number of instruments. However, here, we provide some intuitive explanation for why the Fuller modification works based on certain geometric properties of the high-dimensional sphere. Similar discussion does not appear in Fuller (1977) and does not seem to appear elsewhere in the literature. In addition, the existence of moments result which we give in Hausman et al. (2012) is new, as it generalizes the Fuller (1977) result to IV regression models with heteroskedasticity, non-Gaussian error distributions, and possibly many weak instruments, and it establishes such a result for a new estimator *HFUL*.

In the remainder, we answer each of the questions posed above in turn.

WHY DOES *LIML* NOT HAVE MOMENTS?

Now, to address this question, we note that, under exact identification, we have

$$\hat{\delta}_{LIML} = \hat{\delta}_{2SLS} = \frac{\hat{\pi}_n(z'z)\hat{\phi}_n}{\hat{\pi}_n(z'z)\hat{\pi}_n} = \frac{\hat{\phi}_n}{\hat{\pi}_n}$$

The nonexistence of finite sample moments for this estimator is easily established by the following calculations

$$\begin{aligned}
E\left|\hat{\delta}_{LIML}\right|^p &= \int_{-\infty}^{\infty}\int_{-\infty}^{\infty}\left|\frac{\hat{\phi}}{\hat{\pi}}\right|^p \frac{n}{(2\pi)}\exp\left\{-\frac{1}{2}\left[n(\hat{\pi}-\pi_0)^2 + n(\hat{\phi}-\phi_0)^2\right]\right\}d\hat{\pi}d\hat{\phi} \\
&= \int_{-\infty}^{\infty}\left|\hat{\phi}\right|^p\sqrt{\frac{n}{2\pi}}\exp\left\{-\frac{n}{2}(\hat{\phi}-\phi_0)^2\right\}d\hat{\phi} \\
&\quad \times \int_{-\infty}^{\infty}|\hat{\pi}|^{-p}\sqrt{\frac{n}{2\pi}}\exp\left\{-\frac{n}{2}(\hat{\pi}-\pi_0)^2\right\}d\hat{\pi} \\
&\geq \int_{-\infty}^{\infty}\left|\hat{\phi}\right|^p\sqrt{\frac{n}{2\pi}}\exp\left\{-\frac{n}{2}(\hat{\phi}-\phi_0)^2\right\}d\hat{\phi} \\
&\quad \times \int_{-|\pi_0|}^{|\pi_0|}|\hat{\pi}|^{-p}\sqrt{\frac{n}{2\pi}}\exp\left\{-\frac{n}{2}(\hat{\pi}-\pi_0)^2\right\}d\hat{\pi} \\
&\geq \int_{-\infty}^{\infty}\left|\hat{\phi}\right|^p\sqrt{\frac{n}{2\pi}}\exp\left\{-\frac{n}{2}(\hat{\phi}-\phi_0)^2\right\}d\hat{\phi} \\
&\quad \times \sqrt{\frac{n}{2\pi}}\exp\{-2n|\pi_0|^2\}\int_{-|\pi_0|}^{|\pi_0|}|\hat{\pi}|^{-p}d\hat{\pi} \\
&= +\infty
\end{aligned} \tag{5}$$

for all p such that $1 \leq p < \infty$ and for each finite n, since

$$\int_{-|\pi_0|}^{|\pi_0|}|\hat{\pi}|^{-p}d\hat{\pi} = +\infty$$

Note that problem here is that part of the integrand (i.e., $|\hat{\pi}|^{-p}$) has a pole at $\hat{\pi} = 0$, so that if there is sufficient probability mass in the neighborhood of $\hat{\pi} = 0$, then the integral does not exist. We will provide more discussion and intuition when we contrast this case with the case where the estimator has been modified in the sense of Fuller (1977). Please see remark in the third section below.

WHY DOES THE FULLER MODIFICATION LEAD TO ESTIMATORS WITH MOMENTS?

To address this question, note first that, under the current setup, Fuller estimator can be written as

$$\hat{\delta}_{FULL} = \frac{\hat{\pi}(z'z)\hat{\phi} + (C/n)x'My}{\hat{\pi}(z'z)\hat{\pi} + (C/n)x'Mx} = \frac{n\hat{\pi}\hat{\phi} + (C/n)v'M\zeta}{n\hat{\pi}^2 + (C/n)v'Mv} = \frac{\hat{\pi}\hat{\phi} + (C/n)(v'M\zeta/n)}{\hat{\pi}^2 + (C/n)(v'Mv/n)} \tag{6}$$

where $M = I_n - z(z'z)^{-1}z' = I_n - zz'/n$. To understand why this estimator solves the moment problems it may be helpful to draw an analogy with ridge-regression. In particular, the ridge version of the least squares estimator has its denominator perturbed by an extra term which ensures that the denominator is nonzero. Similarly, in this case the Fuller modification modifies the denominator of 2SLS/LIML by adding an extra term.

To show that this added term is effective in ensuring the existence of moments, first partition $z = \begin{pmatrix} z_1, & z'_{2\cdot} \\ 1\times 1 & 1\times(n-1) \end{pmatrix}'$ and consider the decomposition

$$M = H^{\perp}H^{\perp'}$$

where

$$\underset{n\times(n-1)}{H^{\perp}} = \begin{pmatrix} -z'_{2\cdot}/z_1 \\ I_{n-1} \end{pmatrix}\left[I_{n-1} + \frac{z_{2\cdot}z'_{2\cdot}}{z_1^2}\right]^{-1/2} \in V_{n-1,n}$$

and where

$$V_{n-1,n} = \left\{ \underset{n\times(n-1)}{X} : X'X = I_{n-1} \right\}$$

denotes the Stiefel manifold. Consider the transformation $v_* = (n-1)^{-1/2} \times H^{\perp'}v$ and $\zeta_* = (n-1)^{-1/2}H^{\perp'}\zeta$, and it is easily verified that in the present case

$$\begin{pmatrix} \zeta_{*,i} \\ v_{*,i} \end{pmatrix} \equiv i.i.d.N(0,(n-1)^{-1}I_2)$$

where $v_{*,i}$ and $\zeta_{*,i}$ are the ith element of v_* and ζ_*, respectively. Moreover, v_* and ζ_* are independent of $\hat{\pi}$ and $\hat{\phi}$ in this case. Using this change of variables, we can rewrite the Fuller estimator in the representation

$$\hat{\delta}_{FULL} = \frac{\hat{\pi}\hat{\phi} + (1-1/n)(C/n)(v_*'\zeta_*)}{\hat{\pi}^2 + (1-1/n)(C/n)(v_*'v_*)}$$

Next, define

$$\xi_1 = \frac{1}{\sqrt{n}} z'\zeta, \xi_2 = \frac{1}{\sqrt{n}} z'v$$

so that

$$\hat{\phi} = \phi_0 + \frac{1}{\sqrt{n}}\xi_1, \hat{\pi} = \pi_0 + \frac{1}{\sqrt{n}}\xi_2$$

and we can further represent the Fuller estimator as

$$\begin{aligned} \hat{\delta}_{FULL} &= \frac{\hat{\pi}\hat{\phi} + (1-1/n)(C/n)(v_*'\zeta_*)}{\hat{\pi}^2 + (1-1/n)(C/n)(v_*'v_*)} \\ &= \frac{\pi_0^2\delta_0 + \pi_0(n^{-1/2}\xi_1) + \pi_0\delta_0(n^{-1/2}\xi_2) + n^{-1}\xi_1\xi_2 + (1-1/n)(C/n)(v_*'\zeta_*)}{\pi_0^2 + 2\pi_0(n^{-1/2}\xi_2) + n^{-1}\xi_2^2 + (1-1/n)(C/n)(v_*'v_*)} \end{aligned} \tag{7}$$

Note that Eq. (7) makes clear that the Fuller estimator can be written as a function of several random components, some of which are linear in the error vectors such as $n^{-1/2}\xi_1$ and $n^{-1/2}\xi_2$ while others are bilinear such as $v_*'\zeta_*$ and $v_*'v_*$. To show the existence of moments for the Fuller estimator, we divide the domain of integration into a region where all of these random components are in some small neighborhood of their asymptotic limit (denoted by the event $\mathcal{A}$ below) and the complement of this region (denoted by $\mathcal{A}^C$). More precisely, let

$$\begin{aligned} \mathcal{A}_1 &= \{|v_*'\zeta_*| < \eta_1\}, \mathcal{A}_2 = \{|v_*'v_* - 1| < \eta_2\}, \\ \mathcal{A}_3 &= \{|n^{-1/2}\xi_1| < \eta_3\}, \mathcal{A}_4 = \{|n^{-1/2}\xi_2| < \eta_4\} \\ \mathcal{A} &= \mathcal{A}_1 \cap \mathcal{A}_2 \cap \mathcal{A}_3 \cap \mathcal{A}_4 \end{aligned}$$

for constants η_1, η_2, η_3, $\eta_4 > 0$ and $\eta_4 < |\pi_0|/2$. Now,

$$
\begin{aligned}
&\left|\hat{\delta}_{FULL}\right|\mathbb{1}_{\mathcal{A}} \\
&= \left|\frac{\pi_0^2\delta_0 + \pi_0(n^{-1/2}\xi_1) + \pi_0\delta_0(n^{-1/2}\xi_2) + n^{-1}\xi_1\xi_2 + (1-1/n)(C/n)(v_*'\zeta_*)}{(\pi_0 + n^{-1/2}\xi_2)^2 + (1-1/n)(C/n)(v_*'v_*)}\right|\mathbb{1}_{\mathcal{A}} \\
&\le \frac{\pi_0^2|\delta_0| + |\pi_0|\left|n^{-1/2}\xi_1\right| + |\pi_0||\delta_0|\left|n^{-1/2}\xi_2\right| + \left|n^{-1/2}\xi_1\right|\left|n^{-1/2}\xi_2\right| + C\left|v_*'\zeta_*\right|}{\pi_0^2 - 2|\pi_0|\left|n^{-1/2}\xi_2\right|} \\
&\le \frac{\pi_0^2|\delta_0| + |\pi_0|\eta_3 + |\pi_0||\delta_0|\eta_4 + \eta_3\eta_4 + C\eta_1}{\pi_0^2 - 2|\pi_0|\eta_4}
\end{aligned}
$$

It follows that for any fixed $p>0$ and any true parameter value (δ_0,π_0) there exists a positive constant C_1, possibly depending on (δ_0,π_0) and p, such that

$$
E\left[\left|\hat{\delta}_{FULL}\right|^p \mathbb{1}_{\mathcal{A}}\right] \le C_1 < \infty \tag{8}
$$

Moreover, suppose that the parameter space of (δ,π) is some bounded set $\mathcal{D} \subset \mathbb{R}^2$, then Eq. (8) holds under some constant not depending on the true value (δ_0,π_0).

Next, consider what happens under the event $\mathcal{A}^C$. In this case, we first form the upper bound

$$
\begin{aligned}
\left|\hat{\delta}_{FULL}\right| &= \left|\frac{\hat{\pi}\hat{\phi} + (C/n)(v_*'\zeta_*/n)}{\hat{\pi}^2 + (C/n)(v_*'v_*/n)}\right| \le \frac{\left|\hat{\pi}\hat{\phi}\right| + (1-1/n)(C/n)(\left|v_*'\zeta_*\right|)}{(1-1/n)(C/n)(v_*'v_*)} \\
&= \left(\frac{n}{n-1}\right)\frac{n\left|\hat{\pi}\hat{\phi}\right|}{Cv_*'v_*} + \frac{\left|v_*'\zeta_*\right|}{v_*'v_*}
\end{aligned}
$$

By Loève's inequality, we have for any fixed $p>0$

$$
E\left[\left|\hat{\delta}_{FULL}\right|^p \mathbb{1}_{\mathcal{A}^C}\right] \le c_p\left\{\left(\frac{n}{n-1}\right)^p E\left|\frac{n\left|\hat{\pi}\hat{\phi}\right|\mathbb{1}_{\mathcal{A}^C}}{Cv_*'v_*}\right|^p + E\left[\frac{\left|v_*'\zeta_*\right|}{v_*'v_*}\mathbb{1}_{\mathcal{A}^C}\right]^p\right\} \tag{9}
$$

To analyze the first term in Eq. (9), note that, by the Cauchy–Schwarz (CS) inequality, we have

$$
E\left|\frac{n\left|\hat{\pi}\hat{\phi}\right|\mathbb{1}_{\mathcal{A}^C}}{Cv_*'v_*}\right|^p \le \frac{n^p}{C^p}\sqrt{\Pr\{\mathcal{A}^C\}}\sqrt{E\left|\frac{\left|\hat{\pi}\hat{\phi}\right|}{v_*'v_*}\right|^{2p}}
$$

Moreover,[1]

$$\begin{aligned}
\Pr\{\mathcal{A}^C\} &= \Pr\{\mathcal{A}_1^C \cup \mathcal{A}_2^C \cup \mathcal{A}_3^C \cup \mathcal{A}_4^C\} \\
&\leq \Pr\{\mathcal{A}_1^C\} + \Pr\{\mathcal{A}_2^C\} + \Pr\{\mathcal{A}_3^C\} + \Pr\{\mathcal{A}_4^C\} \\
&= \Pr\{|v_*'\zeta_*| \geq \eta_1\} + \Pr\{|v_*'v_* - 1| \geq \eta_2\} + \Pr\{|n^{-1/2}\xi_1| \geq \eta_3\} \\
&\quad + \Pr\{|n^{-1/2}\xi_2| \geq \eta_4\} \\
&\leq \frac{E|v_*'\zeta_*|^{4p}}{\eta_1^{4p}} + \frac{E|v_*'v_* - 1|^{4p}}{\eta_2^{4p}} + \frac{E[n^{-1/2}\xi_1]^{4p}}{\eta_3^{4p}} + \frac{E[n^{-1/2}\xi_2]^{4p}}{\eta_4^{4p}} \\
&\quad \text{(by Markov's inequality)} \\
&< \frac{C_p}{n^{2p}\eta_1^{4p}} + \frac{C_p}{n^{2p}\eta_2^{4p}} + \frac{C_p}{n^{2p}\eta_3^{4p}} + \frac{C_p}{n^{2p}\eta_4^{4p}} \\
&\quad \text{(by Lemma 1 below and by the fact that both } \xi_1 \text{ and } \xi_2 \text{ are } N(0,1) \\
&\quad \text{random variables)} \\
&< \frac{\bar{C}}{n^{2p}} \qquad (10)
\end{aligned}$$

Turning our attention now to the expectation $E||\hat{\pi}\hat{\phi}|/(v_*'v_*)|^{2p}$, note that

$$E\left|\frac{|\hat{\pi}\hat{\phi}|}{v_*'v_*}\right|^{2p} = E\left|\hat{\pi}\hat{\phi}\right|^{2p} E\left|v_*'v_*\right|^{-2p}$$

where the equality above follows from the fact that v_* is independent of $\hat{\pi}$ and $\hat{\phi}$, as noted above. Given the joint normality of the OLS estimators as noted in Eq. (4) and given that $\hat{\pi}$ and $\hat{\phi}$ are independent, it is trivial to show (since all moments of the normal distribution exist) that there exists a constant C_p such that

$$E|\hat{\pi}\hat{\phi}|^{2p} = E|\hat{\pi}|^{2p}E|\hat{\phi}|^{2p} \leq C_p < \infty \qquad (11)$$

for any fixed $p>0$. Next, we consider $E\left|v_*'v_*\right|^{-2p}$. To evaluate this expectation, it is helpful to change into (generalized) polar coordinates, viz

$$v_* = hr \text{ with } h = v_*(v_*'v_*)^{-1/2} \text{ and } r = (v_*'v_*)^{1/2} \qquad (12)$$

where $h \in V_{1,n-1}$, so that $h'h = I_{n-1}$. The Jacobian of this transformation is given by

$$(dv_*) = c_n r^{(n-2)} dr[dh] \qquad (13)$$

where $[dh]$ denotes the exterior differential form of the normalized invariant measure on the Stiefel manifold $V_{1,n-1}$ and where

$$c_n = \frac{2\pi^{(n-1)/2}}{\Gamma\left[\frac{1}{2}(n-1)\right]} \tag{14}$$

(See, e.g., Lemma 1.5.2 of Chikuse, 2003). We show in Lemma 2 below that

$$E\left|v_*'v_*\right|^{-2p} = 1 + O(n^{-1}) \tag{15}$$

so that the first term in (9) is bounded for all n sufficiently large, that is,

$$\begin{aligned} E\left|\frac{n\left|\hat{\pi}\hat{\phi}\right|\mathbb{I}_{\mathcal{A}^C}}{Cv_*'v_*}\right|^p &\leq \frac{n^p}{C^p}\sqrt{\Pr\{\mathcal{A}^C\}}\sqrt{E\left|\frac{\left|\hat{\pi}\hat{\phi}\right|}{v_*'v_*}\right|^{2p}} \\ &= \frac{n^p}{C^p}\sqrt{\frac{\bar{C}}{n^{2p}}}\sqrt{E\left|\hat{\pi}\hat{\phi}\right|^{2p} E\left|v_*'v_*\right|^{-2p}} \\ &\leq \frac{n^p}{C^p}\sqrt{\frac{\bar{C}}{n^{2p}}}\sqrt{C_p(1+O(n^{-1}))} \\ &= O(1) \end{aligned} \tag{16}$$

Moreover, it is easy to show that the second term in Eq. (9) is also bounded for all n sufficiently large, that is, $E[\{\left|v_*'\zeta_*\right|/(v_*'v_*)\}\mathbb{I}_{\mathcal{A}^C}]^p = O(1)$. In particular, by making use of various forms of the CS inequality, we have that

$$\begin{aligned} E\left[\frac{\left|v_*'\zeta_*\right|}{v_*'v_*}\mathbb{I}_{\mathcal{A}^C}\right]^p &\leq \sqrt{\Pr(\mathcal{A}^C)}\sqrt{E\left|\frac{\left|v_*'\zeta_*\right|}{v_*'v_*}\right|^{2p}} \leq \sqrt{E[\left|v_*'v_*\right|^{-p}\left|\zeta'_*\zeta_*\right|^p]} \\ &\leq \left(E\left|v_*'v_*\right|^{-2p}\right)^{1/4}\left(E\left|\zeta'_*\zeta_*\right|^{2p}\right)^{1/4} \end{aligned}$$

Now, since ζ_* has the same multivariate normal distribution as v_*, we can apply Lemma 2 (given below) for the case $q = -p < 0$ to obtain

$$E\left|\zeta'_*\zeta_*\right|^{2p} = 1 + O(n^{-1}) \tag{17}$$

Using this result in conjunction with Eq. (15), we have that

$$E\left[\frac{\left|v_*'\zeta_*\right|}{v_*'v_*}\mathbb{I}_{\mathcal{A}^C}\right]^p \leq \sqrt{1+O(n^{-1})}\sqrt{1+O(n^{-1})} = O(1) \tag{18}$$

It follows from Eqs. (8), (16), and (18) that

$$\begin{aligned} E[|\hat{\delta}_{FULL}|^p] &= E[\left|\hat{\delta}_{FULL}\right|^p \mathbb{I}_{\mathcal{A}}] + E[\left|\hat{\delta}_{FULL}\right|^p \mathbb{I}_{\mathcal{A}^C}] \\ &\leq E[\left|\hat{\delta}_{FULL}\right|^p \mathbb{I}_{\mathcal{A}}] + c_p \left\{ \left(\frac{n}{n-1}\right)^p E\left|\frac{n\left|\hat{\pi}\hat{\phi}\right| \mathbb{I}_{\mathcal{A}^C}}{C v_*' v_*}\right|^p + E\left[\frac{\left|v_*'\zeta_*\right|}{v_*' v_*} \mathbb{I}_{\mathcal{A}^C}\right]^p \right\} \\ &= O(1) \end{aligned}$$

which yields the desired existence of moments result for the Fuller estimator.

Remark: Looking back at expression (14), note that

$$c_n = \frac{2\pi^{(n-1)/2}}{\Gamma\left[\frac{1}{2}(n-1)\right]}$$

is the normalization factor for the invariant (uniform) measure on the sphere, and it gives the surface area of the unit sphere (i.e., a sphere with unit radius) in $\mathbb{R}^{n-1}$. By Stirling's approximation one can show that

$$c_n = \frac{2\pi^{(n-1)/2}}{\Gamma\left[\frac{1}{2}(n-1)\right]} \sim \left(\frac{2e\pi}{n}\right)^{(n-2)/2}$$

so that this surface area is very small in high dimension, that is, when n is large. Moreover, the volume of the unit sphere is proportional to $(n-1)^{-1}c_n$, so that it is also small. It follows that in high dimension, the probability of landing within a fixed neighborhood of the origin under the invariant uniform measure is very small. This basic fact of high-dimensional convex geometry provides an intuition for why the Fuller modification is effective in solving the moment problem.[2] In particular, in our simple setting here, the denominator of the Fuller estimator is given by

$$\hat{\pi}^2 + (1-1/n)(c/n)v'_* v_* \sim \hat{\pi}^2 + (C/n)\|v_*\|^2$$

Moreover, the denominator of the $2SLS/LIML$[3] estimator is simply a special case of the expression above with $C=0$. Hence, the $2SLS/LIML$ estimator has denominator that is the square of an one-dimensional random variable $\hat{\pi}$, so that, in particular, its probability of being zero is relatively high given its low dimensionality. This, in turn, leads to the non-existence of moments of the $2SLS/LIML$ estimator, as we have already shown in Eq. (5) above by explicit calculations. On the other hand, as noted above, the Fuller modification amounts to a ridge-regression-type perturbation of the denominator of $2SLS/LIML$, so that the denominator of the modified estimator is now dependent on the square of the norm of a high-dimensional vector v_*, in addition to $\hat{\pi}^2$. In consequence, the probability of the denominator being zero is now very small for finite n sufficiently large, leading to the existence of moments.

IS NORMALITY REQUIRED FOR THE FULLER ESTIMATOR TO HAVE MOMENTS?

Note that although the results here are shown under a Gaussian error assumption as in Fuller (1977), the existence of moments of the Fuller estimator is not hinged upon such an assumption. In particular, such an assumption is not needed to establish the boundedness of the inverse moment $E\left|v_*'v_*\right|^{-2p}$ even though in proving Lemma 2 below, we have evaluated an integral of the form

$$\int_0^{\infty} (2\pi)^{-1/2}(n-1)^{1/2} r^{(n-4p-2)} \exp\left\{-\frac{(n-1)}{2}r^2\right\} dr$$

which may suggest that we need distributions with exponentially decaying tails in order to ensure the existence of all moments as n becomes large. Note, however, that we can easily modify the proof of Lemma 2 by a truncation argument since the existence of $E|v_*'v_*|^{-2p}$ depends only on the behavior of the high-dimensional random vector v_* near the origin. More specifically, note that

$$\begin{aligned} E\left|v_*'v_*\right|^{-2p} &= E[\left|v_*'v_*\right|^{-2p} \mathbb{I}\{\left|v_*'v_*\right| < 1\}] + E[\left|v_*'v_*\right|^{-2p} \mathbb{I}\{\left|v_*'v_*\right| \geq 1\}] \\ &\leq E[\left|v_*'v_*\right|^{-2p} \mathbb{I}\{\left|v_*'v_*\right| < 1\}] + 1 \end{aligned}$$

Hence, changing into polar coordinates, that is, $v_* = hr$ with $h = v_*(v_*'v_*)^{-1/2}$ and $r = (v_*'v_*)^{1/2}$, we have

$$E\left|v_*'v_*\right|^{-2p} \leq E[r^{-4p} \mathbb{I}\{r^2 < 1\}] + 1$$

so that we really only need to specify conditions on the density of r near zero in order to ensure the existence of $E|v_*'v_*|^{-2p}$.

On the other hand, to show the existence of $E[|\hat{\delta}_{FULL}|^p]$ for some $p>0$ (possibly large) we do of course need the error distributions of the IV regression model to have enough (positive order) moments. The assumption of normality ensures that this is not a problem for any p. However, if we are only interested in the existence of $E[|\hat{\delta}_{FULL}|^p]$ for some fixed p, it is sufficient to specify weaker moment conditions on the error distributions, as we do in Hausman et al. (2012).

WHY DO WE NEED A CONDITION SUCH AS HAUSMAN ET AL. (2012), ASSUMPTION 9?

Assumption 9. There exists a positive constant $\bar{C}$ and a positive integer N such that

$$E[(\det[S_{*,n}])^{-2p(1+\eta)/\eta}] \leq \bar{C} < \infty$$

for all $n \geq N$, where $\eta > 0$ is as specified in Assumption 8 (of Hausman et al., 2012) is as follows:

The purpose of this Assumption 9 is to ensure the existence of certain inverse moments. Under Gaussain error assumption, we show explicity in Lemma 2 below that the inverse moments of the form $E[v_*' v_*]^{2p}$ (for $p > 0$) do exist. However, in general under possibly non-normal distribution, it is not true that inverse moments will necessarily exist.

To show that a condition such as Assumption 9 is not superfluous, we give an example of a pathological density under which inverse moments do not exist. To proceed, let w be an $(n-1) \times 1$ random vector, and consider the family of densities

$$f_n(w) = \frac{\Gamma\left[\frac{1}{2}(n-1)\right]}{2^{1/2}\pi^{n/2}} \frac{1}{(w'w)^{(n-2)/2}} \exp\left\{-\frac{1}{2} w'w\right\}, \text{ for } w \in R^{n-1}$$

First, we show that $f_n(w)$ is indeed a density. To proceed, we again change into polar coordinates, viz

$$w = hr, \text{ where } h = w(w'w)^{-1/2} \text{ and } r = (w'w)^{1/2}$$

$$(dw) = c_n r^{(n-2)} dr[dh], \quad \text{where } c_n = \frac{2\pi^{(n-1)/2}}{\Gamma\left[\frac{1}{2}(n-1)\right]}$$

It follows that

$$\begin{aligned}
&\int_{\mathbb{R}^{n-1}} \frac{\Gamma\left[\frac{1}{2}(n-1)\right]}{2^{3/2}\pi^{n/2}} \frac{1}{(w'w)^{(n-2)/2}} \exp\left\{-\frac{1}{2} w'w\right\}(dw) \\
&= \frac{\Gamma\left[\frac{1}{2}(n-1)\right]}{2^{1/2}\pi^{n/2}} \int_{V_{1,n-1}} \int_0^\infty \frac{1}{r^{(n-2)}} \exp\left\{-\frac{1}{2} r^2\right\} c_n r^{(n-2)} dr[dh] \\
&= \frac{\Gamma\left[\frac{1}{2}(n-1)\right]}{2^{1/2}\pi^{n/2}} \frac{2\pi^{(n-1)/2}}{\Gamma\left[\frac{1}{2}(n-1)\right]} \int_{V_{1,n-1}} \int_0^\infty \exp\left\{-\frac{1}{2} r^2\right\} dr[dh] \\
&= \sqrt{\frac{2}{\pi}} \int_{V_{1,n-1}} \int_0^\infty \exp\left\{-\frac{1}{2} r^2\right\} dr[dh] \\
&= 2 \int_{V_{1,n-1}} \int_0^\infty \frac{1}{\sqrt{2\pi}} \exp\left\{-\frac{1}{2} r^2\right\} dr[dh]
\end{aligned}$$

$$= \int_{V_{1,n-1}} [dh] \quad \left(\text{since} \int_0^\infty \frac{1}{\sqrt{2\pi}} \exp\left\{-\frac{1}{2}r^2\right\} dr = \frac{1}{2}\right)$$

$$= \int_{V_{1,n-1}} [dh] = 1 \quad (\text{since } [dh] \text{ defines the differential form for the normalized Haar measure})$$

Moreover, it is easy to see that the inverse moment $E[(w'w)^{-1}]$ does not exist in this case, since by previous calculations

$$E[(w'w)^{-1}] = \int_{R^{n-K}} \frac{\Gamma\left[\frac{1}{2}(n-1)\right]}{2^{3/2}\pi^{n/2}} \frac{1}{(w'w)^{n/2}} \exp\left\{-\frac{1}{2}w'w\right\}(dw)$$

$$= \frac{\Gamma\left[\frac{1}{2}(n-1)\right]}{2^{1/2}\pi^{n/2}} \int_{V_{1,n-1}} \int_0^\infty \frac{1}{r^n} \exp\left\{-\frac{1}{2}r^2\right\} c_n r^{(n-2)} dr[dh]$$

$$= \frac{\Gamma\left[\frac{1}{2}(n-1)\right]}{2^{1/2}\pi^{n/2}} \frac{2\pi^{(n-1)/2}}{\Gamma\left[\frac{1}{2}(n-1)\right]} \int_{V_{1,n-1}} \int_0^\infty \frac{1}{r^2} \exp\left\{-\frac{1}{2}r^2\right\} dr[dh]$$

$$= \sqrt{\frac{2}{\pi}} \int_0^\infty \frac{1}{r^2} \exp\left\{-\frac{1}{2}r^2\right\} dr \int_{V_{1,n-1}} [dh]$$

$$\geq \sqrt{\frac{2}{\pi}} \int_0^\varepsilon \frac{1}{r^2} \exp\left\{-\frac{1}{2}r^2\right\} dr \quad \text{for some } \varepsilon \text{ such that } 0 < \varepsilon < 1$$

$$\geq \sqrt{\frac{2}{\pi}} \exp\left\{-\frac{1}{2}\varepsilon^2\right\} \int_0^\varepsilon \frac{1}{r^2} dr = +\infty$$

so that without ruling out pathological cases such as this one, we will not in general be able to establish the existence of moments of the Fuller estimator.

WHY DO WE HAVE THE ADJUSTMENT FORMULA $\hat{\alpha} = [\tilde{\alpha} - (1-\tilde{\alpha})C/n][1-(1-\tilde{\alpha})C/n]^{-1}$ IN *HFUL*, AND WHAT ARE THE EFFECTS OF *C* ON THE ASYMPTOTIC PROPERTIES OF *HFUL*?

Consider here the more general IV regression model given in the second section of Hausman et al. (2012) with G endogenous regressors and K

instruments. Let X denote the regressors and let Z denote the instruments. In this case, the *HFUL* estimator has the form

$$\hat{\delta} = (X'[P - D_P]X - \hat{\alpha}X'X)^{-1}(X'[P - D_P]y - \hat{\alpha}X'y) \tag{20}$$

where $P = Z(Z'Z)^{-1}Z'$, $D_p = diag(P_{11}, \ldots, P_{nn})$ with P_{ii} being the ith diagonal element of P, and

$$\hat{\alpha} = [\tilde{\alpha} - (1 - \tilde{\alpha})C/n][1 - (1 - \tilde{\alpha})C/n]^{-1} \tag{21}$$

with $\tilde{\alpha}$ being the α value which appears in *HLIM*, the heteroscedasticity robust version of LIML, which was introduced by Hausman et al. (2012). To better understand the adjustment formula (21), note that in Lemma B1 of a supplementary technical appendix to Hausman et al. (2012) (available on the web at http://econweb.umd.edu/~chao/Research/research.html), we show that the *HFUL* estimator Eq. (20) has an equivalent representation of the form

$$\hat{\delta} = \left(X'[P - D_P]X - \left\{\tilde{\kappa} - \frac{C}{n}\right\}X'[M + D_P]X\right)^{-1} \times \left(X'[P - D_P]y - \left\{\tilde{\kappa} - \frac{C}{n}\right\}X'[M + D_P]y\right) \tag{22}$$

where $M = I_n - P$ and $\tilde{\kappa}$ is the smallest root of the determinantal equation

$$\det\{\bar{X}'[P - D_P]\bar{X} - \kappa\bar{X}'[M + D_P]\bar{X}\} = 0$$

with $\bar{X} = [y \quad X]$. From Eq. (22), it is apparent that the adjustment factor $\hat{\alpha}$ allows *HFUL* to be rewritten in a form where the "denominator" also contains a ridge-regression-type perturbation term (i.e., the term (C/n) $X'[M + D_p]X$) analogous to that of the Fuller estimator Eq. (6). As we have shown earlier, this additional term leads to the existence of moments.

C does not affect the first-order asymptotic properties of *HFUL* as can be seen from Theorem 2 of Hausman et al. (2012) and the surrounding discussion. It will have higher-order effects, but that is beyond the scope of this chapter.

Lemmas and Proofs:

Lemma 1. Suppose that $v_* \sim N(0,(n-1)^{-1}I_{n-1})$ and $\zeta_* \sim N(0,(n-1)^{-1}I_{n-1})$; and v_* and ζ_* are independent. Then, for any positive integer p, the following results hold:

$$E[v_*'\zeta_*]^{4p} \leq C_p/n^{2p}; \tag{a}$$

$$E[v_*'v_* - 1]^{4p} \leq C_p/n^{2p}; \tag{b}$$

where C_p is a constant which may be different in parts (a) and (b) above and which may depend on p.

Proof: Define $\tilde{v} = (n-1)^{1/2}v_*$ and $\tilde{\zeta} = (n-1)^{1/2}\zeta_*$, so that $\tilde{v} \sim N(0,I_{n-1})$ and $\tilde{\zeta} \sim N(0,I_{n-1})$. Now, to show part (a), note first that

$$\begin{aligned} E[v_*'\zeta_*]^{4p} &= (n-1)^{-4p}E[\tilde{v}'\tilde{\zeta}]^{4p} \\ &= \frac{1}{(n-1)^{4p}}E\left[\sum_{i=1}^{n-1}\tilde{v}_i\tilde{\zeta}_i\right]^{4p} \\ &\leq \frac{1}{(n-1)^{4p}}E\left[\sum_{i=1}^{n-1}\tilde{v}_i\tilde{\zeta}_i\right]^{4p} \\ &= \frac{1}{(n-1)^{4p}}\sum_{1\leq i_1,\ldots,i_{4p}\leq n-1}E\left[\prod_{j=1}^{4p}(\tilde{v}_{i_j}\tilde{\zeta}_{i_j})\right] \end{aligned} \tag{23}$$

Observe that, $E[\tilde{v}_{i_j}\tilde{\zeta}_{i_\ell}] = 0$ for all $j \neq \ell$, since $E[\tilde{v}_{i_j}] = E[\tilde{\zeta}_{i_j}] = 0$ for all i_j and $\tilde{v}_{i_j}$ is independent of $\tilde{\zeta}_{i_\ell}$ for all $j \neq \ell$. In consequence, each $\tilde{v}_{i_j}\tilde{\zeta}_{i_j}$ must appear at least twice in the product $\prod_{j=1}^{4p}(\tilde{v}_{i_j}\tilde{\zeta}_{i_j})$; otherwise, the expectation of this product is equal to zero. Hence, at most $2p$ distinct factors of the form $\tilde{v}_{i_j}\tilde{\zeta}_{i_j}$ will appear in the product $\prod_{j=1}^{4p}(\tilde{v}_{i_j}\tilde{\zeta}_{i_j})$ if its expectation is nonzero. To account for the different cases, consider a product with $2p-r$ distinct factors, where $r = 0,1,\ldots 2p-1$; and let N_r be the number of such products, i.e., N_r is the number of ways that one can assign $i_1,\ldots,i_{4p}$ from the set $\{1,\ldots,n\}$ such that each i_j appears at least twice and such that exactly $2p-r$ different integers are selected. Moreover, note that since $\tilde{v}_{i_j}$ and $\tilde{\zeta}_{i_j}$ are normally distributed, so that, in particular, moments of all order exist. From these facts, we deduce that there exists some positive constant $\bar{C}_p$ (depending on p) such that

$$E\left[v_*'\zeta_*\right]^{4p} \leq \frac{1}{(n-1)^{4p}}\sum_{1\leq i_1,\ldots,i_{4p}\leq n}E\left[\prod_{j=1}^{4p}(\tilde{v}_{i_j}\tilde{\zeta}_{i_j})\right] \leq \frac{\bar{C}_p}{(n-1)^{4p}}\sum_{r=0}^{2p-1}N_r$$

Now, a crude upper bound for N_r is given by

$$\begin{aligned} N_r &\leq \binom{n}{2p-r}(2p-r)^{4p} \leq \frac{n^{2p-r}}{(2p-r)!}(2p-r)^{4p} \leq (en)^{2p-r}(2p-r)^{2p+r} \\ &\leq (en)^{2p-r}(2p)^{2p+r} \end{aligned}$$

where the third inequality above has made use of the inequality

$$(2p-r)! \geq (2p-r)^{2p-r} e^{-(2p-r)}$$

Applying this upper estimate of N_r, we obtain

$$\begin{aligned}
\frac{1}{(n-1)^{4p}} E\left[\tilde{v}'\tilde{\zeta}\right]^{4p} &\leq \bar{C}_p \frac{1}{(n-1)^{4p}} \sum_{r=0}^{2p-1} (en)^{2p-r}(2p)^{2p+r} \\
&= \bar{C}_p \frac{(2pen)^{2p}}{(n-1)^{4p}} \sum_{r=0}^{2p-1} \left(\frac{2p}{en}\right)^r \\
&= \bar{C}_p \left(\frac{n}{n-1}\right)^{4p} \left(\frac{2pe}{n}\right)^{2p} \sum_{r=0}^{2p-1} \left(\frac{2p}{en}\right)^r \\
&\leq \bar{C}_p \left(\frac{n}{n-1}\right)^{4p} \left(\frac{2pe}{n}\right)^{2p} \left(1-\frac{2p}{en}\right)^{-1} \\
&\quad \left(\text{for } n \text{ sufficiently large so that } \frac{2p}{n} < 1\right) \\
&< 2\bar{C}_p \left(\frac{n}{n-1}\right)^{4p} \left(\frac{2pe}{n}\right)^{2p} \\
&\leq C_p n^{-2p} \qquad (24)
\end{aligned}$$

To show part (b), note that

$$E[v_*'v_* - 1]^{4p} = \frac{1}{(n-1)^{4p}} E\left[\sum_{i=1}^{n-1}(\tilde{v}_i^2 - 1)\right]^{4p} = \frac{1}{(n-1)^{4p}} \sum_{1\leq i_1,\ldots,i_{4p}\leq n} E\left[\prod_{j=1}^{4p}(\tilde{v}_{i_j}^2 - 1)\right]$$

Moreover, observe that $E[(\tilde{v}_{i_j}^2 - 1)(\tilde{v}_{i_\ell}^2 - 1)] = 0$ for all $j \neq \ell$ by mutual independence of the elements of the subsequence $\{\tilde{v}_{i_j}^2\}$ and by the fact that $E[\tilde{v}_{i_j}^2] = 1$ for all i_j. It follows again that each $(\tilde{v}_{i_j}^2 - 1)$ must appear at least twice in the product $\prod_{j=1}^{4p}(\tilde{v}_{i_j}^2 - 1)$ for this product to have a nonzero expectation. Hence, we can bound $E[v_*'v_* - 1]^{4p}$ in a way similar to what has been done in the proof of part (a) to obtain

$$E[v_*'v_* - 1]^{4p} \leq \frac{\bar{C}_p}{(n-1)^{4p}} \sum_{r=0}^{2p-1} N_r \leq C_p n^{-2p} \text{ for } n \text{ sufficiently large} \quad \blacksquare$$

Lemma 2. Suppose that $v_* \sim N(0,(n-1)^{-1} I_{n-1})$. Then, for any real constant q,

$$E\left|v_*'v_*\right|^{-2q} = 1 + O(n^{-1})$$

Proof: Making use of the change-of-variable formulae Eqs. (12)–(14), we can evaluate $E|v_*' v_*|^{-2q}$ as follows:

$$E|v_*'v_*|^{-2q} = \int_{\mathbb{R}^{n-1}} |v_*'v_*|^{-2q} \frac{(n-1)^{\frac{1}{2}(n-1)}}{(2\pi)^{(n-1)/2}} \exp\left\{-\frac{(n-1)}{2} v_*'v_*\right\}(dv_*)$$

$$= \int_{V_{1,n-1}} \int_0^\infty |rh'hr|^{-2q} \frac{(n-1)^{\frac{1}{2}(n-1)}}{(2\pi)^{(n-1)/2}} \exp\left\{-\frac{(n-1)}{2} rh'hr\right\} c_n r^{(n-2)} dr[dh]$$

$$= \int_{V_{1,n-1}} \int_0^\infty r^{-4q} \frac{(n-1)^{\frac{1}{2}(n-1)}}{(2\pi)^{(n-1)/2}} \exp\left\{-\frac{(n-1)}{2} r^2\right\} \frac{2\pi^{(n-1)/2}}{\Gamma\left[\frac{1}{2}(n-1)\right]} r^{(n-2)} dr[dh]$$

$$= \int_{V_{1,n-1}} \frac{2^{-(n-4)/2}\pi^{1/2}(n-1)^{\frac{1}{2}(n-2)}}{\Gamma\left[\frac{1}{2}(n-1)\right]} \int_0^\infty (2\pi)^{-1/2} r^{(n-4q-2)}(n-1)^{1/2}$$

$$\times \exp\left\{-\frac{(n-1)}{2} r^2\right\} dr[dh]$$

Now, the integral

$$\int_0^\infty (2\pi)^{-1/2}(n-1)^{1/2} r^{(n-4q-2)} \exp\left\{-\frac{(n-1)}{2} r^2\right\} dr$$

$$= \frac{1}{2}\int_{-\infty}^\infty (2\pi)^{-1/2}(n-1)^{1/2}|r|^{(n-4q-2)} \exp\left\{-\frac{(n-1)}{2} r^2\right\} dr$$

$$= \frac{1}{2}(n-1)^{-(n-4q-2)/2} \frac{2^{(n-4q-2)/2}\Gamma\left[\frac{1}{2}(n-4q-1)\right]}{\sqrt{\pi}}$$

$$= \frac{2^{(n-4q-4)/2}(n-1)^{-(n-4q-2)/2}\Gamma\left[\frac{1}{2}(n-4q-1)\right]}{\sqrt{\pi}}$$

for n sufficiently large. Plugging this into the original multiple integral we have

$$E|v_*'v_*|^{-2q} = \int_{V_{1,n-1}} \frac{2^{-(n-4)/2}\pi^{1/2}(n-1)^{\frac{1}{2}(n-2)}}{\Gamma\left[\frac{1}{2}(n-1)\right]} \int_0^\infty (2\pi)^{-1/2} r^{(n-4q-2)}(n-1)^{1/2}$$

$$\times \exp\left\{-\frac{(n-1)}{2} r^2\right\} dr[dh]$$

$$= \frac{2^{-(n-4)/2}\pi^{1/2}(n-1)^{\frac{1}{2}(n-2)}}{\Gamma\left[\frac{1}{2}(n-1)\right]} \frac{2^{(n-4q-4)/2}(n-1)^{-(n-4q-2)/2}\Gamma\left[\frac{1}{2}(n-4q-1)\right]}{\sqrt{\pi}}$$

$$\times \int_{V_{1,n-1}} [dh]$$

$$= 2^{-2q}(n-1)^{2q} \frac{\Gamma\left[\frac{1}{2}(n-4q-1)\right]}{\Gamma\left[\frac{1}{2}(n-1)\right]}$$

where the last equality follows from the fact that

$$\int_{V_{1,n-1}} [dh] = 1$$

Next, note that by the Stirling approximation

$$\begin{aligned}
\Gamma\left[\frac{1}{2}(n-4q-1)\right] &= \left(\frac{4\pi}{n-4q-1}\right)^{1/2}\left(\frac{n-4q-1}{2e}\right)^{(n-4q-1)/2}(1+O(n^{-1})) \\
&= (4\pi)^{1/2} n^{(n-4q-2)/2}(2e)^{-(n-4q-1)/2}\left(1-\frac{4q+1}{n}\right)^{n/2}(1+O(n^{-1})) \\
&= (4\pi)^{1/2} n^{(n-4q-2)/2}(2e)^{-(n-4q-1)/2} e^{-(4q+1)/2}(1+O(n^{-1})) \\
&= \left(\frac{n}{2e}\right)^{(n-4q-2)/2}\left(\frac{2\pi}{e^{2(2q+1)}}\right)^{1/2}(1+O(n^{-1}))
\end{aligned}$$

Similarly,

$$\Gamma\left[\frac{1}{2}(n-1)\right] = \left(\frac{n}{2e}\right)^{(n-2)/2}\left(\frac{2\pi}{e^2}\right)^{1/2}(1+O(n^{-1}))$$

Putting things together, we have

$$\begin{aligned}
E\left|v_*'v_*\right|^{-2q} &= \int_{\mathbb{R}^{n-1}} \left|v_*'v_*\right|^{-2q}\frac{(n-1)^{\frac{1}{2}(n-1)}}{(2\pi)^{(n-1)/2}}\exp\left\{-\frac{(n-1)}{2}v_*'v_*\right\}(dv_*) \\
&= 2^{-2q}(n-1)^{2q}\frac{\Gamma\left[\frac{1}{2}(n-4q-1)\right]}{\Gamma\left[\frac{1}{2}(n-1)\right]} \\
&= 2^{-2q}(n-1)^{2q}\left(\frac{n}{2e}\right)^{(n-4q-2)/2}\left(\frac{2\pi}{e^{2(2q+1)}}\right)^{1/2}\left(\frac{n}{2e}\right)^{-(n-2)/2} \\
&\quad\times\left(\frac{2\pi}{e^2}\right)^{-1/2}(1+O(n^{-1})) \\
&= 2^{-2q}(n-1)^{2q}\left(\frac{n}{2e}\right)^{-2q} e^{-2q}(1+O(n^{-1})) \\
&= \left(1-\frac{1}{n}\right)^{2q}(1+O(n^{-1})) \\
&= 1+O(n^{-1}).
\end{aligned}$$

■

ACKNOWLEDGEMENT

We all are indebted to Jerry for his advice, insights, wisdom, and wit. We thank James Fisher for helpful comments.

NOTES

1. These moment bounds are obtained by using fairly standard arguments commonly used to establish certain large deviation inequalities. See in particular Chapter 2 of Tao (2012). For completeness sake, we give the explicit calculations of these bounds in the proof of Lemma 1 below. Note, however, that more complicated bounds are actually needed for the more general IV regression setting considered in Hausman et al. (2012) and so a different method of proof is used there.
2. The study of high-dimensional spheres with unit radius has a long history. An elegant modern account can be found in Ball (1997). Our chapter, however, seems to be the first to apply the basic results and concepts of high-dimensional convex geometry to provide an intuitive explanation for the eixtence of moments of the Fuller estimator.
3. Here, we consider the case of just identification, for which the *LIML* and *2SLS* estimators are equivalent.

Assumption 9. There exists a positive constant $\bar{C}$ and a positive integer N such that

$$E[(\det[S_{*,n}])^{-2p(1+\eta)/\eta}] \leq \bar{C} < \infty \tag{19}$$

for all $n \geq N$, where $\eta > 0$ is as specified in Hausman et al. (2012), Assumption 8.

REFERENCES

Ball, K. (1997). An elementary introduction to modern convex geometry. In S. Levy (Ed.), *Flavors of geometry*. MSRI Lecture Notes. Cambridge: Cambridge University Press.

Bekker, P. A. (1994). Alternative approximations to the distributions of instrumental variable estimators. *Econometrica*, *62*, 657–681.

Chikuse, Y. (2003). Statistics on special manifolds. In *Lecture notes in statist* (Vol. 174). New York, NY: Springer.

Fuller, W. A. (1977). Some properties of a modification of the limited information estimator. *Econometrica*, *45*, 939–954.

Hahn, J., Hausman, J. A., & Kuersteiner, G. M. (2004). Estimation with weak instruments: Accuracy of higher-order Bias and MSE approximations. *Econometrics Journal*, *7*, 272–306.

Hausman, J. A., Newey, W. K., Woutersen, T., Chao, J. C., & Swanson, N. R. (2012). Instrumental variable estimation with heteroskedasticity and many instruments. *Quantitative Economics*, *3*, 211–255.

Kunitomo, N. (1980). Asymptotic expansions of distributions of estimators in a linear functional relationship and simultaneous equations. *Journal of the American Statistical Association, 75*, 693–700.

Tao, T. (2012). Topics in random matrix theory. *Graduate studies in mathematics*. Providence, RI: American Mathematical Society.

OVERCOMING THE MANY WEAK INSTRUMENT PROBLEM USING NORMALIZED PRINCIPAL COMPONENTS

Nicky Grant

ABSTRACT

Principal component (PC) techniques are commonly used to improve the small sample properties of the linear instrumental variables (IV) estimator. Carrasco (2012) argue that PC type methods provide a natural ranking of instruments with which to reduce the size of the instrument set. This chapter shows how reducing the size of the instrument based on PC methods can lead to poor small sample properties of IV estimators. A new approach to ordering instruments termed 'normalized principal components' (NPCs) is introduced to overcome this problem. A simulation study shows the favourable small samples properties of IV estimators using NPC, methods to reduce the size of the instrument relative to PC. Using NPC we provide evidence that the IV setup in Angrist and Krueger (1992) may not suffer the weak instrument problem.

Essays in Honor of Jerry Hausman
Advances in Econometrics, Volume 29, 107–147

ISSN: 0731-9053/doi:10.1108/S0731-9053(2012)0000029010

Keywords: Many weak instruments; principal components; instrument selection

JEL classification: C13; C31; C51; C52

INTRODUCTION

The many weak instrument bias for linear instrumental variables (IV) estimators[1] is now widely recognized and understood in the literature. The small sample (higher order) bias of IV estimators is a function of both the size and the strength of a set of instruments. In general this bias is increasing with the size and decreasing in the strength of a set of instruments[2] (Chao & Swanson, 2005; Hahn, Hausman, & Yogo, 2003; Hahn, Hausman, & Kuersteiner, 2004; Hahn, Hausman, & Newey, 2008; Hausman, Newey, Woutersen, Chao, & Swanson, 2012; Newey & Smith, 2004; Newey & Windmeijer, 2009; Okui, 2010; Rothenberg, 1984; Staiger & Stock, 1997; Stock, Wright, & Yogo, 2002).

The strength of an instrument is related to the degree of correlation it possesses with the endogenous variable. Weak instruments are those instruments which have zero to little correlation with the endogenous variable. The weak instrument problem is the poor properties of IV estimators when instruments are weak (Staiger & Stock, 1997). The many instrument problem is the poor small sample properties of IV using large instruments sets (Han & Phillips, 2006). Hence, the many weak instrument problem is the poor small sample properties posed by using many instrument where some may be weak (Chao & Swanson, 2005).

Within a large set of instruments there may be at least one linear combination of instruments which is strongly correlated with the endogenous variable. If we could (asymptotically) identify those linear combinations which are highly correlated with the endogenous variable, we could base IV estimation on these, omitting those linear combinations of instruments weakly correlated to the endogenous variable. This will reduce the small sample bias from many instruments while not increasing the limiting variance of IV estimators. We may be able to overcome or at least reduce the many instrument bias.

Ideally we would like a method to do just this: condense a large set of instruments in to a smaller set, preserving the correlation with the endogenous variable. A common instrument reduction technique utilized in IV settings is principal components (PCs). The PC method applied to IV models is now well documented in both theoretical and applied research (Amemiya, 1966; Carrasco, 2012; Carrasco & Tchuente, 2012; Doran & Schmidt, 2006; Kloek & Mennes, 1960; Winekelreid & Smith, 2011).

Doran and Schmidt (2006) consider the small sample properties of dynamic panel generalized method of moments (GMM) estimators. They provide a heuristic argument why dropping those PCs that explain the least amount of variation within a set of moments could improve small sample properties of GMM. When a subset of PCs are (almost) irrelevant, Doran and Schmidt (2006) argue the PC method may be able reduce the dimension of the moments used for estimation with potentially little loss in efficiency. This logic underlies much of the literature utilizing PCs to reduce the size of the moments to improve small sample properties of GMM type estimators.

Carrasco (2012) and Carrasco and Tchuente (2012) derive higher order mean squared error (MSE) approximations similar to Donald and Newey (2001); though for a potentially infinite number of instruments. Various regularization methods are considered to invert the sample covariance matrix of the instruments in finite samples. PCs and related regularization techniques are considered in both papers. When the size of the instrument set is less than the sample size, the MSE approximations in Carrasco (2012) and Carrasco and Tchuente (2012) collapse to a modified version of the MSE approximations in Donald and Newey (2001).

Irrespective of the size of the instrument set, the underlying premise of Carrasco (2012) and Carrasco and Tchuente (2012) is the same as much of the other literature on PC type methods for instrument reduction. Namely that transforming instruments in to their PCs and ranking each PC by their variance provide a good ranking of these PCs in terms of their correlation with the endogenous variable.

Though at first seemingly intuitive, the premise of PC methods when applied to reducing the size of the instrument set can be crucially flawed. PC methods generally reduce the dimension of the instrument set by keeping those PCs with the largest variance (i.e. those linear combinations of the instruments that explain most of the variation within the instrument set).

This chapter demonstrates how those PCs that explain most of the variation from within the instrument set need not explain any of the variation in the endogenous variable. In fact it is possible that the total variation of the endogenous variable explained by the total variation of instrument set lies in those PCs with the smallest variance.

However, these are exactly the PCs that are dropped using PC methods of instrument reduction. Hence, it is entirely plausible that selecting instruments based on PC methods may lead to poor small sample properties of IV estimators. This situation could arise even when there exist linear combinations of instruments with a strong correlation to the endogenous variable. As such we provide an adapted method of ordering instruments to overcome this problem. We term this method of instrument dimension reduction 'normalized principal components' (NPCs).

NPC transforms the instrument set in such a way that we can rank these transformed instruments (the NPCs) by the amount of variation of the endogenous variable that they explain. To do this, NPC normalizes all PCs to have equal variance. NPC then estimates parameters from a least squares regression of the endogenous variable on the NPCs. The square of these estimated parameters (under regularity conditions) are shown to form a consistent ranking of the variation each corresponding NPC explains of the total variation in the endogenous variable.

NPC provides a natural and clear way to order a set of instruments in terms of their strength. We could then use this ranking with which to select instruments to improve the small sample properties of IV. For example, we could adopt adhoc rules, select all those NPCs that have t-values in the first stage regression above a certain threshold. NPCs also provide a natural ordering of instruments with which to minimize the MSE approximations of Donald and Newey (2001). This is useful as Donald and Newey (2001) point out the practical use of MSE approximations with large instrument sets are limited without some a priori ranking of instrument strength.

The NPC method has a very natural interpretation and is extremely useful as a basis for inference and visualization of the correlation structure between a set of instruments and the endogenous variable. We argue it may be better to view the strength of a set of instruments as a whole. Namely a given set of instruments will explain a certain proportion of the variation in the endogenous variable. If the total instrument set explains none of the variation, in the endogenous variable, we have a weak instruments problem (or a many weak instruments problem if the dimension of the instrument set is large).

When the total instrument set has a non-negligible correlation with endogenous variable, then we do not have a weak instrument problem. When there are many instruments in this set, we may suffer the many instrument bias which may cause IV estimators to have poor small sample properties (Han & Phillips, 2006). It may then be the case that the many instrument problem is mistakenly thought to be a weak instrument problem in applied work.

The NPC method allows us to estimate which linear combinations from this instrument set are most correlated with the endogenous variable. Often the number of relevant linear combinations may be much smaller than the size of the total instrument. Dropping out those irrelevant linear combinations of instruments (asymptotically) reduces the many instrument problem while maintaining the correlation with the endogenous variable.

In order to implement NPC in practice, we need a precise estimate of both the variance matrix of the instruments and the first-stage parameters from a regression of the endogenous variable on the NPCs. When the sample size is small relative to the number of instruments, these estimates may be imprecise. The NPC method of ranking of instruments may be poor in this case. However, the PC method of Carrasco (2012) and other similar methods suffer this drawback also, in that PC methods rely upon a precise estimate of the covariance matrix of the instruments. PC methods, as we demonstrate, also suffer the further drawback that ordering PCs by their variances (eigenvalues) may be a poor indicator of their correlation with the endogenous variable even asymptotically.

There exist many classic examples of many weak instrument problems where the sample size far outweighs the number of instruments, such as the returns to education data of Angrist and Krueger (1992) that use the Vietnam War Lottery dummies as in instrument for education attainment. The sample size is over 25,000 with only 130 IV. Another example is the Angrist and Krueger (1991) wage-education data using quarter of birth as instrument with a sample size of over 300,000 and 180 instruments. With such data sets we may expect precise estimates of the covariance matrix of the instruments and the relevant first-stage parameters.

It is widely regarded in the literature that the Vietnam War Lottery as an instrument for educational attaintment is weak (Angrist & Krueger, 1995; Bound, Jaeger, & Baker, 1995). However, using the NPC method applied to this set of instrument, we in fact demonstrate that there exist up to 14 statistically significant linear combinations from the total 130 instruments considered in Angrist and Krueger (1992). As such this IV problem may not suffer the weak instruments problem. The poor small sample properties in Angrist and Krueger (1992) may be due to the poor small sample properties of two-stage least squares (2SLS) with many instruments.

The poor properties of 2SLS in Angrist and Krueger (1992) may have been caused by using a larger instrument set than was necessary. Various estimators based on a reduced set of instruments selected by using various criteria based on the NPC ordering estimates a return to education much lower than the corresponding OLS estimator in Angrist and Krueger (1992). This conforms with our a priori notion of the sign of the bias in wage-education regressions, unlike 2SLS based on all 130 instruments which estimates a return to education much larger than that of OLS.

A simulation experiment compares ordering instruments using the NPC ranking relative to that of PC. We use both the NPC and PC method with which to minimize small sample MSE approximations of Donald and Newey (2001). The simulation study demonstrates the favourable small sample properties of IV based on ranking PCs by the NPC method as opposed to that of PC. The PC approach to selecting instruments is shown in some cases to yield IV estimators with extremely poor small sample properties when the PC ranking of instruments is poor.

The second section recaps the literature on instrument selection. The third section details the potential problem of PC and shows how the NPC method of ranking instruments overcomes this. The fourth section presents a small simulation study to show the performance of NPC as an ordering of instruments to minimize the MSE of Donald and Newey (2001) relative to the PC methods considered in Carrasco (2012). The fifth section applies the NPC method of choosing instruments to Angrist and Krueger (1992). The sixth section provides concluding remarks. Definitions used throughout the chapter and proof of Lemmas along with details on how to practically implement the NPC method detailed in the chapter (along with R code) are collected in an Appendix.

INSTRUMENT SELECTION METHODS

The poor small sample properties of IV estimators with many (weak) instruments is now well documented in the literature. In light of this problem, a thriving area of research considers methods to select instruments to reduce this many (weak) instrument bias (Carrasco, in press; Donald & Newey, 2001; Donald, Imbens, & Newey, 2009; Hall, Rudebusch, & Wilcox, 1996; Hall & Peixe, 2003; Kuersteiner & Okui, 2010; Shea, 1997).

The literature on methods to select instruments is now vast. This chapter focuses mainly on the methods derived in Donald and Newey (2001) and Carrasco (2012), providing a compact review of the instrument selection techniques from each paper. Donald and Newey (2001) derive an approximation to the small sample MSE of the linear homoscedastic IV estimator as a function of any given instrument set.

A large drawback as mentioned by the authors is that for m instruments there are 2^m possible combinations of instruments to choose from. Even for moderately sized m the number of combinations can be large. This is both computationally demanding and also may lead to fragile estimators when minimizing the MSE over a large and discrete parameter space. As such Donald and Newey (2001) argue an a priori ordering of instruments is needed, though they did not provide such an ordering.

Carrasco (2012) argue that a natural way to order a set of instruments can be achieved using PCs. Carrasco (2012) derives MSE approximations as a function of the PCs[3] of the instruments. Implicitly the good small properties of the estimator in Carrasco (2012) rely upon the variance of the PCs providing a good ranking in terms of their correlation with the endogenous variable. In general this may not be the case. This is also the idea that underlies the adhoc moment selection procedure based upon PCs in Doran and Schmidt (2006) and much of the other literature that uses PCs to improve small sample properties of IV estimators.

As we discuss in section 'Problem with the PC Method of Instrument Reduction' this logic though seemingly intuitive is flawed. The PC from the instrument set which explains most of the variation within the instrument set may not necessarily explain most of the variation of the endogenous variable. It may in fact be uncorrelated with the endogenous variable. In general ranking, PCs by their variances yield a correct ordering in terms of their strength only under quite stringent conditions. When these conditions do not hold, the small sample properties of the Carrasco (2012) estimator and others in the literature may be very poor. The results of the simulation experiment in the fourth section demonstrate this.

This motivates the NPC ranking of instruments to overcome this problem. NPC transforms the instruments in some way in order to get a ranking of instruments in terms of how much of the variation of the endogenous variable they explain. The same logic can also be applied to general moment problems, though this is beyond the scope of this chapter. Hence, we have to be cautious when ranking instruments using the PC method. We propose the NPC method as an alternative ranking of instruments, which we detail in section 'Normalized Principal Components'.

We now sketch the MSE type approximations of Donald and Newey (2001). Essentially these expansions provide an approximation to the small sample MSE of various estimators based on a given set of instruments. As such they provide a natural criterion with which to select instruments to efficiently reduce the dimension of the instrument set.

MSE Approximations of Donald and Newey (2001)

Donald and Newey (2001) [DN] consider the following linear IV model.

$$y_i = x_i'\beta + \varepsilon_i \tag{1}$$

$$x_i = f(z_i) + \eta_i \tag{2}$$

where x_i is a $px1$ vector of endogenous/exogenous variables and z_i is a $m^* \times 1$ vector of variables such that $\mathbb{E}[\eta_i|z_i] = 0$; $\mathbb{E}[\varepsilon_i^2|z_i] = \sigma^2$. $\sigma_{\eta\varepsilon}$ is a $p \times 1$ vector and $\sigma^2 > 0$. $f(\cdot)$ is a $p \times 1$ function of the excluded exogenous variables z_i. We have an $mx1$ vector of instruments $Z_i = \varphi(z_i)$ where $\varphi(\cdot)$ is some $m \times 1$ function of the exogenous variables z_i. Common examples include polynomials of z_i.

$$x_i = \Pi_m Z_i + m(Z_i) + \eta_i \tag{3}$$

where $m(Z_i)$ is a $p \times 1$ vector containing the approximation error for a given instrument set Z_i (i.e. $m(Z_i) = f(z_i) - \Pi_m Z_i$). The assumption is that as $m \to \infty$ some linear $p \times m$ linear combination Π_m of Z_i approximate $f(z_i)$ with arbitrary precision (i.e. $\mathbb{E}[||m(Z_i)||^2] \to 0$ as $m \to \infty$ at some rate). Define $Z = (Z_1', \ldots, Z_n')'$.

The MSE approximation is a function of the number of instruments m and the form of the instruments Z. For every set of instrument set of size m, the asymptotic variance is estimated by the usual estimate of the semiparametric lower bound (SPLB) and the bias is estimated as some function of m and Z. DN derive higher order expansions for the 2SLS, Limited Information Maximum Likelihood (LIML) and bias corrected 2SLS. We focus upon the MSE approximation for 2SLS for brevity.

For each of the estimators under certain restrictions on the growth rate of m relative to the n the MSE is of the form

$$n(\hat{\beta} - \beta_0)(\hat{\beta} - \beta_0)' = \sigma^2 H^{-1} + S(m) + r(m) \tag{4}$$

where $S(m)$ varies for the different estimators, $r(m)$ is asymptotically negligible and $\sigma^2 H^{-1}$ is the asymptotic variance (SPLB) where $H := \mathbb{E}[f(z_i)f(z_i)']$.

For 2SLS under the assumption that $m^2/n \to 0$ along with other regularity conditions, DN show that the above approximation holds with

$$S(m) = H^{-1}\left(\sigma_{\eta\varepsilon}\sigma_{\eta\varepsilon}'\frac{m^2}{n} + \sigma^2\frac{f'(I-P)f}{n}\right)H^{-1} \tag{5}$$

where $P := Z'(Z'Z)^{-1}Z$ is the projection matrix of the instruments Z, $f := (f(z_1), \ldots, f(z_n))'$. In practice we estimate $\sigma^2 H^{-1}$ (the asymptotic variance of 2SLS) and $S(m)$ (the higher order bias) using their sample counterparts; see Donald and Newey (2001) for a discussion. Section 'R Code for NPC Instrument Selection' in the appendix provides the R code for the estimating $\sigma^2 H^{-1} + S(m)$.[4]

If we consider m instruments then there are 2^m sets of instruments to minimize over and we have a discrete optimization problem. The number of instrument sets over which to choose increases exponentially with m and becomes computationally challenging. Optimizing over such a large set of potential instruments combination may also lead to unstable estimates and give poor second-stage estimators. In light of this, DN argue we need some a priori notion of which instruments are strongest to reduce the size of the problem. This knowledge is not often known or predicted by theory in general.

The regularization approach of Carrasco (2012) and Carrasco and Tchuente (2012) provide one such ranking based on PCs and related techniques. They also generalize the expansions of Donald and Newey (2001) for 2SLS and LIML for the case where $m > n$ and possibly infinite.

The Regularization MSE Approach

Carrasco (2012) considers the same linear IV setup as in DN detailed in section 'MSE Approximations of Donald and Newey (2001)'. Carrasco (2012) considers the case where m may be greater than n and possibly infinite. When we have an infinite dimensional problem (or more generally when $m > n$), the problem is ill posed since the sample covariance of the instruments is singular. Carrasco (2012) uses various regularization methods to approximate the sample covariance matrix of the instruments and generalizes the MSE approximations in DN (2001) for 2SLS. Carrasco and Tchuente (2012) provide similar results for the LIML estimator.

Carrasco (2012) uses a regularized inverse of the instrument sample covariance matrix. We will highlight the intuition for the PCs and spectral cut-off regularization. Define K_n as the (potentially infinite dimensional) sample covariance matrix of Z, λ_{jn} the j'th sample eigenvalue and φ_{jn} the corresponding sample eigenvector ($<,.,>$ is the inner product with respect to the Euclidean Norm) such that for any vector r (conformable with the dimension of K_n)

$$K_n^{-1} r := \sum_{j=1}^{\infty} \frac{1}{\lambda_{jn}} < r, \varphi_{jn} > \varphi_{jn} \tag{6}$$

In finite samples we need to truncate the (infinite dimensional) sample covariance matrix to form a problem which is tractable and that yields an asymptotically valid approximation.

The different truncations uses correspond to the different methods of regularization. For example the spectral cut-off regularization approximates the K_n using eigenvectors with eigenvalues greater than some threshold α (using eigenvectors with the largest eigenvalues first as these correspond to most of the variation within the instrument).

$$(K_n^{\alpha})^{-1}r := \sum_{\lambda_{jn}^2 \geq \alpha} \frac{1}{\lambda_{jn}} < r, \varphi_{jn} > \varphi_{jn} \tag{7}$$

K_n^{α} is the truncated approximation to the K_n. α is the tuning parameter and as discussed in Carrasco (2012) can be viewed as the counterpart to the tuning parameter in non-parametric estimation. See Carrasco (2012) for details on regularizing potentially infinite dimensional matrices and for other forms of regularization.

The PC regularization is directly linked to the Spectral Cutoff (SC) method approximates K_n using those eigenvectors with corresponding eigenvalues less than or equal to $1/\alpha$. Then for $\alpha \to 0$ fast enough relative to $n \to \infty$, Carrasco (2012) shows the linear IV-GMM estimator based on this regularization will reach the SPLB and be consistent and asymptotically normal under certain regularity conditions. Here the tuning parameter α is playing the role of m, the number of instruments in DN. Carrasco (2012) derives the MSE as a function of α for $\frac{\alpha^2}{n} \to 0$:

$$n(\hat{\beta}-\beta_0)(\hat{\beta}-\beta_0)' = \sigma^2 H^{-1} + S(\alpha) + r(\alpha) \tag{8}$$

where $r(\alpha)$ is asymptotically negligible and

$$S(\alpha) = H^{-1}\left[\sigma_{\eta\varepsilon}\sigma_{\eta\varepsilon}' \frac{\left(\sum q(\alpha, \lambda_j^2)\right)}{n} + \sigma^2 \frac{f'(I-P^{\alpha})f}{n}\right] H^{-1} \tag{9}$$

where for PCs $q(\alpha, \lambda_j^2) = I\left(j \leq \frac{1}{\alpha}\right)$ and P^{α} is the projection on the space spanned by the first n eigenvectors of the truncated sample covariance matrix. Note the similarity with DN where now we have the tuning parameter α instead of m.

We consider a special case of Carrasco (2012) where $m \leq n$. In this case the MSE approximations in Carrasco (2012) for PC collapse to those of DN where the MSE approximations in DN are evaluated at the PCs as opposed to the original instruments Z. This is the setting we consider in the simulation experiment in the fourth section. Though the Carrasco (2012) MSE approximations are more general in allowing $m > n$, PCs are ordered by their eigenvalues which as we show in section 'Normalized Principal Components' may not be sensible and could lead to poor small sample properties of the IV-GMM estimator.

INSTRUMENT REDUCTION TECHNIQUES

Increasing the size of instrument set m in general reduces the variance of an IV estimator but increases the small sample bias. The trade-off between the two is determined by the strength of the instruments incrementally added to the existing set. Adding an irrelevant instrument to a given set of instruments does not reduce the asymptotic variance of the IV estimator but increases to the small sample bias. We would like to keep m as small as possible while preserving the strongest linear combinations of instruments from within the instrument set. The NPC method is designed to (asymptotically) achieve this.

The basic idea of NPC is that the amount of information within a large set of instruments could be collapsed into a smaller set that preserves most of this information. By information we mean the amount of variation in the instrument set that overlaps with the variation of the endogenous variable.

Essentially we are using some set of instruments $Z_i = \varphi(z_i)$ of approximating functions to estimate the unknown optimal instrument $f(z_i)$. We would like a method to be able to condense all the relevant information from a potentially large set of instruments into a smaller set that incurs a small loss in efficiency for a large reduction in the small sample bias of linear IV estimators.

There are two sides to choosing instruments to improve the small sample efficiency of IV. First, we require some method to transform the instruments in such a way to form a ranking of the transformed instruments in terms of their strength. Second, we require some method with which to select among these transformed instruments. The second section describes methods with which to choose from any set of instruments. The remainder of this section provides methods with which to transform instruments to rank them in terms of their relevance.

The PC method is one such way of doing this which we discuss in detail in section 'Principal Component Ranking of Instruments'. In section 'Problem with the PC Method of Instrument Reduction', we argue why this method of ranking instruments may be a poor one. The NPC method of transforming and ranking instruments is laid out in section ‘Normalized Principal Components’.

Principal Component Ranking of Instruments

Suppose we have an $m \times 1$ vector of instruments Z_i then it is plausible there exists some linear combination of these variables that explain a large portion of the variation within Z_i. PC is a method that identifies which linear combinations of the variables Z_i explain most of the total variation in Z_i.

Define $\Sigma := Var(Z_i)$ the unknown population covariance matrix of the instruments. Define P_j is the j'th eigenvector corresponding to the eigenvalue λ_j (i.e. $P_j'\Sigma P_j = \lambda_j$) for $j = \{1,\ldots,m\}$, $P := (P_1',\ldots,P_{m'})'$ and Λ an $m \times m$ diagonal matrix where $[\Lambda]_{jj} = \lambda_j$. Since Σ is symmetric (by construction) and positive definite, we can eigen-decompose Σ as $\Sigma = P\Lambda P'$ where $P'P = I_{m\times m}$.

The j'th PC is defined as $Z_{ij}^{pc} = P_j'Z_i$. The PC with the largest variance is the one with the largest eigenvalue. Since $Var(Z_{ij}^{pc}) = P_j'Var(Z_i)P_j = P_j'\Sigma P_j = \lambda_j$. Hence, the variance of the PC Z_{ij}^{pc} (which is a linear combination of Z_i using as weights the eigenvector P_j) is λ_j. See Jolliffe (2002) for a great discussion on the method of PCs.

The method of PC as applied to IV is to transform the instrument set using the eigenvectors P and rank this transformed set of instruments by their corresponding eigenvalues. Namely we order PCs by the size of their variance. This is then used as a basis for dimension reduction of the instrument set. Without loss of generality, the PCs are ordered such that $\lambda_1 \geq \lambda_2 \ldots \geq \lambda_m$.

To implement the method in practice we require a consistent estimate of Σ with which to estimate P (the matrix of PC weighings) and Λ (the diagonal matrix with the eigenvalues of Σ along the diagonal). Natural estimates can be formed taking the sample variance of Z_i as an estimate of Σ. Namely $\hat{\Sigma} := \frac{1}{n}\sum_{i=1}^{n}(Z_i - \bar{Z})(Z_i - \bar{Z})'$ where $\bar{Z} := \frac{1}{n}\sum_{i=1}^{n} Z_i$.

We can spectrally decompose $\hat{\Sigma} = \hat{P}\hat{\Lambda}\hat{P}'$ where $\hat{P}'\hat{P} = I_{m\times m}$ and $\hat{\Lambda}$ is a diagonal matrix with sample eigenvalues $\hat{\lambda}_j$ where $\hat{P}_{j'}\hat{\Sigma}\hat{P}_j = \hat{\lambda}_j (j = \{1,\ldots,m\})$ along the diagonal.

When $||\hat{\Omega} - \Omega|| = O_p(n^{-1/2})$ (a sufficient condition being that Z_i is i.i.d. $(i = 1,\ldots,n\})$, we can show that $||\hat{P}' - P'|| = O_p(mn^{-1/2})$ and $||\hat{\Lambda} - \Lambda|| = O_p(mn^{-1/2})$ (e.g. Bosq, 2000). So long as $m^2/n \to 0$ (along with some regularity conditions) then $\hat{P}_j$ and $\hat{\lambda}_j$ consistently estimate P_j and λ_j respectively for $j = \{1,\ldots,m\}$.

A common sample PC method then estimates Z_{ij}^{npc} as $\hat{Z}_{ij}^{pc} = \hat{P}_j' Z_i$ which we can show has sample variance equal to $\hat{\lambda}_j$ similar to the population analogue above. The sample PCs are then ranked based on the size of the sample eigenvalues (i.e. their sample variance).

Carrasco (2012) considers $m > n$ in general, hence $\hat{\Sigma}$ is singular. As such the regularization techniques in section 'The Regularization MSE Approach' are required. The MSE approximations in Carrasco (2012) based on PC collapse to those of DN estimated as a function of the estimated PCs when $m < n$. In the simulation experiment in the fourth section, we consider the MSE expansions using the PC regularization of Carrasco (2012) where $m < n$ as a point of comparison with the NPC method in section 'Normalized Principal Components' which is developed for $m < n$.

Though the Carrasco (2012) regularization with $m > n$ is a generalization of the expansions in DN, the regularization will still suffer the drawback we detail in section 'Problem with the PC Method of Instrument Reduction'. Namely the ranking over the $m > n$ PCs is based on their variances (eigenvalues) which are shown to have some potentially undesirable properties in section 'Problem with the PC Method of Instrument Reduction'.

Problem with the PC Method of Instrument Reduction

In order to illustrate this problem we utilize the linear IV set up in section 'MSE Approximations of Donald and Newey (2001)' with one endogenous variable and no exogenous variables (i.e. $p = 1$). This result easily extends to the case of many endogenous and exogenous variables.[5]

$$x_i = \pi' Z_i + \eta_i \tag{10}$$

where π is an $m \times 1$ vector of first stage coefficients.

Take the population PCs $Z_i^{pc} = P' Z_i$ (where $Z_{ij}^{pc} = P_j' Z_i$ as defined above). Defining $\pi_{pc} := P'\pi$ where π_{pcj} is the j'th element of π_{pc} then

$$x_i = \pi' Z_i + \eta_i = \pi' P P' Z_i + \eta_i = \pi_{pc}' Z_i^{pc} + \eta_i \tag{11}$$

Since $P'P = I$ and hence $P' = P^{-1}$. So π_{pcj} is the population coefficient from a regression of x_i on the of the j'th PC. We now derive the variation each PC explains to the total variation in x_i explained by the all PCs (i.e. decompose the total variation in x_i explained by the whole instrument set for the PCs).

$$Var(\pi' Z_i) = \pi' \Sigma \pi = \pi' P \Lambda P' \pi = \pi_{pc}' \Lambda \pi_{pc} = \sum_{j=1}^{m} \pi_{pcj}^2 \lambda_j \tag{12}$$

The PC method then (asymptotically) ranks the transformed instruments Z_{ij}^{pc} by λ_j. However, the variation that the j'th PC Z_{ij}^{pc} contributes to the total variation of x_i explained by all m instruments ($Var(\pi' Z_i)$) is $\pi_{pcj}^2 \lambda_j$. If $\pi_{pcj} = 0$ then the j'th PC is irrelevant, irrespective of the size of λ_j.

In fact basing dimension reduction using a ranking based on the eigenvalues could give a reverse ranking. Take for example the simple case where $\pi_{pcj} = \lambda_j^{-\delta} \forall j = \{1,\ldots,m\} \forall j = \{1,\ldots,m\}$ where $\delta > 1/2$. A simple example where the PC ranking provides a correct ranking of the strength of the PCs is where $\pi_{pcj} = \pi_{pci}$ for all $i,j \in \{1,\ldots,m\}$.

In fact it could be the case that all the variation in x_i explained by all PCs lie within the components with the smallest eigenvalues. Take the extreme example where $\pi_{pcj} = 0, \forall\ j \in \{1,\ldots(m-1)\}$ and $\pi_{pcm} \neq 0$. However, in general the PC with the smallest eigenvalues would be dropped using the PC method of dimension reduction.

Normalized Principal Components

A more intuitive way to transform the instrument set with which to form an ordering of the new instruments is to normalize all the PCs to have equal variance.

Define $Z_i^{npc} = \Lambda^{-1/2} Z_i^{pc}$.

Then $Var(Z_i^{npc}) = \Lambda^{-1/2} Var(Z_i^{pc}) \Lambda^{-1/2} = \Lambda^{-1/2} \times \ \Lambda\Lambda^{-1/2} = I_{m\times m}$.Then Z_i^{npc} are the NPCs.

Define $\pi_{npc} := \Lambda^{1/2} P' \pi$

$$x_i = \pi' Z_i + \eta_i = \pi_{npc}' Z_i^{npc} + \eta_i \tag{13}$$

since $\pi_{npc}' Z_i^{npc} = \pi' P \Lambda^{1/2} \Lambda^{-1/2} P' Z_i = \pi' Z_i$.

Letting π_{npcj} denote the j'th element of π_{npc} then the variation in x_i explained the m NPCs can be expressed as

$$Var(\pi' Z_i) = Var(\pi_{npc}' Z_i^{npc}) = \pi_{npc}' Var(Z_i^{npc}) \pi_{npcj} = \pi_{npc}' \pi_{npc} = \sum_{j=1}^{m} \pi_{npcj}^2 \tag{14}$$

We now have a natural ordering of instruments based on NPC. Since π_{npcj}^2 is the contribution of the j'th NPC to the total variation in x_i explained by all NPCs. Hence, we can rank NPCs by the absolute size of their parameters in the first stage. A natural measure of the strength of NPC j

$$S_j := \frac{\pi_{npcj}^2}{\sum_{l=1}^{m} \pi_{npcl}^2} \tag{15}$$

The proportion of the total variation is explained by NPC j. A natural way of then ordering NPCs is by S_j. Arrange NPCs with S_j from largest to smallest, hence $S_1 \geq S_2 \ldots \geq S_m$. The amount of the total variation in x_i is explained by the whole set of NPCs (and hence the total váriation in the original instrument set) by the first k NPCs $C_{\leq k}$

$$C_{\leq k} := \frac{\sum_{l=1}^{k} \pi_{npcl}^2}{\sum_{l=1}^{m} \pi_{npcl}^2} = \sum_{j=1}^{k} S_j \tag{16}$$

$C_{\leq k}$ is the proportion of the total variation in the endogenous variable explained by the whole instrument set captured by the first k NPCs. This is an extremely useful tool for visualizing how the informative content in a set of instruments is spread across the instrument set. If $C_{\leq k}$ grows quickly with k, then a small number of linear combinations explain most of the variation in the endogenous variable explained by the total instrument set. This is desirable since it implies that the variation in the endogenous variable explained by the whole instrument set can be captured by a smaller number of linear combinations of these instruments.

The curvature of C_k against $k = \{1, \ldots, m\}$ is a direct measure of how much we can reduce the instrument set while preserving its strength using NPC. If C_k is the 45 degree line, the informative content within the set of instrument is spread out equally among the NPCs. Interestingly in this case, in light of the instrument averaging results of Kapetanios and Marcellino (2006), the average across the NPCs used as one instrument may (asymptotically) suffer no reduction in efficiency. This is an interesting avenue for future research.

In general we do not know the true NPC Z_i^{npc} or the population parameter π_{npc} with which to estimate S_j for $j = \{1, \ldots, m\}$. Section 'Sample NPC Method' shows how to form a sample version of the infeasible NPC method outlined here. Some sufficient conditions and a sketch of a proof that the sample NPC mimic the population NPC are provided. We do not go into unnecessary technical detail providing an outline of a proof. A crucial assumption is that m does not grow too fast relative to n. An assumption also required for sample PC method to mimic the population PC asymptotically.

If these regularity conditions do not hold, NPC in terms of providing instruments for estimation is still valid, since any linear combination of instruments is a potentially relevant instrument. It does however mean that the properties we detailed for the population NPC above may not hold in the sample, even asymptotically.

Sample NPC Method
To perform the NPC method of instrument reduction we need estimators of both the NPCs ($Z_i^{npc} = \Lambda^{-1/2}P'Z_i$) and coefficient vector π_{npc} with which to form an estimate of the relevance of the NPCs (S_j for $j \in \{1,\ldots,m\}$).

We estimate the population NPC using the sample versions of P and Λ (similar to how we estimated the population PCs). Namely the estimated NPCs are $\hat{Z}_i^{npc} := \hat{\Lambda}^{-1/2}\hat{P}'Z_i$. Define the sample matrix of estimated NPCs $\hat{Z}^{npc} := (\hat{Z}_1^{npc'},\ldots,\hat{Z}_m^{npc'})'$ and the population version $Z^{npc} := (Z_1^{npc'},\ldots,Z_m^{npc'})'$.

We can form an estimate of π_{npc} using an OLS regression of x_i on $\hat{Z}_i^{npc}$

$$\hat{\pi}_{npc} := \left(\frac{1}{n}\hat{Z}^{npc'}\hat{Z}^{npc}\right)^{-1}\frac{1}{n}\hat{Z}^{npc'}X \tag{17}$$

where $X := (x_1,\ldots,x_n)'$.

We sketch some sufficient conditions in Lemma 1 for which the sample NPC mimics the population NPC asymptotically.

Lemma 1. (i) $||\frac{1}{n}(\hat{Z}^{npc} - Z^{npc})|| \xrightarrow{p} 0$, (ii) $\hat{\pi}_{npc} \xrightarrow{p} \pi_{npc}$.

Proof. See the appendix.

Lemma 1 (i) establishes that the estimated NPCs approach the population NPCs w.p.a.1 and (ii) that the estimated variation that the NPC explains of x_i forms a consistent estimate of the true variation. Using Lemma 1 we may form a consistent estimate of S_j, and hence form a consistent correct ranking of NPCs asymptotically. Define $\hat{S}_j = \hat{\pi}_{npcj}^2/\sum_{l=1}^m \hat{\pi}_{npcl}^2$. Then by Lemma 1 (ii) and an application the continuous mapping theorem

$$\hat{S}_j \xrightarrow{p} S_j \tag{18}$$

For any $j, \in \{1,\ldots,m\}$. Likewise we can define a consistent estimator of $C_{\leq k}$ for any $k \in \{1,\ldots,m\}$ as $\hat{C}_{\leq k} := \sum_{j=1}^k \hat{S}_j$. Here $\hat{C}_{\leq k}$ is a consistent estimator of the total variation of the endogenous variable explained by the first k NPCs.

This measure can be useful for deriving adhoc rules. For example, choosing the size of the instrument set k such is the minimum k such that $\hat{C}_{\leq k} \geq \alpha_n$ for some (possibly data dependent α_n) where $0 < \alpha_n \leq 1$. $\hat{C}_{\leq k}$ $k \in \{1,\ldots,m\}$ is plotted for the Vietnam War Lottery instrument of Angrist and Krueger (1992) in Figs. 1 and 3.

Sufficient conditions for the sample NPC approach to mimic that of the population NPC (Z_i,x_i,η_i) ($i = 1,\ldots,n$) are i.i.d., $\sup_{i \leq n}||Z_i|| = o_p(n^{1/2}/m^2)$

and $||X||/n = O_p(1)$. This approach does not rule out unbounded instruments; however, we require $m^4/n \to 0$. This is stronger than that of $m^2/n \to 0$ required for the sample PC approach, which mimics the population PC approach asymptotically.

However, for m not too large relative to n, by Lemma 1 the sample NPC should estimate well the unknown population NPCs and their corresponding ranking in terms of instrument relevance. The main benefit to the NPC method as we demonstrated in section 'Normalized Principal Components' is that it (asymptotically) provides a means to construct and rank the strongest linear combinations of instruments. This overcomes the potential problem with PC, where even the population ranking may be incorrect. This could lead to poor small sample properties of IV estimators which use sample PC methods to reduce the size of the instrument set.

The fourth section in a simulation compares the two approaches – the ordering of instruments by the sample NPC and sample PC, with which to minimize the MSE approximations of DN estimated as a function of both set of instruments respectively. The NPC method ranks the NPCs using $\hat{\pi}^2_{npcj}$ and PC method of Carrasco (2012) orders the PCs by the eigenvalues $\hat{\lambda}_j$ for $j \in \{1, \ldots, m\}$.

As to be expected in light of section 'Problem with the PC Method of Instrument Reduction', the Carrasco (2012) method performs very poorly when the PC ranking of instruments based on the eigenvalues of Σ does not correspond to those PCs that explain most of the variation in x_i. The NPC ranking provides a robust stable estimator in all settings considered even for cases when NPC may be imprecise, that is when m^4/n is large.

SIMULATION

In this section we compare the two methods of ordering instruments PC and NPC. In order to make comparison clear, we consider choosing instruments based on both rankings to minimize the MSE approximations of DN.

The aim of the simulation is not to study the different small sample properties of more robust estimators based on all instruments. The performance of different estimators on a given set of instruments has been well documented (Newey & Smith, 2004). We are more interested at which transformation and ranking of instruments provide a better basis for instrument reduction for any given estimator. As such we only consider the IV-GMM estimator. It would however be interesting to see how using NPC to rank instruments to minimize the estimated MSE for more robust estimators affects their small sample distribution.

We consider the IV setup in section 'MSE Approximations of Donald and Newey (2001)' with $f(z_i) = \frac{cp}{\sqrt{2.9}}\sinh(z_i)$ for $cp = \{0.1, 1, 10\}$.

$$y_i = \beta_0 x_i + \varepsilon_i \tag{19}$$

$$x_i = \frac{cp}{\sqrt{2.9}}\sinh(z_i) + \eta_i \tag{20}$$

where $\beta_0 = 1,\ z_i \overset{d}{\sim} N(0,1)$. Since $Var(\sinh(z_i)) = 2.9$ we divide by $\sqrt{2.9}$ so that cp in Eq. (20) refers to the concentration parameter (the variation in x_i explained by the instrument z_i), where η_i and ε_i are i.i.d. normally distributed

$$\begin{pmatrix} \varepsilon_i \\ \eta_i \end{pmatrix} \overset{d}{\sim} N\left(\begin{pmatrix} 0 \\ 0 \end{pmatrix}, \begin{pmatrix} 1 & 0.5 \\ 0.5 & 1 \end{pmatrix}\right) \tag{21}$$

We set the sample size n small ($n = 100$). For both PC and NPC we consider choosing from instrument sets with up to polynomial order m for $m = \{3, 4, 5, 6, 7, 8\}$ where the transformed instruments (PC or NPC) are then estimated for any m and added incrementally using their respective rankings.

We minimize the MSE functions for any m by incrementally adding in PCs governed by their respective rankings. For any m, cp and both PC and NPC we estimate the MSE approximations of DN for each ranking and for every m.

For both NPC and PC we select the size of the instrument set in each case to minimize the estimated MSE. We then estimate β_0 based on this optimally selected instrument set (for both PC and NPC) using 2SLS. The simulation is repeated 10,000 times.

By the Taylor series expansion, we have that

$$\sinh(z_i) = z_i + \frac{1}{3!}z_i^3 + \frac{1}{5!}z_i^5 + \frac{1}{7!}z_i^7 + \dots \tag{22}$$

In this setup the remainder is negligible for $m = \{6, 7, 8\}$ and is still relatively small for lower order polynomial approximations.

Tables 1 and 2 show the squared transformed first-stage coefficients π_{pc} and the eigenvalues (λ_j) of the instruments for $m = \{3, 4, 5, 6, 7, 8\}$. For any m we have seen the variance in x_i explained by all the PCs for a given m is $\sum_{j=1}^{m} \pi_{pcj}^2 \lambda_j$. The instrument selection using a PC ranking such as Carrasco (2012) will perform poorly for m even since by Table 1 we see that the PC

Table 1. First-Stage Parameters Squared for PC (π^2_{pcj}).

	3	4	5	6	7	8
1	0.059225	0.000000	0.000642	0.000000	0.000003	0.000000
2	0.000001	0.059226	0.000000	0.000642	0.000000	0.000003
3	0.177036	0.000001	0.087644	0.000007	0.002889	0.000000
4	–	0.177040	0.000031	0.087698	0.000010	0.002900
5	–	–	0.248724	0.000249	0.154490	0.000052
6	–	–	–	0.248396	0.000112	0.154666
7	–	–	–	–	0.163050	0.001010
8	–	–	–	–	–	0.161939

Table 2. Eigenvalues of Principal Components (λ_j).

	3	4	5	6	7	8
1	15.6	107	959.12	10442	132610	1896566
2	3.00	15.6	107	958	10431	132185
3	0.38	0.84	3.85	20	140	1185
4	–	0.38	0.84	3.85	20	139
5	–	–	−0.19	0.34	1.50	5.64
6	–	–	–	0.19	0.34	1.50
7	–	–	–	–	0.10	0.15
8	–	–	–	–	–	0.10

with the highest variation is uncorrelated with x_i. For m odd the ranking is improved, especially for $m=3$.

Table 3 presents values given in Tables 1 and 2 multiplied element by element.

For brevity, in Table 3 we consider the case $cp=1$; however, the corresponding parameters for $cp=0.1$ or $cp=10$ can be found by scaling relevant entries in Table 3 by cp. Each element (for a given m) in Table 3 shows the proportion of the variance each PC explains for the total variance, since the total variance is normalized to 1. We can see for $m=3$ that the first PC explains over 92% of the variation explained by the first three instruments. Hence, the PC method we expect to perform relatively well in this case.

We can see that for $m=\{4,6,8\}$ the PC with the largest eigenvalue is irrelevant in explaining x_i. This highlights how the Carrasco (2012)

Table 3. Variation in x_i Explained by Principal Components $\pi^2_{pcj}\lambda_j$.

	3	4	5	6	7	8
1	0.9264	0.0000	0.6154	0.0000	0.3477	0.0001
2	0.0000	0.9264	0.0000	0.6154	0.0003	0.3481
3	0.0681	0.0000	0.3377	0.0001	0.4046	0.0005
4	–	0.0681	0.0000	0.3376	0.0002	0.4042
5	–	–	0.0483	0.0001	0.2322	0.0003
6	–	–	–	0.0482	0.0000	0.2318
7	–	–	–	–	0.0164	0.0002
8	–	–	–	–	–	0.0162

method of selecting instruments is sensitive to the number and form of instruments from which to select from. In some cases the ranking could be very poor and can lead to very unstable estimation as we shall see.

Simulation Results

The results are presented in Table 4 in each case. MAD, MSE and IQR refer to the mean absolute deviation, MSE and interquartile range of the 2SLS with instruments selected as detailed above for both NPC and PC.

The NPC ranking provides a stable estimate for all m and reaches the lowest MSE when selecting from $m = \{3,4\}$, which is to be expected given the first four polynomials explain most of the variation in $f(z_i)$ and n is small. As m increases, relative to n we showed in Lemma 1 how in this case the NPC may provide a poor ranking of instruments. The MSE , MAD and IQR do increase slightly as m increases, though only marginally. Using NPC as a ranking for instrument selection yields a robust estimate across all m,cp.

For $m = 3$ the PC ranking provides a reasonable ranking but is still massively outperformed by NPC. For even number instrument sets we have seen in Table 3 that the first PC is irrelevant. When the PC method selects only the first PC the estimator is unidentified, hence the poor small sample properties appear, as shown in Table 4.

The NPC overcomes this issue by estimating the relevance of each PC and then ranking accordingly. Essentially, the NPC ranking works directly with Table 3. For example, for $m = 3$ the correct ranking of relevance of PCs is (1,3,2) and this is the way the NPC estimator would (asymptotically) rank the PCs when minimizing the small sample MSE approximations.

Table 4. Simulation Results.

		$cp=0.1$			$cp=1$			$cp=10$		
		MSE	MAD	IQR	MSE	MAD	IQR	MSE	MAD	IQR
NPC	$m=3$	0.2043	0.3151	0.4470	0.0145	0.0929	0.1515	0.0013	0.0281	0.0462
	$m=4$	0.1874	0.3224	0.4707	0.0163	0.0989	0.1602	0.0016	0.0313	0.0510
	$m=5$	0.1946	0.3298	0.4650	0.0184	0.1042	0.1655	0.0018	0.0327	0.0541
	$m=6$	0.1933	0.3387	0.4794	0.0222	0.1145	0.1790	0.0022	0.0364	0.0596
	$m=7$	0.1985	0.3423	0.4739	0.0225	0.1164	0.1857	0.0023	0.0371	0.0594
	$m=8$	0.2039	0.3535	0.4881	0.0268	0.1271	0.1997	0.0027	0.0405	0.0648
PC	$m=3$	5.559	0.4436	0.4698	0.0145	0.0929	0.1514	0.0013	0.0281	0.0462
	$m=4$	1766	2.031	0.9192	33.14	0.5171	0.2885	5.508	0.1597	0.0775
	$m=5$	7.329	0.5605	0.5484	0.0194	0.1055	0.1667	0.0018	0.0327	0.0540
	$m=6$	122.5	1.484	0.9030	21.73	0.4336	0.2915	52.98	0.1977	0.0814
	$m=7$	58.32	0.7552	0.5999	0.0268	0.1220	0.1910	0.0023	0.0371	0.0593
	$m=8$	73.85	1.449	0.9014	12.44	0.4186	0.3039	0.8134	0.1089	0.0857

PC performs well for m odd relative to m even as we expected given the results in Table 3. When $cp = 10$ then PC and NPC have almost equivalent MSE, MAD and IQR for m odd. This is because the first PC is very strongly identified in each case. PC performs poorly relative to NPC when $cp = 0.1$ for m odd, because even though the first PC is not irrelevant, it gets the ranking incorrect for the remaining PCs.

When $cp = 0.1$ for m odd, the first PC has a very small coefficient; therefore, including further relevant PCs may help to improve the small sample properties of the IV estimator in this case. For example, using the PC ranking for $m = 3$ the second PC is irrelevant and we would need to include all three PCs using the sequential method of choosing instruments utilized here and in Carrasco (2012). When the minimum of the estimated MSE for PC is at 2 in this case, then the final PC which could improve small sample properties is not included. Also we need to include all three PCs in this case, whereas only two are relevant. The NPC has the ability to include only the two relevant PCs and hence reduces the many instrument bias.

NPC overcomes this by providing an estimated ranking of relevance of NPCs and adding them sequentially so as to not (asymptotically) include irrelevant PCs first. In sum, the NPC ranking works well for all forms of instrument set and for very weak and very strong instruments. This was also found in further simulations looking at different forms of $f(z_i)$, and it seems the NPC is a stable and reliable estimator that helps provide the best possible inference from a set of many (weak) instruments.

The principal drawback of NPC is that it requires a reliable ranking of first-stage coefficients. We have sketched in Lemma 1 why NPC will work asymptotically if $m^4/n \to 0$. In this simulation we considered selecting from instrument sets up to order $m = 8$ where $m^4/n = 8^4/100 = 4096/100 \approx 4$. The NPC method is shown to produce estimators with stable and very favourable small sample properties relative to PC even with small n. Note that the PC method relies upon m not being too large relative to n and so suffers a similar drawback to NPC.

In sum, the PC methods to minimize MSE considered in Carrasco (2012) could lead to very poor inference unless the PC provides a good ranking of instruments. When this is not the case, we have seen in Table 4 the small sample properties of these estimators may be extremely poor. The MSE, MAD and IQR of the estimator based on instruments selected by NPC matches or outperforms the PC method of Carrasco (2012) for all m and cp, even for sample sizes as small as 100.

APPLICATION TO ANGRIST AND KRUEGER (1992)

In this section, we re-analyse the returns to education data of Angrist and Krueger (1992) [AK] using Vietnam War Lottery draft as an instrument for educational attainment. Those in or going into education were exempt from the draft and some men tried avoiding subscription by extending length of their course . AK argue this may have led to exogenous changes in levels of education and hence may satisfy the IV exclusion restriction.

A set of controls are used including region of birth, marital status, year of birth, veteran status and ethnicity dummies. Two sets of instruments are considered, one of which utilizes 130 instruments generated by interacting 13 lottery dummies with the 9 year of birth dummies. As such we have a potentially large number of IV, we demonstrate only around 10% of potential linear combinations of these instruments that may be correlated with education.

We also expand this instrument set by interacting each lottery dummy with all the remaining control variables as these too are potentially valid instruments. In this scenario we have 364 instruments with which to choose from. This instrument set was not considered in the original AK paper. In doing this we find a large increase in the number of significant linear combination instruments (found by NPC). Hence, potentially we can gain more efficient inference by increasing the amount of exogenous variation in education explained by this expanded instrument set.

During the time of publication the issue of weak instruments had received little attention, especially in applied work. It has been suggested subsequently that the AK IV setup suffers from a weak instrument problem and as such inference from their original paper is dubious. Bound et al. (1995) showed that in simulations generating instruments at random yielded qualitatively similar results as of AK. This is because when instruments are irrelevant the 2SLS estimator tends in probability to the limit of the biased OLS estimator (Buse, 1992).

In the original paper itself first stage partial F-stats of around 1 were reported for the various specifications they considered. The general rule of thumb is that the if the Partial F stat from the first stage regression less than 10 corresponds to the 2SLS being weakly identified (Staiger & Stock, 1997). More formal methods of testing for weak identification based on the partial F stat are laid out in Stock and Yogo (2002). The underlying idea of these forms of test are that a lower first-stage partial F indicates that a set of instruments may be weak.

However this logic is too rigid when using large instruments sets where no attempt is made to reduce the instrument set has been carried out. Using the NPC method we find 14 statistically significant NPCs at the 10% level, one of which is highly significant with a *p*-value of 0.0007. As such there exist some highly statistically significant linear combinations from within the 130 instruments.

The partial *F*-stats are based on first-stage regressions with all 130 instruments. The null hypothesis is that all 130 parameters are equal to zero. In the case of one endogenous variable we only need one or more valid (linear combinations of) instruments in order for IV estimators to be strongly identified. The *F*-stat is then not always a reliable indicator no matter how small we could possibly make the finite sample bias of the IV estimator. Namely that if we use a set of instruments with a low partial *F*-stat the resulting IV estimator may have poor finite sample properties. However, by reducing the instrument set using methods to preserve the variation of the endogenous variable explained by a smaller set, we could possibly yield an estimator with good finite sample properties.

In other words, even when there are strongly correlated linear combinations of instruments, increasing the instrument set by adding in more potentially irrelevant instruments could lead to a low *F*-stat. This is a signal that this set of instruments would have poor small sample properties. However, if there exist a smaller number of linear combinations of these instruments correlated with the endogenous variable, and we could identify these linear combinations, we can reduce the instrument set to irradiate the many instrument bias.

NPC is one method which asymptotically achieves this. In practise when using large sets of instruments, some means should be used to efficiently reduce this instrument set. As such we shouldn't see the size of the instrument set as fixed when performing the usual rule-of-thumb analysis based on first-stage regressions.

The null hypothesis for strong identification is that at least (linear combinations of) the instruments are corrected with the endogenous variable. Using NPCs this allows us to naturally set up this hypothesis. The squared first-stage parameters based on NPCs, we have seen, estimate the proportion of the variance in the endogenous variable explained by that NPC (i.e. that particular linear combination of instruments). Hence, if at least one of the NPCs from the first-stage regression is found to be highly statistically significant, we do not (with high probability) have a weak instrument problem.

For AK given that at least one NPC is highly statistically significant, it suggests the poor small sample properties of 2SLS based on all 130 instruments suffer a lot as opposed to a weak instrument problem. Out of the 130 instruments, around 10% of the NPCs (i.e. certain linear combinations of all 130 instruments) are statistically significant at the 10% significance level. AK may have used many more instruments, than they needed to, given the identifying power of the instruments seems to be captured by a much smaller set of instruments. Given the poor bias properties of 2SLS with many instruments, this could explain the poor small sample properties and why AK is widely considered in the literature to be a weak instrument problem.

We consider the same set of controls as used in the original AK and estimate the return to education using the IV, GMM and empirical likelihood (EL). The OLS estimator is known to be biased given the likely endogeneity of education in determining wages. The IV and GMM estimators both suffer relatively larger (higher order) bias from many instruments. This problem is amplified even further given the potential weakness of the instruments. As such we also consider the EL estimator (Smith, 1997) that in many situations is shown to have a smaller bias than IV and GMM (Newey & Smith, 2004). As we use the whole set of instruments, those NPCs are relevant at the 10% significance level, and those selected using the NPC ranking of instruments to minimize the estimated MSE of DN which we label 'Relevant' and 'Optimal' respectively in Table 7.

Table 5 reports the estimated first-stage parameters based on the sample NPCs (namely $\hat{\pi}_{npcj}$ for $j = \{1, \ldots, 30\}$). The square of the entries in Table 5 provide an estimate of the amount of variation the corresponding NPC contributes to the total variation in education. Thefirst NPC is highly

Table 5. First Stage NPC Parameter Estimates (130 instruments).

	Estimate	$Pr(>\|t\|)$		Estimate	$Pr(>\|t\|)$		Estimate	$Pr(>\|t\|)$
1	−0.0608	0.0007	11	0.0325	0.0704	21	0.0254	0.1583
2	−0.0580	0.0012	12	−0.0309	0.0857	22	0.0252	0.1601
3	−0.0467	0.0094	13	0.0306	0.0882	23	−0.0250	0.1646
4	−0.0458	0.0107	14	0.0304	0.0904	24	0.0249	0.1665
5	−0.0446	0.0131	15	−0.0278	0.1219	25	0.0234	0.1927
6	0.0394	0.0282	16	−0.0275	0.1259	26	−0.0234	0.1931
7	0.0336	0.0618	17	−0.0273	0.1291	27	−0.0234	0.1934
8	0.0335	0.0622	18	−0.0262	0.1449	28	0.0233	0.1940
9	−0.0334	0.0629	19	0.0259	0.1498	29	−0.0232	0.1971
10	0.0333	0.0640	20	−0.0254	0.1570	30	−0.0218	0.2251

statistically significant, suggesting in fact IV setting here is not weakly identified.

Fig. 1 plots $\hat{C}_{\leq m}$ for $m \in \{1, \ldots, 130\}$ and shows the amount of variation in education by the total set of instruments explained by using the first m NPCs. We see a very sharp incline for the first 10–15 NPCs. The amount of variation in education explained by adding in more NPCs after around 60 is marginal. As such the original AK specification using all 130 instruments likely suffered from the many instrument bias, amplified further by the fact the majority of these instruments are weak.

Fig. 2 plots sample estimates of the MSE approximations of DN from Eq. (4) based on the inclusion of the NPCs from 1 to m. In other words, the figure plots the small sample MSE changes as we sequentially include NPCs governed by the ranking in Table 5. There is a sharp decline in MSE for the first 20 instruments; however, after around 40 instruments the approximate MSE increases quite sharply. Fig. 2 suggests instrument sets of size 40–60 minimize the small sample MSE of the IV estimator.

In fact the partial F-stat based on the first 14 most significant NPCs is 5.38. The partial F-stat using all 130 instruments is 1.1. This is likely due to the fact around 90% of the NPCs are irrelevant and hence the true

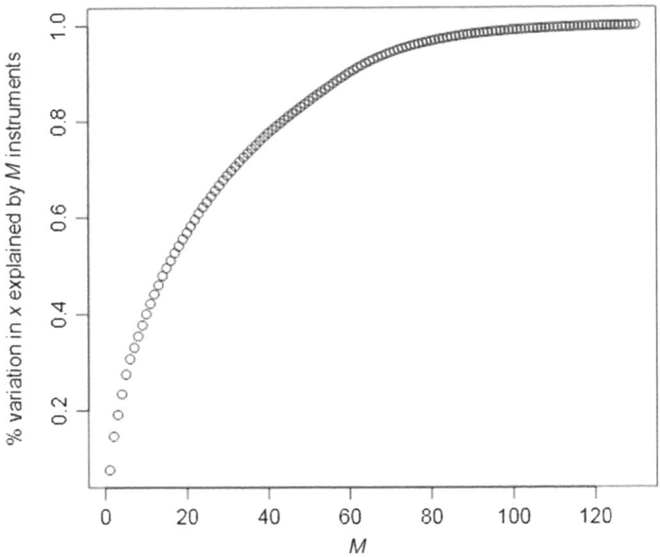

Fig. 1.

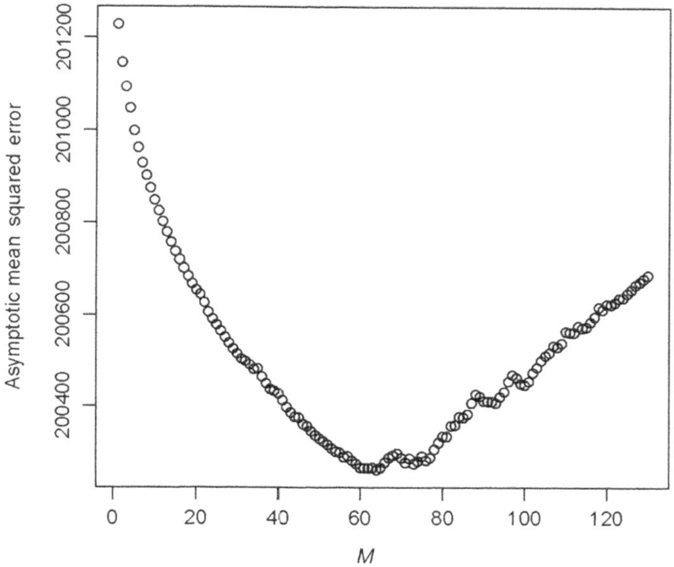

Fig. 2.

parameters are quite close to the boundary of the null of all zero. This is likely to provide incorrect guidance on the potential strength of the instrument set when transformed and reduced to ameliorate the many moment bias while preserving the strength of the original set of instruments.

We now repeat the analysis in Table 6 and Figs. 3 and 4 by using an extended set of instruments generating extra instruments by interacting all the 13 lottery dummies with all the exogenous control variables yielding 364 instruments in total. Table 6 reports the first-stage coefficients of the NPCs with their corresponding p-values. Forty of the NPCs from the potential 364 are statistically significant at the 10% significance level, which suggests expanding the instrument set has captured more of the variation in education and as such could reduce the variance of IV estimators.

Fig. 3 shows the steep incline each additional NPCs contributes to the variation in education for the first 30–40 NPCs. After 50–60 NPCs (which explain around 75% of the total variation in education by all 364 instruments), adding in NPCs to the instrument set provides little increase in explanatory power. This is again matched in Fig. 4 by the estimated small sample MSE. After inclusion of about 80 NPCs, the addition of more NPCs increases the estimated small sample MSE of IV.

Table 6. First Stage NPC Parameter Estimates (364 instruments).

	Estimate	$Pr(>\|t\|)$		Estimate	$Pr(>\|t\|)$		Estimate	$Pr(>\|t\|)$
1	0.0534	0.0029	16	−0.0386	0.0316	31	0.0327	0.0690
2	−0.0515	0.0042	17	−0.0382	0.0336	32	−0.0324	0.0714
3	−0.0509	0.0046	18	−0.0372	0.0383	33	0.0318	0.0766
4	0.0504	0.0050	19	−0.0360	0.0449	34	−0.0314	0.0803
5	0.0500	0.0054	20	−0.0353	0.0493	35	−0.0311	0.0831
6	0.0492	0.0062	21	−0.0349	0.0518	36	−0.0309	0.0852
7	0.0439	0.0146	22	0.0346	0.0541	37	−0.0305	0.0896
8	−0.0429	0.0169	23	−0.0345	0.0550	38	0.0301	0.0940
9	0.0426	0.0178	24	−0.0342	0.0567	39	−0.0299	0.0963
10	−0.0411	0.0222	25	0.0342	0.0573	40	−0.0298	0.0977
11	0.0411	0.0223	26	0.0339	0.0589	41	−0.0296	0.0993
12	−0.0407	0.0234	27	−0.0333	0.0640	42	0.0293	0.1026
13	0.0395	0.0280	28	0.0331	0.0654	43	−0.0291	0.1052
14	−0.0390	0.0301	29	−0.0330	0.0661	44	0.0285	0.1121
15	−0.0387	0.0311	30	−0.0327	0.0687	45	0.0285	0.1124

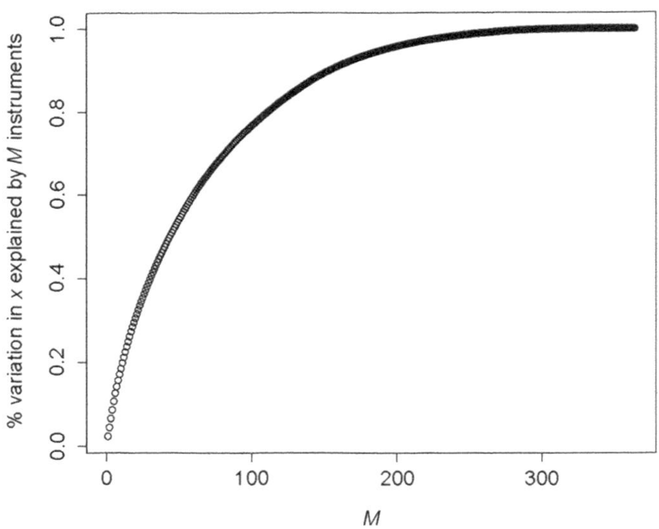

Fig. 3.

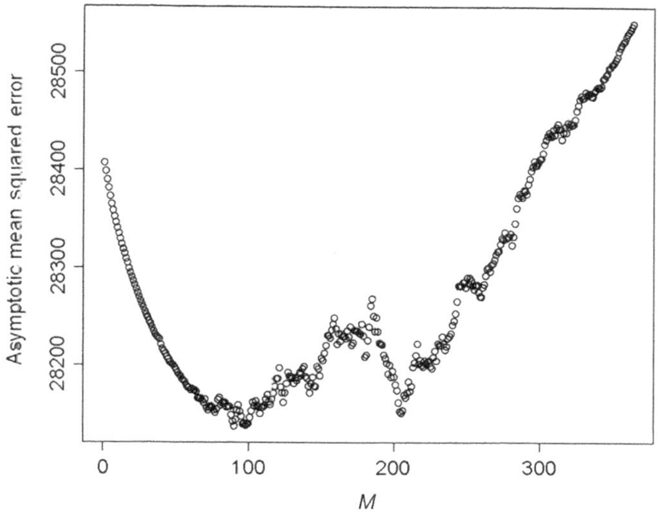

Fig. 4.

Table 7. Estimates of Returns to Education.

Instrument Set	All	Optimal	Relevant
2SLS (130)	0.703 (0.0158)	0.60 (0.0161)	0.518 (0.0221)
GMM (130)	0.0698 (0.0157)	0.597 (0.0161)	0.501 (0.0221)
EL (130)	0.5142 (0.157)	0.5157 (0.0162)	0.511 (0.0221)
F-stat	1.1	2.75	5.14
J-stat	0.394	0.141	0.23
2SLS (364)	0.7064 (0.0096)	0.689 (0.0112)	0.533 (0.0139)
GMM (364)	0.741 (0.0094)	0.692 (0.0112)	0.538 (0.0138)
EL (364)	0.4931 (0.00946)	0.5159 (0.01168)	0.05108 (0.01389)
F-stat	1.05	3.33	4.57
J-stat	0.387	0.098	0.267

Given the potential poor properties of the Carrasco (2012) estimator, we decide not to consider this here. Table 7 reports the results estimating the returns to education using the various instrument sets and estimators highlighted above-estimating with all instruments, those selected by NPC to minimize small sample MSE and those that are relevant at the 10% level from both sets of instruments. Standard errors are presented in parentheses with the corresponding p-value for the Hansen J-test presented beneath. For brevity, we just report the J-stat from the GMM estimator. The F-stat is the partial F-stat from regression of education on the relevant number of NPCs. As shown in AK, the OLS estimator is 0.59 with standard error 0.011 and the 2SLS estimate with all 130 instruments is 0.7(0.0158).

Interestingly, for all specifications the moment restrictions are not rejected at the 10% level suggesting validity of instruments. This is bolstered further by the fact that using 40 or 14 significant instruments suggests the J-stat may not suffer poor size properties found with many weak instruments (Hahn, Hausman & Yogo, 2002). Also, for both the GMM and 2SLS based on relevant instruments the return to education is estimated to be around 0.5, which is much lower than that based on all instruments and the OLS estimator.

The 2SLS estimate of the return to education is much larger than that of OLS which does not reconcile with our a priori notion of direction of bias in the wage-education regression. This along with the non-rejection of the instruments may suggest that the instruments are indeed valid and also not so weak as to be useless as suggested by AK.

Interestingly, the 2SLS and GMM estimators based on those NPCs that are statistically significant are very similar to those based on EL. The EL is relatively robust to the many instrument problem (Newey & Smith, 2004). This is encouraging as it suggests that the NPC method of instrument reduction may have overcome the many instrument problem for the GMM/IV estimator.

It also suggests the NPC reduction of instruments may improve considerably the small properties of EL, especially for very large instruments sets. Under certain conditions EL is first-order unbiased with a higher order bias that grows at a slower rate with the instrument set (relative to GMM). The benefit in terms of reducing the bias of the EL estimator relative to GMM will often be less when utilizing small- to medium-sized instrument sets.

However, when selecting from much larger instrument sets, the EL estimator will eventually suffer the many instrument bias and as such the NPC method may improve the small sample properties in this case. Also, the EL estimated standard errors are often undersized with large instrument sets (Newey & Windmeijer, 2009). As such the EL estimator based on the relevant NPCs in Table 7 may provide more reliable inference.

CONCLUSION

The many (weak) instrument bias is a common problem encountered in empirical work. The properties of 2SLS (and related estimators) are known to have poor small sample (higher order) bias properties when m is large relative to n. This bias is amplified if many of these instruments are weak. If every instrument we have is weak then it is difficult to evade the poor small sample properties of the IV type estimators, irrespective of the sample size.

In order to overcome the many weak instrument bias, much research has focused on methods to select instruments to minimize this small sample bias. A leading example is DN who derive higher order expansions of the MSE for a given instrument set. The MSE approximations then form a natural criterion function with which to choose an instrument set to minimize the small sample MSE. A problem with this approach as pointed out by the authors is that for large instrument sets some a priori ranking of instruments is required in practice.

A commonly used method to rank instruments in the literature is that of PCs. Carrasco (2012) and others argue that PCs provide a natural ranking of instruments. This idea is also embellished in general moment settings by Doran and Schmidt (2006). However as we demonstrate, this logic, though at first sight intuitive, is potentially flawed. Namely that the PC with the highest variance need not explain most (if any) of the variation in the endogenous variable.

The NPC does not suffer this problem asymptotically. NPC forms a ranking of m distinct linear combinations of instruments selecting those linear combinations of instruments (asymptotically) that are with the highest correlation with the endogenous variable, down to the lowest. To achieve this, NPC normalizes each PC so they have equal variance. A regression of the endogenous variable on the NPCs is shown to yield estimates that when squared provide a consistent estimate of the amount of variation the NPC explains of the total variation in the endogenous variable. The performance of this ranking depends crucially on the size of the instrument set not being too large relative to the sample size, a shortfall also of the PC method.

NPC transforms the instrument set to allow the formation of a clear ranking across this transformed instrument set in terms of their strength. There are two main benefits to this approach. First, it provides a natural ordering of instruments with which to minimize the small sample MSE approximations of DN or otherwise. It also lends itself well to adhoc rules, such as selecting NPCs with a t-value above a certain threshold. Given the NPC ranking's intuitive nature, its appeal in econometrics for instrument selection is potentially far reaching.

Second we argue it provides a more reliable means of testing whether our IV model is strongly identified. In the simple case of one endogenous variable, we need that at least one NPC be strongly correlated with the endogenous variable. Commonly in many instrument settings an indicator of the strength of a set of instruments is the partial F-stat based on the null hypothesis that all instruments are irrelevant (Shea, 1997; Stock & Yogo, 2002). However, as we argued, this F-stat in general decreases with the inclusion of an increasing number of irrelevant instruments and is not a reliable indicator of the existence of a potentially smaller number of strong instruments with which to strongly identify the unknown parameter.

It could be the case that there is one (or more) highly correlated linear combination from across the instrument set, though the observed partial F-stat may be small due to the inclusion of large number of linear combinations across the instrument that are (near) irrelevant. A low partial F-stat often is taken as evidence of weak identification, where Stock and Yogo (2002) tabulate critical values for tests of weak identification. We may erroneously believe we have a weak-instrument problem, when in fact we are faced with a many instrument bias which can be avoided to some degree using NPC.

NPC de-tangles the informative content spread across the instrument set (in terms of overlap with the variation of the endogenous variable), transforming the instruments so that this information is clearer to analyse. A lot of theoretical analysis takes size of the instrument set as fixed. In practice any efficient estimation procedure should aim to keep the instrument set as small as possible while preserving the correlation with the endogenous variable. NPC provides a means to achieve this end. As such the methods of testing identification in the literature with many instruments are arguably too rigid.

We posit that many classic empirical examples thought of as weakly identified (where there are also many instruments) may not indeed be. We provided one such example; the Vietnam War Lottery IV estimation of AK. We demonstrated using NPC that of the 130 instruments around 10% of possible linear combinations of across the whole instrument set were statistically significant, 3 of which with a p-value of almost zero. This gives very strong indication that in fact there is enough informative content within the whole instrument set to identify the true parameter, though the poor small sample properties highlighted by Bound et al. (1995) and many others may originate from a many instrument bias. This is especially the case for the 2SLS estimator considered by AK which suffers from a large many instrument bias.

Using 2SLS with the statistically significant NPCs, I estimated a return to education of 0.518, much lower than that based on 2SLS with all instruments estimated to be 0.7, and OLS with an estimate of 0.59. Expanding the instrument set to generate an extra 234 instruments above the 130 used by AK we found 40 NPCs with a non-zero correlation with the endogenous variable at the 10% level. 2SLS based on this set of NPCs estimated the return to education at 0.533. We also considered the EL estimator that is known to have good small sample properties relative to 2SLS. Similar results were found here. Interestingly, the returns to education estimated using EL were all about 0.5 for all instruments sets considered. This agrees with the intuition of this chapter. In that removing those combinations of instruments that are irrelevant we find a return to education based on 2SLS similar to that based on estimators that are relatively robust to the many instrument bias. Hence, the NPC method may have removed the many instrument bias.

The NPC method of instrument reduction will also likely reduce the higher order bias faced by EL and related estimators that remove the first-order estimation bias. In other words, it may reduce their asymptotic variance while maintaining their favourable first-order properties.

An interesting avenue for research would be to extend the methods in this chapter to general non-linear moment conditions. A similar logic will also apply. Removing those linear combinations of moments that have the smallest variance (based upon a first-stage GMM estimate) may not necessarily reduce the variance of the GMM estimator. This was the method considered in Doran and Schmidt (2006). The variance of the GMM estimator moves inversely with the variation of the first order derivative matrix of the moments.

We may wish to drop those combinations of moments that explain a small amount of variation of this first order derivative, not those that explain the least variance within the moment set. Those linear combination of moments with the highest variance may not contribute to the variation in the Jacobian. As such choosing moments using PC methods may face an analogous problem to that found for the linear IV estimator, though this extension would pose a difficult theoretical challenge in that a consistent first-stage estimate of the true parameter is required to estimate the Jacobian in non-linear settings.

ACKNOWLEDGMENTS

I would like to acknowledge financial support of the ESRC studentship (2008–2011) which part by helped in funding this research. The usual disclaimer applies.

NOTES

1. Throughout the chapter when referring to an IV estimator we refer in general to any estimator based on a set of instruments (e.g. two-stage least squares (2SLS), generalized method of moments (GMM), generalized empirical likelihood (GEL)) unless specifically stated otherwise.
2. For ease of exposition, this chapter will illustrate ideas based on the one endogenous variable, many exogenous variables IV setup. The ideas generalize naturally to the case of many endogenous regressors.
3. Carrasco (2012) also considers other related regularization methods, some of which are discussed in section 'The Regularization MSE Approach'.
4. Specifically the code allows one to perform the NPC ranking detailed in section 'Sample NPC Method' and estimates the MSE expansions of DN evaluated as a function of NPCs. It would be easy to modify the code and evaluate the MSE approximations with a different form of instruments.
5. The idea extends readily to more than one endogenous variables and with exogenous controls. This result easily extends to the case of many endogenous and exogenous variables.
6. The full rank assumption on Σ is trivial, since if it were not full rank some linear combination of instruments would be redundant for any sample size.

REFERENCES

Amemiya, T. (1966). On the use of principal components of independent variables in two-stage least-squares estimation. *International Economic Review*, *7*(3), 283–303.

Angrist, J. D., & Krueger, A. B. (1991). Does compulsory schooling attendance affect schooling and earnings? *Quarterly Journal of Economics*, *106*(November 1991), 979–1014.

Angrist, J.D. & Krueger, A.B. (1992). *Estimating the Payo to schooling using the Vietnam-era draft lottery*. NBER Working Papers 4067, National Bureau of Economic Research.

Angrist, J. D., & Krueger, A. B. (1995). Split-sample instrumental variables estimates of the return to schooling. *Journal of Business & Economic Statistics*, *13*(2), 225–235.

Bound, J., Jaeger, D. A., & Baker, R. M. (1995). Problems with instrumental variables estimation when the correlation between the instruments and the endogenous explanatory variable is weak. *Journal of the American Statistical Association*, *90*(430), 443–450.

Bosq, D. (2000). *Linear processes in function spaces*. New York, NY: Springer - Verlag.

Buse, A. (1992). The bias of instrumental variable estimators. *Econometrica*, *60*(1), 173–180.

Carrasco, M. (2012) A regularization approach to the many instruments problem, *Journal of Econometrics*, *170*, 383–398.

Carrasco, M. & Tchuente, G. (2012). *Regularized LIML for many instruments*. Working Paper, May 2012. University of Montreal, CIREQ, CIRANO.

Chao, J. C., & Swanson, N. R. (2005). Consistent estimation with a large number of weak instruments. *Econometrica*, *73*, 1673–1692.

Donald, S. G., Imbens, G. W., & Newey, W. K. (2009). Choosing instrumental variables in conditional moment restriction models. *Journal of Econometrics*, *152*, 28–36.
Donald, S. G., & Newey, W. K. (2001). Choosing the number of instruments. *Econometrica*, *69*(5), 1161–1191.
Doran, H. E., & Schmidt, P. (2006). GMM estimators with improved finite sample properties using principal components of the weighting matrix, with an application to the dynamic panel data model. *Journal of Econometrics*, *133*(1), 387–409.
Hahn, J., Hausman, J., & Kuersteiner, G. (2004). Estimation with weak instruments: Accuracy of higher order bias and MSE approximations. *Econometrics Journal*, *7*(1), 272–306.
Hahn, J., Hausman, J., & Yogo, M. (2002). A new specification test for the validity of instrumental variables. *Econometrica*, *70*(1), 163–189.
Hahn, J., Hausman, J., & Yogo, M. (2003). Weak instruments: Diagnosis and cures in empirical econometrics. *American Economic Review*, *93*(2), 118–125.
Hall, A., & Peixe, F. (2003). A consistent method for the selection of relevant instruments. *Econometric Reviews*, *22*(3), 269–287.
Hall, A. R., Rudebusch, G. D., & Wilcox, D. W. (1996). Judging instrument relevance in instrumental variables estimation. *International Economic Review*, *37*(2), 283–298.
Han, C., & Phillips, P. C. B. (2006). GMM with many moment conditions. *Econometrica*, *74*(1), 147–192.
Hausman, J., Newey W.K., Woutersen, T., Chao, J., & Swanson, N.R. (2012). IV estimation with heteroscedasticity and many instruments. *Quantitative Economics*, *3*, 211–255.
Jolliffe, I. T. (2002). *Principal component analysis* (2nd ed.). New York, NY: Springer-Verlag.
Kapetanios, G., & Marcellino, M. (2006). Cross-sectional averaging and instrumental variable estimation with many weak instruments. *Economics Letters*, *108*(1), 36–39.
Kloek, T., & Mennes, B. M. (1960). Simultaneous equations estimation based on principal components of predetermined variables. *Econometrica*, *28*(1), 45–61.
Kuersteiner, G., & Okui, R. (2010). Constructing optimal instruments by first-stage prediction averaging. *Econometrica*, *78*(2), 697–718.
Newey, W. N., & Smith, R. J. (2004). Higher order properties of GMM and generalized empirical likelihood estimators. *Econometrica*, *72*(1), 219–255.
Newey, W. N., & Windmeijer, F. (2009). Generalized method of moments with many weak moment conditions. *Econometrica*, *77*(3), 687–719.
Okui, R. (2010). Instrumental variable estimation in the presence of many moment conditions. *Journal of Econometrics*, *165*, 70–86.
Rothenberg, T. J. (1984). Approximating the distributions of econometric estimators and test statistics. In Z. Griliches & M. D. Intriligator (Eds.), *Handbook of econometrics* (Vol. 2, pp. 881–935). Amsterdam: North-Holland.
Shea, J. (1997). Instrument relevance in multivariate linear models: A simple measure. *Review of Economics and Statistics*, *79*(2), 348–352.
Smith, R. J. (1997). Alternative semi-parametric likelihood approaches to generalized method of moments estimation. *The Economic Journal*, *107*, 503–519.
Staiger, D., & Stock, J. H. (1997). Instrumental variables regression with weak instruments. *Econometrica*, *65*(3), 557–586.
Stock, J. H., Wright, J. H., & Yogo, M. (2002). A survey of weak instruments and weak identification in generalized method of moments. *Journal of Business & Economic*

Statistics, *20*(4), 518–529. (Twentieth Anniversary Issue on the generalized method of moments).
Stock, J. H., & Yogo, M. (2002). Testing for weak instruments in linear IV regression. In D. W. K. Andrews & J. H. Stock (Eds.), *Identification and inference for econometric models: A Festschrift in honor of Thomas J. Rothenberg*. Cambridge: Cambridge University Press.
Winekelreid, D. Q. & Smith, R. J. (2011). *Principal components instrumental variable estimation*. Cambridge Working Papers in Economics No. 1119.

APPENDIX

First we define some notations used throughout the chapter.

For any random vectors x and y then $\mathbb{E}[x]$ refers to the mathematical expectation take w.r.t is the density of x. $\mathbb{E}[x|y]$ is the conditional expectation of x given y. $Var(x) := \mathbb{E}[(x-\mathbb{E}[x])(x-\mathbb{E}[x])']$. Denote $\overset{p}{\to}$,$\overset{d}{\to}$, as convergence in probability and convergence in distribution respectively. For any deterministic sequence a_n and constant b then $a_n \to b$ denotes b as the deterministic limit of a_n. $\overset{d}{\sim}$ is shorthand for 'is distributed as' and 'w.p.a.1' denotes 'with probability approaching 1'. 'i.i.d.' is shorthand for independent and identically distributed. We use $o_p(a)$ to refer to a variable that converges to zero w.p.a.1 when divided by a and similarly $O_p(a)$ a variable bounded in probability when divided by a. $O(a)$ has a similar definition to $O_p(a)$ though for deterministic sequences. Let $\|A\|$ refer to any arbitrary matrix then $||A||$ is the Frobenius norm of a matrix A is equal to $tr(A'A)^{1/2}$ where $tr(A)$ refers to the trace of A. For any $a>0$, $I_{a\times a}$ refers to the $a \times a$ identity matrix. $[A]_{ij}$ is the ij'th element of A.

Proof of Lemma 1.

$$\text{(i)} \sup_{i\leq n} ||\hat{Z}_i^{npc} - Z_i^{npc}|| \leq (||\hat{\Lambda}^{-1/2} - \Lambda^{-1/2}|| + ||\Lambda^{-1/2}||||\hat{P}' - P'||) \sup_{i\leq n} ||Z_i|| \tag{23}$$

Since $||P'|| = m$ (as $P'P = I_{m\times m}$), where $||\Lambda^{-1/2}|| \leq m \sup_{j\leq m}\lambda_j^{-1/2} = O(m)$. Assuming Σ full rank (i.e. $\lambda_j > 0$ $\forall$ $j \in \{1,\ldots,m\}$).[6]

Then if Z_i is i.i.d. (and under some further regularity conditions on the boundedness of Z_i) one can show that $||\hat{P}' - P'|| = O_p(mn^{-1/2})$ and $||\hat{\Lambda}^{-1/2} - \Lambda^{-1/2}|| = O_p(mn^{-1/2})$ (Bosq, 2000).

$$\sup_{i\leq n}\left\| \hat{Z}_i^{npc} - Z_i^{npc} \right\| \leq O_p(m^2 n^{-1/2}) \sup_{i\leq n} ||Z_i|| \tag{24}$$

$$\left\| \frac{1}{n}(\hat{Z}^{npc} - Z^{npc}) \right\| \leq \sup_{i\leq n}\left\| \hat{Z}_i^{npc} - Z_i^{npc} \right\| \leq O_p(m^2/n^{1/2}) \sup_{i\leq n} ||Z_i\| \tag{25}$$

Assuming that $\sup_{i\leq n}||Z_i|| = o_p(n^{1/2}/m^2)$ then by Eq. (25)

$$\left\| \frac{1}{n}(\hat{Z}^{npc} - Z^{npc}) \right\| \overset{p}{\to} 0 \tag{26}$$

The assumption that $\sup_{i \leq n} ||Z_i|| = o_p(n^{1/2}/m^2)$ rules out instruments $Z_i (i = 1, \ldots, n)$ growing at rate $n^{1/2}/m^2$ or faster. A strong sufficient condition is Z_i bounded for all i and $m^4/n \to 0$. This rate condition could possibly be improved under further regularity conditions, though showing this is beyond the scope of this chapter.

(ii) Assume for simplicity that X/n is bounded (i.e. $||X/n|| = O_p(1)$) and given Eq. (26) it is straightforward to establish that

$$\hat{\pi}_{npc} = \hat{\pi}^*_{npc} + o_p(1) \tag{27}$$

where $\hat{\pi}^*_{npc} := \left(\frac{1}{n} Z^{npc\prime} Z^{npc}\right)^{-1} \frac{1}{n} Z^{npc\prime} X$ is the OLS estimator based on the population NPCs Z^{npc}.

Assuming (Z_i, x_i, η_i) $(i = 1, \ldots, n)$ are i.i.d. (though the result will hold under much weaker assumptions) and that Z_i is uncorrelated with η_i (which holds by assumption in the setup of section 'MSE Approximations of Donald and Newey (2001)'), it is easily shown that $\hat{\pi}^*_{npc} \xrightarrow{p} \pi_{npc}$, hence by Eq. (27)

$$\hat{\pi}_{npcj} \xrightarrow{p} \pi_{npcj} \tag{28}$$

IMPLEMENTING NPC TO MINIMIZE MSE OF DN

We discuss how to implement the analysis carried out in the fifth section using NPC for the data set of AK. The notation we use throughout is the same used in the R code below. The explanation of the method of NPC given in section 'Normalized Principal Components' did not consider any exogenous control variables. We need to modify slightly to take into account the potential correlation between the instruments and controls in the first-stage regression so that coefficients of the first-stage regression of x_i on the NPCs and controls satisfy the properties as shown in section 'Normalized Principal Components'. Namely that the magnitude of square of the coefficients on the NPCs form a consistent ranking of the total variation each NPC explains of the variation in x_i.

Consider a scalar endogenous variable x_i, a $p \times 1$ exogenous control variables (w_i) and m instruments z_i for $i \in 1, \ldots, n\}$ where n is the sample size.

Define $x = (x_1, \ldots, x_n)'$ as the $n \times 1$ vector of observations on the endogenous variable, $w = (w_1', \ldots, w_n')'$ the $n \times p$ matrix of data observations on the exogenous control variables and $Z = (z_1', \ldots, z_n')'$ as the $n \times m$ matrix of data observations of the instruments.

$$y_i = \beta x_i + \delta' w_i + \varepsilon_i \tag{29}$$

$$x_i = \pi_z' z_i + \pi_w' w_i + \eta_i \tag{30}$$

where β, δ, π_z, π_w are the true unknown parameters and ε_i and η_i satisfy the conditions as defined in section 'MSE Approximations of Donald and Newey (2001)'. For the following, it is convenient to stack Eqs. (29) and (30) to form

$$y = x\beta + w\delta + \varepsilon \tag{31}$$

$$x = z\pi_z + w\pi_w + \eta \tag{32}$$

where $\eta = (\eta_1, \ldots, \eta_n)'$ and $\varepsilon = (\varepsilon_1, \ldots, \varepsilon_n)'z = m_w z + p_w z$, $p_w = w(w'w)^{-1}w'$ is the projection matrix of w and $m_w = I_{n \times n} - p_w$.

$$x = m_w z\pi_z + p_w z\pi_z + w\pi_w + \eta \tag{33}$$

$m_w z$ projects the instrument z onto the null space of w. It is the variation in z that doesn't overlap with that of w. Hence, we work with $z_w = m_w z$ as our instrument that is uncorrelated with w (since $p_w m_w = 0$ by construction) and by assumption with η_i. The code below then applies NPC method to the instruments z_w that deal with the correlation between z and w. The rest goes through similar to what is given in section 'Normalized Principal Components' and the code below is self explanatory.

Loading your data into R, define from your data set the following: n (the sample size), y (as the dependent variable), x (as the sample vector of the endogenous variable), w (sample matrix of exogenous variables excluding the constant), z (sample matrix of instruments), m (the dimension of the instrument set).

Also pre-specify K, where K is the number of NPCs used to form initial estimate of σ^2 and $\sigma^2_{\eta\varepsilon}$ as defined in section 'MSE Approximations of Donald and Newey (2001)', which are needed to estimate the sample MSE of DN in Eq. (5). A useful approach is to estimate $C_{\leq k}$ for all k and choose K such that $C_{\leq K}$ is above a threshold, e.g. 90%. We may use an iterative procedure, doing a first stage and then repeating.

Once the data has been loaded and saved with the variable names given, then running R mse is an $m \times 1$ vector storing the estimated small sample MSE by iteratively adding in extra NPCs from 1 to m where they have been ordered by their relevance o.

NPC are the sample NPCs based upon zw (the instruments transformed to be uncorrelated with w).

If we then plot(mse) we can choose the size of the instrument set accordingly and perform an analysis similar to that in Fig. 2 and 4. We can also produce $\hat{C}_{\leq k}$ by using the estimated parameters from the regression of x_i on the NPCs pi using the ordering o of their absolute size. Define pi = pi[0] then run sum(pi[c(1:k)]^2)/sum(pi^2).

We can generate the analysis in Tables 5 and 6 by running lm(x ~ NPC + w + 0); this will produce OLS output where the first m coefficients are the NPCs in ascending order of relevance. We can then form t-tests.

R CODE FOR NPC INSTRUMENT SELECTION

```
# Load data, define following variables from data.
# y (1 x n vector of dependent variable)
# x- n x 1 vector (data vector on endogenous variable)
# w- n x p (data matrix of p exogenous variables (excluding the constant))
# z- n x m (data matrix of m of instruments)
# n- sample size
load(sem) # package for 2SLS
load(base)
w = as.matrix(cbind(rep(1,n),w)) # control variables inc. constant
z = as.matrix(z)
delta = as.matrix(lm(z ~ w + 0)$coeff)
zw = z-w%*%delta # instrument projecting out w
m = dim(zw)[2] # number of instruments
mse = rep(0,m) # vector to store MSE for each instrument set
P = eigen(var(zw))$vector # eigenvector matrix of instrument covariance
matrix
L = eigen(var(zw))$value # eigenvalues of covariance matrix of instruments"
Lambda = diag(m)
for(s in c(1:m)){ Lambda[s,s] = L[s]^{-1/2}}
Lambda = as.matrix(Lambda)
NPC =  zw%*%P%*%Lambda # matrix of NPCs
pi = as.vector(lm(x ~ NPC + w + 0)$coeff[c(1:m)]) #OLS estimate of NPC
relevance
o = order(abs(pi),decreasing = TRUE) #ranking of NPCs
NPC = NPC[,c(o)] # NPC rearranged - from most to least relevant
```

```
K= #pre-Select K , cut-off point to form first stage approximation (K<m)
res=tsls(y~x+w+0,~NPC[,c(1:K)]+w+0)$resid
s=t(res)%*%res/n #estimate of σ_ε^2
NPCW=cbind(NPC,w) # all NPC and W for first stage regression
QNPCW=qr.Q(qr(NPCW)) #QR decomposition of NPCW
W=cbind(x,w) #endog variable and controls
H=(t(W)%*%QNPCW%*%t(QNPCW)%*%W/n)
V=solve(H) #component of variance of 2SLS estimator
for(t in c(1:m) ) { # Loop to estimate approx MSE inc. NPC up to t
U=as.logical(c(rep(1,t),rep(0,m-t))) #selection vector (picks first t columns)
NPCU= as.matrix(NPC[,U]) #inst set up to t
rest=as.vector(tsls(y~x+w+0,~NPCU+w+0)$residuals) #estimate of
residuals with instrument set t
Q=qr.Q(qr(cbind (NPCU,w)))
ue=t(W-Q%*%t(Q)%*%W)%*%rest/n
ff=t(W)%*%W- t(W)%*%Q%*%t(Q)%*%W
mse[t]=s*sum(diag(V))+(t^2/n)*sum(diag((V%*%ue%*%t(ue)%*%V)))
+s*sum(diag((V%*%(ff/n)%*%V)))
  #MSE approximation for 2SLS for first t NPCs}
```

ERRORS-IN-VARIABLES AND THE WAVELET MULTIRESOLUTION APPROXIMATION APPROACH: A MONTE CARLO STUDY

Marco Gallegati and James B. Ramsey

ABSTRACT

In this chapter we perform a Monte Carlo simulation study of the errors-in-variables model examined in Ramsey, Gallegati, Gallegati, and Semmler (2010) by using a wavelet multiresolution approximation approach. Differently from previous studies applying wavelets to errors-in-variables problem, we use a sequence of multiresolution approximations of the variable measured with error ranging from finer to coarser scales. Our results indicate that multiscale approximations to the variable observed with error based on the coarser scales provide an unbiased asymptotically efficient estimator that also possess good finite sample properties.

Keywords: Wavelets; IVs; errors-in-variables; Monte Carlo simulations

JEL classification: C14; C26; C53

Essays in Honor of Jerry Hausman
Advances in Econometrics, Volume 29, 149–171

ISSN: 0731-9053/doi:10.1108/S0731-9053(2012)0000029011

INTRODUCTION

Although highly likely to be observed in practice due to inaccuracy in data recording or because the measured variable is different from the true variable, the problem of measurement error is largely disregarded in empirical works. The solution adopted to overcome the problem of measurement error is generally provided by the application of the Instrumental variables (IVs) technique under the assumption of instruments correlated with the true value of the variable measured with error and uncorrelated with the measurement error. When these assumptions hold, IV estimation, in contrast to OLS, provides consistent estimates in the linear regression models with measurement errors.

In the application of the IV technique, empirical researcher must deal with the cumbersome search for suitable instruments. Indeed, as evidenced by the recent econometric literature, using "weak, or poor, instruments" is likely to produce biased and inconsistent estimates that are potentially worse than the OLS estimator using the variable suspected of being observed with error (e.g., Bound, Jaeger, & Baker, 1995; Hahn & Hausman, 2003; Staiger & Stock, 1997; Stock, Wright, & Yogo, 2002).[1] Since finding such "good instruments" may not be an easy task and clear guidelines are difficult to provide, traditional IV methods rely mainly on economic theory or intuition, so that the choice is often influenced by what variables are available. Also the assumed non-correlation with the error term is usually taken on faith; at the worse many, if not most, choices of instrument can be categorized as solving the problem by assumption.

From this perspective, wavelet analysis can provide an effective solution to the problem of finding valid instruments. Wavelets are functions localized in both the time and frequency domains that can provide a multiscale analysis of a signal. The adaptive time-frequency resolution of wavelet signal processing is suitable for analyzing nonstationary signals at different scales, reducing noise, and extracting the local features of signals such as peaks, discontinuities, and breakdown points. One of the most effective application areas of wavelets in signal processing is reducing noise in a signal or denoising. By retaining the structural component of a signal after denoising, the wavelet transform is able to decompose the observed time series into the sum of a structural component and a random error component. Such denoised signal can provide a feasible IV for a variable measured with error whose properties as an instrument can be easily verified. Specifically, wavelet multiresolution approximation, by sequentially approximating the underlying structural component of a variable, can provide a natural and obvious solution to IV problems.

Several recent papers have demonstrated the usefulness of wavelet analysis in providing additional IV (Michis & Sapatinas, 2007), and dealing with measurement error problems (Gencay & Gradejovic, 2011; Ramsey et al., 2010) and simultaneous equations misspecification (Ramsey et al., 2010). Specifically, the Monte Carlo simulation results obtained in Michis and Sapatinas (2007) and in Gencay and Gradejovic (2011) indicate that using wavelet IV can reduce the estimation bias and lead to significant gains in efficiency with respect to standard methods, respectively. Moreover, Ramsey et al. (2010) using some simulated models show that the structural component revealed by wavelet analysis yields nearly ideal IV for variables observed with error and for co-endogenous variables in simultaneous equation models.

Since the results in Ramsey et al. (2010) were obtained using just one randomly generated dataset, in this chapter we perform a Monte Carlo simulation study in order to assess the robustness of their numerical results and the validity of the proposed methodology. Specifically, by extracting several random samples from a simulated data set generated from the errors-in-variables model analyzed in Ramsey et al. (2010), we compare the performance of various wavelet-based estimators with those of standard OLS method by looking at the distributional properties of the various estimators for different sample sizes. Differently from previous studies using wavelet-based estimators, that is Ramsey et al. (2010) and Gencay and Gradejovic (2011), we use a sequence of wavelet estimators varying from finer to coarser approximation levels.

The results of the simulation experiment indicate that wavelets can provide a valid "feasible" IV for dealing with measurement error in explanatory variables of regression models. Specifically, we provide evidence that wavelet estimators based on the coarser scale approximations provide an unbiased and asymptotically efficient estimator for the errors-in-variables case. In addition, and in contrast to IV estimators with instruments weakly correlated with the regressors, these wavelet-based estimators appear to possess also good finite sample properties.

The chapter is organized as follows. In the second section, we provide a brief description of wavelet analysis and its main properties. The third section provides the theoretical underpinnings for the wavelet multiresolution approach to provide suitable instruments. In the fourth section, a Monte Carlo simulation study of the distributional finite sample properties of wavelet-based estimators relative to OLS in the errors-in-variables case is performed. The last section concludes.

BRIEF DESCRIPTION OF WAVELETS AND THEIR PROPERTIES

We begin this section by recalling the basic structure of the wavelet approach to modeling time series data.[2] For a more complete and insightful development of the theory and use of wavelets, see Percival and Walden (2000), Bruce and Gao (1996), Gencay, Selcuk, and Whitcher (2002), and Ramsey (2008). At the simplest level, a "wavelet" is a function $\psi(.)$ such that

$$\int_{-\infty}^{\infty} \psi(t)dt = 0 \tag{1}$$

$$\int_{-\infty}^{\infty} \psi(t)^2 dt = 1 \tag{2}$$

We see from these relationships that wavelets involve weighted differences, integral of $\psi(.)$ is zero, and has a normalized scale. The import of the latter is that for any $\varepsilon > 0$, there exists a finite T such that

$$\int_{-T}^{T} \psi(t)^2 dt < 1 - \varepsilon \tag{3}$$

In short, the squared contribution to the variance is vanishingly small outside the range $(-T, T)$. In addition, there is a requirement on the choice of wavelet function that is called the "admissibility condition" which ensures that the original function can be reconstructed from the wavelet decomposition (Percival & Walden, 2000).[3]

For any arbitrary mother wavelet function ψ, the continuous wavelet transform (CWT) of a given function $f(t)$ is

$$W_x(\lambda, \tau) = \int_{-\infty}^{\infty} \psi_{\lambda,\tau}(t) f(t)dt \tag{4}$$

where

$$\psi_{\lambda,\tau}(t) \equiv \frac{1}{\sqrt{\lambda}} \psi\left(\frac{t-\tau}{\lambda}\right)$$

represents a set of wavelet daughters obtained by scaling and translating the mother wavelet ψ (Percival & Walden, 2000). In the definition, parameters

λ and τ denote the dilation (scale factor) and translation (time shift), respectively.

Since the CWT is a highly information redundant transform, the general formulation for a CWT can be restricted to the definition of the " discrete wavelet transform" (DWT) by discretizing the parameters λ and τ. In order to obtain an orthonormal basis, a transform of the scaling parameter, $\lambda = \lambda_0^j$, and the Nyquist sampling rule, $\tau = k\lambda_0^j T$, are used.[4] The generating wavelet functions are then

$$\psi_{j,k}(t) = \lambda_0^{-j/2}\psi\left(\frac{t-k\lambda_0^j T}{2^j}\right) \tag{5}$$

where j and k are integers. If T is small enough and the computation is done octave by octave, i.e., $\lambda_0 = 2$, the " mother wavelet" results in the following equation:

$$\psi_{j,k}(t) = 2^{-j/2}\psi\left(\frac{t-2^j k}{2^j}\right) \tag{6}$$

This function represents a sequence of rescalable functions at a scale of $s = 2^j$, $j = 1, 2, ..., J$, and with time index k, $k = 1, 2, 3, ..., N/2^j$. The wavelet transform coefficient of the projection of the observed function, $f(t)$, $k = 1, 2, 3, ..., N, N = 2^J$ on the wavelet $\psi_{j,k}(t)$ is given by

$$d_{j,k} \approx \int \psi_{j,k}(t)f(t)dt, \quad j = 1, 2, .., J \tag{7}$$

For a complete reconstruction of a signal $f(t)$, one requires a scaling function, $\phi(.)$, that represents the smoothest component of the signal. While the wavelet coefficients represent weighted "differences" at each scale, the scaling coefficients represent averaging at each scale. The scaling function, also known as the "father wavelet," is defined by

$$\phi_{J,k}(t) = 2^{-J/2}\phi\left(\frac{t-2^J k}{2^J}\right) \tag{8}$$

and the scaling function coefficient is given by

$$s_{J,k} \approx \int {}_{J,k}(t)f(t)dt \tag{9}$$

The DWT re-expresses a time series in terms of coefficients that are associated with a particular time and a particular dyadic scale. For the

DWT, where the number of observations is $N = 2^J$, the number of coefficients at each dyadic scale is

$$N = N/2^J + N/2^J + N/2^{J-1} + \ldots + N/4 + N/2 \tag{10}$$

that is, there are $N/2^J$ coefficients $s_{J,k}$, $N/2^J$ coefficients $d_{J,k}$, $N/2^{J-1}$ coefficients $d_{J-1,k}$, ..., and $N/2$ coefficients $d_{1,k}$.

By construction, we have an orthonormal set of basis functions, whose detailed properties depend on the choices made for the functions $\phi(.)$ and $\psi(.)$; see, for example, the references cited above as well as Daubechies (1992), Silverman (1998), and Strang and Nguyen (1996).[5]

At each scale, the entire real line is approximated by a sequence of "non-overlapping" wavelets. The deconstruction of the function $f(t)$ is therefore

$$f(t) \approx \sum_k s_{J,k}\phi_{J,k}(t) + \sum_k d_{J,k}\psi_{J,k}(t) + \ldots + \sum_k d_{j,k}\psi_{j,k}(t) + \ldots + \sum_k d_{1,k}\psi_{1,k}(t) \tag{12}$$

The degree of relative error in many cases of economic variables is approximately on the order of 10^{-13}, so that one can reasonably claim that the wavelet decomposition in Eq. (11) is very good. Further, the approximation can be re-written in terms of collections of coefficients at given scales as:

$$\begin{aligned} S_J f(t) &= \sum_k s_{J,k}\phi_{J,k}(t) \\ D_J f(t) &= \sum_k d_{J,k}\psi_{J,k}(t) \\ D_{J-1} f(t) &= \sum_k d_{J-1,k}\psi_{J-1,k}(t) \\ &\vdots \\ D_1 f(t) &= \sum_k d_{1,k}\psi_{1,k}(t) \end{aligned} \tag{13}$$

Finally, in terms of coefficient crystals, the approximating equation can be restated as

$$f(t) \approx S_J f(t) + D_J f(t) + D_{J-1} f(t) + \ldots + D_2 f(t) + D_1 f(t) \tag{14}$$

where $S_J f(t)$ contains the "smooth component" of the signal, and the $D_j f(t)$, $j = 1, 2, .., J$, the detail signal components at ever increasing levels of detail. Hence, $S_J f(t)$ provides the large-scale road map, while $D_1 f(t)$ shows the pot-holes. Since any term in Eq. (14) represents a component of the signal $f(t)$ with a different resolution, the previous equation indicates what is termed the multiresolution decomposition (MRD).

From the previous equation, one can easily derive the recursive equations:

$$R_j f(t) = \begin{cases} 0, & j = 0 \\ \sum_{k=1}^{j} D_k f(t) & 1 \leq j \leq J \end{cases} \tag{15}$$

For any signal $f(t)$: $f(t) = S_j f(t) + R_j f(t)$ and as is easily deduced:

$$S_{j-1} f(t) = S_j f(t) + D_j f(t) \tag{16}$$

Therefore, adding each detail component $D_j f(t)$ in turn we can produce a refinement of the $S_j f(t)$ approximation which represents the scale 2^{j-1} approximation to the signal. The collection of approximations $S_J f(t)$, $S_{J-1} f(t)$, ..., $S_j f(t)$, ..., $S_1 f(t)$, ranging from coarser to finer scales, provides a set of multiresolution approximation of the original signal $f(t)$.

Finally, in this introduction to wavelet analysis, we might mention the maximum overlap, or non-decimated wavelet transform, MODWT (Daubechies, 1992). This transform is a compromise between the CWT, with continuous variations in scale, and DWT, where the power of the transform is highly localized. The MODWT is highly redundant, so that the transformations at each scale are not orthogonal, but the offsetting gain is that applying the transform leaves the phase invariant, a very useful property in analyzing transformations, and the transform is not restricted to limitations imposed by the dyadic expansion used by the DWT.

STRUCTURAL/NOISE DECOMPOSITION AND WAVELET MULTIRESOLUTION ANALYSIS

All of the above equations can be swiftly summarized in terms of one equation. Let $\mathbf{w}$ represent the N-dimensional vector of wavelet coefficients, W an NxN matrix of orthonormal wavelet transforms, and $\mathbf{x}$, the N-dimensional vector of observations on a signal, then we have

$$\mathbf{w} = W\mathrm{x} \tag{17}$$

$\mathbf{w}$ is a $Nx1$ vector of wavelet coefficients, which can be redefined by

$$\mathbf{w}' = \{\mathbf{w}'_1,\ \mathbf{w}'_2,\ ..., \mathbf{w}'_j,\ \mathbf{v}'_J\} \tag{18}$$

where $\mathbf{v}^J$ is a length, $N/2^J$ vector of scaling coefficients and $\mathbf{w}_j$ is a length $N/2^j$ vector of wavelet coefficients.

If the observed vector $\mathbf{x}$ is composed of two components, a structural one, x_s, and a "noise" term, with or without transients, *i.e.*, $\mathbf{x} = x_s + \varepsilon$, then

$$\mathbf{w} = W\mathbf{x}_s + W\varepsilon \tag{19}$$

from which one sees that all coefficient estimates are contaminated by the noise component. However, although noise contaminates wavelet coefficients at all scales, the relative magnitude of the error components as compared to the structural terms rapidly diminishes with scale (Ramsey, 1999). Since this contamination effect is likely to diminish with increases in scale, we can expect noise effects to be larger at shortest scales, and smallest, although not zero, at longest scales.

The coefficient vector $\mathbf{w}$ is said to be sparse in that very many coefficients are zero or very close to it. In practice, cross-scale correlations diminish rapidly as the scales are separated. Further, in many instances quite complex signals can be represented by the largest 15–20 coefficients; in practice very high degrees of approximation for observations numbering in the thousands are often achieved with only 100 coefficients (see e.g., Donoho & Johnstone, 1995, 1998; Percival & Walden, 2000; Ramsey & Zhang, 1996, 1997).

The key insight is that through wavelet multiresolution analysis any random variable can be decomposed approximately and non-parametrically into the sum of a structural component and a noise component. This separation can be of great benefit in analyzing data with unknown structure. Indeed, the structural/noise deconstruction facilitates alternative analysis techniques of many types (see e.g., Ramsay & Ramsey, 2002; Ramsay & Silverman, 2005, on the use of functional data analysis).

A brief review of an example discussed in Ramsey (1999) can illustrate the situation. Consider a regression of "consumption" on "income" after allowing for time scale. The "income" and "consumption" variables are defined as

$$\begin{aligned} \mathbf{y} &= y(\exp) + y(\sin) \\ \mathbf{y}(\exp) &= \exp[2(i/512)], \quad i = 1, 512 \\ \mathbf{y}(\sin) &= \sin[(\pi/7.8)] \\ \text{cons} &= 0.9\mathbf{y}(\exp) + 0.6\mathbf{y}(\sin) + \varepsilon \\ \varepsilon N(0,\sigma^2), \sigma &= 0.3MAD[\mathbf{y}(\sin)] \end{aligned} \tag{20}$$

where MAD is the median absolute deviation.

The wavelet that was used to analyze the data was the *Symmlet*, designated as "S12" to reflect the relative smoothness of the income series with noise restricted to the $D_1f(t)$ level and possibly up to the $D_2f(t)$ level.[6] The time scale decomposition revealed that the constituent time scales in a simulation of the above model were the following:

- y(exp) was approximated very closely by $S_4f(t)$;
- y(sin) was approximated very closely by the sum of $D_4f(t)$ and $D_3f(t)$;
- the noise was contained in the sum of $D_2f(t)$ and $D_1f(t)$;
- Gaussianity of the estimators and of the "residuals" was maintained;
- correlations across time scales were "low" being on the order of 10^{-6} to 10^{-9}; and
- the regression coefficients were correctly estimated to three decimal places with small standard errors.

The analysis was repeated for an error distribution that was log-normal and similar results were obtained; the regression estimates were still within three decimals of the true values with small standard errors, and correlations across time scales were nearly as small, on the order of 10^{-5} to 10^{-8}.

The results presented above provide the background for the critical assumption of the wavelet-based structural/noise decomposition approach, i.e., that "noise" $\{\varepsilon\}$, represents a short-scale phenomenon. It was remarked at the beginning of this section that the presence of error affects all wavelet coefficients, but that the relative degree of effect diminishes with increases in scale. Hence, the effect of noise, although affecting the coefficients at all levels, is likely to be influential, especially at shorter time scales. Thus, the component of a given signal $f(t)$ represented by the wavelet decomposition $D_1f(t)$ is composed of wavelet transformations of irregular very short scale innovations to the series $f(t)$. In some situations, it may well be true that the noise component is remarkable in the crystal $D_2f(t)$ as well as in $D_1f(t)$.

Therefore, the wavelet approximations

$$\begin{aligned}
S_1f(t) &= S_Jf(t) + D_Jf(t) + \ldots + D_jf(t) + \ldots + D_3f(t) + D_2f(t)\\
S_2f(t) &= S_Jf(t) + D_Jf(t) + \ldots + D_jf(t) + \ldots + D_3f(t)\\
&\vdots\\
S_jf(t) &= S_Jf(t) + D_Jf(t) + \ldots + D_{j+1}f(t)\\
&\vdots\\
S_{J-1}f(t) &= S_Jf(t) + D_Jf(t)
\end{aligned} \tag{21}$$

represent a sequence of increasingly coarser approximations to the smooth component $S_J f(t)$ that can provide natural IVs for the originally observed time series $f(t)$.

These results can be improved by thresholding when the variable to be approximated is distinctly non-smooth (see Donoho & Johnstone, 1995, 1998; Percival & Walden, 2000). Consider hard thresholding in which wavelet coefficient estimates below a threshold bound are set to zero and retain their observed values for estimates above the bound (see e.g., Bruce & Gao, 1996; Donoho & Johnstone, 1995; Donoho, Johnstone, Keryachariam, & Picard, 1995). The second-order effects of random errors can be mitigated by thresholding without affecting the details of the main structural features. If we label the thresholded crystals as $D_j^{th} f(t)$, the thresholded structural component of the signal, is given by

$$\hat{\mathbf{x}}^{th} f(t) = \mathbf{S}_J^{th} f(t) + D_J^{th} f(t) + D_{J-1}^{th} f(t) + \ldots + D_2^{th} f(t) \tag{22}$$

In principle, the DWT is only one of the various filtering/smoothing techniques that may be used to capture patterns of observed data without imposing any rigid functional form to the relationship and yielding a less variable signal where noise is reduced.[7] But while the various techniques of smoothing like loess, kernel, or splines are, at varying degree, sensitive to irregular data, one of the main advantage of wavelets is its ability to handle very irregular signals. This characteristic feature of the wavelet transform is important in that the usual process of smoothing the relationship to improve the approximation to the coefficient estimates is ill-advised when the function itself is not smooth.

THE ERRORS-IN-VARIABLES PROBLEM: A MONTE CARLO SIMULATION STUDY

The IV method is the most popular approach to obtain consistent regression coefficients estimates in linear "errors-in-variables" models with classical measurement errors. A classical errors-in-variables problem, where while we may wish to observe the aggregate variable x_i it is most likely that we will instead observe $x_i^* = x_i + \varepsilon$, ε has been recently analyzed in Ramsey et al. (2010).

The aim of this section is to investigate the robustness of their results and of the proposed wavelet methodology by performing a Monte Carlo simulation study based on the same linear regression model with measurement errors.[8] The motivation is that the numerical results presented in that chapter using some simulated models were produced using just one randomly generated dataset.

Following Ramsey et al. (2010), the "true" model is specified by an equation with a constant and two explanatory variables of the following form:

$$y_t = \alpha_0 + \alpha_1 x_{1t}^* + \alpha_2 x_{2t} + u_t \tag{23}$$

where the errors u_t are independent, normally distributed variables with mean zero and variance σ_u^2. However, as in the classical errors-in-variables problem x_{1t}^* is not observed; only its contaminated counterpart x_{1t} is observed as

$$x_{1t} = x_{1t}^* + v_t \tag{24}$$

where the measurement error v_t is a normally distributed zero mean disturbance with variance σ_v^2, i.e., $v_t \sim i.i.d.(0,\sigma_v^2)$.

In the simulation experiment, the estimated regression model is:

$$\begin{aligned} y_t &= \alpha_0 + \alpha_1 x_{1t} + \alpha_2 x_{2t} + w_t \\ w_t &= u_t - \alpha_1 v_t \end{aligned} \tag{25}$$

where the values of the dependent variable y_t are generated by using the values of the explanatory variables as

$$x_{1t} = 2\sin\left(\frac{\pi i}{64}\right), \quad x_{2t} = \exp\left(\frac{2i}{512}\right) \tag{26}$$

and the parameter values are set to $\alpha = (10, 0.6, 0.9)$, $\sigma_u^2 = 0.6$, and $\sigma_v^2 = 0.3$, as in Ramsey et al. (2010). The simulation experiment includes generation of sample sizes of 256, 512, and 1024 observations in order to study the finite sample properties of the wavelet-based estimators represented by the multiresolution approximations to the structural component.[9]

The application of the wavelet multiresolution approximation (WMRA) method to the errors-in-variables problem consists in first obtaining different levels of approximation representing a sequence of increasingly coarser approximations to the structural component of the variable observed with error $x_{1,t}$, as in Eq. (21), and then estimating the errors-in-variables model using these sequential approximations as instruments. Given the practical limitations of DWT, we perform the wavelet multiresolution analysis by applying the MODWT.[10] The application of the MODWT with a number of levels $J = 4$ produces four wavelet details vectors $D_4(x_{1,t})$, $D_3(x_{1,t})$, $D_2(x_{1,t})$, $D_1(x_{1,t})$ and one wavelet smooth vector, $S_4(x_{1,t})$, each associated with a specific time scale.[11] In particular, for the error contaminated variable $x_{1,t}$ the multi resolution decomposition analysis can be expressed in terms of the crystals $D_j(x_{1,t})$, $j = 1, 2, .., 4$ as

$$x_{1,t} \cong S_4(x_{1,t}) + D_4(x_{1,t}) + D_3(x_{1,t}) + D_2(x_{1,t}) + D_1(x_{1,t}) \tag{27}$$

Since we consider a sequential fine to coarse approach that involves first examining the data at the finest approximation level and then moving to coarser approximation levels, different approximations to the error contaminated variable $x_{1,t}$ can be obtained by subtracting cumulatively from the error contaminated variable $x_{1,t}$ the crystals $D_1(x_{1,t})$, $D_2(x_{1,t})$, and $D_3(x_{1,t})$ so as to obtain closer approximations to the structural component of $x_{1,t}$. Specifically, we can obtain three sequential regressors, *i.e.*, $S_1(x_{1,t})$, $S_2(x_{1,t})$, $S_3(x_{1,t})$,[12] that represent increasingly coarser approximations to the structural component of $x_{1,t}$. Moreover, as in Gencay and Gradejovic (2011), we also consider the coarsest approximation level corresponding to the smooth component of $x_{1,t}$, i.e. $S_4(x_1, t)$.[13]

The results of the Monte Carlo simulation study are summarized in Tables 1–3. The first column reports the explanatory variable used in regression Eq. (25) to estimate the parameter α_1, while the last three columns report, for each estimated parameter, the mean of the simulated distribution along with its standard deviation (in parentheses).

Table 1. Monte Carlo Simulation Results for the Errors-in-Variables Model ($N = 1024$).

Variable	Mean ($\hat{\alpha}_0$)	Mean ($\hat{\alpha}_1$)	Mean ($\hat{\alpha}_2$)
$x_{1,t}$	10.020	**0.5280**	0.8941
	(0.0542)	(0.0161)	(0.0149)
$S_1(x_{1,t})$	10.008	**0.5686**	0.8977
	(0.0527)	(0.0175)	(0.0144)
$S_2(x_{1,t})$	10.003	**0.5838**	0.8993
	(0.0512)	(0.0179)	(0.0143)
$S_3(x_{1,t})$	10.001	**0.5922**	0.8996
	(0.0543)	(0.0186)	(0.0147)
$S_4(x_{1,t})$	10.002	**0.5960**	0.8995
	(0.0550)	(0.0181)	(0.0151)

Note: OLS estimates with standard errors in parentheses.
Bold values refer to the estimated coefficient of the error contaminated variable (true value = 0.6).

Table 2. Monte Carlo Simulation Results for the Errors-in-Variables Model (N = 512).

Variable	Mean ($\hat{\alpha}_0$)	Mean ($\hat{\alpha}_1$)	Mean ($\hat{\alpha}_2$)
$x_{1,t}$	10.070	**0.5265**	0.8594
	(0.1332)	(0.0234)	(0.0740)
$S_1(x_{1,t})$	10.031	**0.5674**	0.8829
	(0.1383)	(0.0255)	(0.0788)
$S_2(x_{1,t})$	10.020	**0.5836**	0.8892
	(0.1340)	(0.0263)	(0.0743)
$S_3(x_{1,t})$	10.011	**0.5923**	0.8937
	(0.1359)	(0.0257)	(0.0763)
$S_4(x_{1,t})$	10.007	**0.5950**	0.8961
	(0.1373)	(0.0269)	(0.0773)

Note: See footnote text in Table 1.

Table 3. Monte Carlo Simulation Results for the Errors-in-Variables Model (N = 256).

Variable	Mean ($\hat{\alpha}_0$)	Mean ($\hat{\alpha}_1$)	Mean ($\hat{\alpha}_2$)
$x_{1,t}$	10.280	**0.5202**	0.6847
	(0.3781)	(0.0350)	(0.2894)
$S_1(x_{1,t})$	10.151	**0.5638**	0.7831
	(0.3947)	(0.0380)	(0.3017)
$S_2(x_{1,t})$	10.098	**0.5817**	0.8237
	(0.3951)	(0.0375)	(0.3034)
$S_3(x_{1,t})$	10.023	**0.5930**	0.8821
	(0.4119)	(0.0404)	(0.3151)
$S_4(x_{1,t})$	10.015	**0.5984**	0.8876
	(0.3893)	(0.0394)	(0.2967)

Note: See footnote text in Table 1.

Table 1 presents the results for a sample size N = 1024. The regression estimates for the error-free coefficients, i.e., α_0 and α_2, remain within a fraction of a standard deviation of the correct values, a result not unexpected given that our error contaminated variable $x_{1,t}$ is uncorrelated with all other variables. On the other hand, as expected, OLS estimation for the error contaminated variable, $x_{1,t}$ is downward biased, with a difference of the estimated coefficient as to the true value equal to 0.072, four times its standard deviation. In the subsequent rows of Table 1, we present the coefficient estimates for α_1 obtained by replacing the error contaminated variable with a sequence of multiresolution approximations to $x_{1,t}$, with such approximations varying from finer to coarser scales. Interestingly, there is a noticeable impact on the coefficient estimates when we use the fine-to coarse approximations to the error contaminated variable. With $S_1(x_{1,t})$ the difference of the estimated coefficient as to the true value equal one and a half standard deviation, and with $S_2(x_{1,t})$ the difference is within a fraction of a standard error. This result is consistent with what was remarked in the previous section about noise effects since noise is likely to contaminate the coefficients at all scales, but with a decreasing relative effect from higher to shorter time scales. To summarize, the results clearly indicate that moving from fine tocoarse scale approximation levels yields more accurate estimates of the estimated coefficient of the variable measured with error.

Tables 2 and 3 show that the results are similar for any sample size examined. As the level of the approximation to the smooth component of $x_{1,t}$ increases, that is moving from fine tocoarse scale levels, so does the convergence of the "near structural" estimates. Indeed, the results show that using fine-to coarse multiscale approximations to the variable observed with error yields increasingly accurate estimates of the true parameter value. For example, in samples with 512 and 256 observations, the downward bias using the error contaminated variable $x_{1,t}$ is again very large, with a difference of .735 and .798, respectively, with respect to the true value, which is three and two times the standard deviation of the two coefficient estimates. By contrast, estimates using wavelet multiresolution approximations provide, once more, coefficient estimates that become increasingly closer to the true value of the parameter as the approximation moves from fine to coarse scale levels. As an example, at the approximation scale level $S_2(x_{1,t})$ the downward bias of the coefficient estimate reduces to a fraction of its standard deviation, while at $S_3(x_{1,t})$ the downward bias reduces to less than one-third. Finally, the comparison of Monte Carlo simulation results among different samples indicates that such wavelet multiresolution approximations also possess good finite sample properties. Indeed, the coefficient estimates for the error contaminated variable obtained using the wavelet multiscale approximations remain strikingly stable across different sample sizes.

In Fig. 1. we present the distribution of the estimated coefficient of the regressor measured with error, $\hat{\alpha}_1$, using various alternative estimators, i.e., OLS (longdash line), S_1 (dotdash line), S_2 (dotted line), S_3 (dashed line) and S_4 (solid line), for different sample sizes, $N = 1024$ (top panel), $N = 512$

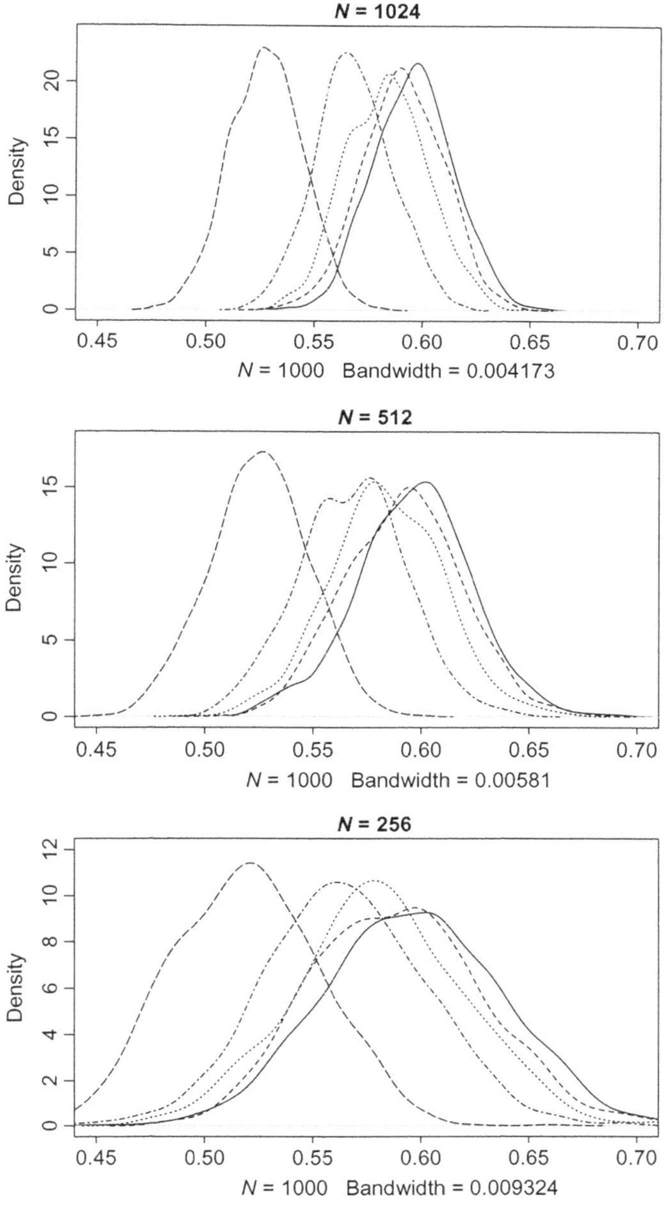

Fig. 1. Distribution of $\hat{\alpha}_1$ for $(x_{1,t})$ (longdash), $S_1(x_{1,t})$ (dotdash), $S_2(x_{1,t})$ (dotted), $S_3(x_{1,t})$ (dashed), and $S_4(x_{1,t})$ (solid) with $N = 1024$ (top panel), $N = 512$ (middle panel), and $N = 256$ (bottom panel).

(middle panel) and $N = 256$ (bottom panel). From the sampling distributions it is easily detectable the large reduction in bias of the wavelet-based estimators, especially at the coarser approximation levels $S_3(x_{1,t})$ and $S_4(x_{1,t})$. Indeed, the absolute bias relative to the true parameter value gets smaller as the degree of approximation to the structural component increases, being minimum for the smooth component $S_4(x_{1,t})$ which is the coarsest approximation level to the variable measured with error.[14] Moreover, the comparison of the distributional properties indicates that wavelet-based estimators, especially at the coarser scale approximation levels, are asymptotically efficient. Finally, in terms of the magnitude of measurement errors at different scale levels, our results seem to suggest that although such errors can be quite large at the shortest scales, their influence is likely to vanish at the highest scale approximation levels.

In sum, the evidence provided by Monte Carlo simulation results reported in this section indicates that IVs obtained from the multiresolution approximation approach can provide unbiased and asymptotically efficient estimators for linear "errors-in-variables" models with classical measurement errors. Moreover, wavelet estimators constructed through the wavelet multiresolution approximation of the variable measured with error appear to possess in finite samples those desirable properties that IVs estimators generally have only asymptotically, especially when the instruments are only weakly correlated with the regressors (*e.g.*, Bound et al., 1995; Nelson & Startz, 1990; Staiger & Stock, 1997).

CONCLUSIONS

In this chapter, we show that wavelet multiresolution analysis, by approximating the underlying structural component of a variable measured with error, can provide a useful "IV" to deal with measurement errors in the explanatory variable of a regression model. Specifically, the results from a Monte Carlo simulation study of the errors-in-variables example examined in Ramsey et al. (2010) indicate that wavelet estimators based on coarse scale approximation levels of the explanatory variable measured with error can provide unbiased and asymptotically efficient estimators with also good finite sample properties. The evidence provided in this chapter confirms that the wavelet structural approximation represents a promising direction of research to overcome the problem of "weak instruments" for the errors-in-variables case.

While the theory underlying this approach is straightforward, the key is the pragmatic one of the degree of approximation that can be achieved without extensive "fine-tuning" of the algorithms, especially in light of the alternatives. Some alternative approaches are to substitute for a suspected errors in variables model, a different variable that is correlated with the variable measured with error, but not with the regression's error term; one might call this approach "solution by assumption" in that the critical property needed is untestable, unless one can extract the error component, but then one is back in the realm of wavelets. Other alternatives consist in substituting smoothed series to the variable measured with error using one of the various smoothing techniques, e.g., kernel or spline smoothing, locally weighted smoothers, etc. However, this approach relies on the assumption that the structural model is itself smooth relative to the error component. Signals with substantial rapid oscillations cannot be handled effectively by smoothing procedures and in these circumstances the wavelet approach is a logical choice.

As an aside, the reader might recognize that the same procedure of choosing the set of $\{D_j\}$ to model the error component of the dependent variable is viable and provides a separate assessment of the structural and error components of the dependent variable. This opportunity may well be very advantageous in practice. For example, suppose that a regressor x_i is missing, or not measurable directly, and a theoretically relevant corresponding variable z_j has been suggested as instrument. Using the approach developed here, one can separate the variable z_j into its structural and error components and similarly for the dependent variable. One can check directly whether the suggested instrument is nearly uncorrelated with the regression error term (checking the degree of correlation between the instrument, and the missing variable is not available, of course). However, these remarks indicate that there might also be an advantage to analyzing regression results, even in the context of linear models, by reducing all variables, including the dependent variable, to their structural and error components, before exploring regression relationship.'

NOTES

1. In finite samples, the IV estimates are biased in the same direction as OLS, with the magnitude of the bias being inversely related with the correlation between the instrument and the endogenous explanatory variable (Bound et al., 1995).

2. Although spectral methods have been by far the most important filter processing tool in economics for many years (e.g., Engle, 1974, 1978), the role of wavelets has by now become familiar in empirical economic analysis. For details about mathematical similarities and differences between Fourier and wavelet transforms, see Strang (1993).

3. By means of the inverse transform, the original signal can be recovered by integrating over all scales λ and locations τ, respectively.

4. The key difference between the CWT and the DWT lies in the fact that the DWT uses only a limited number of translated and dilated versions of the mother wavelet to decompose the original signal.

5. The orthonormal properties can be demonstrated by the equations:

$$\int \phi_{J,k}(t)\phi_{J,k^*}(t)dt = \delta_{k,k^*}$$

$$\int \psi_{j,k}(t)\psi_{j^*,k^*}(t)dt = \delta_{j,j^*}\delta_{k,k^*}$$

$$\int \psi_{j,k}(t)\phi_{J,k^*}(t)dt = 0 \tag{11}$$

where $\delta_{i,j}$ is the Kronecker delta.

6. For the details the reader is referred to Ramsey (1999).

7. Examples of well-known smoothing techniques used in non-parametric analyses are the simple moving average, the local regression smoother (loess), the kernel smoother, and the spline function (see Cleveland, 1979, for a review of smoothing techniques).

8. In our simulation experiment the "treatment of interest" is given by the ability of wavelet approximation analysis to yield nearly ideal IVs for measurement error problems. The "effect of interest" is the comparison of the precision of the estimates obtained using the wavelet multiresolution approximation to the structural component with respect to those obtained using OLS.

9. The number of observations are chosen on the basis of the length mostly found in economic and finance empirical analysis and double from one sample to the next one. The values of x_{2t} were held fixed in the subsequent 1,000 replications of the experiment.

10. The MODWT is a non-orthogonal variant of the classical DWT that, unlike the DWT, is translation invariant, as shifts in the signal do not change the pattern of coefficients, can be applied to data sets of length not divisible by 2^J and returns at each scale a number of coefficients equal to the length of the original series. In applying the MODWT we retain the number of scales at 4, and use the Daubechies "least symmetric" wavelet, *LA*(8), based on eight non-zero coefficients (Daubechies, 1992) with reflecting boundary conditions.

11. Since the J components obtained by the application of MODWT are not orthogonal, they do not sum up to the original variable.

12. $S_1(x_{1,t})=x_{1,t}-D_1(x_{1,t})$, $S_2(x_{1,t})=x_{1,t}-(D_1(x_{1,t})+D_2(x_{1,t}))$ and $S_3(x_{1,t})=x_{1,t}-(D_1(x_{1,t})+D_2(x_{1,t})+D_3(x_{1,t}))$.

13. Gencay and Gradejovic (2011) assume that noise coincides with wavelet coefficients so that only scaling coefficients are used in their regression estimates.

14. This finding is consistent with Gencay and Gradejovic's (2011) assumption about the structural/noise decomposition in terms of scaling and wavelet coefficients.

REFERENCES

Bound, J., Jaeger, D. A., & Baker, R. M. (1995). Problems with instrumental variables estimation when the correlation between the instruments and the endogenous explanatory variable is weak. *Journal of the American Statistical Association, 90*(430), 443–450.

Bruce, A., & Gao, H. (1996). *Applied wavelet analysis with S-plus*. New York, NY: Springer-Verlag.

Cleveland, W. S. (1979). Robust locally weighted regression and smoothing scatterplots. *Journal of the American Statistical Association, 74*, 829–836.

Daubechies, I. (1992). *Ten lectures on wavelets*. Philadelphia, PA: SIAM.

Donoho, D. L., & Johnstone, I. M. (1995). Adapting to unknown smoothness via wavelet shrinkage. *Journal of the American Statistical Association, 90*, 1200–1224.

Donoho, D. L., & Johnstone, I. M. (1998). Minimax estimation by wavelet shrinkage. *Annals of Statistics, 26*, 879–921.

Donoho, D. L., Johnstone, I. M., Keryachariam, G., & Picard, D. (1995). Wavelet shrinkage: Asymptopia? *Journal of the Royal Statistical Society B, 57*, 301–369.

Dougherty, C. (2007). *Introduction to econometrics*. Oxford: Oxford University Press.

Engle, R. F. (1974). Band spectrum regression. *International Economic Review, 15*, 1–11.

Engle, R. F. (1978). Testing price equations for stability across spectral frequency bands. *Econometrica, 46*, 869–881.

Friedman, M. (1957). *A theory of the consumption function*. Princeton, NJ: Princeton University Press.

Gencay, R., & Gradojevic, G. (2011). Errors-in-variables estimation with wavelets. *Journal of Statistical Computation and Simulation, 81*(11), 1545–1564.

Gencay, R., Selcuk, F., & Whitcher, B. (2002). *An introduction to wavelets and other filtering methods in finance and economics*. New York, NY: Academic Press.

Hahn, J., & Hausman, J. (2003). Weak instruments: Diagnosis and cures in empirical economics. *American Economic Review, 93*(2), 118–125.

Michis, A., & Sapatinas, T. (2007). Wavelet instruments for efficiency gains in generalized method of moment models. *Studies in Nonlinear Dynamics & Econometrics, 11*(4), 4.

Nelson, C. R., & Startz, R. (1990). Some further results on the exact small sample properties of the instrumental variable estimator. *Econometrica, 58*, 967–976.

Percival, D. B., & Walden, A. T. (2000). *Wavelet methods for time series analysis*. Cambridge: Cambridge University Press.

Ramsay, J. O., & Ramsey, J. B. (2002). Functional data analysis of the dynamics of the monthly index of nondurable goods production. *Journal of Econometrics, 107*, 327–344.

Ramsay, J. O., & Silverman, B. W. (2005). *Functional data analysis. Springer series in statistics*. New York, NY: Springer.

Ramsey, J. B. (1999). Regression over time scale decompositions: A sampling analysis of distributional properties. *Economic Systems Research, 11*(2), 163–183.

Ramsey, J. B. (2008). Wavelets. In S. N. Durlauf & L. E. Blume (Eds.), *The new Palgrave dictionary of economics* (2nd ed.). Basingstoke: Palgrave Macmillan.

Ramsey, J. B., & Zhang, Z. (1996). The application of waveform dictionaries to stock market index data. In Y. A. Kravtsov & J. Kadtke (Eds.), *Predictability of complex dynamical systems* (pp. 189–208). New York: Springer-Verlag.

Ramsey, J. B., & Zhang, Z. (1997). The analysis of foreign exchange rates using waveform dictionaries. *Journal of Empirical Finance*, *4*, 341–372.

Ramsey, J. B., Gallegati, M., Gallegati, M., & Semmler, W. (2010). Instrumental variables and wavelet decomposition. *Economic Modeling*, *27*(6), 1498–1513.

Silverman, B. W. (1998). Wavelets in statistics: some recent developments. In R. Payne & P. Green (Eds.) *Compstat: Proceedings in Computational Statistics* (pp. 15–26). Heidelberg: Physica-Verlag.

Staiger, D., & Stock, J. H. (1997). Instrumental variables regression with weak instruments. *Econometrica*, *65*, 557–586.

Stock, J. H., Wright, J. H., & Yogo, M. (2002). A survey of weak instruments and weak identification in generalized method of moments. *Journal of Business & Economic Statistics*, *20*(4), 518–529.

Strang, G. (1993). Wavelet transforms versus Fourier transforms. *Bulletin (New Series) of the American Mathematical Society*, *28*, 288–305.

Strang, G., & Nguyen, T. (1996). *Wavelets and filter banks*. Cambridge: Wellesley-Cambridge Press.

APPENDIX A: THE APPLICATION OF WAVELET ESTIMATORS TO A TEXTBOOK EXAMPLE

The errors-in-variables model analyzed in this chapter assume a particular set up for the explanatory variables, that is a sine function for the explanatory variable measured with error and an exponential function for the other one. Given this setup one can question whether our results are linked to the particular functional form chosen. Hence, to check the robustness of our results to different functional forms for the explanatory variables, in this appendix we apply the wavelet structural approximation approach to a well-known prototype model for the errors-in-variables problem: the permanent income hypothesis (Friedman, 1957). Friedman's permanent income hypothesis (PIH) states is that consumption is proportionally related to permanent income, not current income:

$$c_t = \beta y_t^P \tag{A.1}$$

where permanent income is defined as that part of actual income that does not have transitory nature, that is

$$y_t^P = y_t - y_t^T \tag{A.2}$$

Thus, when one estimates the Keynesian consumption function regressing current consumption on current income the marginal propensity to consume will be underestimated because the explanatory variable y_t is subject to measurement error y_t^T. A textbook example (Dougherty, 2007) can illustrate the problems with OLS estimate and the benefits of using wavelet structural approximations for the variable measured with error. Suppose that permanent income increases by 100 each year and that transitory income is given by

$$y_t^T = 200u_t \tag{A.3}$$

where u_t is a random number drawn from a normal distribution with zero mean and unit variance and that the true value of β is equal to 0.9. The results of a Monte Carlo simulation analysis using a number of observations $N = 100$ and $N = 200$ with 1,000 replications are presented in Table A.1. They closely resemble those obtained previously. Indeed, as expected, estimates of the marginal propensity to consume using y_t are downward biased. This is particularly true for the smallest sample where the bias in absolute value is twice than that of the bad performing wavelet approximation to y_t, i.e., $S_1(y_t)$. By contrast, the other wavelet

Table A.1. Monte Carlo Simulation Results for the PIH Model ($N = 100$ and $N = 200$).

Variable	Mean(β) $N = 100$	Mean (β) $N = 200$
y_t	0.8059	0.8739
	(0.0254)	(0.0110)
S1(yt)	0.8575	0.8887
	(0.0286)	(0.0110)
$S_2(y_t)$	0.8804	0.8950
	(0.0300)	(0.0114)
$S_3(y_t)$	0.8906	0.8976
	(0.0302)	(0.0112)
$S_4(y_t)$	0.8966	0.8992
	(0.0301)	(0.0108)

Note: See footnote text in Table 1.

approximations, especially $S_3(y_t)$ and $S_4(y_t)$, provide estimates of the marginal propensity to consume very close to the true value, equal to 0.9, with the size of the absolute bias being a decreasing function of the degree of approximation to the smooth component. Moreover, we find that an increase in the sample size produces a positive effect on the efficiency of the wavelet-based estimates.

The distributions of the estimated parameter β using y_t and various approximations to its structural components $S_{(.)}(y_t)$ for two different sample sizes are shown in Fig. A.1. The results resemble those presented in Fig. 1 in terms of the wide reduction of the estimated downward bias obtainable through wavelet approximations $S_{(.)}(y_t)$ even at small samples, with such gains getting larger as the sample size gets smaller. Indeed, with the only exception of $S_1(y_t)$, whose downward bias tends to remain quite large even when sample size gets larger, estimates accuracy tends to increase the closer the level of approximation to the smooth component. Finally, as regards efficiency we find that as the sample gets larger, the variance of the wavelet estimators gets smaller. In sum, the evidence provided by this textbook example suggests that the kind of results obtained using the wavelet structural approximation approach cannot be considered exclusive to the specific errors-in-variables model examined in Ramsey et al. (2010).

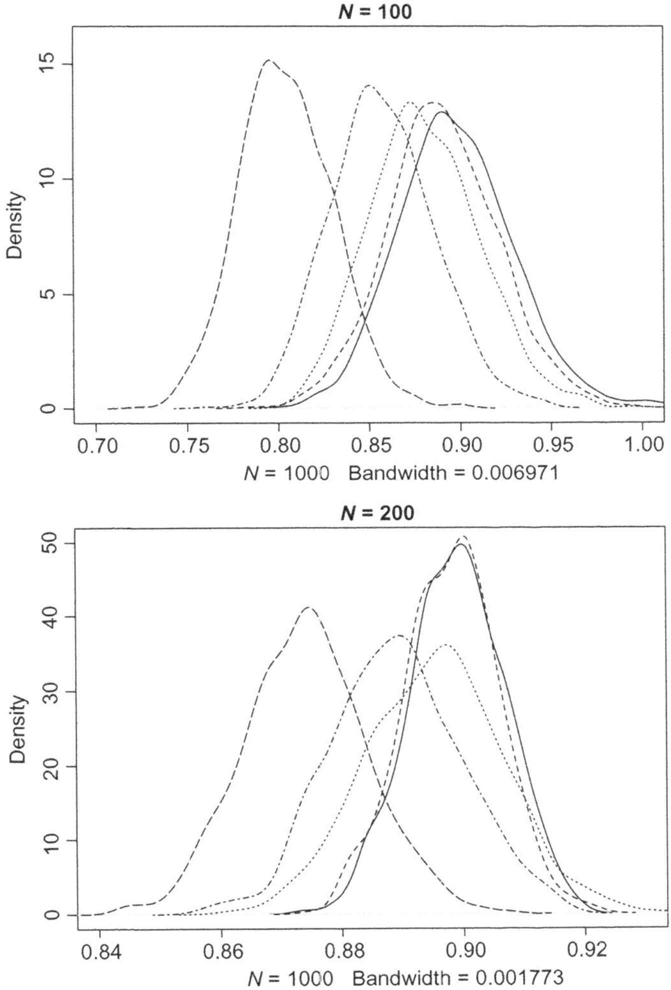

Fig. A.1. Distribution of $\hat{\beta}$ for $(x_{1,t})$ (longdash), $S_1(x_{1,t})$ (dotdash), $S_2(x_{1,t})$ (dotted), $S_3(x_{1,t})$ (dashed), and $S_4(x_{1,t})$ (solid) for 1,000 replications with $N = 100$ (top panel) and $N = 200$ (bottom panel).

PART II
PANEL DATA

A ROBUST HAUSMAN–TAYLOR ESTIMATOR

Badi H. Baltagi and Georges Bresson

ABSTRACT

This chapter suggests a robust *Hausman and Taylor (1981), hereafter HT, estimator that deals with the possible presence of outliers. This entails two modifications of the classical HT estimator. The first modification uses the Bramati and Croux (2007) robust Within MS estimator instead of the Within estimator in the first stage of the HT estimator. The second modification uses the robust Wagenvoort and Waldmann (2002) two-stage generalized MS estimator instead of the 2SLS estimator in the second step of the HT estimator. Monte Carlo simulations show that, in the presence of vertical outliers or bad leverage points, the robust HT estimator yields large gains in MSE as compared to its classical Hausman–Taylor counterpart. We illustrate this robust version of the HT estimator using an empirical application.*

Keywords: Bad leverage points; Hausman–Taylor; panel data; two-stage generalized MS estimator; vertical outliers

JEL classification: C23; C26

Essays in Honor of Jerry Hausman
Advances in Econometrics, Volume 29, 175–214

ISSN: 0731-9053/doi:10.1108/S0731-9053(2012)0000029012

INTRODUCTION

It is well known in the statistical literature that the presence of outlying observations can strongly distort the classical least squares estimator and lead to unreliable inference. Three types of outliers that influence the least squares estimator are vertical outliers, good leverage points and bad leverage points (Rousseeuw & Leroy, 2003). Vertical outliers are observations that have outlying values for the corresponding error term (the y-dimension) but are not outlying in the design space (the X-dimension). They contaminate the estimation of the intercept but only mildly influence that of the regression coefficients. Good leverage points are observations that are outlying in the design space but are located close to the regression line. They marginally influence the estimation of both the intercept and the regression coefficients but they affect inference. In contrast, bad leverage points are observations located far away from the regression line. They contaminate the least squares estimation for both the intercept and the slopes (Dehon, Gassner, & Verardi, 2009).

The focus of this chapter is on panel data regression methods based on estimators such as fixed effects (FE) or random effects least squares that control for heterogeneity of the individuals, but are sensitive to data contamination and outliers like any least squares procedure (Ronchetti & Trojani, 2001). This sensitivity can be characterized by measures of robustness such as the breakdown point, which evaluates the smallest contaminated fraction of a sample that can arbitrarily change the estimates (see, e.g., Donoho & Huber, 1983; Huber, 1981; Huber & Ronchetti, 2009).[1] Since the breakdown point of linear estimators such as least squares is asymptotically zero, the statistical literature has stressed the importance of robust and positive breakdown-point methods (e.g. Čížek, 2008; Maronna, Martin, & Yohai, 2006; Wagenvoort & Waldmann, 2002).

Panel data also suffer from data contamination and outliers. Besides paying attention to vertical outliers or bad leverage points, one has to pay attention to block-concentrated outliers (block-concentrated bad leverage points). In the latter case, the vertical outliers (bad leverage points) are concentrated on few individuals, but these individuals are observed for most of the time periods. There are only few studies dealing with these problems using panel data. Wagenvoort and Waldmann (2002) and Lucas van Dijk, and Kloek (2007) studied the bounded-influence estimation of static and dynamic panel data models, respectively. Wagenvoort and Waldmann (2002) developed two estimation procedures: the two-stage generalized M (2SGM) estimator and the robust generalized method of moments

(RGMM) estimator. Both estimators are B-robust, i.e. their associated influence function is bounded, consistent and asymptotically normally distributed. For dynamic panel data models, Lucas et al. (2007) proposed a variant of the GMM estimator which is less sensitive to anomalous observations. Positive breakdown-point methods for static and dynamic panel models were proposed by Bramati and Croux (2007), Dhaene and Zhu (2009) and Aquaro and Čížek (2010). The Within MS (WMS) estimator proposed by Bramati and Croux (2007) is the robust counterpart of the least squares dummy variables representation of the Within group estimator.[2] Using Monte Carlo simulations, they observe that, without outliers, the efficiency of the robust estimator is very close to that of the Within group estimator. However, the Within estimator performs badly when there are vertical outliers and even worse in the presence of bad leverage points. In contrast, the WMS estimator performs well and yields stable results over different sampling schemes. The Bramati and Croux (2007) WMS estimator yields large gains in MSE with respect to the classical Within estimator in the presence of outliers, and leads to very small efficiency loss in the absence of outliers.

This chapter proposes a robust version of the Hausman and Taylor (1981), hereafter HT, estimator. Briefly, the HT panel data estimator deals with the common empirical fact that some of our explanatory variables are time varying, while others are time invariant. In addition, some are correlated with the individual effects and some are not. HT proposed a two-step instrumental variables (IV), procedure that is (i) more efficient than the Within estimator and (ii) recaptures the effects of time invariant variables which are wiped out by the Within transformation. The structure of the chapter is as follows: in the second section, we present the HT estimator and in the third section, we briefly review the M, MS and GM robust estimators. The fourth section proposes a robust HT estimator that deals with the possible presence of outliers. This entails two modifications of the classical HT estimator. The first modification uses the Bramati and Croux (2007) robust WMS estimator instead of the Within estimator in the first stage of the HT estimator.[3] The second modification uses the robust Wagenvoort and Waldmann (2002) two-stage generalized MS (2SGMS) estimator instead of the 2SLS estimator in the second step of the HT estimator. In the fifth section, we run Monte Carlo simulations to study the effects of vertical outliers, bad leverage points, block-concentrated outliers or block-concentrated bad leverage points on the classical and robust HT estimators. We show that the robust HT yields large gains in MSE as compared to its classical Hausman–Taylor counterpart. In the sixth section, we apply our robust Hausman–Taylor estimator to the Cornwell and Rupert (1988) estimation of a Mincer wage equation. Finally, the seventh section concludes.

THE HAUSMAN–TAYLOR ESTIMATOR

Hausman and Taylor (1981), hereafter HT, considered the following model where some of the explanatory variables are time varying (X_{it}), while others are time invariant (Z_i):

$$y_{it} = X_{it}'\beta + Z_i'\gamma + \mu_i + v_{it}, \quad i = 1, \ldots, N, \quad t = 1, \ldots, T \tag{1}$$

where μ_i is IID $(0, \sigma_\mu^2)$, v_{it} is IID $(0, \sigma_v^2)$ independent of each other and among themselves. HT allowed *some* of the X and Z variables to be correlated with the individual effects μ_i. This is in contrast to the FE estimator where *all* the regressors are correlated with the individual effects, and the random effects estimator where *none* of the regressors are correlated with the individual effects. Using the HT notation: $X = [X_1, X_2]$ and $Z = [Z_1, Z_2]$ where X_1 is $(NT \times k_1)$, X_2 is $(NT \times k_2)$, Z_1 is $(NT \times g_1)$ and Z_2 is $(NT \times g_2)$. X_1 and Z_1 are assumed exogenous in that they are not correlated with μ_i and v_{it}, while X_2 and Z_2 are endogenous because they are correlated with μ_i, but not v_{it}.

HT proposed the following two-step consistent estimator[4] of β and γ:

1. Perform the FE or Within estimator obtained by regressing $\tilde{y}_{it} = (y_{it} - \bar{y}_{i.})$, where $\bar{y}_{i.} = \sum_{t=1}^{T} y_{it}/T$, on a similar Within transformation on the regressors. Note that the Within transformation wipes out the Z_i variables since they are time invariant, and we only obtain an estimate of β which we denote by $\tilde{\beta}_W$.
   - Then, HT average the Within residuals over time

$$\hat{d}_i = \bar{y}_{i.} - \bar{X}_{i.}'\tilde{\beta}_W \tag{2}$$

   - To get an estimate of γ, HT suggest running 2SLS of $\hat{d}_i$ on Z_i with the set of instruments $A = [X_1, Z_1]$. This yields

$$\hat{\gamma}_{2SLS} = (Z'P_A Z)^{-1} Z'P_A \hat{d} \tag{3}$$

where $P_A = A(A'A)^{-1}A'$. It is clear that the order condition has to hold $(k_1 \geq g_2)$ for $(Z'P_A Z)$ to be nonsingular. In fact, if $k_1 = g_2$, then the model is just-identified and one stops here.

2. If $k_1 > g_2$, HT suggest estimating the variance components as follows:

$$\hat{\sigma}_v^2 = (y_{it} - X_{it}'\tilde{\beta}_W)' Q (y_{it} - X_{it}'\tilde{\beta}_W)/N(T-1) \tag{4}$$

and

$$\hat{\sigma}_1^2 = (y_{it} - X_{it}'\tilde{\beta}_W - Z_i'\gamma_{2SLS})' P (y_{it} - X_{it}'\tilde{\beta}_W - Z_i'\gamma_{2SLS})/N \tag{5}$$

where $\sigma_1^2 = T\sigma_\mu^2 + \sigma_v^2$. $P = I_N \otimes \bar{J}_T$ and $\bar{J}_T = J_T/T$, with I_N being an identity matrix of dimension N, and J_T is a matrix of ones of dimension T. P is a matrix which averages the observations across time for each individual. $Q = I_{NT} - P$. Once the variance-components estimates are obtained, the model is transformed using $\hat{\Omega}^{-1/2}$ where (see Baltagi, 2008).

$$\Omega^{-1/2} = \frac{1}{\sigma_1} P + \frac{1}{\sigma_v} Q \tag{6}$$

Note that $y^* = \hat{\sigma}_v \hat{\Omega}^{-1/2} y$ has a typical element $y_{it}^* = y_{it} - \hat{\theta}\bar{y}_{i.}$ where $\hat{\theta} = 1 - (\hat{\sigma}_v/\hat{\sigma}_1)$ and X_{it}^* and Z_i^* are defined similarly. In fact, the transformed regression becomes

$$\hat{\sigma}_v \hat{\Omega}^{-1/2} y_{it} = \hat{\sigma}_v \hat{\Omega}^{-1/2} X_{it}\beta + \hat{\sigma}_v \hat{\Omega}^{-1/2} Z_i \gamma + \hat{\sigma}_v \hat{\Omega}^{-1/2} u_{it} \tag{7}$$

where $u_{it} = \mu_i + v_{it}$. The asymptotically efficient HT estimator is obtained by running 2SLS on this transformed model using $A_{HT} = [\tilde{X}, \bar{X}_1, Z_1]$ as the set of instruments. In this case, $\tilde{X}$ denotes the Within transformed X, and $\bar{X}_1$ denotes the time average of X_1. More formally, the HT estimator under over-identification is given by

$$\begin{pmatrix} \hat{\beta} \\ \hat{\gamma} \end{pmatrix}_{HT} = \left[\begin{pmatrix} X^{*\prime} \\ Z^{*\prime} \end{pmatrix} P_{A_{HT}} (X^*, Z^*) \right]^{-1} \begin{pmatrix} X^{*\prime} \\ Z^{*\prime} \end{pmatrix} P_{A_{HT}} y^* \tag{8}$$

where $P_{A_{HT}}$ is the projection matrix on $A_{HT} = [\tilde{X}, \bar{X}_1, Z_1]$ (see also Breusch, Mizon, & Schmidt, 1989).

A BRIEF REVIEW OF M, MS AND GM ROBUST ESTIMATORS

To robustify the HT estimator for the possible presence of outliers, we used two MS estimators: the one proposed by Bramati and Croux (2007) for the first step of the HT estimator and a 2SGMS estimator inspired from

Wagenvoort and Waldmann (2002) for the second step of the HT estimator. In this section, we briefly review M and S and MS estimators from the robust statistics literature.

Huber (1964) generalized the median regression to a wider class of estimators, called M estimators, by considering other functions besides the absolute value of the residuals. This increases Gaussian efficiency while keeping robustness with respect to vertical outliers. Consider the panel data FE regression disturbances: $r_{it}(\alpha, \beta) \equiv r_{it} = y_{it} - X'_{it}\beta - \alpha_i$. The M estimator is defined as

$$\hat{\theta}_M(\equiv (\alpha', \beta')') = \arg\min_{\alpha,\beta} \sum_{i=1}^{N} \sum_{t=1}^{T} \rho\left(\frac{r_{it}}{\sigma}\right) \tag{9}$$

To guarantee scale equivariance (i.e. independence with respect to the measurement units of the dependent variable), residuals are standardized by a measure of dispersion σ. This can be implemented as an iterative weighted least squares. The M estimator of θ based on the function $\rho(\cdot)$ is the vector $\hat{\theta}_M$ of size $(K \times 1)$ which is the solution of the following system:

$$\min_{\theta} \sum_{i=1}^{N} \sum_{t=1}^{T} \psi\left(\frac{r_{it}}{\sigma}\right) \frac{d(r_{it})}{d\theta_j} = 0, \quad j = 1, \ldots, K \tag{10}$$

$\psi(u) = \rho'(u)$ is called the influence function. If we define a weight function $W_r(u) = \psi(u)/u$, then $\hat{\theta}_M$ is a weighted least squares estimator:

$$\hat{\theta}_M = \arg\min_{\theta} \sum_{i=1}^{N} \sum_{t=1}^{T} W_r(r_{it}) r_{it}^2 \tag{11}$$

and the first order condition which defines the class of M estimators is given by

$$\sum_{i=1}^{N} \sum_{t=1}^{T} X'_{it} r_{it} W_r(r_{it}) = 0 \tag{12}$$

The loss function $\rho(\cdot)$ is a symmetric, positive-definite function with a unique minimum at zero. There are several constraints that a robust M estimator should meet: (a) the first is of course to have a bounded influence function $\psi(r_{it}/\sigma)$; (b) second, the robust estimator should be unique. This requires that the function $\rho(\cdot)$ is convex in θ. The literature on robust statistics proposed several specifications for the ρ-function. The choice of the loss function $\rho(\cdot)$ is crucial to having good robustness properties and high Gaussian efficiency. The Tukey biweight function is a common choice[5]:

$$\rho(u) = \begin{cases} \frac{u^2}{2} - \frac{u^4}{2c^2} + \frac{u^6}{6c^4} & \text{if} \quad |u| \leq c \\ \frac{c^2}{6} & \text{if} \quad |u| > c \end{cases} \tag{13}$$

The associated influence function and weight function are defined as

$$\psi(u) = \begin{cases} u\left[1 - \left(\frac{u}{c}\right)^2\right]^2 & \text{if} \quad |u| \leq c \\ 0 & \text{if} \quad |u| > c \end{cases} \quad \text{and} \quad W_r(u) = \begin{cases} \left[1 - \left(\frac{u}{c}\right)^2\right]^2 & \text{if} \quad |u| \leq c \\ 0 & \text{if} \quad |u| > c \end{cases} \tag{14}$$

In this case, the high breakdown point M estimator is defined as

$$\hat{\theta}_M = (X' W_r X)^{-1} X' W_r y \tag{15}$$

where y is the $(NT \times 1)$ vector denoting the dependent variable, and X is the $(NT \times K)$ matrix of the explanatory variables. W_r is an $(NT \times NT)$ matrix with diagonal elements given by

$$W_r(r_{it}) = \begin{cases} \left[1 - \left(\frac{r_{it}}{c\sigma}\right)^2\right]^2 & \text{if} \quad \left|\frac{r_{it}}{\sigma}\right| \leq c \\ 0 & \text{if} \quad \left|\frac{r_{it}}{\sigma}\right| > c \end{cases} \tag{16}$$

For the tuning constant $c = 2.937$ (or $c = 1.547$), the corresponding M-estimator resists contamination up to 25% (or up to 50%) of outliers. In other words, it is said to have a breakdown point of 25% (or 50%). Unfortunately, this M-estimator suffers from some deficiencies. If it is able to identify isolated outliers, it is inappropriate in case of the existence of clusters of outliers, i.e. where one outlier can mask the presence of another. Hence, it is not guaranteed to identify all leverage points. Furthermore, the initial values for the iterative reweighted least squares algorithm are monotone M-estimators that are not robust to bad leverage points and may cause the algorithm to converge to a local instead of a global minimum (Croux & Verardi, 2008).[6]

Rousseeuw and Yohai (1987) proposed minimizing a measure of dispersion of the residuals that is less sensitive to extreme values. They call this class of estimators the S-estimators. In order to increase robustness, they suggest finding the smallest robust scale of the residuals. This robust dispersion, that will be called $\hat{\sigma}^S$, satisfies

$$\frac{1}{NT}\sum_{i=1}^{N}\sum_{t=1}^{T}\rho\left(\frac{r_{it}(\alpha,\beta)}{\hat{\sigma}_S}\right) = b \tag{17}$$

where $b = E[\rho(Q)]$ with $Q \sim N(0,1)$. The value of θ that minimizes $\hat{\sigma}_S$ is then called an S-estimator defined as

$$\hat{\theta}_M^S = \arg\min_{\theta} \hat{\sigma}_S\,(r_{11}(\theta),\ldots,r_{NT}(\theta)) \tag{18}$$

with the corresponding $\hat{\sigma}_S$ being the robust estimator of scale.

Rousseeuw and Yohai (1987) computed the asymptotic efficiency of the S-estimator of a Gaussian model for different values of the breakdown point (see Appendix B). Unfortunately, this S-estimator has a Gaussian efficiency of only 28.7%. If the tuning constant (c) of the Tukey biweight loss function $\rho(\cdot)$ is high, for instance $c = 5.182$, the Gaussian efficiency climbes to 96.6% but the breakdown point drops to 10%.[7]

To cope with this, Yohai (1987) introduced M-estimators that combine high-breakdown point and high efficiency. These estimators are redescending M-estimators, but where the scale is fixed at $\hat{\sigma}_S$. The preliminary S-estimator guarantees a high breakdown point and the final M-estimator allows a high Gaussian efficiency. Following the proposition of Rousseeuw and Yohai (1987), the tuning constant can be set to $c = 1.547$ for the S-estimator to guarantee a 50% breakdown point, and it can be set to $c = 5.182$ for the second-step M-estimator to guarantee 96% efficiency of the final estimator.

Generally, the S- and M-estimator use the algorithm of Salibian-Barrera and Yohai (2006) (see also Maronna & Yohai, 2006). The algorithm starts by randomly picking p-subsets of K observations where K is the number of regression parameters to estimate. For each of the p-subsets, residuals are computed and a scale estimate $\hat{\sigma}_S$ is obtained. An approximation for the final scale estimate $\hat{\sigma}_S$ is then given by the value that leads to the smallest scale over all p-subsets.[8] Maronna and Yohai (2006) introduce the MS-estimator that alternates an S-estimator and an M-estimator, until convergence. This estimator has been adapted for the FE panel data case by Bramati and Croux (2007). They call this estimator the WMS estimator. This will be our estimator in place of the classical Within estimator in the first step of our robust HT estimator.

Hinloopen and Wagenvoort (1997) proposed further protection against observations with a high leverage. They suggest using location weights indirectly proportional to the values of covariates:

$$W_x(X_{it}) = \min\left(1, \frac{\sqrt{\chi^2_{K,0.975}}}{RD_{it}}\right) \tag{19}$$

where $\chi^2_{K,0.975}$ is the upper 97.5% quantile of a chi-squared distribution with K degrees of freedom.

$$RD_{it} = \sqrt{(X_{it} - \hat{\mu}_x)' V_x^{-1} (X_{it} - \hat{\mu}_x)} \tag{20}$$

is a robust version of the Malahanobis distance (or Rao's distance) and $\hat{\mu}_x$ and V_x are the robust estimates of the location and variance matrix[9] of X_{it}. Wagenvoort and Waldmann (2002) proposed the use of this class of generalized M-estimators (GM estimators hereafter).[10] The first-order condition which defines this class of GM estimators is

$$\sum_{i=1}^{N} \sum_{t=1}^{T} X'_{it} W_x(X_{it}) r_{it} W_r(r_{it}) = 0 \tag{21}$$

In this case, the high breakdown point GM estimator is defined as

$$\hat{\theta}_{GM} = (X' W_x W_r X)^{-1} X' W_x W_r y \tag{22}$$

where W_x is the $(NT \times NT)$ matrix with diagonal elements given by $W_x(X_{it})$.

THE ROBUST HAUSMAN–TAYLOR ESTIMATOR

To robustify the HT estimator for the possible presence of outliers, two MS estimators are successively used: the one proposed by Bramati and Croux (2007) for the first step of the HT estimator and a 2SGMS estimator inspired from Wagenvoort and Waldmann (2002) for the second step of the HT estimator.

The WMS Estimator

The WMS $\tilde{\beta}_{WMS}$ estimator proposed by Bramati and Croux (2007) is then defined as

$$\tilde{\beta}_{WMS} = \arg\min_{\beta} \hat{\sigma}_S(r_{11}(\beta), ..., r_{NT}(\beta)) \tag{23}$$

with

$$r_{it}(\beta) = (y_{it} - X'_{it}\beta) - \text{median}_{t=1}^{T}(y_{it} - X'_{it}\beta) \tag{24}$$

Given an initial estimate β_0, they use an iterative algorithm to get closer to the minimum of Eq. (23). This algorithm is based upon the generation of random subsamples suggested by Maronna and Yohai (2006) to compute the robust scale estimate of the residuals $\hat{\sigma}_S$. They suggest iterating a fixed number of times ($\max m = 20$), and to choose the $\tilde{\beta}^{(m)}_{WMS}$ which produces the minimum value of the objective function in Eq. (23).

Unfortunately, for the HT model, the WMS estimator, like the Within estimator, gives us only an estimate of β and not γ. Once again, the Z_i variables drop out as they are time invariant. The variance-covariance matrix of the WMS estimate $\tilde{\beta}_{WMS}$ is given by

$$Var(\tilde{\beta}_{WMS}) = \hat{\sigma}^2_S(\hat{X}'D_1\hat{X})^{-1}\hat{X}'D_2\hat{X}(\hat{X}'D_1\hat{X})^{-1} \tag{25}$$

where D_1 and D_2 are diagonal matrices with diagonal elements given by

$$D_{1,it} = \frac{d}{du_{it}}[u_{it}W_r(u_{it})] \text{ and } D_{2,it} = [u_{it}W_r(u_{it})]^2 \text{ with } u_{it} = \frac{r_{it}}{c\hat{\sigma}_S} \tag{26}$$

The Two-Stage Generalized MS Estimator

Instead of averaging the Within residuals over time as HT suggest (see Eq. (2)), we take the *median* of the resulting residuals over time:

$$\hat{r}_i = \text{median}_{t=1}^{T}(y_{it} - X'_{it}\tilde{\beta}_{WMS}) \tag{27}$$

and instead of the 2SLS procedure suggested by HT, we propose a 2SGMS estimator following Wagenvoort and Waldmann (2002).

More specifically:

1. *Stage 1*: Suppose that there are m_1 instrumental variables A_{it} which are correlated with the explanatory factors Z_i but independent of the

error term ε_{it} $(= \mu_i + v_{it})$. The explanatory variable Z_k (the kth column of Z) is regressed on the instrumental variables $A = [X_1, Z_{1,}] : Z_{it,k} = A_{it}\eta_k + \xi_{it,k}$. The high breakpoint GM estimate and the prediction of the kth column of Z is computed according to[11]

$$\hat{Z}_k = A(A'W_A(A)W_r(r_{1,k})A)^{-1}A'W_A(A)W_r(r_{1,k})Z_k \tag{28}$$

where $W_A(A)$ and $W_r(r_{1,k})$ are the diagonal matrices comprising the weight functions $W_A(A_{it})$ and $W_r(r_{1it,k})$. $r_{1,k}$ are the first-stage GM residuals associated with Z_k $(r_{1,k} = Z_k - A\hat{\eta}_k)$, and $W_r(r_{1,k})$ differs for every distinct column of Z. Thus $(g_1 + g_2)$ separate GM regressions are performed if $dim(Z) = g_1 + g_2$. Contrary to Wagenvoort and Waldmann (2002), we suggest using the residuals $(r_{1,k})$ to estimate a new robust scale estimator of the residuals $\hat{\sigma}_S$, which is then used to re-estimate a new weight function $W_r(r_{1it,k})$, and so on. Following the suggestion of Maronna and Yohai (2006), we compute this iterated MS procedure using a maximum of 20 iterations.

2. *Stage 2*: Replacing the explanatory variables of the original equation by their robust projection on A. This returns the high breakpoint 2SGMS estimator:

$$\tilde{\gamma}_{2SGMS} = (\hat{Z}'W_Z(\hat{Z})W_r(r_2)\hat{Z})^{-1}\hat{Z}'W_Z(\hat{Z})W_r(r_2)\hat{r}_2 \tag{29}$$

where $W_Z(\hat{Z})$ and $W_r(r_2)$ are diagonal matrices containing the second-step GMS weights and r_2 are the second-stage GMS residuals $(r_2 = y - \tilde{Z}\tilde{\gamma}_{2SGMS})$.

The Second Step: A Two-Stage Generalized MS Estimator
The variance-components estimates are obtained as follows:

$$\tilde{\sigma}_v^2 = \frac{(y_{it} - X_{it}'\tilde{\beta}_{WMS})'Q(y_{it} - X_{it}'\tilde{\beta}_{WMS})}{N(T-1)} \tag{30}$$

and

$$\tilde{\sigma}_1^2 = \frac{(y_{it} - X_{it}'\tilde{\beta}_{WMS} - Z_i'\tilde{\gamma}_{2SGMS})'P(y_{it} - X_{it}'\tilde{\beta}_{WMS} - Z_i'\tilde{\gamma}_{2SGMS})}{N} \tag{31}$$

where $\sigma_1^2 = T\sigma_\mu^2 + \sigma_v^2$. Once the variance-components estimates are obtained, we compute

$$y_{it}^* = y_{it} - \tilde{\theta}\bar{y}_{i.} \tag{32}$$

where $\tilde{\theta} = 1 - \tilde{\sigma}_v/\tilde{\sigma}_1$ and X_{it}^* and Z_i^* are defined similarly. The 2SGMS procedure applied to this transformed model can be described as follows:

1. *Stage 1*: Each explanatory variable of $V = [X_{it}^*, Z_i^*]$ is regressed on the m_2 instrumental variables $A_{HT} = [\tilde{X}, \bar{X}_1, Z_1]$. The kth explanatory variable V_k is regressed on the IV: $V_{it,k} = A_{HT_{it}}\delta_k + \xi_{it,k}$. This returns the GM estimate, and the prediction of the kth column of $V = [X_{it}^*, Z_i^*]$ is computed according to

$$\hat{V}_k = A_{HT}(A'_{HT}W_{A_{HT}}(A_{HT})W_r(r_{1,k})A_{HT})^{-1} \times A'_{HT}W_{A_{HT}}(A_{HT})W_r(r_{1,k})V_k \tag{33}$$

$W_{A_{HT}}(A)$ and $W_r(r_{1,k})$ are the diagonal matrices comprising the weight functions $W_{A_{HT}}(A_{HT,it})$ and $W_r(r_{1it,k})$. $r_{1,k}$ are the first-stage GM residuals associated with V_k ($r_{1,k} = V_k - A_{HT}\hat{\delta}_k$), and $W_r(r_{1,k})$ differs for every distinct column of V.

Thus ($K = k_1 + k_2 + g_1 + g_2$) separate GM regressions are performed if $dim(V) = K$. With these residuals ($r_{1,k}$), we estimate a new robust scale estimator of the residuals $\hat{\sigma}_S$ which is used to re-estimate a new weight function $W_r(r_{1it,k})$, and so on. Following the suggestion of Maronna and Yohai (2006), we compute this iterated MS procedure up to a maximum of 20 iterations.

2. *Stage 2*: Replacing the explanatory variables of the original equation by their robust projection on A_{HT} and applying the GM technique one more time provides the 2SGMS estimates:

$$\tilde{\lambda}_{2SGM} = \begin{pmatrix} \tilde{\beta} \\ \tilde{\gamma} \end{pmatrix}_{2SGMS} = (\hat{V}'W_V(\hat{V})W_r(r_2)\hat{V})^{-1} \times \hat{V}'W_V(\hat{V})W_r(r_2)y^* \tag{34}$$

$W_V(\hat{V})$ and $W_r(r_2)$ are diagonal matrices containing the second-step GMS weights and r_2 are the second-stage GMS residuals ($r_2 = y^* - \hat{V}\hat{\lambda}_{2SGMS}$).

Following Wagenvoort and Waldmann (2002), the variance-covariance matrix of the 2SGMS estimate $\tilde{\lambda}_{2SGMS}$ is given by

$$Var(\tilde{\lambda}_{2SGMS}) = \hat{D}^{-1}M(\hat{D}^{-1})' \tag{35}$$

with

$$\hat{D} = \hat{V}'W_V(\hat{V})D_1\hat{V} \text{ and } M = GG' \tag{36}$$

where

$$G = (\hat{V}' W_V(\hat{V}) W_r(r_2)\hat{V})(R_2 + R_3) \\ - \hat{\Lambda}'(A'_{HT} W_V(\hat{V}) W_r(r_2) A_{HT}) BAC \tag{37}$$

and where $R_2, R_3, A, \hat{\Lambda}, B$ and C are $(NT \times NT), (NT \times NT), (Km_2 \times Km_2), (m_2 \times K), (m_2 \times Km_2), (Km_2 \times NT)$, matrices defined as follows:

$$\begin{aligned} R_2 &= diag(y_{it} - V_{it}\tilde{\lambda}_{2SGMS}) \\ R_3 &= diag((V_{it} - \hat{V}_{it})\tilde{\lambda}_{2SGMS}) \end{aligned} \tag{38}$$

$$A = diag[\{A'_{HT} W_{A_{HT}}(A_{HT}) W_r(r_{1,it,k}) A_{HT}\}^{-1}], \quad k = 1, ..., K \tag{39}$$

$$\hat{\Lambda} = [\delta_1, \delta_2, \ldots, \delta_K] \tag{40}$$

$$B = \tilde{\lambda}'_{2SGMS} \otimes I_{m_2} \tag{41}$$

$$C = [C_{11}, ..., C_{NT}] \tag{42}$$

where C_{ij} is a $(Km_2 \times 1)$ vector given by

$$C_{ij} = \begin{pmatrix} A'_{HT_{ij}} W_{A_{HT}}(A_{HT_{ij}})(V_{ij,1} - \hat{V}_{ij,1}) W_r(r_{1,it,1}) \\ \vdots \\ \vdots \\ A'_{HT_{ij}} W_{A_{HT}}(A_{HT_{ij}})(V_{ij,K} - \hat{V}_{ij,K}) W_r(r_{1,it,K}) \end{pmatrix} \tag{43}$$

For ease of comparison, the next table gives the steps for the HT and the corresponding robust HT estimator.

Hausman–Taylor

$$\text{Step 1}\begin{cases} \text{FE}\tilde{\beta}_W = (\tilde{X}'\tilde{X})^{-1}\tilde{X}'\tilde{y} \\ \hat{d}_i = \bar{y}_{i.} - \bar{X}'_{i.}\tilde{\beta}_W \\ \text{2SLS}\begin{cases} Z = [Z_1, Z_2], A = [X_1, Z_1] \\ \text{stage 1: } \hat{Z} = P_A Z \\ \text{stage 2: } \hat{\gamma}_{2SLS} = (\hat{Z}'\hat{Z})^{-1}\hat{Z}'\hat{d} \end{cases} \end{cases}$$

$$
\text{Step 2}\begin{cases}
\hat{\sigma}_v^2, \hat{\sigma}_1^2, \hat{\theta} \\
y_{it}^* = y_{it} - \hat{\theta}\bar{y}_{i.} \\
\text{2SLS}\begin{cases}
Z^* = [Z_1^*, Z_2^*], A_{HT} = [\tilde{X}, \bar{X}_1, Z_1] \\
\text{stage 1: } \hat{Z}^* = P_{A_{HT}} Z^* \\
\text{stage 2: } \begin{pmatrix} \hat{\beta} \\ \hat{\gamma} \end{pmatrix}_{HT} = (\hat{Z}^{*\prime}\hat{Z}^*)^{-1}\hat{Z}^{*\prime} y^*
\end{cases}
\end{cases}
$$

Robust Hausman–Taylor

$$
\text{Step 1}\begin{cases}
\text{WMS}\tilde{\beta}_{WMS} \\
\hat{r}_i = \text{median}_{t=1}^{T}(y_{it} - X_{it}'\tilde{\beta}_{WMS}) \\
\text{2SGMS}\begin{cases}
Z = [Z_1, Z_2], A = [X_1, Z_1] \\
\text{stage 1: } \hat{Z}_k = P_{A_{ROB}} Z_k \\
\text{with } P_{A_{ROB}} = A(A' W_A(A) W_r(r_{1,k})A)^{-1} \\
\qquad \times A' W_A(A) W_r(r_{1,k}) \\
\text{stage 2: } \hat{\gamma}_{2SGM} = (\hat{Z}' W_Z(\hat{Z}) W_r(r_2)\hat{Z})^{-1} \\
\qquad \times \hat{Z}' W_Z(\hat{Z}) W_r(r_2)\hat{r}_2 \\
\text{with } r_2 = y - \hat{Z}\tilde{\gamma}_{2SGMS}
\end{cases}
\end{cases}
$$

$$
\text{Step 2}\begin{cases}
\tilde{\sigma}_v^2, \tilde{\sigma}_1^2, \tilde{\theta} \\
y_{it}^* = y_{it} - \tilde{\theta}\bar{y}_{i.} \\
\text{2SGMS}\begin{cases}
V = [X_{it}^*, Z_i^*], A_{HT} = [\tilde{X}, \bar{X}_1, Z_1] \\
\text{stage 1: } \hat{V}_k = P_{A_{HTROB}} V_k \\
\text{with } P_{A_{HTROB}} = A_{HT}(A_{HT}' W_{A_{HT}}(A_{HT}) W_r(r_{1,k}) A_{HT})^{-1} \\
\qquad \times A_{HT}' W_{A_{HT}}(A_{HT}) W_r(r_{1,k}) \\
\text{stage 2: } \begin{pmatrix} \tilde{\beta} \\ \tilde{\gamma} \end{pmatrix}_{2SGMS} = (\hat{V}' W_V(\hat{V}) W_r(r_2)\hat{V})^{-1} \\
\qquad \times \hat{V}' W_V(\hat{V}) W_r(r_2) y^*
\end{cases}
\end{cases}
$$

THE SIMULATION STUDY

We first simulate a Hausman–Taylor world (see below) and in the next step, contamination is carried out on the y's only (vertical outliers) and then on both the y and the X variables (leverage) and last on the y, X and Z variables (leverage).

The DGP of a Hausman–Taylor World

We consider the following panel data regression model with one-way error component disturbances:

$$y_{i,t} = \beta_1 X_{1,i,t} + \beta_2 X_{2,i,t} + \eta_{11} Z_{11,i} + \eta_{12} Z_{12,i} + \eta_2 Z_{2,i} + \mu_i + v_{it} \tag{44}$$

with $X_{1,i,t} = [X_{11,i,t} X_{12,i,t}]$, $\beta_1 = [\beta_{11}\beta_{12}]'$, $X_{1,it}$ is $1 \times k_1$ (here $k_1 = 2$), $X_{2,i,t}$ is $1 \times k_2$ (here $k_2 = 1$), $Z_{1,i}$ is $1 \times g_1$ (here $g_1 = 2$, $Z_{1,i} = [Z_{11,i}, Z_{12,i}]$) and $Z_{2,i}$ is $1 \times g_2$ (here $g_2 = 1$). The $Z_{11,i}$ is a constant ($Z_{11,i} \equiv 5$), $Z_{12,i}$ is a cross-sectional time-invariant $(0, 1)$ dummy variable and $Z_{2,i}$ is a cross-sectional time-invariant variable. Our experiments are designed as follows:

- $\beta_{11} = \beta_{12} = \beta_2 = \eta_{11} = \eta_{12} = \eta_2 = 1$.
- μ_i is IIN $(0, \sigma_\mu^2)$, v_{it} is IIN $(0, \sigma_v^2)$, the total variance is fixed $\sigma_u^2 = \sigma_\mu^2 + \sigma_v^2 = 3$. The proportion of the total variance due to the individual effects is set at $\rho = \sigma_\mu^2/\sigma_u^2 = 0.5$.
- $N = 100, 200$, and $T = 5,10$.
- The number of replications is 1000.

The $X_{j,i,t}$ variables are generated by

$$\begin{aligned} X_{11,i,t} &= \delta_i + \zeta_{i,t} \\ X_{12,i,t} &= \theta_i + w_{i,t} \\ X_{2,i,t} &= \mu_i + \tau_{i,t} \end{aligned} \tag{45}$$

where $\delta_i, \zeta_{i,t}, \theta_i, w_{i,t}, \tau_{i,t}$ are uniform on $[-2, 2]$. It is clear that X_2 is correlated with μ_i by construction. The cross-sectional time-invariant $(0, 1)$ dummy variable $Z_{12,i}$ has been generated randomly such that its mean is 0.2.

The HT world is defined with Z_2 correlated with μ_i, X_{11}, X_{12} and X_2.

$$Z_{2,i} = \mu_i + \delta_i + \theta_i + \xi_i \tag{46}$$

where ξ_i is uniform on $[-2, 2]$. So, the $Z_{2,i}$ variable is correlated with $X_{11,i,t}$ (by the term δ_i) with $X_{12,i,t}$ (by the term θ_i) and with $X_{2,i,t}$ (by the term μ_i).

Contamination

Once the observations are generated for our model in Eq. (44), contamination is carried out as follows:

- the y's only (vertical outliers);
- both y and the time-varying explanatory variables (X) by introducing bad leverage points;
- y, X and Z_{12} by introducing bad leverage points;
- y, X, Z_{12}, and Z_2 by introducing bad leverage points;

Contamination is generated in either of the two different ways:

- completely randomly over all observations (*random contamination*);
- concentrating the contamination in a number of blocks such that half of the observations in the affected time series are contaminated (*concentrated contamination*). In other words, only a small number of individuals in the sample have 50% of their data corrupted while the remaining individuals have clean observations.[12]

Outliers generated by random contamination are either vertical outliers or leverage points, whereas in the case of concentrated contamination, they are either block-concentrated vertical outliers or block-concentrated leverage points.

Vertical outliers are obtained by adding a term $\sim N(5\bar{y}, \sigma_y^2/40)$ to the y's originally generated.

Bad leverage points are obtained by replacing X-values (and the Z_{12} and Z_2) corresponding to the observations already contaminated in the y-direction, by points coming from a K-variate normal distribution $N(e_K, 0.5I_K)$, where e_K is a $K \times 1$ vector of ones and I_K is a $K \times K$ identity matrix. We use the Tukey biweight functions $W_r(\cdot)$ for the WMS estimator (Eq. (23)), for the first stage (Eq. (28)) and the second stage (Eq. (29)) of step 1 of the 2SGMS, and for the first stage (Eq. (33)) and the second stage (Eq. (34)) of step 2 of the 2SGMS.[13] For all these functions, we need to define the breakdown points and the associated tuning constants. We used the same breakdown point of 25% with a tuning constant $c = 2.937$ yielding an asymptotic efficiency of 76%.[14]

The percentages of contamination considered are 5% and 10%. We report results for the case of no outliers as well as eight different cases of contamination:

Case 1: vertical outliers (y)
Case 2: leverage points (y, X_1, X_2)

Case 3: concentrated vertical outliers (y)
Case 4: concentrated leverage points (y, X_1, X_2)
Case 5: leverage points with Z_{12} (y, X_1, X_2, Z_{12})
Case 6: concentrated leverage points with Z_{12} (y, X_1, X_2, Z_{12})
Case 7: leverage points with Z_{12} and Z_2 (y, X_1, X_2, Z_{12}, Z_2)
Case 8: concentrated leverage points with Z_{12} and Z_2 (y, X_1, X_2, Z_{12}, Z_2)

The Results

Table 1 reports the MSE of the coefficients for the HT estimator and its robust counterpart (robust HT) based on 1,000 replications.[15] The results in Table 1 pertain to $N=100$, $T=5$, with no outliers as well as eight different cases of contamination, where the level of contamination is 5% or 10%.

When no outliers are present, the robust HT shows loss in MSE relative to the standard HT estimator. The absolute magnitudes are small (except for η_{12}, the coefficient of Z_{12}), but the relative MSE of robust HT with respect to classical HT could be as small as 1 and as big as 2, depending on the coefficient. Contrasting that to the various types of 5% and 10% contaminations considered, it is clear that the gain in absolute as well as relative MSE is huge for the robust HT estimator compared to the classical HT estimator. Note also that the largest absolute magnitude of this MSE is for η_{12} (the coefficient of Z_{12}, which is the exogenous time-invariant dummy variable). This is 0.12 for the HT estimator compared to 0.20 for our robust HT estimator in case of no outliers. However, when we introduce 5% contamination and vertical outliers, the MSE of HT rises to 0.62 compared to 0.20 for the robust HT estimator. In case of bad leverage points, the MSE of HT rises to 0.48 compared to 0.20 for the robust HT estimator. But when you add bad leverage points in Z_{12}, the MSE of HT becomes really bad, 31.7 compared to 0.39 for the robust HT estimator. This is true for contamination cases 5, 6, 7 and 8 with bad leverage points and concentrated leverage points. The gains in absolute and relative MSE of robust HT over HT can be huge. For example, in the presence of vertical outliers, the robust HT estimator with 5% contamination, yields large gains in MSE with respect to the classical HT procedure. The HT MSE is 8–9 times higher than its robust counterpart for the coefficient estimates of X_1, X_2; 23 times higher for the intercept (Z_{11}) and 3–5 times higher for the coefficient estimates of Z_{12} and Z_2. Similarly, for bad leverage points, these MSE are respectively 74–107 times higher for the coefficient estimates of X_1, X_2; 18 times higher

Table 1. MSE of Coefficients $N = 100$, $T = 5$, 5% and 5% Contamination (1,000 Replications).

		β_{11}	β_{12}	β_2	η_{11}	η_{12}	η_2
No outlier	HT	0.0023	0.0026	0.0028	0.0010	0.1235	0.0102
	Robust HT	0.0042	0.0049	0.0046	0.0014	0.2010	0.0164
Contamination (5%)							
Vertical outliers	HT	0.0453	0.0446	0.0554	0.0663	0.6205	0.0882
	Robust HT	0.0054	0.0058	0.0056	0.0028	0.1981	0.0181
Leverage points	HT	0.6299	0.6357	0.7643	0.0420	0.4827	0.5856
	Robust HT	0.0084	0.0064	0.0071	0.0023	0.2027	0.0239
Concentrated vertical outliers	HT	0.0446	0.0435	0.0542	0.0581	0.6984	0.0942
	Robust HT	0.0067	0.0055	0.0058	0.0044	0.2198	0.0217
Concentrated leverage points	HT	0.5142	0.4460	0.6145	0.0383	0.5567	0.3740
	Robust HT	0.0087	0.0098	0.0094	0.0041	0.2411	0.0338
Leverage points with Z_{12}	HT	0.3464	0.3683	0.3964	0.0227	31.7112	0.3983
	Robust HT	0.0080	0.0087	0.0078	0.0026	0.3851	0.0239
Concentrated leverage points with Z_{12}	HT	0.2693	0.2994	0.3147	0.0232	33.5696	0.2638
	Robust HT	0.0089	0.0078	0.0090	0.0040	0.4215	0.0324
Leverage points with Z_{12} and Z_2	HT	0.3356	0.3710	0.3387	0.0205	29.8074	0.3845
	Robust HT	0.0089	0.0085	0.0077	0.0025	0.4621	0.0236
Concentrated leverage points with Z_{12} and Z_2	HT	0.2782	0.2821	0.3120	0.0211	31.3235	0.2694
	Robust HT	0.0084	0.0076	0.0087	0.0029	0.4787	0.0296
Contamination (10%)							
Vertical outliers	HT	0.0718	0.0770	0.1111	0.2481	0.9964	0.1379
	Robust HT	0.0067	0.0076	0.0056	0.0103	0.2523	0.0197
Leverage points	HT	1.6804	1.6431	1.9832	0.1348	0.7264	1.5328
	Robust HT	0.0120	0.0112	0.0117	0.0087	0.2242	0.0481
Concentrated vertical outliers	HT	0.0707	0.0682	0.0914	0.2116	1.5824	0.1503
	Robust HT	0.0073	0.0064	0.0051	0.0225	0.4390	0.0327
Concentrated leverage points	HT	1.2417	1.2015	1.3094	0.1189	1.0429	0.7424
	Robust HT	0.0204	0.0211	0.0209	0.0194	0.4306	0.1102
Leverage points with Z_{12}	HT	0.7343	0.7314	0.7407	0.0503	64.7983	0.8470
	Robust HT	0.0231	0.0225	0.0197	0.0095	1.1644	0.0609
Concentrated leverage points with Z_{12}	HT	0.5671	0.6129	0.6127	0.0620	70.5724	0.5393
	Robust HT	0.0244	0.0261	0.0276	0.0198	0.8332	0.1154
Leverage points with Z_{12} and Z_2	HT	0.7279	0.8791	0.8224	0.0535	63.8211	0.8714
	Robust HT	0.0208	0.0192	0.0168	0.0087	0.9404	0.0486
Concentrated leverage points with Z_{12} and Z_2	HT	0.6235	0.5389	0.5822	0.0567	67.5897	0.4981
	Robust HT	0.0195	0.0218	0.0221	0.0189	0.8958	0.1032

for the intercept (Z_{11}) and 2–24 times higher for the coefficient estimates of Z_{12} and Z_2.

When the outliers are block-concentrated vertical outliers, we get similar results but when the outliers are block-concentrated leverage points, the gain in MSE of the robust HT estimate becomes more pronounced. Whatever the sampling scheme, the MSE of η_{12} – the parameter of the dummy variable Z_{12} – is always more affected than that of the other parameters. Of course, the robust version yields better results than HT no matter what type of contamination.

When we increase the level of contamination from 5% to 10%, the classical HT estimator yields much larger MSE and the gains from relative MSE using the robust HT procedure are much larger than the 5% contamination case no matter what sampling scheme is used.

When we increase the size of N and T, we get similar conclusions. Table 2 keeps N fixed at 100, but double T from 5 to 10, while Table 3 keeps T fixed at 5 and doubles N from 100 to 200. Table 4 doubles both N and T from $(100, 5)$ to $(200,10)$. While the magnitudes of the MSE are different, the gains in MSE as we go from HT to robust HT are maintained throughout the experiments and for various types of contamination. Once again the largest values for the MSE are reported for η_{12} (the coefficient of Z_{12}).

These results may be conditional on the fact that we only have 10% contamination. What happens if we increase the percentage of corrupted data? In order to investigate this, we used the largest allowable values of the breakdown points (i.e. 50% and $c = 1.547$) for each estimator (WMS and 2SGMS). We ran simulations for $N = 100, T = 5$, for case 2 (leverage points (y, X_1, X_2) and for 5%, 10%, 15%, 20%, 25%, 30%, 35% and 40% contamination.[16] Results in Table 5 show that the robust HT estimator resists quite well the increase in the percentage of contamination up to 35%. When the level of contamination is even higher, the gain in relative MSE decreases quickly even if the robust HT estimator is a little bit better than the classical HT estimator. However, when 40% of the data are corrupted, the MSE for the time invariant variable Z_2 converges and even exceeds that of the MSE of HT. Figs. 1–4 show average HT and robust HT estimates with their 95% confidence intervals for the coefficients of X_{11}, X_2, X_{12} and Z_2 respectively. For the time varying variables (X_{11} and X_2), Figs. 1 and 2 show that the robust HT estimator is stable with narrow confidence intervals showing a small bias and a good precision of the estimators leading to a relatively small MSE. For time invariant

Table 2. MSE of Coefficients $N = 100$, $T = 10$, 5% and 10% Contamination (1,000 Replications).

		β_{11}	β_{12}	β_2	η_{11}	η_{12}	η_2
No outlier	HT	0.0012	0.0011	0.0013	0.0009	0.1065	0.0081
	Robust HT	0.0019	0.0018	0.0023	0.0012	0.1921	0.0107
Contamination (5%)							
Vertical outliers	HT	0.0189	0.0219	0.0278	0.0662	0.3180	0.0382
	Robust HT	0.0030	0.0033	0.0028	0.0063	0.1967	0.0140
Leverage points	HT	0.5893	0.5989	0.7037	0.0401	0.3378	0.5309
	Robust HT	0.0043	0.0040	0.0037	0.0064	0.1717	0.0144
Concentrated vertical outliers	HT	0.0183	0.0184	0.0216	0.0563	0.6558	0.0566
	Robust HT	0.0028	0.0027	0.0023	0.0141	0.3836	0.0270
Concentrated leverage points	HT	0.3703	0.3607	0.4397	0.0368	0.4525	0.2016
	Robust HT	0.0053	0.0052	0.0058	0.0123	0.3808	0.0468
Leverage points with Z_{12}	HT	0.3273	0.3369	0.3962	0.0393	43.6259	0.3550
	Robust HT	0.0040	0.0041	0.0032	0.0056	0.2905	0.0159
Concentrated leverage points with Z_{12}	HT	0.2457	0.2362	0.2591	0.0608	61.7257	0.2023
	Robust HT	0.0057	0.0054	0.0058	0.0126	0.5750	0.0481
Leverage points with Z_{12} and Z_2	HT	0.3564	0.3147	0.3327	0.0387	43.4782	0.3588
	Robust HT	0.0035	0.0045	0.0033	0.0050	0.4028	0.0146
Concentrated leverage points with Z_{12} and Z_2	HT	0.2185	0.2282	0.2452	0.0529	54.5255	0.1640
	Robust HT	0.0047	0.0049	0.0049	0.0112	0.5467	0.0389
Contamination (10%)							
Vertical outliers	HT	0.0375	0.0365	0.0486	0.2450	0.4764	0.0641
	Robust HT	0.0033	0.0036	0.0030	0.0380	0.2535	0.0158
Leverage points	HT	1.6572	1.7292	1.8854	0.1332	0.5636	1.4878
	Robust HT	0.0064	0.0067	0.0064	0.0304	0.2079	0.0272
Concentrated vertical outliers	HT	0.0255	0.0256	0.0255	0.1703	1.8336	0.1151
	Robust HT	0.0025	0.0028	0.0019	0.0244	0.7454	0.0480
Concentrated leverage points	HT	0.6623	0.7548	0.7656	0.1007	1.0182	0.1882
	Robust HT	0.0092	0.0103	0.0112	0.0282	0.7329	0.1434
Leverage points with Z_{12}	HT	0.7021	0.7079	0.8027	0.0958	86.4403	0.7952
	Robust HT	0.0091	0.0080	0.0079	0.0326	0.6247	0.0364
Concentrated leverage points with Z_{12}	HT	0.3648	0.3919	0.3797	0.1376	118.2726	0.2568
	Robust HT	0.0106	0.0124	0.0124	0.0278	1.2446	0.1568
Leverage points with Z_{12} and Z_2	HT	0.7350	0.7159	0.7651	0.1029	88.9891	0.7858
	Robust HT	0.0077	0.0080	0.0065	0.0292	0.7635	0.0322
Concentrated leverage points with Z_{12} and Z_2	HT	0.3989	0.3785	0.3601	0.1410	112.4906	0.2629
	Robust HT	0.0111	0.0107	0.0109	0.0275	1.1932	0.1431

Table 3. MSE of Coefficients $N = 200$, $T = 5$, 5% and 10% Contamination (1,000 Replications).

		β_{11}	β_{12}	β_2	η_{11}	η_{12}	η_2
No outlier	HT	0.0013	0.0013	0.0014	0.0004	0.0514	0.0048
	Robust HT	0.0025	0.0020	0.0026	0.0007	0.0833	0.0073
Contamination (5%)							
Vertical outliers	HT	0.0250	0.0221	0.0298	0.0649	0.2665	0.0422
	Robust HT	0.0032	0.0033	0.0030	0.0023	0.0959	0.0091
Leverage points	HT	0.5862	0.5724	0.7283	0.0404	0.2227	0.5624
	Robust HT	0.0043	0.0045	0.0046	0.0019	0.1042	0.0145
Concentrated vertical outliers	HT	0.0204	0.0188	0.0272	0.0595	0.3678	0.0468
	Robust HT	0.0032	0.0028	0.0029	0.0043	0.1171	0.0092
Concentrated leverage points	HT	0.4848	0.5399	0.5920	0.0388	0.2185	0.3857
	Robust HT	0.0060	0.0061	0.0062	0.0039	0.1107	0.0239
Leverage points with Z_{12}	HT	0.3718	0.3591	0.3730	0.0194	30.7602	0.3762
	Robust HT	0.0044	0.0040	0.0040	0.0017	0.1660	0.0125
Concentrated leverage points with Z_{12}	HT	0.2909	0.2907	0.3192	0.0273	36.0306	0.2600
	Robust HT	0.0060	0.0061	0.0059	0.0032	0.2196	0.0239
Leverage points with Z_{12} and Z_2	HT	0.3208	0.3391	0.3504	0.0190	31.4212	0.3545
	Robust HT	0.0044	0.0046	0.0038	0.0013	0.2090	0.0124
Concentrated leverage points with Z_{12} and Z_2	HT	0.2935	0.2786	0.3013	0.0225	32.2625	0.2621
	Robust HT	0.0048	0.0043	0.0042	0.0027	0.2308	0.0169
Contamination (10%)							
Vertical outliers	HT	0.0363	0.0371	0.0483	0.2444	0.4273	0.0634
	Robust HT	0.0035	0.0028	0.0029	0.0095	0.1089	0.0088
Leverage points	HT	1.6679	1.6053	1.8884	0.1283	0.3845	1.5108
	Robust HT	0.0088	0.0086	0.0084	0.0077	0.1066	0.0297
Concentrated vertical outliers	HT	0.0389	0.0377	0.0456	0.2128	0.7118	0.0750
	Robust HT	0.0032	0.0035	0.0030	0.0237	0.2230	0.0161
Concentrated leverage points	HT	1.2614	1.2761	1.3243	0.1183	0.5092	0.7000
	Robust HT	0.0182	0.0179	0.0189	0.0188	0.2231	0.1007
Leverage points with Z_{12}	HT	0.7173	0.8023	0.8121	0.0490	63.7971	0.8610
	Robust HT	0.0137	0.0136	0.0131	0.0082	0.4565	0.0410
Concentrated leverage points with Z_{12}	HT	0.5688	0.6160	0.6019	0.0583	69.9450	0.4638
	Robust HT	0.0196	0.0198	0.0207	0.0189	0.4322	0.1037
Leverage points with Z_{12} and Z_2	HT	0.7576	0.7869	0.7428	0.0442	61.7973	0.8441
	Robust HT	0.0101	0.0102	0.0099	0.0071	0.5515	0.0312
Concentrated leverage points with Z_{12} and Z_2	HT	0.5793	0.5650	0.6015	0.0587	67.0209	0.4536
	Robust HT	0.0151	0.0165	0.0166	0.0162	0.3982	0.0962

Table 4. MSE of Coefficients $N = 200$, $T = 10$, 5% and 10% Contamination (1,000 Replications).

		β_{11}	β_{12}	β_2	η_{11}	η_{12}	η_2
No outlier	HT	0.0006	0.0006	0.0007	0.0004	0.0589	0.0042
	Robust HT	0.0009	0.0008	0.0010	0.0006	0.0820	0.0056
Contamination (5%)							
Vertical outliers	HT	0.0103	0.0102	0.0145	0.0662	0.1621	0.0179
	Robust HT	0.0016	0.0014	0.0014	0.0060	0.0864	0.0060
Leverage points	HT	0.6265	0.6294	0.6866	0.0387	0.1558	0.5890
	Robust HT	0.0024	0.0023	0.0019	0.0056	0.0827	0.0089
Concentrated vertical outliers	HT	0.0088	0.0081	0.0094	0.0536	0.3951	0.0311
	Robust HT	0.0014	0.0013	0.0009	0.0138	0.2244	0.0134
Concentrated leverage points	HT	0.3720	0.3862	0.4201	0.0349	0.2455	0.1966
	Robust HT	0.0039	0.0050	0.0047	0.0117	0.2508	0.0363
Leverage points with Z_{12}	HT	0.3106	0.3373	0.3943	0.0341	43.9376	0.3435
	Robust HT	0.0025	0.0023	0.0019	0.0051	0.1343	0.0089
Concentrated leverage points with Z_{12}	HT	0.2284	0.2518	0.2546	0.0563	60.5669	0.1669
	Robust HT	0.0043	0.0047	0.0045	0.0117	0.3075	0.0348
Leverage points with Z_{12} and Z_2	HT	0.3290	0.3300	0.3460	0.0371	42.8320	0.3779
	Robust HT	0.0024	0.0024	0.0016	0.0042	0.1872	0.0074
Concentrated leverage points with Z_{12} and Z_2	HT	0.2292	0.2334	0.2245	0.0622	59.7633	0.1554
	Robust HT	0.0036	0.0032	0.0036	0.0096	0.3200	0.0348
Contamination (10%)							
Vertical outliers	HT	0.0198	0.0217	0.0234	0.2441	0.2536	0.0293
	Robust HT	0.0019	0.0019	0.0013	0.0383	0.1061	0.0084
Leverage points	HT	1.7081	1.5612	1.9221	0.1305	0.2831	1.5793
	Robust HT	0.0050	0.0046	0.0044	0.0301	0.1096	0.0223
Concentrated vertical outliers	HT	0.0125	0.0120	0.0163	0.1670	0.9008	0.0571
	Robust HT	0.0012	0.0012	0.0010	0.0220	0.4063	0.0233
Concentrated leverage points	HT	0.7113	0.6753	0.7371	0.1019	0.5339	0.1489
	Robust HT	0.0083	0.0077	0.0087	0.0264	0.3498	0.1061
Leverage points with Z_{12}	HT	0.7000	0.7468	0.7239	0.1062	93.9170	0.8229
	Robust HT	0.0057	0.0059	0.0057	0.0309	0.2828	0.0245
Concentrated leverage points with Z_{12}	HT	0.3691	0.3613	0.3495	0.1540	120.1300	0.2022
	Robust HT	0.0091	0.0094	0.0104	0.0250	0.6855	0.1190
Leverage points with Z_{12} and Z_2	HT	0.6805	0.6756	0.7437	0.0955	88.5690	0.7853
	Robust HT	0.0046	0.0043	0.0038	0.0279	0.3611	0.0206
Concentrated leverage points with Z_{12} and Z_2	HT	0.3536	0.3545	0.3616	0.1317	114.3700	0.2204
	Robust HT	0.0086	0.0084	0.0091	0.0250	0.6182	0.1260

Table 5. MSE of Coefficients for Leverage Points, from 5% to 40% Contamination, $N = 100$, $T = 5$ (1,000 Replications).

Contamination		β_{11}	β_{12}	β_2	η_{11}	η_{12}	η_2
5%	HT	0.6299	0.6357	0.7643	0.0420	0.4827	0.5856
	Robust HT	0.0084	0.0064	0.0071	0.0023	0.2027	0.0239
10%	HT	1.6804	1.6431	1.9832	0.1348	0.7264	1.5328
	Robust HT	0.0120	0.0112	0.0117	0.0087	0.2242	0.0481
15%	HT	2.6447	2.8059	3.1403	0.2324	1.1057	2.4817
	Robust HT	0.0202	0.0236	0.0222	0.0284	0.3318	0.0865
20%	HT	3.6674	3.7195	4.0780	0.3833	1.2714	3.4245
	Robust HT	0.0364	0.0356	0.0306	0.0768	0.4462	0.1649
25%	HT	4.6089	4.4924	4.9189	0.5097	1.4811	3.9350
	Robust HT	0.0757	0.0812	0.0880	0.1507	0.6847	0.4081
30%	HT	5.0355	5.0298	5.5646	0.6478	1.7890	4.7209
	Robust HT	0.0980	0.0885	0.0917	0.2959	1.8805	0.5418
35%	HT	5.5962	5.5722	6.6318	0.8208	1.7701	4.7974
	Robust HT	0.1924	0.2178	0.1897	0.5065	2.8786	0.9733
40%	HT	6.3150	6.1837	6.9899	0.9517	1.9593	5.5632
	Robust HT	3.3007	3.2071	3.2774	0.9650	5.8274	3.2028

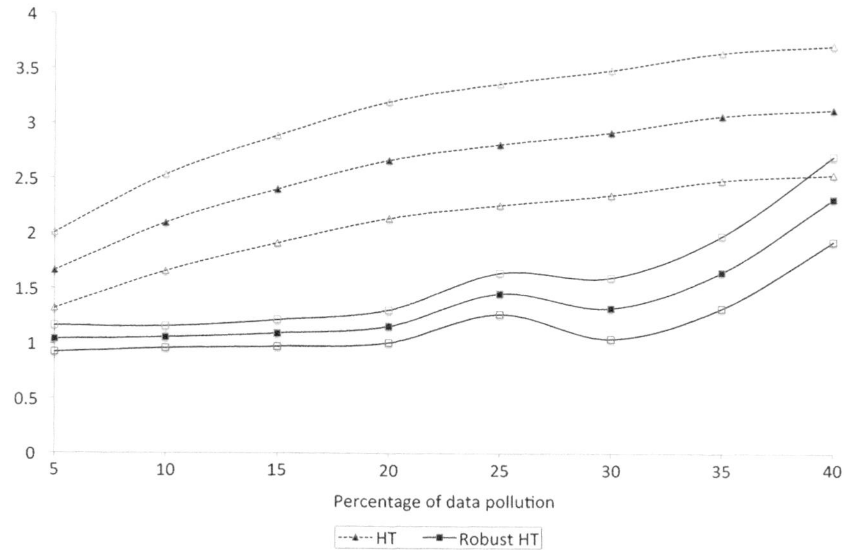

Fig. 1. Average HT and Robust HT Estimates of β_{11} with Corresponding 95% Confidence Intervals.

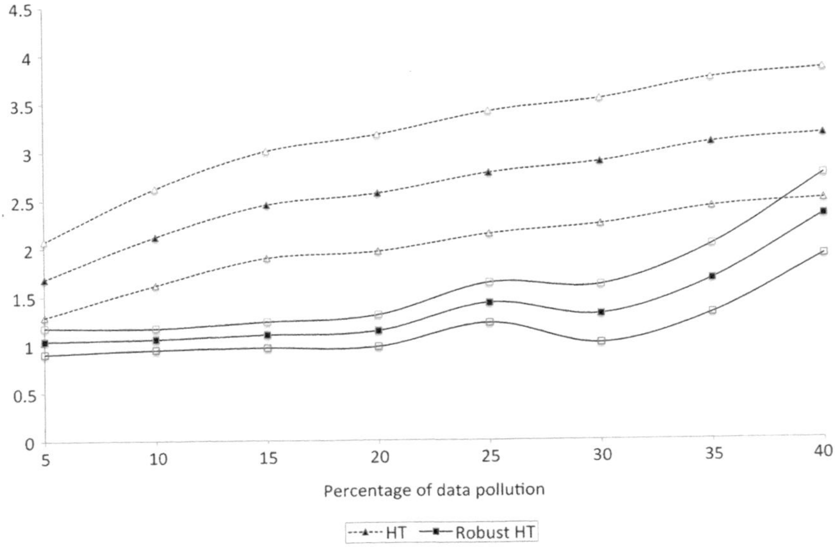

Fig. 2. Average HT and Robust HT Estimates of β_2 with Corresponding 95% Confidence Intervals.

variables (Z_{12} and Z_2), Figs. 3 and 4 show good stability of the robust HT estimator associated with narrow confidence intervals up to 25% of contamination. When the percentage of data pollution is higher, the confidence interval for the dummy variable Z_{12} widens appreciably. For the time invariant variable Z_2, both bias and confidence interval increase remaining always lower than the corresponding magnitudes for the standard HT estimator.

In order to evaluate the potential impact of the breakdown point values on the final 2SGMS estimator, we run simulations for $N = 100$, $T = 5$ for case 2 (leverage points (y, X_1, X_2) for 10% and 25% contamination but with several breakdown point (*bdp*) values. We define $bdp_{WMS,S}$ ($bdp_{WMS,M}$) as the breakdown point for the S-estimator (M-estimator) of the WMS. We also define $bdp_{2SGMS\_1\_j,S}$ ($bdp_{2SGMS\_1\_j,M}$) as the breakdown point for the first stage of step j ($j = 1, 2$) for the S-estimator (M-estimator) of 2SGMS; and $bdp_{2SGMS\_2\_j,S}$ ($bdp_{2SGMS\_2\_j,M}$) as the breakdown point for the second stage of step j ($j = 1, 2$) for the S-estimator (M-estimator) of 2SGMS. We studied the

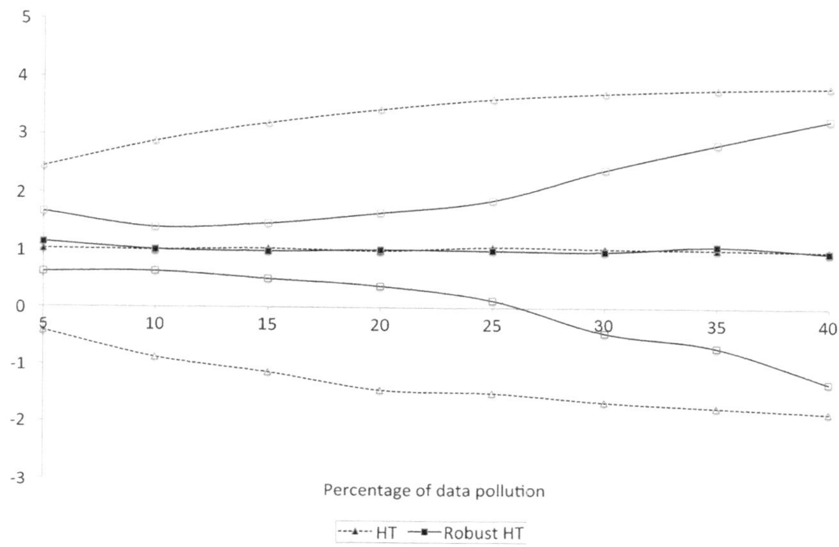

Fig. 3. Average HT and Robust HT Estimates of η_{12} with Corresponding 95% Confidence Intervals.

following five cases to check the sensitivity of our results to different breakdown point values[17]:

	Case A	Case B	Case C	Case D	Case E
$bdp_{WMS,S}$	0.50	0.25	0.50	0.50	0.50
$bdp_{WMS,M}$	0.25	0.25	0.25	0.25	0.25
$bdp_{2SGMS\_1\_j,S}$	0.25	0.50	0.50	0.25	0.50
$bdp_{2SGMS\_1\_j,M}$	0.25	0.25	0.25	0.25	0.25
$bdp_{2SGMS\_2\_j,S}$	0.25	0.50	0.25	0.50	0.50
$bdp_{2SGMS\_2\_j,M}$	0.25	0.25	0.25	0.25	0.25

In case A, we used different values of the breakdown points only for WMS. As suggested by Rousseeuw and Yohai (1987), we set the tuning constant to $c = 1.547$ for the S-estimator to guarantee a 50% breakdown point and

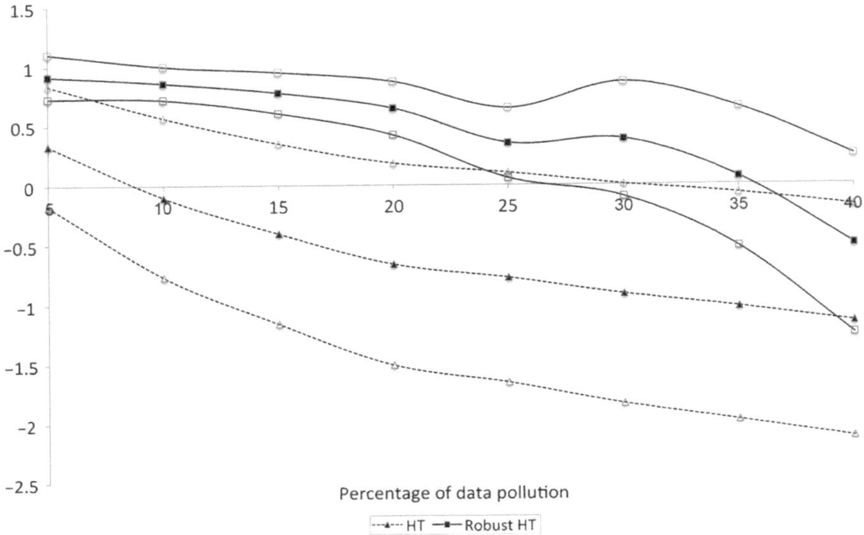

Fig. 4. Average HT and Robust HT Estimates of η_2 with Corresponding 95% Confidence Intervals.

we set the tuning constant to $c = 2.937$ for the second-step M-estimator to guarantee a higher efficiency of 76% for the final estimator. Results in Table 6 for 10% contamination are similar to those of Table 1 for which all the breakdown points are 25%. When only 10% of the data are corrupted, there is no significant differences between cases A to E. But, when we increase the percentage of data pollution up to 25%, the results deteriorate for cases A and C. In these two cases, the breakdown point values of the second stage of step j ($j = 1,2$) for the S-estimator of 2SGMS $bdp_{2SGMS\_2\_j,S}$ are small (0.25 as compared to 0.5 in the three other cases). Cases B, D and E give similar results showing that the crucial values are those of $bdp_{2SGMS\_2\_j,S}$ and not necessarily those of bdp_{WMS} or $bdp_{2SGMS\_1\_j}$.

What about the interesting case where outliers only exist in the time invariant variables (for instance in Z_2)?[18] To check this potential negative influence, we run simulations for $N = 100$, $T = 5$ and for 20% contamination for leverage points. First, we suppose that only y and Z_2 are randomly contaminated or block-contaminated and second, we suppose that only Z_2 is randomly contaminated or block-contaminated. In Table 7, results for leverage points for both y and Z_2 show that the robust HT estimator yields

Table 6. MSE of Coefficients for Leverage Points from 10% to 25% Contamination, $N = 100$, $T = 5$ (1,000 Replications).

		β_{11}	β_{12}	β_2	η_{11}	η_{12}
Contamination (10%)						
HT	1.6804	1.6431	1.9832	0.1348	0.7264	1.5328
Robust HT – case A	0.0119	0.0130	0.0119	0.0094	0.2493	0.0496
Robust HT – case B	0.0132	0.0139	0.0140	0.0090	0.2885	0.0414
Robust HT – case C	0.0130	0.0138	0.0135	0.0096	0.2649	0.0395
Robust HT – case D	0.0144	0.0118	0.0134	0.0096	0.2969	0.0497
Robust HT – case E	0.0122	0.0137	0.0127	0.0102	0.2796	0.0493
Contamination (25%)						
HT	4.6089	4.4924	4.9189	0.5097	1.4811	3.9350
Robust HT – case A	2.0403	1.9726	1.9137	0.0776	1.2611	2.0880
Robust HT – case B	0.0841	0.0841	0.0879	0.1469	0.7055	0.4223
Robust HT – case C	2.1863	2.1296	2.1639	0.0862	1.4104	2.2172
Robust HT – case D	0.0837	0.0863	0.0883	0.1480	0.7856	0.4094
Robust HT – case E	0.0757	0.0812	0.0880	0.1507	0.6847	0.4081

Case A: $bdp_{WMS,M} = 0.25$, $bdp_{2SGMS\_1\_j,S} = 0.25$, $bdp_{2SGMS\_1\_j,M} = 0.25$, $bdp_{2SGMS\_2\_j,S} = 0.25$, $bdp_{2SGMS\_2\_j,M} = 0.25$, $j = 1,2$.

Case B: $bdp_{WMS,S} = 0.25$, $bdp_{WMS,M} = 0.25$, $bdp_{2SGMS\_1\_j,S} = 0.50$, $bdp_{2SGMS\_1\_j,M} = 0.25$, $bdp_{2SGMS\_2\_j,S} = 0.50$, $bdp_{2SGMS\_2\_j,M} = 0.25$, $j = 1,2$.

Case C: $bdp_{WMS,S} = 0.50$, $bdp_{WMS,M} = 0.25$, $bdp_{2SGMS\_1\_j,S} = 0.50$, $bdp_{2SGMS\_1\_j,M} = 0.25$, $bdp_{2SGMS\_2\_j,S} = 0.25$, $bdp_{2SGMS\_2\_j,M} = 0.25$, $j = 1,2$.

Case D: $bdp_{WMS,S} = 0.50$, $bdp_{WMS,M} = 0.25$, $bdp_{2SGMS\_1\_j,S} = 0.25$, $bdp_{2SGMS\_1\_j,M} = 0.25$, $bdp_{2SGMS\_2\_j,S} = 0.50$, $bdp_{2SGMS\_2\_j,M} = 0.25$, $j = 1,2$.

Case E: $bdp_{WMS,S} = 0.50$, $bdp_{WMS,M} = 0.25$, $bdp_{2SGMS\_1\_j,S} = 0.50$, $bdp_{2SGMS\_1\_j,M} = 0.25$, $bdp_{2SGMS\_2\_j,S} = 0.50$, $bdp_{2SGMS\_2\_j,M} = 0.25$, $j = 1,2$.

Table 7. MSE of Coefficients $N=100$, $T=10$, 5% and 10% Contamination (1,000 Replications).

		β_{11}	β_{12}	β_2	η_{11}	η_{12}	η_2
Leverage points	HT	0.1273	0.1322	0.1729	0.8234	1.3979	0.2124
(Y and Z_2 only)	Robust HT	0.0088	0.0101	0.0078	0.1072	0.5063	0.0357
Concentrated leverage	HT	0.0963	0.1019	0.1051	0.6144	2.6819	0.2728
points (Y and Z_2 only)	Robust HT	0.0097	0.0096	0.0069	0.1165	1.0016	0.0831
Leverage points (only Z_2)	HT	0.0028	0.0030	0.0026	0.0027	0.1316	0.0105
	Robust HT	0.0048	0.0039	0.0049	0.0029	0.2000	0.0165
Concentrated leverage	HT	0.0026	0.0025	0.0028	0.0023	0.1384	0.0089
points (only Z_2)	Robust HT	0.0043	0.0042	0.0046	0.0025	0.2121	0.0185

better results than HT no matter what type of contamination. In contrast, when we simulate contamination only on Z_2, the impact of this contamination appears to be marginal.

Last, we tried an hybrid setup where we have a quasi-robust HT estimator where only one of the two robust estimators is deployed.[19] Two cases are possible: either the robust Within estimator is followed by the generic IV regression, or either the classic Within estimator is followed by the 2SGMS estimator. We only run these two quasi-robust HT estimators for $N = 100, T = 5$, for case 2 (leverage points (y, X_1, X_2)) and for 10% contamination. The results in Table 8 show that the second quasi-robust estimator (labeled quasi-robust HT (Within, 2SGMS)) gives similar results as compared to the robust HT estimator whatever the type of contamination (vertical outliers, leverage points, random or block-contamination). In contrast, the first quasi-robust estimator (labelled quasi-robust HT (WMS, HT)) does not seem to clean effectively the negative effects of contamination as there seems to be no significant gain in absolute or relative MSE as compared to the standard HT estimate. This gives further evidence that a robust version of the second step of the HT estimator is necessary and highly recommended.

AN EMPIRICAL EXAMPLE: THE CORNWELL–RUPERT (1988) MINCER WAGE EQUATION

Cornwell and Rupert (1988) applied the HT estimator to a returns to schooling example based on a panel of 595 individuals observed over the

Table 8. MSE of Coefficients $N = 100$, $T = 5$, 10% Contamination, Robust and Quasi-Robust HT Estimators (1,000 Replications).

		β_{11}	β_{12}	β_2	η_{11}	η_{12}	η_2
No outlier	HT	0.0023	0.0026	0.0028	0.0010	0.1235	0.0102
	Robust HT	0.0042	0.0049	0.0046	0.0014	0.2010	0.0164
	Quasi-robust HT (WMS, HT)	0.0027	0.0026	0.0025	0.0008	0.1183	0.0105
	Quasi-robust HT (Within, 2SGMS)	0.0043	0.0042	0.0045	0.0015	0.1950	0.0152
Contamination (10%)							
Vertical outliers	HT	0.0718	0.0770	0.1111	0.2481	0.9964	0.1379
	Robust HT	0.0067	0.0076	0.0056	0.0103	0.2523	0.0197
	Quasi-robust HT (WMS, HT)	0.0843	0.0848	0.1173	0.2512	0.9760	0.1348
	Quasi-robust HT (Within, 2SGMS)	0.0070	0.0072	0.0069	0.0042	0.2315	0.0180
Leverage points	HT	1.6804	1.6431	1.9832	0.1348	0.7264	1.5328
	Robust HT	0.0120	0.0112	0.0117	0.0087	0.2242	0.0481
	Quasi-robust HT (WMS, HT)	1.7202	1.6030	1.9746	0.1312	0.8288	1.5557
	Quasi-robust HT (Within, 2SGMS)	0.0174	0.0163	0.0118	0.0152	0.2835	0.0650
Concentrated vertical outliers	HT	0.0707	0.0682	0.0914	0.2116	1.5824	0.1503
	Robust HT	0.0073	0.0064	0.0051	0.0225	0.4390	0.0327
	Quasi-robust HT (WMS, HT)	0.0745	0.0809	0.1009	0.2187	1.3779	0.1685
	Quasi-robust HT (Within, 2SGMS)	0.0064	0.0072	0.0054	0.0161	0.3855	0.0335
Concentrated leverage points	HT	1.2417	1.2015	1.3094	0.1189	1.0429	0.7424
	Robust HT	0.0204	0.0211	0.0209	0.0194	0.4306	0.1102
	Quasi-robust HT (WMS, HT)	1.2562	1.2113	1.3700	0.1187	0.9489	0.7312
	Quasi-robust HT (Within, 2SGMS)	0.0193	0.0215	0.0177	0.0157	0.3987	0.1083

Table 8. *(Continued)*

		β_{11}	β_{12}	β_2	η_{11}	η_{12}	η_2
	HT	0.7343	0.7314	0.7407	0.0503	64.7983	0.8470
Leverage points with Z_{12}	Robust HT	0.0231	0.0225	0.0197	0.0095	1.1644	0.0609
	Quasi-robust HT (WMS, HT)	0.7181	0.7615	0.7533	0.0479	61.4710	0.7458
	Quasi-robust HT (Within, 2SGMS)	0.0253	0.0263	0.0203	0.0209	0.9807	0.0917
	HT	0.5671	0.6129	0.6127	0.0620	70.5724	0.5393
Concentrated leverage points with Z_{12}	Robust HT	0.0244	0.0261	0.0276	0.0198	0.8332	0.1154
	Quasi-robust HT (WMS, HT)	0.5920	0.5941	0.6386	0.0854	81.9930	0.5391
	Quasi-robust HT (Within, 2SGMS)	0.0231	0.0251	0.0216	0.0159	0.8725	0.1028
	HT	0.7279	0.8791	0.8224	0.0535	63.8211	0.8714
Leverage points with Z_{12} and Z_2	Robust HT	0.0208	0.0192	0.0168	0.0087	0.9404	0.0486
	Quasi-robust HT (WMS, HT)	0.7456	0.8357	0.8438	0.0513	57.6370	0.8320
	Quasi-robust HT (Within, 2SGMS)	0.0242	0.0212	0.0182	0.0233	0.9265	0.0906
	HT	0.6235	0.5389	0.5822	0.0567	67.5897	0.4981
Concentrated leverage points	Robust HT	0.0195	0.0218	0.0221	0.0189	0.8958	0.1032
with Z_{12} and Z_2	Quasi-robust HT (WMS, HT)	0.6550	0.5567	0.6400	0.0731	76.7050	0.4874
	Quasi-robust HT (Within, 2SGMS)	0.0227	0.0213	0.0200	0.0173	0.8710	0.0899

period 1976–1982 drawn from the Panel Study of Income Dynamics (PSID). In particular, log wage is regressed on years of education (ED), weeks worked (WEEKS), years of full-time work experience (EXP) and its square (EXP2), occupation (OCC = 1, if the individual is in a blue-collar occupation), residence (SOUTH = 1, SMSA = 1, if the individual resides in the South, or in a standard metropolitan statistical area), industry (IND = 1, if the individual works in a manufacturing industry), marital status (MAR = 1, if the individual is married), sex and race (FEM = 1, BLK = 1, if the individual is female or black), union coverage (UNION = 1, if the individual's wage is set by a union contract). Table 9 reports the Within, WMS, HT and robust HT estimators for this Mincer wage equation in which the X_1 variables are OCC, SOUTH, SMSA, IND, the X_2 variables are EXP, EXP2, WKS, MAR, UNION, the Z_1 variables are FEM, BLK and the Z_2 variable is ED. In this specification, there are 8 dummies for 12 explanatory variables. As Croux and Verardi (2008) note, the need of random picking p-subsets of K observations become Achille's heel of the MS algorithm when several dummy variables are present. Subsampling algorithms can easily lead to collinear subsamples if various dummies are present. A rough solution is to use subsets of size a little bit larger than K. For this empirical example, we generated 500 random subsets of $(T{\cdot}K)$ observations.[20] If we compare the Within and WMS estimators, we see that all the coefficients of WMS are statistically significant contrary to those of the Within estimator. MAR switches sign and becomes significant. Weeks worked has a larger effect that is now statistically significant. The HT estimator indicates that an additional year of schooling yields a 13.8% wage gain, and that gender discrimination (FEM) is statistically insignificant. An additional year of schooling yields almost the same effect as for HT, 13.5%, but with lower standard errors. The FEM coefficient estimate yields a lower but statistically significant effect on wages. Interestingly, SOUTH is insignificant for both HT and robust HT, while MAR is significant only for the robust HT estimator. In fact, with the robust HT estimator, industry and weeks worked are also statistically significant. Only a small proportion of the observations (2.5% and 8.4%) change values for SOUTH and MAR over the period observed. This indicates that these variables would have been eliminated using the Within transformation since the proportion of observations switching values is close to zero. To check the sensitivity of our results, we removed SOUTH and MAR, and the results are reported at the bottom of Table 9. For the robust HT estimator deleting these two dummy variables, the returns to education is about the same and the FEM coefficient is smaller but statistically significant.

Table 9. Cornwell and Rupert (1988) Mincer Wage Equation.

	WITHIN			WMS		
	Coefficient	Standard Errors	*T*-stat	Coefficient	Standard Errors	*T*-stat
OCC	−0.0215	0.0138	−1.5581	−0.0224	0.0027	−8.2684
SOUTH	−0.0019	0.0343	−0.0543	−0.0975	0.0025	−38.8978
SMSA	−0.0425	0.0194	−2.1859	−0.0209	0.0024	−8.6947
IND	0.0192	0.0154	1.2437	−0.0177	0.0024	−7.3852
EXP	0.1132	0.0025	45.8141	0.1105	0.0005	220.0491
EXP2	−0.0004	0.0001	−7.6629	−0.0005	0.0000	−42.4252
WKS	0.0008	0.0006	1.3940	0.0020	0.0001	16.9810
MAR	−0.0297	0.0190	−1.5659	0.0345	0.0032	10.9441
UNION	0.0328	0.0149	2.1970	0.0363	0.0025	14.2990

	HT			ROBUST HT		
	Coefficient	Standard Errors	*T*-stat	Coefficient	Standard Errors	*T*-stat
OCC	−0.0207	0.0138	−1.5024	−0.0184	0.0038	−4.8763
SOUTH	0.0074	0.0320	0.2328	−0.0162	0.0130	−1.2451
SMSA	−0.0418	0.0190	−2.2066	−0.0327	0.0069	−4.7163
IND	0.0136	0.0152	0.8928	−0.0205	0.0045	−4.5335
EXP	0.1131	0.0025	45.7850	0.1077	0.0007	164.1500
EXP2	−0.0004	0.0001	−7.6718	−0.0004	0.0000	−26.5820
WKS	0.0008	0.0006	1.3963	0.0009	0.0002	5.4072
MAR	−0.0299	0.0190	−1.5728	−0.0121	0.0052	−2.3474
UNION	0.0328	0.0149	2.1982	0.0116	0.0050	2.3116
INTERCEPT	2.9127	0.2837	10.2690	3.1716	0.0690	45.9800
FEM	−0.1309	0.1267	−1.0337	−0.0650	0.0254	−2.5564
BLK	−0.2858	0.1557	−1.8352	−0.0832	0.0347	−2.3970
ED	0.1379	0.0212	6.4919	0.1320	0.0051	25.8780

Table 9. *(Continued)*

	WITHIN			WMS		
	Coefficient	Standard Errors	*T*-stat	Coefficient	Standard Errors	*T*-stat
OCC	−0.0216	0.0137	−1.5712	−0.0286	0.0027	−10.4797
SMSA	−0.0445	0.0193	−2.3059	−0.0265	0.0024	−11.0088
IND	0.0189	0.0154	1.2222	0.0007	0.0024	0.2778
EXP	0.1133	0.0025	45.8456	0.1134	0.0005	224.5598
EXP2	−0.0004	0.0001	−7.6682	−0.0004	0.0000	−38.5920
WKS	0.0008	0.0006	1.3819	0.0026	0.0001	23.9203
UNION	0.0327	0.0149	2.1944	−0.0148	0.0025	−5.9975

	HT			ROBUST HT		
	Coefficient	Standard Errors	*T*-stat	Coefficient	Standard Errors	*T*-stat
OCC	−0.0210	0.0137	−1.5279	−0.0155	0.0039	−3.9153
SMSA	−0.0434	0.0189	−2.3013	−0.0287	0.0069	−4.1785
IND	0.0133	0.0152	0.8746	−0.0195	0.0047	−4.1591
EXP	0.1132	0.0025	45.8140	0.1077	0.0007	157.6600
EXP2	−0.0004	0.0001	−7.6728	−0.0004	0.0000	−24.5100
WKS	0.0008	0.0006	1.3789	0.0009	0.0002	5.9036
UNION	0.0331	0.0149	2.2196	0.0095	0.0051	1.8813
INTERCEPT	2.8666	0.2839	10.0960	3.0986	0.0717	43.2180
FEM	−0.1046	0.1257	−0.8322	−0.0535	0.0271	−1.9760
BLK	−0.2789	0.1559	−1.7896	−0.0729	0.0375	−1.9419
ED	0.1396	0.0214	6.5265	0.1365	0.0054	25.3530

CONCLUSION

This chapter applies the useful robust panel data methods suggested by Bramati and Croux (2007) and Wagenvoort and Waldmann (2002) to the Hausman and Taylor (1981) estimator. We demonstrate using Monte Carlo experiments the substantial gains in efficiency as measured by MSE of this robust HT estimator over its classical counterpart. The magnitude of the gains in MSE depends upon the *type* and *degree* of contamination of the observations.[21] We illustrate this robust HT method by applying it to the classical Mincer wage equation using the empirical study of Cornwell and Rupert (1988). For this empirical study, the returns to education seem to be robust to outliers, while the magnitude and significance of the female coefficient are sensitive to robustification of the HT estimator. We performed several sensitivity analysis but there remains a lot of questions for future research. For example, we did not prove that the proposed robust HT estimator is scale, regression and affine equivariant. There is also a need to derive formal tests or metrics to use in applied panel data setting to determine the presence of outliers. This analysis can also be extended to dynamic HT type models, where one can check the sensitivity of using the difference transformation, rather than a Within transformation that subtracts a mean or a median to get rid of the individual effects, on the performance of the contaminated classical dynamic panel data estimators.

ACKNOWLEDGMENTS

We would like to thank three referees for helpful comments and suggestions. Many thanks to the participants of the 11th Advances in Econometrics Conference: Essays in Honor of Jerry Hausman, Louisiana State University, Baton Rouge, February 17–19, 2012 and the participants of the 18th International Panel Data Conference held at the Banque de France, Paris, July 5–6, 2012. We thank Christophe Croux for providing his Matlab codes and for helpful discussion on the Within MS estimator. We dedicate this chapter to the memory of Halbert L. White Jr.

NOTES

1. See Appendix A.
2. M, S and MS estimators are discussed in detail in the robust statistics literature, see Huber (1964), Rousseeuw and Yohai (1987) and Maronna and Yohai (2006) to

mention a few. The corresponding WMS estimator for panel data is discussed in detail in the section entitled 'The WMS Estimator'.

3. Aquaro and Čížek (2010) use a first difference rather than a Within transformation. Their simulations reveal superior performance over the median difference estimator. However, differencing eliminates the first wave, and in micro-panels that is a loss of N observations. Differencing is usually not employed in panel data unless the model is dynamic. In keeping with the spirit of the HT approach that uses the Within estimator in the first stage, and in order not to waist N observations, we use a robust Within approach rather than an approach based on first differences or pairwise differences.

4. See Cornwell and Rupert (1988), Egger and Pfaffermayr (2004) and Serlenga and Shin (2007) to mention a few applications of the HT estimator.

5. For the advantages and disadvantages of several influence functions considered in this literature, see Rousseeuw and Leroy (2003).

6. M-estimators are called monotone if the loss function ρ is convex over the entire domain and are called redescending if the influence function ψ is bounded. Redescending M-estimators have high breakdown points (close to 0.5) and their influence function can be chosen to redescend smoothly to 0 as in the Tukey biweight function.

7. Monotone M-estimators are robust to outliers in the response variable, but are not resistant to outliers in the explanatory variables (leverage points). In contrast, redescending M-estimators are resistant to bad leverage points but are difficult to implement from a computational point of view. S-estimation, which finds an hyperplane that minimizes a robust estimate of the scale of the residuals, is highly resistant to leverage points, and is robust to outliers in the response. However, this method can be inefficient. MM-estimation (not used here) tries to capture both the robustness and resistance of S-estimation, while at the same time gaining the efficiency of M-estimation. The method proceeds in three steps: (a) with a first loss function, we get an initial M-estimate, (b) we obtain an M-estimate of the scale of the residuals, (c) the estimated scale is then held constant while an M-estimate of the parameters is located with a new loss function. MM-estimators are robust and efficient.

8. From Eq. (18), the algorithm calculates the hyperplane of K observations that fits all points perfectly if all K points are regular observations and do not contain outliers. For each subset, the residuals are defined as the vertical distance separating each observation from the hyperplane. Using these residuals, a scale estimate $\hat{\sigma}_S$ is obtained as in Eq. (17) for each p-subset. Salibian-Barrera and Yohai (2006) proposed the following number of generated subsamples N_{sub}:

$$N_{sub} = \left\lceil \frac{\log(1 - P)}{\log(1 - (1 - v)^K)} \right\rceil$$

where v is the maximal expected proportion of outliers. P is the desired probability of having at least one p-subset without outliers among the N_{sub} subsamples and $\lceil x \rceil$ is the ceiling operator of x, i.e. the smallest integer not less than x. The number of subsamples is chosen to guarantee that at least one p-subset without outliers is selected with high probability (Croux & Verardi, 2008; Maronna & Yohai, 2006; Salibian-Barrera & Yohai, 2006). In our Monte Carlo study, we use $N_{sub} = 500$. As

Croux and Verardi (2008) warn, subsampling algorithms can easily lead to collinear subsamples if various dummies are present. A rough solution is to use subsets of size a little bit larger than K. An exact solution is given by Maronna and Yohai (2006) who introduce the MS-estimator that alternates an S-estimator (for continuous variables) and an M-estimator (for dummy ones) till convergence.

9. The robust estimates $\hat{\mu}_x$ and V_x can be obtained using the Minimum Covariance Determinant (MCD) estimator (Rousseeuw, 1984). The MCD method looks for the $h(>NT/2)$ observations whose classical covariance matrix has the lowest possible determinant. The raw MCD estimate of location $\hat{\mu}_x$ is then the average of these h points, whereas the raw MCD estimate of the scatter V_x is their covariance matrix, multiplied by a consistency factor. The MCD estimates can resist $(NT-h)$ outliers and a value of $h=0.75NT$ is recommended to obtain a high finite-sample efficiency. The computation of the MCD estimator is non-trivial. Rousseeuw and Van Driessen (1999) suggest a fast resampling algorithm (FAST-MCD) that we use. Several other algorithms have been proposed (Olive, 2008, Chapter 10 for a discussion).

10. Bramati and Croux (2007) also use this GM estimator for FE panel data model and call it the Within GM (or WGM) estimator. They show that this estimator gives similar results when compared to the WMS estimator.

11. In our specific case, $Z=[Z_1,Z_2]$ and $A=[Z_1,X_{11},X_{12}]$, so $\hat{Z}_1 \equiv Z_1$ and $\hat{Z}_2 = A(A'W_A(A)W_r(r_{1,2})A^{-1})A'W_A(A)W_r(r_{1,2})Z_2$.

12. For instance, if $N=100, T=10$ and 10% of the observations are corrupted, it means that 20 individuals have all five time period observations corrupted.

13. There are several weighting functions defined in the robust statistics literature. Since the Tukey biweight function is widely used, we only test the properties of the robust HT estimator with this weight function.

14. Bramati and Croux (2007) used a unique breakdown point of 20% with a tuning constant $c=3.420$, for their Monte Carlo study on samples of $N=100, T=4$, 20, and 5% or 10% contamination.

15. Following Kapoor, Kelejian and Prucha (2007), our measure of dispersion is closely related to the standard measure of the MSE, but it is based on quantiles rather than moments because, unlike moments, quantiles are assured to exist. For ease of presentation, we also refer to our measure as MSE. It is defined by

$$MSE = bias^2 + \left[\frac{IQ}{1.35}\right]^2$$

where *bias* is the difference between the median and the true value and IQ is the interquantile range Q_3-Q_1 where Q_3 is the 0.75 quantile and Q_1 is the 0.25 quantile. If the distribution is normal, the median is the mean and, aside from a slight rounding error, $IQ/1.35$ is the standard deviation.

16. We thank a referee for this suggestion.

17. We thank a referee for this suggestion.

18. We thank a referee for this suggestion.

19. We thank a referee for this suggestion.

20. One can also use the exact solution proposed by Maronna and Yohai (2006) who introduce the MS-estimator that alternates an S-estimator (for continuous variables) and an M-estimator (for dummy ones) till convergence.

21. We focus on contamination in balanced panels for ease of notation.
22. The $T/2$ corrupted time data can be randomly chosen between $t = 1$ and $t = T$.

REFERENCES

Aquaro, M., & Čížek, P. (2010). *One-step robust estimation of fixed-effects panel data models*. Working Paper CentER No. 2010–110. Department of Econometrics, Tilburg University, The Netherlands.

Baltagi, B. H. (2008). *Econometric analysis of panel data* (4th ed.). Chichester: Wiley.

Bramati, M. C., & Croux, C. (2007). Robust estimators for the fixed effects panel data model. *Econometrics Journal, 10*, 521–540.

Breusch, T. S., Mizon, G. E., & Schmidt, P. (1989). Efficient estimation using panel data. *Econometrica, 57*, 695–700.

Čížek, P. (2008). Robust and efficient adaptive estimation of binary-choice regression models. *Journal of the American Statistical Association, 103*, 687–696.

Cornwell, C., & Rupert, P. (1988). Efficient estimation with panel data: An empirical comparison of instrumental variables estimators. *Journal of Applied Econometrics, 3*, 149–155.

Croux, C., & Verardi, V. (2008). Robust regression in Stata. *The Stata Journal, 9*, 439–453.

Dehon, C., Gassner, M., & Verardi, V. (2009). Beware of 'good' outliers and overoptimistic conclusions. *Oxford Bulletin of Economics and Statistics, 71*, 437–452.

Dhaene, G., & Zhu, Y. (2009). *Median-based estimation of dynamic panel models with fixed effects*. Working Paper. Faculty of Business and Economics, Catholic University of Leuven, Belgium.

Donoho, D. L., & Huber, P. J. (1983). The notion of breakdown point. In P. J. Bickel, K. A. Doksum & J. L. Hodges (Eds.), *A. Festschrift for Erich L. Lehmann* (pp. 157–184). Belmont, CA: Wadsworth.

Egger, P., & Pfaffermayr, M. (2004). Distance, trade and FDI: a SUR Hausman–Taylor approach. *Journal of Applied Econometrics, 19*, 227–246.

Hausman, J. A., & Taylor, W. E. (1981). Panel data and unobservable individual effects. *Econometrica, 49*, 1377–1398.

Hinloopen, J., & Wagenvoort, J. L. M. (1997). On the computation and efficiency of a HBP-GM estimator: Some simulation results. *Computational Statistics and Data Analysis, 25*, 1–15.

Huber, P. (1964). Robust estimation of a location parameter. *Annals of Mathematical Statistics, 35*, 73–101.

Huber, P. J. (1981). *Robust statistics, Series in probability and mathematical statistics* (1st ed.). New York, NY: Wiley.

Huber, P. J., & Ronchetti, E. M. (2009). *Robust statistics, Series in probability and mathematical statistics* (2nd ed.). New York, NY: Wiley.

Kapoor, M., Kelejian, H. H., & Prucha, I. R. (2007). Panel data models with spatially correlated error components. *Journal of Econometrics, 140*, 97–130.

Lucas, A., van Dijk, R., Kloek, T. (2007). Outlier robust GMM estimation of leverage determinants in linear dynamic panel data models, Vrije Universiteit, Amsterdam, the Netherlands. Unpublished manuscript.

Maronna, R. A., Martin, R. D., & Yohai, V. J. (2006). *Robust statistics*. New York, NY: Wiley.

Maronna, R., & Yohai, V. (2006). Robust regression with both continuous and categorical predictors. *Journal of Statistical Planning and Inference*, *89*, 197–214.

Olive, D. J. (2008). *Applied robust statistics*, Department of Mathematics, Southern Illinois University. Unpublished manuscript.

Ronchetti, E., & Trojani, F. (2001). Robust inference with GMM estimators. *Journal of Econometrics*, *101*, 37–69.

Rousseeuw, P. J. (1984). Least median of squares regression. *Journal of the American Statistical Association*, *79*, 87–780.

Rousseeuw, P. J., & Leroy, A. M. (2003). *Robust regression and outlier detection*. New York, NY: Wiley.

Rousseeuw, P. J., & Van Driessen, K. (1999). A fast algorithm for the minimum covariance determinant estimator. *Technometrics*, *41*, 212–223.

Rousseeuw, P. J., & Yohai, V. (1987). Robust regression by means of S-estimators. In J. Franke, W. Härdle & D. Martin (Eds.), *Robust and nonlinear time series analysis* (pp. 256–272). Berlin: Springer-Verlag.

Salibian-Barrera, M., & Yohai, V. (2006). A fast algorithm for S-regression estimates. *Journal of Computational and Graphical Statistics*, *15*, 414–427.

Serlenga, L., & Shin, Y. (2007). Gravity models of intra-EU trade: Application of the CCEP-HT estimation in heterogeneous panels with unobserved common time-specific factors. *Journal of Applied Econometrics*, *22*, 361–381.

Wagenvoort, R., & Waldmann, R. (2002). On B-robust instrumental variable estimation of the linear model with panel data. *Journal of Econometrics*, *106*, 297–324.

Yohai, V. (1987). High breakdown-point and high efficiency estimates for regression. *The Annals of Statistics*, *15*, 642–665.

APPENDIX A

Definition of the Breakdown Point

As Bramati and Croux (2007, p. 523) noted, the breakdown point of an estimator is defined as the smallest fraction of outlying observations that can cause a 'breakdown' of the estimator. Let our panel data sample be composed of NT observations $\Omega = \{y_{it}, X_{it}\}$ and let $\theta(\Omega)$ be our estimator. Let $\tilde{\Omega} = \{\tilde{y}_{it}, \tilde{X}_{it}\}$ be a contaminated set of NT observations, any m of the original points of Ω are replaced by arbitrary values, and $\tilde{\theta}(\tilde{\Omega})$ is our estimator of the corrupted sample $\tilde{\Omega}$. If $\omega(m, \theta, \Omega)$ is the supremum of $||\tilde{\theta}(\tilde{\Omega}) - \theta(\Omega)||$, then the breakdown point of θ at Ω is defined as:

$$\begin{aligned} \varepsilon^*_{NT}(m, \theta, \Omega) &= \min\left\{\frac{m}{NT}; \omega(m, \theta, \Omega) \text{ is infinite}\right\} \\ &= \min\left\{\frac{m}{NT}; \sup_{\tilde{\Omega}} ||\tilde{\theta}(\tilde{\Omega}) - \theta(\Omega)|| = \infty\right\} \end{aligned}$$

The breakdown point of the estimator θ at Ω is the smallest proportion of observations replaced by outliers which can cause the estimator θ to take on values arbitrarily far from $\theta(\Omega)$ (Bramati & Croux, 2007; Croux & Verardi, 2008). In case of block-contaminated data, we suppose that for some individuals half of the time, the data is contaminated. In particular, $\tilde{\Omega} = \{\tilde{y}_{it}, \tilde{X}_{it}\}$ where for some individuals $\tilde{y}_{it}, \tilde{X}_{it}$ are contaminated for $t = 1, 2, ..., T/2$ and not for $t = (T/2) + 1, ..., T)$.[22] For instance, if $N = 100, T = 10$ and 10% of the observations are corrupted, it means that we had 20 individuals all of whom had five time period observations corrupted.

APPENDIX B

Breakdown Point and Asymptotic Efficiency

Rousseeuw and Yohai (1987) computed the asymptotic efficiency of the S-estimator of a Gaussian model for different values of the breakdown point for the Tukey biweight function:

Breakdown Point ε^*	Asymptotic Efficiency *as.eff*	Tuning Constant c	Expected Loss b
50%	28.7%	1.547	0.1995
45%	37.0%	1.756	0.2312
40%	46.2%	1.988	0.2634
35%	56.0%	2.251	0.2957
30%	66.1%	2.560	0.3278
25%	75.9%	2.937	0.3593
20%	84.7%	3.420	0.3899
15%	91.7%	4.096	0.4194
10%	96.6%	5.182	0.4475

Source: Rousseeuw and Yohai (1987), Table 3, p. 268.

where $as.eff = (\int \psi' d\Phi)^2 / (\int \psi^2 d\Phi)$ in which Φ is the cumulative distribution function of $N(0, 1)$ and $b = E[\rho(Q)]$ with $Q \sim N(0, 1)$.

SMALL SAMPLE PROPERTIES AND PRETEST ESTIMATION OF A SPATIAL HAUSMAN–TAYLOR MODEL

Badi H. Baltagi, Peter H. Egger and Michaela Kesina

ABSTRACT

Purpose – *This chapter considers a Hausman and Taylor (1981) panel data model that exhibits a Cliff and Ord (1973) spatial error structure.*

Methodology/approach – *We analyze the small sample properties of a generalized moments estimation approach for that model. This spatial Hausman–Taylor estimator allows for endogeneity of the time-varying and time-invariant variables with the individual effects. For this model, the spatial fixed effects estimator is known to be consistent, but its disadvantage is that it wipes out the effects of time-invariant variables which are important for most empirical studies.*

Findings – *Monte Carlo results show that the spatial Hausman–Taylor estimator performs well in small samples.*

Essays in Honor of Jerry Hausman
Advances in Econometrics, Volume 29, 215–236

ISSN: 0731-9053/doi:10.1108/S0731-9053(2012)0000029013

Keywords: Hausman–Taylor estimator; spatial random effects; small sample properties

JEL classification: C23; C31

INTRODUCTION

Hausman and Taylor (1981) proposed a random effects (RE) panel data model which allows for endogeneity of time-varying and time-invariant variables with the individual effects. For this model, fixed effects (FE) is known to be consistent, but its disadvantage is that it wipes out the effects of time-invariant variables which are important for most empirical studies. In an earnings equation, the time-invariant variable could be schooling and this is correlated with the unobservable individual effect (see Cornwell & Rupert, 1988). In this case, FE would not deliver an estimate of the returns to schooling, but the alternative Hausman–Taylor estimator will provide an asymptotically efficient estimator of this effect. The order condition of identification requires that there are as many exogenous time-variant regressors as there are endogenous time-invariant regressors. Other applications of this estimator include the effect of an individual's birth year on wages (Light & Ureta, 1995); the effect of health on wages (Contoyannis & Rice, 2001); the effect of distance on bilateral trade (Egger, 2004) or foreign direct investment (Egger & Pfaffermayr, 2004); the effect of common language on bilateral trade (Serlenga & Shin, 2007); and the effect of public ownership of firms on productivity (Baltagi, Egger, & Kesina, 2011). The last paper introduces spatial spillovers in total factor productivity by allowing the error term across firms to be spatially interdependent. This model is estimated by extending the Hausman–Taylor estimator to allow for spatial correlation in the error term. Baltagi et al. (2011) find evidence of positive spillovers across firms and a large and significant detrimental effect of public ownership on total factor productivity.

This is a follow-up paper that studies the small sample performance of various estimators applied to this *spatial* Hausman–Taylor model using Monte Carlo experiments. We will refer to the spatial Hausman–Taylor model by the acronym SHT. This chapter also studies the small sample performance of a pretest estimator which is based on two Hausman tests usually carried out by the empirical researcher in practice. It is well known that the choice between FE and RE estimators can be based on the Hausman (1978) test. Baltagi, Bresson, and Pirotte (2003) suggest an alternative pretest estimator based on the Hausman–Taylor model. This pretest estimator reverts to the RE estimator if the standard Hausman test based on the FE versus the RE estimators is not rejected. It reverts to the HT estimator if the choice of strictly exogenous regressors is not rejected by a second Hausman over-identification test based on the difference between the FE and HT estimators. If both tests are rejected, then the pretest estimator reverts to the FE estimator. See Baltagi (2008) for a textbook treatment of this subject. This chapter generalizes this pretest estimator to account for spatial correlation. In the first step, a standard Hausman (1978) test is performed based on the contrast between spatial fixed effects (SFE) and spatial random effects (SRE),[1] and in the second step a Hausman–Taylor over-identification test is performed based on the contrast between SFE and the SHT estimator. The spatial pretest (SPT) estimator becomes the SRE estimator if the Hausman test is not rejected in the first step. It becomes the SHT estimator if the first Hausman test is rejected but the second Hausman–Taylor over-identification test is not rejected. If both tests are rejected, then the SPT estimator reverts to the SFE estimator.

This chapter performs Monte Carlo experiments to compare the performance of this SPT estimator with the spatial panel data estimators under various designs. The estimators considered are OLS, SFE, SRE, and SHT, respectively.

In the experiments, we let some regressors be correlated with the individual effects and the error to be spatially correlated, i.e., a SHT world. Our results show that the SPT estimator is a viable estimator and performs reasonably well in terms of root mean squared error (RMSE). However, it does not perform well for simple tests of hypotheses. The SFE estimator is a consistent estimator in the SHT world, but its disadvantage is that it does not allow the estimation of the coefficients of the time-invariant regressors. When there is endogeneity among the regressors, we show that there is a substantial bias in the OLS and SRE estimators and both yield misleading inference.

The remainder of the chapter is organized as follows. The next section briefly reviews the estimator for the SHT model which will be employed in the Monte Carlo analysis. The subsequent section introduces the Monte Carlo design and discusses the results. The last section concludes with a brief summary of our main findings.

ECONOMETRIC MODEL

In this section, we briefly review the Hausman and Taylor (1981) model with spatial correlation (Baltagi et al., 2011). Let $i = 1, ..., N$ refer to individual units and $t = 1, ..., T$ refer to time periods. In what follows, we are interested in analyzing a Cliff and Ord (1973) spatial model for period t of the form

$$\boldsymbol{y}_t = \mathbf{X}_t\boldsymbol{\beta} + \mathbf{Z}\gamma + \boldsymbol{u}_t = \mathfrak{Z}_t\boldsymbol{\delta} + \boldsymbol{u}_t \tag{1}$$

$$\boldsymbol{u}_t = \rho\mathbf{W}\boldsymbol{u}_t + \boldsymbol{\varepsilon}_t, \quad \boldsymbol{\varepsilon}_t = \boldsymbol{\mu} + \boldsymbol{v}_t \tag{2}$$

where $\mathfrak{Z}_t = [\mathbf{X}_t, \mathbf{Z}]$, and $\boldsymbol{\delta} = [\boldsymbol{\beta}', \gamma']'$. Here, $\boldsymbol{y}_t = (y_{1t}, ..., y_{Nt})'$ is an $N \times 1$ vector of observations on the dependent variable at time t, $\mathbf{X}_t$ is an $N \times K$ matrix of time-varying regressors for period t, $\mathbf{Z}$ is an $N \times R$ matrix of time-invariant regressors. The regressors may be decomposed into $\mathbf{X}_t = [\mathbf{X}_{Ut}, \mathbf{X}_{Ct}]$ and $\mathbf{Z} = [\mathbf{Z}_U, \mathbf{Z}_C]$, where subindex C denotes regressors which are *correlated* with $\boldsymbol{\mu}$ while subindex U indicates regressors which are *uncorrelated* with $\boldsymbol{\mu}$. $\mathbf{W}$ is an $N \times N$ observed non-stochastic spatial weights matrix. $\boldsymbol{u}_t = (u_{1t}, ..., u_{Nt})'$ is the $N \times 1$ vector of disturbances, and $\boldsymbol{\varepsilon}_t = (\varepsilon_{1t}, ..., \varepsilon_{Nt})'$ is an $N \times 1$ vector of innovations which consists of two components: a time-invariant $\boldsymbol{\mu} = (\mu_1, ..., \mu_N)'$ and a time-variant $\boldsymbol{v}_t = (v_{1t}, ..., v_{Nt})'$ component, where $\mu_i \sim IID(0, \sigma_\mu^2)$ and $v_{it} \sim IID(0, \sigma_v^2)$. The vector $\mathbf{W}\boldsymbol{u}_t$ represents a spatial lag of $\boldsymbol{u}_t$. The scalar ρ denotes the spatial autoregressive parameter, while $\boldsymbol{\beta}$ and γ are $K \times 1$ and $R \times 1$ vectors of regression parameters.[2]

When stacking the model for all time periods $t = 1, .., T$, it reads

$$\boldsymbol{y} = \mathbf{X}\boldsymbol{\beta} + (\iota_T \otimes \mathbf{Z})\gamma + \boldsymbol{u} = \mathfrak{Z}\boldsymbol{\delta} + \boldsymbol{u} \tag{3}$$

$$\boldsymbol{u} = \rho(\mathbf{I}_T \otimes \mathbf{W})\boldsymbol{u} + \boldsymbol{\varepsilon}, \quad \boldsymbol{\varepsilon} = \mathbf{Z}_\mu\boldsymbol{\mu} + \boldsymbol{v} \tag{4}$$

where $\mathbf{X} = [\boldsymbol{x}_1', \ldots, \boldsymbol{x}_T']'$, $\mathfrak{Z} = [\mathfrak{Z}_1', \ldots, \mathfrak{Z}_T']'$, $\boldsymbol{u} = [\boldsymbol{u}_1', \ldots, \boldsymbol{u}_T']'$ and $\boldsymbol{\varepsilon} = [\boldsymbol{\varepsilon}_1', \ldots, \boldsymbol{\varepsilon}_T']'$. $\boldsymbol{\iota}_T$ denotes a $T \times 1$ vector of ones and $\mathbf{I}_T$ denotes a $T \times T$ identity matrix. $\mathbf{Z}_\mu = \boldsymbol{\iota}_T \otimes \mathbf{I}_N$ is an $NT \times N$ selector matrix of ones and zeroes.

For estimation, we employ moment conditions derived in Kapoor, Kelejian, and Prucha (2007) for the SRE model. These moment conditions are given by $\frac{1}{N(T-1)}E(\boldsymbol{\varepsilon}'\mathbf{Q}\boldsymbol{\varepsilon}) = \sigma_v^2$, $\frac{1}{N(T-1)}E(\bar{\boldsymbol{\varepsilon}}'\mathbf{Q}\bar{\boldsymbol{\varepsilon}}) = \sigma_v^2\frac{1}{N}tr(\mathbf{W}'\mathbf{W})$, $\frac{1}{N(T-1)}E(\bar{\boldsymbol{\varepsilon}}'\mathbf{Q}\boldsymbol{\varepsilon}) = 0$, $\frac{1}{N}E(\boldsymbol{\varepsilon}'\mathbf{P}\boldsymbol{\varepsilon}) = \sigma_1^2$, $\frac{1}{N}E(\bar{\boldsymbol{\varepsilon}}'\mathbf{P}\bar{\boldsymbol{\varepsilon}}) = \sigma_1^2\frac{1}{N}tr(\mathbf{W}'\mathbf{W})$, $\frac{1}{N}E(\bar{\boldsymbol{\varepsilon}}'\mathbf{Q}\boldsymbol{\varepsilon}) = 0$, where $\bar{\boldsymbol{\varepsilon}} \equiv (\mathbf{I}_T \otimes \mathbf{W})\boldsymbol{\varepsilon}$ and $\sigma_1^2 = T\sigma_\mu^2 + \sigma_v^2$. $\mathbf{P} = \mathbf{I}_N \otimes \bar{\mathbf{J}}_T$ is the (between) projection matrix, where $\bar{\mathbf{J}}_T = T^{-1}\mathbf{J}_T$ and $\mathbf{J}_T$ is a matrix of ones of dimension T. $\mathbf{Q} = \mathbf{I}_{NT} - \mathbf{P}$ denotes the within transformation matrix. The moment conditions can be rewritten in terms of $\boldsymbol{u}$ using the fact that $\boldsymbol{\varepsilon} = (\mathbf{I}_T \otimes [\mathbf{I}_N - \rho\mathbf{W}])\boldsymbol{u} = \boldsymbol{u} - \rho\bar{\boldsymbol{u}}$ whereby $\bar{\boldsymbol{u}} \equiv (\mathbf{I}_T \otimes \mathbf{W})\boldsymbol{u}$ and $\bar{\boldsymbol{\varepsilon}} \equiv (\mathbf{I}_T \otimes \mathbf{W})(\mathbf{I}_T \otimes [\mathbf{I}_N - \rho\mathbf{W}])\boldsymbol{u} = \bar{\boldsymbol{u}} - \rho\bar{\bar{\boldsymbol{u}}}$ with $\bar{\bar{\boldsymbol{u}}} \equiv (\mathbf{I}_T \otimes \mathbf{W})\bar{\boldsymbol{u}}$.

The resulting moment conditions are then stacked and solved as a solution to the system of six equations in three unknowns. More formally, $\gamma - \boldsymbol{\Gamma}\boldsymbol{\alpha} = 0$, where $\boldsymbol{\alpha} = (\rho, \rho^2, \sigma_v^2, \sigma_1^2)'$ and

$$\gamma = \begin{pmatrix} \frac{1}{N(T-1)}\boldsymbol{u}'\mathbf{Q}\boldsymbol{u} \\ \frac{1}{N(T-1)}\bar{\boldsymbol{u}}'\mathbf{Q}\bar{\boldsymbol{u}} \\ \frac{1}{N(T-1)}\boldsymbol{u}'\mathbf{Q}\bar{\boldsymbol{u}} \\ \frac{1}{N}\boldsymbol{u}'\mathbf{P}\boldsymbol{u} \\ \frac{1}{N}\bar{\boldsymbol{u}}'\mathbf{P}\bar{\boldsymbol{u}} \\ \frac{1}{N}\boldsymbol{u}'\mathbf{P}\bar{\boldsymbol{u}} \end{pmatrix},$$

$$\boldsymbol{\Gamma} = \begin{pmatrix} \frac{2}{N(T-1)}\boldsymbol{u}'\mathbf{Q}\bar{\boldsymbol{u}} & \frac{-1}{N(T-1)}\bar{\boldsymbol{u}}'\mathbf{Q}\bar{\boldsymbol{u}} & 1 & 0 \\ \frac{2}{N(T-1)}\bar{\bar{\boldsymbol{u}}}'\mathbf{Q}\bar{\boldsymbol{u}} & \frac{-1}{N(T-1)}\bar{\bar{\boldsymbol{u}}}'\mathbf{Q}\bar{\bar{\boldsymbol{u}}} & \frac{1}{N}tr\mathbf{W}'\mathbf{W} & 0 \\ \frac{1}{N(T-1)}(\boldsymbol{u}'\mathbf{Q}\bar{\bar{\boldsymbol{u}}} + \bar{\boldsymbol{u}}'\mathbf{Q}\bar{\boldsymbol{u}}) & \frac{-1}{N(T-1)}\bar{\boldsymbol{u}}'\mathbf{Q}\bar{\bar{\boldsymbol{u}}} & 0 & 0 \\ \frac{2}{N}\boldsymbol{u}'\mathbf{P}\bar{\boldsymbol{u}} & \frac{-1}{N}\bar{\boldsymbol{u}}'\mathbf{P}\bar{\boldsymbol{u}} & 0 & 1 \\ \frac{2}{N}\bar{\bar{\boldsymbol{u}}}'\mathbf{P}\bar{\boldsymbol{u}} & \frac{-1}{N}\bar{\bar{\boldsymbol{u}}}'\mathbf{P}\bar{\bar{\boldsymbol{u}}} & 0 & \frac{1}{N}tr\mathbf{W}'\mathbf{W} \\ \frac{1}{N}(\boldsymbol{u}'\mathbf{P}\bar{\bar{\boldsymbol{u}}} + \bar{\boldsymbol{u}}'\mathbf{P}\bar{\boldsymbol{u}}) & \frac{-1}{N}\bar{\boldsymbol{u}}'\mathbf{P}\bar{\bar{\boldsymbol{u}}} & 0 & 0 \end{pmatrix}.$$

We replace $\boldsymbol{u}, \bar{\boldsymbol{u}}$, and $\bar{\bar{\boldsymbol{u}}}$ by their corresponding consistent estimates $\hat{\boldsymbol{u}}, \hat{\bar{\boldsymbol{u}}}$, and $\hat{\bar{\bar{\boldsymbol{u}}}}$. In our case, we replace them by the residuals from a standard HT estimator, ignoring the spatial correlation. This is a consistent but not efficient estimator in the presence of spatial autocorrelation. Kapoor et al. (2007) used standard OLS residuals for their SRE estimator. This estimator is consistent but not efficient in that context. In our case, it would be inconsistent due to the endogeneity of the regressors and the individual effects.

Following Kapoor et al. (2007), we first estimate an initial $\tilde{\rho}$ using only three of the six moment conditions where each moment condition is weighted equally. Define $\boldsymbol{\gamma}_3$ and $\boldsymbol{\alpha}_3$ as the 3×1 subvectors containing the first three elements of $\boldsymbol{\gamma}$ and $\boldsymbol{\alpha}$, respectively, and $\boldsymbol{\Gamma}_3$ as the 3×3 submatrix containing the upper left block of elements of $\boldsymbol{\Gamma}$. Now, solve the first three of the above moment conditions for

$$\tilde{\rho} = \arg \min_{\sigma_v^2 \in S_v, \rho \in S_\rho} [(\hat{\boldsymbol{\gamma}}_3 - \hat{\boldsymbol{\Gamma}}_3 \hat{\boldsymbol{\alpha}}_3)' \mathbf{I}_3 (\hat{\boldsymbol{\gamma}}_3 - \hat{\boldsymbol{\Gamma}}_3 \hat{\boldsymbol{\alpha}}_3)] \quad (5)$$

where S_v and S_ρ denote the respective admissible parameter spaces of σ_v^2 and ρ (see Kapoor et al., 2007, for details). We can estimate $\tilde{\rho}$ and $\tilde{\sigma}_v^2$ consistently by nonlinear least squares. With these estimates at hand, $\tilde{\sigma}_1^2$ can be solved explicitly from the fourth moment condition as $\tilde{\sigma}_1^2 = \frac{1}{N} \hat{\boldsymbol{u}}' \mathbf{P} \hat{\boldsymbol{u}} - \frac{2\tilde{\rho}}{N} \hat{\boldsymbol{u}}' \mathbf{P} \hat{\bar{\boldsymbol{u}}} + \frac{\tilde{\rho}^2}{N} \hat{\bar{\boldsymbol{u}}}' \mathbf{P} \hat{\bar{\boldsymbol{u}}}$. In a second step, following Kapoor et al. (2007) again, we apply a generalized method of moments estimator using all six moment conditions and the weighting matrix $\hat{\boldsymbol{\Upsilon}}$

$$\hat{\boldsymbol{\Upsilon}} = \begin{pmatrix} \frac{1}{T-1} \tilde{\sigma}_v^4 & 0 \\ 0 & \tilde{\sigma}_1^4 \end{pmatrix} \otimes \mathbf{I}_3 \quad (6)$$

Applying nonlinear least squares to

$$\hat{\rho} = \arg \min_{\sigma_v^2 \in S_v, \sigma_1^2 \in S_1, \rho \in S_\rho} [(\hat{\boldsymbol{\gamma}} - \hat{\boldsymbol{\Gamma}} \hat{\boldsymbol{\alpha}})' \hat{\boldsymbol{\Upsilon}} (\hat{\boldsymbol{\gamma}} - \hat{\boldsymbol{\Gamma}} \hat{\boldsymbol{\alpha}})] \quad (7)$$

yields an estimate for ρ.[3] All of the subsequent Monte Carlo simulations are based on the latter procedure. Cliff and Ord type spatial panel data estimators – such as the aforementioned SFE, SHT, and SRE – apply the spatial Cochrane-Orcutt transformation $\boldsymbol{v}_* = (\mathbf{I}_T \otimes [\mathbf{I}_N - \hat{\rho} \mathbf{W}]) \boldsymbol{v}$ to any variable $\boldsymbol{v}$ of size $NT \times 1$ in the model in order to avoid efficiency losses from spatial autocorrelation in the disturbances.[4] Moreover, error components type spatial estimators such as SHT or SRE then transform $\boldsymbol{v}_*$ to obtain $\boldsymbol{v}_{**} = \hat{\sigma}_v \hat{\boldsymbol{\Omega}}^{-1/2} \boldsymbol{v}_*$ with $\boldsymbol{\Omega} = E(\boldsymbol{\varepsilon}\boldsymbol{\varepsilon}')$ and $\hat{\sigma}_v \hat{\boldsymbol{\Omega}}^{-1/2} = \mathbf{Q} + \frac{\hat{\sigma}_v}{\hat{\sigma}_1} \mathbf{P}$. Note that the within counterpart to the SFE estimator replaces $\hat{\sigma}_v \hat{\boldsymbol{\Omega}}^{-1/2}$ by $\mathbf{Q}$ to obtain $\boldsymbol{v}_{**}$.

Besides the aforementioned estimators, we additionally consider the performance of a SPT estimator that decides between SFE, SRE, and SHT in the spirit of Baltagi et al. (2003) but allowing for spatial correlation. This estimator is based on two Hausman test statistics: a Hausman test of SRE vs. SFE and a Hausman–Taylor over-identification test of SHT vs. SFE. If both tests are rejected, then SPT reverts to SFE. If the Hausman test is not rejected, then SPT reverts to SRE. If the first Hausman test is rejected but the Hausman-Taylor over-identification test is not rejected, then SPT reverts to SHT.

MONTE CARLO ANALYSIS

Design

For an assessment of the various estimators of the SHT model including the SPT estimator in small samples, we follow a design which is similar to the one in Baltagi et al. (2003), but we allow for spatial correlation

$$\boldsymbol{y}_t = \mathbf{X}_{U1t}\beta_1 + \mathbf{X}_{U2t}\beta_2 + \mathbf{X}_{Ct}\beta_3 + \mathbf{Z}_U\gamma_1 + \mathbf{Z}_C\gamma_2 + \boldsymbol{u}_t \tag{8}$$

$$\boldsymbol{u}_t = \rho\mathbf{W}\boldsymbol{u}_t + \boldsymbol{\varepsilon}_t, \quad \boldsymbol{\varepsilon}_t = \boldsymbol{\mu} + \boldsymbol{v}_t \tag{9}$$

where $\mu_i \sim IIN(0, \sigma_\mu^2), v_{it} \sim IIN(0, \sigma_v^2)$, and $\mathbf{W}$ is specified as an $N \times N$ nonstochastic, row-normalized spatial weights matrix which is based on the unnormalized counterpart $\mathbf{W}_0$. The latter exhibits zero diagonal elements and otherwise a three-before-and-three-behind neighborhood structure as specified in the appendix. Here, $\boldsymbol{y}_t = (y_{1t}, \ldots, y_{Nt})'$ is an $N \times 1$ vector of observations on the dependent variable at time t, $\boldsymbol{X}_{U1t}$ and $\boldsymbol{X}_{U2t}$ are two $N \times 1$ vectors of time-varying regressors which are *uncorrelated* with $\boldsymbol{\mu}$, the $N \times 1$ vector $\boldsymbol{X}_{Ct}$ is *correlated* with $\boldsymbol{\mu}$, and $\boldsymbol{Z}_U$ is an $N \times 1$ time-invariant regressor which is uncorrelated with $\boldsymbol{\mu}$, while $\boldsymbol{Z}_C$ is an $N \times 1$ time-invariant regressor which is correlated with $\boldsymbol{\mu}$.

We specify the covariates as follows:

- $\boldsymbol{X}_{U1t} = 0.7\boldsymbol{X}_{U1,t-1} + \boldsymbol{\delta} + \boldsymbol{\zeta}_t$, where $\boldsymbol{\delta}$ is time-invariant and uniform on $[-2, 2]$ and $\boldsymbol{\zeta}_t$ is time-variant and uniform on $[-2, 2]$; the initial value $\boldsymbol{X}_{U1,1}$ is defined as $\boldsymbol{X}_{U1,1} = \boldsymbol{\zeta}_1/(1 - 0.7^2)^{1/2} + \boldsymbol{\delta}/(1 - 0.7)$.
- $\boldsymbol{X}_{U2t} = 0.7\boldsymbol{X}_{U2,t-1} + \boldsymbol{\eta} + \boldsymbol{\kappa}_t$, where $\boldsymbol{\eta}$ is time-invariant and uniform on $[-2, 2]$ and $\boldsymbol{\kappa}_t$ is time-variant and uniform on $[-2, 2]$; the initial value $\boldsymbol{X}_{U2,1}$ is defined as $\boldsymbol{X}_{U2,1} = \boldsymbol{\kappa}_1/(1 - 0.7^2)^{1/2} + \boldsymbol{\eta}/(1 - 0.7)$.
- $\boldsymbol{Z}_U = \boldsymbol{\iota}_N$, and, hence, it is a constant as in Baltagi et al. (2003).

Regarding the regression coefficients, we assume $\beta_1 = \beta_2 = \beta_3 = \gamma_1 = \gamma_2 = 1$. We allow for different intensities of spatial autocorrelation and use $\rho \in \{0; 0.2; 0.4; 0.6\}$.

We consider three different sample sizes $N \in \{100; 200; 300\}$ and two time horizons $T \in \{3; 5\}$. We generally set $\sigma_\mu^2 + \sigma_\nu^2 = 3$ but allow the proportion of total variance due to the individual effect to vary by way of $\phi \equiv \frac{\sigma_\mu^2}{\sigma_\mu^2 + \sigma_\nu^2} \in \{0; 0.25; 0.50; 0.75\}$.

In what follows, we consider an (S)HT world where both $\boldsymbol{X}_{Ct}$ and $\boldsymbol{Z}_C$ are correlated with the individual effect $\boldsymbol{\mu}$, and we allow the intensity of this correlation to vary.

- $\boldsymbol{X}_{Ct} = 0.7\boldsymbol{X}_{C,t-1} + \boldsymbol{\vartheta} + \boldsymbol{\lambda}_t$, where $\boldsymbol{\lambda}_t$ is time-variant and uniform on $[-2, 2]$ and the initial value $\boldsymbol{X}_{C,1}$ is defined as $\boldsymbol{X}_{C,1} = \boldsymbol{\lambda}_1/(1 - 0.7^2)^{1/2} + \boldsymbol{\vartheta}/(1 - 0.7)$.

  $\boldsymbol{\vartheta} = \frac{\psi\boldsymbol{\mu} + (1-\psi)\boldsymbol{\theta}}{\sqrt{\psi^2 + (1-\psi)^2}}$ with $\mu_i \sim IIN(0, \sigma_\mu^2)$, $\theta_i \sim IIN(0, \sigma_\theta^2)$, and μ_i and θ_i are independent of each other. When σ_θ^2 equals σ_μ^2, which is what we use in this chapter, then $\vartheta_i \sim IIN(0, \sigma_\mu^2)$. The parameter ψ accounts for the correlation between $\boldsymbol{X}_{Ct}$ and $\boldsymbol{Z}_C$ with the individual effect $\boldsymbol{\mu}$. We allow the intensity to vary and consider $\psi \in \{0; 0.10; 0.25; 0.50; 0.75; 1\}$. Obviously, the case where $\psi = 0$ corresponds to an (S)RE world where the use of instrumental variables unnecessarily reduces efficiency and induces a small sample bias.
- $\boldsymbol{Z}_C = \boldsymbol{\delta} + \boldsymbol{\eta} + \boldsymbol{\vartheta} + \xi$, where ξ is uniform on $[-2, 2]$ and $\boldsymbol{\vartheta}$ is defined above.

In the next section, we focus on the bias, RMSE, and the size of tests for $H_0^a : \beta_3 = 1$, and $H_0^b : \gamma_2 = 1$ at the 5% significance level. We focus on β_3 and γ_2, since they are the coefficients of the endogenous time-variant regressor, and the endogenous time-invariant regressor, respectively.

Results for Bias and RMSE

Table 1 gives the bias, RMSE, and size of tests for $H_0^a : \beta_3 = 1$, and $H_0^b : \gamma_2 = 1$ at the 5% significance level. This is done for $(N = 100, T = 3)$ in an SHT world where $\psi = 1$ in the upper panel of Table 1 and an SRE world where $\psi = 0$ in the lower panel of Table 1. Consider the SHT world configuration where $\rho = 0$ (no spatial correlation) and increasing heterogeneity through $\phi \in \{0; 0.25; 0.50; 0.75\}$ in Table 1. Obviously, with correlation between some regressors and the individual effects, OLS and SRE are consistent only if $\phi = 0$ (no random individual effects correlated with the regressors). If $\phi > 0$, the endogeneity of $\boldsymbol{X}_{Ct}$ and $\boldsymbol{Z}_C$ will lead to parameter

Table 1. Bias, RMSE, and 5% Test Size, $N = 100$ and $T = 3$.

		OLS						Fixed Effects (SFE)			Random Effects (SRE)						Hausman-Taylor (SHT)						Pretest (SPT)					
		β_3			γ_2			β_3			β_3			γ_2			β_3			γ_2			β_3			γ_2		
ρ	ϕ	Bias	RMSE	5% size	Bias	RMSE	5% size	Bias	RMSE	5% size	Bias	RMSE	5% size	Bias	RMSE	5% size	Bias	RMSE	5% size	Bias	RMSE	5% size	Bias	RMSE	5% size	Bias	RMSE	5% size
Estimators for HT World with $\psi = 1$																												
0	0	0.001	0.145	3.9	0.000	0.176	4.8	0.003	0.144	3.7	0.000	0.144	3.3	0.000	0.177	4.8	0.003	0.143	4.4	−0.008	0.151	5.2	0.000	0.144	3.3	0.000	0.176	4.8
	0.25	0.205	0.971	100	0.096	0.289	31.3	−0.006	0.155	6	0.202	0.947	100	0.098	0.298	29.9	−0.005	0.155	6.1	0.006	0.152	5.5	0.124	0.648	64.6	0.066	0.246	21.4
	0.5	0.231	1.492	100	0.107	0.344	49.2	−0.004	0.155	6	0.227	1.444	100	0.111	0.364	46.5	−0.003	0.156	6.3	0.002	0.144	5	0.085	0.650	42.3	0.047	0.234	21.9
	0.75	0.241	2.246	100	0.111	0.419	74.1	−0.003	0.155	6	0.235	2.096	100	0.121	0.493	74.7	−0.001	0.156	6.1	−0.002	0.135	4.5	0.014	0.276	11.9	0.006	0.158	9.2
0.2	0	0.001	0.140	3.7	0.000	0.173	4.8	0.003	0.146	3.7	0.000	0.145	3.8	0.000	0.178	5	0.003	0.145	4.1	−0.007	0.152	5.2	0.000	0.145	3.8	−0.001	0.177	5.0
	0.25	0.206	0.965	100	0.096	0.291	30.9	−0.005	0.150	5.8	0.201	0.930	100	0.098	0.300	29.3	−0.005	0.155	6.4	0.006	0.153	5.5	0.125	0.646	65.6	0.066	0.250	21.1
	0.5	0.232	1.480	100	0.107	0.347	48.4	−0.004	0.150	5.8	0.225	1.487	100	0.111	0.372	47.5	−0.003	0.155	6.5	0.002	0.144	5.2	0.086	0.673	42.8	0.047	0.238	22.6
	0.75	0.242	2.225	100	0.111	0.430	72.9	−0.003	0.150	5.8	0.232	2.068	100	0.121	0.496	73.4	−0.001	0.153	6.1	−0.002	0.134	4.5	0.015	0.285	12.6	0.007	0.161	9.6
0.4	0	0.001	0.135	3.3	0.001	0.171	4.9	0.002	0.149	3.9	0.000	0.147	3.9	−0.001	0.179	5.3	0.002	0.147	4.3	−0.006	0.155	5.4	0.001	0.147	3.9	−0.001	0.178	5.3
	0.25	0.211	0.890	100	0.098	0.286	30.1	−0.004	0.143	5.8	0.197	0.915	100	0.096	0.298	29.3	−0.004	0.153	5.9	0.006	0.152	5.7	0.125	0.644	66.5	0.066	0.250	21.4
	0.5	0.238	1.390	100	0.110	0.336	44.6	−0.004	0.143	5.8	0.220	1.472	100	0.110	0.369	46.2	−0.002	0.153	5.9	0.001	0.145	4.6	0.089	0.690	44.3	0.048	0.240	22.3
	0.75	0.248	2.096	100	0.114	0.410	69.1	−0.002	0.143	5.8	0.226	1.947	100	0.121	0.490	71.9	0.000	0.148	5.7	−0.003	0.134	4.7	0.016	0.280	12.7	0.007	0.162	9.9
0.6	0	0.001	0.130	3.7	0.001	0.171	4.8	0.002	0.153	4	0.000	0.151	3.7	−0.001	0.178	5	0.002	0.151	5	−0.004	0.158	5.1	0.001	0.151	3.7	−0.001	0.177	5.0
	0.25	0.223	0.745	100	0.102	0.250	26.4	−0.004	0.136	5.6	0.191	0.902	100	0.094	0.298	29.1	−0.004	0.147	5.6	0.005	0.152	4.9	0.123	0.640	67.2	0.065	0.250	21.1
	0.5	0.252	1.156	100	0.115	0.286	38.6	−0.003	0.136	5.6	0.213	1.360	100	0.108	0.368	44	−0.002	0.144	5.8	0.001	0.145	4.5	0.089	0.662	45.9	0.049	0.244	22.1
	0.75	0.263	1.483	100	0.120	0.317	57.9	−0.002	0.136	5.6	0.217	1.780	100	0.121	0.475	68.4	0.000	0.141	5.8	−0.004	0.134	4.7	0.019	0.290	14.4	0.008	0.166	10.7

Table 1. *(Continued)*

		OLS						Fixed Effects (SFE)			Random Effects (SRE)						Hausman-Taylor (SHT)						Pretest (SPT)					
		β_3			γ_2			β_3			β_3			γ_2			β_3			γ_2			β_3			γ_2		
ρ	ϕ	Bias	RMSE	5% size	Bias	RMSE	5% size	Bias	RMSE	5% size	Bias	RMSE	5% size	Bias	RMSE	5% size	Bias	RMSE	5% size	Bias	RMSE	5% size	Bias	RMSE	5% size	Bias	RMSE	5% size
Estimators for RE World with $\psi = 0$																												
0	0	0.001	0.145	3.9	0.000	0.176	4.8	0.003	0.144	3.7	0.000	0.144	3.3	0.000	0.177	4.8	0.003	0.143	4.4	−0.008	0.151	5.2	0.000	0.144	3.3	0.000	0.176	4.8
	0.25	0.002	0.147	10.1	0.000	0.165	10.9	−0.006	0.155	6	0.001	0.150	5.3	0.001	0.157	4.4	−0.006	0.154	5.7	0.007	0.166	4.8	0.001	0.150	5.3	0.001	0.158	4.4
	0.5	0.002	0.146	14.8	−0.001	0.161	15.8	−0.004	0.155	6	0.001	0.137	4.5	0.001	0.152	5.3	−0.005	0.154	5.6	0.004	0.160	4.5	0.001	0.138	4.6	0.001	0.152	5.3
	0.75	0.003	0.153	19.4	−0.003	0.155	20	−0.003	0.155	6	0.001	0.128	4.7	0.000	0.150	5.5	−0.004	0.153	5.4	0.000	0.151	4.2	0.000	0.129	4.8	0.000	0.150	5.4
0.2	0	0.001	0.140	3.7	0.000	0.173	4.8	0.003	0.146	3.7	0.000	0.145	3.8	0.000	0.178	5	0.003	0.145	4.1	−0.007	0.152	5.2	0.000	0.145	3.8	−0.001	0.177	5.0
	0.25	0.002	0.148	9.6	0.000	0.162	11.3	−0.005	0.150	5.8	0.002	0.149	4.6	0.001	0.156	4.2	−0.006	0.154	5.8	0.008	0.163	5.4	0.001	0.149	4.7	0.002	0.156	4.3
	0.5	0.002	0.147	14.7	−0.002	0.158	16.4	−0.004	0.150	5.8	0.001	0.133	4.8	0.001	0.149	4.6	−0.005	0.153	5.5	0.004	0.156	4.4	0.001	0.134	4.8	0.001	0.149	4.6
	0.75	0.003	0.154	19.3	−0.003	0.154	20.4	−0.003	0.150	5.8	0.001	0.123	4.8	0.000	0.151	5	−0.003	0.152	5.3	0.001	0.151	4.4	0.001	0.125	4.8	0.000	0.151	5.0
0.4	0	0.001	0.135	3.3	0.001	0.171	4.9	0.002	0.149	3.9	0.000	0.147	3.9	−0.001	0.179	5.3	0.002	0.147	4.3	−0.006	0.155	5.4	0.001	0.147	3.9	−0.001	0.178	5.3
	0.25	0.002	0.150	9.4	0.000	0.160	10.9	−0.004	0.143	5.8	0.002	0.149	4.8	0.001	0.155	4	−0.005	0.153	5.6	0.008	0.161	5.1	0.001	0.149	4.9	0.002	0.155	4.0
	0.5	0.003	0.149	14.2	−0.002	0.156	16.6	−0.004	0.143	5.8	0.001	0.131	4.5	0.001	0.147	4.9	−0.004	0.153	5.3	0.005	0.155	4.4	0.001	0.132	4.6	0.001	0.147	4.9
	0.75	0.003	0.155	20	−0.003	0.153	20.4	−0.002	0.143	5.8	0.001	0.120	5.1	0.000	0.153	4.5	−0.003	0.151	5.5	0.001	0.152	4.6	0.001	0.122	5.1	0.000	0.153	4.5
0.6	0	0.001	0.130	3.7	0.001	0.171	4.8	0.002	0.153	4	0.000	0.151	3.7	−0.001	0.178	5	0.002	0.151	5	−0.004	0.158	5.1	0.001	0.151	3.7	−0.001	0.177	5.0
	0.25	0.002	0.151	9.5	−0.001	0.161	10.3	−0.004	0.136	5.6	0.002	0.151	5.3	0.002	0.155	3.7	−0.005	0.147	5.7	0.008	0.161	5.2	0.001	0.150	5.3	0.002	0.155	3.8
	0.5	0.003	0.150	14.6	−0.003	0.157	16.7	−0.003	0.136	5.6	0.001	0.130	4.4	0.001	0.146	4.4	−0.004	0.146	5.7	0.005	0.155	4.5	0.001	0.131	4.5	0.001	0.146	4.4
	0.75	0.003	0.156	20.6	−0.004	0.157	21.4	−0.002	0.136	5.6	0.001	0.118	4.7	0.000	0.151	4.5	−0.003	0.143	5.9	0.001	0.152	4	0.001	0.119	4.8	0.000	0.151	4.5

bias. Note that the bias and RMSE for OLS and SRE increase with ϕ and the size of the tests for $H_0^a : \beta_3 = 1$ and $H_0^b : \gamma_2 = 1$ is unacceptable, rejecting the null when true up to 100% of the time, especially when $\phi > 0.5$. This confirms the results in Baltagi et al. (2003). SFE performs well for β_3 but does not yield estimates for γ_2. The SHT estimator yields a low RMSE for both β_3 and γ_2.

If $\rho \neq 0$ (spatial correlation), OLS is consistent but inefficient at $\phi = 0$. Of course, OLS is inconsistent if $\phi > 0$ with endogenous regressors. SHT delivers consistent and asymptotically efficient estimates of both β_3 and γ_2 at $\phi > 0$ and $\rho \neq 0$, while SFE yields consistent estimates for β_3 only. In Table 1, for $\rho = 0.6$ and $\phi = 0.5$, the RMSE of β_3 for OLS is 1.156 compared to 0.136 for SFE, 1.360 for SRE, and 0.144 for SHT. The corresponding RMSE of γ_2 for OLS is 0.286 compared to 0.368 for SRE and 0.145 for SHT. Tests of hypotheses are misleading with OLS and SRE unless $\phi = 0$ but are properly sized for SFE and SHT at $\phi > 0$ and $\rho \neq 0$.

In an SRE world as in the lower panel of Table 1, there is no correlation between the regressors and the individual effects ($\psi = 0$). In this case, the SRE estimator gives a lower RMSE for β_3 than OLS, SFE, or SHT, especially with $\phi > 0$ and as ϕ increases. This is also true for γ_2 when comparing SRE to OLS or SHT. However, SHT is not far behind SRE in RMSE performance even if the true world is SRE.

In Table 2, we hold N constant at 100 and increase T from 3 to 5, while in Table 3, we hold T constant at 3 but increase N from 100 to 300. The purpose of these tables is to see how different sample sizes and time periods affect the performance of the estimators. By and large, we observe the same results as in Table 1, but with different bias and RMSE magnitudes. In general, the SHT and SFE estimators perform best in an SHT world, and the SRE and SHT estimators perform best in an SRE world in terms of RMSE.

In Tables 1–3, we considered the two cases of $\psi = 0$ or 1. In Table 4, we repeat the results from those tables for two alternative values of spatial autocorrelation, $\rho \in \{0.2, 0.4\}$, and for a sample size of $N = 100$ and $T = 3$ but at values of $\psi \in \{0, 0.1, 0.25, 0.5, 1\}$. The purpose of this table is to illustrate how the performance of the estimators changes with the degree of correlation between the regressors and the individual effects. In fact, the average correlation between $\boldsymbol{\mu}$ and $\boldsymbol{X}_{Ct}$ and $\boldsymbol{Z}_C$ amounts to 0.928 and 0.519, respectively, at a true value of $\psi = 1$ and $\phi = 0.5$ and to 0.652 and 0.365, respectively, at a true value of $\psi = 0.5$ and $\phi = 0.5$. The results suggest that the SHT estimator outperforms the SRE and OLS estimators as ψ increases.

Table 2. Bias, RMSE, and 5% Test Size, $N=100$ and $T=5$.

		OLS						Fixed Effects (SFE)			Random Effects (SRE)						Hausman-Taylor (SHT)						Pretest (SPT)					
		β_3			γ_2			β_3			β_3			γ_2			β_3			γ_2			β_3			γ_2		
ρ	ϕ	Bias	RMSE	5% size	Bias	RMSE	5% size	Bias	RMSE	5% size	Bias	RMSE	5% size	Bias	RMSE	5% size	Bias	RMSE	5% size	Bias	RMSE	5% size	Bias	RMSE	5% size	Bias	RMSE	5% size
		Estimators for HT World with $\psi=1$																										
0	0	−0.003	0.158	4.8	0.002	0.163	4.8	−0.006	0.152	4.7	−0.003	0.159	5	0.002	0.162	4.9	−0.006	0.153	5.1	−0.002	0.159	5.2	−0.003	0.159	5.0	0.002	0.162	4.9
	0.25	0.205	1.209	100	0.095	0.311	46.3	0.000	0.164	4.9	0.199	1.180	100	0.100	0.318	44.2	0.001	0.166	5	0.000	0.145	4	0.041	0.370	24.1	0.022	0.182	12.6
	0.5	0.231	1.822	100	0.107	0.381	70.7	0.000	0.164	4.9	0.223	1.703	100	0.116	0.413	69.8	0.002	0.165	5.1	0.000	0.146	4.4	0.008	0.211	7.9	0.004	0.154	6.5
	0.75	0.241	2.609	100	0.111	0.478	90.6	0.000	0.164	4.9	0.228	2.239	100	0.131	0.568	94.3	0.002	0.165	5.1	0.000	0.121	5.6	0.002	0.165	5.1	0.000	0.121	5.6
0.2	0	−0.003	0.157	4.9	0.002	0.162	4.4	−0.006	0.153	4.7	−0.003	0.160	5.3	0.002	0.162	5.1	−0.006	0.157	5	−0.002	0.161	5.1	−0.003	0.159	5.3	0.002	0.162	5.1
	0.25	0.206	1.240	100	0.096	0.290	46.3	−0.001	0.162	4.9	0.197	1.192	100	0.099	0.321	44.1	0.001	0.162	5.4	0.000	0.148	3.6	0.040	0.368	24.3	0.021	0.185	12.2
	0.5	0.232	1.993	100	0.108	0.344	69.4	−0.001	0.162	4.9	0.221	1.683	100	0.116	0.413	69.3	0.001	0.161	5.3	−0.001	0.142	4.6	0.009	0.217	8.8	0.004	0.152	7.2
	0.75	0.242	2.733	100	0.112	0.414	90.4	0.000	0.162	4.9	0.225	2.194	100	0.132	0.568	94.2	0.002	0.161	5.3	−0.001	0.117	4.9	0.002	0.161	5.3	−0.001	0.117	4.9
0.4	0	−0.003	0.158	4.5	0.002	0.164	4	−0.005	0.149	4.6	−0.002	0.161	5.2	0.002	0.160	5.1	−0.005	0.157	4.4	−0.002	0.163	4.7	−0.003	0.161	5.2	0.002	0.160	5.1
	0.25	0.211	1.224	100	0.099	0.265	45.2	−0.001	0.158	5	0.193	1.168	100	0.098	0.327	43.2	0.000	0.158	5.5	−0.001	0.152	3.8	0.040	0.366	24.9	0.021	0.190	12.3
	0.5	0.237	1.950	100	0.111	0.303	67.8	−0.001	0.158	5	0.215	1.649	100	0.116	0.423	68.7	0.001	0.157	5.6	−0.002	0.138	4.2	0.010	0.218	9.4	0.004	0.150	7.0
	0.75	0.248	2.487	100	0.115	0.351	85.5	−0.001	0.158	5	0.217	2.109	100	0.135	0.591	93.1	0.002	0.158	5.4	−0.002	0.114	5	0.001	0.158	5.4	−0.002	0.114	5.0
0.6	0	−0.004	0.160	4.6	0.002	0.166	4.2	−0.005	0.147	4.5	−0.002	0.162	5.1	0.002	0.159	4.8	−0.005	0.159	4.7	−0.002	0.162	5.3	−0.002	0.162	5.1	0.002	0.159	4.8
	0.25	0.223	1.136	100	0.105	0.234	41.1	−0.001	0.155	5	0.186	1.127	100	0.096	0.335	41.7	0.000	0.155	5.1	−0.001	0.153	4.1	0.041	0.373	26.4	0.022	0.196	12.9
	0.5	0.251	1.520	100	0.118	0.259	60.7	−0.001	0.155	5	0.206	1.600	100	0.115	0.441	66.8	0.001	0.154	4.9	−0.002	0.135	4	0.011	0.223	9.5	0.004	0.151	7.2
	0.75	0.262	1.819	100	0.123	0.290	74.9	−0.001	0.155	5	0.205	1.965	100	0.138	0.600	93.1	0.001	0.154	5.3	−0.003	0.111	4.7	0.001	0.154	5.3	−0.003	0.111	4.7

Table 2. *(Continued)*

		OLS						Fixed Effects (SFE)			Random Effects (SRE)						Hausman-Taylor (SHT)						Pretest (SPT)					
		β_3			γ_2			β_3			β_3			γ_2			β_3			γ_2			β_3			γ_2		
ρ	ϕ	Bias	RMSE	5% size	Bias	RMSE	5% size	Bias	RMSE	5% size	Bias	RMSE	5% size	Bias	RMSE	5% size	Bias	RMSE	5% size	Bias	RMSE	5% size	Bias	RMSE	5% size	Bias	RMSE	5% size
														Estimators for RE World with $\psi = 0$														
0	0	0.002	0.131	4.4	0.001	0.159	4.9	0.000	0.154	4.6	0.002	0.131	4.4	0.001	0.155	4.8	0.000	0.154	4.7	0.005	0.150	4.6	0.002	0.132	4.4	0.002	0.155	4.8
	0.25	0.000	0.157	14.8	−0.002	0.157	15.8	0.001	0.156	5.5	0.000	0.132	6.2	−0.003	0.154	5.7	0.001	0.155	5.7	−0.006	0.161	5.4	0.000	0.133	6.2	−0.003	0.154	5.7
	0.5	0.000	0.156	23.4	−0.003	0.151	24	0.001	0.156	5.5	0.000	0.129	5.8	−0.004	0.150	5.1	0.001	0.156	5.9	−0.006	0.162	5	0.000	0.130	5.8	−0.004	0.151	5.1
	0.75	0.000	0.157	29.6	−0.004	0.152	31.1	0.000	0.156	5.5	0.000	0.132	5.5	−0.005	0.152	5.5	0.000	0.156	5.9	−0.005	0.146	4.9	0.000	0.134	5.5	−0.005	0.152	5.5
0.2	0	0.002	0.130	4	0.001	0.153	4.6	0.000	0.152	4.6	0.002	0.133	4.3	0.002	0.163	4.6	0.000	0.152	5	0.006	0.151	4.9	0.002	0.134	4.3	0.002	0.162	4.6
	0.25	0.000	0.156	15.5	−0.002	0.154	15.6	0.001	0.153	5.5	0.000	0.133	6.1	−0.003	0.158	5.7	0.001	0.153	5.8	−0.006	0.161	5.2	0.000	0.134	6.1	−0.003	0.158	5.7
	0.5	0.000	0.154	22.9	−0.003	0.148	24.6	0.001	0.153	5.5	0.000	0.130	5.7	−0.004	0.151	4.9	0.001	0.153	5.8	−0.006	0.161	5.2	0.000	0.131	5.7	−0.004	0.152	4.9
	0.75	0.000	0.153	29.6	−0.004	0.149	31.9	0.000	0.153	5.5	0.000	0.133	5.3	−0.005	0.152	5.5	0.000	0.153	5.9	−0.005	0.148	4.7	0.000	0.134	5.3	−0.005	0.152	5.5
0.4	0	0.002	0.130	4.6	0.001	0.149	4.8	0.000	0.150	4.6	0.002	0.135	4.3	0.002	0.164	4.4	0.000	0.150	5	0.007	0.153	4.7	0.002	0.136	4.3	0.002	0.164	4.4
	0.25	0.000	0.156	15.7	−0.002	0.151	15.7	0.001	0.152	5.5	0.000	0.134	5.7	−0.003	0.160	5.7	0.001	0.151	5.9	−0.005	0.162	5.2	0.000	0.135	5.7	−0.003	0.161	5.7
	0.5	0.000	0.152	23.3	−0.003	0.146	23.8	0.001	0.152	5.5	0.000	0.132	5.4	−0.004	0.153	4.9	0.001	0.151	5.7	−0.005	0.158	5.2	0.000	0.133	5.4	−0.004	0.153	4.9
	0.75	0.001	0.150	29.3	−0.003	0.147	32.8	0.001	0.152	5.5	0.000	0.132	5.1	−0.005	0.152	5	0.001	0.152	5.8	−0.005	0.150	4.4	0.000	0.133	5.1	−0.005	0.152	5.0
0.6	0	0.002	0.134	4.7	0.000	0.138	4.4	0.000	0.150	4.8	0.002	0.140	4.1	0.002	0.161	4.3	0.000	0.150	5.1	0.007	0.153	4.8	0.001	0.140	4.2	0.002	0.161	4.3
	0.25	0.000	0.157	14.8	−0.001	0.147	16	0.001	0.152	5.5	0.000	0.136	5.5	−0.003	0.161	5.4	0.001	0.151	5.8	−0.005	0.162	5.1	0.000	0.137	5.5	−0.003	0.161	5.4
	0.5	0.000	0.150	22.2	−0.002	0.144	23.6	0.001	0.152	5.5	0.000	0.132	5.1	−0.004	0.151	5	0.001	0.151	5.9	−0.005	0.153	5.1	0.000	0.133	5.1	−0.004	0.151	5.0
	0.75	0.001	0.145	27.9	−0.003	0.143	32	0.001	0.152	5.5	0.000	0.132	4.9	−0.005	0.150	5.1	0.001	0.151	5.8	−0.005	0.148	4.1	0.000	0.133	4.9	−0.005	0.150	5.1

Table 3. Bias, RMSE, and 5% Test Size, $N = 300$ and $T = 3$.

		OLS						Fixed Effects (SFE)			Random Effects (SRE)						Hausman-Taylor (SHT)						Pretest (SPT)					
		β_3			γ_2			β_3			β_3			γ_2			β_3			γ_2			β_3			γ_2		
ρ	ϕ	Bias	RMSE	5% size	Bias	RMSE	5% size	Bias	RMSE	5% size	Bias	RMSE	5% size	Bias	RMSE	5% size	Bias	RMSE	5% size	Bias	RMSE	5% size	Bias	RMSE	5% size	Bias	RMSE	5% size
														Estimators for HT World with $\psi = 1$														
0	0	−0.001	0.165	4.8	0.001	0.176	6.8	−0.002	0.167	6.3	−0.001	0.166	4.9	0.001	0.176	5.9	−0.002	0.168	6.5	0.001	0.142	5	−0.001	0.166	5.0	0.001	0.175	5.9
	0.25	0.207	1.615	100	0.095	0.454	71.8	−0.003	0.157	4.8	0.204	1.596	100	0.097	0.477	70.9	−0.002	0.155	5.1	0.003	0.162	5	0.031	0.390	20.5	0.020	0.217	16.7
	0.5	0.232	2.492	100	0.106	0.591	91.5	−0.002	0.157	4.8	0.228	2.496	100	0.110	0.619	91.6	−0.002	0.156	5.1	0.003	0.167	4.5	0.001	0.179	6.0	0.004	0.172	5.4
	0.75	0.242	3.735	100	0.110	0.755	99.7	−0.002	0.157	4.8	0.236	3.558	100	0.120	0.796	99.7	−0.001	0.157	4.9	0.003	0.171	4.5	−0.001	0.157	4.9	0.003	0.171	4.5
0.2	0	−0.001	0.167	4.9	0.001	0.173	6.4	−0.002	0.166	5.7	−0.001	0.167	5.2	0.000	0.177	5.9	−0.002	0.167	5.9	0.000	0.142	5.2	−0.001	0.167	5.2	0.000	0.175	5.9
	0.25	0.208	1.622	100	0.096	0.461	71.6	−0.003	0.152	5.4	0.203	1.585	100	0.096	0.459	70.6	−0.003	0.151	5.7	0.003	0.160	4.9	0.031	0.385	21.1	0.019	0.212	16.2
	0.5	0.233	2.507	100	0.107	0.583	90.9	−0.002	0.152	5.4	0.227	2.400	100	0.110	0.618	90.3	−0.002	0.152	5.6	0.003	0.160	4.9	0.001	0.176	6.6	0.004	0.165	5.9
	0.75	0.243	3.729	100	0.111	0.746	99.5	−0.002	0.152	5.4	0.233	3.486	100	0.120	0.794	99.7	−0.001	0.152	5.4	0.003	0.162	5.1	−0.001	0.152	5.4	0.003	0.162	5.1
0.4	0	−0.001	0.172	5.5	0.001	0.172	6.2	−0.002	0.167	5.1	−0.001	0.169	5	0.000	0.176	5.4	−0.002	0.167	5.6	−0.001	0.142	5.6	−0.001	0.169	5.0	0.000	0.175	5.4
	0.25	0.214	1.559	100	0.098	0.450	69.5	−0.003	0.149	5.4	0.199	1.534	100	0.094	0.441	69.3	−0.003	0.149	5.8	0.002	0.156	4.8	0.031	0.380	21.5	0.018	0.206	16.1
	0.5	0.240	2.453	100	0.110	0.561	89.5	−0.003	0.149	5.4	0.222	2.317	100	0.108	0.591	89.1	−0.002	0.149	5.7	0.002	0.154	5	0.001	0.179	7.0	0.004	0.160	6.2
	0.75	0.250	3.481	100	0.114	0.649	98.2	−0.002	0.149	5.4	0.227	3.365	100	0.119	0.787	99.6	−0.001	0.149	5.8	0.002	0.155	5.2	−0.001	0.149	5.8	0.002	0.155	5.2
0.6	0	−0.001	0.163	4.9	0.002	0.172	6.4	−0.002	0.167	5.3	−0.001	0.167	5.2	0.000	0.174	4.7	−0.002	0.166	5.7	−0.002	0.142	5.8	−0.001	0.167	5.2	0.000	0.173	4.7
	0.25	0.227	1.473	100	0.105	0.412	64	−0.003	0.147	5.5	0.192	1.500	100	0.091	0.422	66.3	−0.003	0.147	5.8	0.002	0.152	4.7	0.030	0.380	22.0	0.018	0.200	15.8
	0.5	0.255	2.243	100	0.117	0.475	83.1	−0.003	0.147	5.5	0.214	2.284	100	0.105	0.564	87.3	−0.002	0.147	5.8	0.002	0.148	5.5	0.002	0.188	7.6	0.004	0.157	7.1
	0.75	0.265	2.567	100	0.122	0.514	93.8	−0.002	0.147	5.5	0.217	3.357	100	0.118	0.784	99.5	−0.001	0.147	5.7	0.002	0.150	5.2	−0.001	0.147	5.7	0.002	0.150	5.2

Table 3. (*Continued*)

		OLS						Fixed Effects (SFE)			Random Effects (SRE)						Hausman-Taylor (SHT)						Pretest (SPT)					
		β_3			γ_2			β_3			β_3			γ_2			β_3			γ_2			β_3			γ_2		
ρ	ϕ	Bias	RMSE	5% size	Bias	RMSE	5% size	Bias	RMSE	5% size	Bias	RMSE	5% size	Bias	RMSE	5% size	Bias	RMSE	5% size	Bias	RMSE	5% size	Bias	RMSE	5% size	Bias	RMSE	5% size
												Estimators for RE World with $\psi = 0$																
0	0	−0.001	0.165	4.8	0.001	0.176	6.8	−0.002	0.167	6.3	−0.001	0.166	4.9	0.001	0.176	5.9	−0.002	0.168	6.5	0.001	0.142	5	−0.001	0.166	5.0	0.001	0.175	5.9
	0.25	−0.001	0.129	9.8	0.001	0.158	10.9	−0.003	0.157	4.8	−0.001	0.134	5	0.001	0.154	5.8	−0.003	0.157	5.1	0.003	0.162	5.2	−0.001	0.135	5.0	0.001	0.155	5.8
	0.5	−0.001	0.131	15.3	0.000	0.159	15.3	−0.002	0.157	4.8	−0.001	0.139	5.5	0.001	0.160	5.5	−0.002	0.157	5.1	0.003	0.159	4.5	−0.001	0.139	5.5	0.001	0.160	5.5
	0.75	−0.001	0.144	19	0.000	0.160	19.3	−0.002	0.157	4.8	−0.001	0.159	5.4	0.001	0.155	5.7	−0.002	0.157	5	0.003	0.155	4.7	−0.001	0.159	5.4	0.001	0.155	5.7
0.2	0	−0.001	0.167	4.9	0.001	0.173	6.4	−0.002	0.166	5.7	−0.001	0.167	5.2	0.000	0.177	5.9	−0.002	0.167	5.9	0.000	0.142	5.2	−0.001	0.167	5.2	0.000	0.175	5.9
	0.25	−0.001	0.128	9.3	0.001	0.154	11	−0.003	0.152	5.4	−0.001	0.133	5.5	0.001	0.161	5.5	−0.003	0.153	5.7	0.003	0.160	4.7	−0.001	0.134	5.5	0.001	0.161	5.5
	0.5	−0.001	0.129	15.6	0.001	0.154	15.2	−0.002	0.152	5.4	−0.001	0.139	5.6	0.001	0.163	5.2	−0.003	0.153	5.5	0.003	0.156	5	−0.001	0.140	5.6	0.001	0.163	5.2
	0.75	−0.001	0.141	18.8	0.000	0.159	18.9	−0.002	0.152	5.4	−0.001	0.160	5.4	0.001	0.157	5.6	−0.002	0.153	5.6	0.003	0.153	4.7	−0.001	0.159	5.4	0.001	0.156	5.6
0.4	0	−0.001	0.172	5.5	0.001	0.172	6.2	−0.002	0.167	5.1	−0.001	0.169	5	0.000	0.176	5.4	−0.002	0.167	5.6	−0.001	0.142	5.6	−0.001	0.169	5.0	0.000	0.175	5.4
	0.25	−0.001	0.129	9.2	0.001	0.150	11.2	−0.003	0.149	5.4	−0.001	0.133	5.2	0.001	0.168	5.4	−0.003	0.149	5.7	0.003	0.157	4.8	−0.001	0.134	5.2	0.001	0.168	5.4
	0.5	−0.001	0.128	15.9	0.001	0.149	14.9	−0.003	0.149	5.4	−0.001	0.141	5.3	0.001	0.165	5.5	−0.003	0.150	5.7	0.003	0.154	5	−0.001	0.141	5.3	0.001	0.164	5.5
	0.75	−0.001	0.138	20.4	0.001	0.155	19	−0.002	0.149	5.4	−0.002	0.161	5	0.001	0.159	5	−0.002	0.149	5.4	0.003	0.152	4.6	−0.002	0.160	5.0	0.001	0.159	5.0
0.6	0	0.000	0.179	4	0.000	0.138	4	−0.001	0.150	4.1	0.000	0.152	5	0.001	0.150	5.5	−0.001	0.151	4.4	0.010	0.145	4.3	0.000	0.152	5.0	0.001	0.150	5.5
	0.25	0.000	0.163	10.8	0.001	0.137	8.7	−0.002	0.145	5.7	0.000	0.157	6.2	0.001	0.125	3.5	−0.002	0.147	5.6	−0.009	0.150	4.8	0.000	0.156	6.2	0.000	0.125	3.5
	0.5	0.000	0.155	15.8	0.001	0.156	13.9	−0.001	0.145	5.7	0.000	0.151	6.2	0.000	0.134	3.2	−0.001	0.148	5.6	−0.008	0.152	4.7	0.000	0.151	6.2	0.000	0.135	3.3
	0.75	0.000	0.157	22	0.000	0.156	19.6	−0.001	0.145	5.7	0.000	0.152	5.6	0.000	0.152	3.8	−0.001	0.148	5.6	−0.007	0.154	4.2	0.000	0.151	5.6	0.000	0.152	3.8

Table 4. Bias, RMSE, and 5% Test Size, $N = 100$ and $T = 3$, at Different Correlation Levels ψ.

			OLS						Fixed Effects (SFE)			Random Effects (SRE)						Hausman-Taylor (SHT)						Pretest (SPT)					
			β_3			γ_2			β_3			β_3			γ_2			β_3			γ_2			β_3			γ_2		
ρ	ψ	ϕ	Bias	RMSE	5% size	Bias	RMSE	5% size	Bias	RMSE	5% size	Bias	RMSE	5% size	Bias	RMSE	5% size	Bias	RMSE	5% size	Bias	RMSE	5% size	Bias	RMSE	5% size	Bias	RMSE	5% size
0.2	0	0	0.001	0.140	3.7	0.000	0.173	4.8	0.003	0.146	3.7	0.000	0.145	3.8	0.000	0.178	5	0.003	0.145	4.1	−0.007	0.152	5.2	0.000	0.145	3.8	−0.001	0.177	5.0
		0.25	0.002	0.148	9.6	0.000	0.162	11.3	−0.005	0.150	5.8	0.002	0.149	4.6	0.001	0.156	4.2	−0.006	0.154	5.8	0.008	0.163	5.4	0.001	0.149	4.7	0.002	0.156	4.3
		0.5	0.002	0.147	14.7	−0.002	0.158	16.4	−0.004	0.150	5.8	0.001	0.133	4.8	0.001	0.149	4.6	−0.005	0.153	5.5	0.004	0.156	4.4	0.001	0.134	4.8	0.001	0.149	4.6
		0.75	0.003	0.154	19.3	−0.003	0.154	20.4	−0.003	0.150	5.8	0.001	0.123	4.8	0.000	0.151	5	−0.003	0.152	5.3	0.001	0.151	4.4	0.001	0.125	4.8	0.000	0.151	5.0
	0.1	0	−0.003	0.148	5	−0.001	0.163	4.4	0.002	0.165	4.5	−0.003	0.144	4.7	−0.001	0.164	4.7	0.002	0.164	5.2	−0.015	0.144	5.9	−0.002	0.144	4.7	−0.002	0.163	4.7
		0.25	0.024	0.184	17	0.012	0.156	10.7	0.002	0.149	5.2	0.022	0.183	9.7	0.014	0.147	6.5	0.002	0.151	5	0.016	0.167	4.6	0.020	0.181	9.4	0.014	0.148	6.4
		0.5	0.026	0.192	24.3	0.014	0.156	15.6	0.002	0.149	5.2	0.022	0.200	10.6	0.019	0.143	7.3	0.002	0.151	5.1	0.014	0.169	4.5	0.021	0.197	10.3	0.019	0.144	7.2
		0.75	0.027	0.196	30.9	0.015	0.165	21.7	0.001	0.149	5.2	0.019	0.205	9.6	0.026	0.149	7.4	0.001	0.151	5.2	0.010	0.165	4.4	0.018	0.201	9.3	0.025	0.149	7.3
	0.25	0	0.001	0.140	3.7	0.000	0.173	4.8	0.003	0.146	3.7	0.000	0.145	3.8	0.000	0.178	5	0.003	0.145	4.1	−0.007	0.152	5.2	0.000	0.145	3.8	−0.001	0.177	5.0
		0.25	0.067	0.280	47.2	0.030	0.168	12.2	−0.005	0.150	5.8	0.062	0.306	32.1	0.033	0.174	6.8	−0.005	0.154	5.8	0.008	0.161	5.5	0.055	0.291	29.6	0.032	0.173	6.7
		0.5	0.075	0.310	67.4	0.031	0.166	17.6	−0.004	0.150	5.8	0.065	0.306	42.2	0.044	0.172	7.5	−0.004	0.154	5.3	0.004	0.154	4.2	0.057	0.288	37.9	0.040	0.170	7.2
		0.75	0.079	0.340	76	0.031	0.161	21.9	−0.003	0.150	5.8	0.058	0.274	41.7	0.060	0.182	9.6	−0.003	0.153	5.3	0.000	0.145	4.3	0.049	0.256	36.1	0.052	0.177	8.9
	0.5	0	0.001	0.140	3.7	0.000	0.173	4.8	0.003	0.146	3.7	0.000	0.145	3.8	0.000	0.178	5	0.003	0.145	4.1	−0.007	0.152	5.2	0.000	0.145	3.8	−0.001	0.177	5.0
		0.25	0.147	0.686	97.9	0.067	0.211	19.4	−0.005	0.150	5.8	0.139	0.633	95.1	0.071	0.225	16	−0.005	0.155	5.9	0.007	0.159	5.4	0.107	0.526	75.2	0.059	0.212	13.9
		0.5	0.165	0.812	100	0.074	0.213	26.1	−0.004	0.150	5.8	0.150	0.756	99.4	0.090	0.247	21	−0.003	0.155	5.7	0.003	0.148	4.5	0.097	0.547	66.9	0.062	0.215	15.7
		0.75	0.172	0.764	100	0.075	0.204	32	−0.003	0.150	5.8	0.141	0.742	99.6	0.118	0.279	32.6	−0.002	0.153	5.9	−0.001	0.138	4.2	0.056	0.392	43.8	0.050	0.199	16.4
	1	0	0.001	0.140	3.7	0.000	0.173	4.8	0.003	0.146	3.7	0.000	0.145	3.8	0.000	0.178	5	0.003	0.145	4.1	−0.007	0.152	5.2	0.000	0.145	3.8	−0.001	0.177	5.0
		0.25	0.206	0.965	100	0.096	0.291	30.9	−0.005	0.150	5.8	0.201	0.930	100	0.098	0.300	29.3	−0.005	0.155	6.4	0.006	0.153	5.5	0.125	0.646	65.6	0.066	0.250	21.1
		0.5	0.232	1.480	100	0.107	0.347	48.4	−0.004	0.150	5.8	0.225	1.487	100	0.111	0.372	47.5	−0.003	0.155	6.5	0.002	0.144	5.2	0.086	0.673	42.8	0.047	0.238	22.6
		0.75	0.242	2.225	100	0.111	0.430	72.9	−0.003	0.150	5.8	0.232	2.068	100	0.121	0.496	73.4	−0.001	0.153	6.1	−0.002	0.134	4.5	0.015	0.285	12.6	0.007	0.161	9.6

Table 4. *(Continued)*

			OLS						Fixed Effects (SFE)			Random Effects (SRE)						Hausman-Taylor (SHT)						Pretest (SPT)					
			β_3			γ_2			β_3			β_3			γ_2			β_3			γ_2			β_3			γ_2		
ρ	ψ	ϕ	Bias	RMSE	5% size	Bias	RMSE	5% size	Bias	RMSE	5% size	Bias	RMSE	5% size	Bias	RMSE	5% size	Bias	RMSE	5% size	Bias	RMSE	5% size	Bias	RMSE	5% size	Bias	RMSE	5% size
0.4	0	0	0.001	0.135	3.3	0.001	0.171	4.9	0.002	0.149	3.9	0.000	0.147	3.9	−0.001	0.179	5.3	0.002	0.147	4.3	−0.006	0.155	5.4	0.001	0.147	3.9	−0.001	0.178	5.3
		0.25	0.002	0.150	9.4	0.000	0.160	10.9	−0.004	0.143	5.8	0.002	0.149	4.8	0.001	0.155	4	−0.005	0.153	5.6	0.008	0.161	5.1	0.001	0.149	4.9	0.002	0.155	4.0
		0.5	0.003	0.149	14.2	−0.002	0.156	16.6	−0.004	0.143	5.8	0.001	0.131	4.5	0.001	0.147	4.9	−0.004	0.153	5.3	0.005	0.155	4.4	0.001	0.132	4.6	0.001	0.147	4.9
		0.75	0.003	0.155	20	−0.003	0.153	20.4	−0.002	0.143	5.8	0.001	0.120	5.1	0.000	0.153	4.5	−0.003	0.151	5.5	0.001	0.152	4.6	0.001	0.122	5.1	0.000	0.153	4.5
	0.1	0	−0.003	0.149	5.2	−0.002	0.165	4.5	0.002	0.167	4.4	−0.003	0.138	4.8	−0.001	0.165	4.8	0.002	0.163	5.6	−0.015	0.138	6.4	−0.002	0.139	4.8	−0.002	0.165	4.8
		0.25	0.024	0.196	16.8	0.011	0.156	10.7	0.002	0.150	4.7	0.021	0.180	9.7	0.014	0.146	6.4	0.002	0.152	5.2	0.016	0.165	4.2	0.020	0.178	9.4	0.014	0.147	6.3
		0.5	0.027	0.204	23.6	0.013	0.159	15.8	0.001	0.150	4.7	0.022	0.195	10.8	0.019	0.142	7.4	0.002	0.151	5	0.014	0.169	4.2	0.020	0.193	10.5	0.019	0.142	7.3
		0.75	0.028	0.196	29.6	0.014	0.166	21.9	0.001	0.150	4.7	0.019	0.203	9.4	0.026	0.148	7.7	0.001	0.152	5.1	0.011	0.168	4.3	0.018	0.200	9.1	0.026	0.149	7.6
	0.25	0	0.001	0.135	3.3	0.001	0.171	4.9	0.002	0.149	3.9	0.000	0.147	3.9	−0.001	0.179	5.3	0.002	0.147	4.3	−0.006	0.155	5.4	0.001	0.147	3.9	−0.001	0.178	5.3
		0.25	0.069	0.271	45.8	0.030	0.165	12	−0.004	0.143	5.8	0.061	0.305	32.3	0.033	0.179	6.9	−0.005	0.153	5.7	0.008	0.159	5.2	0.055	0.291	29.9	0.031	0.177	6.8
		0.5	0.077	0.302	66.1	0.032	0.167	17.2	−0.004	0.143	5.8	0.063	0.307	41.1	0.043	0.173	6.8	−0.004	0.153	5.4	0.004	0.153	4.1	0.056	0.289	37.0	0.039	0.171	6.5
		0.75	0.081	0.326	74	0.032	0.161	22.7	−0.002	0.143	5.8	0.057	0.270	41.1	0.059	0.182	9.4	−0.002	0.151	5.6	0.000	0.145	3.8	0.048	0.252	35.8	0.051	0.178	8.7
	0.5	0	0.001	0.135	3.3	0.001	0.171	4.9	0.002	0.149	3.9	0.000	0.147	3.9	−0.001	0.179	5.3	0.002	0.147	4.3	−0.006	0.155	5.4	0.001	0.147	3.9	−0.001	0.178	5.3
		0.25	0.150	0.657	97.9	0.068	0.205	18.2	−0.004	0.143	5.8	0.136	0.627	94.4	0.071	0.233	15.4	−0.004	0.154	5.6	0.007	0.158	5.5	0.105	0.523	74.9	0.058	0.218	13.5
		0.5	0.169	0.778	100	0.075	0.211	25.4	−0.004	0.143	5.8	0.147	0.729	99.3	0.089	0.244	20.8	−0.003	0.153	5.4	0.003	0.149	4.1	0.095	0.531	67.1	0.061	0.214	15.5
		0.75	0.176	0.734	100	0.077	0.196	31.6	−0.002	0.143	5.8	0.138	0.724	99.5	0.117	0.276	32.5	−0.001	0.150	5.5	−0.001	0.138	3.9	0.057	0.389	44.7	0.050	0.198	16.3
	1	0	0.001	0.135	3.3	0.001	0.171	4.9	0.002	0.149	3.9	0.000	0.147	3.9	−0.001	0.179	5.3	0.002	0.147	4.3	−0.006	0.155	5.4	0.001	0.147	3.9	−0.001	0.178	5.3
		0.25	0.211	0.890	100	0.098	0.286	30.1	−0.004	0.143	5.8	0.197	0.915	100	0.096	0.298	29.3	−0.004	0.153	5.9	0.006	0.152	5.7	0.125	0.644	66.5	0.066	0.250	21.4
		0.5	0.238	1.390	100	0.110	0.336	44.6	−0.004	0.143	5.8	0.220	1.472	100	0.110	0.369	46.2	−0.002	0.153	5.9	0.001	0.145	4.6	0.089	0.690	44.3	0.048	0.240	22.3
		0.75	0.248	2.096	100	0.114	0.410	69.1	−0.002	0.143	5.8	0.226	1.947	100	0.121	0.490	71.9	0.000	0.148	5.7	−0.003	0.134	4.7	0.016	0.280	12.7	0.007	0.162	9.9

Table 5. Number of Times the Pretest Estimator Took on the Spatial Fixed Effects (SFE), Spatial Random Effects (SRE), and Spatial Hausman-Taylor (SHT) in 1000 Simulations.

		$N=100$, $T=3$			$N=100$, $T=5$			$N=300$, $T=3$		
ρ	ϕ	SFE	SRE	SHT	SFE	SRE	SHT	SFE	SRE	SHT
					Configuration with $\psi = 1$					
0	0	15	947	38	19	941	40	21	943	36
	0.25	42	623	335	61	201	738	79	163	758
	0.5	57	384	559	64	30	906	69	10	921
	0.75	67	62	871	69	0	931	79	0	921
0.2	0	15	946	39	22	938	40	21	944	35
	0.25	37	633	330	58	200	742	50	163	787
	0.5	55	389	556	64	37	899	59	11	930
	0.75	62	69	869	61	0	939	66	0	934
0.4	0	17	947	36	26	934	40	21	940	39
	0.25	35	644	321	50	206	744	48	167	785
	0.5	43	408	549	52	41	907	48	14	938
	0.75	51	74	875	54	0	946	58	0	942
0.6	0	13	952	35	26	938	36	19	943	38
	0.25	27	653	320	48	224	728	43	172	785
	0.5	43	426	531	50	48	902	49	19	932
	0.75	41	91	868	52	0	948	52	0	948
					Configuration with $\psi = 0$					
0	0	15	947	38	26	946	28	21	943	36
	0.25	23	935	42	12	950	38	13	960	27
	0.5	19	940	41	14	951	35	16	959	25
	0.75	19	938	43	9	951	40	14	954	32
0.2	0	15	946	39	25	947	28	21	944	35
	0.25	20	934	46	10	957	33	16	957	27
	0.5	19	938	43	14	953	33	13	960	27
	0.75	16	944	40	10	954	36	15	950	35
0.4	0	17	947	36	24	946	30	21	940	39
	0.25	22	935	43	12	955	33	19	951	30
	0.5	19	940	41	11	959	30	13	956	31
	0.75	18	940	42	9	950	41	14	954	32
0.6	0	13	952	35	20	944	36	22	952	26
	0.25	19	936	45	14	950	36	16	953	31
	0.5	20	938	42	12	957	31	20	946	34
	0.75	18	936	46	11	948	41	19	943	38

The Spatial Pretest Estimator

Table 5 shows the choice of the SPT estimator for various values of ρ and ϕ corresponding to the results in Tables 1–3 at values of $\psi = 1$ (SHT world) and $\psi = 0$ (SRE world). The upper-left panel in Table 5 provides the results for $(N = 100, T = 3)$ for an SHT world. For example, at $\rho = 0.4$ and $\phi = 0.75$, the SPT estimator is an SHT estimator in 875 out of 1000 replications, an SFE estimator in 51 replications, and an SRE estimator in the remaining 74 replications. As ϕ, N, or T increases, the SPT estimator picks the SHT estimator more frequently. The performance of the SPT estimator reported in the upper panel of Table 1 is in between the SHT and the SRE estimators in terms of RMSE for both β_3 and γ_2. The size of tests for $H_0^a : \beta_3 = 1$, and $H_0^b : \gamma_2 = 1$ for SPT are obviously affected by the pretesting and are not recommended in practice.[5]

In the lower panel of Table 5, we show the choice of the SPT estimator for various values of ρ and ϕ corresponding to the results in Tables 1–3 in an SRE world. For example, at $\rho = 0.4$, $\phi = 0.75$, and $(N = 100, T = 3)$, the SPT estimator is an SRE estimator in 940 out of 1000 replications, an SFE estimator in 18 replications, and an SHT estimator in the remaining 42 replications. As N or T increases, the SPT estimator picks the SRE estimator more frequently. The performance of the SPT estimator reported in the lower panel of Table 1 is in between the SRE and the SFE estimator in terms of RMSE for β_3. Again, the size of tests for $H_0^a : \beta_3 = 1$, and $H_0^b : \gamma_2 = 1$ for SPT are obviously affected by the pretesting.

CONCLUSIONS

This chapter provides Monte Carlo evidence on the small sample performance of Cliff and Ord (1973) type spatial panel data estimators. We focus on Hausman and Taylor (1981) type panel data models with spatial disturbances. We find that the SHT estimator performs well in terms of RMSE in comparison to the SFE, the SRE, and the OLS estimators. An added advantage of the SHT estimator is that it delivers estimates of endogenous time-invariant variables, unlike the SFE model. Unlike the SRE or the pooled OLS model, it allows regressors in the model to be correlated with the individual-specific effects.

We also investigate the performance of a SPT estimator based on two Hausman tests. We find that the SPT estimators perform particularly well if the heterogeneity due to the individual effects is relatively important and the associated problem of endogeneity of the regressors with the individual effects becomes more pertinent. The SPT estimator guards against a possible misspecified choice of estimator and its RMSE performance is satisfactory, but tests of hypotheses using the SHT estimator are not recommended. Instead one should use the one-step SFE in practice, but unfortunately this applies to the time-varying regressor coefficients only.[6]

ACKNOWLEDGMENTS

The authors gratefully acknowledge numerous helpful comments on an earlier version of the chapter by two anonymous reviewers and conference participants at the 11th Advances in Econometrics Conference in honor of Jerry Hausman, held at Louisiana State University, Baton Rouge, Louisiana, February 18–19, 2012.

NOTES

1. See Mutl and Pfaffermayr (2011) for the large and small sample properties of the Hausman test statistic in a Cliff and Ord type spatial panel data model. See also Debarsy (2012) who tested for the endogeneity of the regressors and their spatially weighted counterparts with the individual effects using a likelihood ratio test.

2. We aim at extending the Hausman and Taylor (1981) estimator and thus focus on spatial autocorrelation in the error term. In the spirit of Hausman and Taylor, there is no other endogeneity besides the correlation of the regressors with the individual effects. Including a spatial lag of the dependent variable in the model is realistic and important (Ertur & Koch, 2007, 2011; Pfaffermayr, 2009), but causes additional endogeneity and is not in the spirit of Hausman and Taylor (1981).

3. Kapoor et al. (2007) illustrate that either type of weighting of the moment conditions performs well even in small samples.

4. The SFE estimates of ρ and σ_v^2 are based on the first three moment conditions in Eq. (5) and replacing $\boldsymbol{u}$ by the FE residuals ignoring the spatial correlation. The SRE estimates of ρ, σ_v^2, and σ_1^2 are based on all six moment conditions in Eq. (7) and replacing $\boldsymbol{u}$ by OLS residuals ignoring the spatial correlation as in Kapoor et al. (2007).

5. It is well known that the pretest estimator (based on the Hausman test in the first step and a simple hypothesis test in the second step) displays poor size and power properties (see Guggenberger, 2010). This is confirmed by Baltagi et al. (2003) using standard panel data Monte Carlo experiments and by our results here for their spatial counterparts. In fact, Guggenberger's (2010) recommendation of using a (one-step) t-test procedure based on the FE estimator instead of a two-step procedure is a good idea even under the presence of spatial correlation. In this

case, the researcher would use the t-test based on the SFE estimator instead of the two-stage procedure.

6. Modern approaches to causal influence queries should be defined dynamically and should recognize the role of time in causality. This is an important problem for future research but is beyond the scope of this chapter.

REFERENCES

Baltagi, B. H. (2008). *Econometric analysis of panel data*. Chichester, UK: Wiley.

Baltagi, B. H., Bresson, G., & Pirotte, A. (2003). Fixed effects, random effects or Hausman-Taylor? A pretest estimator. *Economics Letters*, *79*, 361–369.

Baltagi, B. H., Egger, P. H., & Kesina, M. (2011). *Firm-level productivity spillovers in China's chemical industry: A spatial Hausman-Taylor approach*. Working Paper. University of Syracuse.

Cliff, A. D., & Ord, J. K. (1973). *Spatial autocorrelation*. London, UK: Pion.

Contoyannis, P., & Rice, N. (2001). The impact of health on wages: Evidence from the British household panel survey. *Empirical Economics*, *26*, 599–622.

Cornwell, C., & Rupert, P. (1988). Efficient estimation with panel data: An empirical comparison of instrumental variables estimators. *Journal of Applied Econometrics*, *3*, 149–155.

Debarsy, N. (2012). The Mundlak approach in the spatial Durbin panel data model. *Spatial Economic Analysis*, *7*, 109–131.

Egger, P. H. (2004). On the problem of endogenous unobserved effects in the estimation of gravity models. *Journal of Economic Integration*, *19*, 182–191.

Egger, P. H., & Pfaffermayr, M. (2004). Distance, trade and FDI: A Hausman-Taylor SUR approach. *Journal of Applied Econometrics*, *19*, 227–246.

Ertur, C., & Koch, W. (2007). Growth, technological interdependence and spatial externalities: Theory and evidence. *Journal of Applied Econometrics*, *22*, 1033–1062.

Ertur, C., & Koch, W. (2011). A contribution to the Schumpeterian growth theory and empirics. *Journal of Economic Growth*, *16*, 215–255.

Guggenberger, P. (2010). The impact of a Hausman pretest on the size of a hypothesis test: The panel data case. *Journal of Econometrics*, *156*, 337–343.

Hausman, J. A. (1978). Specification tests in econometrics. *Econometrica*, *46*, 1251–1271.

Hausman, J. A., & Taylor, W. E. (1981). Panel data and unobservable individual effects. *Econometrica*, *49*, 1377–1398.

Kapoor, M., Kelejian, H. H., & Prucha, I. R. (2007). Panel data models with spatially correlated error components. *Journal of Econometrics*, *140*, 97–130.

Light, A., & Ureta, M. (1995). Early-career work experience and gender wage differentials. *Journal of Labor Economics*, *13*, 121–154.

Mutl, J., & Pfaffermayr, M. (2011). The Hausman test in a Cliff and Ord panel model. *Econometrics Journal*, *14*, 48–76.

Pfaffermayr, M. (2009). Conditional beta and sigma convergence in space: A maximum likelihood approach. *Regional Science and Urban Economics*, *39*, 63–78.

Serlenga, L., & Shin, Y. (2007). Gravity models of intra-EU trade: Application of the CCEP-HT estimation in heterogeneous panels with unobserved common time-specific factors. *Journal of Applied Econometrics*, *22*, 361–381.

APPENDIX

All of the Monte Carlo runs employ the following unnormalized weights matrix based on a three-before-and-three-behind design of neighborhood

$$\mathbf{W}_0 = \begin{pmatrix} 0 & 1 & 1 & 1 & 0 & \cdots & 0 & 1 & 1 & 1 \\ 1 & 0 & 1 & 1 & 1 & 0 & \cdots & 0 & 1 & 1 \\ 1 & 1 & 0 & 1 & 1 & 1 & 0 & \cdots & 0 & 1 \\ 1 & 1 & 1 & 0 & 1 & 1 & 1 & 0 & \cdots & 0 \\ 0 & 1 & 1 & 1 & 0 & 1 & 1 & 1 & 0 & 0 \\ \vdots & \vdots & \vdots & \vdots & \vdots & 0 & \vdots & \vdots & \vdots & \vdots \\ 0 & \cdots & 0 & 1 & 1 & 1 & 0 & 1 & 1 & 1 \\ 1 & 1 & \cdots & 0 & 1 & 1 & 1 & 0 & 1 & 1 \\ 1 & 1 & 0 & \cdots & 0 & 1 & 1 & 1 & 0 & 1 \\ 1 & 1 & 1 & 0 & \cdots & 0 & 1 & 1 & 1 & 0 \end{pmatrix}.$$

Each row of this matrix exhibits a row-sum of 6. Hence, the row-normalized as well as the maximum row-sum normalized counterpart of that matrix is

$$\mathbf{W} = \begin{pmatrix} 0 & 1/6 & 1/6 & 1/6 & 0 & \cdots & 0 & 1/6 & 1/6 & 1/6 \\ 1/6 & 0 & 1/6 & 1/6 & 1/6 & 0 & \cdots & 0 & 1/6 & 1/6 \\ 1/6 & 1/6 & 0 & 1/6 & 1/6 & 1/6 & 0 & \cdots & 0 & 1/6 \\ 1/6 & 1/6 & 1/6 & 0 & 1/6 & 1/6 & 1/6 & 0 & \cdots & 0 \\ 0 & 1/6 & 1/6 & 1/6 & 0 & 1/6 & 1/6 & 1/6 & 0 & 0 \\ \vdots & \vdots & \vdots & \vdots & \vdots & 0 & \vdots & \vdots & \vdots & \vdots \\ 0 & \cdots & 0 & 1/6 & 1/6 & 1/6 & 0 & 1/6 & 1/6 & 1/6 \\ 1/6 & 1/6 & \cdots & 0 & 1/6 & 1/6 & 1/6 & 0 & 1/6 & 1/6 \\ 1/6 & 1/6 & 0 & \cdots & 0 & 1/6 & 1/6 & 1/6 & 0 & 1/6 \\ 1/6 & 1/6 & 1/6 & 0 & \cdots & 0 & 1/6 & 1/6 & 1/6 & 0 \end{pmatrix}.$$

The latter is utilized in all experiments in that paper.

QUANTILE REGRESSION ESTIMATION OF PANEL DURATION MODELS WITH CENSORED DATA

Matthew Harding and Carlos Lamarche

ABSTRACT

This paper studies the estimation of quantile regression panel duration models. We allow for the possibility of endogenous covariates and correlated individual effects in the quantile regression models. We propose a quantile regression approach for panel duration models under conditionally independent censoring. The procedure involves minimizing ℓ_1 convex objective functions and is motivated by a martingale property associated with survival data in models with endogenous covariates. We carry out a series of Monte Carlo simulations to investigate the small sample performance of the proposed approach in comparison with other existing methods. An empirical application of the method to the analysis of the effect of unemployment insurance on unemployment duration illustrates the approach.

Keywords: Quantile regression; duration models; panel data; unemployment insurance

JEL classification: C23; C33

Essays in Honor of Jerry Hausman
Advances in Econometrics, Volume 29, 237–267

ISSN: 0731-9053/doi:10.1108/S0731-9053(2012)0000029014

INTRODUCTION

This paper focuses on econometric methods for longitudinal, or panel data durations consisting of repeated measurements on the same subject, which are commonly encountered in applied economics research. Han and Hausman's (1990) work on duration and competing risk models introduced flexible approaches to duration analysis, while also emphasizing the importance of controlling for unobserved heterogeneity. The recent econometric literature has built on these two fundamental ideas. On the one hand, there has been a growing literature on flexible approaches including semiparametric duration and censored models (e.g., Chen & Khan, 2001; Fitzenberger & Wilke, 2006; Honoré & de Paula, 2010; Horowitz & Lee, 2004; Khan & Tamer, 2007; Khan & Tamer, 2009; Lee, 2008; Wang & Fygenson, 2009, among others). Endogenous treatments in a hazard model were investigated in Eberwein, Ham and Lalonde (1997) and Abbring and van der Berg (2003). At the same time new approaches to controlling for unobserved heterogeneity in more general settings are being explored (Burda, Harding, & Hausman, 2012; Hausman & Woutersen, 2005).

However, existing quantile regression approaches have not been developed for survival data when the covariates are endogenous and the latent unobserved heterogeneity is associated with the independent variables. For example, this situation arises in studies of firms' entry and exit of a market (e.g., Audretsch, 1991; Audretsch & Mahmood, 1995; De Silva, Kosmopoulou, & Lamarche, 2009; Geroski, 1995). These studies include a small number of firms in business for a relatively long period of time. In these papers, it is important to account for the presence of a censored duration, unobserved heterogeneity, and the possibility that market duration affects non-duration explanatory variables.

The quantile regression model considered in this paper represents a more general version of several specifications recently proposed in the literature. Several econometric approaches exist for the case of one measure for each subject in the sample and exogenous covariates. While a quantile regression model with uncensored data can be estimated following Koenker and Geling (2001), a quantile regression model with censored data can be estimated using the methods developed by Portnoy (2003) and Peng and Huang (2008). Chernozhukov and Hansen (2005, 2006, 2008) estimator might be used when the model includes endogenous covariates and a monotone transformation for the dependent variable. This estimator, however, does not accommodate for the possibility of censored data. In cases with more than one measure per subject and no censor data, the

Koenker (2004) fixed effects estimator offers the possibility of estimating a quantile regression model with correlated individual effects. Alternatively, the practitioner can employ the Harding and Lamarche (2009) panel data estimator in a quantile regression model with potentially endogenous covariates. However, these methods are not designed to estimate a censored quantile regression model that simultaneously consider endogenous covariates and correlated individual effects.

This paper proposes a new approach to quantile regression survival analysis for longitudinal data. We allow for the possibility of endogenous covariates and correlated individual effects in the quantile regression model under conditionally independent censoring. The procedure involves minimizing ℓ_1 convex objective functions and is motivated by a martingale property associated with survival data in models with endogenous covariates. The proposed new estimator is similar in spirit to the Peng and Huang (2008) estimator, although their estimator fails to accommodate for correlated individual effects and endogenous covariates. Moreover, the performance of Peng and Huang (2008) estimator in small samples dramatically deteriorates when the model includes a large number of parameters and the degree of censoring is high. Our approach is also related to Chernozhukov and Hansen (2006, 2008), Harding and Lamarche (2009), and Koenker (2008). We carry out simulations to investigate the small sample performance of the proposed approach in comparison with other existing methods. Considering several Monte Carlo designs, we find that the finite sample performance of the proposed method is satisfactory in all the variants of the models.

The method is applied to a panel duration model of unemployment to investigate how unemployment insurance benefits affect the duration of unemployment. We use data on unemployed workers who participated in a federal unemployment program from 1997 until 2001. Our data set offers the possibility of observing multiple spells, where the number of spells per worker ranges from 1 to 6. Motivated by the early work of Jerry Hausman on duration data, we consider that unobserved individual heterogeneity could be potentially correlated with whether the worker received unemployment benefits and other important covariates in the model. All the variants of the quantile regression models estimated in this paper suggest that workers receiving unemployment benefits tend to be unemployed for a longer period of time than workers not receiving unemployment benefits. The estimated effect is largest at the lower tail of the conditional duration distribution, suggesting that workers' incentives to seek jobs are mostly influenced by the policy intervention among workers with low durations.

Moreover, our approach offers different policy prescriptions relative to other competing approaches. The application illustrates the importance of controlling for unobserved heterogeneity in a quantile regression model when practitioners use multiple-spell duration data.

The paper is organized as follows. The next section introduces the model and the proposed quantile regression estimator. The subsequent section offers Monte Carlo evidence. The fourth section demonstrates how the estimator can be used in an empirical application. The last section concludes.

MODEL AND METHOD

This paper investigates the estimation of quantile regression panel duration models. Specifically, we consider the following model:

$$h(T_{ij}) = \boldsymbol{d}'_{ij}\gamma + \boldsymbol{x}'_{ij}\boldsymbol{\beta} + \alpha_i + u_{ij}, \qquad i = 1, \ldots, n; \; j = 1, \ldots, m_i \tag{1}$$

$$\boldsymbol{d}_{ij} = \boldsymbol{w}'_{ij}\boldsymbol{\pi}_0 + \boldsymbol{x}'_{ij}\boldsymbol{\pi}_1 + \boldsymbol{v}_{ij} \tag{2}$$

$$Y_{ij} = C_{ij} \wedge T_{ij} \tag{3}$$

where $h(\cdot)$ is a known monotone transformation and T_{ij} is the (potentially) latent j-th response for the i-th subject. In this paper, we will adopt the logarithmic transformation, $h(T) = \log(T)$. In the first equation, the variable $\boldsymbol{d}_{ij}$ is a vector of k_1 endogenous variables, $\boldsymbol{x}_{ij}$ is a vector of k_2 exogenous independent variables, α_i is an individual effect potentially correlated with the independent variable $\boldsymbol{d}_{ij}$, and u_{ij} is the error term. We allow for dependence between the endogenous variable $\boldsymbol{d}_{ij}$ and the individual effect α_i. The parameter of interest is γ. The second equation indicates that $\boldsymbol{d}_{ij}$ is correlated with a vector of $k_w \geq k_1$ instruments $\boldsymbol{w}_{ij}$, the exogenous variables $\boldsymbol{x}_{ij}$, and a variable $\boldsymbol{v}_{ij}$ that is stochastically dependent on u_{ij}. Although we can consider the case of over-identification, for simplicity we concentrate on the case of exact identification. Thus, $k_w = k_1$ in what it follows. The last equation simply indicates that Y_{ij} represents observed values, with C_{ij} indicating censoring times. Additionally, we define $\delta_{ij} = I(T_{ij} \leq C_{ij})$, taking the value 1 when the event $T_{ij} \leq C_{ij}$ is true. We focus on the case where n and $min(m_1, ..., m_n)$ are both large.

We begin by describing three examples of interest in the theoretical and empirical literature which can be thought of as special cases of the model in Eqs. (1)–(3). We then consider the general version of the model and the identification strategy.

Example 1: Cross-sectional quantile regression models are investigated in Koenker and Geling (2001), Portnoy (2003), and Peng and Huang (2008). This case arises by setting $m_i = 1$ for all i and assuming that u and v are stochastically independent. Model (1)–(3) reduces to

$$h(T_i) = \boldsymbol{d}'_i\gamma + x'_i\boldsymbol{\beta} + u_i, \qquad i = 1, \ldots, n \tag{4}$$

$$Y_i = C_i \wedge T_i \tag{5}$$

While Portnoy (2003) and Peng and Huang (2008) propose approaches for the censored data case, Koenker and Geling (2001) consider the case of $\delta_i = I(T_i \leq C_i) = 1\ \forall i$.

Example 2: Chernozhukov and Hansen (2006, 2008) discuss the importance of addressing the endogeneity of d_{ij} when $m_i = 1$ for all i and $Y_{ij} = T_{ij}$ for all (i,j). They developed an approach that can be applied to the estimation of the following model:

$$h(T_i) = \boldsymbol{d}'_i\gamma + \boldsymbol{x}'_i\boldsymbol{\beta} + u_i, \qquad i = 1, \ldots, n \tag{6}$$

$$\boldsymbol{d}_i = \boldsymbol{w}'_i\boldsymbol{\pi}_0 + \boldsymbol{x}'_i\boldsymbol{\pi}_1 + \boldsymbol{v}_i \tag{7}$$

This model can be consistently estimated in the case of no censoring (e.g., $\delta_i = I(T_i \leq C_i) = 1$ for all subjects in the sample).

Example 3: Panel duration models arise in the case of $m > 1$. Under the assumption that u and v are stochastically independent and no censoring, we can apply the procedure in Koenker (2004) to estimate the following model:

$$h(T_{ij}) = \boldsymbol{d}'_{ij}\gamma + \boldsymbol{x}'_{ij}\boldsymbol{\beta} + \boldsymbol{\alpha}_i + u_{ij}, \qquad i = 1, \ldots, n;\ j = 1, \ldots, m_i \tag{8}$$

$$Y_{ij} = T_{ij} = C_{ij} \wedge T_{ij} \tag{9}$$

This approach estimates the quantile regression version of the previous model under large n, large m conditions. The case of dependence between u and v can be addressed by the method proposed by Harding and Lamarche (2009).

Estimating a Quantile Regression Duration Model

This paper develops an estimation procedure for the following quantile regression model:

$$Q_{T_{ij}}(\tau|\boldsymbol{d}_{ij}, \boldsymbol{x}_{ij}, \boldsymbol{z}_{ij}) = \exp(\boldsymbol{d}'_{ij}\boldsymbol{\gamma}(\tau) + \boldsymbol{x}'_{ij}\boldsymbol{\beta}(\tau) + \boldsymbol{z}'_{ij}\boldsymbol{\alpha}(\tau)) \tag{10}$$

where the quantile $\tau \in (0,1)$, the variable $z_{ij} = (0, ..., 1, ..., 0)'$ is a $n \times 1$ indicator for the individual effect α_i, and $\boldsymbol{\alpha}(\tau) = (\alpha_1(\tau), \ldots, \alpha_n(\tau))'$ is a $n \times 1$ vector of nuisance parameters. Given the logarithmic transformation $h(T) = \log(T)$, model (10) is equivalent to $Q_{\log T_{ij}}(\tau|\boldsymbol{d}_{ij}, \boldsymbol{x}_{ij}, \boldsymbol{z}_{ij}) = \boldsymbol{d}'_{ij}\gamma(\tau) + \boldsymbol{x}'_{ij}\boldsymbol{\beta}(\tau) + \boldsymbol{z}'_{ij}\boldsymbol{\alpha}(\tau)$. Then, model (10) can be seen as the quantile regression version of Eq. (1) after the logarithmic transformation is adopted and α_i is replaced by $\boldsymbol{z}'_{ij}\boldsymbol{\alpha}$. The alternative notation is used in this section because it is convenient for introducing conditional quantile functions and estimating equations.

We assume that $P(T_{ij} \leq Q_{T_{ij}}(\tau|\boldsymbol{d}_{ij}, \boldsymbol{x}_{ij}, \boldsymbol{z}_{ij})|\boldsymbol{w}_{ij}, \boldsymbol{x}_{ij}, \boldsymbol{z}_{ij})$ is equal to the quantile τ. This assumption is equivalent to require that $u_{ij}(\tau) \equiv T_{ij} - Q_{T_{ij}}(\tau|\boldsymbol{d}_{ij}, \boldsymbol{x}_{ij}, \boldsymbol{z}_{ij})$ has zero τ-th quantile conditional on $\boldsymbol{w}_{ij}$, $\boldsymbol{x}_{ij}$, and $\boldsymbol{z}_{ij}$. Our parameter of interest, $\gamma(\tau)$, is the effect of the endogenous variable on the quantile τ of the conditional distribution of the latent response variable $\log(T)$. The parameter $\gamma(\tau)$ provides an opportunity for investigating how the endogenous factors influence the location, scale, and shape of the conditional distribution of the response variable.

The model also includes exogenous variables and individual effects. We assume that the individual effect, $\alpha_i(\tau)$, represents a distributional shift since we are focusing on estimating large m_i survival models. In other circumstances, when m_i is relatively small, it is appropriate to impose the condition that $\alpha_i(\tau) = \alpha_i$ for all $\tau \in (0,1)$ (see, e.g., Koenker, 2004). The individual specific effect is then a location shift, implying that the conditional quantiles of T for each subject can have different locations and equal shapes. An additional advantage of this condition is that the assumption facilitates the interpretation of α_i as a fixed effect. Our specification allows for different locations and shapes, which appears to be a more flexible model.

Our method estimates a quantile regression model (10) considering *iid* samples, $\{(Y_{ij}, \delta_{ij}, \boldsymbol{d}_{ij}, \boldsymbol{x}_{ij}, \boldsymbol{w}_{ij}) : i = 1, \ldots, n;\ j = 1, \ldots, m_i\}$. Consider for simplicity the case of balanced designs with $m_i = m$ for all i. We solve a linear programming problem corresponding to the following estimating equations:

$$E\left\{ (nm)^{-1/2} \sum_{i=1}^{n} \sum_{j=1}^{m} (\boldsymbol{x}'_{ij}, \boldsymbol{z}'_{ij}, \boldsymbol{w}'_{ij})' N_{ij}(\exp(\boldsymbol{d}'_{ij}\gamma(\tau) + \boldsymbol{x}'_{ij}\boldsymbol{\beta}(\tau) + \boldsymbol{z}'_{ij}\boldsymbol{\alpha}(\tau) + \boldsymbol{w}'_{ij}\boldsymbol{\lambda}(\tau))) \right.$$
$$\left. - \int_0^{\tau} I(Y_{ij} \geq \exp((\boldsymbol{d}'_{ij}\gamma(\upsilon) + \boldsymbol{x}'_{ij}\boldsymbol{\beta}(\upsilon) + \boldsymbol{z}'_{ij}\boldsymbol{\alpha}(\upsilon) + \boldsymbol{w}'_{ij}\boldsymbol{\lambda}(\upsilon)))\, dH(\upsilon) \right\} = 0 \qquad (11)$$

where $H(\upsilon) = -\log(1-\upsilon)$ for $\upsilon \in [0,1)$ and the counting process $N_{ij} = I(Y_{ij} \leq t, \delta_{ij} = 1)$. It is possible to show that solving Eq. (11) is equivalent to finding the argument that minimizes an ℓ_1 convex objective function. The left-hand side of Eq. (11) can be interpreted as the gradient of the convex objective function defined in Eq. (12). (See Remark 2 for details on related ideas for cross-sectional data.)

Our convex objective function is defined as the sum of convex functions of the form

$$Q_{ij}(\tau, \gamma, \boldsymbol{\beta}, \boldsymbol{\alpha}, \boldsymbol{\lambda}) = \varrho_\tau(h(y_{ij}) - \mathbf{d}'_{ij}\gamma - \mathbf{x}'_{ij}\boldsymbol{\beta} - \mathbf{z}'_{ij}\boldsymbol{\alpha} - \mathbf{w}'_{ij}\boldsymbol{\lambda}) \tag{12}$$

where the function $\varrho_\tau(u) = u(\vartheta(\tau) - \delta \times I(u \leq 0))$, and

$$\vartheta_{ij}(\tau) = \sum_{k=0}^{q-1} I(h(y_{ij}) - \mathbf{d}'_{ij}\gamma \geq \mathbf{x}_{ij}\hat{\boldsymbol{\beta}} + \mathbf{z}'_{ij}\hat{\boldsymbol{\alpha}} + \mathbf{w}'_{ij}\hat{\boldsymbol{\lambda}})(H(\tau_{k+1}) - H(\tau_k)) \tag{13}$$

First, we minimize the objective function above for $\boldsymbol{\beta}$, $\boldsymbol{\alpha}$, and $\boldsymbol{\lambda}$ as functions of τ and γ:

$$\{\hat{\boldsymbol{\beta}}(\tau, \gamma), \hat{\boldsymbol{\alpha}}(\tau, \gamma), \hat{\boldsymbol{\lambda}}(\tau, \gamma)\} = \underset{\beta, \alpha, \lambda \in \mathcal{B} \times \mathcal{A} \times \mathcal{L}}{\arg\min} \sum_{i=1}^{n} \sum_{j=1}^{m_i} Q_{ij}(\tau, \gamma; \boldsymbol{\beta}, \boldsymbol{\alpha}, \boldsymbol{\lambda}). \tag{14}$$

Then we estimate the coefficient on the endogenous variable by finding the value of γ, which minimizes a weighted distance function defined on $\boldsymbol{\lambda}$:

$$\hat{\gamma}(\tau) = \underset{\gamma \in \mathcal{G}}{\arg\min} \left\{ \hat{\boldsymbol{\lambda}}(\tau, \gamma)' \hat{\boldsymbol{A}}(\tau) \hat{\boldsymbol{\lambda}}(\tau, \gamma) \right\} \tag{15}$$

for a positive definite matrix $\boldsymbol{A}$. The parameter estimates are then given by,

$$\hat{\boldsymbol{\theta}}(\tau) \equiv (\hat{\gamma}(\tau), \hat{\boldsymbol{\beta}}(\tau), \hat{\boldsymbol{\alpha}}(\tau)) = (\hat{\gamma}(\tau), \hat{\boldsymbol{\beta}}(\hat{\gamma}(\tau), \tau)), \hat{\boldsymbol{\alpha}}(\hat{\gamma}(\tau), \tau))) \tag{16}$$

Remark 1: To address the possibility of endogenous covariates, the estimator could be alternatively defined by integrating the approaches considered in Koenker (2004), Blundell and Powell (2007), and Peng and Huang (2008). The control function approach proposed in Blundell and Powell (2007) offers a convenient alternative for addressing the possibility of endogenous regressors. Our approach can be seen within the recent developments on quantile regression for the structural equations model (see, e.g., Chernozhukov & Hansen, 2005; Harding & Lamarche, 2009) to estimate the conditional quantile function. Alternatively, it can be seen as an extension of the ideas behind existing methods developed for the classical case of endogenous covariates in duration models (see, e.g., Chesher, 2002; Lancaster, 1985; Olsen & Farkas, 1988).

Remark 2: The condition that leads to the modified version of the quantile regression check function, denoted by $\varrho_\tau(\cdot)$, is motivated by the martingale property of counting processes presented in Fleming and Harrington (1991) and employed by Peng and Huang (2008). Peng and Huang's estimator however fails to accommodate for endogenous individual effects and endogenous covariates. In the cross-sectional case with no endogenous covariates and no unobserved heterogeneity, Peng and Huang's estimating equations are

$$\mathbb{E}\left\{ n^{-1/2} \sum_{i=1}^{n} \boldsymbol{x}'_i N_i(\exp(\boldsymbol{x}'_i \boldsymbol{\beta}(\tau))) - \int_0^{\tau} I(Y_i \geq \exp(\boldsymbol{x}'_i \boldsymbol{\beta}(s))) dH(s) \right\} = 0 \quad (17)$$

As pointed by Peng and Huang (2008), the monotonicity of (17) facilitates the computation of the estimator. Koenker (2008) provides important insights on the implementation of the approach, and Koenker (2010) offers an efficient estimation method based on simplex and interior point methods.

Remark 3: It is interesting to note that when there is no censoring, the method is similar to the panel data approach proposed by Harding and Lamarche (2009). In the one sample case considered in Peng and Huang (2008), the second term in Eq. (17) is $-\log(1-\tau) \approx \tau$, and therefore it follows that

$$Q_{ij}(\tau, \gamma, \boldsymbol{\beta}, \boldsymbol{\alpha}, \boldsymbol{\lambda}) = \varrho_\tau h(y_{ij}) - \boldsymbol{d}'_{ij}\gamma - \boldsymbol{x}'_{ij}\boldsymbol{\beta} - \boldsymbol{z}'_{ij}\boldsymbol{\alpha} - \boldsymbol{w}'_{ij}\boldsymbol{\lambda} \quad (18)$$

where $\varrho_\tau(u) = \rho_\tau(u) = u(\tau - I(u \leq 0))$, the standard quantile regression check function (Koenker, 2005).

Panel Implementation

The implementation of the estimator defined in (14) and (15) relies heavily on the sparsity of the design. Koenker (2008) shows that the solution of Peng and Huang's (2008) generalized equations (17) can be obtained as a solution of a linear programming problem. It is natural then to use existing simplex methods, and/or interior point methods. The key idea behind the implementation is a dual formulation of the linear minimization problem. However, finding the solution of this problem can be challenging when the number of estimated parameters is large and the degree of censoring is high. To overcome these difficulties, we use sparse matrix methods to take advantage of the sparsity of the design. This dramatically increases the algorithm's speed of convergence and significantly reduces memory requirements. The practitioner interested in single spell duration data should consider Koenker (2010), which offers several procedures for estimating a censored quantile regression model with cross-sectional data.

Inference and Asymptotic Considerations

We propose to use the bootstrap to provide inference about $\hat{\boldsymbol{\theta}}$. Peng and Huang (2008) highlight that the bootstrap seems to have advantages over the estimation of the covariance matrices of the limiting process $(nm)^{-1/2}(\hat{\boldsymbol{\theta}}-\boldsymbol{\theta})$. It might be possible to follow the quantile regression literature by considering the pair bootstrap by replacing pairs $\{(h(\boldsymbol{Y}_{i\bullet}), \boldsymbol{d}'_{i\bullet}, \boldsymbol{x}'_{i\bullet}, \boldsymbol{w}'_{i\bullet}) : 1 = 1, \ldots n\}$ over subject units i.[1] In the case of panel duration data we proceed by drawing a sample (with replacement) of n subjects including their m_i observations. Using these new pairs $(h(\boldsymbol{Y}^*_{i\bullet}), \boldsymbol{d}^*_{i\bullet}, \boldsymbol{x}^*_{i\bullet}, \boldsymbol{w}^*_{i\bullet}))$, we obtain $\boldsymbol{\theta}^*$ as the argument that minimizes (14) and (15). We reiterate this procedure B times to obtain a large sample of realizations $\{\boldsymbol{\theta}^*_b\}_{b=1}^B$. For a given quantile, we can obtain the variance of $\hat{\boldsymbol{\theta}}(\tau)$ as the sample variance of $\{\boldsymbol{\theta}^*_b\}_{b=1}^B$.

In this paper, we follow the resampling method described in Section 4.1 of Peng and Huang (2008), which was initially proposed by Jin, Ying, Wei (2001) and considered in Ma and Kosorok (2005). Peng and Huang propose a simple resampling approach designed to perturb the objective function (14). They suggest drawing $\zeta_{11}, \ldots, \zeta_{nm}$ independent variables from a non-negative distribution with mean 1 and variance 1. We consider the exponential distribution, drawing $\{\zeta_{i\bullet} : i = 1, \ldots n\}$ over subjects. One can then obtain $\boldsymbol{\theta}^*$ as the argument that minimizes a perturbed Eq. (14) (see Section 4.1 of Peng and Huang (2008) for additional details). As before, we reiterate this procedure B times to obtain a large sample of realizations $\{\boldsymbol{\theta}^*_b\}_{b=1}^B$ and compute its sample variance. Moreover, a $100(1-2q)$ confidence interval can be obtained by constructing the q-th quantile and $(1-q)$th quantile of $\{\boldsymbol{\theta}^*_b\}_{b=1}^B$. This procedure, which is applied in the empirical application considered in section "Empirical Results," works under fairly general conditions. Because it maintains the endogenous structure of the model, it can be accommodated to include the use of instrumental variables (IV).

It is possible also to employ a Wald-type statistic (see, e.g., Koenker & Bassett, 1982; Koenker, 2005) for testing a basic general linear hypothesis on a vector $\boldsymbol{\xi}$ of the form $H_0 : \boldsymbol{R\xi} = \boldsymbol{r}$, where $\boldsymbol{R}$ is a matrix that depends on the type of restrictions imposed. We evaluate the null hypothesis of equality of effects across quantiles considering a vector $\boldsymbol{\xi} = (\boldsymbol{\theta}(\tau_1), \ldots, \boldsymbol{\theta}(\tau_J))'$. In the special case of $\delta_{ij} = 1$ and $\hat{\boldsymbol{v}}_{ij} = c$ for all (i,j), it is possible to evaluate the vector over a range of quantiles by extending the framework developed in Koenker and Xiao (2002). The null hypothesis is $H_0 : \theta_k(\tau) = \mu_k + \sigma_k \theta(\tau)$, where k indicates the covariate, μ_k is the location parameter, and σ_k is the scale parameter. Note that $\sigma_k = 0$ implies that the covariate effect affects only the location of the conditional distribution of survival time. Alternatively, if $\sigma_k > 0$, the covariate effect affects both the location and scale of the conditional distribution of the response.

The derivation of the asymptotic results including asymptotic covariance matrices raises several issues that are worth mentioning. First, the existence of a vector of dimension n that tends to infinity was noted by Koenker (2004). This issue is typically avoided by concentrating out the Bahadur's representation of the individual effects in the objective function (see, e.g., Koenker, 2004; Lamarche, 2010). Second, the derivation of asymptotic results is facilitated by letting n and m tend to infinity, although it is possible that the estimator is biased in cases of low, fixed m (see Graham, Hahn, & Powell, 2009, for a discussion when $\delta_{ij} = 1$ for all (i,j) and the independent variables are exogenous). We emphasize this point because m_i ranges between 3 and 6 unemployment spells in the application considered in the fourth section. Let τ_U be a deterministic constant subject to some identifiability restrictions by the presence of censoring (Peng & Huang, 2008). If regularity conditions are met, for $\tau \in (0,\tau_U)$, it is possible to show that the quantile regression estimator $\hat{\theta}(\tau)$ converges weakly to a Gaussian process. The result can be shown using results and arguments in Chernozhukov and Hansen (2006, 2008), Koenker (2004), and Peng and Huang (2008).

MONTE CARLO EVIDENCE

This section reports the results of several simulation experiments designed to evaluate the performance of the proposed method in finite samples.

We generate the dependent variable considering the following equations:

$$T_{ij} = \beta_0 + \beta_1 d_{ij} + \beta_2 x_{ij} + \alpha_i + (1 + \delta d_{ij}) u_{ij} \tag{19}$$

$$d_{ij} = \pi_0 + \pi_1 w_{ij} + v_{ij} \tag{20}$$

$$\alpha_i = \gamma_1 \bar{d}_i + \gamma_2 \varepsilon_i \tag{21}$$

$$w_{ij} = \mu \eta_i + e_{ij} \tag{22}$$

and $Y_{ij} = C_{ij} \wedge T_{ij}$, where C_{ij} indicates censoring times and $\bar{d}_i = m^{-1}\sum_j d_{ij}$ is the individual specific sample mean of d. The model presented in Eqs. (19)–(22) is estimated using different sample sizes $n = 10, 20, 50$ and $m = 5, 20, 50$. In models with $m = 5$, we consider the following fixed and random censoring times: $C_{im} = 4$ and $C_{im} = 4 + \xi_{im}$, where ξ_{im} is a uniform random variable. When $m > 5$, we assume that the fixed censoring point is $C_{ij} = 7.5$ and the random censoring point is $C_{ij} = 6.5 + 0.25\xi_{ij}$, where ξ_{ij} is a Gaussian random variable. As a result of these variants of the model, the proportion of censoring in the simulations ranges from 6 to 25. The random variable $\varepsilon_i \sim \mathcal{N}(0, 0.5)$, and the variables $(e, x, \eta)'$ are Gaussian independent random variables. The error terms in the first two equations (Eqs. (19) and (20)) are $(u_{it}, v_{it})' \sim \mathcal{N}(0,\Omega)$, where $\Omega_{11} = \Omega_{22} = 1$. The parameters are assumed to be $\beta_0 = 5$, $\beta_1 = \beta_2 = \pi_1 = 1$, $\pi_0 = 0$, $\gamma_2 = -0.5$, and $\mu = 0.25$.

We consider four basic variations of the model:

Design I: The endogenous variable d_{ij} is not correlated with the α_i's, and the variables u_{ij} and v_{ij} are independent Gaussian variables. We assume $\gamma_1 = 0$ and $\Omega_{12} = \Omega_{21} = 0$.

Design II: The endogenous variable d_{ij} is not correlated with the α_i's, and the variables u_{ij} and v_{ij} are not independent. We assume $\gamma_1 = 0$ and $\Omega_{12} = \Omega_{21} = -0.5$.

Design III: The endogenous variable d_{ij} is correlated with the α_i's, and the variables u_{ij} and v_{ij} are independent Gaussian variables. We assume $\gamma_1 = -0.5$ and $\Omega_{12} = \Omega_{21} = 0$.

Design IV: The variable u_{it} is correlated with v_{it} and the individual effect α_i is correlated with the independent variable d_{ij}. We assume that $\gamma_1 = -0.5$ and $\Omega_{12} = \Omega_{21} = -0.5$.

Finally, we evaluate the method under fixed and random censoring in the location-shift model ($\delta = 0$) and the location-scale shift model ($\delta = 0.1$). By allowing δ to be different than zero, we consider models where the slope parameter β_1 changes across the quantiles of the conditional distribution of the response variable T. We report results at two different quantiles $\tau = \{0.25, 0.50\}$.

Tables 1–4 present the percentage of censored data, bias, and root mean square error (RMSE) of the simulation experiments. For instance, Table 1 shows results for model (19)–(22) under fixed censoring when $\delta = 0$. While the upper panel of the table presents results for the case that $\tau = 0.5$, the lower panel of the table presents results for the case of $\tau = 0.25$. The tables show results from (i) a quantile regression approach that uses the latent variable T (Omni), (ii) a quantile regression approach that uses the variable

Table 1. Monte Carlo Results for Model (19)–(22) Under Fixed Censoring in the Location Shift Model.

Sample		Design	Censoring	Omni		Naive		Peng–Huang		Panel	
n	m			Bias	RMSE	Bias	RMSE	Bias	RMSE	Bias	RMSE
					τ= 0.5 quantile						
50	5	I	0.106	−0.005	0.075	−0.086	0.116	−0.003	0.078	0.011	0.102
		II	0.104	−0.260	0.269	−0.323	0.331	−0.257	0.267	0.010	0.100
		III	0.118	−0.165	0.175	−0.243	0.251	−0.168	0.179	−0.002	0.088
		IV	0.097	−0.394	0.398	−0.456	0.460	−0.392	0.396	0.003	0.092
20	5	I	0.120	−0.011	0.115	−0.090	0.152	−0.012	0.118	−0.005	0.156
		II	0.123	−0.262	0.283	−0.322	0.342	−0.259	0.281	0.016	0.159
		III	0.153	−0.150	0.181	−0.220	0.243	−0.149	0.182	−0.019	0.155
		IV	0.128	−0.406	0.416	−0.461	0.473	−0.407	0.418	−0.009	0.149
20	20	I	0.097	−0.004	0.057	−0.087	0.102	−0.002	0.059	0.002	0.071
		II	0.063	−0.240	0.246	−0.287	0.292	−0.243	0.249	0.023	0.079
		III	0.110	−0.053	0.071	−0.148	0.154	−0.049	0.071	0.006	0.075
		IV	0.079	−0.302	0.304	−0.346	0.348	−0.298	0.301	0.035	0.086
10	50	I	0.099	0.005	0.058	−0.086	0.102	0.007	0.062	0.000	0.062
		II	0.086	−0.230	0.236	−0.287	0.291	−0.228	0.234	0.029	0.070
		III	0.113	−0.023	0.046	−0.130	0.135	−0.025	0.052	0.003	0.065
		IV	0.083	−0.264	0.267	−0.319	0.321	−0.263	0.266	0.034	0.075

			τ= 0.25 quantile								
50	5	I	0.106	−0.005	0.073	−0.166	0.185	−0.002	0.075	0.006	0.112
		II	0.104	−0.256	0.266	−0.394	0.402	−0.253	0.262	0.010	0.102
		III	0.118	−0.161	0.173	−0.386	0.395	−0.163	0.175	−0.005	0.101
		IV	0.097	−0.391	0.395	−0.585	0.589	−0.388	0.393	0.002	0.098
20	5	I	0.120	−0.008	0.123	−0.135	0.199	−0.007	0.128	−0.014	0.172
		II	0.123	−0.261	0.288	−0.378	0.400	−0.262	0.289	0.002	0.160
		III	0.153	−0.147	0.186	−0.301	0.329	−0.153	0.191	−0.009	0.166
		IV	0.128	−0.407	0.421	−0.525	0.538	−0.407	0.421	−0.006	0.161
20	20	I	0.097	0.001	0.060	−0.062	0.081	0.001	0.060	−0.002	0.078
		II	0.063	−0.242	0.249	−0.271	0.276	−0.243	0.250	0.017	0.083
		III	0.110	−0.037	0.060	−0.119	0.127	−0.036	0.061	0.003	0.069
		IV	0.079	−0.285	0.289	−0.333	0.336	−0.286	0.290	0.027	0.081
10	50	I	0.099	−0.001	0.056	−0.075	0.091	0.000	0.058	−0.001	0.059
		II	0.086	−0.230	0.236	−0.265	0.270	−0.228	0.235	0.020	0.068
		III	0.113	−0.033	0.057	−0.104	0.112	−0.033	0.059	0.004	0.075
		IV	0.083	−0.304	0.307	−0.331	0.333	−0.304	0.307	0.018	0.069

Table 2. Monte Carlo Results for Model (19)–(22) Under Random Censoring in the Location Shift Model.

Sample		Design	Censoring	Omni		Naive		Peng–Huang		Panel	
n	m			Bias	RMSE	Bias	RMSE	Bias	RMSE	Bias	RMSE
					$\tau = 0.5$ quantile						
50	5	I	0.085	0.001	0.074	−0.076	0.108	−0.001	0.075	0.009	0.086
		II	0.085	−0.255	0.264	−0.318	0.326	−0.253	0.263	0.016	0.088
		III	0.100	−0.194	0.204	−0.259	0.266	−0.192	0.203	−0.005	0.098
		IV	0.097	−0.428	0.432	−0.480	0.483	−0.426	0.430	0.002	0.093
20	5	I	0.104	−0.013	0.115	−0.080	0.140	−0.007	0.116	−0.016	0.147
		II	0.103	−0.262	0.283	−0.312	0.333	−0.256	0.279	0.005	0.142
		III	0.125	−0.144	0.178	−0.215	0.239	−0.146	0.180	0.009	0.159
		IV	0.128	−0.399	0.411	−0.450	0.460	−0.403	0.416	0.022	0.170
20	20	I	0.186	−0.007	0.061	−0.185	0.194	−0.009	0.071	0.002	0.076
		II	0.175	−0.245	0.251	−0.370	0.373	−0.242	0.249	0.064	0.114
		III	0.226	−0.060	0.074	−0.273	0.276	−0.058	0.077	0.001	0.078
		IV	0.187	−0.300	0.303	−0.430	0.432	−0.296	0.300	0.066	0.108
10	50	I	0.217	−0.004	0.050	−0.227	0.234	−0.004	0.063	0.003	0.071
		II	0.152	−0.241	0.246	−0.342	0.346	−0.237	0.244	0.052	0.093
		III	0.233	−0.036	0.058	−0.270	0.273	−0.026	0.060	0.010	0.078
		IV	0.196	−0.288	0.291	−0.429	0.431	−0.286	0.289	0.073	0.109

						τ= 0.25 quantile					
50	5	I	0.085	0.009	0.079	−0.128	0.154	0.008	0.080	0.011	0.097
		II	0.085	−0.252	0.262	−0.362	0.371	−0.253	0.264	0.016	0.106
		III	0.100	−0.181	0.193	−0.320	0.329	−0.179	0.193	0.005	0.106
		IV	0.097	−0.419	0.424	−0.531	0.535	−0.420	0.424	0.005	0.097
20	5	I	0.104	−0.004	0.120	−0.131	0.181	−0.004	0.126	−0.022	0.168
		II	0.103	−0.259	0.280	−0.364	0.381	−0.258	0.280	−0.005	0.161
		III	0.125	−0.144	0.179	−0.263	0.286	−0.144	0.181	0.009	0.181
		IV	0.128	−0.400	0.412	−0.492	0.503	−0.402	0.414	0.020	0.178
20	20	I	0.186	0.013	0.068	−0.130	0.142	0.014	0.071	0.004	0.077
		II	0.175	−0.223	0.231	−0.302	0.306	−0.222	0.231	0.043	0.090
		III	0.226	−0.044	0.068	−0.239	0.243	−0.041	0.071	0.006	0.084
		IV	0.187	−0.299	0.303	−0.397	0.399	−0.297	0.301	0.057	0.108
10	50	I	0.217	−0.005	0.066	−0.139	0.150	−0.003	0.067	0.002	0.079
		II	0.152	−0.254	0.262	−0.325	0.329	−0.253	0.261	0.048	0.094
		III	0.233	−0.042	0.062	−0.231	0.234	−0.040	0.066	0.004	0.073
		IV	0.196	−0.287	0.290	−0.398	0.400	−0.286	0.289	0.055	0.100

Table 3. Monte Carlo Results for Model (19)–(22) Under Fixed Censoring in the Location-Scale Shift Model.

Sample		Design	Censoring	Omni		Naive		Peng–Huang		Panel	
n	m			Bias	RMSE	Bias	RMSE	Bias	RMSE	Bias	RMSE
				τ= 0.5 quantile							
50	5	I	0.105	−0.005	0.074	−0.095	0.123	−0.001	0.076	0.007	0.100
		II	0.102	−0.253	0.263	−0.319	0.326	−0.245	0.254	0.016	0.099
		III	0.116	−0.164	0.174	−0.261	0.269	−0.166	0.179	0.000	0.086
		IV	0.114	−0.429	0.432	−0.510	0.513	−0.419	0.423	0.003	0.098
20	5	I	0.118	−0.007	0.111	−0.100	0.154	−0.010	0.116	−0.004	0.154
		II	0.120	−0.253	0.276	−0.327	0.345	−0.249	0.272	0.017	0.157
		III	0.152	−0.154	0.184	−0.236	0.259	−0.152	0.185	−0.024	0.163
		IV	0.139	−0.406	0.415	−0.467	0.477	−0.410	0.420	−0.030	0.154
20	20	I	0.090	0.002	0.057	−0.083	0.099	0.002	0.058	−0.002	0.065
		II	0.062	−0.232	0.238	−0.274	0.279	−0.231	0.237	0.022	0.072
		III	0.112	−0.039	0.060	−0.140	0.145	−0.038	0.060	0.002	0.065
		IV	0.078	−0.272	0.275	−0.319	0.322	−0.269	0.272	0.039	0.080
10	50	I	0.115	0.001	0.053	−0.102	0.114	0.002	0.056	0.001	0.059
		II	0.085	−0.225	0.231	−0.278	0.282	−0.221	0.227	0.027	0.067
		III	0.107	−0.035	0.055	−0.129	0.134	−0.032	0.055	0.002	0.065
		IV	0.069	−0.288	0.291	−0.326	0.328	−0.284	0.287	0.029	0.077

			τ= 0.25 quantile								
50	5	I	0.105	0.009	0.071	−0.154	0.172	0.012	0.075	0.025	0.106
		II	0.102	−0.231	0.241	−0.358	0.364	−0.223	0.233	0.035	0.107
		III	0.116	−0.153	0.163	−0.380	0.388	−0.152	0.164	0.014	0.100
		IV	0.114	−0.373	0.377	−0.552	0.555	−0.370	0.375	0.025	0.106
20	5	I	0.118	0.001	0.126	−0.128	0.187	0.004	0.127	0.007	0.174
		II	0.120	−0.240	0.269	−0.347	0.369	−0.242	0.270	0.023	0.167
		III	0.152	−0.143	0.185	−0.298	0.324	−0.148	0.187	0.001	0.168
		IV	0.139	−0.394	0.406	−0.497	0.508	−0.397	0.409	0.010	0.166
20	20	I	0.090	0.013	0.061	−0.039	0.065	0.014	0.061	0.003	0.072
		II	0.062	−0.213	0.220	−0.234	0.239	−0.213	0.219	0.018	0.079
		III	0.112	−0.037	0.060	−0.104	0.113	−0.035	0.059	0.004	0.066
		IV	0.078	−0.274	0.277	−0.301	0.304	−0.272	0.276	0.021	0.073
10	50	I	0.115	0.010	0.056	−0.052	0.073	0.012	0.057	0.001	0.058
		II	0.085	−0.208	0.215	−0.233	0.238	−0.206	0.213	0.018	0.067
		III	0.107	−0.031	0.055	−0.090	0.099	−0.029	0.054	0.005	0.071
		IV	0.069	−0.280	0.283	−0.298	0.300	−0.278	0.281	0.019	0.079

Table 4. Monte Carlo Results for Model (19)–(22) Under Random Censoring in the Location-Scale Shift Model.

Sample		Design	Censoring	Omni		Naive		Peng–Huang		Panel	
n	m			Bias	RMSE	Bias	RMSE	Bias	RMSE	Bias	RMSE
				$\tau = 0.5$ quantile							
50	5	I	0.087	0.001	0.075	−0.086	0.115	0.003	0.074	0.010	0.086
		II	0.082	−0.251	0.261	−0.317	0.326	−0.245	0.256	0.019	0.088
		III	0.098	−0.196	0.205	−0.273	0.280	−0.192	0.202	−0.005	0.095
		IV	0.094	−0.425	0.429	−0.486	0.489	−0.419	0.423	0.006	0.097
20	5	I	0.102	−0.016	0.112	−0.090	0.148	−0.010	0.117	−0.013	0.148
		II	0.101	−0.259	0.281	−0.319	0.339	−0.251	0.276	0.008	0.152
		III	0.123	−0.145	0.179	−0.227	0.251	−0.147	0.183	0.002	0.161
		IV	0.124	−0.395	0.407	−0.454	0.465	−0.396	0.409	0.023	0.169
20	20	I	0.181	0.006	0.057	−0.178	0.186	0.009	0.062	0.000	0.073
		II	0.169	−0.241	0.247	−0.356	0.360	−0.232	0.239	0.056	0.105
		III	0.248	−0.061	0.075	−0.296	0.299	−0.055	0.075	−0.004	0.078
		IV	0.179	−0.288	0.291	−0.409	0.411	−0.276	0.280	0.055	0.096
10	50	I	0.189	−0.009	0.059	−0.198	0.204	−0.008	0.066	−0.007	0.064
		II	0.146	−0.233	0.239	−0.327	0.330	−0.225	0.232	0.043	0.081
		III	0.218	−0.024	0.046	−0.247	0.250	−0.023	0.049	0.002	0.066
		IV	0.188	−0.277	0.280	−0.409	0.411	−0.267	0.270	0.064	0.097

						$\tau = 0.25$ quantile					
50	5	I	0.087	0.021	0.081	−0.115	0.141	0.022	0.083	0.027	0.103
		II	0.082	−0.231	0.241	−0.331	0.339	−0.226	0.238	0.039	0.112
		III	0.098	−0.173	0.184	−0.314	0.322	−0.172	0.185	0.018	0.110
		IV	0.094	−0.403	0.408	−0.506	0.509	−0.400	0.405	0.027	0.107
20	5	I	0.102	0.006	0.118	−0.118	0.169	0.010	0.121	−0.009	0.180
		II	0.101	−0.238	0.260	−0.332	0.348	−0.236	0.259	0.016	0.164
		III	0.123	−0.139	0.174	−0.257	0.279	−0.140	0.175	0.028	0.183
		IV	0.124	−0.381	0.393	−0.469	0.478	−0.381	0.393	0.038	0.182
20	20	I	0.181	0.012	0.065	−0.110	0.122	0.011	0.066	0.004	0.073
		II	0.169	−0.194	0.203	−0.259	0.264	−0.192	0.201	0.040	0.086
		III	0.248	−0.055	0.072	−0.196	0.200	−0.053	0.071	−0.002	0.069
		IV	0.179	−0.279	0.282	−0.354	0.356	−0.271	0.276	0.050	0.101
10	50	I	0.189	0.010	0.056	−0.140	0.150	0.012	0.056	0.009	0.068
		II	0.146	−0.229	0.237	−0.281	0.287	−0.226	0.235	0.040	0.086
		III	0.218	−0.021	0.048	−0.168	0.172	−0.019	0.052	0.007	0.073
		IV	0.188	−0.270	0.273	−0.356	0.357	−0.263	0.265	0.046	0.090

Y (Naive), (iii) the survival approach for a censored quantile regression model (Peng–Huang) proposed by Peng and Huang (2008), and (iv) the quantile regression estimator for a panel duration model with individual effects (Panel). Note that the first three procedures being compared are in effect cross-sectional methods.

We can compare the different estimators for Design I in the absence of endogeneity or correlated individual effects. Our estimator performs very similarly to the Peng–Huang estimator and both are a substantial improvement relative to the Naive estimator. As we introduce endogeneity in Designs II–IV however, the performance of the Peng–Huang estimator decreases substantially and becomes comparable to that of the Naive estimator. Our proposed estimator, by contrast, continues to perform very well. This indicates that, relatively to each other, endogeneity and correlated individual effects induce biases, which are an order of magnitude larger than the biases induced by censoring which is unaccounted for.

Our estimator performs exceptionally well in Design III, which has correlated individual specific effects but no additional source of endogeneity. This highlights the effectiveness of using a panel data approach to controlling for unobserved heterogeneity when such data is in fact available. Removing additional endogeneity using IV induces a small amount of bias (less than 5% in almost all cases, and less than 2% in most cases). In our simulations, we have also considered the case where $n = 10$ and $m = 50$. Strictly speaking, this corresponds to a multiple time-series scenario rather than the more common longitudinal data format encountered in microeconometrics. Notice that in this setting under Design III, the Peng–Huang estimator also performs quite well in the sense that it has substantially lower bias than the Naive estimator. This might be explained by noting that Naive does not account for censoring and $\gamma_1/m \approx -0.01$ generates a small correlation between α_i and the zero-mean variables d_{ij}'s. Nevertheless, the bias of the Peng–Huang estimator is larger than that of the Panel estimator proposed in this paper. In terms of RMSE, however, it performs better than the Panel estimator. This is to be expected since the Panel estimator includes individual effects and also performs an additional IV step and is thus not efficient. The multiple time-series case, however, is unlikely to be encountered in applied econometrics as typically in duration analysis data on multiple individuals is easier to obtain than data on a few individuals over a long period of time.

The good performance of the Panel estimator relative to the other competing estimators is also observed for sample size (n, m) equal to (10, 20) and (20, 50). The results were qualitatively similar to the ones reported in

Tables 1–4, and they are not reported in the paper. They are, however, available upon request from the authors.

The simulations indicate that the proposed Panel estimator performs very well under both random and fixed censoring and is thus to be preferred over the Peng–Huang estimator when endogeneity and correlated individual effects are of concern.

AN EMPIRICAL APPLICATION

In this section, we analyze data for unemployed workers who received unemployment insurance, to study how insurance benefits affects the duration of unemployment.[2] The effect of unemployment insurance on the duration of unemployment has also been investigated by Han and Hausman (1990), Ham and Rea (1987), Meyer (1990), and Hausman and Woutersen (2005). This paper is, however, the first one to estimate the impact of unemployment insurance using repeated unemployment spells. Our results indicate that workers receiving unemployment benefits tend to be unemployed for a longer period of time than workers not receiving unemployment benefits. The quantile approach reveals that the estimated effect is largest at the lower tail of the conditional duration distribution, suggesting that workers' incentives to seek jobs among workers with low durations are more susceptible to the effect of unemployment insurance. The application illustrates the importance of controlling for unobserved heterogeneity in (quantile) survival analysis.

Data

The data used here includes unemployed workers who were eligible for receiving unemployment insurance during the period 1997–2001. The sample includes information obtained from administrative records and telephone interviews with unemployed workers eligible for unemployment insurance. The data contains information on the recipient's exhaustee status, the date when the unemployment spell began, and the date when the unemployment spell ended. With this information, we construct the duration of repeated spells. Table 5 shows the duration of the unemployment spells and the frequency distribution of spells, which ranges from 1 to 6 spells per worker. The sample offers a range of unemployment durations. While the average unemployment duration is more than 1 year for workers

Table 5. Distribution of Spells and Durations.

Number of Spells	Duration (in days)	Number of Workers	Number of Observations
1	442	2213	2213
2	186	722	1444
3	118	271	813
4	97	78	312
5	82	37	185
6	66	8	48
Total	–	3329	5015

Table 6. Variable Description and Summary Statistics.

Variable	Description	Mean	Std.Dev.	Min	Median	Max
Duration	Length of the spell in days	273.98	300.52	10.00	145.00	1365.00
UI	= 1, if received unemployment benefit	0.69	0.46	0.00	1.00	1.00
Age	Age of the unemployed worker	40.25	10.90	21.00	39.84	63.00
Perm	= 1, if permanent job before unemployment 0.78	0.41	0.00	1.00	1.00	
Unemp	State rate of unemployment	4.52	0.92	2.20	4.60	6.90
Censored	= 1, if the observation is not censored	0.74	0.44	0.00	1.00	1.00

who were unemployed once in the period of analysis, it reduces to approximately 2 months for workers who have a maximum of six unemployment spells between 1997 and 2001.

The sample consists of 3329 workers and 5015 observations. In the regression analysis that we will perform later in this section, we restrict attention to workers who were unemployed between 3 and 6 times in the period of analysis. This leads to a data set of 1358 observations on multiple unemployment spells of 394 workers. Moreover, we limit the sample to include workers between the ages of 20 and 65. We have information on the duration of the spells, whether the worker received unemployment benefits, the age of the worker at the beginning of the unemployment spell, whether the worker had a permanent employment before unemployment, and the state where the worker collects her benefits. Variable definitions and sample means are introduced in Table 6.

Workers generally receive unemployment insurance in their first unemployment spell, and the proportion of workers receiving benefits decreases dramatically after the first spell. The workers considered in this sample do not appear to necessarily be part-time workers, since approximately 78% lost a permanent job before unemployment. We also have information on whether the observation is censored. As shown in Table 6, the sample includes 26% of censored observations.

Preliminary evidence on the effect of unemployment benefits on the duration of unemployment is offered in Fig. 1. We classify states into groups

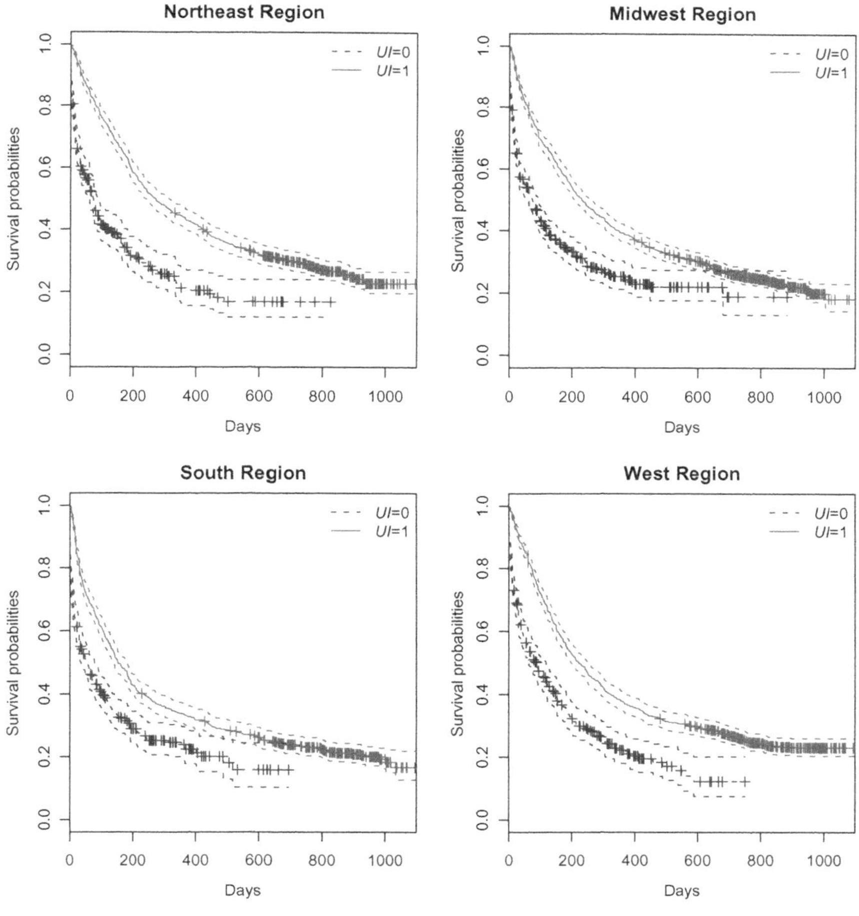

Fig. 1. Survival Functions for the Duration of Unemployment. The Dashed Lines Represent 95% Confidence Intervals.

according to the definition of the U.S. Census Bureau. The evidence presented by regions allows us to examine if important regional differences of the effect of unemployment benefits on the duration of unemployment may exist across regions. The figures present Kaplan–Meier estimators of survival functions for the number of days of unemployment, separately for workers who receive unemployment insurance ($UI = 1$) and workers who do not receive unemployment insurance ($UI = 0$). The effect of unemployment benefit on short unemployment durations appears to be important and significantly different for workers not receiving unemployment insurance and workers receiving unemployment insurance. The effect of unemployment benefits tends to decrease at higher unemployment durations. The effect, however, remains statistically significant at standard levels. The evidence also suggests that regional differences in terms of the duration of unemployment and the effect of unemployment benefits are relatively minor quantitatively. The South exhibits the smallest difference in the estimated distributions between workers who receive unemployment insurance and those who do not.

Empirical Results

We estimate the following panel data duration model:

$$\log(T_{ij}) = \boldsymbol{d}'_{ij}\gamma + \boldsymbol{x}'_{ij}\boldsymbol{\beta} + v_{ij} \tag{23}$$

The vector $\boldsymbol{d}_{ij}$ includes an indicator variable for whether the worker received unemployment benefits (UI), the age of the worker at the beginning of the unemployment spell (Age), and an indicator variable for whether the worker had a permanent job before unemployment (Perm). The vector $\boldsymbol{x}_{ij}$ includes the rate of unemployment in the state where the worker collects unemployment benefits and controls for seasonal effects (i.e., variables indicating the month of the year). In models without individual effects, the vector $\boldsymbol{x}_{ij}$ includes indicator variables to control for the geographical region where the unemployment benefits were collected. These variables were constructed following the definition of the U.S. Census Bureau. In some applications, it may also be advisable to introduce region and/or state effects but here it creates challenges for estimating models since we are faced with both state-invariant variables, and individual-specific variables and in our sample, workers collected benefits in only one geographic location during the period of analysis.

Table 7. Results Based on the Accelerated Failure Time (AFT) Model and Quantile Regression Models Estimated at the Median.

Variables	AFT	Naive	Peng–Huang		Panel		
	(1)	(2)	(3)	(4)	(5)	(6)	(7)
Receiving unemployment insurance	0.203	0.696	0.448	0.451	1.832	1.019	0.550
	(0.137)	(0.178)	(0.152)	(0.204)	(1.332)	(0.752)	(0.196)
Age	0.029	0.019	0.019	0.017	0.013	0.017	0.235
	(0.005)	(0.008)	(0.010)	(0.010)	(0.009)	(0.005)	(0.113)
Permanent employee before unemployment	0.382	0.144	0.352	0.375	0.301	0.235	0.783
	(0.129)	(0.169)	(0.048)	(0.180)	(0.331)	(0.172)	(0.273)
Unemployment	0.483	0.227	0.214	0.185	0.255	0.052	0.360
	(0.050)	(0.105)	(0.130)	(0.181)	(0.379)	(0.059)	(0.226)
Instruments	No	No	No	No	Yes	Yes	No
Time effects	Yes	Yes	Yes	Yes	Yes	Yes	Yes
Region effects	No	No	No	Yes	Yes	No	No
Individual effects	No	No	No	No	No	No	Yes

Standard Errors are in Parentheses.

Table 7 presents regression results derived from estimating several different econometric models. The statistical baseline is given by the accelerated failure time (AFT) model, where $v_{ij} = \alpha_i + u_{ij}$ and u_{ij} is distributed as Weibull. We assume that α_i models unobserved heterogeneity that is distributed as Gamma.

Table 7 also presents the results from three quantile regression models that were estimated at the conditional median. The method labeled Naive is a quantile regression estimator that ignores individual heterogeneity possibly correlated with the independent variables $\boldsymbol{d}_{ij}$ and censoring. The method labeled Peng–Huang is the quantile regression approach proposed by Peng and Huang (2008) for the survival model, and the method labeled Panel is the panel quantile approach developed in the previous sections.

We estimate two versions of the model using Peng–Huang estimator. In column (3), we estimate a model without controlling for workers' latent heterogeneity. In column (4), we estimate a similar model which includes time and region effects to control for the small regional differences suggested in Fig. 1. As expected, columns (3) and (4) do not offer significantly different point estimates. In columns (5), (6), and (7), we employ the proposed approach to estimate a model under different assumptions. Column (5) reports results from a regression that uses unemployment insurance eligibility to instrument the potentially endogenous variable corresponding to whether a worker received unemployment insurance or not. Workers are eligible if they can demonstrate they have lost their jobs through no fault of their own. In column (6), we use a Hausman–Taylor (1981) type instrument obtained within the model, by simply considering differences from worker-specific mean of the indicator variable for whether the worker received unemployment insurance. If the individual effects represent a location shift and u_{ij} and v_{ij} in Eqs. (19) and (20) are independent, this strategy may successfully remove the source of endogeneity. Lastly, in column (7), instead of using instruments, we estimate the model augmented by individual effects.

All the variants of the models estimated in Table 7 suggest that workers receiving unemployment benefits tend to be unemployed for a longer period of time than workers not receiving unemployment benefits. It is also interesting to see that the methods that treat the age of the worker and whether the worker had a permanent job before unemployment as independent of unobserved heterogeneity α, tend to report considerably different effects than the panel approach presented in the last column.

Using Fig. 2, we extend the evidence presented in the last column of Table 7 beyond the median quantile. To obtain the results, we apply the method to estimate a panel-duration quantile version of Eq. (23):

$$Q_{\log(T_{ij})}(\tau|\boldsymbol{d}_{ij}, \boldsymbol{x}_{ij}, \boldsymbol{z}_{ij}) = \boldsymbol{d}'_{ij}\gamma(\tau) + \boldsymbol{x}'_{ij}\boldsymbol{\beta}(\tau) + \boldsymbol{z}'_{ij}\boldsymbol{\alpha}(\tau) \tag{24}$$

for several quantiles τ in the grid (τ_0, τ_U). The quantile τ_0 was set to be zero and the quantile τ_U is a deterministic constant (Peng & Huang, 2008), which is subject to some identifiability restrictions by the presence of censoring. In our application, the constant $\tau_U = 0.62$.

Our model is similar to Eq. (10) under the assumption that the independent variables are not correlated with the error term u_{ij}. Our quantile regression model conditions on individual heterogeneity, and, therefore, we follow the traditional approach of allowing for dependence between unobserved heterogeneity α_i and the independent variable. This is an important concern in this application since individual effects may be correlated with receiving unemployment insurance, losing a permanent job, and the age at the time of unemployment. The figure displays estimates of the effects of interest as a function of the quantiles of the conditional distribution of unemployment duration. We report results for $\tau \in [0.1, 0.6]$.

Fig. 2 indicates that the effect of receiving unemployment benefits is larger at the lower tail of the conditional unemployment duration distribution, and it tends to decrease as we go across quantiles. It is interesting to see that the effect of the age of the worker at the time of being unemployed and whether

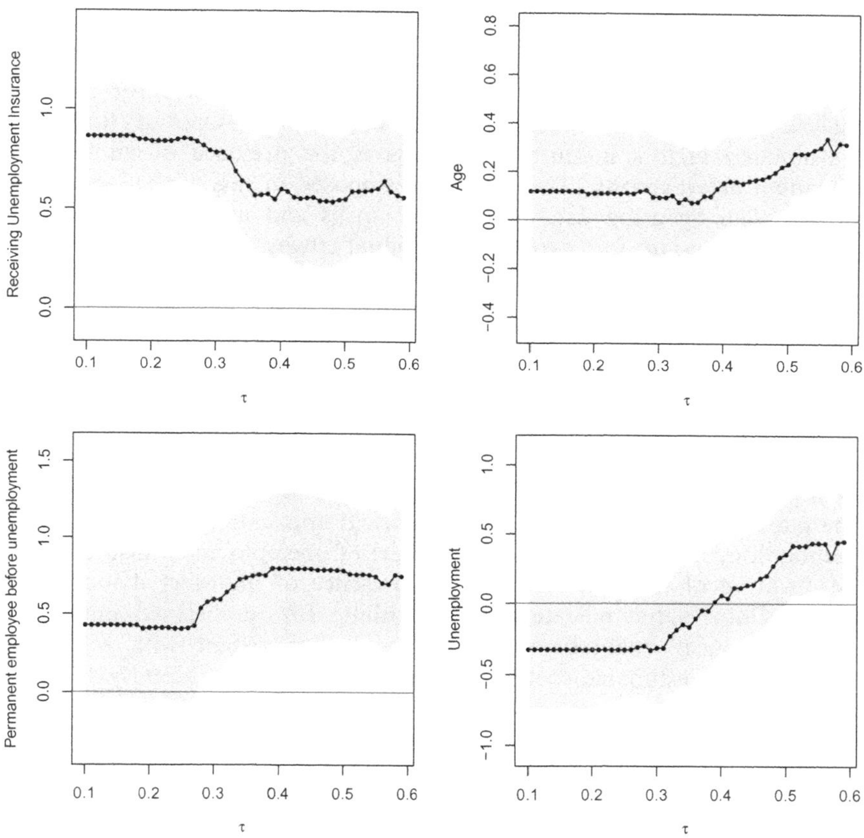

Fig. 2. Results for the Panel Duration Model with Fixed Effects Based on the Quantile Regression Model. The Grey Areas Represent 95% (Pointwise) Confidence Intervals.

the worker had a permanent job before unemployment are significant factors at long (conditional) unemployment durations, while they do not appear to affect short (conditional) unemployment durations. On the other hand, the effect of state unemployment has different signs at the lower and upper tails of the conditional distribution of unemployment duration. While the evidence suggests that an increase in unemployment decreases short unemployment durations, it increases long unemployment durations. It should be noticed, however, that the effect is only statistically significant at standard levels at the upper tail of the conditional distribution.

CONCLUSION

This paper introduces a new quantile regression estimator for survival analysis when the dependent variable is censored. One of the main confounding factors in duration models is the presence of unobserved individual heterogeneity. The estimator proposed in this paper overcomes this problem by using data on multiple spells and using the panel data structure to account for correlated individual effects.

In the analysis of economic durations, the applied economist is also often faced with the presence of additional variables which may be endogenous due to inherent selection issues, such as participation in a government program. Our proposed estimator shows how a two-step procedure using IV can be used to address this problem.

The estimator introduced in this paper has excellent finite sample performance and easily outperforms other estimators such as the Peng and Huang (2008) estimator that do not account for unobserved heterogeneity. The paper also discusses a realistic empirical application of the proposed methodology to the estimation of the effect of unemployment insurance on the duration of unemployment in the presence of unobserved individual effects. Our results indicate that controlling for unobserved individual effects produces qualitatively similar results, consistent with economic theory, but the estimated coefficients are quantitatively sufficiently different and may lead to different policy prescriptions.

ACKNOWLEDGMENTS

We are grateful to Badi Baltagi, Jerry Hausman, Roger Koenker, Shakeeb Khan, Antonio Galvao, and participants at the 11th Advances in Econometrics Conference for insightful conversations and comments.

NOTES

1. Although the wild bootstrap has been used and extensively analyzed by researchers, the vast majority of the existing theory is associated with linear estimators. To the best of our knowledge, the exception is Feng, He and Hu (2011), which propose a wild bootstrap approach for the quantile regression estimator (Koenker & Bassett, 1978). They find that many choices of the weight distribution commonly considered in the literature do not work for estimators with non-linear score functions. While the pair bootstrap works in the presence of heteroskedasticity, there is some evidence that the wild bootstrap may outperform the pair bootstrap in

linear models (Flachaire, 2005). Their relative performance in a quantile regression setting is however not known.

2. The data was originally collected by the Upjohn Institute and is available for purchase from their website.

REFERENCES

Abbring, J. H., & Van Den Berg, G. J. (2003). The nonparametric identification of treatment effects in duration models. *Econometrica*, *71*(5), 1491–1517.

Audretsch, D. B. (1991). New-firm survival and the technological regime. *Review of Economics and Statistics*, *60*, 441–450.

Audretsch, D., & Mahmood, T. (1995). New firm survival: New results using a hazard function. *Review of Economics and Statistics*, *77*, 97–103.

Blundell, R., & Powell, J. L. (2007). Censored regression quantiles with endogenous regressors. *Journal of Econometrics*, *141*, 65–83.

Burda, M., Harding, M., Hausman, J. (2012). *A Bayesian Semiparametric Competing Risk Model with Unobserved Heterogeneity*. mimeo, Stanford University.

Chen, S., & Khan, S. (2001). Semiparametric estimation of a partially linear censored regression model. *Econometric Theory*, *17*, 567–590.

Chernozhukov, V., & Hansen, C. (2005). An IV model of quantile treatment effects. *Econometrica*, *73*(1), 245–262.

Chernozhukov, V., & Hansen, C. (2006). Instrumental quantile regression inference for structural and treatment effect models. *Journal of Econometrics*, *132*(2), 491–525.

Chernozhukov, V., & Hansen, C. (2008). Instrumental variable quantile regression: A robust inference approach. *Journal of Econometrics*, *142*(1), 379–398.

Chesher, A. (2002). *Semiparametric identification in duration models*. CeMMAP Working Paper CWP20/02.

De Silva, D. G., Kosmopoulou, G., & Lamarche, C. (2009). The effect of information on the bidding and survival of entrants in procurement auctions. *Journal of Public Economics*, *93*, 56–72.

Eberwein, C., Ham, J. C., & Lalonde, R. J. (1997). The impact of being offered and receiving classroom training on the employment histories of disadvantaged women: Evidence from experimental data. *The Review of Economic Studies*, *64*(4), 655–682.

Feng, X., He, X., & Hu, J. (2011). Wild bootstrap for quantile regression. *Biometrika*, *98*(4), 995–999.

Fitzenberger, B., & Wilke, R. (2006). Using quantile regression for duration analysis. *Allgemeines Statistisches Archive*, *90*(1), 105–120.

Flachaire, E. (2005). Bootstrapping heteroskedastic regression models: Wild bootstrap vs. pairs boot-strap. *Computational Statistics and Data Analysis*, *49*(2), 361–376.

Fleming, T. R., & Harrington, D. P. (1991). *Counting processes and survival analysis*. New York: Wiley.

Geroski, P. A. (1995). What do we know about entry. *International Journal of Industrial Organization*, *13*, 421–440.

Graham, B. S., Hahn, J., & Powell, J. L. (2009). The incidental parameter problem in a non-differentiable panel data model. *Economics Letters*, *105*, 181–182.

Ham, J. C., & Rea, S. (1987). Unemployment insurance and male unemployment duration in Canada. *Journal of Labor Economics*, *5*(3), 325–353.
Han, A., & Hausman, J. A. (1990). Flexible parametric estimation of duration and competing risk models. *Journal of Applied Econometrics*, *5*(1), 1–28.
Harding, M., & Lamarche, C. (2009). A quantile regression approach for estimating panel data models using instrumental variables. *Economics Letters*, *104*, 133–135.
Hausman, J. A., & Taylor, W. E. (1981). Panel data and unobservable individual effects. *Econometrica*, *49*(6), 1377–1398.
Hausman, J.A., Woutersen, T.M. (2005). *Estimating a semiparametric duration model without specifying heterogeneity*. CeMMAP Working Paper No. CWP11/05.
Honoré, B. E., & de Paula, A. (2010). Interdependent durations. *Review of Economic Studies*, *77*(3), 1138–1163.
Horowitz, J. L., & Lee, S. (2004). Semiparametric estimation of a panel data proportional hazard model with fixed effects. *Journal of Econometrics*, *119*, 155–198.
Jin, Z., Ying, Z., & Wei, L. J. (2001). A simple resampling method by perturbing the minimand. *Biometrika*, *88*(2), 381–390.
Khan, S., & Tamer, E. (2007). Partial rank estimation of transformation models with general forms of censoring. *Journal of Econometrics*, *136*, 251–280.
Khan, S., & Tamer, E. (2009). Inference on endogenously censored regression models using conditional moment in-equalities. *Journal of Econometrics*, *152*, 104–119.
Koenker, R. (2004). Quantile regression for longitudinal data. *Journal of Multivariate Analysis*, *91*, 74–89.
Koenker, R. (2005). *Quantile regression*. Cambridge University Press.
Koenker, R. (2008). Censored quantile regression redux. *Journal of Statistical Software*, *27*, 1–14.
Koenker, R. (2010): quantreg: An R package for quantile regression, Version 4.57. Retrieved from http://CRAN.R-project.org/package = quantreg
Koenker, R., & Bassett, G. (1978). Regression quantiles. *Econometrica*, *46*(1), 33–50.
Koenker, R., & Bassett, G. (1982). Tests of linear hypothesis and l_1 estimation. *Econometrica*, *50*, 1577–1584.
Koenker, R., & Geling, O. (2001). Reappraising medfly longevity: A quantile regression approach. *Journal of the American Statistical Association*, *96*, 458–468.
Koenker, R., & Xiao, Z. (2002). Inference on the quantile regression process. *Econometrica*, *70*, 1583–1612.
Lamarche, C. (2010). Robust penalized quantile regression estimation for panel data. *Journal of Econometrics*, *157*(2), 396–408.
Lancaster, T. (1985). Simultaneous equations models in applied search theory. *Journal of Econometrics*, *28*, 113–126.
Lee, S. (2008). Estimating panel data duration models with censored data. *Econometric Theory*, *24*, 1254–1276.
Ma, S., & Kosorok, M. R. (2005). Robust semiparametric M-estimation and the weighted bootstrap. *Journal of Multivariate Analysis*, *96*(1), 190–217.
Meyer, B. (1990). Unemployment insurance and unemployment spells. *Econometrica*, *58*(4), 757–782.
Olsen, R. J., & Farkas, G. (1988). Endogenous covariates in duration models and the effect of adolescent childbirth on schooling. *Journal of Human Resources*, *24*, 39–53.

Peng, L., & Huang, Y. (2008). Survival analysis with quantile regression models. *Journal of the American Statistical Association, 103*, 637–649.

Portnoy, S. (2003). Censored regression quantiles. *Journal of the American Statistical Association, 98*, 1001–1010.

Wang, H. J., & Fygenson, M. (2009). Inference for censored quantile regression in longitudinal studies. *Annals of Statistics, 37*, 756–781.

LABOR ALLOCATION IN A HOUSEHOLD AND ITS IMPACT ON PRODUCTION EFFICIENCY: A COMPARISON OF PANEL MODELING APPROACHES

Hild Marte Bjørnsen and Ashok K. Mishra

ABSTRACT

The objective of this study is to investigate the simultaneity between farm couples' decisions on labor allocation and production efficiency. Using an unbalanced panel data set of Norwegian farm households (1989–2008), we estimate off-farm labor supply of married farm couples and farm efficiency in a three-equation system of jointly determined endogenous variables. We address the issue of latent heterogeneity between households. We solve the problem by two-stage OLS and GLS estimation where state dependence is accounted for in the reduced form equations. We compare the results against simpler model specifications where we suppress censoring of off-farm labor hours and endogeneity of regressors, respectively. In the reduced form specification, a considerably large number of parameters are statistically significant. Davidson–McKinnon test of exogeneity confirms that both operator and spouse's off-farm labor

Essays in Honor of Jerry Hausman
Advances in Econometrics, Volume 29, 269–303

ISSN: 0731-9053/doi:10.1108/S0731-9053(2012)0000029015

supply should be treated as endogenous in estimating farming efficiency. The parameter estimates seem robust across model specifications. Off-farm labor supply of farm operators and spouses is jointly determined. Off-farm work by farm operator and spouses positively affects farming efficiency. Farming efficiency increases with operator's age, farm size, agricultural subsidises, and share of current investment to total farm capital stock.

Keywords: Labor allocation; farming efficiency; dynamic panel; censoring; endogeneity; unobserved heterogeneity

JEL classification: C33; C34; C52; J22; J43; Q12

INTRODUCTION

Most of the empirical literature in labor economics and time allocation tend to analyze labor allocation decisions of economic agents using cross-sectional data and limited dependent variable models (Maddala, 1983; Tobin, 1958). But such methods implicitly assume that model parameters are stable (constant) across firms and over time. The use of cross-sectional methods is therefore glaringly at odds with the firm-specific aspects of the theoretical models employed in labor economics. Even though Sumner (1991) identified the utilization of longitudinal data to analyze farmers' off-farm work decision as one of the most useful and promising extensions of the early literature, the use of such data is still rare (Ahituv & Kimhi, 2006).

When model parameters vary across firm or over time, a cross-sectional analysis will fail to identify the true model parameters and will lead to parameter estimates that are not efficient (due to heteroskedasticity). Although the issues arising from possible time-varying effects have been noted in the literature, the possibility that model parameters vary across individuals has received scant attention. The unobserved factors that influence the sorting into dual employment (farm and off-farm employment in our case) may also affect wages. It is necessary, therefore, to incorporate the unobserved heterogeneity responsible for the dual decision and explain how it is rewarded in the two sectors (farm and nonfarm sectors).

There is an extensive literature that investigates the determinants of farm households' involvement in nonfarm labor markets. However, increased reliance on off-farm income may have resulted in less time devoted to farming and farm related human capital. In particular, Smith (2002) argues that increased reliance on off-farm employment may have resulted in a reduction in on-farm efficiency. For example, Smith argues that increased off-farm work may have implied less attention to issues of "smart farming" – which could lead to a reduction in variable costs. While Goodwin and Mishra (2004), the only study, have shown that greater involvement in off-farm work increases farming efficiency (defined as the ratio of gross cash farm income to total variable costs), their study has several weaknesses. First, the study ignores the role of spouse in the joint determination of labor supply decision by farm operators and spouses. It is not surprising since most existing analyses of off-farm labor supply in Western economies usually include the decisions of the farm operator and not the joint decision of the spouse (Ahearn, El-Osta, & Dewbre, 2006; Phimister & Roberts, 2006; Weiss, 1997). Second, the data is cross-sectional.

Panel data studies of the labor allocation generally control for endogeneity through fixed effects or alternative instrumental variables (IV) estimators (Baltagi, 2008; Robinson, 1989). These procedures are inflexible in their treatment of worker heterogeneity as they generally assume that the endogeneity is individual-specific and fixed. A preferable approach would decompose the endogeneity underlying farming efficiency and labor allocation into an individual or time-specific effect. Research presented here investigates how farm efficiency is affected by off-farm labor supply and vice versa. Our assumption is that there is simultaneity in the off-farm labor supply decisions between spouses and also with farm efficiency which calls for testing the causality between the variables. It is often assumed that off-farm labor supply affects farm productivity (Lien, Kumbhakar, & Hardaker, 2010) but causality may well go the other way because efficiency in farm production may liberate time to be spent in other income-generating activities, such as off-farm work. This leads us to two main problems that we address in this chapter. First, an endogeneity bias stemming from jointly determined variables (farming efficiency and off-farm labor supply of operator and spouse) and second, the censoring of two of these dependent variables in the context of unbalanced panel data.

Using an unbalanced panel dataset of Norwegian farm households (1989–2008), we estimate off-farm labor supply of married farm couples and farming efficiency in a three-equation system of jointly determined endogenous variables, taking into account the latent heterogeneity between households. Due to the complexity of the model we start with looking at the problem of censoring and endogeneity of regressors partially. We then solve the problem by two-stage OLS and GLS estimation where state dependence is accounted for in the reduced form equations, and compare the results against the simpler, partial model specifications. This is because we want to compare the supposedly inefficient two-stage estimations of the whole system with the simpler specifications and to assess the robustness and efficiency of our proposed modeling techniques.

In the reduced form and two-stage estimations, a considerably large number of parameters are statistically significant. Using a Davidson–McKinnon test of exogeneity on the static two-stage estimations clearly indicates that both operator and spouse's off-farm labor supply should be treated as endogenous in estimating farming efficiency. The parameter estimates seem robust across model specifications and the assumption that the two-stage estimates are inefficient is not apparent. We find that off-farm labor supply of farm operators and spouses is jointly determined. Off-farm work by farm operator and spouses positively affects farming efficiency. Farming efficiency increases with operator's age, farm size, agricultural subsidies, and share of current investment to total farm capital stock.

MODEL FRAMEWORK AND ESTIMATION

The farm household follows a utility maximization framework where it's assumed that the farm operator (O) and spouse (S) comprise the farm household and utility (U) is a function of leisure ($L_i(F, M)$) and income (Y). Utility is assumed to be affected by human capital characteristics (K^O, K^S), other household and local market characteristics (Z_H) that are considered exogenous to current decisions, as well as unobserved heterogeneity in preferences, α_U. Finally, both farm household income and the time spent on leisure are a function of the time devoted to farming activities (F) and off-farm activities (M).

$$Maximize\ U = U(L_i(F^O, M^O), L_i(F^S, M^S), K^O, K^S, Y, Z_H, \alpha_U) \quad (1)$$

subject to

$$T^O = L_o + F^O + M^O(Z_H, M^S) \quad (2)$$

$$T^S = L_s + F^S + M^S(Z_H, M^O) \quad (3)$$

$$P_y Y = P_f Q(X, K^O, K^S, F^O, F^S, R, Z_F, \alpha_Q) + W^O M^O(M^S) + W^S M^S(M^O) + V - pX \quad (4)$$

$$L_o, F^O, M^O(M^S) \geq 0 \qquad L_s, F^S, M^S(M^O) \geq 0 \tag{5}$$

where P_y denotes the price of consumption good Y; L_o is home time (leisure) of the farm operator, O, and L_s is home time (leisure) for the spouse of the farm operator, S; T is the total time endowment, L is the time allocated to leisure, F^i is time allocated to farm work and M^i is time allocated to off-farm work by operator (O) and spouse (S); W^i is the off-farm wage rate. The off-farm wage rates[1] that the operators and spouse face depend on the their respective human capital (K^O, K^S) characteristics, local labor market conditions Z_H, such as local and regional unemployment rate, which are considered as exogenous, as well as unobserved individual heterogeneity, indicated by α_W^O and α_W^S. P_f denotes a vector of farm output prices, X denotes a vector of inputs used in the farm production and p denotes a vector of farm input prices, V signifies other non-labor income including income from government payments/subsidies, K is human capital, and R describes location-specific attributes (e.g., local employment, farm characteristics, and soil conditions). Eq. (4) is the full income constraint, and a non-negativity constraint is represented in Eq. (5). Note that M^O is a function of the off-farm hours worked by the spouse (M^s). This allows for jointness in off-farm labor allocation decisions. The full income constraint is defined as the sum of income from the operator's off-farm labor ($W^O M^O(M^S)$), spouse's off-farm labor ($W^S M^S(M^O)$), farm profits ($P_f Q(.) - pX$) and other household non-labor income (V) minus consumption expenditures ($P_y Y$). Farm output Q depends specifically on the labor hours from operators and spouses (F^O, F^S), which are assumed to be perfect substitutes, a vector of purchased farm inputs (X), human capital (K^O, K^S) attributes, observed farm characteristics, Z_F (includes farming efficiency), as well as unobserved heterogeneity in the technology α_Q. Recall that the utility and the production functions are assumed to be concave, continuous, and twice differentiable. The Lagrangian ($\mathcal{L}$) can be constructed for the outlined maximization problem with the following first-order conditions for off-farm labor:

$$\begin{aligned} U(L_i(F^O, M^O), L_e(F^S, M^S), K^O, K^S, Y, Z_H, \alpha_U) \\ + \delta(P_y Y - (P_f Q(X, K^O, K^S, F^O, F^S, R, Z_F, \alpha_Q) \\ + W^O M^O(M^S) + W^S M^S(M^O) + V - pX)) \\ + \lambda_1(T^O - (L_o + F^O + M^O(Z_M, M^S))) \\ + \lambda_2(T^S - (L_s + F^S + M^S(Z_M, M^O))) \end{aligned} \tag{6}$$

$$\frac{\partial L}{\partial M^O} \Rightarrow MRS^O_{L_o} - W^O = \left(\frac{\partial M^S}{\partial M_O}\right)\{W^S - MRS^S_{L_s,Y}\} \tag{7}$$

$$\frac{\partial L}{\partial M^S} \Rightarrow MRS^S_{L_s} - W^S = \left(\frac{\partial M^O}{\partial M^S}\right)\{W^O - MRS^O_{L_o,Y}\} \tag{8}$$

Per the cross-partial derivative in Eqs. (7) and (8), if the off-farm labor allocation decision of the spouse is independent of the operator, then $\frac{\partial M^S}{\partial M^O} = \frac{\partial M^O}{\partial M^S} = 0$. For the operator, this implies that utility is maximized where the marginal rate of substitution ($MRS^O_{L_o,Y}$) between leisure and the consumption goods is exactly equal to the off-farm wage, and $P_f Q'_{F^O} = W^O$ or that the value of the marginal product of farm labor is equal to the off-farm wage rate. Similarly, spouse's utility is maximized where the marginal rate of substitution ($MRS^S_{L_s,Y}$) between leisure and the consumption goods is exactly equal to the off-farm wage, and $P_f Q'_{F^S} = W^S$ or that the value of the marginal product of farm labor is equal to the off-farm wage rate. Corner solutions are implied if either on-farm or off-farm labor supply is zero. Now if we hold the total amount of labor supplied constant, an increase in the price of output (P_f) or an increase in on-farm labor productivity would yield more labor being supplied to the farm and less to off-farm activities. Similarly, an increase in off-farm wage rate would decrease the number of hours supplied to farming activities. However, it should be noted that the impact of such changes on overall labor supply depends on the competing income and substitution effects.[2]

Differentiating Eq. (6) with respect to $Y, L^O, L^S, M^O, M^S, F^O, F^S, X$ gives the first-order conditions. One can obtain the virtual on-farm labor supply, leisure, and off-farm labor supply functions. The goal of our analysis lies in providing estimates of off-farm labor supply decisions rather than explicit estimation of a structural model of labor supply. Thus, we show and relate off-farm labor supply decisions and on-farm efficiency (Φ) measures to observable and unobservable farm, operator, and spouse characteristics reflected in the determinants of wages, prices, and characteristics of production and utility functions. Specifically, we estimate the following model

$$F^i = \Omega_{F^i}(P_f, p, W^O, W^S, K^O, K^S, Z_F, \alpha_Q) \tag{9}$$

$$L^i = \Omega_{L^i}(P_f, p, W^O, W^S, K^O, K^S, Z_F, V, Z_H, \alpha_U, \alpha_Q) \tag{10}$$

$$M^i = \Omega_{M^i}(P_f, p, W^O, W^S, K^O, K^S, Z_F, V, Z_H, T^i, \alpha_U, \alpha_Q), \quad (i = O, S) \tag{11}$$

$$\Phi = (P_f, p, W^O, W^S, K^O, K^S, V, Z_H, T^i, \alpha_U, \alpha_Q), \quad (i = O, S) \tag{12}$$

Stochastic Specification and Model Estimation

The theoretical behavioral model specified above contains seven specific equations in the seven endogenous variables (or variable vectors) $(F^O, F^S, L^O, L^S, M^O, M^S, \Phi)$, of which the six time allocation variables are subject to censoring as specified in Eq. (5). This is a sizable and complicated system, and to preserve some simplicity we have decided to operationalize only the specification of the three equations which determine off-farm labor supply and farm efficiency in the econometric model version. Our specific assumption therefore is that the couples' off-farm labor supply and the farming efficiency are three jointly determined endogenous variables. All of the three equations include the lag of the specific left-hand-side variable among the right-hand variables. The system becomes more complicated because the causality pattern of the system gives rise to selectivity problems, which also has to be handled in the econometric specification and choice of estimation procedure.

The unbalanced panel design of the data set motivates allowing for unobserved household-specific heterogeneity and state dependence. This further adds to the complexity of the problem, not least with regard to designing an estimation algorithm which can be implemented on available computer software. Standard estimation methods designed for handling, say, only the heterogeneity problem in linear static or first-order autoregressive models, or only the selectivity problem in single-equation or recursive multi-equation models, can at best only provide partial solutions and are very likely to give rise to inconsistent estimates. To our knowledge the entirety of the above problem has not been addressed, at least not for unbalanced data.

The stochastic version of the model consists of two censored time allocation equations for operator's and spouse's off-farm hours (Eqs. (13)–(14)) and one equation for efficiency in farm production (Eq. (15)) which may all include pre-determined endogenous variables, and two observable random variables (Eq. (16)) related to the latent time allocation variables in the labor supply equations. With subscript $i = \text{o,s}$ representing operator and spouse respectively, $h = 1,\ldots,\text{H}$ representing farm household, $t = 1,\ldots,\text{T}$ representing time period, the full simultaneous equations model system can be presented by the following five equations:

$$\mathrm{m}^*_{oht} = \mathrm{x}^{\mathrm{m}}_{oht}\beta^{\mathrm{m}}_o + \mathrm{m}_{oht-1}\delta^{\mathrm{m}}_o + \mathrm{m}_{sht}\gamma^{\mathrm{m}}_o + \varphi_{ht}\theta^{\mathrm{m}}_o + \mathrm{u}^{\mathrm{m}}_{oh} + \mathrm{v}^{\mathrm{m}}_{oht} \tag{13}$$

$$\mathrm{m}^*_{sht} = \mathrm{x}^{\mathrm{m}}_{sht}\beta^{\mathrm{m}}_s + \mathrm{m}_{sht-1}\delta^{\mathrm{m}}_s + \mathrm{m}_{oht}\gamma^{\mathrm{m}}_s + \varphi_{ht}\theta^{\mathrm{m}}_s + \mathrm{u}^{\mathrm{m}}_{sh} + \mathrm{v}^{\mathrm{m}}_{sht} \tag{14}$$

$$\varphi_{ht} = \mathrm{x}^{\varphi}_{ht}\beta^{\varphi} + \varphi_{ht-1}\theta^{\varphi} + \sum_i \mathrm{m}_{iht}\delta^{\varphi}_i + \mathrm{u}^{\varphi}_h + \mathrm{v}^{\varphi}_{ht} \quad i = o, s \tag{15}$$

$$\mathrm{m}_{iht} = \begin{cases} \mathrm{m}^*_{iht} & \text{if } \mathrm{m}^*_{iht} > 0 \\ 0 & \text{otherwise} \end{cases} \quad i = o, s \tag{16}$$

where (m^*_{iht}) is the virtual number of hours spent at off-farm work, as determined by optimization, for individual i and (m_{iht}) is the observed, censored counterpart, (φ_{ht}) is efficiency in farm production defined as farm revenue divided by total variable costs, ($x^{\circ}_{\circ}$) are vectors of observable exogenous variables of which some are time-invariant, some are household-invariant, and most are time- and household-varying, $\mathrm{x}^{\circ}_{ht} = (\mathrm{x}^{\circ}_h, \mathrm{x}^{\circ}_t, \mathrm{x}^{\circ}_{ht})$. The selection of observable exogenous variables may be equation-specific between operator and spouse. Finally, ($\beta^{\circ}_{\circ}$, $\delta^{\circ}_{\circ}$, $\gamma^{\circ}_{\circ}$, $\theta^{\circ}_{\circ}$) are vectors of unknown parameters, ($\mathrm{u}^{\circ}_{\circ}$) are random heterogeneity parameters, and ($\mathrm{v}^{\circ}_{\circ}$) are genuine random disturbances. On the other hand, (v°_{iht}) may be serially correlated, and in a simultaneous equations system, ($\mathrm{u}^{\circ}_{\circ}$, $\mathrm{v}^{\circ}_{\circ}$) may also be correlated with all the jointly endogenous variables in the equation system.

The above specification of the model does not fully consider the time budget of the individuals and households, but time allocation between on- and off-farm hours is assumed implicit in the relationship between farm efficiency and off-farm labor supply. An additional problem not accounted for by the above model description is that off-farm wages is only observed for individuals participating in off-farm work. It is reasonable to assume that market wages are important for determining labor supply, and consequently, we wish to include wages in the vector of explanatory variables. To handle this problem, we postulate separate wage equations, assumed to contain only exogenous covariates, which are then recursive to the rest of the model, so it will not complicate estimation procedures further.

We specifically apply a Heckman two-stage procedure (Heckman, 1974, 1976, 1979) to predict wage rates for individuals not participating in off-farm work. The first step of Heckman's method is to estimate the probability of observing the wage rate, i.e., the probability of participating in off-farm work, $\Pr(m^*_{iht} > 0)$. We let participation be represented by an index dummy variable (I_{iht}) that gives the selection mechanism indicated by

$$I_{iht} = x^I_{iht}\beta^I_i + u^I_{ih} + v^I_{iht} = \begin{cases} 1 & \text{if } m^*_{iht} > 0 \\ 0 & \text{otherwise} \end{cases}, \quad (i = O, S,\ h = 1, \ldots, H,\ t = 1, \ldots, T) \tag{17}$$

and the wage equations by

$$w^{*}_{iht} = x^{w}_{iht}\beta^{w}_{i} + u^{w}_{ih} + v^{w}_{iht} \qquad i = o, s \tag{18}$$

where $(x^{I}_{iht}, x^{w}_{iht})$ are vectors of observed personal, farm, and labor market characteristics, $(\beta^{I}_{i}, \beta^{w}_{i})$ are parameters to be estimated, (u^{I}_{ih}, u^{w}_{ih}) are normally distributed household-specific heterogeneity with zero mean, variances $(\sigma^{2}_{iu^{I}}, \sigma^{2}_{iu^{w}})$, and correlation coefficient θ_i, and $(v^{I}_{iht}, v^{w}_{iht})$ are genuine binormal disturbances with zero means, variances $(\sigma^{2}_{iv^{I}}, \sigma^{2}_{iv^{w}} = 1)$, and correlation coefficient ρ_i. A probit estimation of the participation decision, represented by I_{iht}, provides estimates of Heckman's lambda λ_{ih}, $(\hat{\lambda}_{ih} = \phi(x^{I}_{iht}\hat{\beta}^{I}_{i} + \hat{u}^{I}_{ih})/\Phi(x^{I}_{iht}\hat{\beta}^{I}_{i} + \hat{u}^{I}_{ih}))$, which subsequently are used to produce starting values for $(\hat{\beta}^{w}_{i}, \hat{u}^{w}_{ih})$ to be applied in a final maximum likelihood estimation of the wage equations to predict wage rates for those not participating in off-farm work.

Returning to our primary system of equations, most common solutions applied to handle the joint occurrence of two or more of the relevant problems are extensions of two-step modeling with reduced form solutions. Examples of important contributions for solving simultaneous equation Tobit models by maximum likelihood using cross-sectional data can be found in Amemiya (1974, 1979), Nelson and Olson (1978), Lee, Maddala, and Trost (1980), and Smith and Blundell (1986). Nonlinear and sample selection models in the presence of individual-specific heterogeneity have been addressed by Honoré (1992), Kyriazidou (1997), and Browning and Carro (2010). In linear dynamic panel data models, various IV and generalized method of moments (GMM) techniques have been proposed to correct for endogeneity bias, with different considerations, regarding random (Heckman, 1981; Woolridge, 2005) or fixed (Honoré & Kyriazidou, 2000; Hahn, Hausman, & Kuersteiner, 2007) individual effects.

IV estimation is more complicated in nonlinear models because strong assumptions must be made on the relationship between the endogenous regressors and the instruments. Honoré and Hu (2004) derive moment conditions for censored regression models with pre-determined explanatory variables, a method which is further developed in Honoré and Hu (2010) and Sule, Honoré, Hu, and Leth-Petersen (2011). We will not attempt to follow this line of approach for several reasons.

First, the literature on dynamic panel data censored regression typically relates to one equation models with lagged values of the latent variable which is assumed endogenous, or at least not strictly exogenous. Second, we are interested in the causality between several dependent variables and have thus a system of equations including both continuous and censored endogenous variables, along with lagged dependent variables. Finally, another complication stems from the unbalanced nature of the data sample, where households enter at different time periods and stay in the sample for unequal spells of time. We choose to tackle our problem in a step-wise manner where we initially address simultaneity and selectivity separately before combining the total complexity of the model in a two-step approach where we draw inspiration from the works of Nelson and Olson (1978) and Vella and Verbeek (1999). By doing so, we are able to compare the coefficient estimates between the different specifications to check the robustness of our results.

Assume Exogeneity of Regressors

We start by ignoring simultaneity bias and state dependence and assume that all regressors in the three equations (Eqs. (13)–(16)) are truly exogenous and estimate the three equations separately. The labor supply equations can then be solved by random effects Tobit and the farm efficiency equation by least squares methods. The three equations can be simplified to

$$m^*_{oht} = x^m_{oht}\beta^m_o + u^m_{oh} + v^m_{oht} \tag{13'}$$

$$m^*_{sht} = x^m_{sht}\beta^m_s + u^m_{sh} + v^m_{sht} \tag{14'}$$

$$\varphi_{ht} = x^\varphi_{ht}\beta^\varphi + +u^\varphi_h + v^\varphi_{ht} \tag{15'}$$

$$m_{iht} = \begin{cases} m^*_{iht} & \text{if } m^*_{iht} > 0 \\ 0 & \text{otherwise} \end{cases} \tag{16}$$

The household heterogeneity (u^m_{oh}, u^m_{sh}) and the genuine disturbances (v^m_{oh}, v^m_{sh}) of the Tobit model are unobserved *i.i.d.* random variables with expectation zero and variance $\sigma^2_{u_i}$ and $\sigma^2_{v_i}$, respectively, both conditional on x^m_{iht}, and mutually independent. The model is estimated by adaptive Gauss–Hermite quadrature approximation (with 12 integration points) of the log-likelihood function.

The efficiency equation is linear when the covariates are assumed truly exogenous and can be solved by least squares techniques. We assume usual properties for both $(u^\varphi_h, v^\varphi_{ht})$ of zero mean and covariance, variance (σ^2_u, σ^2_v), no correlation with covariates and no correlation between $(u^\varphi_h, v^\varphi_{ht})$ and apply OLS on $(\varphi_{ht} - \bar{\varphi}_h + \bar{\bar{\varphi}}) = (x^\varphi_{ht} - \bar{x}^\varphi_h + \bar{\bar{x}})\beta^\varphi + (v^\varphi_{ht} - \bar{v}^\varphi_h + \bar{u}) + \bar{\bar{v}}$ where $\bar{\varphi}_h = \sum_{t=1}^T \varphi_{ht}$ and $\bar{\bar{\varphi}} = \sum_{h=i}^H \sum_{t=1}^T \varphi_{ht}$ to produce the consistent fixed effect estimator. Using the same assumptions we apply GLS on

$(\varphi_{ht} - \theta\bar{\varphi}_h) = (x^{\varphi}_{ht} - \theta\bar{x}^{\varphi}_h)\beta^{\varphi} + \{(1-\theta)u^{\varphi}_h + (v^{\varphi}_{ht} - \theta\bar{v}^{\varphi}_h)\}$ where θ is a function of σ^2_u and σ^2_v to produce the random effects estimator.

Disregard Censoring in the Presence of Endogenous Regressors
Allowing for endogenous regressors implies violation of the usual distributional properties, and we have correlation between these covariates and disturbances with the effect that OLS estimates become inconsistent. We make use of IV methods (two-stage OLS or two-stage GLS) to obtain consistency and exclude the households with zero off-farm hours to avoid problems with censored regressors. The system of equation can now be represented by

$$m_{oht} = x^{m}_{oht}\beta^{m}_{o} + m_{sht}\gamma^{m}_{o} + \varphi_{ht}\theta^{m}_{o} + u^{m}_{oh} + v^{m}_{oht} \tag{13''}$$

$$m_{sht} = x^{m}_{sht}\beta^{m}_{s} + m_{oht}\gamma^{m}_{s} + \varphi_{ht}\theta^{m}_{s} + u^{m}_{sh} + v^{m}_{sht} \tag{14''}$$

$$\varphi_{ht} = x^{\varphi}_{ht}\beta^{\varphi} + \sum_{i} m_{iht}\,\delta^{\varphi}_{i} + u^{\varphi}_{h} + v^{\varphi}_{ht} \tag{15''}$$

where $m_{jht}, j \neq i$ and φ_{ht} are included as endogenous variables in the labor supply functions and $m_{iht}, i = o, s$ are endogenous in the farm efficiency equation. Again we keep within a static framework but include first-order lag of the dependent variable among the instruments. The two endogenous variables are allowed to correlate with u°_h and are instrumented by first-order lags in addition to two exogenous variables not included in x°_{ht}, and all three equations are overidentified. The model is solved by two-stage OLS for the fixed effects estimator two-stage GLS for Swamy–Arora random effects estimator. We apply a Davidson–McKinnon test to investigate whether the dependent variables of the two other equations are to be treated as endogenous and test for the efficiency of random effects by means of a Hausman (1978) specification test.

Combine Selectivity and Simultaneity Bias in Two-Step Approach
Finally, we approach our estimation problem through a two-step method where we include lags in the reduced form equations to account for state dependence. When applying two-stage methods in dynamic nonlinear modeling, consistency depends critically on the orthogonality conditions (Abrevaya, Hausman, & Khan, 2010), but the unbalanced nature of the data set complicates the process of deriving initial conditions because period zero varies between households. We simplify by assuming that the

first-period realizations of off-farm hours and farm efficiency are exogenous and thus ignore the initial conditions problem even though this assumption is not realistic in the presence of individual effects. This approach relates to the model version which Vella and Verbeek (*op. cit.*, p. 252) presents as *Dynamic model [A]*. Our model specification is now the original (Eqs. (13)–(16)), and following the reasoning of Nelson and Olson (*op. cit.*) we calculate the reduced-form equations on all exogenous variables where a first-order lag of the dependent variable is included as a pre-determined variable among the regressors.

$$\mathrm{m}^*_{oht} = \mathrm{m}_{oht-1}\pi^{\mathrm{o}}_0 + \mathrm{x}^{\mathrm{m}}_{ht}\pi^{\mathrm{o}}_1 + \mathrm{u}^{\mathrm{o}}_h + \mathrm{v}^{\mathrm{o}}_{ht} \tag{13rf}$$

$$\mathrm{m}^*_{sht} = \mathrm{m}_{sht-1}\pi^{\mathrm{s}}_0 + \mathrm{x}^{\mathrm{m}}_{ht}\pi^{\mathrm{s}}_1 + \mathrm{u}^{\mathrm{s}}_h + \mathrm{v}^{\mathrm{s}}_{ht} \tag{14rf}$$

$$\varphi_{ht} = \varphi_{ht-1}\pi^{\varphi}_0 + \mathrm{x}^{\varphi}_{ht}\pi^{\varphi}_1 + \mathrm{u}^{\varphi}_h + \mathrm{v}^{\varphi}_{ht} \tag{15rf}$$

$$\mathrm{m}_{iht} = \begin{cases} \mathrm{m}^*_{iht} & \text{if } \mathrm{m}^*_{iht} > 0 \\ 0 & \text{otherwise} \end{cases}, \quad i = o, s \tag{16}$$

We assume that the covariance matrices of the genuine errors ($\mathrm{v}^{\mathrm{o}}_{ht}, \mathrm{v}^{\mathrm{s}}_{ht}, \mathrm{v}^{\varphi}_{ht}$) are unrestricted. While estimation of the structural system with two latent and one observed variable is computationally difficult, estimation of the reduced form equations is relatively simple. The reduced form coefficients of the labor supply equations are estimated by random effects Tobit and the efficiency equation by OLS to form instruments for the latent and observed dependent variables ($\hat{\mathrm{m}}^*_{oht}$, $\hat{\mathrm{m}}^*_{sht}$, $\hat{\varphi}_{ht}$) to be used in a second-stage estimation of the structural equations. The instruments ($\hat{\mathrm{m}}^*_{iht} = \mathrm{m}^*_{iht-1}\hat{\pi}^{\mathrm{i}}_0 + \mathrm{x}^{\mathrm{m}}_{ht}\hat{\pi}^{\mathrm{i}}_1$, $i = o, s$) and ($\hat{\varphi}_{ht} = \varphi_{ht-1}\pi^{\varphi}_0 + \mathrm{x}^{\varphi}_{ht}\hat{\pi}^{\varphi}_1$) are then asymptotically uncorrelated with the disturbances. In the second step, the endogenous right-hand-side variables are replaced by their instrumented counterparts in the structural parameters. The two-stage estimates are consistent and asymptotically normal and uncorrelated with the error terms (Nelson and Olson, *op. cit.*) but at a potential cost in efficiency. Proofs of the properties of the two-stage estimates can be found in (Amemiya, 1979).

DATA AND SAMPLE SELECTION

The panel data for this study comes from Norwegian farm households (1989–2008). The data is collected by Norwegian Agricultural Research

Institute (Norsk institutt for landbruksforskning, NILF). This is a yearly survey among approximately 1,000 farm households representing different regions and agricultural products. Most farm household report between 1,800 and 3,100 on-farm hours per year while a standard man-labor year in agriculture is set to 1,875 hours. On-farm hours are normally distributed with mean and median of approximately 2,500 hours. On average, operators work 2,000 hours and spouses 450 hours annually. Hired help is on average 400 hours but with standard deviation of more than 500 hours, and 30 percent of the farm households report no hired help on the farm.

The original panel data set, as well as our final sample, is unbalanced, and some 5–10 percent of the respondents are replaced each year. The extracted sample covers 20 years from 1989 to 2008 and 17,605 observations (total 19,972) were used in the analysis. The attrition of almost 2,400 observations is due to single adult households. The unbalanced panel includes 1,791 unique households which are represented for anything from 3 to 20 years, and on average for 10 years. We find no evidence of potential endogenous sample selection to influence the results but some self-selection may be present because of voluntary participation in the survey and attrition bias from excluding farm units where there is no spouse present.

Variable Definitions and Descriptive Statistics

The variables of particular interest to our study are off-farm work hours and farm efficiency. Multi-employment is common among both farm operators and spouses and many farm operators even have their main income from outside farming. Most farm operators report off-farm work in at least some years, but many only supply a marginal number of hours. As many as 20 percent work between 0 and 37.5 off-farm hours annually. This finding is not surprising because it is well known that many farm operators take on small commissions, e.g., for neighbors (road mending, snow clearing, holiday relief, etc.). For this reason, we define *working off the farm* as having *more than 37.5 annual working hours outside the farm*. This threshold equals to one standard labor week. Operators working less than this are defined as not working off the farm and we rationalize this truncation by the effect on possible measurement error and misclassification in the data.

Although the problem of few reported off-farm hours occurs less frequently for spouses, we choose the same definition for both partners. We see from Table 1 that spouses, on average, work more off-farm hours annually than operators but the variance is greater. Efficiency is defined as

Table 1. Summary Statistics and Definition of Variables.

Variable	Mean	Std. Dev.	Min.	Max.
Operator off-farm hours (annual hours)	491.562	625.658	0	3,751
Spouse off-farm hours (annual hours)	722.45	710.854	0	4,400
Farming efficiency[a]	3.821	1.962	0.634	72.933
Operator age (*years*)	46.062	9.696	12	79
Spouse age (*years*)	44.08	9.914	16	78
Number of children (under the age of 6)	0.229	0.567	0	4
Operator – probability of having a higher education	0.088	0.079	0	0.982
Spouse – probability of having a higher education	0.224	0.1	0.033	0.996
Operator wage rate (*Kr/hr*)	130.284	41.487	60.074	605.396
Spouse wage rate (*Kr/hr*)	129.894	35.583	60.557	534.63
Operator farming experience (*years*)	16.076	9.74	0	60
Operator annual farming hours	2,025.99	798.206	2	7,650
Spouse annual farming hours	449.50	565.843	0	4,970
Hired farm labor hours	397.44	539.074	0	11,000
Milk yield (*1,000 litres*)	57.516	58.872	0	710.312
Agricultural subsidies (*1,000 kroners*)	200.091	103.173	0	1,268.724
Agricultural income, gross farm income (*1,000 kroners*)	735.435	457.242	2.37	7,926.377
Other income (*1,000 kroners*)	45.534	98.915	−239.163	3,604.47
Investments/Capital[b]	0.084	0.125	0	1.306
Total farming area (*hectares*)	22.436	14.489	0	173.8
Rented land (*hectares*)	0.24	0.232	0	2.44
Fallow land (*hectares*)	0.077	0.149	0	1.835
Livestock units (AEU)[c]	40.638	62.171	0	1,440.4
Regional employment/total population in the region (share of regional employment)	0.747	0.081	0.41	1.07
Location Metro 2 area with 10,000 population (= 1, if the farm is located in the Metro 2 area, with 45 minute drive, 0 otherwise)	0.455	0.498	0	1
Location Highland (= 1, if the farm is located in the highland region, 0 otherwise)	0.653	0.476	0	1
Number of observations	17,605			

[a]Defined as ratio of farm revenue to total variable cost.
[b]Total farm investments in a year/total farm capital stock.
[c]AEU (animal equivalent unit): 1 AEU equals 1,000 pounds of animal weight. As an example, a calf that weighs 500 pounds is 0.5 AEUs.

farm revenue divided by total variable cost. On average, revenue is almost four times the total variable cost and median efficiency is 3.5. Approximately 80 percent of the observations lie within the range of 2 and 5. All three endogenous variables show a greater between than within variance, a strong indication of household heterogeneity. Summary statistics and definition of the variables are provided in Table 1 and a graphic presentation of the density of the dependent variables is given in Fig. 1.

ESTIMATION AND TEST RESULTS

This section presents the results in a systematic development. First we will discuss the findings of the wage model, then the reduced form labor supply model, followed by the results of five different model specifications for the off-farm labor supply of operator and spouse, respectively, and six different model specifications for farming efficiency.

Wage Equations

Using a pooled regression we estimate off-farm wages for both the farm operator and the spouse. We assume that the hourly wage rate is determined by age, the probability of having attained higher education, work hours devoted to farming, the centrality of the region, and the regional employment rate; the decision to work off the farm is determined by the number of small children, household income from farming, other income, and implicitly the wage rate through the variables the two equations have in common – age, farming hours, and regional employment rate. The choice of applying a selection model is justified by an LR-test showing that ρ, the correlation between the genuine disturbances, is significantly different from zero for both operator and spouse (see Table A.1) indicating that the results obtained here are consistent and asymptotically efficient. The selection model estimation of the wage equation provides predicted wage rates for individuals not working off the farm.

In general the results show that as age of the operator and spouse increases, they tend to receive lower off-farm wages. However, there is an inverted-U shape quadratic effect of age on off-farm wage rate. This may be due to the fact that age may be a proxy for off-farm work experience. Results also show that educated farmers and their spouses receive higher wages off the farm. Increased work on the farm tends to decrease off-farm

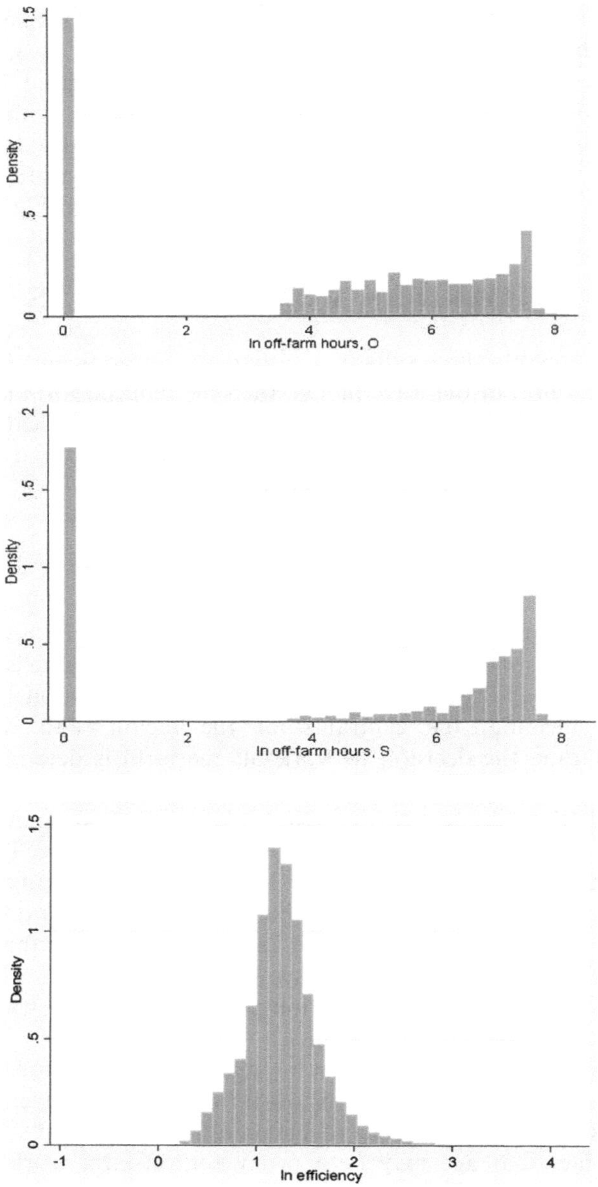

Fig. 1. Density of Endogenous Variables; Operator's Off-Farm Hours, Spouse's Off-Farm Hours and Farming Efficiency.

wages of the farm operator. On the other hand, agricultural income, a proxy for dependence on agriculture, tends to reduce off-farm wages as well. This is consistent with the fact that farm families relying on agricultural income may be more efficient in production agriculture.

Finally, results in Table A.1 show that regional off-farm employment rates play an important role in explaining off-farm wages of both operator and spouses. For example, if the share of regional employment to adult population increases, it leads to an increased opportunity to find off-farm work, while smaller towns have less opportunity for off-farm work.

Labor Supply Functions: Reduced Form

The results from the reduced form estimation are presented in Table A.2. The table presents the parameter estimates of off-farm labor supply, both farm operator and spouse, and farming efficiency models. Columns 1, 3, and 5 represent the model estimation without the lagged dependent variable, while Columns 2, 4, and 6 represent the model estimation with a lagged dependent variable (dynamic). The reduced form equations for off-farm labor supply are estimated by random effects Tobit, and the reduced form farming efficiency is estimated by ordinary least squares (Hausman test rejects random effects for all versions specified). One thing that is obvious from the results is that the coefficient of the static Tobit model is generally higher compared to the parameter estimates obtained from the dynamic Tobit estimation procedure. This can be explained by the large and significant impact of the lagged dependent variable. Presence of the lagged variable is accompanied by smaller random effect variation. Further, some of the variables that were significant in the static model are not significant in the dynamic model (e.g., spouse's age, number of children, farming experience, all in Column 2).

We find that most parameter estimates have expected signs and statistical significance. For example, we find a nonlinear relationship between the age of both operator and spouse off-farm labor supply increases with individual's age and is nonlinear. Further, off-farm labor supply is positively correlated with off-farm wage rate. On the other hand, farm size (agricultural income, a proxy for dependence on agriculture) is negatively correlated with off-farm labor supply for both operator and spouse. Through a simple test – between the observed and predicted values of off-farm hours – the correlation between observed labor supply and the predicted values from the specifications in Column 2 is much higher (0.79 for operator and 0.82 for spouse) than from Column 1 (0.35 for operator and 0.33 for spouse) and we chose to proceed with the results in Columns 2 and 4 in the second stage.

We next examine the labor supply model and the farming efficiency model. The reduced form equations for farming efficiency are estimated by ordinary least squares. Results in Table A.2 show that the lagged dependent variable is statistically significant in the reduced form farming efficiency model. However, inclusion of the lagged dependent variable does little to reduce unexplained inter-household variation. Again we find stronger correlation between the predicted values of efficiency specified with lags and the observed values.

Labor Supply Functions: Approaches to Simultaneity and Censoring

The estimation results of the differently specified labor supply equations for farm operator and spouse are presented in Tables 2 and 3. Column 1 of the tables refers to the simplified model specification where we disregard simultaneity and state dependence, Columns 2 and 3 refer to the simplified version which ignores censoring in the presence of endogenous regressors, and Columns 4 and 5 refer to the results of the two-stage dynamic model which approaches both problems with selectivity and simultaneity bias.

The labor supply equations for operator and spouse are estimated by single equation random effects Tobit as specified in section "Assume Exogeneity of Regressors" where we do not account for the simultaneity of the model system, and all regressors are treated as exogenous. This is a fully static model, but the results are biased even when assuming full exogeneity because of censored right-hand-side variables. The Tobit model relies heavily on the normality assumptions and for this reason, in the empirical model, we have transformed the dependent variables into log-normals. The results for the farm operator's labor supply equation are presented in Column 1 of Table 2 and for the spouse's labor supply equation in Column 1 of Table 3. In general, results in Table 2 show that the operator's off-farm labor supply is positive and significantly affected by spouse's off-farm labor supply and farming efficiency. Similarly, in Table 3 we find that the spouse's off-farm labor supply is positive and significantly affected by operator's off-farm labor supply and farming efficiency.

Consistent with the theory of opportunity cost, regional employment rate has a positive and significant effect on the off-farm labor supply of farm

Table 2. Parameter Estimates of Off-Farm Labor Supply by Operator.

Variable	RE Tobit Static No Endogeneity	2S OLS Static No Censoring	2S GLS Static No Censoring	2S OLS Dynamic Exogenous Correction of Initial Value	2S GLS Dynamic Exogenous Correction of Initial Value
Ln off-hours, spouse	0.0227*	0.0036	0.0114*		
	(0.0091)	(0.0065)	(0.0055)		
Ln farming efficiency	0.2286*	0.8740***	0.4259***		
	(0.0896)	(0.1861)	(0.1005)		
Operator age	0.2953***	0.0993***	0.0902***	0.2900***	0.2843***
	(0.0241)	(0.0102)	(0.0093)	(0.0165)	(0.0155)
Operator age, squared	−0.0034***	−0.0011***	−0.0010***	−0.0035***	−0.0036***
	(0.0003)	(0.0001)	(0.0001)	(0.0002)	(0.0002)
Number of children under	−0.1690***	−0.0421*	−0.0406*	−0.1530***	−0.1464***
the age of 6	(0.0461)	(0.0171)	(0.0164)	(0.0301)	(0.0292)
Operator wage rate	0.0059***	0.0008***	0.0018***	0.0069***	0.0083***
	(0.0007)	(0.0002)	(0.0002)	(0.0004)	(0.0004)
Spouse wage rate	0.0035***	0.0011***	0.0014***	0.0035***	0.0041***
	(0.0009)	(0.0003)	(0.0003)	(0.0006)	(0.0006)
Farm experience, operator	−0.0216***	−0.0127***	−0.0115***	−0.0129**	−0.0096*
	(0.0062)	(0.0027)	(0.0022)	(0.0044)	(0.0038)
Hire labor hours	0.0002***	0.0001***	0.0001***	0.0002***	0.0003***
	(0.0001)	(0.0000)	(0.0000)	(0.0000)	(0.0000)
Agricultural subsidy	−0.0008	−0.0006***	−0.0012***	−0.0012***	−0.0022***
(*1,000 kroners*)	(0.0004)	(0.0002)	(0.0001)	(0.0003)	(0.0003)
Agricultural income	−0.0013***	−0.0005***	−0.0005***	−0.0009***	−0.0010***
(*1,000 kroners*)	(0.0001)	(0.0001)	(0.0000)	(0.0001)	(0.0001)

Table 2. *(Continued)*

Variable	RE Tobit Static No Endogeneity	2S OLS Static No Censoring	2S GLS Static No Censoring	2S OLS Dynamic Exogenous Correction of Initial Value	2S GLS Dynamic Exogenous Correction of Initial Value
Other income	−0.0006**	−0.0002**	−0.0001	−0.0007***	−0.0007***
(1,000 kroners)	(0.0002)	(0.0001)	(0.0001)	(0.0001)	(0.0001)
Total farming area	0.0191***	0.0045**	0.0073***	0.0166***	0.0205***
(hectares)	(0.0037)	(0.0016)	(0.0012)	(0.0029)	(0.0022)
Livestock, units	−0.0003	0.0010***	0.0007**	−0.0003	−0.0003
	(0.0004)	(0.0002)	(0.0002)	(0.0003)	(0.0003)
Share of regional	6.8999***	1.9661***	1.7037***	6.2461***	5.1733***
employment	(0.5702)	(0.2496)	(0.1856)	(0.4377)	(0.3440)
Predicted Ln off-hours,				0.0082	0.0165**
spouse				(0.0063)	(0.0059)
Predicted Ln farming				1.4250***	2.1925***
efficiency				(0.3278)	(0.2659)
Constant	−8.1943***	1.3346***	2.1418***	−8.9327***	−8.9225***
	(0.6631)	(0.3240)	(0.2582)	(0.5552)	(0.4892)
Observations	17,605	11,279	11,279	15,812	15,812
σ_u	3.0810	1.0769	0.8096	1.9297	1.6848
σ_v	2.3144	0.6662	0.6661	1.4250	1.4250
$\rho = \sigma_u^2/(\sigma_u^2 + \sigma_v^2)$	0.6393	0.7232	0.5963	0.6471	0.5830
$\chi^2 \sim x_{ht} = 0$	885.7689	9.0e+05	956.1522	120.55	2628.29
R_o^2		0.0841	0.1438	0.2192	0.2414
R_w^2		0.0025	0.0470	0.1143	0.1124
R_b^2		0.0894	0.1577	0.2894	0.3212

Standard errors in parentheses; $^{*}p<0.05$, $^{**}p<0.01$, $^{***}p<0.001$.

Table 3. Parameter Estimates of Off-Farm Labor Supply by Spouse.

Variable	RE Tobit Static No Endogeneity	2S OLS Static No Censoring	2S GLS Static No Censoring	2S OLS Dynamic Exogenous Correction of Initial Value	2S GLS Dynamic Exogenous Correction of Initial Value
Ln off-hours, operator	0.0382**	−0.1377	0.1151		
	(0.0135)	(0.1102)	(0.0698)		
Ln farming efficiency	0.2757*	3.8424***	1.3382***		
	(0.1137)	(0.6046)	(0.2689)		
Spouse age	0.6091***	0.4010***	0.3775***	0.6077***	0.5890***
	(0.0298)	(0.0311)	(0.0253)	(0.0209)	(0.0192)
Spouse age, squared	−0.0076***	−0.0048***	−0.0047***	−0.0072***	−0.0073***
	(0.0003)	(0.0003)	(0.0003)	(0.0002)	(0.0002)
Number of children under	−0.1596**	−0.1794**	−0.1405**	−0.1305**	−0.1126**
the age of 6	(0.0583)	(0.0550)	(0.0496)	(0.0402)	(0.0391)
Operator wage rate	−0.0016	−0.0021**	−0.0018**	−0.0011	−0.0009
	(0.0008)	(0.0007)	(0.0007)	(0.0006)	(0.0006)
Spouse wage rate	0.0173***	0.0116***	0.0159***	0.0178***	0.0215***
	(0.0011)	(0.0010)	(0.0009)	(0.0008)	(0.0008)
Farm experience, operator	0.0667***	0.0370***	0.0355***	0.0469***	0.0452***
	(0.0070)	(0.0072)	(0.0053)	(0.0046)	(0.0040)
Hire labor hours	0.0000	0.0001	0.0000	0.0000	0.0000
	(0.0001)	(0.0001)	(0.0001)	(0.0000)	(0.0000)
Agricultural subsidy	0.0012*	−0.0012	−0.0007	0.0002	−0.0005
(1,000 kroners)	(0.0005)	(0.0006)	(0.0004)	(0.0004)	(0.0004)
Agricultural income	−0.0013***	−0.0007***	−0.0003*	−0.0011***	−0.0010***
(1,000 kroners)	(0.0001)	(0.0002)	(0.0001)	(0.0001)	(0.0001)

Table 3. *(Continued)*

Variable	RE Tobit Static No Endogeneity	2S OLS Static No Censoring	2S GLS Static No Censoring	2S OLS Dynamic Exogenous Correction of Initial Value	2S GLS Dynamic Exogenous Correction of Initial Value
Other income	−0.0007*	−0.0013***	−0.0012***	−0.0012***	−0.0013***
(*1,000 kroners*)	(0.0003)	(0.0003)	(0.0002)	(0.0002)	(0.0002)
Total farming area	0.0217***	0.0134**	0.0093**	0.0197***	0.0200***
(*hectares*)	(0.0047)	(0.0051)	(0.0034)	(0.0038)	(0.0029)
Livestock, units	−0.0012*	0.0004	−0.0007	−0.0007	−0.0009*
	(0.0006)	(0.0008)	(0.0007)	(0.0004)	(0.0004)
Share of regional	3.3530***	−0.3052	1.7719**	1.5499*	3.3922***
employment	(0.7434)	(0.8473)	(0.5455)	(0.6172)	(0.4620)
Predicted Ln off-hours,				0.0118	0.0274**
operator				(0.0113)	(0.0105)
Predcited Ln farming				0.0581	0.3525
efficiency				(0.4374)	(0.3514)
Constant	−13.7771***	−8.5510***	−8.2414***	−12.2878***	−13.4229***
	(0.8026)	(1.0105)	(0.7143)	(0.7209)	(0.6214)
Observations	17,605	11,279	11,279	15,812	15,812
σ_u	4.0439	2.9521	2.1667	2.5348	2.1509
σ_v	2.8100	2.1342	2.1341	1.9060	1.9060
$\rho = \sigma_u^2/(\sigma_u^2 + \sigma_v^2)$	0.6744	0.6567	0.5076	0.6388	0.5601
$\chi^2 \sim x_{ht} = 0$	1.3e+03	5.3e+04	985.8935	153.80	3045.47
R_o^2		0.0409	0.1135	0.2187	0.2514
R_w^2		.	0.0515	0.1414	0.1382
R_b^2		0.0408	0.1507	0.2583	0.3169

Standard errors in parentheses; $^{*}p<0.05$, $^{**}p<0.01$, $^{***}p<0.001$.

operators and spouses (operator and spouse; Tables 2 and 3, respectively). Consistent with the theory, age has a nonlinear relationship with off-farm labor supply (Ahearn et al. 2006; Mishra & Goodwin, 1997). In the case of farm operator, the number of children under 6, farms specializing in livestock, agricultural subsidies, agricultural income, farming experience, and other income have a significantly negative impact on off-farm labor supply. On the other hand, off-farm wage rate, hired labor, and total land operated (in hectares) have a significantly positive impact on off-farm labor supply of farm operators (Mishra, Morehart, El-Osta, Johnson, & Hopkins, 2002). Also in the case of spouses (Table 3), the number of children under 6, farms specializing in livestock, agricultural income, and other income have a significantly negative impact on off-farm labor supply. Likewise, off-farm wage rate, total land operated (in hectares), and operator's farming experience have a significantly positive impact on off-farm labor supply of spouses.

Columns 2 and 3 of the respective tables present the result from the two-stage IV estimations as described in section "Disregard Censoring in the Presence of Endogenous Regressors." These estimations are partial to the model system in the sense that we exclude all observations of individuals not participating in off-farm work and thus avoid complications caused by censored endogenous variables. As part of the stepwise approach, we have also excluded lags of the dependent variable in these estimations, but give full attention to the simultaneity problem. Correction for state dependence does however appear by the use of first-order lags as instruments. Column 2 in Tables 2 and 3 presents the two-stage fixed effects estimations of operator and spouse's labor supply and Column 3 shows the random effects estimates.

The last two columns in Tables 2 and 3 present the results for the two-stage approach as described in section "Combine Selectivity and Simultaneity Bias in Two-Step Approach" where we incorporate selectivity and endogeneity simultaneously, following the approach specified by Nelson and Olson (1978) and Amemiya (1979). We also account for state dependence by allowing lags of the dependent variables to enter into the reduced form equation following the simplest dynamic specification proposed by Vella and Verbeek (1999). The second-stage estimations are performed with the predicted values of the endogenous variables as instruments which provide consistent but possibly less efficient estimates. The fixed and random effect estimates are presented in Columns 4 and 5, respectively. The first-stage estimations of the reduced form equations are presented in Table A.2.

The parameter estimates of the truly exogenous covariates seem fairly robust across the columns representing different specifications in both tables. With a few exceptions for non-significant coefficients, all coefficients show expected signs and deviate little in value. The static two-stage estimates in Columns 2 and 3 for the labor supply equations (Tables 2 and 3) deviate from the single equation Tobit and the dynamic two-stage estimations (Columns 4 and 5) by lower absolute values for some coefficients, but the differences are not systematic. The coefficients in the random effects specifications (Columns 3 and 5) have smaller standard errors and consequently higher statistical significance than the coefficients from the fixed effects specifications, but again the differences are not decisive.

To test for model specification we use the Hausman (1978) test for estimates in Columns 2 and 3 and between Columns 4 and 5, respectively. Hausman test reveals that in both cases the fixed effects appears as the favored specification. This result also applies for the labor supply equations of both operator and spouse. The results are however not conclusive because the difference in parameter estimates is very small (less than 10^{-3}) for most covariates and it is only for one of the exogenous variables, regional employment rate, that the coefficients are markedly different in value. The *t*-test statistics for this coefficient separately, however, is 3.2 which is still relatively low. A Sargan–Hansen test as proposed by Woolridge (2002) confirms the rejection of the random effects specifications, and we conclude that fixed effects estimates are more consistent for both labor supply equations.

Finally, we perform generalized Hausman tests between the different model specifications to detect systematic differences in the coefficients of the exogenous variables. Tests confirm our naive impression that the results are robust, particularly between the single equation random effects Tobit (Column 1) and the dynamic two-stage specifications (Columns 4 and 5). All pairwise tests favor the single equation Tobit estimates (Column 2) for both the operator and spouse's labor supply equations. However, the chi-square test statistic is relatively small and neither of the coefficients' *t*-statistics exceed 4.8 in the comparison between the Tobit model (Column 1) and the dynamic two-stage (2S) fixed effects model (Column 4) of the operator's labor supply equation in Table 2.

The parameters of the three variables we suspect as being endogenous differ far more between the model specifications than the coefficients for the truly exogenous variables. For the operator's labor supply equation, we find that farming efficiency is highly significant in both two-stage specifications (Columns 4 and 5), but is only significant at the 10 percent level in the single equation Tobit, where efficiency is assumed exogenous. The parameter values are relatively high in the dynamic specifications in Columns 4 and 5.

The spouse's labor hours are also found to have a positively significant effect on the operator's labor supply, but the impact is much smaller and not significant in the fixed effects specifications. The spouse's labor supply is also positively affected by the operator's off-farm hours except for the static two-stage OLS specification. However, only the Tobit estimate in Column 1 of Table 3 and the dynamic two-stage GLS estimate in Column 5 are statistically significant. The cross-effect of off-farm hours is slightly higher for spouse's labor supply than for the operator's labor supply, a finding which is confirmed in previous analyses (see Bjørnsen and Biørn, 2010).

The spouse's labor supply is also positively affected by increased farming efficiency, but less so for the dynamic specifications in Columns 4 and 5 where the coefficients are not statistically significant. We subject the static IV estimations in Column 2 to a Davidson–McKinnon test of exogeneity, and find support for the hypothesis that the partner's labor supply should be treated as endogenous in the estimation of both operator and spouse's labor supply (*p-values of 0.13 and 0.9, respectively*); however, we fail to reject the null hypothesis of exogeneity of the farming efficiency covariate. This result speaks in favor of a bivariate censored regression model for labor supply both operator and spouse's off-farm labor hours are endogenous in the farming efficiency equation (*p-values 0.1 and 0.4*). Confirmation of the assumption that the variables are to be treated as endogenous makes us favor the dynamic two-stage results and the robustness of the results is reassuring.

Labor Supply and Farming Efficiency

Table 4 follows the above logic and presents parameter estimates for farming efficiency. Columns 1 and 2 represent the single equation OLS estimations where endogeneity of regressors is ignored, specified with fixed and random effects, respectively. Columns 3 and 4 present the results from the two-stage estimations where we avoid the selectivity problem by applying a subsample with only positive observations for off-farm work. The fixed and random effects estimates are presented in Columns 3 and 4, respectively. Columns 5 and 6 are the fixed and random effects estimates of the dynamic two-stage specification from section "Combine Selectivity and Simultaneity Bias in Two-Step Approach."

In general, results show that expected hours of off-farm work (Columns 4 and 5) by farm operators and spouses tend to increase farming efficiency. It is reasonable to assume that off-farm wages exceed the marginal value

Table 4. Parameter Estimates of Impact of Labor Allocation on Farming Efficiency.

Variable	OLS Static No Endogeneity	GLS Static No Endogeneity	2S OLS Static No Censoring	2S GLS Static No Censoring	2S OLS Dynamic Exogenous Correction of Initial Value	2S GLS Dynamic Exogenous Correction of Initial Value
Ln off-farm hours, operator	0.0026**	0.0036***	0.0297**	0.0403***		
	(0.0009)	(0.0009)	(0.0099)	(0.0074)		
Ln off-farm hours, spouse	0.0020*	0.0025***	0.0042*	0.0050**		
	(0.0008)	(0.0008)	(0.0021)	(0.0018)		
Hired labor hours	0.0000	0.0000	−0.0000	−0.0000	0.0000***	0.0000***
	(0.0000)	(0.0000)	(0.0000)	(0.0000)	(0.0000)	(0.0000)
Milk yield (liters)	−0.0014***	−0.0014***	−0.0014***	−0.0012***	−0.0015***	−0.0015***
	(0.0001)	(0.0001)	(0.0001)	(0.0001)	(0.0000)	(0.0000)
Farm experience, operator	−0.0002	−0.0007	0.0017*	0.0006	0.0001	0.0001
	(0.0006)	(0.0005)	(0.0008)	(0.0007)	(0.0001)	(0.0001)
Agricultural subsidies (*1,000 krones*)	0.0005***	0.0004***	0.0005***	0.0004***	0.0005***	0.0005***
	(0.0000)	(0.0000)	(0.0001)	(0.0000)	(0.0000)	(0.0000)
Investments/capital[a]	0.0231	0.0225	0.0170	0.0148	0.0234***	0.0236***
	(0.0131)	(0.0133)	(0.0169)	(0.0171)	(0.0024)	(0.0024)
Total land operated (*hectare*)	0.0001	0.0002	0.0006	0.0004	0.0004***	0.0001*
	(0.0004)	(0.0003)	(0.0006)	(0.0004)	(0.0001)	(0.0001)
Share of rented land	−0.0290	−0.0500**	−0.0722**	−0.0951***	−0.0498***	−0.0487***
	(0.0186)	(0.0158)	(0.0258)	(0.0202)	(0.0035)	(0.0030)
Share of land fallow	0.0013	−0.0150	−0.0111	−0.0387	−0.0030	0.0005
	(0.0200)	(0.0188)	(0.0266)	(0.0242)	(0.0037)	(0.0035)
Livestock, units	−0.0002***	−0.0004***	−0.0004***	−0.0009***	−0.0002***	−0.0003***
	(0.0000)	(0.0000)	(0.0001)	(0.0001)	(0.0000)	(0.0000)
Operator age	0.0025	0.0046*	0.0021	0.0045	0.0027***	0.0028***
	(0.0021)	(0.0020)	(0.0034)	(0.0031)	(0.0004)	(0.0004)

Table 4. *(Continued)*

Variable	OLS Static No Endogeneity	GLS Static No Endogeneity	2S OLS Static No Censoring	2S GLS Static No Censoring	2S OLS Dynamic Exogenous Correction of Initial Value	2S GLS Dynamic Exogenous Correction of Initial Value
Operator age, squared	0.0000	−0.0000	−0.0000	−0.0000	0.0000	0.0000
	(0.0000)	(0.0000)	(0.0000)	(0.0000)	(0.0000)	(0.0000)
Regional location, highland	−0.0529	0.0543***	−0.1178**	0.0566***	−0.1020***	−0.0788***
	(0.0292)	(0.0130)	(0.0455)	(0.0156)	(0.0057)	(0.0025)
Predicted Ln off-farm hours, operator					0.0017***	0.0023***
					(0.0002)	(0.0002)
Predicted Ln off-farm hours, spouse					0.0002	0.0006***
					(0.0001)	(0.0001)
Constant	1.1318***	1.0310***	1.0513***	0.8406***	1.1701***	1.1599***
	(0.0502)	(0.0460)	(0.0857)	(0.0728)	(0.0098)	(0.0091)
Observations	17,603	17,603	11,277	11,277	15,812	15,812
σ_u	0.3257	0.2549	0.3419	0.2591	0.0650	0.0468
σ_v	0.2002	0.2002	0.2106	0.2106	0.0346	0.0346
$\rho = \sigma_u^2/(\sigma_u^2 + \sigma_v^2)$	0.7257	0.6184	0.7249	0.6022	0.7796	0.6469
$\chi^2 \sim x_{ht} = 0$	47.33	905.6386	4.2e+05	694.5103	1292.28	2.2e+04
R_o^2	0.0482	0.1053	0.0560	0.1495	0.6028	0.6381
R_w^2	0.0403	0.0369	0.0335	0.0284	0.5636	0.5601
R_b^2	0.0534	0.1319	0.0574	0.1902	0.6252	0.6716

Standard errors in parentheses; $^{*}p<0.05$, $^{**}p<0.01$, $^{***}p<0.001$.

[a]Total farm investments in a year/total farm capital stock.

of an hour spent in farming for most farm households and thus off-farm hours, and the income they generate, may stimulate technical change at the farm. Goodwin and Mishra (2004) found that more intensive participation in off-farm work by farm operators tends to be associated with lower farming efficiency. The higher the potential off-farm wages, the higher the opportunity cost of low farming efficiency, which results in a higher on-farm efficiency. Consistent with the literature, results indicate that agricultural subsidies, farm size (total operated acres), and investment in farming tend to increase farming efficiency. Efficiency also increases with age. This finding is consistent with the fact that younger farm operators are likely to be more educated and use technologies that aid in farm production (Mishra et al., 2002). On the other hand, share of rented land, farms specializing in livestock and dairy enterprises, and farms located in the highland region has lower farming efficiency.

Again, the estimates of the coefficient for the exogenous variables seem fairly robust between model specifications. For the labor supply equations, however, it is the static two-stage estimates represented in Columns 3 and 4 which diverge somewhat from the other specifications. The parameter estimates from the static OLS/GLS method in Columns 1 and 2 and the dynamic two-stage method in Columns 5 and 6 are very similar for all coefficients except operator's farming experience, which is negative in Columns 1 and 2, and the highland dummy variable, for which the estimates are significantly positive in the static GLS estimations represented in Columns 2 and 4, but negative in the other four Columns 1, 3, 5, and 6.

We perform specification tests, similar to the labor supply equations, and the Hausman test (1978) favors fixed effects specifications to random effects. This finding is also confirmed by the Sargan–Hansen test statistic. The generalized Hausman test comparing the different model specifications favors the dynamic two-stage fixed effects specification in Column 5 over both the static single-equation OLS in Column 1 (*p-value* = *0.37*) and over the static two-stage OLS specification in Column 3 (*p-value* = *0.47*). Because the Davidson–McKinnon test of exogeneity clearly indicates that both operator and spouse's off-farm labor should be treated as endogenous in estimating farming efficiency (with *p-values 0.1* and *0.4*), we believe that the dynamic two-stage specification in Column 5 is the best model for our study.

CONCLUSIONS

Empirical literature in household models and time allocation decisions tends to analyze decisions of economic agents using cross-sectional data. Such methods implicitly assume that model parameters are stable (constant) across firms and over time, but this is completely at odds with the firm-specific aspects of the theoretical models employed in labor economics. Model parameters could vary across firm over time and across individuals, which is often unaccounted for in most of the labor economics studies. This study is novel in its attempt to use panel data in modeling the relationship between farm productivity and off-farm labor supply of both partners (farm operator and spouse) in farm households. We evaluate a dynamic panel framework considering individual effects. Panel estimation method is used to capture the unobserved heterogeneity which is apparent between the farm households and to allow for differences in preferences over time and over sectors – farm and nonfarm.

Our assumption is that farming efficiency and off-farm labor supply of farm operator and spouse are three jointly determined endogenous variables and should be modeled simultaneously while allowing for presence of state dependence in the individuals' behavior. When off-farm labor hours are also censored for individuals not participating in off-farm work, the model system becomes rather complex and comprises *censored dependent variables*, *censored* and *continuous endogenous regressors*, *selection bias*, *unobserved heterogeneity*, and *state dependence*, all of which must be dealt with simultaneously. To our knowledge, the entirety of our estimation problem has not been addressed in the literature.

Designing an estimation algorithm to account for all these aspects simultaneously is outside the scope of this study, so we impose some simplifying assumptions for a two-step estimation procedure inspired by the specifications proposed by Nelson and Olson (1978) and Vella and Verbeek (1999), respectively. Specifically, we choose a step-wise approach where we start by addressing the censoring problem separately, assuming all regressors to be exogenous. Second, we address the problem with endogenous regressors when estimating on a subsample where all individuals participate in off-farm work and thus avoiding the selectivity problem. Finally, we include both aspects simultaneously in a two-step procedure where state dependence is accounted for in the reduced form equations. This procedure provides consistent but supposedly not very efficient estimates. Comparisons between the three approaches however, indicates robustness of the parameter estimates and the results from the two-stage estimations appears more efficient than the inconsistent static one-stage estimates where endogeneity is not accounted for in the model estimation.

Results from the dynamic panel modeling approach confirms that the off-farm labor supply of farm operators and spouses are jointly determined. Agricultural subsidies from the government tends to decrease off-farm work by farm operators. Off-farm labor supply of both farm operators and spouses is positively correlated with off-farm wages. However, spouses work less when operators get higher off-farm wages. Finally, the off-farm labor supply of farm operators is positively affected by the hours of off-farm work by spouse and farming efficiency. With regard to farming efficiency, off-farm work by farm operators and spouses is positively affects farming efficiency. Farming efficiency increases with operator's age, farm size, agricultural subsidises, and share of current investment to total farm capital stock. On the other hand, farms specializing in dairy and livestock tend to be less efficient.

ACKNOWLEDGMENTS

The authors would like to thank the participants of the 12th Annual Advances in Econometrics Conference and anonymous reviewers for their suggestions and comment. We would like to thank the editors for their comments and suggestions. All remaining errors are ours. Bjørnsen's time has been financed by the Norwegian Research Council. Mishra's time on this project was supported by the USDA Cooperative State Research Education & Extension Service, Hatch project # 0212495 and Louisiana State University Experiment Station project # LAB 93872.

NOTES

1. $W^i = W^i(K^i, Z_H, \alpha^i_W)(i = O, S)$. We assume flexibility in work schedule in off-arm activities, so that both operators and spouses are price takers and wages are determined independently of the number of hours worked.

2. The issue becomes more complicated as off-farm labor supply of farm operators also depends on how spouses react to changes in their off-farm wages. Notice that M^O, hours spent working off the farm, is a function of the off-farm hours worked by the spouse(M^S).

REFERENCES

Abrevaya, J., Hausman, J. A., & Khan, S. (2010). Testing for causal effects in a generalized regression model with endogenous regressors. *Econometrica*, *78*, 2043–2061.

Ahearn, M. C., El-Osta, H., & Dewbre, J. (2006). The impact of coupled and decoupled government subsidies on off-farm labor participation of U.S. farm operators. *American Journal of Agricultural Economics*, *88*, 393–408.

Ahituv, A., & Kimhi, A. (2006). Simultaneous estimation of work choices and the level of farm activity using panel data. *European Review of Agricultural Economics*, *33*, 49–71.

Amemiya, T. (1974). Multivariate regression and simultaneous-equation models when the dependent variables are truncated normal. *Econometrica*, *42*, 999–1012.

Amemiya, T. (1979). The estimation of a simultaneous-equation Tobit model. *International Economic Review*, *1*, 161–181.

Baltagi, B. (2008). *Econometric analysis of panel data* (. 4th ed.). New York, NY: Wiley.

Bjørnsen, H. M., & Biørn, E. (2010). Interrelated labor decisions of farm couples: A censored response analysis of off-farm work. *Agricultural Economics: An International Journal*, *41*, 595–610.

Browning, M., & Carro, J. M. (2010). Heterogeneity in dynamic discrete choice models. *The Econometric Journal*, *13*, 1–39.

Goodwin, B. K., & Mishra., A. K. (2004). Farming efficiency and the determinants of multiple job holding by farm operators. *American Journal of Agricultural Economics*, *86*, 722–729.

Hahn, J., Hausman, J., & Kuersteiner, G. (2007). Long difference instrumental variables estimation for dynamic panel models with fixed effects. *Journal of Econometrics*, *127*, 574–617.

Hausman, J. A. (1978). Specification tests in econometrics. *Econometrica*, *46*, 1251–1271.

Heckman, J. J. (1974). Shadow prices, market wages, and labour supply. *Econometrica*, *42*, 679–694.

Heckman, J. J. (1976). The common structure of statistical models of truncation, sample selection, and limited dependent variables and a simple estimator for such models. *Annals of Economic and Social Measurement*, *5*, 475–492.

Heckman, J. J. (1979). Sample selection bias as a specification error. *Econometrica*, *47*, 153–161.

Heckman, J. J. (1981). Statistical models for discrete panel data. In C. F. Manski & D. McFadden (Eds.), *Structural analysis of discrete data with econometric applications* (pp. 114–178). Cambridge: MIT Press.

Honoré, B. (1992). Trimmed lad and least squares estimation of truncated and censored regression models with fixed effects. *Econometrica*, *47*, 53–161.

Honoré, B. E., & Kyriazidou, E. (2000). Panel data discrete choice models with lagged dependent variables. *Econometrica*, *68*, 839–874.

Honoré, B. E., & Hu, L. (2004). Estimation of cross sectional and panel data censored regression. *Journal of Econometrics*, *122*, 293–316.

Honoré, B. E., & Hu, L. (2010). Estimation of a transformation model with truncation, interval observation and time-varying covariates. *Econometrics Journal*, *13*(1), 127–144.

Kyriazidou, E. (1997). Estimation of a panel data sample selection model. *Econometrica*, *65*, 1335–1364.

Lee, L. F., Maddala, G. S., & Trost, R. P. (1980). Asymptotic covariance matrices of two-stage probit and two-stage Tobit methods for simultaneous equations models with selectivity. *Econometrica*, *48*, 491–503.

Lien, G., Kumbhakar, S. C., & Hardaker, J. B. (2010). Determinants of off-farm work and its effects on farm performance: The case of Norwegian grain farmers. *Agricultural Economics: An International Journal*, *41*(6), 577–586.

Maddala, G. S. (1983). *Limited-dependent and qualitative variables in econometrics*. Cambridge: Cambridge University Press.

Mishra, A., & Goodwin, B. (1997). Farm income variability and the supply of off-farm labor. *American Journal of Agricultural Economics*, *79*(3), 880–887.

Mishra, A., Morehart, M., El-Osta, H., Johnson, J., & Hopkins., J. (2002). *Income, wealth, and well-being of farm operator households*. Washington, DC: U.S. Department of Agriculture, Economic Research Service.

Nelson, F., & Olson, L. (1978). Specification and estimation of a simultaneous-equation model with limited dependent variables. *International Economic Review*, *3*, 695–709.

Phimister, E., & Roberts, D. (2006). The effect of off-farm work on the intensity of agricultural production. *Environmental and Resource Economics*, *34*, 493–515.

Robinson, C. (1989). The joint determination of union status and union wage effects: Some tests of alternative models. *Journal of Political Economy*, *97*(3), 639–667.

Smith, K. R. (2002). Does off-farm work hinder smart farming? *Agricultural Outlook*, Economic Research Service/USDA, September, 28–30.

Smith, R. J., & Blundell, R. W. (1986). An exogeneity test for a simultaneous equation Tobit model with an application to labor supply. *Econometrica*, *54*, 679–685.

Sule, A., Honoré, B.E., Hu, L., Leth-Petersen, S. (2011). Estimation of panel data regression models with two-sided censoring or truncation. Working Paper Series WP-2011-08. Federal Reserve Bank of Chicago.

Sumner, D. A. (1991). Useful directions for research on multiple job-holding among farm families. In M. C. Hallberg, J. L. Findeis & D. A. Lass (Eds.), *Multiple job-holding among farm families*. Ames, IA: Iowa State University Press.

Tobin, J. (1958). Estimation of relationships for limited dependent variables. *Econometrica*, *26*(1), 24–36.

Vella, F., & Verbeek, M. (1999). Two-step estimation of simultaneous equation panel data models with censored endogenous variables and selection bias. *Journal of Econometrics*, *90*(2), 239–263.

Weiss, C. R. (1997). Do they come back again? The symmetry and reversibility of off-farm employment. *European Review of Agricultural Economics*, *24*, 65–84.

Woolridge, J. (2002). *Econometric analysis of cross-section and panel data. Cambridge, MA*. MIT Press.

Woolridge, J. (2005). Simple solutions to the initial conditions problem in dynamic, non-linear panel-data models with unobserved heterogeneity. *Journal of Applied Econometrics*, *20*, 39–54.

APPENDIX

Table A.1. Heckman Selection and Estimation of Off-Farm Wage Rate.

Variable	Parameter Estimate, Operator	Parameter Estimate, Spouse
Main variables		
Age	−1.6821***	−2.0206***
	(0.2035)	(0.1365)
Age squared	0.0270***	0.0282***
	(0.0022)	(0.0015)
Probability of having a higher education	357.3479***	237.6215***
	(2.7644)	(1.1855)
Total farming hours	−0.0015***	0.0024***
	(0.0003)	(0.0003)
Location Metro 2 area with 10,000 population	−5.3457***	−12.4004***
(= 1, if the farm is located in the Metro 2 area,	(0.4694)	(0.3112)
with 45 minute drive, 0 otherwise)		
Regional employment/total population in the	78.3911***	25.52589***
region (share of regional employment)	(3.0006)	(2.0990)
Constant	62.3678***	92.2644***
	(5.0750)	(3.3221)
Select variables		
Number of children under the age of 6	0.0481*	0.0090
	(0.0194)	(0.0167)
Age	0.0022*	−0.0005
	(0.0011)	(0.0010)
Total farming hours	−0.0002***	−0.0002***
	(0.0000)	(0.0000)
Agricultural income, gross farm income	−0.0001***	−0.0001
(1,000 kroners)	(0.0000)	(0.0000)
Regional employment/total population in the	1.7858***	1.9946***
region (share of regional employment)	(0.1311)	(0.1235)
Other income	−0.0017***	−0.0033***
	(0.0001)	(0.0001)
Constant	−0.3246**	−0.8889***
	(0.1126)	(0.1016)
Observations	17,605	17,605
LL	−70156.88	−55317.68
ρ	−0.2044***	−0.6596***
	(0.0406)	(0.0133)
σ	26.2252***	17.8553***
	(0.1943)	(0.1773)
$\lambda = \rho * \sigma$	−5.3612***	−11.7768***
	(1.0856)	(0.3316)
Wald $\chi^2(6)$	19787.27	44423.76
p	0.0000	0.0000
LR $\chi^2(1)$	15.9958	713.1836
p_c	0.0001	0.0000

Standard errors in parentheses; $^{*}p<0.05$, $^{**}p<0.01$, $^{***}p<0.001$.

Table A.2. Reduced Form Equations for Dynamic Two-Stage Estimation.

Variable	Operator Static, Tobit	Operator Dynamic, Tobit	Spouse Static, Tobit	Spouse Dynamic, Tobit	Efficiency Static, OLS	Efficiency Dynamic, OLS
Operator age	0.0827*	0.0682	0.3571***	0.1143*	0.0027	0.0025
	(0.0420)	(0.0351)	(0.0600)	(0.0464)	(0.0036)	(0.0038)
Spouse age	0.2582***	0.0623	0.3039***	0.1356**	0.0020	0.0001
	(0.0400)	(0.0328)	(0.0576)	(0.0434)	(0.0035)	(0.0036)
Operator age, squared	−0.0016***	−0.0012**	−0.0028***	−0.0008	−0.0000	−0.0000
	(0.0004)	(0.0004)	(0.0006)	(0.0005)	(0.0000)	(0.0000)
Spouse age, squared	−0.0023***	−0.0005	−0.0049***	−0.0023***	−0.0000	0.0000
	(0.0004)	(0.0003)	(0.0006)	(0.0005)	(0.0000)	(0.0000)
Number of children under the age of 6	−0.1651***	−0.0732	−0.1748**	−0.0240	−0.0012	−0.0026
	(0.0460)	(0.0411)	(0.0583)	(0.0491)	(0.0039)	(0.0042)
Operator wage rate	0.0056***	0.0036***	−0.0014	−0.0010	0.0000	0.0001
	(0.0007)	(0.0006)	(0.0008)	(0.0007)	(0.0001)	(0.0001)
Spouse wage rate	0.0034***	0.0015	0.0174***	0.0109***	−0.0001	−0.0000
	(0.0009)	(0.0008)	(0.0011)	(0.0009)	(0.0001)	(0.0001)
Farm experience	−0.0226***	−0.0047	0.0412***	0.0082	−0.0002	0.0003
	(0.0062)	(0.0041)	(0.0081)	(0.0049)	(0.0006)	(0.0006)
Hired labor hours	0.0002***	0.0001*	0.0001	−0.0001	0.0000	0.0000
	(0.0001)	(0.0000)	(0.0001)	(0.0001)	(0.0000)	(0.0000)
Agricultural subsidy (*1,000 kroners*)	0.0000	−0.0004	0.0011*	−0.0008*	0.0006***	0.0005***
	(0.0004)	(0.0003)	(0.0006)	(0.0004)	(0.0000)	(0.0000)
Agricultural income (*1,000 kroners*)	−0.0009***	−0.0003***	−0.0013***	−0.0002	−0.0001***	−0.0000*
	(0.0001)	(0.0001)	(0.0001)	(0.0001)	(0.0000)	(0.0000)
Other income (*1000 kroners*)	−0.0005*	−0.0003	−0.0007*	−0.0008***	0.0001***	0.0001***
	(0.0002)	(0.0002)	(0.0003)	(0.0002)	(0.0000)	(0.0000)
Investments/Capital[a]	0.1606	0.0629	0.4814*	0.2573	0.0151	0.0162
	(0.1581)	(0.1512)	(0.1988)	(0.1786)	(0.0131)	(0.0136)
Total land operated (*hectare*)	0.0179***	0.0104***	0.0181***	0.0055	0.0002	−0.0000
	(0.0041)	(0.0024)	(0.0053)	(0.0029)	(0.0004)	(0.0005)
Share of rented land	0.2507	0.2530*	0.5324*	0.2406	−0.0238	−0.0412*
	(0.1880)	(0.1187)	(0.2423)	(0.1412)	(0.0185)	(0.0199)

Table A.2. *(Continued)*

Variable	Operator Static, Tobit	Operator Dynamic, Tobit	Spouse Static, Tobit	Spouse Dynamic, Tobit	Efficiency Static, OLS	Efficiency Dynamic, OLS
Share of fallow land	0.3094	0.2270	0.8900**	0.3732	−0.0021	0.0018
	(0.2238)	(0.1669)	(0.2795)	(0.1957)	(0.0200)	(0.0212)
Livestock, units	−0.0002	−0.0009	−0.0013*	−0.0004	−0.0001**	−0.0002***
	(0.0004)	(0.0005)	(0.0006)	(0.0006)	(0.0000)	(0.0000)
Milk yield (*liters*)	−0.0089***	−0.0036***	−0.0012	−0.0008	0.0012***	0.0013***
	(0.0010)	(0.0006)	(0.0013)	(0.0007)	(0.0001)	(0.0001)
Share of regional employment	6.6987***	1.7224***	3.4495***	1.1447**	0.2557***	0.2062***
	(0.5778)	(0.3672)	(0.7443)	(0.4186)	(0.0592)	(0.0626)
Regional location, highland	−0.0055	0.1172	0.2611	0.1542	−0.0558	−0.0995**
	(0.1561)	(0.0709)	(0.2055)	(0.0840)	(0.0291)	(0.0325)
Lag of Ln off-farm hours, operator		0.8117***				
		(0.0158)				
Lag of Ln off-farm hours, spouse				0.9349***		
				(0.0152)		
Lag of Ln off-farm hours, efficiency						0.1642***
						(0.0088)
Constant	−8.486***	−3.570***	−15.427***	−7.299***	−0.992***	−0.869***
	(0.6617)	(0.5089)	(0.8548)	(0.6292)	(0.0611)	(0.0668)
Observations	17,603	15,812	17,603	15,812	17,603	15,812
Log likelihood	−3.4e+04	−2.9e+04	−3.4e+04	−2.8e+04	4.3e+03	4.3e+03
σ_u	3.0392	0.8368	4.0539	0.9850	0.3092	0.2764
σ_v	2.3058	2.1791	2.8010	2.4915	0.1996	0.1965
$\rho = \sigma_u^2/(\sigma_u^2 + \sigma_v^2)$	0.6347	0.1285	0.6769	0.1352	0.7059	0.6643
R_o^2					0.1362	0.3591
R_w^2					0.0470	0.0662
R_b^2					0.1735	0.4876

Standard errors in parentheses; $^{*}p<0.05$, $^{**}p<0.01$, $^{***}p<.001$.

[a]Total farm investments in a year/total farm capital stock.

USING PANEL DATA TO EXAMINE RACIAL AND GENDER DIFFERENCES IN DEBT BURDENS

Michael D. S. Morris

ABSTRACT

Debt burdens have risen for US households over the last several decades. As a result, several studies have investigated potential ethnic and gender differences in these debt burdens, along with the risks they pose. However, such estimations can be biased without correctly controlling for individual unobserved heterogeneity, and standard methods to deal with this, such as fixed effects, remove any time-invariant variables from the analysis. In this paper, I use the Hausman–Taylor (HT) estimator to estimate the relationship between these time-invariant demographics and debt burdens, allowing for potential correlation between some variables and the unobserved heterogeneity. I also consider some guidelines in determining the appropriateness of the HT estimation, both in terms of exogeneity assumptions as well as potential problems due to weak instruments. Using data from the National Longitudinal Survey of Youth 1979, the resulting estimates differ substantially from those of a typical random effects GLS estimator. In particular, the HT results find that after controlling for other variables, women are more likely to take on debt, especially nonhousing debt, but those who do take on debt tend to take on a lower amount than their male counterparts. No differences are found for black

Essays in Honor of Jerry Hausman
Advances in Econometrics, Volume 29, 305–325

ISSN: 0731-9053/doi:10.1108/S0731-9053(2012)0000029016

or Hispanic individuals with regard to the amount of debt, though black individuals are found to be slightly less likely to have debt.

Keywords: Debt burdens; gender; race; Hausman–Taylor; panel data

JEL classification: C23; D12; J15; J16

INTRODUCTION

Household debt has been steadily rising in the United States for two decades. In mid-2011, the household debt to after-tax income ratio stood at 1.14, down from a peak of 1.30 in late 2007, but still well above the 0.85 it was in the 1990s (Lahart & Light, 2011). The rise has been attributed to many factors including changes in the availability of debt, low interest rates, demand for assets with rapidly increasing prices such as the stock and housing bubbles (Johnson, 2007), increasing schooling costs, medical costs (Himmelstein, Thorne, Warren, & Woolhandler, 2009), and even cultural factors. In fact, some studies have found that noneconomic demographic factors explain as much of the variation in debt levels as do economic factors (Tippett, 2010). In looking at the rise of household debt and its burden, it is common to consider differences between demographic groups, including ethnic and gender differences (De'Armond & Zhu, 2011; Price, 2004; Rapoport, 1999; Tippett, 2010). However, most typical methods of estimating differences between ethnic and gender groups run a high risk of bias due, in particular, to the potential correlation between these variables and individual-specific unobserved heterogeneity.

In this paper, I use panel data from the National Longitudinal Survey of Youth 1979 (NLSY79) to aid in controlling for unobserved heterogeneity in debt outcomes, applying the Hausman–Taylor (HT) estimator to estimate regressions of time-invariant demographic and other variables on debt. I also discuss steps taken to help determine if the HT estimates are valid. In doing this, I consider both the Hausman test for the exogeneity assumptions, which is common in this setting, and considerations of potential weak instrument problems, which is not considered in most applications of the HT estimator, though the HT estimator is an instrumental variable (IV) estimator. In particular, I look at the Cragg–Donald F-statistic and associated Stock–Yogo critical values in the context of the HT estimator. The results imply that the random effects (RE) estimates are based on an exogeneity assumption that seems not to hold. The HT estimates overcome this problem by using the individual means of time-varying exogenous variables as instrument for an IV procedure, allowing for the appropriate estimation of the time-invariant demographic characteristics. These estimates often differ from those found by RE estimation and indicate that women who hold debt tend to hold less, though they are more likely to hold debt. No significant differences are found for black or Hispanic households regarding the amount of debt, though black individuals appear slightly less likely to hold debt.

The next section of the paper gives a brief overview of the literature on household debt burdens and the estimation of time-invariant variables in a panel setting. Section three presents the empirical methodology used in the paper. Section four reviews the data and how it is applied to the empirical specifications. Section five presents the results and the final section concludes the paper.

BACKGROUND

Household Debt Accumulation

Debt can allow a household investment opportunities and consumption smoothing not available without access to credit markets (Modigliani, 1966); examples of such include home purchases, education financing, and smoothing over temporary income and expense shocks. Several studies have identified changes in these factors as partially explaining rising debt burdens. Policy changes in the early 2000s made credit more available (Johnson, 2007), while, at the same time, debt increases have been associated with the rising costs of housing (Johnson, 2007), medical expenses, and education (Himmelstein et al., 2009). In addition, unemployment spells increase debt levels (Sullivan, 2008), a factor that becomes particularly acute during economic downturns.

Beyond standard economic motivations for debt, additional household demographic factors have been shown to be associated with debt levels including marriage and raising children (Xiao & Yao, 2011) as well as divorce (Fisher & Lyons, 2006). Studies have also found differences in debt levels for black and Hispanic households (De'Armond & Zhu, 2011; Rapoport, 1999; Tippett, 2010), as well as higher nonhousing debt among women (Price, 2004; Xiao & Yao, 2011). In fact, Tippett (2010) finds that heterogeneity among noneconomic characteristics explains variation in debt levels as much as differences in economic characteristics.

Early studies examining these differences were primarily concerned with possible discrimination in credit access and terms (e.g., see Ladd, 1998). More recently, some studies have shifted to considerations of cultural attitudes toward debt (Schooley & Worden, 2010) as well gender differences in management and reporting of debt (Field, 2007; Zargorsky, 2003). In particular, there is a growing body of literature examining gender differences in financial management and behavior. In their survey, Croson & Gnezzy (2009) note that women tend to be more risk averse in their financial choices. Other studies find that women tend to have lower levels of financial literacy (Lusardi & Mitchell, 2008; Lusardi & Tufano, 2009), though it is unclear if this is due to choice of study or a social culture that exposes them less to financial decision making. Lastly, in a study of 2,765 students, Mahnaz Mahdavi finds that women tend to have more credit cards, and be more likely to carry balances over $5,000, pay late fees, and not pay their balances in full (Mahdavi, 2005; Singletary, 2005). These differences could lead to different usage of debt, as well as different access and marketing from lenders in light of such behaviors.

While accessibility to debt can be beneficial, heavy debt burdens pose significant risks to households. Lingering levels of debt can eventually lead to bankruptcy, as well as more subtly restrict future options available to households; for example, Malcolm and Dowd (2009) find such an effect regarding minorities and postgraduate education. Debt burdens have also been shown to reflect strained personal relationships and an increased likelihood of divorce (Dew, 2011) as well as delayed and reduced fertility (Morris & Shreffler, 2011). Furthermore, there have been concerns that debts for minorities and women have risen faster than their incomes and assets, increasing the risk for widening wealth inequality (Shapiro, Meschende, & Sullivan, 2010; Wolff, 2007).

Estimating Coefficients for Time-Invariant Demographic Characteristics

Previous studies regarding differences in debt primarily use regression-based techniques to consider demographic differences in expected levels of debt, or other debt-related dependent variables, while controlling for variables that could mediate these impacts away. It has been pointed out, however, that these estimates are often plagued by unobserved heterogeneity issues and bias (e.g., Berkovec, Canner, Gabriel, & Hannan, 1994; Yezer, Phillips, &

Trost, 1994). The issue is that there are unobserved individual level preferences that cannot be fully controlled for by the observable cross-section variables. Panel data can potentially be used to help control for unobserved heterogeneity by estimating individual level variation as separate from idiosyncratic variation. However, using a method such as fixed effects (FEs) or first differences to fully control for this heterogeneity does not allow for coefficient estimation of time-invariant characteristics such as gender and race. The HT estimator (Hausman & Taylor, 1981) can potentially estimate these characteristics while effectively controlling for individual level unobserved heterogeneity. The technique has been used, for example, to consider the impact of education (Baltagi & Khanti-Akom, 1990) and health (Contoyannis & Rice, 2001) on wages. In this paper, I will use the HT estimator to estimate differences in debt burdens across race and gender.

EMPIRICAL METHODOLOGY

The primary focus here is using panel data to examine debt burden differences related to time-invariant demographics such as gender and ethnicity. The panel regression model for $i = 1, \ldots, N$ individuals, with each individual observed across $t = 1, \ldots, T_i$ time periods, expressed in the terms of Hausman and Taylor (1981), is given by the following equation:

$$D_{it} = X'_{it}\beta + Z'_i\gamma + \mu_i + v_{it} \tag{1}$$

where μ_i is the iid $(0, \sigma_\mu^2)$ and v_{it} is the iid $(0, \sigma_v^2)$. The first element of the error term, μ_i, measures a time-invariant, individual-specific unobserved heterogeneity, while v_{it} is an idiosyncratic variation, uncorrelated with μ_i. D_{it} is a measure of debt burden, X_{it} is a vector of time-varying regressors, and Z_i is a vector of time-invariant regressors.

If all the regressors in Eq. (1) are uncorrelated with μ_i and v_{it}, the ordinary least squares (OLS) estimator is consistent. Using the standard RE Generalized Least Squares (GLS) estimation to estimate and account for σ_μ^2 can gain efficiency and improve on the estimators. However, the consistency of both the RE and OLS estimates hinge on none of the observed regressors being correlated with the unobserved heterogeneity, μ_i (as well as also being uncorrelated with the idiosyncratic v_{it}). If there is such correlation, then these estimators are biased and inconsistent (Baltagi, 2008).

To deal with potential correlation between the regressors and the unobserved heterogeneity, the FE estimator can be used, which just performs a regression on the individual time-demeaned transformation of the variables:

$$\tilde{D}_{it} = \tilde{X}'_{it}\beta + \tilde{\upsilon}_{it} \tag{2}$$

where the operator ($\sim$) just time-demeans variables within individuals (e.g., $\tilde{D}_{it} = D_{it} - \bar{D}_i$ where $\bar{D}_i = \sum_{t=1}^{T_i} D_{it}/T_i$). The FE estimator is consistent as long as the regressors are strictly exogenous, that is, $E[v_{it}|X_{i1}, X_{i2} \ldots] = 0$. However, any time-invariant variables will reduce to zero when time-demeaned, so the FE estimator is of no use when the coefficients of interest are on time-invariant variables.

The HT estimator is an IV estimator that can be used to consistently estimate the full set of parameter estimates in Eq. (1) when some of the variables are correlated with μ_i. Following the notation of Hausman and Taylor, let $X_{it} = [X_{1it}, X_{2it}]$ and $Z_i = [Z_{1i}, Z_{2i}]$, where X_{1it} and Z_{1i} are assumed to be exogenous (i.e., uncorrelated with μ_i and v_{it}) while X_{2it} and Z_{2i} are assumed to be endogenous (i.e., allowed to be correlated with μ_i, though still uncorrelated with v_{it}). Fundamentally, the HT estimator works by using information in X_1 to instrument for Z_2, so the identification condition requires the number of variables in X_1, say k_1, be at least as large the number of variables in Z_{2i}, say g_2 (so we need $k_1 \geq g_2$). More specifically, the HT estimator employs a GLS transformation of Eq. (1):

$$\ddot{D}_{it} = \ddot{X}'_{it}\beta + \ddot{Z}'_{it}\gamma + \ddot{\mu}_{it} + \ddot{\upsilon}_{it} \tag{3}$$

using $(\tilde{X}_{it}, \bar{X}_{1i}, Z_1)$ as instruments to estimate the coefficients. The operator (..) performs the panel GLS transformation (e.g., $\ddot{D}_{it} = D_{it} - \theta\bar{D}_i$, with $\theta = 1 - \sqrt{\sigma_v^2/(\sigma_v^2 + T_i\sigma_\mu^2)}$).

To implement this feasibly, it remains to estimate the error component variances. As suggested by Hausman and Taylor, σ_v^2 can be estimated from the residuals of the FE regression Eq. (2), giving $\hat{\sigma}_v^2 = \text{RSS}/(N - n)$, where RSS is the residual sum of squares, N is the total number of observations and n is the number of individuals. Also from the FE regression, we can get predictions of the individual-specific intercepts, $\hat{\alpha}_{it} = \bar{y}_i - \bar{X}'_i\hat{\beta}_{\text{FE}}$. Then γ can be consistently estimated by IV estimation of

$$\hat{\alpha}_{it} = [Z_{i1}, Z_{i2}]'\gamma + v_{it} \tag{4}$$

using (X_1, Z_1) as instruments. The resulting parameter estimates, $\hat{\gamma}_{\mathrm{IV}}$, along with $\hat{\beta}_{\mathrm{FE}}$, can be used to estimate the two-way residual from Eq. (1), $\hat{e}_{it} = D_{it} - X'_{it}\hat{\beta}_{\mathrm{FE}} - Z'_i\hat{\gamma}_{\mathrm{IV}}$, whose variance can be estimated as $\hat{\sigma}_e^2 = (1/N)\sum_{i=1}^{n}\sum_{t=1}^{T_i}(1/T_i)(\sum_{t=1}^{T_i}\hat{e}_{it})^2$. Hausman and Taylor also proved that we can use the above calculated $\hat{\sigma}_v^2$ and $\hat{\sigma}_e^2$ to estimate $\hat{\sigma}_\mu^2 = (\hat{\sigma}_e^2 - \hat{\sigma}_v^2)\bar{T}^{-1}$, where $\bar{T}$ is the harmonic mean of the number of periods have observations of individuals.

The HT estimates also provide an easy way to conduct an over-identification test of the assumption that X_{1it} is not correlated with μ_i by just conducting a standard Hausman (1978) test between the FE estimates (consistent with or without the exogeneity but less efficient if the exogeneity holds) and the HT estimates (inconsistent without the exogeneity, but consistent and more efficient if the exogeneity holds). In fact, Baltagi, Bresson, and Pirotte (2003) suggest using this as part of a pretest estimation procedure to select between RE, FE, and HT estimates. The first step is to run the RE and FE estimators and then conduct the Hausman specification test on the exogeneity of the regressors to μ_i based on the difference in the estimates. If the exogeneity assumption cannot be rejected, then the RE estimator is the one to use. However, if the exogeneity assumption is rejected, then the RE is inconsistent. In this case, the HT estimator is considered and the Hausman test between it and the FE estimates is run. If the test is not rejected, then the HT estimates are preferred, while if it is rejected then only leaves the FE estimates.[1]

Beyond just satisfying the exogeneity, since the HT estimator is an IV estimator, there is still a concern that there could be problems due to a weak set of instruments, in which case the resulting estimates could be biased and/or have incorrect standard errors as has been well documented. However, studies implementing the HT estimator do not tend to consider this extensively. In the feasible implementation of the HT estimator, there are actually two IV regressions run: the final estimates in Eq. (3) and the intermediate step in Eq. (4) to get an unbiased GLS transformation correctly. The Cragg and Donald (1993) minimum eigenvalue F-Statistic can be calculated from each of these and then the critical values calculated by Stock and Yogo (2005) can be considered; though since Eq. (3) will typically contain many variables being instrumented, there will not be critical values available as Stock and Yogo considered only one to three variables being instrumented.[2] Still, the guidelines from their results can be used to help infer something about the strength of the instruments.

DATA

The data come from the NLSY79. The original panel consisted of 12,686 men and women aged 14–22 years in 1979, making them 43–52 years in 2008, the last wave used for analysis in this study. These individuals were interviewed annually until 1994, and biennially since. While the stated primary focus of the data is on labor force behavior, the data contain a relatively rich set of information including demographic variables, marriage and fertility, and asset and debt information. For a summary of the variables used in this study, see Table 1. The variables include debt levels, ethnicity, and gender along with additional variables previously found to be important in determining debt levels including income, education, unemployment, marriage, children, interest rates, and other controls. Since debt,

Table 1. Summary Statistics.

	Mean	Std. Dev.	Min.	Max.
Have debt?	0.52	0.50	0	1
Debt (if have debt)[a]	34,252	65,884	125	1,073,651
Have NH debt?	0.47	0.50	0	1
NH debt (if have NH debt)[a]	13,985	40,270	125	955,116
Black	0.39	0.49	0	1
Hispanic	0.17	0.38	0	1
Female	0.49	0.50	0	1
Employed	0.83	0.38	0	1
Weeks unemployed	3.82	9.58	0	52
Health problem	0.09	0.28	0	1
Newly divorced	0.07	0.26	0	1
Children	1.01	1.32	0	7
HGC	12.65	2.31	0	20
Age	30.53	6.83	20	51
Assets[a]	58,201	201,513	0	4,125,919
Assets net HD[a]	47,644	281,036	−29,817	4,029,117
Income[a]	37,837	53,401	0	1,287,623
Own home	0.16	0.36	0	1
Mortgage Int.	8.04	1.56	2.24	8.82
Prime Int.	5.53	1.22	1.29	6.75
Urban	0.83	0.37	0	1
Northeast	0.19	0.39	0	1
North-central	0.22	0.42	0	1
West	0.19	0.39	0	1

[a]Measured in 2008 dollars NH; NH debt refers to nonhousing debt.

asset, and some other information were collected only at the household level, it is unclear whether to consider married couples male or female when looking at the impact of gender on debt. This is similarly true for race when couples who are of differing racial backgrounds. As such, only single households are used in the analysis. The final sample size used for panel estimation consists of 6,658 individuals observed 1–14 times giving almost 23,000 respondent-year observations.[3]

The NLSY79 first collected information on household debt and assets in 1985 and regularly thereafter. Amounts of mortgage and property debts, along with car, business and "other debt" was collected each time, though there is not regularly detailed information on the nature of the other debt (whether it consists of credit cards, education loans, etc.).[4] For this study, I examine total nonbusiness debt (*Debt*) as well as nonhousing debt (*NH Debt*), which is measured as all nonbusiness debt excluding real-estate debt. The debt amounts were adjusted into 2008 dollar values using the Consumer Price Index (CPI).

Consideration must be taken as to the appropriate debt measurement and relationship to use in estimating Eq. (1). It seems unlikely, for example, that differences in gender would result in the same dollar difference in expected debt for all values of other variables including income. It is much more likely that gender differences would manifest as a different percentage change from the baseline predicted by those other variables. To account for this, the natural log of the debt measures (*lnDebt* and *lnNH Debt*) can be used as dependent variables and hence the coefficients estimate the percentage change in the debt resulting from a change in the independent variables. However, as shown in Table 1, a sizeable portion of the sample has no debt, so we cannot compute *lnDebt* for those individuals. One common solution for this in the applied literature is to use ln(*Debt*+1) and continue to use the percentage change interpretation. However, the percentage change at zero debt is actually undefined in the untransformed data, and when the data are dominated by zeros, this becomes a problem for using these data and interpreting the results as a typical percentage change, so this approach is not recommended when the dependent variable has many zeros (Wooldridge, 2000, p. 185). One approach in this situation would be a mixture model of the probability of having debt along with the amount of debt conditional on taking out debt. However, the standard HT model, as a linear panel IV estimator, does not translate easily into such a nonlinear environment. Due to this, the estimates that follow will focus on the amount of debt conditional on having debt (using lnDebt for those with debt) and separately a linear probability of having debt. While the linear probability model is flawed, when using robust standard errors it can be adequate in getting the general direction and significance of the average marginal effect (Wooldridge, 2010, p. 563).

Information on income, assets, and interest rates are also used, as these financial variables can clearly impact debt decisions. Income is measured from the household income key variable in the NLSY79 and assets are computed as the sum of all nonbusiness assets reported.[5] For estimations on the amount of NH Debt, assets net of real-estate debt will be considered (*Assets Net HD*). All income and assets are adjusted into 2008 dollars using the CPI, and when a natural log of debt is used as a dependent variable, the natural log of income and assets will be used.[6] Interest rates are the annualized average interest rates given by the Federal Reserve Board (2011) for 30-year fixed rate mortgages and the prime interest rates in the year the household showed an increase in housing or nonhousing debt as appropriate.

Two employment variables are used. First, *Employed* is an indicator measuring whether the respondent worked for pay in the last week. Second, *Weeks Unemployed* measures how many weeks the respondent was unemployed over the past year. Listing zero for both indicates that the respondent was not in the labor force; therefore, to be considered unemployed you must be actively seeking work. A variable gauging health, *Health Problem*, is an indicator of whether the respondent's health limited the work they were able to do.

Demographic information regarding education and family situation is also considered. Education is measured as the highest grade the respondent completed (*HGC*). *Newly Divorced* indicates that the respondent became divorced between interviews, since divorce has been shown to lead to short-term spikes in debt (Fisher & Lyons, 2006). Further demographic variables used include the gender and racial variables that are to be investigated (*Female*, *Black*, and *Hispanic*), the number of *Children* the respondent has, *Age*, Age^2, and the current living location (*Northeast*, *North-Central*, or *West*; zero on all three indicates living in the south) and whether the respondent lives in an urban location.

One remaining issue relating to the data and variables is determining which variables to consider exogenous to μ_i in Eq. (1) and which to consider correlated with μ_i. Consider μ_i as an individual's unobserved tendency to take out debt (unaccounted for by the observed variables). For time-invariant variables, race might be considered exogenous, but given the evidence discussed from previous studies on gender differences in debt and financial management (due to either risk preferences, financial literacy, etc.), it seems better to consider female to be correlated. So the default in the estimation will be Z_1=(*Black, Hispanic*). As for the time-varying variables, the default estimation below will consider age, age squared, newly divorced, and income as exogenous, that is, $X_1 = (Age, Age^2, Newly\ divorced, lnIncome)$. Age and age squared would be unrelated to an individual's time-invariant debt preference. While possible, it seems unlikely that unobserved debt preferences play a strong role in determining the choices to be newly divorced. Furthermore, while decisions to work or not might be correlated, the type of job and hence the average income earned seem much less likely to be correlated. The remaining variables will be considered endogenous by default. Choice of living location seems likely to be correlated given differences in cost of living; education is likely related since it might be debt financed; owning a home is clearly related to debt preferences; and even the interest rates under which you agree to acquire debt are likely correlated with your taste for debt (i.e., if more averse to debt would be even less likely to take out a higher interest loan). Robustness checks for some variation in the choice of instruments will be conducted to see if results hinge on a particular partitioning of the variables into endogenous and exogenous.

RESULTS

Table 2 shows the results for OLS, RE, FE, and HT estimates on the natural log of debt. The OLS and RE estimates give similar magnitude coefficient estimates, as expected, though they differ occasionally on statistical significance. They both indicate greater amounts of debt for women who take out loans, less for blacks, and no statistically significant difference for Hispanics. However, the Hausman test on the exogeneity of the regressors in the RE estimation with regard to the unobserved heterogeneity is easily rejected at $p < 0.001$, so the results cannot be used with confidence. The Hausman test of the HT estimator does not reject the exogeneity assumption. The HT estimate for female is negative and strongly statistically significant, which is very different from the results of the RE estimation. In fact, it indicates a 50% decrease in debt for women compared to men after controlling for the same level of other observables.[7] Furthermore, there is no statistically significant impact found for Black, which again differs from the RE model.

Considering some of the other variables in the estimation, having a health problem that prevents you from working increases expected debt for those who hold debt (7.4%), as does recently divorced (6.7%) and children (6.1% per child). For this age group of singles (late teens until late forties), age is not a statistically significant factor after considering the other variables. A 1% increase in income is associated with a 0.03% increase in debt and a 1%

Table 2. Results for lnDebt.

	OLS	RE	FE	HT[a]
Female	0.0684***	0.0505*		−0.5012***
	(0.0141)	(0.0199)		(0.1519)
Black	−0.0654***	−0.0925***		−0.0163
	(0.0170)	(0.0239)		(0.0356)
Hispanic	−0.0220	−0.0141		0.0716
	(0.0206)	(0.0288)		(0.0423)
Employed	0.1186***	0.1083**	0.0617	0.0622
	(0.0340)	(0.0342)	(0.0425)	(0.0402)
Weeks unemployed	−0.0176	−0.0107	−0.0090	−0.0091
	(0.0105)	(0.0103)	(0.0120)	(0.0114)
Health problem	0.0409	0.0558	0.0740*	0.0740*
	(0.0286)	(0.0295)	(0.0362)	(0.0342)
Newly divorced	0.0984***	0.0864***	0.0640*	0.0672**
	(0.0246)	(0.0236)	(0.0281)	(0.0247)
Children	0.0041	0.0140	0.0594**	0.0608***
	(0.0069)	(0.0088)	(0.0193)	(0.0178)
Age	0.0116	0.0086	−0.0061	−0.0064
	(0.0087)	(0.0086)	(0.0105)	(0.0100)
Age^2	−0.0036**	−0.0036**	−0.0026	−0.0026
	(0.0013)	(0.0012)	(0.0015)	(0.0014)
HGC	0.0625***	0.0707***	0.0773***	0.0770***
	(0.0033)	(0.0044)	(0.0143)	(0.0135)
lnIncome	0.0974***	0.0690***	0.0255*	0.0259*
	(0.0097)	(0.0100)	(0.0126)	(0.0118)
lnAssets	0.3934***	0.3947***	0.3955***	0.3957***
	(0.0060)	(0.0063)	(0.0080)	(0.0076)
Own home	0.8339***	0.8511***	0.8714***	0.8711***
	(0.0247)	(0.0257)	(0.0316)	(0.0299)
Mortgage Int.	−0.1059***	−0.1194***	−0.1477***	−0.1478***
	(0.0063)	(0.0066)	(0.0084)	(0.0079)
Prime Int.	−0.0701***	−0.0714***	−0.0772***	−0.0772***
	(0.0055)	(0.0055)	(0.0065)	(0.0062)
Urban	0.1174***	0.0791***	−0.0235	−0.0236
	(0.0183)	(0.0211)	(0.0303)	(0.0286)
Northeast	0.0766***	0.0576*	−0.0702	−0.0719
	(0.0207)	(0.0273)	(0.0702)	(0.0662)
North-central	0.0049	0.0010	0.0539	0.0533
	(0.0181)	(0.0245)	(0.0624)	(0.0590)
West	0.1259***	0.1087***	0.0527	0.0514
	(0.0197)	(0.0266)	(0.0664)	(0.0627)
Constant	−1.5992***	−1.5104***	−0.9206***	−0.6990**
	(0.1688)	(0.1748)	(0.2613)	(0.2702)
Hausman test		$\chi^2_{(17)} = 136.09$ * **		$\chi^2_{(3)} = 0.08$
Cragg–Donald				28.45

Note: Standard errors in parentheses.

*$p<0.05$; **$p<0.01$; ***$p<0.001$.

[a] $X_1 =$ (Age, Age^2, Newly divorced, lnIncome), $Z_1 =$ (Black, Hispanic).

increase in assets is associated with a 0.40% increase in debt, both statistically significant. Owning a home is estimated to increase debt by 87%, clearly the dominant debt for those who own homes. Higher education increases debt, not surprising given it is often debt financed, and higher interest rates are associated with having less debt as would be expected.

Table 2 also reports the Cragg–Donald minimum eigenvalue F-statistic for Eq. (3) of 28.45. What to directly conclude from this is a bit unclear. None of the variables in Eq. (3) are directly included as instruments, and hence they are technically all being instrumented for giving 21 variables in the regression not included as instruments, with an even greater number of instruments, which is beyond the range of the Stock–Yogo calculated critical values. However, the Stock–Yogo critical values allow for a rejection at the $p<0.05$ level of a greater than 5% bias relative to OLS once the critical value exceeds roughly 20 for a wide range of the number of variable instrumented for and the number of instruments. The second critical value computed by Stock–Yogo is for a rejection of a greater than 10% size for a 5% Wald test, which can be rejected at a $p<0.05$ level if the Cragg–Donald statistic exceeds their calculated critical value. These critical values can get large with many instruments, but it declines a lot between one and two variables not included in the instruments. The 28.45 Cragg–Donald value for this estimation could reject a greater than 15% size even if there was only one variable not in the instrument set, and likely would easily be fine for many. Hence, there does not seem to be indication of a weak instrument problem.

Table 3 expands upon the examination of the weak instruments as well as considering the robustness of the HT estimation presented in Table 2. Here, the coefficients for female, black, and Hispanic are presented for several different partitions of the variables into Z_1 and X_1. Along with the coefficient estimates, the Hausman test of the HT model versus the FE model is presented along with the Cragg–Donald statistic for Eq. (3) as well as the earlier intermediate Cragg–Donald statistic for Eq. (4). In the intermediate-step estimation done in Eq. (4), the Stock–Yogo critical values can be reported and are shown as well. Column 1 is the default HT estimation from Table 2. You can see that the intermediate stage clearly shows no signs of weak instruments, as the Cragg–Donald statistic is well above the critical values to reject a greater than 5% relative bias or a greater than 10% size on a 5% Wald test. Column 2 considers including children as exogenous as well. The results hardly change at all. Column 3 considers black endogenous while keeping children exogenous, and again the results are very similar. In column 4, where we try considering female as exogenous, the results shift, but the Hausman test rejects the assumption of exogeneity

Table 3. Robustness Checks for lnDebt.

	HT 1[a]	HT 2[b]	HT 3[c]	HT 4[d]	HT 5[e]	HT 6[f]
Female	−0.5012***	−0.5079***	−0.4495**	0.0722**	−0.0679	0.4959**
	(0.1519)	(0.1514)	(0.1671)	(0.0262)	(0.1419)	(0.1635)
Black	−0.0163	−0.0124	−0.1448	−0.3587*	−0.0622	−0.1057**
	(0.0356)	(0.0349)	(0.1785)	(0.1541)	(0.0356)	(0.0333)
Hispanic	0.0716	0.0748	0.0278	−0.0396	0.0588	0.0405
	(0.0423)	(0.0416)	(0.0759)	(0.0682)	(0.0428)	(0.0387)
Hausman test	$\chi^2_{(3)} = 0.08$	$\chi^2_{(4)} = 0.41$	$\chi^2_{(3)} = 0.01$	$\chi^2_{(4)} = 10.56^*$	$\chi^2_{(5)} = 46.45^{***}$	$\chi^2_{(1)} = 14.64^{***}$
Cragg–Donald	28.45	26.74	19.05	31.40	25.75	19.81
Interm. Cragg–Donald	277.37	344.92	196.68	507.40	177.22	97.21
Interm. Stock–Yogo 5% bias	16.85	18.37	13.97	18.37	19.28	–
Interm. Stock–Yogo 10% size	24.58	26.87	19.45	26.87	29.18	19.93

Note: Standard errors in parentheses.
$^*p<0.05$; $^{**}p<0.01$; $^{***}p<0.001$.
[a]HT specification 1 has $X_1 =$ (Age, Age^2, Newly divorced, lnIncome), $Z_1 =$ (Black, Hispanic).
[b]HT specification 2 has $X_1 =$ (Age, Age^2, Newly divorced, lnIncome, Children), $Z_1 =$ (Black, Hispanic).
[c]HT specification 3 has $X_1 =$ (Age, Age^2, Newly divorced, lnIncome, Children), $Z_1 =$ (Hispanic).
[d]HT specification 4 has $X_1 =$ (Age, Age^2, Newly divorced, lnIncome, Children), $Z_1 =$ (Female, Hispanic).
[e]HT specification 5 has $X_1 =$ (Age, Age^2, Newly divorced, lnIncome, Mortgage Int., Prime Int.), $Z_1 =$ (Black, Hispanic).
[f]HT specification 6 has $X_1 =$ (Age, Age^2), $Z_1 =$ (Black, Hispanic).

indicating that indeed gender is correlated with the unobserved heterogeneity in this model. Column 5 returns female to endogenous and black to exogenous, and adds the interest rates at which the debt was financed as exogenous. Again the results change, but the Hausman test strongly rejects the exogeneity assumption. Columns 6 reduces the number of exogenous variables to only Age and Age^2 and once again the results change but are rejected by the Hausman test.

Table 4 presents results for estimating the natural log of nonhousing debt, where assets are now measured as assets net of real-estate debt. The Hausman test again rejects the RE specification, but not the proposed HT estimation. Again we see the HT estimates suggesting women who take out debt take out a lower amount (39%) which was not indicated by the RE estimates and there is no statistically significant impact for black or Hispanic while the RE estimations found a negative impact for black.

Tables 5 and 6 show the linear probability estimates for having debt and having nonhousing debt, respectively. In both cases, the RE estimates are

Table 4. Results for lnNH Debt.

	OLS	RE	FE	HT[a]
Female	0.0513**	0.0392		−0.3939*
	(0.0157)	(0.0201)		(0.1635)
Black	−0.0437*	−0.0690**		−0.0242
	(0.0188)	(0.0242)		(0.0356)
Hispanic	−0.0356	−0.0252		0.0165
	(0.0228)	(0.0292)		(0.0423)
Employed	0.1556***	0.1512***	0.1106*	0.1118*
	(0.0379)	(0.0384)	(0.0498)	(0.0472)
Weeks unemployed	−0.0345**	−0.0283*	−0.0187	−0.0189
	(0.0117)	(0.0116)	(0.0142)	(0.0135)
Health problem	0.0176	0.0404	0.0640	0.0638
	(0.0319)	(0.0331)	(0.0428)	(0.0406)
Newly divorced	0.1151***	0.1121***	0.0748*	0.0865**
	(0.0278)	(0.0273)	(0.0342)	(0.0291)
Children	0.0084	0.0137	0.0728**	0.0776***
	(0.0078)	(0.0094)	(0.0235)	(0.0215)
Age	−0.0365***	−0.0324***	−0.0382**	−0.0388**
	(0.0097)	(0.0097)	(0.0125)	(0.0119)
Age^2	0.0052***	0.0045**	0.0047**	0.0048**
	(0.0014)	(0.0014)	(0.0018)	(0.0017)
HGC	0.0688***	0.0728***	0.0745***	0.0732***
	(0.0037)	(0.0046)	(0.0167)	(0.0158)
lnIncome	0.0833***	0.0632***	0.0186	0.0199
	(0.0107)	(0.0111)	(0.0147)	(0.0139)
lnAssets net HD	0.2355***	0.2476***	0.2677***	0.2682***
	(0.0057)	(0.0061)	(0.0084)	(0.0080)
Prime Int.	−0.0929***	−0.0936***	−0.0992***	−0.0993***
	(0.0062)	(0.0063)	(0.0076)	(0.0072)
Urban	0.0485*	0.0339	−0.0285	−0.0286
	(0.0205)	(0.0231)	(0.0365)	(0.0346)
Northeast	0.0136	−0.0052	−0.1416	−0.1479
	(0.0230)	(0.0283)	(0.0821)	(0.0775)
North-central	−0.0464*	−0.0659**	−0.0512	−0.0543
	(0.0203)	(0.0253)	(0.0725)	(0.0686)
West	0.0326	0.0141	0.0027	−0.0021
	(0.0219)	(0.0273)	(0.0768)	(0.0726)
Constant	−2.2057***	−2.3004***	−2.0708***	−1.8771***
	(0.1760)	(0.1809)	(0.2895)	(0.3012)
Hausman test		$\chi^2_{(15)} = 58.87$ * **		$\chi^2_{(3)} = 0.51$
Cragg–Donald				22.03

Note: Standard errors in parentheses.

*$p<0.05$; **$p<0.01$; ***$p<0.001$.

[a]$X_1 =$ (Age, Age^2, Newly divorced, Income), $Z_1 =$ (Black, Hispanic).

Table 5. Results for Have Debt?

	OLS	RE	FE	HT[a]
Female	0.0729***	0.0659***		0.1602**
	(0.0047)	(0.0066)		(0.0553)
Black	−0.0338***	−0.0397***		−0.0328**
	(0.0056)	(0.0079)		(0.0105)
Hispanic	−0.0135*	−0.0160		−0.0010
	(0.0069)	(0.0096)		(0.0131)
Employed	0.1096***	0.0925***	0.0680***	0.0687***
	(0.0095)	(0.0097)	(0.0115)	(0.0111)
Weeks unemployed	−0.0138***	−0.0135***	−0.0148***	−0.0148***
	(0.0031)	(0.0030)	(0.0034)	(0.0033)
Health problem	0.0420***	0.0350***	0.0278*	0.0273*
	(0.0093)	(0.0097)	(0.0115)	(0.0111)
Newly divorced	0.0069	0.0050	0.0004	0.0057
	(0.0087)	(0.0083)	(0.0095)	(0.0086)
Children	0.0079***	0.0097***	0.0119*	0.0140*
	(0.0022)	(0.0028)	(0.0058)	(0.0055)
Age	0.0089**	0.0079**	0.0036	0.0032
	(0.0028)	(0.0028)	(0.0033)	(0.0032)
Age^2	−0.0033***	−0.0031***	−0.0026***	−0.0025***
	(0.0004)	(0.0004)	(0.0005)	(0.0005)
HGC	0.0111***	0.0128***	0.0352***	0.0350***
	(0.0011)	(0.0015)	(0.0045)	(0.0044)
lnIncome	0.0216***	0.0146***	0.0075*	0.0083*
	(0.0029)	(0.0030)	(0.0036)	(0.0034)
lnAssets	0.0675***	0.0742***	0.0805***	0.0807***
	(0.0017)	(0.0018)	(0.0022)	(0.0021)
Own home	0.1026***	0.0957***	0.0903***	0.0896***
	(0.0085)	(0.0088)	(0.0104)	(0.0101)
Mortgage Int.	−0.0213***	−0.0201***	−0.0208***	−0.0212***
	(0.0021)	(0.0022)	(0.0027)	(0.0026)
Prime Int.	−0.0758***	−0.0644***	−0.0525***	−0.0525***
	(0.0020)	(0.0020)	(0.0024)	(0.0023)
Urban	−0.0225***	−0.0201**	−0.0186	−0.0187
	(0.0062)	(0.0071)	(0.0100)	(0.0097)
Northeast	−0.0703***	−0.0691***	−0.0649**	−0.0669**
	(0.0067)	(0.0088)	(0.0217)	(0.0210)
North-central	−0.0032	−0.0024	−0.0235	−0.0254
	(0.0061)	(0.0082)	(0.0202)	(0.0196)
West	−0.0251***	−0.0251**	−0.0261	−0.0282
	(0.0066)	(0.0089)	(0.0215)	(0.0209)
Constant	1.1556***	1.0971***	0.8749***	0.8184***
	(0.0551)	(0.0573)	(0.0816)	(0.0893)
Hausman test		$\chi^2_{(17)} = 198.29**$		$\chi^2_{(3)} = 2.12$
Cragg–Donald				31.52

Note: Standard errors in parentheses.
*$p<0.05$; **$p<0.01$; ***$p<0.001$.
[a] $X_1 =$ (Age, Age^2, Newly divorced, lnIncome), $Z_1 =$ (Black, Hispanic).

Table 6. Results for Have lnNH Debt?

	OLS	RE	FE	HT[a]
Female	0.0795***	0.0724***		0.2366***
	(0.0051)	(0.0070)		(0.0611)
Black	−0.0270***	−0.0330***		−0.0254*
	(0.0061)	(0.0084)		(0.0117)
Hispanic	−0.0095	−0.0139		0.0079
	(0.0075)	(0.0102)		(0.0146)
Employed	0.1249***	0.1049***	0.0757***	0.0771***
	(0.0103)	(0.0105)	(0.0125)	(0.0121)
Weeks unemployed	−0.0164***	−0.0155***	−0.0160***	−0.0161***
	(0.0033)	(0.0033)	(0.0037)	(0.0036)
Health problem	0.0468***	0.0390***	0.0291*	0.0283*
	(0.0101)	(0.0105)	(0.0125)	(0.0121)
Newly divorced	0.0230*	0.0175	0.0054	0.0159
	(0.0094)	(0.0090)	(0.0103)	(0.0093)
Children	0.0085***	0.0102***	0.0110	0.0152*
	(0.0024)	(0.0031)	(0.0063)	(0.0059)
Age	0.0033	0.0009	−0.0056	−0.0064
	(0.0031)	(0.0030)	(0.0036)	(0.0035)
Age^2	−0.0026***	−0.0022***	−0.0014**	−0.0013**
	(0.0004)	(0.0004)	(0.0005)	(0.0005)
HGC	0.0129***	0.0145***	0.0411***	0.0408***
	(0.0012)	(0.0016)	(0.0049)	(0.0048)
lnIncome	0.0251***	0.0179***	0.0100**	0.0115**
	(0.0032)	(0.0033)	(0.0039)	(0.0037)
lnAssets net HD	0.0457***	0.0530***	0.0616***	0.0621***
	(0.0016)	(0.0017)	(0.0022)	(0.0021)
Prime Int.	−0.0963***	−0.0846***	−0.0713***	−0.0715***
	(0.0021)	(0.0022)	(0.0026)	(0.0025)
Urban	−0.0266***	−0.0222**	−0.0197	−0.0198
	(0.0068)	(0.0077)	(0.0109)	(0.0106)
Northeast	−0.0765***	−0.0744***	−0.0499*	−0.0539*
	(0.0073)	(0.0095)	(0.0237)	(0.0230)
North-central	−0.0177**	−0.0176*	−0.0326	−0.0363
	(0.0067)	(0.0088)	(0.0221)	(0.0213)
West	−0.0292***	−0.0298**	−0.0350	−0.0394
	(0.0072)	(0.0095)	(0.0235)	(0.0227)
Constant	1.0870***	1.0627***	0.8260***	0.7340***
	(0.0568)	(0.0583)	(0.0842)	(0.0937)
Hausman test		$\chi^2_{(15)} = 239.90^{**}$		$\chi^2_{(3)} = 6.72$
Cragg–Donald				35.81

Note: Standard errors in parentheses.

$^{*}p<0.05$; $^{**}p<0.01$; $^{***}p<0.001$.

[a] $X_1 =$ (Age, Age^2, Newly divorced, Income), $Z_1 =$ (Black, Hispanic).

strongly rejected by the Hausman test while the proposed HT estimates are not. Unlike on the amount of debt, however, the stories painted by the estimates are not as drastically different. In both cases, all of the estimates find that blacks are 3% less likely to take on debt. Furthermore, all of the estimates find that women are more likely to take on some debt. However, on this account, the estimates differ on magnitude. The RE estimate indicates women are 7% more likely to take on debt while the HT estimates show women 16% more likely to have some kind of debt and 24% more likely to have some nonhousing debt. This suggest that, relative to men, women are more likely to have debt, particularly driven by nonhousing-related debt, though as estimated above the amount that they take out tends to be less.

CONCLUSION

In this paper, panel data and the HT estimator are used to estimate the relationship between time-invariant demographic characteristics and household debt burdens. The results suggest that typical estimation methods regarding these variables may be biased due to correlations with unobserved heterogeneity, which the HT estimator can help deal with. This is particularly useful since the Hausman test typically rejects the exogeneity of variables in panel RE models of household behavior and FE estimates are unable to estimate the impact of time-invariant characteristics. Furthermore, for some of the results, the coefficient estimates change sign, magnitude, and significance when the HT estimates are used instead. The validity of the HT estimates can be considered using the Cragg–Donald F-statistic and the associated Stock–Yogo critical values to investigate potential problems with weak instruments, along with the additional Hausman test of the exogeneity of the overidentified instruments used.

As for the estimated difference in debt burdens for those who hold debt, the results indicate women tend to have lower amounts of debt when controlling for other factors. No significant difference was found for black or Hispanic households when considering the amount of debt once other factors were controlled for. At the same time, women were found to be more likely to have some debt, especially nonhousing debt. Blacks were slightly less likely to have debt, and again no difference was found for Hispanic. As with other demographic studies, it is difficult to interpret these results beyond the indication that differences remain after accounting for the controls used. In the cases where women were found to be more likely to have debt, it could indicate they are in a potentially higher need financial situation. They could also find themselves in higher risk financial situations with regard to negative shocks, since they also tend to have lower incomes, though the results do indicate they are more cautions with the amount of debt they take on. Additionally, more can be gleaned from the fact that the results suggest there are some time-invariant unobserved characteristics correlated with gender, as would be expected given prior research on gender differences in risk aversion and investment and debt decisions.

NOTES

1. Note that the degrees of freedom for the Hausman test comparing the HT estimates to the FE estimates is only k_1-g_2, the number of overidentified regressors, and not the full number of coefficients.
2. While packages such as Stata have Hausman–Taylor estimation as a separate routine and IV estimation routines including postestimation tests based on the Craig–Donald F-statistic, it remains to get the variables needed to run Eqs. (3) and (4). While Eq. (4) is straightforward after running the FE regression, Eq. (3) is a bit trickier. However, the estimates of $\hat{\sigma}_{\mu}^2$ and $\hat{\sigma}_{v}^2$ can be retrieved from the saved results of Stata's Hausman–Taylor estimation and then the GLS transformation of the variables can be done directly. The transformed data can be used to conduct the IV estimation of Eq. (3), with care taken to make sure and use a GLS transformed intercept instead of a standard intercept.
3. To be included, a respondent must provide information on all variables used in a given year. In addition, a few extreme outliers were removed (less than 0.25% of the sample).
4. Beginning in 2004, more detailed information regarding credit card debt and outstanding student loans was collected.
5. Similar to debt information, information on housing, vehicle, business, and "other" assets are regularly collected. In later years, the "other" category received some more detailed breakdown into retirement assets, other stocks, and so on.
6. For households that have debt, only 2% have zero income, assets, or negative assets net real estate debts; so for estimations taking the log, these observations were dropped. Including them by giving them $1 of positive assets or income instead of zero did not change the results in any substantial way.
7. Given the natural log specification of the dependent variable, the percentage impact of a dummy variable can be calculated as $100^*(\exp(\hat{\beta})-1)$ (see, e.g., Wooldridge, 2000, p. 184).

ACKNOWLEDGMENTS

I would like to thank participants at the 11th Advances in Econometrics conference as well as participants at the LSU economics seminar series and Carter Hill in particular for their valuable comments.

REFERENCES

Baltagi, B. H. (2008). *Econometric analysis of panel data* (4th Ed). Chinchester, UK: Wiley.

Baltagi, B. H., & Khanti-Akom, S. (1990). On efficient estimation with panel data: An empirical comparison of instrumental variables estimators. *Journal of Applied Econometrics*, *5*, 402–406.

Baltagi, B. H., Bresson, G., & Pirotte, A. (2003). Fixed effects, random effects or Hausman – Taylor? A pretest estimator. *Economics Letters*, *79*, 361–369.

Berkovec, J. A., Canner, G. B., Gabriel, S. A., & Hannan, T. H. (1994). Race, redlining, and residential mortgage loan performance. *Journal of Real Estate Finance and Economics*, *9*(3), 263–294.

Contoyannis, P., & Rice, N. (2001). The impact of health on wages: Evidence from the British household panel survey. *Empirical Economics*, *26*, 599–622.

Cragg, J. G., & Donald, S. G. (1993). Testing identifiability and specification in instrumental variables models. *Econometric Theory*, *9*, 222–240.

Croson, R., & Gnezzy, U. (2009). Gender differences in preferences. *Journal of Economic Literature*, *47*(2), 448–474.

De'Armond, D., & Zhu, D. (2011). Determinants of consumer debt: An examination of individual credit management variables. *Journal of Finance and Accountancy*, 7, 1–17.

Dew, J. (2011). The association between consumer debt and the likelihood of divorce. *Journal of Family and Economic Issues*, *32*, 554–565.

Federal Reserve Board. (2011). Data from http://www.federalreserve.gov/releases/h15/data.htm

Field, N. (2007). Debt and the gender gap. *Money Magazine*, October 5.

Fisher, J. D., & Lyons, A. C. (2006). Till debt do us part: A model of divorce and personal bankruptcy. *Review of Economics of the Household*, *4*, 35–52.

Hausman, J. A. (1978). Specification test in econometrics. *Econometrica*, *46*, 1251–1272.

Hausman, J. A., & Taylor, W. E. (1981). Panel data and unobservable individual effects. *Econometrica*, *49*, 1377–1398.

Himmelstein, D. U., Thorne, D., Warren, E., & Woolhandler, S. (2009). Medical bankruptcy in the United States, 2007: Results of a national study. *The American Journal of Medicine*, *122*(8), 741–746.

Johnson, K. W. (2007). Recent developments in the credit card market and the financial obligations ratio. In S. Agarwal & B. W. Ambrose (Eds.), *Household credit usage: Personal debt and mortgages*. New York: Palgrave Macmillan.

Ladd, H. F. (1998). Evidence on discrimination in mortgage lending. *The Journal of Economic Perspectives*, *12*(2), 41–62.

Lahart, J., & Light, J. (2011). U.S. household net worth climbs 1.2%. *The Wall Street Journal*, June 10.

Lusardi, A., & Mitchell, O. S. (2008). Planning and financial literacy: How do women fare? *American Economic Review*, *98*(2), 413–417.

Lusardi, A., & Tufano, P. (2009). *Debt literacy, financial experiences, and overindebtedness*. NBER Working Paper No. 14808, The National Bureau of Economic Research, Cambridge, MA.

Mahdavi, M. (2005). 2005 Survey of Financial Knowledge and Practice among College Students. Retrieved from http://www.smith.edu/wfi/research_2005survey.php

Malcolm, L. E., & Dowd, A. C. (2009). *College student debt as opportunity or disadvantage?* A Reconceptualization and Application to STEM Graduate Enrollment. Center for Urban Education Working Paper, University of Southern California.
Modigliani, F. (1966). The life cycle hypothesis of saving, the demand for wealth, and the supply of capital. *Social Research*, *33*(2), 150–217.
Morris, M. D. S., & Shreffler, K. (2011). *Household debt and meeting fertility expectations*. Working Paper. Oklahoma State University.
Price, D. V. (2004). Educational debt burden among student borrowers: An analysis of the baccalaureate and beyond panel, 1997 follow-up. *Research in Higher Education*, *45*, 7.
Rapoport, A. I. (1999). *Does the educational debt burden of science and engineering doctorates differ by race/ethnicity and sex?* National Science Foundation Issues Brief, NSF 99-341.
Schooley, D. K., & Worden, D. D. (2010). Fueling the credit crisis: Who uses consumer credit and what drives debt burden?. *Business Economics*, *45*(4), 266–276.
Shapiro, T. M., Meschende, T., & Sullivan, L. (2010). *The racial wealth gap increases fourfold*. Institute on Assets and Social Policy Research and Policy Brief, May.
Singletary, M. (2005). Hitting the books on personal finance. *The Washington Post*, August 25.
Stock, J. H., & Yogo, M. (2005). Testing for weak instruments in linear IV regression. In D. W. K. Andrews & J. H. Stock (Eds.), *Identification and inference in econometric models: Essays in honor of Thomas Rothenberg*. New York: Cambridge University Press.
Sullivan, J. X. (2008). Borrowing during unemployment: Unsecured debt as safety net. *The Journal of Human Resources*, *43*(2), 383–412.
Tippett, R. M. (2010). *Household debt across the life course: An analysis of the late Baby Boomers*. Dissertation. Duke University.
Wooldridge, J. M. (2000). *Introductory econometrics: A modern approach*. USA: South-Western College Publishing.
Wooldridge, J. M. (2010). *Econometric analysis of cross section and panel data* (2nd ed). USA: Massachusetts Institute of Technology.
Wolff, E. N. (2007). *Recent trends in household wealth in the United States: Rising debt and the middle-class squeeze*. Levy Economics Institute Working Paper No. 502.
Xiao, J. J., & Yao, R. (2011). *Debt holding and burden by family structure in 1989–2007*. Working Paper 2011-WP-04, Networks Financial Institute, Indiana State University.
Yezer, A. M. J., Phillips, R. F., & Trost, R. P. (1994). Bias in estimates of discrimination and default in mortgage lending: The effects of simultaneity and self-selection. *Journal of Real Estate Finance and Economics*, *9*(3), 196–215.
Zargorsky, J. L. (2003). Husbands' and wives' view of the family finances. *Journal of Socio-Economics*, *21*, 127–146.

SOVEREIGN BOND SPREAD DRIVERS IN THE EU MARKET IN THE AFTERMATH OF THE GLOBAL FINANCIAL CRISIS

Iuliana Matei and Angela Cheptea

ABSTRACT

Recently the world economy was confronted to the worst financial crisis since the great depression. This unprecedented crisis started in mid-2007 had a huge impact on the European government bond market. But what are the main drivers of this "perfect storm" that since 2009 affects EU government bond market as well? To answer this question, we propose an empirical study of the determinants of the sovereign bond spreads of EU countries with respect to Germany during the period 2003–2010. Technically, we address two main questions. First, we ask what share of the change in sovereign bond spreads is explained by changes in the fundamentals, liquidity, and market risks. Second, we distinguish between EU member states within and outside the Euro area and question whether long-term determinants of spreads affect EU members uniformly. To these ends, we employ panel data techniques in a regression model where spreads to Germany (with virtually no default risk) are explained by set of traditional variables and a number of policy variables. Results reveal that large fiscal deficits and public debt as well as political risks and to a

Essays in Honor of Jerry Hausman
Advances in Econometrics, Volume 29, 327–352

ISSN: 0731-9053/doi:10.1108/S0731-9053(2012)0000029017

lesser extent the liquidity are likely to put substantial upward pressures on sovereign bond yields in many advanced European economies.

Keywords: Debt; Euro zone crisis; financial contagion; panel models

JEL classification: F33; E42; G15

INTRODUCTION

The last three years the world economy faced the worst financial crisis since the great depression. Started in mid-2007, this unprecedented crisis had huge impacts on the Euro zone government bond market. A mix of deteriorating economic prospects, failing commodity prices, growing risk aversion, and huge financial stress have raised the concerns about the risk of a sharp increases of fiscal deficits and government debt in many countries. In the early 2009, market interest rates on sovereign debt have started to spike upward across a number of EU countries and have affected initially countries with large and vulnerable banking sectors. Accordingly, the rising share of sovereign bond flows in total capital inflows, especially in the times of crisis, has become an issue of deep concern for many countries around the world.

With respect to the recent crisis, while the sovereign debt increases have been most pronounced only in a few Euro area countries, they have become a real problem for the area as a whole. An increase in the gap between the yields of sovereign bonds issued by European Monetary Union (EMU) countries and the yields of bonds with similar characteristics issued by the German economy, assumed as virtually free of default risk, generates a similar shift in the market perceptions of the default risk in non-EMU economies as well. Hence, spreads on the yields of European bonds reflect the premiums required by investors to hold these securities and are a component of the costs that countries have to pay when borrowing on external markets. If one combines this with the foreign currency risk faced by EU countries outside the Euro zone, one adds to the potential threat.

Given the economic importance of yield spreads, it is not surprising that there is a large literature focusing on the determinants of yield spreads. A central issue closely investigated by this literature is how the market assesses sovereign default risk. This question has been addressed essentially for emerging countries: see, for example, Edwards (1984); Cline and Barnes

(1997); Kamin and Von Kleist (1999); Mody (2009); Jahjah and Zhanwei Yue (2010); Bellas, Papaioannou, and Petrova (2010). Although the evidence presented in these studies clearly suggests some empirical regularities for emerging markets, the debate about the "real" empirical model on driving forces of spreads is far from being settled.

More recently, an increasing number of papers focus on the determinants of the spreads on sovereign bond yields in the Euro area: see, for example, Cordogno et al. (2003); Bernoth, von Hagen, and Schuknecht (2006); Manganelli and Wolswijk (2009); Barbosa and Costa (2010); Oliveira, Curto, and Nunes (2011); and Maltritz (2011). Results revealed by this strand of literature differ not only across time periods and country panels but also for similar periods due to the use of different variables or methodologies.

Our contribution to this existing literature is threefold. First, we consider a much larger country panel than previous studies. Existing works employ panel data techniques on (very) small data samples (up to 15 countries), which limits the validity of obtained results. Differently, we investigate the key drivers of yield spreads on government bonds issued by 25 EU countries. In line with the literature, we consider bonds issued by Germany to be free of risk and compute spreads as the difference between each country's interest rate and German interest rate. Our analysis carries on an eight-year period (from 2003 to 2010), with special emphasis on years corresponding to the crisis period (2008–2010). Second, we distinguish between Euro area members and other EU countries to explore the differences between the two groups and to test the robustness of our results across different panels of countries. Previous works ignore the role of exchange rate risks in explaining yield spreads. The use of a panel combining both EMU and non-EMU countries allows us to address the role of exchange rate policy in the assessment of sovereign default risk. Third, apart from factors identified in the literature, we test the presence of a new driving force of EU spreads, political instability.

More precisely, we estimate an empirical model in which spreads to Germany are explained by a set of explanatory variables including traditional determinants of spreads, such as gross domestic product (GDP) growth, inflation, debt, liquidity, and other fiscal measures, as well as new sources of risk, namely, the exchange rate regime, the political risk perception, and the financial crisis. We apply panel data estimation techniques and test the difference in impacts for EMU and non-EMU countries, before and during the crisis. We test several hypotheses regarding the driving forces of EU spreads. This strategy is justified by the fact that there is no consensus about "an appropriate model" regarding the relevant drivers of yield spreads. Each work in the literature uses a different set of explanatory variables. In accordance to the panel structure of our data, we employ a fixed-effects model to estimate our results.

Our results suggest that large fiscal deficits, public debt, political risks, and, to a lesser extent, liquidity risks are likely to put substantial upward pressures on sovereign bond yields in many advanced European economies. Thus, our analysis reveals ways for national and regional governments to ease/avoid financial stress.

The remainder of the chapter is structured as follows. The second section presents a brief review of the existing literature on the determinants of interest rate spreads on EU sovereign bonds. In the third section, we identify the main determinants of EU yield differentials, discuss their expected influence on the yield spreads, and formulate the hypothesis that will be tested. The fourth section describes the empirical specification and presents our data sources. In the fifth section, results from the econometric estimations are reported and the last section resumes our conclusions.

RELATED LITERATURE

This section reviews the existing literature on EU government bond yields or their spreads against a benchmark country (most often Germany).

Recent studies on EU government bond yields can be divided into two broad categories: studies analyzing the period preceding and following the recent financial crisis and studies concerned with creation of the European single currency and monetary union. Both strands of this literature investigate the determinants of government bond yield spreads in the absence of exchange rate risk in the Euro area since the creation of EMU.

Three drivers of yield spreads are found in all recent papers in the field: credit risk, liquidity indicators, and changes in general risk aversion or international risk factor. Although the global financial crisis revealed all these types of risk, existing research – starting with Codogno, Favero, and Missale (2003) and Bernoth, von Hagen, and Schuknecht (2004) and including more recent studies such as Manganelli and Wolswijk (2009); Haugh, Ollivaud, and Turner (2009); Schuknecht, von Hagen, and Wolswijk (2009); Barrios, Iversen, Lewandowska, & Setzer (2009); Von Hagen, Schuknecht, and Wolswijk (2011); Pozzi and Wolswijk (2011); Maltritz (2011); Gibson, Hall, and Tavlas (2011); and Oliveira et al. (2011) – highlights the difficulty to distinguish between these interpretations of yield spreads.

The existing literature reports three types of *credit risks*: (1) the default risk, (2) the credit spread risk, and (3) the downgrades risk. The default risk refers to the probability that the issuer fails to meet its financial obligations; the credit spread risk reflects the situation in which the bond market value does not exceed the value of other comparable quality bonds; and the downgrades risk is the fear to being downgraded by a credit rating agency. This literature includes a growing number of papers focusing on the role of credit risk traditionally captured by variables reflecting past or projections of future fiscal performance. Still, the findings on this component differ according to the considered period. Studies prior to the financial crisis (e.g., Bernoth et al., 2004, and Codogno et al., 2003) find evidence for credit risk as a major driving force of yield spreads. More precisely, Cordogno et al. (2003) explore the role of international risk in explaining yield spreads for nine EU countries from 1999 to 2002 period. They relate US corporate bond spread, US swap spreads to country-specific default risk factors, and find that the default risk, although relatively small, is a significant element of yield differentials, given its capacity to influence countries' fiscal discipline. Using data on EU Eurobonds issued between 1991 and 2002 (but ignoring the exchange rate risk), Bernoth et al. (2004) study the determinants of EU yield spreads against Germany and the United States and show that international risk factors (measured by US corporate risk) influence spreads while interactions of global risk with local fundamentals or liquidity indicators are less evident. In a different paper (Bernoth et al., 2006), authors examine the effects of the monetary union on the risk premiums relative to Germany or the United States for 14 EU countries before and after the creation of the EMU. They find that the default risk premium is positively affected by debt and debt service ratios of the issuing country. Schuknecht et al. (2009) arrive to a similar conclusion, showing that the default risk is an essential component of yield spreads on a panel off 13 EU countries over the period 1991–2005.

The credit risk stands for a key driving force of yield spreads also in studies following the global financial crisis, too. Using time series cointegration techniques to analyze the determinants of Greek spreads relative to Germany from January 2000 to September 2010, Gibson, Hall, and Tavlas (2011) study the role of credit risk in explaining Greek spreads after the crisis erupted in 2009. They also present evidence on the share of risk premium unexplained by the credit rating of the Greek sovereign and point out that, despite the improvement in Greece's macroeconomic fundamentals in 2010, the widening of spreads was translated into a self-fulfilling crisis. Using panel data models, Schuknecht, von Hagen, and

Wolswijk (2010) highlight the role of credit risk in determining yield spreads for 15 EU countries over the period 1991–2009. The fact that credit risk appears as a major component of EU yield spreads has been interpreted as evidence of the credibility of the Stability and Growth Pact, its goal being to enforce fiscal discipline among EMU members. However, findings of Manganelli and Wolswijk (2009) suggest that penalties imposed by financial markets were not sufficiently high to prevent fiscal imbalances in certain EU countries. They show that some ratings and short-term interest rates are pertinent spread drivers for 15 EU countries from 1991 to 2009.

Another key component of yield spreads is *risk aversion* (international risk factor), often associated with the willingness of investors to take risk. Haugh et al. (2009) point out the importance of the risk aversion in explaining yield spreads particularly in times of financial uncertainty as those known by Euro zone since 2009. To assess the drivers of spreads for 10 Euro area countries, they apply a static panel model on quarterly spreads against Germany from 2005 to 2009. They identify the effects of fiscal policies on future deficits and the debt service ratio as relevant spread determinants. Looking at the government bond yield spreads in the US and Euro bond markets during two periods (pre-crisis and crisis periods – from 1991 to mid-2009), Von Hagen et al. (2011) study the role of risk aversion versus fiscal criteria to account for credit risk. Similarly to Haugh et al. (2009) and Barrios et al. (2009), they find evidence that fiscal imbalances are more penalized by markets since the 2008 Lehman Brothers' default. Manganelli and Wolswijk (2009) find evidence in favor of a positive relation between international risk aversion, short-term interest rates, and government bond spreads. They also point out the role of liquidity, and to a lesser extent of credit risks as factors of yield spreads on government bonds.

The role of *liquidity* in explaining government bond yield differentials across EMU members is somewhat contentious in the literature, especially on the pre-crisis period. The liquidity risk premium measures the extra interest rate an investor requires in compensation for bearing the risk of having to liquidate the security at a lower price than the benchmark. Studies such as Codogno et al. (2003); Bernoth et al. (2004); Geyer, Kossmeier, and Pichler (2004); and Schuknecht et al. (2009) find evidence of a weak liquidity effect on EMU spreads, while Haugh et al. (2009); Beber, Brandt, and Kavajecz (2009); and Manganelli and Wolswijk (2009) show that liquidity is a strong driving force of spreads. By contrast, Favero, Pagano, and von Thadden (2010) find that interaction between liquidity demand and risk is negative. A possible explanation of their finding is that econometric estimations take into account not only the dimension of country-specific risk but also that of aggregate risk factors. The other three papers do not pay attention to the last group. Oliveira et al. (2011) arrive at a similar conclusion as Favero et al. (2010) and find no evidence of a significant liquidity effect before or during the 2007 financial crisis period for seven EMU countries during the 2000–2010 period and three yield maturities – 5-, 10-, and 15-year maturity.

As a final point, there is a common consensus in the literature that not only the fiscal discrepancies but also other macroeconomic imbalances have been strongly penalized by financial markets during the global financial crisis. Macrofundamentals (e.g., trade balance, degree of openness, and terms of trade), international risk conditions (e.g., US interest rates) or market sentiments (e.g., corporate bond spreads), and fiscal conditions are relevant drivers of yield spreads for Maltritz (2011). These results are obtained by applying a Bayesian approach to annual panel data from 1990 to 2009 in order to study the determinants of sovereign yield spreads of EMU member states. Using state space methods for weekly data over the period 1995–2009, Pozzi and Wolswijk (2011) look at the bond risk premium and the financial integration of government bond markets for five EMU countries: Belgium, France, Italy, Germany, and the Netherlands. Their findings show that idiosyncratic factors were eliminated by 2006 in all countries, except Italy, since the beginning of the recent financial crisis and that country-specific exposures to common international risk factors converged over the whole period across countries. The role played by the macroeconomic variables in the spreads dynamics has been revealed by other studies as well – see, for instance, Ang and Piazzesi (2003), Lemke (2008), and Mesonnier, Borgy, Laubach, and Renne (2011).

Based on this succinct overview of the literature and on the theoretical arguments of benefits and costs of monetary unions, the next section identifies key drivers of EU yield differentials, discusses their expected influence on yield spreads, and formulates some hypothesis.

DETERMINANTS OF EU YIELD DIFFERENTIALS AND HYPOTHESIS

Understanding what fundamentally drives the developments in EU yield spreads and why the driving forces of sovereign bond spreads could be different in EMU and non-EMU countries is an issue of interest to policymakers and practitioners alike.

The academic literature on government bond yield is consensual in establishing three main forces that drive the yield differentials: the credit risk, the liquidity risk, and the investors' risk aversion. Therefore, theoretical explanations of EU government bond differentials should be revolved around the theoretical arguments of benefits and costs of currency unification, financial integration, and market discipline as well.

The adoption of the Euro conferred several benefits to EMU members. First, there is a consensus in the literature that high inflation and inflation variability raise costs on the economy creating uncertainty and an inefficient allocation of resources. Higher price differentials lead to losses in competitiveness, to difficulties with debt service mainly for countries that lack an independent monetary policy (e.g., for pegged currencies or even common currencies), increasing the default risks. Dealing with inflation is not an easy task for EMU countries, as they have to achieve the optimal inflation criterion of the Maastricht Treaty without an independent monetary policy. Furthermore, countries troubled in the past by episodes of high inflation achieve easier low inflation rates by integrating a monetary union. Hence, the status of Euro area member guaranties low inflation rates, and should be a major benefit for EU countries with regular histories of high inflation. The first hypothesis to be tested is given as follows:

H1. Higher inflation rates are associated with higher default risks, and accordingly with higher government bond spreads.

Furthermore, low inflation rates – underpinning by European Central Bank's (ECB) monetary policy – are associated with reduced nominal interest rate which encourages borrowing and lending at longer maturities and therefore stimulates investment and growth and reduces yield spreads. Monetary policy can substantially affect the incentives to take risk via the interest rate. In this sense, Manganelli and Wolswijk (2009) report two main channels showing the link between investor's risk aversion and short-term interest rate. First, low interest rates rise funding liquidity and the incentives of investors to take additional risks to boost their returns. If interest rates are high, investors are interested in safer assets, whereas if interest rates are low, investors assume growing risks to maximize the return on their investments. Second, interest rates affect the state of the economy, which in turn is known to be related to agents' risk aversion. We formulate the second hypothesis as:

H2. Lower interest rates are related with lower degrees of risk aversion, and therefore with lower government bond spreads.

Another important dimension often revealed by the existing literature and designed as stability criterion in the Maastricht Treaty is the government debt and deficit. The debt situation describes the payment obligations that governments have to perform. Higher government indebtedness increases the default risk and yield spreads. This implies that the country has to spend additional money for debt service, increasing the default probability of the country and accordingly the credit risk.

H3. Higher levels of debt and of deficit raise the country's default risks and therefore its yield spreads.

The state of the economy is a key feature for a country desiring to fulfill easier the debt service requirements. The most important indicator used to capture this situation is the growth of GDP accepted to have a negative effect on spreads. Theoretical arguments around the sustainability of the country's debt (e.g., Domar, 1950) underline the relationship between the growth rate of GDP and the growth rate of debt, pointing out that growing debt is not a problem as long as debt rises at a slower rate than the GDP. For EMU and non-EMU members of the European Union, we formulate the following hypothesis:

H4. GDP growth rates reduces, ceteris paribus, the country's default risk.

The introduction of the Euro also impacted the yield curves of Euro zone countries. First, new Euro-denominated debt was issued and, simultaneously, all outstanding debt was redenominated in the new currency, which involved the disappearance of currency risk premiums of inflation and devaluation. Therefore, the elimination of the exchange rate fluctuations and of the competitive devaluations among participating countries is a key benefit of joining the Euro area. By contrast, non-EMU members are more exposed to exchange rate uncertainty and risk premiums, some of them experiencing in the past a chain of exchange rate crises (e.g., Czech Republic, Hungary).

Taking into account the standardization of a large Euro-denominated bond market and the reduction in risk premium in "normal" times, recent literature highlights that market expectations should be that different public debt issues of equal maturity would become perfect substitutes. This interesting finding implies an increasing process of financial integration of the Euro area financial markets with two main consequences: first, a diminishing liquidity effect on spreads involved by increasing "cross border trade in securities"; second, a hamper effect on the market ability to discriminate the quality of EU fiscal policies. In this case, integrated financial markets do not allow a correct appreciation by market participants of bonds issued by different governments. Most of the studies considers that financial integration is a necessary condition for markets to work properly and exert their disciplinary effects (see, Manganelli & Wolswijk, 2009). It is important to highlight here that despite the increasing convergence process of yield on public debt in the pre-crisis period, the yield differentials against Germany do not disappear completely. Furthermore, during the recent financial crisis, spreads increased more because of the deterioration of some macroeconomic fundamentals.

Although Euro area bond market has already achieved a high degree of integration, liquidity risk is still priced in by investors. In the case of non-EMU members, we expect a higher liquidity effect to explain some of the movements in yield spreads not accounted for by fiscal imbalance variables capturing the credit risk:

H5. Liquidity risk is higher for non-EMU members than EMU members.

Finally, the countries' political stability may have an influence on yield differential. In this sense, market expectations that governments destabilized or overthrown by unconstitutional means (including politically motivated violence and terrorism) are not able to correctly fulfill their financial obligations, which may increase interest rates and lead to a higher market perception of the default risk. The next hypothesis will be tested:

H6. Higher political instability leads to a widening of yield spreads.

The reduction in risk premia and in the nominal interest rates, the increase of GDP growth, and political stability contribute to lower the costs of servicing the public sector debt, facilitating fiscal adjustment and a more responsible allocation of resources.

METHODOLOGY AND DATA

This section deals with the empirical specifications that will be tested with empirical data.

The Empirical Specification

The present paper examines the main drivers of European sovereign bond spreads to Germany in the aftermath of the recent global crisis. To this end, we consider the following equation:

$$\text{Spread}_{it} = \mu + \beta \cdot \text{HYP}_{it} + \delta \cdot \text{CV}_{it} + v_i + \varepsilon_{it} \quad (1)$$

where $Spread_{it}$ is the difference between the yields of 10-year sovereign bonds issued by country i in year t and the yields of similar bonds issued by Germany. When spreads go up, market perceptions of the risks of default of other EU economies increases. Hence, the yields spreads measure the premium required by investors to hold such securities and they are a component of the costs that these less developed countries should pay when borrowing on the external markets. If one combines this with the foreign currency risk for EU countries that do not belong to the Euro zone, one adds to the potential threat. HYP is the vector of our hypothesis variables: political stability, crisis, and Euro zone membership. CV is a vector of control variables drawn from the recent empirical literature on long-term spreads determinants: GDP growth, inflation, liquidity ratio, budget balance (surplus or deficit), and government debt. The term v_i is the country-specific disturbance and ε_{it} is the disturbance component varying across both time and countries. To get the most out of the variation in the data and in line with the existing literature, we choose to log-linearize the variables. Some of our variables have a negative sign on the considered period, which does not allow the use of a simple logarithmic transformation. Instead, we employ the following transformation that permits to keep observations with negative-sign values for any variable X taking both positive and negative values within the panel (Busse & Hefeker, 2007):

$$Y = \ln(X + \sqrt{X^2 + 1}) \tag{2}$$

There are two main approaches to analyze the determinants of sovereign yield spreads in the recent empirical literature, both with their pros and cons (Maltritz, 2011). The first one relates both dependent and independent variables to an "anchor" country (in this paper, Germany) by taking the difference between observed values for each variable and its corresponding value for the anchor country. By doing so, this approach considers that the anchor country is not completely free of default risk. The second approach accepts the "free-risk" assumption regarding the benchmark country and consequently explains the sovereign yield spreads with respect to the "anchor country" by the observed data for the selected explaining variables. The second approach implicitly assumes that the benchmark country is risk free or that its bond yield is the safest measure for a risk-less rate. We run the estimations by assuming the second approach where German bond yield is considered as the best approximation for a free-risk interest rate. This choice is reasonably motivated by recent movements in German yields that touched zero or a negative territory near to zero. The existing literature usually analyzes the first approach and checks the robustness of the estimations by applying the latter. We take the opposite way by considering the second approach that uses the observed data for the analyzed countries and the yield differentials against Germany.

The benchmark model becomes

$$\begin{aligned}\ln \text{Spread}_{it} = \alpha_0 + \alpha_1 \ln \text{GDP growth}_{it} + \alpha_2 \ln \text{Inflation}_{it} + \alpha_3 \ln \text{Debt}_{it} \\ + \alpha_4 \ln \text{Liquidity}_{it} + \alpha_5 \ln \text{Deficit}_{it} + \alpha_6 \ln \text{Stability}_{it} + v_i + \varepsilon_{it} \quad (3)\end{aligned}$$

where α_1 to α_6 are the estimated parameters. Furthermore, to test how EMU membership affects the impact of different variables on the bond yield spreads, we take an additional step and add interaction terms between explanatory *variables* and the Euro zone dummy EMU_{it}:

$$\begin{aligned}\ln \text{Spread}_{it} = \alpha_0 + \alpha_1 \ln \text{GDP growth}_{it} + \alpha_2 \ln \text{Inflation}_{it} + \alpha_3 \ln \text{Debt}_{it} \\ + \alpha_4 \ln \text{Liquidity}_{it} + \alpha_5 \ln \text{Balance}_{it} + \alpha_6 \ln \text{Stability}_{it} + \beta_1 \text{EMU}_{it} \\ \times \ln \text{Debt}_{it} + \beta_2 \text{EMU}_{it} \times \ln \text{Liquidity}_{it} + \beta_3 \text{EMU}_{it} \times \ln \text{Balance}_{it} \\ + v_i + \varepsilon_{it} \quad (4)\end{aligned}$$

Similarly, to test the impact of these variables during the 2008–2010 financial crisis, we add interaction terms with a crisis dummy, which takes the value one for the last three years of our panel and zero elsewhere:

$$\begin{aligned}\ln \text{Spread}_{it} = \alpha_0 + \alpha_1 \ln \text{GDP growth}_{it} + \alpha_2 \ln \text{Inflation}_{it} \\ + \alpha_3 \ln \text{Debt}_{it} + \alpha_4 \ln \text{Liquidity}_{it} + \alpha_5 \ln \text{Balance}_{it} + \alpha_6 \ln \text{Stability}_{it} \\ + \gamma_1 \text{Crisis}_t \times \ln \text{Debt}_{it} + \gamma_2 \text{Crisis}_t \times \ln \text{Liquidity}_{it} + \gamma_3 \text{Crisis}_t \\ \times \ln \text{Balance}_{it} + v_i + \varepsilon_{it} \quad (5)\end{aligned}$$

This is a convenient alternative to estimating Eq. (3) on the 2008–2010 subpanel, as it does not induce a large drop in the number of observations, nor losses in terms of degrees of freedom.

Data and Variables

The data panel contains observations from 25 EU countries and covers the 2003–2010 period. We included all countries for which the ECB publishes sovereign bond yields, that is, all EU members except Estonia. Our panel does not include Germany, since it is taken as reference. To study the main determinants of bond yield spreads, we take into account both time series and cross-country variation in our data set. Our data are in annual frequency, meaning that the effects we identify below correspond to long-term determinants of spreads.

Table 1 presents a brief summary of employed variables and data sources. Spreads on government bonds are computed as the difference between the yields on 10-year bonds issued by each country in our panel and Germany. We employ monthly data provided by the ECB and take annual averages. GDP growth and inflation are obtained from the World Bank's World Development Indicators (WDI) database. The liquidity ratio is computed as money and quasi-money (M2) divided by reserves exclusive of gold, both from the WDI database. It measures the access to credit relative to national reserves. According to the literature (e.g., Cartapanis, 2002), this ratio is also a good indicator for the capacity of the economies and central banks to face speculative attacks. Data on government debt and budget balance (deficit or surplus) come from the Eurostat. Finally, to assess countries' political stability, we use the Political Stability and Absence of Violence/Terrorism ranking indicator from the World Bank's Worldwide Governance Indicators (WGI) database, computed by Kaufmann, Kraay, and Mastruzzi (2009). It measures the perceptions of the likelihood that the government will be destabilized or overthrown by unconstitutional or violent means, including politically motivated violence and terrorism. It corresponds to the

Table 1. Data Sources of Explained and Explanatory Variables.

Variable	Explanation, Computation	Data Source
Spread	Difference between yields on 10-year bonds of a given country and Germany, annual average obtained from monthly data	European Central Bank (ECB) statistics, monthly data
GDP growth	Annual GDP growth (%)	World Development Indicators (WDI), World Bank
Inflation	Annual inflation rate in terms of consumer prices (%)	WDI, World Bank
Government debt	Total government debt as % of GDP	Eurostat
Liquidity ratio	Money (M2) to reserves (without gold) ratio (%)	WDI, World Bank
Budget balance	Public administration financing capacity (+) or needs (−) as % of GDP	Eurostat
Political stability	The political stability and absence of violence percentile rank of countries: the higher the index, the lower the political risk and the higher the stability	Worldwide Governance Indicators (WGI), World Bank

Table 2. Labels and Transformations of Explained and Explanatory Variables.

Variable	Variable Label	Transformation
Spread	Spread_{it}	$\ln(\text{Spread}_{it} + \sqrt{\text{Spread}_{it}^2 + 1})$
GDP growth	GDP growth_{it}	$\ln(\text{GDP growth}_{it} + \sqrt{\text{GDP growth}_{it}^2 + 1})$
Inflation	Inflation_{it}	$\ln(\text{Inflation}_{it} + \sqrt{\text{Inflation}_{it}^2 + 1})$
Government debt	Debt_{it}	$\ln \text{Debt}_{it}$
Liquidity ratio	Liquidity_{it}	$\ln \text{Liquidity}_{it}$
Budget balance	Balance_{it}	$\ln(\text{Balance}_{it} + \sqrt{\text{Balance}_{it}^2 + 1})$
Political stability	Stability_{it}	$\ln \text{Stability}_{it}$

percentile rank among all countries and ranges from 0 (lowest) to 100 (highest) rank or political stability. (See http://info.worldbank.org/governance/wgi/index.asp for additional information.) This is an inverse measure of political insecurity and political risk. Unlike the spread, explanatory variables are expressed in levels rather than as differences with respect to Germany, which virtually is considered here as free of default risk.

Table 2 summarizes the labels and logarithmic transformations of variables used for estimating the model presented in the previous section. As explained earlier, variables that take both positive and negative values need a more specific transformation. Table 3 exposes the main descriptive statistics of variables integrated in estimations.

ECONOMETRIC RESULTS

In this section, we look at the determinants of spreads on sovereign bond yields of EU countries with respect to Germany over the entire 2003–2010 period and during the 2008–2010 crisis. The Hausman test statistics is always significant at the 1% level, pleading in favor of a fixed-effects model. Results displayed in this section correspond to fixed-effects estimators. The appendix displays correlation estimates for all variables considered in the empirical specifications (see the correlation matrix in the appendix). We observe that interaction terms are highly correlated with each other and also with dummy variables. Consequently, interaction terms will be added separately in the considered equations.

Table 3. Descriptive Statistics of Explained and Explanatory Variables.

	2003–2010					2008–2010				
Observed Values	Obs.	Mean	Std. Dev.	Min.	Max.	Obs.	Mean	Std. Dev.	Min.	Max.
Spread	198	1.03	1.61	−1.19	10.78	75	1.77	2.14	−0.10	10.78
GDP growth	200	2.32	4.16	17.95	12.23	75	−0.74	4.57	17.95	9.43
Inflation	200	3.01	2.58	−4.48	15.40	75	2.85	2.92	−4.48	15.40
Government debt	200	50.80	27.65	6.10	144.90	75	56.01	29.57	13.40	144.90
Liquidity ratio	198	103.16	243.69	1.32	2235.76	73	105.77	192.72	1.42	1025.38
Budget balance	200	−2.98	4.22	31.30	5.30	75	−5.26	4.93	31.30	4.20
Political stability	200	73.92	15.98	34.12	100.00	75	73.06	16.47	34.12	100.00

	2003–2010					2008–2010				
Logarithmic Transformations	Obs.	Mean	Std. Dev.	Min.	Max.	Obs.	Mean	Std. Dev.	Min.	Max.
Spread	198	0.66	0.72	−1.01	3.07	75	1.04	0.76	−0.10	3.07
GDP growth	200	1.17	1.60	−3.58	3.20	75	−0.11	1.84	−3.58	2.94
Inflation	200	1.58	0.80	−2.20	3.43	75	1.44	1.01	−2.20	3.43
Government debt	200	3.75	0.64	1.81	4.98	75	3.87	0.59	2.60	4.98
Liquidity ratio	198	2.96	1.95	0.28	7.71	73	3.27	1.91	0.35	6.93
Budget balance	200	−1.24	1.50	−4.14	2.37	75	−1.94	1.29	−4.14	2.14
Political stability	200	4.28	0.23	3.53	4.61	75	4.26	0.25	3.53	4.61

Notes: Logarithmic transformations correspond to the last column on Table 2.

Table 4 summarizes the effects of different determinants over the entire period. Column 1 shows parameter estimates of Eq. (3). The rest of columns report the point estimates of Eq. (4) parameters with each EMU interaction term added separately in the equation.

The state of the economy captured by the GDP growth has a negative and significant (at the 1% level) impact on sovereign bond yield spreads with respect to Germany. This finding is in line with theoretical literature predictions stating that growing economies are more able to respect payment obligations than stagnating countries. The inflation rate affects spreads positively, but the effect is not statistically significant. High inflation rates reveal structural problems in government's finance reducing the real level of the accumulated debt. If investors anticipate high inflation, they will demand high interest rates on government debt, making public borrowing more expensive. Furthermore, in the case of countries without independent monetary policy (with pegged currencies or in a monetary union), which is

Table 4. Determinants of Sovereign Bond Yield Spreads: 2003–2010.

	(1)	(2)	(3)	(4)	(5)	(6)
GDP growth	−0.11***	−0.10***	−0.10***	−0.10***	−0.10***	−0.10***
	(0.02)	(0.02)	(0.02)	(0.02)	(0.02)	(0.02)
Inflation	0.02	0.02	0.02	0.03	0.01	−0.00
	(0.04)	(0.04)	(0.04)	(0.04)	(0.04)	(0.04)
Government debt	0.80***	0.77***	0.77***	0.63***	0.78***	0.77***
	(0.13)	(0.13)	(0.13)	(0.14)	(0.13)	(0.13)
Liquidity ratio	0.07	0.06	0.10	0.09	0.16	0.11*
	(0.04)	(0.04)	(0.06)	(0.06)	(0.17)	(0.06)
Budget balance	−0.07**	−0.07**	−0.07**	−0.05*	−0.07**	−0.13***
	(0.03)	(0.03)	(0.03)	(0.03)	(0.03)	(0.04)
Political stability		−0.54*	−0.53*	−0.53*	−0.54*	−0.61**
		(0.29)	(0.29)	(0.28)	(0.29)	(0.28)
EMU member			−0.17	−1.87***	−0.07	−0.01
			(0.21)	(0.74)	(0.32)	(0.22)
EMU*Gov. debt				0.45**		
				(0.19)		
EMU*Liquidity ratio					−0.07	
					(0.17)	
EMU*Budget balance						0.12**
						(0.05)
Constant term	−2.56***	−0.10	−1.82	0.35	−0.22	0.07
	(0.54)	(1.40)	(1.41)	(1.40)	(1.41)	(1.39)
No. obs.	196	196	196	196	196	196
R^2 within	0.541	0.551	0.553	0.568	0.553	0.568
R^2 between	0.052	0.018	0.019	0.005	0.024	0.017
Corr $(u_i, X_{it}\beta)$	−0.684	−0.662	−0.658	−0.691	−0.674	−0.662
$\rho = \sigma_u^2/(\sigma_u^2 + \sigma_e^2)$	0.878	0.871	0.870	0.880	0.874	0.874

Notes: The explained variable is expressed as change with respect to yields on German bonds. Fixed-effects estimators. Standard errors in parentheses.
$^{*}p<0.10$; $^{**}p<0.05$; $^{***}p<0.01$.

the case of the most of the countries of our sample, price differentials may lead to losses in competitiveness which increases the default risk. The total government debt to GDP ratio raises significantly (at the 1% level) the spreads. The high absolute value of this effect confirms that debt level is an essential component of the risk premium incorporated in sovereign bond yields. The budget balance to GDP ratio has a negative and significant coefficient (at the 5% level) on spreads. A high surplus (or financing capacity) or a low deficit (or financing needs) depicts a higher capacity of the country to honor payments on issued bonds and keeps the cost of sovereign debt (yields on new bonds) down, close to that of the free-risk reference. We also find that political stability reduces the cost differential on new bonds, although the effect is significant only at the 10% level. The effects of all these variables are in line with theoretical predictions and are robust across different specifications.

On the opposite, we do not find evidence of a negative effect of liquidity, as suggested by the theory. In all specifications, but the last, the liquidity ratio effect is not significantly different from zero. In column 6, however, this ratio enters the equation with a positive and significant coefficient, revealing that an increase in liquidity of EMU countries has not been always positively appreciated by the market. One possible explanation is the fact that most EMU countries severely affected by the 2008–2010 crisis saw their liquidity ratio increase significantly in the years preceding the crisis.[1]

By including interaction terms between the EMU membership dummy and debt, liquidity, and fiscal variables in columns 4–6, we are able to test whether the effects of these variables differ for EMU and non-EMU countries, or as a country integrates the Euro zone. We find a significant effect only for the budget balance and government debt. According to our findings, the government surplus or deficit is reflected only in the level of spreads of non-EMU countries or prior to joining the EMU. The positive coefficient on the interaction term between the budget balance deficit and EMU membership is not in line with theoretical predictions. One possible explanation is related to the market discipline view (see Manganelli & Wolswijk, 2009). Accordingly, market participants may perceive the Stability and Growth Pact as not credible or inefficient, in which case Brussels' decisions and recommendations concerning fiscal performances of EMU countries would have no impact on yield differentials. An alternative explanation is that the public finances of EMU countries were not in sufficiently good shape after the financial crisis erupted in 2008. Alternatively, this may be related to the fact that public finances of EMU countries were not in sufficiently good shape after the financial crisis erupted in 2008.

In Table 5, we test whether the effect of macroeconomic fundamentals changes during the crisis. In the first two columns, we restrict the sample to the crisis period, that is, the last three years of our panel, and report estimates of our benchmark model given by Eq. (3). Accordingly, we end up with fewer observations and degrees of freedom for our estimation. Only three of the control variables included in the equation impact significantly the spread and all of them have the expected sign. Differently from results for the entire period, we find a larger positive effect for government debt and a negative effect for liquidity.

Table 5. Determinants of Sovereign Bond Yield Spreads: The Crisis.

	2008–2010		2003–2010			
	(1)	(2)	(3)	(4)	(5)	(6)
GDP growth	-0.07^{***}	-0.08^{**}	-0.07^{***}	-0.06^{***}	-0.07^{***}	-0.09^{**}
	(0.03)	(0.02)	(0.03)	(0.02)	(0.02)	(0.02)
Inflation	0.06	0.02	0.06	−0.02	−0.01	0.01
	(0.06)	(0.04)	(0.06)	(0.04)	(0.04)	(0.04)
Government debt	1.00^{***}	0.67^{***}	1.00^{***}	0.65^{***}	0.65^{***}	0.71^{***}
	(0.27)	(0.13)	(0.27)	(0.13)	(0.13)	(0.13)
Liquidity ratio	-0.42^{**}	0.02	-0.39^{**}	−0.02	−0.01	0.03
	(0.17)	(0.05)	(0.17)	(0.05)	(0.05)	(0.05)
Budget balance	0.01	−0.02	0.02	−0.03	−0.04	-0.06^{***}
	(0.05)	(0.03)	(0.06)	(0.03)	(0.03)	(0.03)
Political stability		-0.57^{**}	−0.39	-0.69^{***}	-0.63^{***}	-0.54^{**}
		(0.28)	(0.72)	(0.28)	(0.28)	(0.28)
Crisis			0.29^{***}			
			(0.08)			
Crisis*Gov. debt				0.07^{***}		
				(0.02)		
Crisis*Liquidity ratio					0.03	
					(0.02)	
Crisis*Budget balance						-0.09^{***}
						(0.03)
Constant term	−1.54	0.52	0.05	1.17	0.87	0.19
	(1.28)	(1.39)	(3.20)	(1.39)	(1.39)	(1.41)
N	73	196	73	196	196	196
R^2 within	0.520	0.570	0.524	0.588	0.581	0.557
R^2 between	0.176	0.000	0.198	0.026	0.000	0.009
Corr (u_i, $X_{it}\beta$)	−0.544	−0.538	−0.520	−0.480	−0.511	−0.604
$\rho = \sigma_u^2/(\sigma_u^2 + \sigma_e^2)$	0.864	0.839	0.854	0.828	0.834	0.855

Notes: The explained variable is expressed as change with respect to yields on German bonds. Fixed-effects estimators. Standard errors in parentheses.
$^{*}p<0.10$; $^{**}p<0.05$; $^{***}p<0.01$.

This confirms the common belief that during a crisis, markets follow closely the dependence of economies on debt. A 1% increase in the debt-to-GDP ratio results in an equal increase in spreads. During the crisis, the liquidity ratio of most countries decreased, picturing a more constrained access to credit relative to national reserves. This increased the pressure on the credit market and pushed up the cost of newly issued bonds, countries with the largest drop in liquidity suffering the largest spread escalation.

Estimates from the second column also confirm the role of a country's political stability in reducing the cost of its sovereign debt. This aspect is important since the political risk generally increases during a crisis. For example, the Economist Intelligence Unit argues that the level of threat posed to governments by social protests has increased in most European countries since 2007.

Alternatively, we can test the effect of control variables during the crisis by adding the interaction between each variable and a crisis dummy as in Eq. (5). An important advantage of this approach is that estimations are performed on the entire panel. As previously, interaction terms are highly correlated with each other and, therefore, introduced one by one in the equation, point estimates of parameters are displayed in columns 2–4 of Table 5. Again, we find that in times of crisis, an economy's dependence on debt is more severely reflected in the spreads on the new sovereign bonds it issues.

Our results suggest that markets penalize governments with large budget deficits only during the crises, while the impact of liquidity is not statistically significantly different from zero.

For robustness checks, we have also computed the liquidity ratio as M2 (money and quasi-money) over reserves including gold. Similarly, we used different measures of budget balance: the central administration (primary) budget balance and the public administration surplus or deficit, both computed as percentage of GDP. We obtain very similar results to those in Tables 4 and 5 for all specifications. In addition, we estimate the model without making the risk-free assumption. For that both dependent and independent variables are related to the "anchor" country (Germany), that is, all are expressed as deviations from values for Germany. Results confirm main previous findings, although some estimates loose in significance, due to a lower variance in explanatory variables in this case.

In Table 6, we add interaction terms between the drivers of yield spreads identified above and EMU membership and crisis variables. The first column shows parameter estimates of Eq. (3) augmented with an EMU membership and a crisis dummy. We find a positive and significant impact on EU yield differentials for the crisis dummy and a negative and statistically no significant effect for EMU membership. This result suggests that the recent financial crisis produced an important structural break in determining the evolutions of sovereign spreads. As previously, GDP growth, budget balance, government debt, and political stability are important drivers of differentials in EU bond yields. In a next step, we

Table 6. Determinants of Sovereign Bond Yield Spreads: 2003–2010.

	(1)	(2)	(3)	(4)	(5)
GDP growth	−0.06***	−0.06***	−0.07***	−0.11*	−0.06***
	(0.02)	(0.02)	(0.02)	(0.06)	(0.02)
Inflation	−0.02	0.03	−0.10*	0.11***	−0.02
	(0.04)	(0.04)	(0.06)	(0.04)	(0.04)
Gov. debt	0.65***	0.65***	0.67***	0.50***	0.65***
	(0.13)	(0.13)	(0.13)	(0.13)	(0.13)
Liquidity ratio	0.03	0.11	0.01	0.03	0.04
	(0.06)	(0.14)	(0.05)	(0.06)	(0.06)
Budget balance	−0.03**	−0.03	−0.04	−0.02	−0.03
	(0.03)	(0.03)	(0.03)	(0.03)	(0.03)
Political stability	−0.67**	−0.69**	−0.65**	−0.80***	−0.68***
	(0.28)	(0.28)	(0.28)	(0.27)	(0.28)
EMU member	−0.23		−0.31	1.44	
	(0.20)		(0.20)	(2.15)	
Crisis	0.29***		0.29***	0.24	
	(0.08)		(0.12)	(1.02)	
EMU*Liquidity ratio		−0.11			
		(0.10)			
EMU*Inflation			0.05		
			(0.06)		
Crisis*Inflation			−0.15***		
			(0.04)		
EMU*GDP growth				−0.03	
				(0.03)	
Crisis*GDP growth				0.05	
				(0.06)	
EMU*Political risk					−0.06
					(0.05)
Crisis*Political risk					0.07***
					(0.02)
Constant	1.09	1.04	1.03	2.45*	1.13
	(1.39)	(1.39)	(1.39)	(1.42)	(1.41)
N	196	196	196	196	196
R^2 within	0.591	0.590	0.590	0.615	0.590
R^2 between	0.003	0.000	0.000	0.006	0.003
Corr (u_i, $X_{it}\beta$)	−0.465	−0.518	0.517	−0.360	−0.471
$\rho = \sigma_u^2/(\sigma_u^2 + \sigma_e^2)$	0.825	0.840	0.840	0.811	0.826

Notes: The explained variable is expressed as change with respect to yields on German bonds. Fixed-effects estimators. Standard errors in parentheses.
$^{*}p<0.10$; $^{**}p<0.05$; $^{***}p<0.01$.

add separately in all interaction terms of these explanatory variables with the EMU dummy, and with the crisis dummy. We exclude terms that are highly correlated with other interaction terms or other left hand side variables (see the correlation matrix in the appendix). Thus, in column 2, we keep only the interaction term between EMU membership and the liquidity ratio.

We overcome this difficulty by including alternatively, for each of the above factors, the interaction terms with the EMU and the crisis dummies in the same specification. Estimation results are reported in the last three columns of the table. In columns 3 and 4, we test whether inflation and, respectively, GDP growth have larger positive effects for EMU member countries. We find a significant effect only for inflation. Although the coefficient of the interaction term between inflation and EMU membership is not statistically significant, its positive sign suggests that price differentials may lead to losses in competitiveness for EMU countries. The negative coefficient on the interaction term with the crisis dummy shows that during the global financial crisis, markets pay special attention to countries with high inflation rates. Estimates from the last column allow us to differentiate the role of political stability in decreasing the costs of a country's sovereign debt before and during the crisis, and the importance of this factor for EMU and non-EMU countries. Results are in line with the predictions of the Economist Intelligence Unit, highlighting that political risk increases during the crisis periods.

CONCLUSIONS

This paper aims to identify the key drivers of sovereign bond spreads in EU countries from an ex-post perspective. Two main questions are addressed. First, we ask what proportion of the change in market spreads is explained by changes in the underlying fundamentals, external factors, liquidity, and market risk. Second, we distinguish between Euro zone members and other EU countries and test how effects vary across the two groups.

To answer these questions, we use a data panel of 25 EU countries from 2003 to 2010. We estimate an empirical model in which spreads to Germany on 10-year government bonds are explained by a set of variables including the exchange rate regimes, the political risk perception, and traditional determinants of spreads, such as GDP growth, inflation, debt, liquidity, and fiscal measures. The data suggest the use of a fixed-effect estimator. We find significant effects in line with theoretical predictions for all variables except inflation. The only difference in impacts between EMU and non-EMU countries is obtained for the budget balance. According to our results, the government surplus or deficit is reflected only in the level of spreads of non-EMU countries.

We also test the difference in the impacts of different explanatory variables before and during the 2008–2010 crisis. We conclude that during the crisis, markets penalize more a high dependence on debt and a large drop in liquidity. As for large budget deficits, they are reflected in spread escalation only in times of crises.

ACKNOWLEDGMENTS

We thank the editor and two anonymous reviewers for their insightful suggestions and constructive comments, which helped us to improve the manuscript. We are also grateful to the participants at the 73rd International Atlantic Economic Conference and 61th Annual Conference of the AFSE for helpful comments. The usual disclaimer applies. The views expressed in the paper are those of the authors.

NOTE

1. The econometric estimations on the pre-crisis period for the non-EMU members show that coefficients for liquidity ratio are negative and statistically nonsignificant.

REFERENCES

Ang, A., & Piazzesi, M. (2003). A no-arbitrage vector autoregression of term structure dynamics with macroeconomic and latent variables. *Journal of Monetary Economics*, *50*(4), 745–787.

Barbosa, L., & Costa, S. (2010). *Determinants of sovereign bond yield spreads in the euro area in the context of the economic and financial crisis*. Working Papers w201022, Banco de Portugal, Economics and Research Department.

Barrios, S., Iversen, P., Lewandowska, M., & Setzer, R. (2009). *Determinants of intra-Euro area government bond spreads during the financial crisis*. European Economy, Economic Papers No. 388.

Beber, A., Brandt, M., & Kavajecz, K. (2009). Flight-to-quality or flight-to-liquidity? Evidence from the euro-area bond market. *Review of Financial Studies*, *22*(3), 925–957.

Bellas, D., Papaioannou, M. G., & Petrova, I. (2010). *Determinants of emerging market sovereign bond spreads*. IMF Working Paper 10/281.

Bernoth, K., von Hagen, J., & Schuknecht, L. (2004). *Sovereign risk premia in the European government bond market*. ECB Working Paper No. 369.

Bernoth, K., von Hagen, J., & Schuknecht, L. (2006). *Sovereign risk premia in the European government bond market*. University of Mannheim Paper.

Busse, M., & Hefeker, C. (2007). Political risk, institutions and foreign direct investment. *European Journal of Political Economy*, *23*, 397–415.

Cartapanis, A. (2002). Les crises de change, qu'avons-nous appris depuis dix ans? *Economie Internationale*, *88*(4), 1–16.

Codogno, L., Favero, C., & Missale, A. (2003). Yield spreads on EMU government bonds. *Economic Policy*, *October*, 503–532.

Cline, W., & Barnes, K. (1997). *Spreads and risk in emerging market lending*. IIF Working Paper No. 97–1.

Domar, E. (1950). The effect of foreign investment on the balance of payments. *American Economic Review*, *40*, 805–826.

Edwards, S. (1984). LDC foreign borrowing and default risk: An empirical investigation, 1976–80. *The American Economic Review*, *74*(4), 726–734.

Favero, C., Pagano, M., & von Thadden, E.-L. (2010). How does liquidity affect government bond yields? *Journal of Financial and Quantitative Analysis*, *45*(1), 107–134.

Haugh, D., Ollivaud, P., Turner, D. (2009). *What drives sovereign risk premiums? An analysis of recent evidence from the Euro area*. OECD Economics Department Working Papers No. 718.

Geyer, A., Kossmeier, S., & Pichler, S. (2004). Measuring systematic risk in EMU government yield spreads. *Review of Finance*, *8*, 171–197.

Gibson, H. D., Hall, S. G., & Tavlas, G. S. (2011). The Greek financial crisis: Growing imbalances and sovereign spreads. *Journal of International Money and Finance*, *31*(3), 498–516.

Jahjah, S., Wei, B., & Zhanwei Yue, V. (2010). *Exchange rate policy and sovereign bond spreads in developing countries*. IMF Working Paper No. 04/210.

Kamin, S., & Von Kleist, K. (1999). *The evolution and determinants of emerging market credit spreads in the 1990s*. BIS Working Paper No. 68.

Kaufmann D., Kraay, A., & Mastruzzi, M. (2009). *Governance matters VIII: Aggregate and individual governance indicators*. Policy Research Working Paper No. 4978, World Bank, Washington, DC.

Lemke, W. (2008). An affine macro-finance term structure model for the Euro area. *North American Journal of Economics and Finance*, *19*, 41–69.

Maltritz, D. (2011). Determinants of sovereign yield spreads in the Euro zone: A Bayesian approach. *Journal of International Money and Finance*, doi:10.1016/j.jimonfin.2011.10.010

Manganelli, S., & Wolswijk, G. (2009). What drives spreads in the Euro area government bond market?. *Economic Policy*, *24*, 191–240.

Mesonnier, J. S., Borgy, V., Laubach, T., & Renne, J.-P. (2011). Soutenabilité de la dette publique, risque de défaut et écarts de rendements obligataires souverains dans la zone euro. Banque de France Document de travail No. 350, Novembre.

Mody, A. (2009). *From Bear Stearns to Anglo Irish: How Euro zone sovereign spreads related to financial sector vulnerability*. IMF Working Paper No. 09/108.

Oliveira, L., Curto, J. D., & Nunes, J. P. (2011). The determinants of sovereign credit spread changes in the euro-Zone. *Journal of International Financial Markets, Institutions and Money*, *22*(2), 278–304.

Pozzi, L., & Wolswijk, G. (2011). The time-varying integration of Euro area government bond markets. *European Economic Review*, doi: 10.1016/j.euroecorev.2011.05.006.

Schuknecht, L., von Hagen, J., & Wolswijk, G. (2009). Government risk premiums in the bond market: EMU and Canada. *European Journal of Political Economy*, *25*, 371–384.

Schuknecht, L., von Hagen, J., & Wolswijk, G. (2010). *Government risk premiums in the EU revisited – The impact of the financial crisis*. ECB Working Paper Series No. 1152.

Von Hagen, J., Schuknecht, L., & Wolswijk, G. (2011). Government bond risk premiums in the EU revisited: The impact of the financial crisis. *European Journal of Political Economy*, *27*, 36–43.

APPENDIX. CORRELATION MATRIX

	GDP Growth	Debt Gov.	Budget	Liquid	Polit. Stab.	Crisis	EMU*GDP Growth	EMU* Inflation	EMU* Debt Gov.	EMU*Liquid
GDP growth	1									
Debt gov.	−0.2948	1								
Budget	0.3860	−0.3986	1							
Liquid	−0.1990	0.2475	0.0398	1						
Polit. Stab.	0.0954	−0.1458	0.2971	0.0463	1					
Crisis	−0.6254	0.1482	−0.3535	0.1231	−0.0586	1				
EMU*GDP growth	0.5441	−0.0576	0.3688	0.3168	0.1674	−0.3590	1			
EMU*inflation	0.0586	0.2109	0.1428	0.6972	0.0388	−0.0136	0.6009	1		
EMU*debt gov.	−0.2293	0.4967	−0.0785	0.7756	0.0002	0.1477	0.3132	0.7620	1	
EMU*liquid	−0.1840	0.2206	0.0257	0.9198	0.0578	0.1242	0.3600	0.7813	0.8914	1
Crisis*debt gov.	−0.6297	0.2497	−0.3864	0.1684	−0.0774	0.9822	−0.3689	0.0118	0.2105	0.1663
Crisis*liquid	−0.5445	0.2589	−0.2925	0.4501	−0.0553	0.8072	−0.3430	0.1868	0.4142	0.4277
Crisis*budget	0.6041	−0.2560	0.6078	−0.1028	0.2168	−0.7629	0.3980	0.1161	−0.1657	−0.1164
EMU*budget	0.4036	−0.5366	0.6358	−0.3905	0.2157	−0.3331	0.2497	−0.2316	−0.5820	−0.4449
EMU*inflation	0.0586	0.2109	0.1428	0.6972	0.038	−0.0136	0.6009	1.0000	0.7620	0.7813
Crisis*inflation	−0.2901	−0.0065	−0.1621	−0.0359	−0.0990	0.7497	−0.0775	0.1569	−0.0320	−0.0382
EMU*polit. stab.	−0.1812	0.3029	0.0452	0.8301	0.1503	0.1176	0.3955	0.7959	0.9597	0.9418
Crisis*polit. stab.	−0.6134	0.1412	−0.3367	0.1218	−0.0093	0.9972	−0.3497	−0.0124	0.1468	0.1239
EMU*growth	0.5441	−0.0576	0.3688	0.3168	0.1674	−0.3590	1.0000	0.6009	0.3132	0.3600
Crisis*growth	0.7246	−0.0728	0.1651	−0.0635	0.1321	−0.0491	0.4761	0.1881	−0.0462	−0.0566
EMU	−0.1924	0.3324	0.0221	0.8361	0.0851	0.1229	0.3823	0.8020	0.9722	0.9476
Crisis	−0.6254	0.1482	−0.3535	0.1231	−0.0586	1.0000	−0.3590	−0.0136	0.1477	0.1242

APPENDIX. *(Continued)*

	Crisis*Debt Gov.	Crisis*Liquid	Crisis Budget	EMU Budget	EMU Inflation	Crisis Inflation	EMU Polit. Stab.	Crisis Polit. Stab.	EMU Growth	Crisis Growth	EMU
Crisis debt gov.	1										
Crisis liquid	0.8401	1									
Crisis budget	−0.7977	−0.6247	1								
EMU budget	−0.4012	−0.5070	0.4995	1							
EMU inflation	0.0118	0.1868	0.1161	−0.2316	1						
Crisis inflation	0.6965	0.4779	−0.4448	−0.0380	0.1569	1					
EMU polit. stab.	0.1612	0.3863	−0.0961	−0.4460	0.7959	−0.0465	1				
Crisis polit. stab.	0.9772	0.8041	−0.7412	−0.3215	−0.0124	0.7414	0.1243	1			
EMU growth	−0.3689	−0.3430	0.3980	0.2497	0.6009	−0.0775	0.3955	−0.3497	1		
Crisis growth	−0.0705	−0.0968	0.2201	0.1610	0.1881	0.2201	−0.0239	−0.0343	0.4761	1	
EMU	0.1703	0.3966	−0.1131	−0.4755	0.8020	−0.0430	0.9964	0.1255	0.3823	−0.0328	1
Crisis	0.9822	0.8072	−0.7629	−0.3331	−0.0136	0.7497	0.1176	0.9972	−0.3590	−0.0491	0.1229

PART III
SPECIFICATION TESTING

CONDITIONAL INDEPENDENCE SPECIFICATION TESTING FOR DEPENDENT PROCESSES WITH LOCAL POLYNOMIAL QUANTILE REGRESSION

Liangjun Su and Halbert L. White

ABSTRACT

We provide straightforward new nonparametric methods for testing conditional independence using local polynomial quantile regression, allowing weakly dependent data. Inspired by Hausman's (1978) specification testing ideas, our methods essentially compare two collections of estimators that converge to the same limits under correct specification (conditional independence) and that diverge under the alternative. To establish the properties of our estimators, we generalize the existing nonparametric quantile literature not only by allowing for dependent heterogeneous data but also by establishing a weak consistency rate for the local Bahadur representation that is uniform in both the conditioning variables and the quantile index. We also show that, despite our nonparametric approach, our tests can detect local alternatives to conditional independence that decay to zero at the parametric rate. Our

Essays in Honor of Jerry Hausman
Advances in Econometrics, Volume 29, 355–434

ISSN: 0731-9053/doi:10.1108/S0731-9053(2012)0000029018

approach gives the first nonparametric tests for time-series conditional independence that can detect local alternatives at the parametric rate. Monte Carlo simulations suggest that our tests perform well in finite samples. We apply our test to test for a key identifying assumption in the literature on nonparametric, nonseparable models by studying the returns to schooling.

Keywords: Conditional exogeneity; conditional independence; empirical process; local polynomial; quantile regression; specification test

INTRODUCTION

Hausman's (1978) seminal paper on specification testing opened the way to a broad array of methods for assessing the validity of econometric models and their resulting insights. The fundamental idea of comparing two estimators, both consistent under correct specification, but divergent under misspecification, applies not only to detecting incorrect parametric functional form for conditional means, variances, or other aspects of the conditional distribution of a variable of interest, but also to detecting failures of exogeneity – the stochastic orthogonality condition between observable and unobservable drivers of the dependent variable of interest ensuring that structural features of interest can be recovered from observable data.

Although functional form misspecification can be considerably mitigated using nonparametric methods, exogeneity in one form or another remains a crucial assumption; its failure results in estimators being largely uninformative about structural objects of interest (see, e.g., White & Chalak, forthcoming). There remains a clear need to develop convenient nonparametric methods for exogeneity specification testing; Hausman's (1978) approach provides a valuable foundation on which to construct such tests.

Over the years since Hausman's paper appeared, various alternatives to strict exogeneity (observable causes (W) independent of unobservable causes (U)) useful for identifying economic structure of interest have emerged. One important alternative is that introduced by Barnow, Cain, and Goldberger (1980), termed " selection on observables," namely that observable causes are independent of unobservable causes, conditional on some further observables, say X. We write this conditional independence as $W \perp U|X$, following Dawid (1979). This condition plays an important role in both micro and macro econometrics where U is usually observed in the latter case.

Example 1. (Identification and estimation of treatment effects) Unconfoundedness is central to identifying treatment effects. See Heckman, Ichimura, and Todd (1997), Imbens (2004), Imbens and Wooldridge (2009), White and Lu (2011), and White and Chalak (forthcoming), among others. Consider a binary treatment W and potential outcomes of interest Y_0 and Y_1, corresponding to the possibilities $W=0$ and $W=1$, respectively. Unconfoundedness requires the existence of a vector X of observable characteristics such that $W \perp U|X$, where $U=(Y_0, Y_1)$. Similar conditions play a key role in recovering structural features in many other contexts, as catalogued by Chalak and White (2011). Because U is unobservable and, in the general case, not estimable, indirect methods for testing $W \perp U|X$ have been developed, based on the fact that, under additional plausible assumptions, $W \perp U|X$ implies certain conditional independence relations among observables, for example, $W \perp S|X$, where S is observable (White & Chalak, 2010). Imbens (2004) discusses two sets of indirect tests for the unconfoundedness assumption. One focuses on estimating the causal effect of a treatment that is known not to have an effect, relying on the presence of multiple control groups; the other on estimating the causal effect of the treatment on a variable known to be unaffected by it. More recently, Donald, Hsu, and Lieli (2011) propose a test for the unconfoundedness assumption via the inverse probability weighted estimators of the local average treatment effect for the treated under instrumental variable assumptions with covariates.

Example 2. (Identification of nonparametric nonseparable models) Conditional exogeneity is a key identifying assumption in the context of nonparametric and nonseparable structural equations. Assume that $Y=m(W, U)$ where m is an unknown smooth function, W is observable, while U is unobservable. To identify various objects associated with m, it is commonly assumed that $W \perp U|X$ for some observable X. See Matzkin (2003), Altonji and Matzkin (2005), Hoderlein and Mammen (2007), Imbens and Newey (2009), Lu and White (2011), Hoderlein, Su, and White (2012), and Su, Tu, and Ullah (2012), among others. Imbens and Newey's (2009) control function approach also provides us with a control variable X that satisfies the conditional exogeneity assumption under suitable conditions.

Example 3. (Test for asymmetric information) Since Akerlof (1970) asymmetric information, comprising adverse selection and moral hazard, has become one of the most important notions in economics. As Chiappori, Jullien, Salanié, and Salanié (2006) argue, asymmetric information is present in all markets but irrelevant or inconsequential in most of the time. Various tests have been proposed to test for it. Dionne, Gourieroux, and Vanasse (2001, 2006) first note that a test for the absence of asymmetric information can be reformulated as a test for conditional independence. Let X denote a vector of exogenous control variables, Y a decision or choice variable, and Z a "performance" variable. For example, in insurance market, X usually includes variables that are used for risk classification by the insurance company, Y could be the choice of deductibles, and Z could be the number of accidents or claims or the sum of reimbursements caused by accidents. There is no asymmetric information in the market if and only if the prediction of the endogenous variable Z based on X and Y jointly coincides with its prediction based on X alone, that is, $Z \perp Y|X$. Based on this formulation Su and Spindler (2012) propose a nonparametric test for asymmetric information and apply them to two insurance datasets.

Example 4. (Test for Granger noncausality) Conditional independence also plays a key role in macroeconomics. For example, tests of Granger non-causality in distribution (Granger, 1969; Granger & Newbold, 1986) are tests of conditional independence among observables. Let $\{(Y_t, X_t)\}$ denote a time series. $\{X_t\}$ does not Granger-cause $\{Y_t\}$ if $Y_t \perp (X_{t-1}, \ldots, X_{t-p_x})|(Y_{t-1}, \ldots, Y_{t-p_y})$ for any lags p_x and p_y. Su and White (2007, 2008) propose tests for Granger noncausality based on conditional characteristic functions and Hellinger distance measure of conditional densities, respectively. More recently, White and Lu (2011) show, such tests can be used to test structural noncausality under appropriate conditions.

For other potential use of conditional independence in economics, we refer the readers to Linton and Gonzalo (1997), Su and White (2007, 2008), and Huang and White (2010).

Accordingly, our main goal and contribution here is to provide straightforward and powerful new nonparametric methods for testing conditional independence. Hausman's (1978) ideas provide the basic foundation for our approach; however, as is now often the case, our methods compare two *collections* of estimators that converge to the same limits under correct specification (conditional independence) and that diverge under the alternative.

We construct our tests using local polynomial quantile regression, allowing weakly dependent data. This yields specification testing methods suitable for either cross-section or time-series data. In pursuing our main goal in this way, we make a number of further related contributions. Specifically, we generalize the existing nonparametric quantile literature not only by allowing for dependent heterogeneous data but also by establishing a weak consistency rate for the local Bahadur representation that is uniform in *both* the conditioning variables and the quantile index. We also show that, despite our nonparametric approach, our tests can detect local alternatives to conditional independence that decay to zero at the *parametric* rate, in contrast to the tests of Huang (2010) and of Su and White (2007, 2008, 2012). Although other tests can also detect local alternatives at the parametric rate (Delgado & González-Manteiga, 2001; Huang & White, 2010; Linton & Gonzalo, 1997; Song, 2009), those tests are for independent identically distributed (IID) data and do not necessarily extend easily to the time-series case. Our tests are thus the first for time series conditional independence that can detect local alternatives at the parametric rate.

The rest of the paper is organized as follows. In Section "Quantile regression and conditional independence" we describe quantile regression and its relation to conditional independence. Section "Local polynomial quantile regression and uniform Bahadur representation" introduces the local polynomial quantile regression estimator and studies its uniform local Bahadur representation. We apply this representation result to testing conditional independence in Section "Testing conditional independence", where we also conduct some Monte Carlo simulations to evaluate the finite sample performance of our tests. Section "Conclusion" provides a summary and conclusion. All proofs are provided in the appendix. Matlab codes that are used to implement our tests are available from the first author upon request.

QUANTILE REGRESSION AND CONDITIONAL INDEPENDENCE

Let $\{(Y_t, X_t)\}$ denote a time series of random vectors, with Y_t a scalar for simplicity. Let $m_t(\tau, x)$ define the τth conditional quantile function of Y_t given $X_t = x \in \mathbb{R}^d$, that is, the τth conditional regression quantile. Specifically,

$$m_t(\tau, x) \equiv \inf\{y : F_t(y|x) \geq \tau\}$$

where $F_t(\cdot|x)$ denotes the conditional cumulative distribution function (CDF) of Y_t given $X_t = x$. Let $\rho_\tau(z) = z(\tau - \mathbf{1}(z \leq 0))$ be the "check" function, with $\mathbf{1}(\cdot)$ being the usual indicator function. It is well known that the τth conditional quantile $m_t(\tau, x)$ solves the minimization problem

$$m_t(\tau, x) = \arg\min_{q \in \mathcal{Q}} E[\rho_\tau(Y_t - q(X_t)|X_t = x)] \tag{1}$$

where $\mathcal{Q}$ is a given space of measurable functions defined on $\mathbb{R}^d$. As is common, we assume that the solution to this minimization problem is unique.

Often, the distribution of $\{(X_t, Y_t)\}$ is assumed to be stationary, so the conditional quantile function $m_t(\tau, x)$ is not time-varying; in this case, we write $m_t(\tau, x) = m(\tau, x)$ for all $t \geq 1$. Here, we do not assume stationarity; however, under conditional stationarity of Y_t given X_t, we again have $m_t = m$.

Koenker and Bassett (1978) pioneered quantile regression, treating the linear parametric case where $\mathcal{Q} = \{q : q(x) = \beta^T x,\ \beta \in \mathbb{R}^d\}$ and T denotes the transpose operator. Subsequently, nonparametric quantile regression has been studied by Bhattacharya and Gangopadhyay (1990), Chaudhuri (1991), White (1992), Fan, Hu, and Truong (1994), He and Shao (1996), Welsh (1996), Yu and Jones (1998), Honda (2000), and Lu, Hui, and Zhao (2001), among others. Here, we apply local polynomial methods, as described in the next section.

Our main focus of interest is the conditional independence of Y_t and Z_t given X_t, that is, $Y_t \perp Z_t | X_t$. Let $m(\tau, x)$ and $m(\tau, x, z)$ define the τth conditional quantile functions of Y_t given $X_t = x$ and $(X_t, Z_t) = (x, z)$, respectively. Then $Y_t \perp Z_t | X_t$ if and only if the following null hypothesis holds:

$$H_0 : \Pr[m(\tau, X_t, Z_t) = m(\tau, X_t)] = 1 \quad \text{for all } \tau \in (0, 1) \tag{2}$$

An important special case is that of Granger noncausality (1969). Let $\mathcal{X}_{t-1} = (X_{t-1}, \ldots, X_{t-p_x})^T$ and $\mathcal{Y}_{t-1} = (Y_{t-1}, \ldots, Y_{t-p_y})^T$, and let $m(\tau, \mathcal{Y}_{t-1})$ and $m(\tau, \mathcal{X}_{t-1}, \mathcal{Y}_{t-1})$ denote the τth conditional quantiles of Y_t given $\mathcal{Y}_{t-1}$ and $(\mathcal{X}_{t-1}, \mathcal{Y}_{t-1})$, respectively. Finite-order Granger noncausality in distribution is the condition that $Y_t \perp \mathcal{X}_{t-1} | \mathcal{Y}_{t-1}$ (for additional related concepts, see White and Lu, 2010). Then $Y_t \perp \mathcal{X}_{t-1} | \mathcal{Y}_{t-1}$ if and only if

$$H_0^G : \Pr[m(\tau, \mathcal{X}_{t-1}, \mathcal{Y}_{t-1}) = m(\tau, \mathcal{Y}_{t-1})] = 1 \text{ for all } \tau \in (0, 1)$$

Recently, Jeong and Härdle (2008) proposed a test of a version of this hypothesis with fixed τ by extending the work of Zheng (1998) from the IID case to the time-series case.

An important feature of H_0 is that it involves all quantiles $\tau \in (0,1)$ and all values in the joint support of the conditioning variables. This generally requires the convergence of the quantile estimators underlying the test to be uniform in both τ and the conditioning variables.

LOCAL POLYNOMIAL QUANTILE REGRESSION AND UNIFORM BAHADUR REPRESENTATION

The local polynomial quantile regression estimator

When the distribution of Y_t given X_t is stationary, and if $m(\tau,x)$ is a sufficiently smooth function of x, for any $\tilde{x}$ in a neighborhood of x, we have

$$m(\tau, \tilde{x}) = m(\tau, x) + \sum_{1 \le |j| \le p} \frac{1}{j!} D^{|j|} m(\tau, x)(\tilde{x} - x)^j + o(||\tilde{x} - x||^p)$$

$$\equiv \sum_{0 \le |j| \le p} \beta_j(\tau, x; h)((\tilde{x} - x)/h)^j + o(||\tilde{x} - x||^p), \text{ say}$$

Here, we use the notation of Masry (1996): Letting $j_1, \ldots, j_d$ be nonnegative integers, $\boldsymbol{j} \equiv (j_1, \ldots, j_d)$, $|\boldsymbol{j}| \equiv \sum_{i=1}^{d} j_i, x^{\boldsymbol{j}} \equiv \Pi_{i=1}^{d} x_i^{j_i}$, $\sum_{0 \le |j| \le p} \equiv \sum_{k=0}^{p} \times \sum_{j_1=0}^{k} \cdots \sum_{\substack{j_d=0 \\ j_1+\cdots+j_d=k}}^{k}$ $D^{|j|} m(\tau, x) \equiv \frac{\partial^{|j|} m(\tau, x)}{\partial^{j_1} x_1 \cdots \partial^{j_d} x_d}$, $\beta_j(\tau, x; h) \equiv \frac{h^{|j|}}{j!} D^{|j|} m(\tau, x)$, where $\boldsymbol{j}! \equiv \Pi_{i=1}^{d_1} j_i!$, and $h = h(n)$ is a bandwidth parameter that scales the distance between $\tilde{x}$ and x.

With observations $\{(Y_t, X_t)\}_{t=1}^{n}$, we estimate the quantile regression function by local polynomial quantile regression. For this, let $\boldsymbol{\beta}$ denote the vector formed by stacking the vectors β_j in lexicographic order. Define

$$\hat{\beta}(\tau, x; h) \equiv \arg\min_{\boldsymbol{\beta}} \; Q_n(\tau, x; \boldsymbol{\beta}) \equiv n^{-1} \sum_{t=1}^{n} \rho_\tau \left(Y_t - \sum_{0 \le |j| \le p} \beta_j((X_t - x)/h)^j \right) \times K((x - X_t)/h) \qquad (3)$$

where K is a nonnegative kernel function on $\mathbb{R}^d$. The conditional quantile $m(\tau, x)$ and its derivatives up to pth order are then estimated respectively by

$$\hat{m}(\tau, x) = \hat{\beta}_0(\tau, x; h) \text{ and } \hat{D}^{|j|} m(\tau, x) = (j!/h^{|j|})\hat{\beta}_j(\tau, x; h), \quad 0 \le |j| \le p$$

In particular, a local linear approach obtains when $p = 1$ See Fan et al. (1994) and Yu and Jones (1998), among many others.

To proceed, we introduce some notation. Let $N_l = (l + d - 1)!/(l!(d - 1)!)$ be the number of distinct d-tuples $\boldsymbol{j}$ with $|\boldsymbol{j}| = l$. This denotes the number of distinct lth order partial derivatives of $m(\tau, x)$ with respect to x. Arrange the N_l d-tuples as a sequence in a lexicographical order (with highest priority to last position), so that $\phi_l(1) \equiv (0, 0, ..., l)$ is the first element in the sequence and $\phi_l(N_l) \equiv (l, 0, ..., 0)$ is the last element, and let ϕ_l^{-1} denote the mapping inverse to ϕ_l. Let $N = \sum_{l=1}^{p} N_l$. For each $\boldsymbol{j}$ with $0 \le |\boldsymbol{j}| \le 2p$, let $\mu_{\boldsymbol{j}} = \int_{\mathbb{R}^d} x^{\boldsymbol{j}} K(x) dx$, and define the $N \times N$ dimensional matrix $\mathbb{H}$ and $N \times 1$ matrix $\mathbb{B}$ by

$$\mathbb{H} = \begin{bmatrix} \mathbb{H}_{0,0} & \mathbb{H}_{0,1} & \cdots & \mathbb{H}_{0,p} \\ \mathbb{H}_{1,0} & \mathbb{H}_{1,1} & \cdots & \mathbb{H}_{1,p} \\ \vdots & \vdots & \ddots & \vdots \\ \mathbb{H}_{p,0} & \mathbb{H}_{p,1} & \cdots & \mathbb{H}_{p,p} \end{bmatrix}, \mathbb{B} = \begin{bmatrix} \mathbb{H}_{0,p+1} \\ \mathbb{H}_{1,p+1} \\ \vdots \\ \mathbb{H}_{p,p+1} \end{bmatrix} \tag{4}$$

where $\mathbb{H}_{i,j}$ are $N_i \times N_j$ dimensional matrices whose (l, s) elements are $\mu_{\phi_i(l)+\phi_j(s)}$.

Assumptions

A Bahadur representation is an approximation of the sample quantiles by the empirical distribution function (Bahadur, 1966). Local Bahadur representations of conditional quantiles have been previously considered in a number of papers, including He and Shao (1996), Honda (2000), Lu et al. (2001). In particular, Honda (2000) establishes a Bahadur representation that is uniform in the conditioning variables. More recently, Kong, Linton, and Xia (2010) establish a strong uniform consistency rate for the Bahadur representation of local polynomial M-regression estimates; there, too, the uniform rate is obtained only in the conditioning variables. In this section, we provide conditions sufficient to obtain a local Bahadur representation for $\hat{\beta}(\tau, x; h)$, uniform in both τ and the conditioning variables.

For given n, let $\{(Y_{nt}, X_{nt}) \in \mathbb{R} \times \mathbb{R}^d\}_{t=1}^{n}$ be a sequence of time-series random vectors. The triangular-array notation $\{(Y_{nt}, X_{nt})\}_{t=1}^{n}$ facilitates the study of asymptotic local power properties of many testing problems, including ours. Nevertheless, to avoid complicated notation we will suppress reference to the n subscript in what follows; in particular, we write $Y_t = Y_{nt}$, $X_t = X_{nt}$. For example, we will denote the conditional CDF of Y_{nt} given X_{nt} as $F_t(\cdot|X_t)$, instead of $F_{nt}(\cdot|X_{nt})$.

Next, let $\mathcal{T} \subset (0,1)$ and for $(\tau, u) \in \mathcal{T} \times \mathbb{R}$, define

$$\psi_\tau(u) \equiv \tau - \mathbf{1}(u \leq 0)$$

For simplicity, we let the supports of the X_t's and Y_t's be time-invariant. For simplicity, we also suppose that the conditional support of Y_t given X_t coincides with Y_t's unconditional support. These restrictions can be straightforwardly relaxed, but with a considerable proliferation of notation. We thus let $\mathcal{X}$ denote the common support of the X_t's and $\mathcal{Y}$ denote the common support of the Y_t's. We let $||\cdot||$ denote the Euclidean norm. Although n is implicit for Y_t and X_t in what follows, the stated conditions hold for $n = 1,2,\ldots$, and the referenced bounding constants or functions do not depend on n.

Assumption 1. $\{(Y_t, X_t)\}$ is a strong mixing process with mixing coefficients $\alpha(s)$ such that $\sum_{s=0}^{\infty} s^3 \alpha(s)^{\eta/(4+\eta)} \leq C < \infty$ for some $\eta > 0$ with $\eta/(4+\eta) \leq 1/2$.

Assumption 2. (i) X_t is continuously distributed, with probability density function (PDF) $f_t(\cdot)$ bounded with bounded first-order derivatives on $\mathcal{X}$ for each $t = 1, 2, \ldots$. (ii) The conditional CDF $F_t(\cdot|X_t)$ of Y_t given X_t has Lebesgue density $f_t(\cdot|X_t)$ such that $\sup_{y:F_t(y|X_t)\in\mathcal{T}} f_t(y|X_t) \leq C_1 < \infty$ for all t, and for all $y_1, y_2 \in \mathcal{Y}, \left|f_t(y_1|X_t) - f_t(y_2|X_t)\right| \leq C_2(X_t)\left|y_1 - y_2\right|$ a.s. for all t, where $C_2(\cdot)$ is a continuous function. (iii) The joint PDF $f_{ts}(\cdot,\cdot)$ of (X_t, X_s) is bounded for all $t, s = 1, 2, \ldots$.

Assumption 3. For all $(\tau, x) \in \mathcal{T} \times \mathcal{X}$, the conditional quantile function defined by $m_t(\tau, x) \equiv \inf\{y \in \mathcal{Y} : F_t(y|x) \geq \tau\}$ satisfies: (i) $m_t(\tau, x) = m(\tau, x) + n^{-1/2} c(\tau, x, t/n)$ where $c(\tau, x, t/n)$ is uniformly bounded for all $(\tau, x) \in \mathcal{T} \times \mathcal{X}$ and $t \leq n$; (ii) $m(\tau, x)$ is bounded uniformly in $(\tau, x) \in \mathcal{T} \times \mathcal{X}$. It is Lipschitz continuous in (τ, x) and for each $\tau \in \mathcal{T}$ has all partial derivatives with respect to x up to order $p+1$; (iii) The $(p+1)$th order partial derivatives with respect to x, that is, $D^{\mathbf{k}} m(\tau, x)$ with $|\boldsymbol{k}| = p+1$, are uniformly bounded in $(\tau, x) \in \mathcal{T} \times \mathcal{X}$ and are Hölder continuous in (τ, x) with exponent $\gamma_0 > 0$: $|D^{\mathbf{k}} m(\tau, x) - D^{\mathbf{k}} m(\tilde{\tau}, \tilde{x})| \leq C_3(|\tau - \tilde{\tau}|^{\gamma_0} + ||x - \tilde{x}||^{\gamma_0})$ for some constant $C_3 < \infty$, and for all $\tau, \tilde{\tau} \in \mathcal{T}$ and $x, \tilde{x} \in \mathcal{X}$ and all $\mathbf{k}$ such that $|\mathbf{k}| = p+1$.

Assumption 4. $\lim_{n\to\infty} n^{-1} \sum_{t=1}^{n} f_t(m(\tau, x)|x) f_t(x) > 0$ uniformly in $(\tau, x) \in \mathcal{T} \times \mathcal{X}$.

Assumption 5. The kernel function $K(\cdot)$ is a product kernel of $k(\cdot)$, which is a symmetric density function with compact support $\mathcal{A} \equiv [-c_k, c_k]$. $\sup_{a\in\mathcal{A}} \left|k(a)\right| \leq \bar{c}_1 < \infty$, and $|k(a) - k(\tilde{a})| \leq \bar{c}_2 |a - \tilde{a}|$ for all $a, \tilde{a} \in \mathbb{R}$ and some $\bar{c}_2 < \infty$. The functions $H_j(x) = x^j K(x)$ for all $\boldsymbol{j}$ with $0 \leq |j| \leq 2p+1$ are Lipschitz continuous. $\mathbb{H}$ defined in Eq. (4) is positive definite.

Assumption 6. As $n \to \infty$, (i) $h \to 0$, $nh^{2d}/(\log n)^2 \to \infty$, $nh^{d+2(p+1)} \to c \in [0,\infty)$, $h^{d/2}/(\kappa_n \log\log n) \to 0$, and $h^{(p+1)}/\kappa_n \to 0$ for some nonincreasing positive sequence κ_n. (ii) Let $h = n^{-1/\varsigma_1}$ and $\kappa_n = n^{-\varsigma_\kappa}$ where $\varsigma_1 > 0$, $\varsigma_\kappa \geq 0$ and $4\varsigma_\kappa + d/\varsigma_1 - 1 < 0$. There exists $\upsilon \in (\varsigma_\kappa, (1 - d/\varsigma_1)/2)$ such that $16/\eta > [5/2 + d + 2\upsilon + 3d/(2\varsigma_1) + (2N+1)\varsigma_\kappa]/(1 - 2\upsilon - d/\varsigma_1) - 1$.

Assumption 1 restricts the process $\{(Y_t, X_t)\}$ to be strong mixing with mixing rates decaying sufficiently fast. Significantly, it does not require the stationarity of the process. Assumption 2 imposes smoothness conditions on the functions $f_t(\cdot)$,$f_t(\cdot|X_t)$, and $f_{ts}(\cdot,\cdot)$. Assumptions 3 and 4 are required to establish the uniform local Bahadur representation for our local polynomial estimates. In particular, Assumption 3 requires the process $\{(Y_t, X_t)\}$ be asymptotically stationary, implying that our uniform Bahadur representation obtained in the next section is applicable to the case of asymptotically stationary process, which is needed, say, in the local power analysis for testing structural changes based on conditional quantile regressions. Assumptions 5 and 6 specify typical conditions on the kernel and bandwidth used in local polynomial regression. In particular, Assumption 6 implies that $nh^d\kappa_n^2 \to \infty$ as $n \to \infty$.

Uniform local Bahadur representation

We now show that with the above assumptions, the local polynomial quantile estimator $\hat{\boldsymbol{\beta}}(\tau, x; h)$ has a Bahadur representation uniform in both τ and x. For this, we introduce some additional notation. Let $\mu((X_t - x)/h)$ be an $N \times 1$ vector that contains the regressors $((X_t - x)/h)^j$ in the local polynomial quantile regression (see Eq. (3)) in the lexicographical order. For example, if $p = 1$, then $\mu((X_t - x)/h) = (1, (X_t - x)^T/h)^T$. Let $\mu_{tx} \equiv \mu((X_t - x)/h)$. Define

$$H_n(\tau, x) \equiv \frac{1}{nh^d} \sum_{t=1}^{n} K((x - X_t)/h) f_t(m(\tau, X_t)|X_t) \mu_{tx} \mu_{tx}^T \text{ and}$$

$$J_n(\tau, x) \equiv \frac{1}{\sqrt{nh^d}} \sum_{t=1}^{n} K((x - X_t)/h) \mu_{tx} \psi_\tau(Y_t - \boldsymbol{\beta}_0(\tau, x; h)^T \mu_{tx})$$

Theorem 1. Suppose Assumptions 1-6 hold. Then $\sqrt{nh^d}\,(\hat{\boldsymbol{\beta}}(\tau, x; h) - \boldsymbol{\beta}(\tau, x; h)) = H_n(\tau, x)^{-1} J_n(\tau, x) + o_P(\kappa_n)$ uniformly in $(\tau, x) \in \mathscr{T} \times \mathscr{X}$. In particular,

$\sqrt{nh^d}(\hat{m}(\tau,x) - m(\tau,x)) = e_1^T H_n(\tau,x)^{-1} J_n(\tau,x) + o_P(\kappa_n)$ uniformly in $(\tau,x) \in \mathcal{T} \times \mathcal{X}$,
where $e_1 = (1,0,\ldots,0)^T$ is an N-vector.

Remark 1. Theorem 1 generalizes the local Bahadur representation results in the literature. This uniform result is useful for many statistical applications, where one usually requires κ_n to be 1 or $h^{d/2}$. If $\kappa_n = 1$, we can choose $\varsigma_\kappa = 0$ in Assumption 6(ii), and the last two conditions in Assumption 6(i) are automatically satisfied. To construct a conditional quantile-based test that can detect deviations from the null at the parametric rate, one typically needs $\kappa_n = h^{d/2}$. In this case, $\varsigma_\kappa = d/(2\varsigma_1)$, and the first condition in Assumption 6(ii) implies that $nh^{3d} \to \infty$.

Remark 2. Guerre and Sabbah (2012) also consider uniform Bahadur representation for local polynomial estimators of the conditional quantile function where the order of the local polynomial estimator is higher than the differentiability order of the conditional quantile function. For IID observations, they establish the uniform order of the bias and Bahadur remainder terms where the uniformity is taken with respect to the quantile index $\tau \in \mathcal{T} \subset (0,1)$, the covariate $x \in \mathcal{X}_0$, and the smoothing parameter h, and $\mathcal{X}_0$ is a compact subset of the interior of $\mathcal{X}$. In contrast, we limit our attention to the case where the order of local polynomial estimator is no bigger than the differentiability order of the conditional quantile function, but we allow nonstationary time series observations. Our results hold uniformly with respect to $\tau \in \mathcal{T} \subset (0,1)$ and $x \in \mathcal{X}$ but not with respect to h. We conjecture that it is possible to extend the uniform results to allow for uniformity with respect to h but that extension is beyond the scope of this chapter. Undoubtedly, the permission of nonstationary time series is important for the local power analysis of a variety of test statistics based on conditional quantile functions, and the uniformity over the whole support $\mathcal{X}$ of the covariate will make some trimming device unnecessary.

Remark 3. Like Guerre and Sabbah (2012) we restrict our attention to a compact subset $\mathcal{T}$ of (0,1) for the quantile index τ. It is well known the estimator of the (conditional) quantile function at the extreme quantile index (i.e., $\tau \to 0$ or 1) has distinctive behavior than that at the interior of (0,1). The estimation of $m(\tau,x)$ when τ is in the vicinity of 0 has been considered by Chernozhukov (2005) for the parametric quantile regression. That is, he considers the specification that $m(\tau,x) = \beta'_\tau x$ for some

$\beta_\tau \in \mathbb{R}^d$. He provides a complete asymptotic characterization of the quantile regression estimator of β_τ for the case where the distribution F of the error term lies in the domain of attraction of any extreme value distribution by allowing τ to approach 0 at a speed that is slower than or proportional to the sample size. Recently, Martins-Filho, Yao, and Torero (2012) consider a two-stage estimation of the nonparametric quantile function in a conditionally homoskedastic nonparametric regression model when the quantile index τ is in the vicinity of 1, but they limit their attention to the case where F belongs to the domain of attraction of a Fréchet distribution and τ approaches 1 at a speed slower than the sample size. They estimate first the conditional mean function nonparametrically and then the finite dimensional parameters associated with the distribution of the error term, based on which the estimate of the conditional quantile function is constructed. It is unclear whether one can extend the results of Chernozhukov (2005) to local polynomial estimators of the conditional quantile function by allowing τ tending to either 0 or 1 as the sample sizes increases to infinity.

The following corollary is handy for deriving the asymptotic properties of our test statistic.

Corollary 1. Suppose Assumptions 1–6 hold with κ_n and ς_κ in Assumption 6 replaced by $h^{d/2}$ and $d/(2\varsigma_1)$, respectively. Suppose $nh^{2(p+1)} = o(1)$. Then, uniformly in $(\tau, x) \in \mathcal{T} \times \mathcal{X}$,

$$\sqrt{nh^d}(\hat{m}(\tau,x) - m(\tau,x)) = e_1^T H(\tau,x)^{-1}\bar{J}_n(\tau,x)[1 + o_P(1)] + o_P(h^{d/2})$$

where $\bar{J}_n(\tau,x) \equiv n^{-1/2}h^{-d/2}\sum_{t=1}^n K((x-X_t)/h)\mu_{tx}\psi_\tau(Y_t - m(\tau,X_t))$, $H(\tau,x) \equiv \bar{f}(\tau,x)\mathbb{H}$, $\bar{f}(\tau,x) \equiv \lim_{n\to\infty}\bar{f}_n(\tau,x)$, and $\bar{f}_n(\tau,x) \equiv n^{-1}\sum_{t=1}^n f_t(m(\tau,x)|x)f_t(x)$.

If we assume the process $\{(X_t, Y_t)\}$ is stationary, then the conditional and marginal PDFs $f_t(m(\tau,x)|x)$ and $f_t(x)$ can be written $f(m(\tau,x)|x)$ and $f(x)$, so that $H(\tau,x) = f(m(\tau,x)|x)f(x)\mathbb{H}$. This result is frequently used in the next section.

TESTING CONDITIONAL INDEPENDENCE

Motivation and the test statistic

As discussed in Section "Quantile regression and conditional independence", we wish to test

$$H_0 : \Pr[m(\tau, X_t, Z_t) = m(\tau, X_t)] = 1 \text{ for all } \tau \in (0, 1)$$

where X_t and Z_t are random vectors of dimension d_X and d_Z, respectively. An obvious way to test this hypothesis would be to compare estimators of $m(\tau, X_t, Z_t)$ and $m(\tau, X_t)$ for all $\boldsymbol{\tau}$ and all admissible $W_t \equiv (X_t^T, Z_t^T)^T$. This approach clearly would give a form of Hausman test. As White (1994, Chapter 9) shows, however, Hausman tests can also be formulated as m-tests, that is, tests of specific moment restrictions that hold under correct specification and fail otherwise. Such m-tests are often especially convenient, both for analysis and computation.

To formulate a corresponding m-test for H_0 let $u_{t\tau} \equiv Y_t - m(\tau, X_t)$ and $\varepsilon_{t\tau} \equiv Y_t - m(\tau, X_t, Z_t)$, and recall that $\psi_\tau(u) \equiv \tau - \mathbf{1}(u<0)$. Then $u_{t\tau} = \varepsilon_{t\tau}$ under H_0 and H_0 holds if and only if

$$H_0^* : E[\psi_\tau(u_{t\tau})|W_t] = 0 \ \text{ a.s. for all } \tau \in (0, 1)$$

This hypothesis has the form of a conditional moment restriction, involving the generalized residuals $\psi_\tau(u_{t\tau})$. Two challenges are apparent here. First, for each τ there is an infinite number of unconditional moment restrictions implied by $E[\psi_\tau(u_{t\tau})|W_t] = 0$. Second, we must accommodate the fact that $\boldsymbol{\tau}$ can take a continuum of values.

Results of Stinchcombe and White (1998, SW) allow us to convert conditional to unconditional moment restrictions in a convenient way. Specifically, SW provide conditions under which

$$\begin{gathered} E\left[\psi_\tau(u_{t\tau})|W_t\right] = 0 \text{ a.s. for all } \tau \in (0, 1) \\ \text{if and only if} \\ E\left[\psi_\tau(u_{t\tau})\varphi(W_t, \gamma)\right] = 0 \text{ almost every where (a.e.) in } (\tau, \gamma) \in (0, 1) \times \Gamma \end{gathered} \tag{5}$$

where $\Gamma \subset \mathbb{R}^{d_\Gamma}$ is a properly chosen set with typical choices $d_\Gamma = d_X + d_Z$ or $d_X + d_Z + 1$, and φ is a *generically comprehensively revealing* (GCR) or *comprehensively revealing* (CR) function. Examples of GCR functions include (1) $\varphi(W_t, \gamma) = \exp(i\gamma^T W_t)$, (2) $\varphi(W_t, \gamma) = \sin(\gamma^T W_t)$, and (3) $\varphi(W_t, \gamma) = \exp(\gamma^T W_t)$, where $i = \sqrt{-1}$. The following CR functions are frequently used in the literature: (1) $\varphi(W_t, \gamma) = \mathbf{1}(W_t \leq \gamma)$, (5) $\varphi(W_t, \gamma) = \mathbf{1}(\beta^T W_t \leq \alpha)$ with $\gamma = (\alpha, \beta^T)^T$, where $\mathbf{1}(W_t \leq \gamma) = \Pi_{i=1}^{d_X+d_Z} \mathbf{1}(W_{ti} \leq \gamma_i)$, and W_{ti} and γ_i are the ith elements of W_t and γ respectively. See SW for primitive conditions for GCR or CR functions.

A remarkable property of GCR functions is that if φ is GCR, then deviations from the null hypothesis can be detected by essentially any choice of $\gamma \in \Gamma$, where Γ can be chosen as any small compact set with nonempty interior. In contrast, for CR functions the set Γ may have to be $\mathbb{R}^{d_\Gamma}$ in order to ensure consistency of the associated test. Also, different choices of φ result in different local power properties. There is no general way to choose the "optimal" φ to conduct a test because such a function φ will depend on the underlying data generating process or the true alternative. For this reason, it is desirable to establish a general theory that covers a large class of (G)CR functions φ.

Given a sample $\{(Y_t, W_t)\}_{t=1}^n$, define the empirical process

$$S_n^{(1)}(\tau,\gamma) \equiv n^{-1/2}\sum_{t=1}^n \psi_\tau(u_{t\tau})\varphi(W_t,\gamma)$$

Since $u_{t\tau}$ is not observable, in practice we replace it with $\hat{u}_{t\tau}$, where $\hat{u}_{t\tau} \equiv Y_t - \hat{m}(\tau, X_t)$, and $\hat{m}(\tau, x)$ denotes the pth order local polynomial quantile regression estimate of $m(\tau, x)$. A practical test of CI can be based on the process

$$S_n^{(2)}(\tau,\gamma) \equiv n^{-1/2}\sum_{t=1}^n \psi_\tau(\hat{u}_{t\tau})\varphi(W_t,\gamma)$$

The limiting distribution of $S_n^{(2)}(\tau,\gamma)$ is different from that of $S_n^{(1)}(\tau,\gamma)$, a consequence of the "parameter estimation error" problem. As we explain shortly, this causes great difficulty in proposing a bootstrap test statistic whose limiting distribution coincides with the limiting null distribution of the test statistic. In addition, the indicator function in $\psi_\tau(\cdot)$ is not a smooth function, which makes the asymptotic analysis of $S_n^{(2)}(\tau,\gamma)$ intractable: even if we assume that the conditional quantile function $m(\tau,x)$ belongs to a certain smooth class of functions (e.g., Van der Vaart & Wellner (1996, p. 154)) so that $S_n^{(1)}(\tau,\gamma)$ obeys a version of the Donsker theorem, it is hard (if even possible) to ensure that the local polynomial quantile estimate $\hat{m}(\tau,x)$ also belongs to the same class. We, therefore, cannot apply empirical process theory to study $S_n^{(2)}(\tau,\gamma)$ directly. Instead, we propose to approximate the indicator function by a smooth function $G(\cdot)$ and consider the stochastic process

$$S_n(\tau,\gamma) \equiv n^{-1/2}\sum_{t=1}^n [\tau - G(-\hat{u}_{t\tau}/\lambda_n)]\varphi(W_t,\gamma)$$

where $G(\cdot)$ is a function that behaves like a CDF with uniformly bounded derivatives up to third order and $\lambda_n \to 0$ is a smoothing parameter.

The process $S_n(\tau,\gamma)$ will be the main ingredient of our test statistic. Under some regularity conditions, it converges to a mean-zero Gaussian process under the null and diverges for some value(s) of (τ, γ) under the alternative. Consequently, we accommodate the continuum of values for τ and γ using the Cramér-von Mises test statistics

$$CM_n \equiv \int_\Gamma \int_{\mathscr{T}} |S_n(\tau, \gamma)|^2 \Psi_1(d\tau)\Psi_2(d\gamma) \tag{6}$$

where $\mathscr{T} = [\underline{\tau}, \bar{\tau}]$ is a subset of (0,1), and $\Psi_1(\cdot)$ and $\Psi_2(\cdot)$ are weighting functions satisfying some mild conditions.

One can also consider the Kolmogorov-Smirnoff test statistic

$$KS_n \equiv \sup_{\tau \in \mathscr{T}} \sup_{\gamma \in \Gamma} |S_n(\tau, \gamma)|$$

But KS_n is much more computationally demanding than CM_n so we focus on the CM_n statistic.

As we show next, despite the nonparametric quantile regression, our tests can detect local alternatives that decay to zero at the parametric rates, in sharp contrast with the tests of Su and White (2007, 2008, 2012). More importantly, since our tests only involve d_X-dimensional smoothing, it is less severely subject to the "curse of dimensionality" problem than some of the earlier tests. In addition, our tests allow for weakly dependent data, and they are asymptotically pivotal under the null hypothesis for independent or martingale difference sequence (m.d.s.) data.

Asymptotic Null Distribution

We make the following assumptions.

Assumption 7. For all $\tau \in (0, 1)$, $E[\psi_\tau(Y_t - m(\tau, W_t))|W_t] = 0$ a.s.

Assumption 8. (i) $\{(Y_t, W_t)\}$ is a strictly stationary strong mixing process with mixing coefficients $\alpha(s)$ such that $\sum_{s=0}^{\infty} s^5 \alpha(s)^{\eta/(6+\eta)} \leq C < \infty$ and $\frac{\eta}{2+\eta} + \frac{1+v}{6\bar{v}} < 1$ for some $\eta > 0$ with $\eta/(6+\eta) \leq 1/2$ where $\bar{v} = 1 \wedge (rv)$, and r and v are specified in Assumption 10. (ii) Assumptions 2 and 3 hold for the stationary process $\{(Y_t, W_t)\}$, where the PDF of X_t can be written as $f(\cdot)$ in A(i), the conditional CDF and PDF of Y_t given X_t can be written as $F(\cdot|X_t)$ and $f(\cdot|X_t)$, respectively in A(ii), and the τth conditional quantile function of Y_t given $X_t = x$ can be written as $m(\tau, x)$ in Assumption 3 so that 3(i) holds with $c = 0$. (iii) $f(\cdot)$ is bounded away from 0 on its support $\mathscr{X}$ and $\inf_{(\tau,x) \in \mathscr{T} \times \mathscr{X}} f(m(\tau, x)|x) > 0$.

Assumption 9. (i) The conditional CDF of Y_t given W_t, $F_{Y|W}(\cdot|W_t)$, and its Lebesgue density function $f_{Y|W}(\cdot|W_t)$ have continuous derivatives up to qth order denoted respectively by $F_{Y|X}^{(s)}(\cdot|X_t)$ and $f_{Y|W}^{(s)}(\cdot|W_t)$, $s = 1, \ldots, q$. $f_{Y|W}(\cdot|W_t)$ is Lipschitz continuous a.s., and $F_{Y|W}^{(q)}(\cdot|W_t)$ and $f_{Y|W}^{(q)}(\cdot|W_t)$ are bounded and uniformly continuous on $\mathbb{R}$ a.s. (ii) Let $V_t \equiv (Y_t, W_t^T)^T$. The joint PDF $f_{t_1,\ldots,t_{12}}(\cdot)$ of $(V_{t_1}, \ldots, V_{t_{12}})$ exists and is bounded for all $t_1, \ldots, t_{12} \in 1, 2, \ldots, n\}$.

Assumption 10. $\varphi(\cdot, \cdot)$ is uniformly bounded by c_φ on the support of W_t and Γ. For some constants $r \geq 2$ and $v \in (0, 1]$, either one of the following conditions holds: (i) $\varphi(\cdot, \gamma)$ is Holder continuous with respect to γ in the sense that for some measurable function $C_\varphi(\cdot)$ with $E(|C_\varphi(W)|^r) < \infty$,

$$|\varphi(W, \gamma) - \varphi(W, \gamma')| \leq C_\varphi(W)||\gamma - \gamma'||^v$$

for all $\gamma, \gamma' \in \Gamma$; (ii) $\varphi(\cdot, \gamma)$ is locally uniformly L_r-continuous with respect to γ in the sense that for some constant $C_\varphi > 0$,

$$\left\{E\left[\sup_{\gamma':||\gamma-\gamma'||\leq\delta} |\varphi(W_t, \gamma) - \varphi(W_t, \gamma')|^r\right]\right\}^{1/r} \leq C_\varphi \delta^v$$

for all $\gamma \in \Gamma$ and all small positive $\delta = o(1)$.

Assumption 11. (i) $\sup_{u \in \mathbb{R}} |G(u)| \leq \bar{c}_G$ for some $\bar{c}_G < \infty$, $\lim_{u \to -\infty} G(u) = 0$, and $\lim_{u \to \infty} G(u) = 1$. (ii) $G(\cdot)$ is three times differentiable with derivatives denoted by $G^{(s)}(\cdot)$ for $s = 1, 2, 3$; $G(\cdot)$ and its first derivative $G^{(1)}(\cdot)$ are uniformly bounded, and the integrals $\int_{-\infty}^{\infty} |G^{(s)}(u)| du$, $s = 1, 2, 3$, are finite. (iii) $g(\cdot) \equiv G^{(1)}(\cdot)$ is symmetric over its support. There exists an integer $q \geq 2$ such that $\int_{-\infty}^{\infty} u^s g(u) du = \delta_{s0}$ for $s = 0, 1, \ldots, q-1$ and $\int_{-\infty}^{\infty} u^q g(u) \, du < \infty$, where δ_{s0} is Kronecker's delta. (iv) For some $c_G < \infty$ and $A_G < \infty$, either $G^{(3)}(u) = 0$ for $|u| > A_G$ and for $u, u' \in \mathbb{R}$, $|G^{(3)}(u) - G^{(3)}(u')| \leq c_G |u - u'|$, or $G^{(3)}(u)$ is differentiable with $|G^{(4)}(u)| \leq c_G$ and for some $\gamma_0 > 1$ and $|G^{(4)}(u)| \leq c_G |u|^{-\gamma_0}$ for all $|u| > A_G$.

Assumption 12. (i) Assumption 6 holds with κ_n and ς_κ replaced by $h^{d/2}$ and $d/(2\varsigma_1)$, respectively. (ii) As $n \to \infty$, $nh^{2(p+1)} \to 0$, $\lambda_n \to 0$, $n\lambda_n^{2q} \to 0$, $n^2 \lambda_n^3 h^{7d_X/2} / \log n \to \infty$, and $n^3 \lambda_n^6 h^{4d_X} / (\log n)^4 \to \infty$.

Assumption 7 says that for each τ, $m(\tau, W_t)$ is the τth conditional quantile function of Y_t given W_t. Assumption 8(i) strengthens the mixing conditions in Assumption 2. The first part of Assumptions 8(i) (i.e., the summability condition) is used to determine the sixth moment of a second-order

U-statistic, whereas the second part is used together with Assumption 10 to prove the stochastic equicontinuity of a certain empirical process. Assumptions 8(ii) and (iii) are variants of Assumptions 2–4. Assumption 9 imposes some smoothness conditions on the conditional CDF $F_{Y|W}(\cdot|W_t)$ and PDF $f_{Y|W}(\cdot|W_t)$. The uniform boundedness of the joint PDF $f_{t_1,\cdots,t_{12}}(\cdot)$ facilitates the determination of the six moments of certain U-statistics. Assumptions 10(i) and (ii) parallel Conditions (3.1) and (3.2) in Chen, Linton, and Van Keilegom (2003). It is easy to verify that the five examples after Eq. (5) satisfy either condition (i) or (ii) in Assumption 10. In all but Example 3, $\varphi(\cdot,\cdot)$ is uniformly bounded no matter whether we allow the support of W_t to be compact or not. In the case where W_t is compactly supported, $\varphi(\cdot,\cdot)$ is also uniformly bounded in Example 3. Assumption 11(i) is required because we use G to approximate the indicator function. Nevertheless, G does not need to be bounded between 0 and 1, nor does it need to be monotone. Assumptions 11(ii)-(iv) specify smoothness conditions on G. In particular, Assumption 11(iii) requires that the first derivative function g behaves like a symmetric q th order kernel and Assumption 11(iv) is used in studying the remainder term of a third-order Taylor expansion. If $q=2$, the CDF for the standard normal distribution meets all the conditions on G if $q=4$, one can use the integral of the fourth-order Gaussian or Epanechnikov kernel as G. Assumption 12 specifies conditions on the smoothing parameters λ_n and h. Note that the last requirement Assumption 12(ii) implies that $n^{-1/2}h^{-d_X/2}\sqrt{\log n} = o(\lambda_n)$, that is $n\lambda_n^2 h^{d_X}/\log n \to \infty$. If we set $h = n^{-1/\varsigma_1}$ and $\lambda_n \propto n^{-1/\varsigma_2}$ so that the conditions in Assumption 12(i)–(ii) are all satisfied, we then need

$$\max\left(\frac{6\varsigma_1}{4\varsigma_1 - 7d_X}, \frac{6\varsigma_1}{3\varsigma_1 - 4d_X}\right) < \varsigma_2 < 2q$$

When the dimension d_X of the conditioning variable X_t is small and η is small enough in Assumption 8(i), $q = 2$ will suffice. For example, if $d_X = 1$, $p = 1$, $q = 2$, $h \propto n^{-1/3.5}$, then one can choose $\varsigma_2 \in (42/13, 4)$; if $d_X = 2$, $p = 2$, $q = 2$, $h \propto n^{-1/5.75}$, then one can choose $\varsigma_2 \in (23/6, 4)$; if $d_X = 2$, $p = 3$, $q = 2$, $h \propto n^{-1/7}$, then one can choose $\varsigma_2 \in (42/13, 4)$.

Let $\eta_t(\gamma, \tau) = [\varphi(W_t, \gamma) - c_0 b(X_t, \gamma)]\psi_\tau(\varepsilon_{t\tau})$, where $c_0 = e_1^T \mathbb{H}\mathbb{B}$ and $b(X_t, \gamma) \equiv E[\varphi(W_t, \gamma)|X_t]$. Let $\Rightarrow$ denote weak convergence and a^c to denote the complex conjugate of a. The following theorem shows that $S_n(\cdot,\cdot)$ converges weakly to a Kiefer process under the null hypothesis.

Theorem 2. Suppose Assumptions 5 and 7–12 hold. Then under H_0

$$S_n(\cdot,\cdot) \Rightarrow S_\infty(\cdot,\cdot)$$

where $S_\infty(\cdot,\cdot)$ is a mean-zero Gaussian process with covariance kernel $\Upsilon(\tau,\tau';\gamma,\gamma') \equiv E[S_\infty(\tau,\gamma)\,S_\infty(\tau',\gamma')] = E[\eta_1(\gamma,\tau)\,\eta_1^c(\gamma',\tau')] + \sum_{i=1}^{\infty} E[\eta_1(\gamma,\tau) \times \eta_{1+i}^c(\gamma',\tau')] + E[\eta_{1+i}(\gamma,\tau)\eta_1^c(\gamma',\tau')]$.

Remark 4. Theorem 2 indicates that the process $\{S_n(\tau,\gamma) : \tau \in \mathscr{T}, \gamma \in \Gamma, n \geq 1\}$ converges to a zero-mean Gaussian process under the null hypothesis of CI. By the continuous mapping theorem,

$$CM_n \Rightarrow \int_\Gamma \int_{\mathscr{T}} \left|S_\infty(\tau,\gamma)\right|^2 \Psi_1(d\tau)\Psi_2(dw)$$

provided Ψ_1 and Ψ_2 are well behaved. The covariance kernel of the limiting process $\{S_\infty(\tau,\gamma) : \tau \in \mathscr{T}, \gamma \in \Gamma\}$ depends on the (G)CR function $\varphi(\cdot,\cdot)$ and the dependence structure in the data. There is thus no way to tabulate the critical values for our test, so we will provide a method to obtain bootstrap p-values. Note that the term $c_0 b(X_t,\gamma)$ in the definition of $\eta_t(\gamma,\tau)$ reflects the cost paid for replacing $m(\tau,X_t)$ with its local polynomial estimate. (We can show that $c_0 = 1$ for the local linear quantile regression estimate and lies strictly between 0 and 1 for general local polynomial regression with $p \geq 2$.) This term has to be taken into account when one proposes a bootstrap procedure to obtain the p-values.

Remark 5. Let $\mathfrak{F}_{t-1} \equiv \sigma(W_t, Y_{t-1}, W_{t-1}, Y_{t-2}, W_{t-2}, \cdots)$. If $\{\psi_\tau(\varepsilon_{t\tau}), \mathfrak{F}_t\}$ is an m.d.s. for each τ (e.g., when $\{(Y_t, W_t)\}$ is an independent sequence), then

$$\Upsilon(\tau,\tau';\gamma,\gamma') = E[\eta_1(\gamma,\tau)\eta_1^c(\gamma',\tau')]$$

In this special case, the limiting process $\{S_\infty(\tau,\gamma) : \tau \in \mathscr{T}, \gamma \in \Gamma\}$ is asymptotically pivotal. But this still depends on the chosen (G)CR and kernel functions.

Consistency and Asymptotic Local Power Properties

Now we study the consistency and asymptotic local power properties of tests based on $S_n(\cdot,\cdot)$. First, we show that the tests are consistent.

Theorem 3. Suppose Assumptions 5 and 7–12 hold. Then under $H_1 : H_0$ is false, for each $(\tau,\gamma) \in \mathscr{T} \times \Gamma$

$$n^{-1/2} S_n(\tau,\gamma) \xrightarrow{P} E\{f(m(\tau,W_t)|W_t)\varphi(W_t,\gamma)[m(\tau,W_t) - m(\tau,X_t)]\}$$

Consequently, the (G)CR nature of the function φ implies that $E\{f(m(\tau, W_t)|W_t)\varphi(W_t, \gamma)[m(\tau, W_t) - m(\tau, X_t)]\} \neq 0$ in a set with positive measure, so the CM_n test statistic will diverge to ∞ under the alternative.

To study the local power properties of the tests based upon $S_n(\cdot, \cdot)$, we consider the quantile regression model Eq. (3) with the following class of local alternatives:

$$H_{1n} : m(\tau, W_t) = m(\tau, X_t) + n^{-1/2}\delta(\tau, W_t) \tag{7}$$

where $\delta(\cdot, \cdot)$ is a non-constant measurable function. To facilitate our analysis, we add the following assumption.

Assumption 13. (i) $\delta(\tau, W)$ is uniformly bounded and uniformly continuous on $\mathcal{T}$ and the support of W_t. (ii) $n^{-1}\sum_{t=1}^{n} E\{f(m(\tau, W_t)|W_t)\delta(\tau, W_t) \times [\varphi(W_t, \gamma) - c_0 b(X_t, \gamma)]\} = \mathbf{\Delta}(\tau, \gamma) + o(1)$ uniformly in $(\tau, \gamma) \in \mathcal{T} \times \Gamma$.

The above assumption is not minimal. The uniform boundedness and continuity of $\delta(\tau, W)$ greatly simplify our proofs.

Theorem 4. Suppose Assumptions 5 and 7–13 hold. Then under H_{1n},

$$S_n(\cdot, \cdot) \Rightarrow S_\infty(\cdot, \cdot) + \mathbf{\Delta}(\cdot, \cdot)$$

Theorem 4 implies that the CM_n test has nontrivial power in detecting $n^{-1/2}$-local alternatives provided $\mathbf{\Delta}(\tau, \gamma) \neq 0$ for (τ, γ) in a set of positive measure on $\mathcal{T} \times \Gamma$.

A Bootstrap Version of the Test

From the previous section, we see that the asymptotic null distributions of the CM_n test statistics are generally not asymptotically pivotal, so the critical values for these tests cannot be tabulated. In this section, we propose a bootstrap version of our test, which is in the spirit of the block bootstrap (e.g., Bühlmann, 1994) but differs from the latter in several ways.

Let $\hat{b}(X_j, \gamma)$ denote a local linear estimate of $b(X_j, \gamma)$ with kernel $K(\cdot)$ and bandwidth h_b. Let

$$S_n^*(\tau, \gamma) \equiv n^{-1/2} \sum_{i=1}^{n-L+1} \zeta_i \sum_{j=i}^{i+L-1} [\tau - G(-\hat{u}_{j\tau}/\lambda_n)][\varphi(W_j, \gamma) - c_0\hat{b}(X_j, \gamma)]$$

where $L \equiv L(n)$ denotes the block length and $\{\zeta_i\}_{i=1}^{n-L+1}$ is a sequence of random variables. The requirements on L and ζ_i are stated in the next assumption.

Assumption 14. (i) $\{\zeta_t\}_{t=1}^{n-L+1}$ are IID and independent of the process $\{(Y_t, W_t)\}$. (ii) $E(\zeta_t) = 0$, $E(\zeta_t^2) = 1/L$, and $E(\zeta_t^4) = O(1/L^2)$. (iii) As $n \to \infty$, $L \to \infty$ and $L/n^{1/2} \to 0$.

Like Inoue (2001), we will generate ζ_t independently from $N(0, 1/L)$. Using $S_n^*(\cdot,\cdot)$, we construct the bootstrap version CM_n^* of the test statistic CM_n. We repeat this procedure B times to obtain the sequence $\{CM_{n,j}^*\}_{j=1}^B$. We reject the null when, for example, $p^* = B^{-1}\sum_{j=1}^B 1(CM_n \leq CM_{n,j}^*)$ is smaller than the desired significance level. Let $\overset{p}{\Rightarrow}$ denote weak convergence in probability, as defined by Giné and Zinn (1990).

Theorem 5. Suppose Assumptions 5 and 7–14 hold. Then under either H_0 or H_{1n}

$$S_n^*(\cdot,\cdot) \overset{p}{\Rightarrow} S_\infty(\cdot,\cdot)$$

Remark 6. First, if $\{\psi_\tau(\varepsilon_{t\tau}), \mathfrak{F}_t\}$ is an m.d.s., we do not need to mimic the dependence structure in the data so we can take $L = 1$ and our bootstrap is essentially a wild bootstrap:

$$S_n^W(\tau,\gamma) \equiv n^{-1/2} \sum_{i=1}^{n} \zeta_i [\tau - G(-\hat{u}_{j\tau}/\lambda_n)]\varphi(W_j,\gamma)$$

and there is also no need to account for the parameter estimation error by recentering $\varphi(W_j,\gamma)$ around $c_0\hat{b}(X_j,\gamma)$ Second, if $\{\psi_\tau(\varepsilon_{t\tau}), \mathfrak{F}_t\}$ is not an m.d.s., the limiting Gaussian process under the null hypothesis has the long-run covariance kernel defined in Theorem 2 and the wild bootstrap does not work, because it ignores the dependence structure of the data. Third, the parameter estimation error generally cannot be ignored in the bootstrap procedure. To see why, consider the following "naive" bootstrap process:

$$S_n^\dagger(\tau,\gamma) \equiv n^{-1/2} \sum_{i=1}^{n-L+1} \zeta_i \sum_{j=i}^{i+L-1} [\tau - G(-\hat{u}_{j\tau}/\lambda_n)]\varphi(W_j,\gamma)$$

One can decompose $\frac{1}{\sqrt{L}}\sum_{j=i}^{i+L-1} [\tau - G(-\hat{u}_{j\tau}/\lambda_n)]\varphi(W_j,\gamma)$ into

$$\frac{1}{\sqrt{L}} \sum_{j=i}^{i+L-1} \psi_\tau(\varepsilon_{j\tau})\varphi(W_j,\gamma) + \frac{1}{\sqrt{L}} \sum_{j=i}^{i+L-1} [1(\varepsilon_{j\tau} \leq 0) - G(-\varepsilon_{j\tau}/\lambda_n)]\varphi(W_j,\gamma)$$
$$+ \frac{1}{\sqrt{L}} \sum_{j=i}^{i+L-1} [G(-\varepsilon_{j\tau}/\lambda_n) - G(-\hat{u}_{j\tau}/\lambda_n)]\varphi(W_j,\gamma)$$

where the first term is our main object of interest, the second term represents the error due to the approximation of the indicator function by the smooth function $G(\cdot)$, and the third term reflects the parameter estimation error due to the estimation of $m(\tau, X_j)$ by $\hat{m}(\tau, X_j)$ (under the local alternative H_{1n}, the difference between $m(\tau, X_j)$ and $m(\tau, W_j)$ does not enter the asymptotics of $S_n^{\dagger}(\tau, \gamma)$). Under weak conditions, we can show that the second term is $o_P(1)$ uniformly in (τ, γ), and the third term is also $o_P(1)$ uniformly in (τ, γ) provided $L^{1/2}\upsilon_n = o(1)$ where $\upsilon_n \equiv n^{-1/2}h^{-d_X/2}\sqrt{\log n} + h^{p+1}$ is the uniform probability order of the estimation error, that is, $\max_{1 \le j \le n} \sup_{\tau \in \mathscr{T}} |\hat{m}(\tau, X_j) - m(\tau, X_j)| = O_P(\upsilon_n)$. [In the decomposition of $S_n(\tau, \gamma)$, the above third term corresponds to $\frac{1}{\sqrt{n}}\sum_{j=1}^{n} [G(-\varepsilon_{j\tau}/\lambda_n) - G(-\hat{u}_{j\tau}/\lambda_n)]\varphi(W_j, \gamma)$, which is $O_P(1)$ instead.] It follows that

$$\begin{aligned} E[S_n^{\dagger}(\tau, \gamma)S_n^{\dagger c}(\tau', \gamma')|\mathfrak{D}_n] &= n^{-1}\sum_{i=1}^{n-L+1}\frac{1}{L}\sum_{j=i}^{i+L-1}[\tau - G(-\hat{u}_{j\tau}/\lambda_n)]\varphi(W_j, \gamma) \\ &\quad \times [\tau' - G(-\hat{u}_{j\tau'}/\lambda_n)]\varphi^c(W_j, \gamma') \\ &= n^{-1}\sum_{i=1}^{n-L+1}\frac{1}{L}\sum_{j=i}^{i+L-1}\psi_\tau(\varepsilon_{j\tau})\varphi(W_j, \gamma)\psi_{\tau'}(\varepsilon_{j\tau'}) \\ &\quad \times \varphi^c(W_j, \gamma') + o_P(1) \\ &\nrightarrow \Upsilon(\tau, \tau'; \gamma, \gamma') \text{ in probability} \end{aligned}$$

where $\mathfrak{D}_n \equiv \{(Y_t, W_t)\}_{t=1}^{n}$. That is, conditional on $\mathfrak{D}_n$, $S_n^{\dagger}(\cdot, \cdot)$ cannot converge to $S_\infty(\cdot, \cdot)$, as it does not have the correct covariance kernel $\Upsilon(\cdot, \cdot; \cdot, \cdot)$. Fourth, as an alternative one can replace our bootstrap procedure by the block bootstrap of Bühlmann (1994):

$$S_n^{\ddagger}(\tau, \gamma) = n^{-1/2}\sum_{i=1}^{n-L+1}\sum_{j=s_i}^{s_i+L-1}[\tau - G(-\hat{u}_{j\tau}/\lambda_n)][\varphi(W_j, \gamma) - c_0\hat{b}(X_j, \gamma)]$$

where the s_i's are IID Uniform $(\{1, 2, \ldots, n - L + 1\})$. We conjecture that such a block bootstrap procedure is asymptotically equivalent to ours but the proof strategy will be quite different.

Remark 7. Theorem 5 shows that each bootstrapped process $\{S_n^*(\cdot, \cdot)\}$ converges weakly to the relevant Gaussian process, thus providing a valid asymptotic basis for approximating the limiting null distribution of test statistics based on $\{S_n(\cdot, \cdot)\}$. But we are only able to prove the above theorem under the sequence of local alternatives converging to 0 at the $n^{-1/2}$-rate (see H_{1n}). This is a phenomenon associated with many bootstrap versions of tests that aim not to re-estimate the model under investigation and are thus computationally attractive.

Monte Carlo Simulations

In this subsection we conduct some Monte Carlo experiments to evaluate the finite sample performance of our tests.

Data generating processes
We consider four data generating processes (DGPs):
DGP 1.

$$Y_t = \beta Z_t + X_t + \varepsilon_{Yt}$$
$$Z_t = X_t + 0.25X_t^2 + \varepsilon_{Zt}$$

where X_t is IID $U(-1, 1)$, ε_{Yt} is IID $N(0, 1)$, ε_{Zt} is IID, computed as the sum of 48 independent random variables, each uniformly distributed on $[-0.25, 0.25]$, $\{X_t\}, \{\varepsilon_{Yt}\}$, and $\{\varepsilon_{Zt}\}$ are mutually independent, and $\beta = \rho/(2\sqrt{1-\rho^2})$. It is easy to verify that ρ characterizes the conditional correlation coefficient of Y_t and Z_t given X_t.
DGP 2.

$$\begin{pmatrix} Y_t \\ Z_t \end{pmatrix} | X_t \sim N\left(\mathbf{0}, \begin{pmatrix} 1 + X_t^2 & \rho\sqrt{(1+X_t^2)(0.5+2X_t^2)} \\ \rho\sqrt{(1+X_t^2)(0.5+2X_t^2)} & 0.5 + 2X_t^2 \end{pmatrix}\right)$$

where $X_t = 0.5 + 0.5X_{t-1} + \varepsilon_{Xt}$, and ε_{Xt} is generated in the same way that ε_{Zt} is generated in DGP 1. Note that ρ is also the conditional correlation coefficient of Y_t and Z_t given X_t.
DGP 3.

$$Y_t = 0.1 + \phi(Y_{t-1})Y_{t-1} + \beta Z_{t-1} + \varepsilon_{Yt}$$
$$Z_t = 0.5Z_{t-1} + \sqrt{1 - 0.5^2}\varepsilon_{Zt}$$

where $\varepsilon_{Yt} = 0.5\varepsilon_{Yt-1} + \sqrt{1-0.5^2}e_{Y_t}$, e_{Y_t} and ε_{Zt} are independently generated in the same way that ε_{Zt} is generated in DGP 1, $\phi(\cdot)$ is the standard normal PDF, and $\beta = \rho/(2\sqrt{1-\rho^2})$ with ρ denoting the conditional correlation coefficient of Y_t and Z_{t-1} given Y_{t-1}.
DGP 4.

$$Y_t = \frac{2}{1 + \exp(1 - 0.5X_t^2)} + \sqrt{\vartheta_{Yt}}\varepsilon_{Yt}$$
$$\vartheta_{Yt} = 0.05 + 0.9\vartheta_{Y,t-1} + 0.05Y_{t-1}^2 + 0.1X_t^2$$

$$Z_t = 1 + X_t + \sqrt{\vartheta_{Zt}}\varepsilon_{Zt}$$

$$\vartheta_{Zt} = 0.05 + 0.7\vartheta_{Z,t-1} + 0.2Z_{t-1}^2 + 0.2X_t^2$$

where $X_t = 0.5X_{t-1} + \sqrt{1 - 0.5^2}\varepsilon_{Xt}$, ε_{Yt} and ε_{Zt} are both $t(3)/\sqrt{3}$ and have correlation given by ρ, and ε_{Xt} is generated as X_t in DGP 1, independently of $(\varepsilon_{Yt}, \varepsilon_{Zt})$.

Clearly, DGP 1 generates IID data $\{(Y_t, Z_t, X_t)\}$ as in typical microeconomic applications. All other DGPs generate time-series observations where the usual m.d.s. conditions on the error term may or may not be satisfied. In particular, $\{\psi_\tau(\varepsilon_{t\tau}), \mathfrak{F}_t\}$ forms an m.d.s. in both DGPs 1 and 2, but not in DGPs 3 and 4. It is worth emphasizing that the main advantage of our nonparametric test is twofold. First, despite its nonparametric nature, it can detect local alternatives that converge to the null at the usual $n^{-1/2}$-rate which the tests of Su and White (2007, 2008) and Huang (2010) cannot achieve. Second, we allow serial dependence in the error process. Some existing tests can also detect local alternatives at the parametric rate (Delgado & González-Manteiga, 2001; Huang & White, 2010; Linton & Gonzalo, 1997; Song, 2009), but these tests are applicable only to IID data and do not necessarily extend to the time-series case. In particular, when the error process does not form an m.d.s., one has to use the block bootstrap to obtain the bootstrap p-values. For this reason, it is worthwhile to focus mainly on time-series observations to examine the finite sample performance of our test and check how the proposed block bootstrap procedure works in this situation.

Note that our test is based on local polynomial quantile regressions, which typically require compactly supported conditioning variables. This motivates the otherwise awkward way we generate ε_{Zt} in DGP 1, ε_{Xt} in DGP 2, and e_{Y_t} and ε_{Zt} in DGP 3. According to the central limit theorem, we can treat these variables as being nearly standard normal random variables but with compact support $[-12, 12]$. In all DGPs except DGP 3, we are interested in testing whether Y_t and Z_t are conditionally independent given X_t. In DGP 3, we test whether Y_t and Z_{t-1} are independent conditional on Y_{t-1}; that is, the null hypothesis in this case is that Z_t does not Granger-cause Y_t at the first-order distributional level. Obviously, in all DGPs, the null hypotheses are satisfied if and only if the parameter ρ takes the value 0. The larger the value of $|\rho|$, the stronger the conditional dependence between Y_t and Z_t (or Z_{t-1} in DGP 3).

Implementation
To construct the test statistics, we estimate the conditional quantile function $m(\tau, x)$ using locally linear quantile regression ($p = 1$). We choose the normalized Epanechnikov kernel (with variance 1): $K(u) = \frac{3}{4}(1 - \frac{1}{5}u^2)\mathbf{1}(|u| \leq \sqrt{5})$. Since there is no data-driven procedure to choose the bandwidth for quantile regression, to estimate the τ th conditional quantile of Y_t given X_t, we choose a preliminary bandwidth according to the rule of thumb recommended by Yu and Jones (1998):

$$h_{0\tau} = s_X n^{-1/(d_X+1)}\{\tau(1-\tau)[\phi(\Phi^{-1}(\tau))]^{-2}\}^{1/(d_X+1)}$$

where s_X is the standard deviation of X_t, and ϕ and Φ are the standard normal PDF and CDF, respectively. Since undersmoothing is required for our test, we modify the above choice of bandwidth to

$$h_{0\tau} = s_X n^{-1/\theta}\{\tau(1-\tau)[\phi(\Phi^{-1}(\tau))]^{-2}\}^{1/(d_X+1)}$$

where $3 < \theta < 4$ for the case $d_X = 1$. We study the behavior of our tests with different choices of λ_n in order to examine the sensitivity of our test to the bandwidth sequence. Robinson (1991, p. 448) and Lee (2003, p. 16) propose very similar devices. Note that these choices for $h_{0\tau}$ and the kernel function meet the requirements for our test. Through a preliminary simulation study, we find our bootstrap-based test is not sensitive to the choice of θ when we take $\theta \in (3, 4)$. So we fix $\theta = 3.5$ for our simulation results. When $d_X = 2$ as in the applications below, we use $\theta = 5.75$. See the remark after Assumption 12.

To construct the bootstrap tests, we need to estimate $b(X_t, \gamma)$. Again, we apply the local linear estimation method by regressing $\varphi(W_t, \gamma)$ on X_t to obtain the estimate $\hat{b}(X_t, \gamma)$. We choose the bandwidth by the rule of thumb: $h_b = 2s_X n^{-1/(d_X+1)}$. To construct the CM_n test statistics, we consider five cases of the (G)CR functions φ listed after Eq. (5). We also need to choose the integrating functions $\Psi_1(\cdot)$ and $\Psi_2(\cdot)$ (see Eq. (6)). We treat all quantiles τ as equally important, so we choose $\Psi_1(d\tau) = 1/(\bar{\tau} - \underline{\tau})$ if $\tau \in [\underline{\tau}, \bar{\tau}]$ and 0 otherwise. Following the common practice in the parametric quantile regression literature, we set $\underline{\tau} = 0.1$ and $\bar{\tau} = 0.9$. Note that in order for our test to have correct size, we cannot choose too small $\underline{\tau}$ or too high $\bar{\tau}$. The desirable minimum value of $\underline{\tau}$ and maximum value of $\bar{\tau}$ depend on the number of observations on hand. In the simulations reported below, we have only $n = 100$ or 200 observations so that the effective number of observations for estimating the conditional quantile function at $\tau = 0.1$ or

0.9 is about 10–20 and one cannot estimate it reasonably accurately with smaller number of observations without adversely affecting the size of our tests. Additional simulations suggest that for moderately large sample sizes, say, $n = 400-800$, it is fine to specify $\underline{\tau} = 0.05$ and $\bar{\tau} = 0.95$. We conjecture that for even larger sample sizes, it is also fine to use smaller value of $\underline{\tau}$ and larger value of $\bar{\tau}$.

The choice of $\Psi_2(\cdot)$ depends on the nature of the (G)CR function φ and the ease of implementation. To obtain the CM_n test statistics, we need to compute the integral

$$I_{ts} \equiv \int \varphi(W_t, \gamma)\varphi^c(W_s, \gamma)d\Psi_2(\gamma)$$

Even though numerical integration is possible, it is computationally costly, especially when the dimension of γ is high. To save time in computation, we choose Ψ_2 to ensure that I_{ts} can be calculated analytically. Let $N(\mathbf{0}, \Sigma)$ denote a multivariate normal distribution with mean zero and variance-covariance matrix Σ. Corresponding to the five choices of the GCR (or CR) functions, we consider the following integrating functions $\Psi_2(\cdot)$:

1. When $\varphi(W_t, \gamma) = \exp(iw^T W_t)$, choose Ψ_2 to be the multivariate standard normal CDF. Then $I_{ts} = \exp(-\sum_{i=1}^{d_X+d_Z}(W_{ti} - W_{si})^2/2)$, and we denote the resulting test statistic as CM_{1n}. Here I is an identity matrix and W_{ti} denotes the ith element of W_t.
2. When $\varphi(W_t, \gamma) = sin(\gamma^T W_t)$, choose Ψ_2 to be the multivariate standard normal CDF. Then $I_{ts} = [\exp(-\sum_{i=1}^{d_X+d_Z}(W_{ti} - W_{si})^2/2) - \exp(-\sum_{i=1}^{d_X+d_Z} \times (W_{ti} + W_{si})^2/2)]/2$, and we denote the resulting test statistic as CM_{2n}.
3. When $\varphi(W_t, \gamma) = \exp(\gamma^T W_t)$, we need to ensure that the values of $\gamma^T W_t$ are not too large or small in absolute value. (Note that $\exp(u)$ is close to linear if $|u|$ is close to 0, close to 0 if u is too small, and explodes quickly when u is too large. In such cases, the test will not be well behaved. See Bierens (1990). We thus follow Bierens's (1990) advice and transform W_t to make sure each element W_{ti} of W_t lies between 0 and 1: $\bar{W}_{ti} = 1/(1 + \exp(-W_{ti}))$, $i = 1, \ldots, d_X + d_Z$. Then we choose $\Psi_2 \sim N(\mathbf{0}, 1/(d_X + d_Z)I)$. In this case, $I_{ts} = \exp(\sum_{i=1}^{d_X+d_Z}(\bar{W}_{ti} + \bar{W}_{si})^2/(2(d_X + d_Z)))$. We denote the resulting test statistic as CM_{3n}.
4. When $\varphi(W_t, \gamma) = \mathbf{1}(W_t \leq \gamma)$, we consider two choices for $\Psi_2(\cdot)$. First, we choose Ψ_2 to be the multivariate standard normal CDF. Then $I_{ts} = \prod_{i=1}^{d_X+d_Z}[1 - \Phi(W_{ti} \vee W_{si})]$, and we denote the resulting test statistic as CM_{4n}. Second, we choose Ψ_2 to be the empirical distribution of W_t;

then $I_{ts} \equiv \frac{1}{n}\sum_{l=1}^{n} \Pi_{i=1}^{d_X+d_Z} \mathbf{1}(W_{ti} \vee W_{si} \leq W_{li})$, and we denote the resulting test statistic as CM_{4bn}.

5. When $\varphi(W_t, \gamma) = \mathbf{1}(\beta^T W_t \leq \alpha)$ with $\gamma = (\alpha, \beta^T)^T$, we follow Escanciano (2006) and set

$$\Psi_2(dw) = F_{n,\beta}(d\alpha)d\beta$$

where $F_{n,\beta}(\cdot)$ denotes the empirical distribution function of $\{\beta^T W_t\}_{t=1}^n$ and $d\beta$ denotes the uniform density on the unit sphere. Then I_{ts} can be calculated analytically, but the exact formula is cumbersome. See Appendix B in Escanciano (2006) for a simple algorithm to compute I_{ts}. We denote the resulting test statistic as CM_{5n}. Admittedly, it takes much more time to calculate CM_{5n} than $CM_{1n}, CM_{2n}, CM_{3n}, CM_{4n}$, and CM_{4bn}.

To save on computation, we will consider two sample sizes, namely $n =$ 100 and 200. For each sample size n, we use 1000 replications and 500 bootstrap resamples in each replication. To examine the sensitivity of our tests to the choice of block size L and the smoothing parameter λ_n, we set $\lambda_n = 0, 0.001$, and 0.01, and choose $L = \lceil cn^{1/4} \rfloor$ for three choices of c: 1, 2, 4. When $\lambda_n = 0$, we effectively replace the approximating function $G(-\hat{u}_{t\tau}/\lambda_n)$ by the indicator function $\mathbf{1}(\hat{u}_{t\tau} \leq 0)$. This allows us to examine whether the use of the indicator function can be justified in practice when one needs to estimate the conditional quantile function but is not sure whether the estimate belongs to the same class of smooth functions as the original quantile function.

Test results

We first focus on the finite sample performance of our tests under the null. Tables 1–4 report the empirical rejection frequencies of the CM_n tests at the 5% nominal level for DGPs 1–4, respectively, where $\rho = 0$. We summarize some important findings from Tables 1–4. First, when $\lambda_n = 0$, the sizes of our tests are highly distorted, whereas for $\lambda_n = 0.001$ or 0.01, they are reasonably well behaved. This indicates that the use of indicator function is questionable and thus we only focus on the case where $\lambda_n = 0.001$ or 0.01. Second, our tests depend on the choice of block size L (or equivalently c in the table): when $\lambda_n = 0.001$ or 0.01, the tests tend to be oversized for smaller values of block size ($c = 1, 2$) and close to the nominal levels or a little bit undersized when $c = 4$. Third, there is some level variation due to different choices of φ, but this is not large: the levels of CM_{3n} and CM_{5n} tend to be inflated more often than for the other tests. Fourth, as the sample size doubles, the levels of all tests improve.

Figs. 1–4 display the powers of our tests at the 5% level for the block size $L = \lceil cn^{1/4} \rfloor (c= 2)$ and smoothing parameter $\lambda_n= 0.01$. To compare the tests

Table 1. Finite Sample Rejection Frequency under the Null (DGP 1, Nominal Level: 0.05).

n	Tests	$\lambda_n = 0, L = \lceil cn^{1/4} \rfloor$			$\lambda_n = 0.001, L = \lceil cn^{1/4} \rfloor$			$\lambda_n = 0.01, L = \lceil cn^{1/4} \rfloor$		
		c = 1	c = 2	c = 4	c = 1	c = 2	c = 4	c = 1	c = 2	c = 4
100	CM_1	0.128	0.099	0.063	0.062	0.045	0.019	0.061	0.045	0.020
	CM_2	0.054	0.050	0.028	0.059	0.052	0.028	0.064	0.055	0.031
	CM_3	0.290	0.296	0.298	0.100	0.095	0.088	0.096	0.092	0.086
	CM_4	0.273	0.243	0.210	0.080	0.077	0.038	0.086	0.072	0.048
	CM_{4b}	0.359	0.321	0.269	0.100	0.080	0.042	0.102	0.082	0.050
	CM_5	0.589	0.539	0.455	0.102	0.076	0.044	0.097	0.082	0.045
200	CM_1	0.094	0.083	0.058	0.056	0.048	0.024	0.055	0.046	0.029
	CM_2	0.061	0.053	0.036	0.057	0.058	0.034	0.055	0.051	0.040
	CM_3	0.177	0.191	0.183	0.090	0.084	0.081	0.079	0.084	0.078
	CM_4	0.173	0.150	0.132	0.067	0.058	0.035	0.066	0.057	0.040
	CM_{4b}	0.217	0.203	0.171	0.079	0.063	0.045	0.080	0.064	0.042
	CM_5	0.326	0.315	0.253	0.091	0.076	0.060	0.085	0.076	0.050

Table 2. Finite Sample Rejection Frequency under the Null (DGP 2, Nominal Level: 0.05).

n	Tests	$\lambda_n = 0, L = \lceil cn^{1/4} \rfloor$			$\lambda_n = 0.001, L = \lceil cn^{1/4} \rfloor$			$\lambda_n = 0.01, L = \lceil cn^{1/4} \rfloor$		
		c = 1	c = 2	c = 4	c = 1	c = 2	c = 4	c = 1	c = 2	c = 4
100	CM_1	0.145	0.119	0.065	0.071	0.050	0.017	0.066	0.045	0.018
	CM_2	0.062	0.050	0.033	0.055	0.045	0.026	0.054	0.045	0.028
	CM_3	0.285	0.282	0.299	0.064	0.067	0.060	0.062	0.063	0.064
	CM_4	0.332	0.316	0.264	0.082	0.069	0.040	0.073	0.065	0.032
	CM_{4b}	0.487	0.443	0.366	0.089	0.067	0.032	0.078	0.070	0.030
	CM_5	0.704	0.678	0.613	0.093	0.074	0.045	0.088	0.076	0.047
200	CM_1	0.109	0.089	0.071	0.059	0.056	0.033	0.059	0.059	0.034
	CM_2	0.065	0.050	0.040	0.061	0.049	0.034	0.057	0.049	0.036
	CM_3	0.223	0.224	0.232	0.066	0.065	0.058	0.068	0.064	0.063
	CM_4	0.243	0.221	0.186	0.076	0.065	0.045	0.070	0.062	0.044
	CM_{4b}	0.344	0.322	0.267	0.079	0.056	0.034	0.068	0.060	0.033
	CM_5	0.502	0.484	0.451	0.085	0.076	0.061	0.084	0.076	0.055

Table 3. Finite Sample Rejection Frequency under the Null (DGP 3, Nominal Level: 0.05).

n	Tests	$\lambda_n = 0, L = \lceil cn^{1/4} \rfloor$			$\lambda_n = 0.001, L = \lceil cn^{1/4} \rfloor$			$\lambda_n = 0.01, L = \lceil cn^{1/4} \rfloor$		
		c = 1	c = 2	c = 4	c = 1	c = 2	c = 4	c = 1	c = 2	c = 4
100	CM_1	0.156	0.125	0.068	0.061	0.046	0.016	0.063	0.044	0.019
	CM_2	0.075	0.066	0.038	0.067	0.060	0.034	0.071	0.057	0.031
	CM_3	0.457	0.469	0.466	0.094	0.081	0.078	0.092	0.081	0.080
	CM_4	0.288	0.270	0.228	0.062	0.047	0.024	0.063	0.049	0.019
	CM_{4b}	0.277	0.261	0.224	0.055	0.045	0.018	0.060	0.048	0.021
	CM_5	0.817	0.795	0.721	0.103	0.085	0.054	0.096	0.080	0.050
200	CM_1	0.089	0.084	0.064	0.052	0.048	0.028	0.053	0.047	0.031
	CM_2	0.053	0.049	0.037	0.050	0.054	0.031	0.045	0.048	0.035
	CM_3	0.332	0.338	0.350	0.070	0.072	0.062	0.079	0.072	0.065
	CM_4	0.212	0.199	0.170	0.062	0.052	0.035	0.058	0.053	0.040
	CM_{4b}	0.211	0.200	0.171	0.059	0.050	0.036	0.057	0.047	0.038
	CM_5	0.623	0.598	0.545	0.071	0.072	0.049	0.067	0.068	0.044

Table 4. Finite Sample Rejection Frequency under the Null (DGP 4, Nominal Level: 0.05).

n	Tests	$\lambda_n = 0, L = \lceil cn^{1/4} \rfloor$			$\lambda_n = 0.001, L = \lceil cn^{1/4} \rfloor$			$\lambda_n = 0.01, L = \lceil cn^{1/4} \rfloor$		
		c = 1	c = 2	c = 4	c = 1	c = 2	c = 4	c = 1	c = 2	c = 4
100	CM_1	0.162	0.122	0.054	0.081	0.050	0.012	0.079	0.053	0.013
	CM_2	0.067	0.044	0.028	0.054	0.039	0.019	0.054	0.038	0.022
	CM_3	0.274	0.273	0.295	0.082	0.076	0.056	0.078	0.074	0.054
	CM_4	0.241	0.217	0.190	0.064	0.050	0.029	0.068	0.052	0.027
	CM_{4b}	0.258	0.243	0.207	0.062	0.056	0.026	0.062	0.051	0.028
	CM_5	0.784	0.755	0.682	0.090	0.078	0.030	0.093	0.072	0.038
200	CM_1	0.217	0.180	0.096	0.088	0.069	0.057	0.082	0.700	0.050
	CM_2	0.052	0.049	0.030	0.046	0.044	0.033	0.049	0.045	0.034
	CM_3	0.249	0.250	0.249	0.084	0.071	0.063	0.078	0.076	0.064
	CM_4	0.226	0.216	0.192	0.074	0.058	0.040	0.076	0.060	0.041
	CM_{4b}	0.218	0.214	0.190	0.073	0.058	0.042	0.072	0.056	0.036
	CM_5	0.622	0.594	0.550	0.081	0.070	0.057	0.084	0.073	0.055

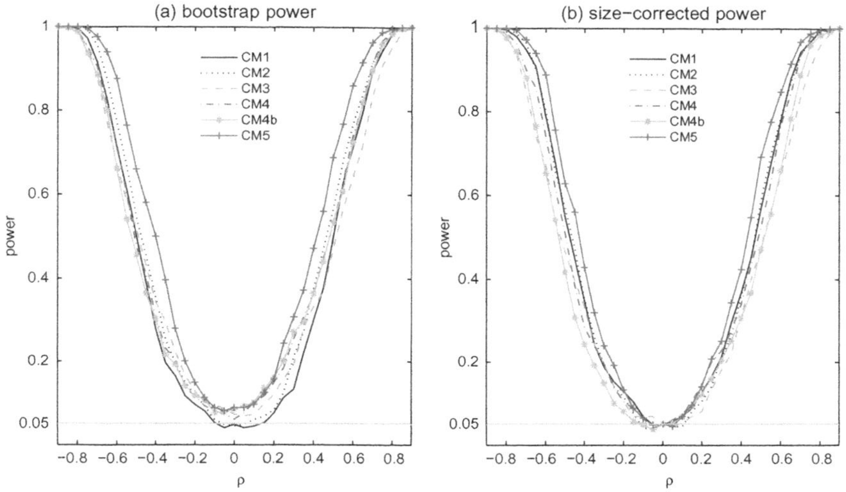

Fig. 1. Power Function for DGP 1 ($n = 100$, $\lambda_n = 0.01$, Nominal Level: 0.05).

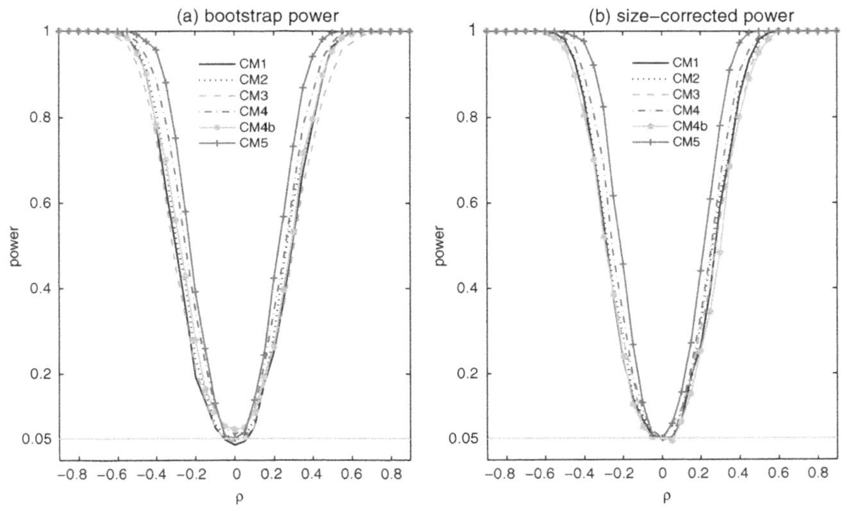

Fig. 2. Power Function for DGP 2 ($n = 100$, $\lambda_n = 0.01$, Nominal Level: 0.05).

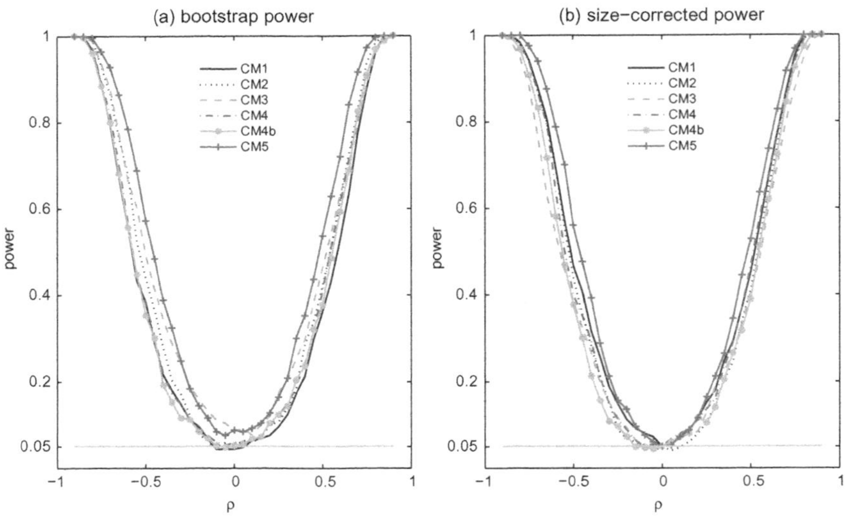

Fig. 3. Power Function for DGP 3 ($n = 100$, $\lambda_n = 0.01$, Nominal Level: 0.05).

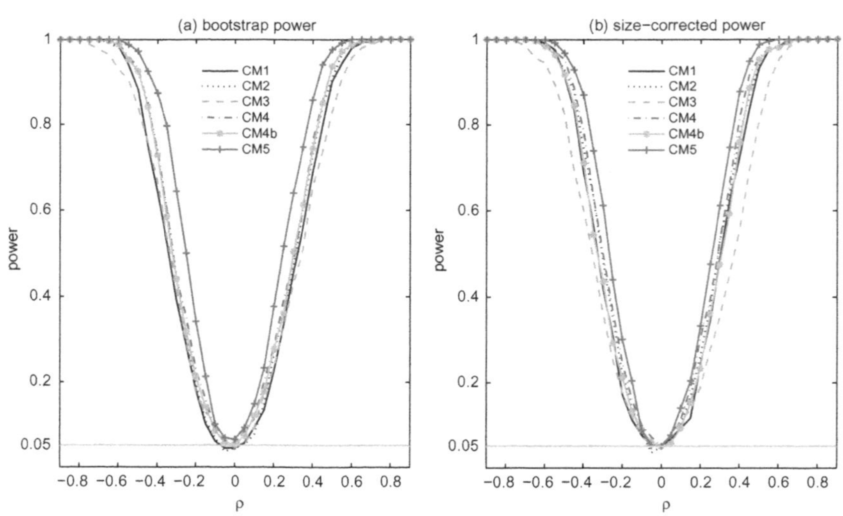

Fig. 4. Power Function for DGP 4 ($n = 100$, $\lambda_n = 0.01$, Nominal Level: 0.05).

on an equal basis, we consider not only the power of bootstrap-based tests but also the size-corrected power obtained by using critical values simulated from 250 replications under the null hypothesis of conditional independence ($\rho = 0$) for the four DGPs introduced above. In either case, we use 250 replications for each value of $\rho \in [-0.9, 0.9]$; the bootstrap tests are based on 500 bootstrap resamples in each replication. We summarize some of the main findings: (a) As the degree of conditional dependence ($|\rho|$) increases, the powers of all tests increase. (b) With or without size correction, the CM_{5n} test dominates the other tests in terms of power for all DGPs examined here. (c) The CM_{4bn} and CM_{3n} tests tend to be dominated by other tests in terms of size-corrected power. (d) The performance of the other tests tends to be DGP-dependent. Overall, CM_{5n} with $L = \lceil 2n^{1/4} \rfloor (c = 2)$ provide reliable level and power performance.

Application to the Returns to Schooling

In this subsection we apply our test to test for one key identifying assumption in the study of marginal returns to schooling. Specifically, we consider the following nonparametric nonseparable structural model:

$$\ln(Ahe_i) = g(S_i, Exp_i, Race_i, Male_i, U_i) \tag{8}$$

where the subscript i stands for individuals, *Ahe* denotes average hourly earnings, S denotes years of schooling, *Exp* denotes working experience, *Race* is a categorical variable which takes three values (0, 1, and 2 for black, Hispanic and white, respectively), *Male* is a dummy variable, and U is an unobservable error term. As the error term contains the unobserved inherent *ability*, it is typically correlated with the variable S. To identify the marginal effect of schooling on average hourly earnings, two key assumptions have been made in the literature: (i) the left-hand-side variable $\ln(Ahe_i)$ is a monotonic function of U_i for any potential values of the observables on the right-hand-side of Eq. (8), and (ii) there exists an instrumental variable (IV) Q_i such that

$$U_i \perp S_i | (Q_i, Exp_i, Race_i, Male_i). \tag{9}$$

Hoderlein and Mammen (2007, 2009) study identification and estimation of the average marginal effects without the first assumption but maintaining the second one. Here we want to test whether Eq. (9) holds.

The difficulty is that U_i is not observable and it seems impossible to test the identifying hypothesis in Eq. (9) directly even if we know the proper choice of Q_i. Over the years applied researchers frequently tackle the unobserved ability problem by finding proxies, for example, IQ or AFQT scores, and including them as regressors. For example, Neal and Johnson (1996) use the 1980 AFQT score as a proxy for ability. Hoderlein et al. (2012) argue that such a proxy can serve as the proper IV Q_i in Eq. (9). This means that whatever is not exactly accounted for in U_i by using AFQT and the other control variables in the regression is independent of schooling. Below we choose Q_i as the 1980 AFQT score. Following White and Chalak (2010) and Huang and White (2010), if we could find another proxy for ability, say TS, such that

$$\begin{aligned} TS_i &= h(Exp_i, Race_i, Male_i, AFQT_i, U_i, V_i) \\ V_i &\perp S_i | (Exp_i, Race_i, Male_i, AFQT_i, U_i), \end{aligned} \tag{10}$$

then Eq. (9) implies that

$$TS_i \perp S_i | (AFQT_i, Exp_i, Race_i, Male_i). \tag{11}$$

Here h denotes some unknown function and V_i is an error term in the equation for TS_i. Note that all variables in Eq. (11) are observable and one can test it by using our test statistics and treating $(AFQT_i, Exp_i, Race_i, Male_i)$, S_i, and TS_i as our X, Y, and Z, respectively.

A side problem occurs when one realizes that $Race_i$ and $Male_i$ are discrete variables whereas our previous theory requires that all variables in X be continuous. Nevertheless, easy modification can be done. Write $X_i = (X_i^c, X_i^d)^T$ where X_i^c and X_i^d are d_c- and d_d-vector of continuous and discrete variables, respectively. We can estimate $m(\tau, (x^c, x^d))$ by the minimizing intercept term in the following minimization problem:

$$\begin{aligned} \min_{\boldsymbol{\beta}} Q_n(\tau, (x^c, x^d); \boldsymbol{\beta}) \equiv n^{-1} \sum_{i=1}^{n} \rho_\tau \left(Y_t - \sum_{0 \le |j| \le p} \beta_j ((X_t^c - x)/h)^j \right) \\ \times K((x - X_i^c)/h) \mathbf{1}(X_i^d = x^d). \end{aligned} \tag{12}$$

Then the asymptotic theory for our test goes through with obvious modification.

We now follow Huang and White (2010) and apply our test to test the implied hypothesis in Eq. (11). We use the same dataset as Huang and White

Table 5. Summary Statistics for the Returns to Schooling.

Variables	Min	Mean	Median	Max	St. Dev.	Number of obs
	Full sample					
Hourly wage in 2010 ($)	1	16.108	13	653.84	15.109	6147
Schooling beyond high school (yrs)	0	1.734	1	8	1.726	5875
Working experience in 2010 (yrs)	0.058	15.256	16.404	23.058	5.199	6147
Male	0	0.505	1	1	0.500	6147
White	0	0.482	0	1	0.500	6147
Hispanic	0	0.191	0	1	0.393	6147
Black	0	0.306	0	1	0.461	6147
AFQT1980	−1.601	0.000	−0.178	2.435	1.000	5922
Math score	200	443.6	420	760	124.6	518
Verbal score	200	406.2	390	770	123.4	515
	Subsample with observations for both math and verbal scores					
Hourly wage in 2010 ($)	1.15	18.30	15	192.3	14.692	501
Schooling beyond high school (yrs)	0	1.92	1	8	1.759	501
Experience in 2010 (yrs)	0.94	15.97	16.96	22.87	4.94	501
Male	0	0.535	1	1	0.499	501
White	0	0.790	1	1	0.407	501
Hispanic	0	0.056	0	1	0.230	501
Black	0	0.130	0	1	0.336	501
AFQT1980	−1.411	0.304	0.260	2.435	1.020	501
Math score	200	462.9	460	690	102.8	501
Verbal score	200	422.8	415	610	99.4	501

(2010),[1] that is, the National Longitudinal Survey of Youth 1997 (NLSY97) with the survey year 2000. TS_i includes math score and verbal score for preliminary scholastic aptitude test (SAT) from high school transcript survey in 1981. S_i denotes the years of schooling beyond high school so that TS_i should not be affected by S_i. Table 5 provides some summary statistics for the dataset. From Table 5 we see that even though the full sample is large and contains 6,147 observations for most variables of interest, the subsample that contains both math and verbal scores is only moderate, containing only 501 observations.

Huang and White (2010) implement their test for the subsample of male whites with both math and verbal scores, which contains 148 observations. To compare with their test result, we also implement our test for the same subsample and the subsample of female whites with both math and verbal scores. The latter subsample contains 152 observations. In this case, the conditioning information set in Eq. (11) contains only $(AFQT_i, Exp_i)$. Table 6 reports the test results where λ_n takes value 0.001 or 0.010, $[\underline{\tau}, \bar{\tau}] = [0.05, 0.95]$, or [0.10, 0.90] and the choices of bandwidth and kernels are as described in the simulation study. In all cases, we cannot reject the null hypothesis in Eq. (11) at the 5% nominal level. This is consistent with the findings in Huang and White (2010). Nevertheless, one may wonder whether the failure of rejection of the null hypothesis may be due to the

Table 6. p-values of Our Tests Based on the Subsamples for Male and Female Whites.

λ_n	$[\underline{\tau}, \bar{\tau}]$	CM_1	CM_2	CM_3	CM_4	CM_{4b}	CM_5
		Subsample of male whites ($n = 148$)					
0.001	[0.05, 0.95]	0.593	0.665	0.088	0.074	0.096	0.119
0.010	[0.05, 0.95]	0.597	0.672	0.087	0.076	0.100	0.114
		Subsample of female whites ($n = 152$)					
0.001	[0.05, 0.95]	0.593	0.665	0.088	0.074	0.096	0.119
0.010	[0.05, 0.95]	0.597	0.672	0.087	0.076	0.100	0.114
		Subsample of male whites ($n = 148$)					
0.001	[0.1, 0.9]	0.966	0.771	0.334	0.091	0.132	0.336
0.010	[0.1, 0.9]	0.963	0.765	0.317	0.087	0.130	0.318
		Subsample of female whites ($n = 152$)					
0.001	[0.1, 0.9]	0.769	0.711	0.203	0.191	0.244	0.286
0.010	[0.1, 0.9]	0.776	0.716	0.201	0.192	0.248	0.285

Note: Total number of bootstrap resamples = 1000 and $L = 1$.

Table 7. p-Values of Our Tests Based on the Full Subsamples with 501 Observations on Both Math and Verbal Scores.

λ_n	$[\underline{\tau}, \tau]$	CM_1	CM_2	CM_3	CM_4	CM_{4b}	CM_5
0.001	[0.05, 0.95]	0.001	0.383	0.001	0.001	0.001	0.001
0.010	[0.05, 0.95]	0.001	0.376	0.001	0.001	0.001	0.001
0.001	[0.05, 0.95]	0.023	0.682	0.001	0.001	0.001	0.001
0.010	[0.05, 0.95]	0.021	0.664	0.001	0.001	0.001	0.001

Note: Total number of bootstrap resamples = 1,000 and $L = 1$.

small subsample sizes for both the white male and white female subsamples. For this reason, we also consider the full subsample with 501 observations for both math and verbal scores by controlling the gender and race. Table 7 reports the test results. Interestingly all tests but CM_2 suggest that we can reject the null hypothesis in Eq. (11) at the 5% nominal level. This indicates either Eq. (9) or Eq. (10) may not hold. Further studies are required in order to conclude whether the key identifying hypothesis in Eq. (9) holds or not.

CONCLUSION

We provide straightforward new nonparametric methods for testing conditional independence using local polynomial quantile regression, allowing for weakly dependent data. Inspired by Hausman (1978), our methods essentially compare two collections of estimators that converge to the same limits under correct specification (conditional independence) and that diverge under the alternative.

In addition, we generalize the existing nonparametric quantile literature not only by allowing for dependent heterogeneous data but also by establishing a weak consistency rate for the local Bahadur representation that is uniform in both the conditioning variables and the quantile index. We also show that, despite our nonparametric approach, our tests can detect local alternatives to conditional independence that decay to zero at the parametric rate. Our tests are the first for time-series conditional independence that can detect local alternatives at the parametric rate. Monte Carlo simulations suggest that our tests perform well in finite samples. Our tests have a variety of uses in applications, such as testing for failure of conditional exogeneity or for Granger noncausality.

ACKNOWLEDGMENTS

The authors sincerely thank the editors and the two anonymous referees for their many insightful comments and suggestions that lead to a substantial improvement of the chapter. The first author gratefully acknowledges the financial support from a research grant (Grant number: C244/MSS8E004) from SMU.

NOTE

1. We are grateful to Meng Huang and Xun Lu for sharing their dataset with us.

REFERENCES

Akerlof, G. (1970). The market for lemons: Quality uncertainty and the market mechanism. *Quarterly Journal of Economics*, *84*, 488–500.

Altonji, J. G., & Matzkin, R. L. (2005). Cross section and panel data estimators for nonseparable models with endogenous regressors. *Econometrica*, *73*, 1053–1102.

Andrews, D. W. K., & Pollard, D. (1994). An introduction to functional central limit theorems for dependent stochastic processes. *International Statistical Review*, *62*, 119–132.

Bahadur, R. R. (1966). A note on quantiles in large samples. *Annals of Mathematical Statistics*, *37*, 577–580.

Barnow, B., Cain, G., & Goldberger, A. (1980). Issues in the analysis of selectivity bias. In E. W. Stromsdorfer & G. Farkas (Eds.), *Evaluation Studies Review Annual* (Vol. 5, pp. 43–59). Beverly Hills, CA: Sage.

Bhattacharya, P. K., & Gangopadhyay, A. K. (1990). Kernel and nearest-neighbor estimation of a conditional quantile. *Annals of Statistics*, *18*, 1400–1415.

Bierens, H. J. (1990). A consistent conditional moment test of functional form. *Econometrica*, *58*, 1443–1458.

Bosq, D. (1996). *Nonparametric statistics for stochastic processes: Estimation and prediction*. New York, NY: Springer.

Bühlmann, P. (1994). Blockwise bootstrapped empirical process for stationary sequences. *Annals of Statistics*, *22*, 995–1012.

Chalak, K., & White, H. (2011). An extended class of instrumental variables for the estimation of causal e ects. *Canadian Journal of Economics*, *44*, 1–51.

Chaudhuri, P. (1991). Nonparametric estimates of regression quantiles and their local Bahadur representation. *Annals of Statistics*, *19*, 760–777.

Chen, X., Linton, O., & van Keilegom, I. (2003). Estimation of semiparametric models when the criterion function is not smooth. *Econometrica*, *71*, 1591–1608.

Chernozhukov, V. (2005). Extreme quantile regression. *Annals of Statistics*, *33*, 806–839.

Chiappori, P.-A., Jullien, B., Salanié, B., & Salanié, F. (2006). Asymmetric information in insurance: General testable implications. *Rand Journal of Economics*, *37*, 783–798.

Dawid, A. D. (1979). Conditional independence in statistical theory. *Journal of the Royal Statistical Society, Series B, 41*, 1–31.
Delgado, M. A., & González-Manteiga, W. (2001). Significance testing in nonparametric regression based on the bootstrap. *Annals of Statistics, 29*, 1469–1507.
Dionne, G., Gourieroux, C., & Vanasse, C. (2001). Testing for evidence of adverse selection in the automobile insurance market: A comment. *Journal of Political Economy, 109*, 444–453.
Dionne, G., Gourieroux, C., & Vanasse, C. (2006). Informational content of household decisions with applications to insurance under asymmetric information. In P. A. Chiappori & C. Gollier (Eds.), *In competitive failures in insurance markets: Theory and policy implications* (pp. 159–184). Cambridge, MA: MIT Press.
Donald, S. G., Hsu, Y.-C., Lieli, R. P. (2011). Testing the unconfoundedness assumption via inverse probability weighted estimators of (L)ATT. Working Paper, University of Texas, Austin.
Escanciano, J. C. (2006). A consistent diagnostic test for regression models using projections. *Econometric Theory, 22*, 1030–1051.
Fan, J., Hu, T.-C., & Truong, Y. K. (1994). Robust non-parametric function estimation. *Scandinavian Journal of Statistics, 21*, 433–446.
Giné, E., & Zinn, J. (1990). Bootstrapping general empirical measures. *Annals of Probability, 18*, 851–869.
Granger, C. W. J. (1969). Investigating causal relations by econometric models and cross-spectral methods. *Econometrica, 37*, 424–438.
Granger, C. W. J., & Newbold, P. (1986). *Forecasting economic time series* (2nd ed.). Orlando, FL: Academic Press.
Guerre, E., & Sabbah, C. (2012). Uniform bias study and Bahadur representation for local polynomial estimators of the conditional quantile function. *Econometric Theory, 28*, 87–129.
Hall, P., & Heyde, C. C. (1980). *Martingale limit theory and its applications*. San Diego, CA: Academic Precess.
Hansen, B. E. (2008). Uniform convergence rates for kernel estimation with dependent data. *Econo-metric Theory, 24*, 726–748.
Hausman, J. (1978). Specification tests in econometrics. *Econometrica, 78*, 1251–1271.
He, X., & Shao, Q.-M. (1996). A general Bahadur representation of M-estimators and its application to linear regression with nonstochastic design. *Annals of Statistics, 24*, 2608–2630.
Heckman, J. J., Ichimura, H., & Todd, P. (1997). Matching as an econometric evaluation estimators: Evidence from evaluating a job training programme. *Review of Economic Studies, 64*, 605–654.
Hoderlein, S., & Mammen, E. (2007). Identification of marginal effects in nonseparable models without monotonicity. *Econometrica, 75*, 1513–1518.
Hoderlein, S., & Mammen, E. (2009). Identification and estimation of local average derivatives in non-separable models without monotonicity. *Econometrics Journal, 12*, 1–25.
Hoderlein, S., Su, L., White, H. (2012). Specification testing for nonparametric structural models with monotonicity in unobservables. Working Paper, Department of Economics, UCSD.
Honda, T. (2000). Nonparametric estimation of a conditional quantile for mixing processes. *Annals of Institute of Statistical Mathematics, 52*, 459–470.

Huang, T.-M. (2010). Testing conditional independence using maximal nonlinear conditional indepen-dence. *Annals of Statistics*, *38*, 2047–2091.

Huang, M., White, H. (2010). A flexible test for conditional independence. Working Paper. Department of Economics, UCSD.

Imbens, G. W. (2004). Nonparametric estimation of average treatment effects under exogeneity: A review. *Review of Economics and Statistics*, *86*, 4–29.

Imbens, G. W., & Newey, W. K. (2009). Identification and estimation of triangular simultaneous equations models without additivity. *Econometrica*, *77*, 1481–1512.

Imbens, G. W., & Wooldridge, J. M. (2009). Recent developments in the econometrics of program evaluation. *Journal of Economic Literature*, *47*, 5–86.

Inoue, A. (2001). Testing for distributional change in time series. *Econometric Theory*, *17*, 156–187.

Jeong, K., Härdle, W. K. (2008). A consistent nonparametric test for causality in quantile. Working Paper. Center for Applied Statistics and Economics, Humboldt-Universität zu Berlin.

Koenker, R., & Bassett, G. (1978). Regression quantiles. *Econometrica*, *46*, 33–50.

Koenker, R., & Zhao, Q. (1996). Conditional quantile estimation and inference for ARCH models. *Econometric Theory*, *12*, 793–813.

Kong, E., Linton, O., & Xia, Y. (2010). Uniform Bahadur representation for local polynomial estimates of M-regression and its application to the additive model. *Econometric Theory*, *26*, 1529–1564.

Lee, S. (2003). Efficient semiparametric estimation of partially linear quantile regression model. *Econometric Theory*, *19*, 1–31.

Linton, O., Gozalo, P. (1997). Conditional independence restrictions: Testing and estimation. Discussion Paper. Cowles Foundation for Research in Economics, Yale University.

Lu, X., White, H. (2011). Testing for separability in structural equations. Discussion Paper. Departmet of Economics, UCSD.

Lu, Z., Hui, Y. V., & Zhao, Q. (2001). *Local linear quantile regression under dependence: Bahadur representation and applications*. City University of Hong Kong: Mimeo.

Martins-Filho, C., Yao, F., Torero, M. (2012) High order conditional quantile estimation based on nonparametric models of regression. Working Paper, University of Colorado, Boulder.

Masry, E. (1996). Multivariate local polynomial regression for time series: Uniform strong consistency rates. *Journal of Time Series Analysis*, *17*, 571–599.

Matzkin, R. L. (2003). Nonparametric estimation of nonadditive random functions. *Econometrica*, *71*, 1339–1375.

Neal, D., & Johnson, W. (1996). The role of premarket factors in black-white wage di erences. *Journal of Political Economy*, *104*, 869–895.

Pollard, D. (1990). Empirical processes: Theory and applications (Vol. 2). NSF-CBMS Regional Conference Series in Probability and Statistics. Institute of Mathematical Statistics, Hayward, California.

Robinson, P. M. (1991). Consistent nonparametric entropy-based testing. *Review of Economic Studies*, *58*, 437–453.

Ruppert, D., & Carroll, R. J. (1980). Trimmed least squares estimation in the linear model. *Journal of the American Statistical Association*, *75*, 828–838.

Shen, J., & Huang, Y.-M. (1998). Nonparametric estimation in a model with a trend. *Statistical Inference for Stochastic Processes*, *1*, 43–60.

Song, K. (2009). Testing conditional independence via Rosenblatt transform. *Annals of Statistics*, *37*, 4011–4045.

Stinchcombe, M. B., & White, H. (1998). Consistent specification testing with nuisance parameters present only under the alternative. *Econometric Theory*, *14*, 295–325.

Su, L., Spindler, M. (2012). Nonparametric testing for asymmetric information. Working Paper. Singapore Management University.

Su, L., Tu, Y., Ullah, A. (2012). Testing additive separability of error term in nonparametric structural models. Working Paper. Singapore Management University.

Su, L., & White, H. (2007). A consistent characteristic-function-based test for conditional independence. *Journal of Econometrics*, *141*, 807–834.

Su, L., & White, H. (2008). A nonparametric Hellinger metric test for conditional independence. *Econometric Theory*, *24*, 829–864.

Su, L., & White, H. (2012). Testing conditional independence via empirical likelihood. Working Paper. Department of Economics, UCSD.

Sun, S., & Chiang, C.-Y. (1997). Limiting behavior of the perturbed empirical distribution functions evaluated at U-statistics for strongly mixing sequences of random variables. *Journal of Applied Mathematics and Stochastic Analysis*, *10*, 3–20.

Van der Vaart, A., & Wellner, J. A. (1996). *Weak convergence and empirical processes: With applications to statistics*. New York, NY: Springer.

Welsh, A. H. (1996). Robust estimation of smooth regression and spread functions and their derivatives. *Statistica Sinica*, *6*, 347–366.

White, H. (1992). Nonparametric estimation of conditional quantiles using neural networks. In Proceedings of the Symposium on the Interface, Springer-Verlag, New York, NY (pp. 190–199).

White, H. (1994). *Estimation, inference and specification analysis*. New York, NY: Cambridge University Press.

White, H., & Chalak, K. (2010). Testing a conditional form of exogeneity. *Economic Letters*, *109*, 88–90.

White, H. & Chalak, K. (2013). Identification and identification failure for treatment effects using structural systems. *Econometric Reviews*, *32*, 273–317.

White, H., & Lu, X. (2010). Granger causality and dynamic structural systems. *Journal of Financial Econometrics*, *8*, 193–243.

White, H., & Lu, X. (2011). Causal diagrams for treatment effect estimation with application to efficient covariate selection. *Review of Economics and Statistics*, *93*, 1453–1459.

Yu, K., & Jones, M. C. (1998). Local linear quantile regression. *Journal of American Statistical Association*, *93*, 228–237.

Zheng, J. X. (1998). A consistent nonparametric test of parametric regression models under conditional quantile restrictions. *Econometric Theory*, *14*, 123–138.

APPENDIX A: PROOF OF THE MAIN RESULTS

Let $\mu_{ix} \equiv \mu(X_i - x)/h$ and $K_{ix} \equiv K\big((x - X_i)/h\big)$. Let E_i denote expectation conditional on X_i. We use C to signify a generic constant whose exact value may vary from case to case and a^T to denote the transpose of a unless otherwise stated. We write $A_n \simeq B_n$ to signify that $A_n = B_n[1 + o_P(1)]$ as $n \to \infty$.

First we state a lemma that is used in the proof of Theorem 1.

Lemma A.1. Let $\mathscr{V}_n(\tau, x; \Delta)$ be a vector function that satisfies (i) $-\Delta^T \mathscr{V}_n(\tau, x; \lambda\Delta) \geq -\Delta^T \mathscr{V}_n(\tau, x; \Delta)$ for all $\lambda \geq 1$ and $(\tau, x) \in \mathscr{T} \times \mathscr{X}$, (ii) $\sup_{(\tau,x)\in\mathscr{T}\times\mathscr{X}} \sup_{\|\Delta\|\leq M} \|\mathscr{V}_n(\tau, x; \Delta) + \mathscr{H}_n(\tau, x)\Delta - \mathscr{A}_n(\tau, x)\| = o_{\mathscr{P}}(\kappa_n)$, where Δ may depend on (τ, x), $0 < M < \infty$, $\inf_{(\tau,x)\in\mathscr{T}\times\mathscr{X}} \lambda_{\min}(\mathscr{H}_n(\tau, x)) > 0$ a.s. as $n \to \infty$, and $\|\mathscr{A}_n(\tau, x)\| = O_P(1) \forall (\tau, x) \in \mathscr{T} \times \mathscr{X}$. Suppose that $\Delta_{n\tau x}$ satisfies $\sup_{(\tau,x)\in\mathscr{T}\times\mathscr{X}} \|\mathscr{V}_n(\tau, x; \Delta_{n\tau x})\| = o_P(\kappa_n)$. Then

(a) $\sup_{(\tau,x)\in\mathscr{T}\times\mathscr{X}} \|\Delta_{n\tau x}\| = O_P(1)$;
(b) $\Delta_{n\tau x} = \mathscr{H}_n(\tau, x)^{-1} \mathscr{A}_n(\tau, x) + o_P(\kappa_n)$ uniformly in $(\tau, x) \in \mathscr{T} \times \mathscr{X}$.

This extends the pointwise result of Koenker and Zhao (1996, p. 809) to a uniform result.

To prove Theorem 1, we need some additional notation. Let $\boldsymbol{\beta}_{0\tau x} = \boldsymbol{\beta}(\tau, x; h)$ denote the vector that contains the true value of $m(\tau, x)$ and its scaled partial derivatives with respect to x. Let $\boldsymbol{\beta}_{\tau x}$ denote the stack of the quantile regression coefficients $\boldsymbol{\beta}_j, 0 \leq |j| \leq p$, in the lexicographical order (see Eq. (3)), where the dependence of $\boldsymbol{\beta}_j$ on (τ, x) is made explicitly, but we suppress the dependence of both $\boldsymbol{\beta}_{0\tau x}$ and $\boldsymbol{\beta}_{\tau x}$ on h. Define

$$a_n \equiv \sqrt{nh^d}, \hat{\Delta}_{\tau x} \equiv a_n(\hat{\beta}(\tau, x; h) - \beta_{0\tau x}), \text{ and } \Delta_{\tau x} \equiv a_n(\beta(\tau, x; h) - \beta_{0\tau x})$$

It follows that

$$\hat{\Delta}_{\tau x} = \arg \min_{\Delta_{\tau x}\in\mathbb{R}^N} \sum_{i=1}^{n} \rho_\tau(Y_i - (\boldsymbol{\beta}_{0\tau x} + a_n^{-1}\Delta_{\tau x})^T \mu_{ix}) K_{ix} \tag{A.1}$$

Let $V_n(\tau, x; \Delta) \equiv a_n^{-1} \sum_{i=1}^n \psi_\tau(Y_i - (\boldsymbol{\beta}_{0\tau x} + a_n^{-1}\Delta)^T \mu_{ix}) \mu_{ix} K_{ix}$, and $\bar{V}_n(\tau, x; \Delta) \equiv a_n^{-1} \sum_{i=1}^n E_i[\psi_\tau((Y_i - (\boldsymbol{\beta}_{0\tau x} + a_n^{-1}\Delta)^T \mu_{ix})] \mu_{ix} K_{ix}$. The following lemmas constitute the main steps in the proof of Theorem 1.

Lemma A.2. Suppose Assumptions 1–6 hold. Then $\| V_n(\tau, x; 0)\| = O_P(1)$ for each $(\tau, x) \in \mathscr{T} \times \mathscr{X}$.

Lemma A.3. Suppose Assumptions 1–6 hold. Then

$$\sup_{\tau\in\mathscr{T}}\sup_{x\in\mathscr{X}}\sup_{\|\Delta\|\leq M}\| V_n(\tau, x; \Delta) - V_n(\tau, x; 0) - [\bar{V}_n(\tau, x; \Delta) - \bar{V}_n(\tau, x; 0)]\| = o_P(\kappa_n).$$

Lemma A.4. Suppose Assumptions 1–6 hold. Then

$$\sup_{\tau\in\mathscr{T}}\sup_{x\in\mathscr{X}}\sup_{\|\Delta\|\leq M}\| \bar{V}_n(\tau, x; \Delta) - \bar{V}_n(\tau, x; 0) + H_n(\tau, x)\Delta\| = o_P(\kappa_n).$$

Lemma A.5. Suppose Assumptions 1–6 hold. Then $\sup_{\tau\in\mathscr{T}}\sup_{x\in\mathscr{X}}\times ||V_n(\tau, x; \hat{\Delta}_{\tau x})|| = o_P(\kappa_n)$.

Proof of Theorem 1. We prove the theorem by checking that the conditions of Lemma A.1 hold with $\mathscr{A}_n(\tau, x) = V_n(\tau, x; 0)$, $\mathscr{V}_n(\tau, x; \Delta) = V_n(\tau, x; \Delta)$, $\mathscr{H}_n(\tau, x) = H_n(\tau, x)$, and $\Delta_{n\tau x} = \hat{\Delta}_{\tau x}$. By Assumption 4, $\mathscr{H}_n(\tau, x)$ is positive definite a.s. as $n \to \infty$ for each $(\tau, x) \in (\mathscr{T}, \mathscr{X})$. By Lemma A.2, $||\mathscr{A}_n(\tau, x)|| = O_P(1)\forall(\tau, x) \in \mathscr{T} \times \mathscr{X}$. By Lemma A.5, $\sup_{\tau\in\mathscr{T}}\sup_{x\in\mathscr{X}}||\mathscr{V}_n(\tau, x, \hat{\Delta}_{\tau x})|| = o_P(\kappa_n)$. By Lemmas A.3 and A.4,

$$\sup_{\tau\in\mathscr{T}}\ \sup_{x\in\mathscr{X}}\ \sup_{\|\Delta\|\leq M}\left|V_n(\tau, x; \Delta) - V_n(\tau, x; 0) + H_n(\tau, x)\Delta\right| = o_P(\kappa_n),$$

so that condition (ii) in Lemma A.1 is satisfied. Noting that $\psi_\tau(y)$ is a nondecreasing function of y, the function

$$-\Delta^T V_n(\tau, x; \lambda\Delta) = a_n^{-1}\sum_{i=1}^{n}\psi_\tau(Y_{ni} - \boldsymbol{\beta}_{0\tau x}^T\mu_{ix} - \lambda a_n^{-1}\Delta^T\mu_{ix})(-\Delta^T\mu_{ix})K_{ix}$$

is also nondecreasing in λ. This implies that condition (i) in Lemma A.1 holds. Consequently, we have $\sqrt{nh^d}(\hat{\boldsymbol{\beta}}(\tau, x) - \boldsymbol{\beta}_{0\tau x}) = H_n(\tau, x)^{-1}V_n(\tau, x; 0) + o_P(\kappa_n)$ uniformly in $(\tau, x) \in \mathscr{T} \times \mathscr{X}$. ∎

Proof of Corollary 1. We prove the corollary by showing (i) $\sup_{(\tau,x)\in\mathscr{T}\times\mathscr{X}}\times \|H_n(\tau, x) - H(\tau, x)\| = O_P(n^{-1/2}h^{-d/2}\sqrt{\log n} + h^{\gamma_0}) = o_P(1)$ and (ii) $J_n(\tau, x) = \bar{J}_n(\tau, x) + o_P(h^{d/2})$. Then $\sqrt{nh^d}(\hat{m}(\tau, x) - m(\tau, x)) = e_1^T H(\tau, x)^{-1}\bar{J}_n(\tau, x)[1 + o_P(1)] + o_P(h^{d/2})$. The proof of (i) is similar to but simpler than that of Corollary 2 in Masry (1996) because we only need convergence in probability, whereas Masry proved almost sure convergence. For (ii), let

$$R_n(\tau, x) = \frac{1}{\sqrt{nh^d}}\sum_{t=1}^{n}\{1(Y_t \leq m(\tau, X_t)) - 1(Y_t \leq \boldsymbol{\beta}_0(\tau, x; h)^T\mu_{ix})\}\mu_{ix}K_{ix}.$$

Then $J_n(\tau,x) = \bar{J}_n(\tau,x) + R_n(\tau,x)$. We can write $R_n(\tau,x)$ as $\{R_n(\tau,x) - E[R_n(\tau,x)]\} + E[R_n(\tau,x)]$. The last term is $O(\sqrt{nh^d}h^{p+1})$ uniformly in (τ,x). Following the proof for W_{n1} in Lemma A.3, we can show the first term is $o_P(h^{d/2})$. Then $J_n(\tau,x) = \bar{J}_n(\tau,x) + o_P(h^{d/2})$ because $O(\sqrt{nh^d}h^{p+1}) = o_P(h^{d/2})$ by assumption. ■

Proof of Lemma A.1. To save space, let $\mathscr{A}_{n\tau x} \equiv \mathscr{A}_n(\tau,x)$ and $\sup_{\tau,x} \equiv \sup_{(\tau,x)\in\mathscr{T}\times\mathscr{X}}$. Fix $\varepsilon > 0$, $\sigma > 0$.

$$
\begin{aligned}
&P\left(\sup_{\tau,x}\inf_{\|\Delta\|=M}[-\Delta^T\mathscr{V}_n(\tau,x;\Delta)] < \sigma M\right)\\
&\leq P\Bigg(\sup_{\tau,x}\inf_{\|\Delta\|=M} -\Delta^T\mathscr{V}_n(\tau,x;\Delta) < \sigma M, \sup_{\tau,x}\inf_{\|\Delta\|=M}\\
&\quad -\Delta^T[-\mathscr{H}_n(\tau,x)\Delta + \mathscr{A}_{n\tau x}] \geq 2\sigma M\Bigg)\\
&\quad + P\left(\sup_{\tau,x}\inf_{\|\Delta\|=M} -\Delta^T[\mathscr{A}_{n\tau x} - \mathscr{H}_n(\tau,x)\Delta] < 2\sigma M\right)\\
&\equiv A_{1n} + A_{2n}, \text{say.}
\end{aligned}
\tag{A.2}
$$

Noting that $\sup_{\tau,x}\inf_{\|\Delta\|=M} - \Delta^T\mathscr{V}_n(\tau,x;\Delta) < \sigma M$ and $\sup_{\tau,x}\inf_{\|\Delta\|} = M - \Delta^T[-\mathscr{H}_n(\tau,x)\Delta + \mathscr{A}_{n\tau x}] \geq 2\sigma M$ implies that

$$
\begin{aligned}
&\sup_{\tau,x}\left[\sup_{\|\Delta\|=M}\{-\Delta^T[-\mathscr{H}_n(\tau,x)\Delta + \mathscr{A}_{n\tau x}] - (-\Delta^T\mathscr{V}_n(\tau,x;\Delta))\}\right]\\
&= \sup_{\tau,x}\sup_{\|\Delta\|=M}(-\Delta^T[-\mathscr{H}_n(\tau,x)\Delta + \mathscr{A}_{n\tau x}]) - \inf_{\tau,x}\inf_{\|\Delta\|=M}(-\Delta^T\mathscr{V}_n(\tau,x;\Delta))\\
&\geq 2\sigma M - \sigma M = \sigma M,
\end{aligned}
$$

we have

$$
\begin{aligned}
A_{1n} &\leq P\left(\sup_{\tau,x}\sup_{\|\Delta\|=M}\Delta^T[\mathscr{V}_n(\tau,x;\Delta) + \mathscr{H}_n(\tau,x)\Delta - \mathscr{A}_{n\tau x}] \geq \sigma M\right)\\
&\leq P\left(\sup_{\tau,x}\sup_{\|\Delta\|=M}\|\mathscr{V}_n(\tau,x;\Delta) + \mathscr{H}_n(\tau,x)\Delta - \mathscr{A}_{n\tau x}\| \geq \sigma\right)
\end{aligned}
\tag{A.3}
$$

where the last line follows from the fact $\|\Delta^T B\| \leq \|\Delta\|\|B\|$. For A_{2n}, noting that

$$
\begin{aligned}
&-\Delta^T[\mathscr{A}_{n\tau x}-\mathscr{H}_n(\tau,x)\Delta] \\
&=-\Delta^T\mathscr{A}_{n\tau x}+\Delta^T\mathscr{H}_n(\tau,x)\Delta\geq-||\Delta||\;||\mathscr{A}_{n\tau x}||\;+c_1\;||\Delta||^2\,\forall\,(\tau,x)\in\mathscr{T}\times\mathscr{X},
\end{aligned}
$$

where $c_1\equiv\inf_{(\tau,x)\in\mathscr{T}\times\mathscr{X}}\lambda_{\min}(\mathscr{H}_n(\tau,x))>0$ a.s. As $n\to\infty$, we have

$$
\sup_{\tau,x}\inf_{\|\Delta\|=M}\{-\Delta^T[\mathscr{A}_{n\tau x}-\mathscr{H}_n(\tau,x)\Delta]\}\geq-M\|\mathscr{A}_{n\tau x}\|+c_1M^2.
$$

It follows that

$$
\begin{aligned}
A_{2n}&=P\left(\sup_{\tau,x}\inf_{\|\Delta\|=M}\{-\Delta^T[\mathscr{A}_{n\tau x}-\mathscr{H}_n(\tau,x)\Delta]\}<2\sigma M\right) \\
&\leq P(-\|\mathscr{A}_{n\tau x}\|+c_1M<2\sigma)=P(\|\mathscr{A}_{n\tau x}\|>c_1M-2\sigma).
\end{aligned}
\tag{A.4}
$$

This, together with Eqs. (A.2) and (A.3), implies that

$$
\begin{aligned}
&P\left(\sup_{\tau,x}\inf_{\|\Delta\|=M}[-\Delta^T\mathscr{V}_n(\tau,x;\Delta)]<\sigma M\right) \\
&\qquad\leq P\left(\sup_{\tau,x}\sup_{\|\Delta\|=M}\|\mathscr{V}_n(\tau,x;\Delta)+\mathscr{H}_n(\tau,x)\Delta-\mathscr{A}_{n\tau x}\|\geq\sigma\right) \\
&\qquad+P(\|\mathscr{A}_{n\tau x}\|\geq c_1M-2\sigma).
\end{aligned}
$$

Given condition (ii) and the fact that $\|\mathscr{A}_{n\tau x}\|=O_P(1)$, one can choose $M>0$ and $n_0>0$ such that for $n\geq n_0$,

$$
P\left(\sup_{\tau,x}\inf_{\|\Delta\|=M}[-\Delta^T\mathscr{V}_n(\tau,x;\Delta)]<\sigma M\right)<\varepsilon.
\tag{A.5}
$$

Next, consider the case $\|\Delta\|\geq M$. Let $\lambda^*\equiv\|\Delta\|/M$ and $\Delta^*\equiv\Delta/\lambda^*$. Then $||\Delta^*||=M$. By condition (i), we have

$$
-\Delta^{*T}\mathscr{V}_n(\tau,x;\Delta)=-\Delta^{*T}\mathscr{V}_n(\tau,x;\lambda^*\Delta^*)\geq-\Delta^{*T}\mathscr{V}_n(\tau,x;\Delta^*).
$$

It follows that $\|\mathscr{V}_n(\tau,x;\Delta)\|\geq-\Delta^{*T}\mathscr{V}_n(\tau,x;\Delta^*)/M$. This, together with (A.5), implies

$$
P\left(\sup_{\tau,x}\inf_{\|\Delta\|\geq M}\|\mathscr{V}_n(\tau,x;\Delta)\|<\sigma\right)\leq P\left(\sup_{\tau,x}\inf_{\|\Delta^*\|=M}-\Delta^{*T}\mathscr{V}_n(\tau,x;\Delta^*)<\sigma M\right)<\varepsilon.
$$

Noting that $\sup_{\tau,x}\|\mathscr{V}_n(\tau,x;\Delta_{n\tau x})\|=o_P(\kappa_n)$, we have $P(\kappa_n^{-1}\sup_{\tau,x}\times\|\mathscr{V}_n(\tau,x;\Delta_{n\tau x})\|\geq\sigma)\leq\varepsilon$ for large enough n, say $n\geq n_1$. It follows that when $n\geq n_0\vee n_1$, we have

$$P\left(\sup_{\tau,x}\|\Delta_{n\tau x}\|\geq M\right)\leq P\left(\sup_{\tau,x}\|\Delta_{n\tau x}\|\geq M,\kappa_n^{-1}\sup_{\tau,x}\|\mathscr{V}_n(\tau,x;\Delta_{n\tau x})\|<\sigma\right)$$
$$+P\left(\kappa_n^{-1}\sup_{\tau,x}\|\mathscr{V}_n(\tau,x;\Delta_{n\tau x})\|\geq\sigma\right)$$
$$\leq P\left(\kappa_n^{-1}\sup_{\tau,x}\inf_{\|\Delta\|\geq M}\|\mathscr{V}_n(\tau,x;\Delta)\|<\sigma\right)+\varepsilon\leq 2\varepsilon.$$

That is, $\sup_{\tau,x}\|\Delta_{n\tau x}\|=O_P(1)$. Then by condition (ii), we have

$$\mathscr{V}_n(\tau,x;\Delta_{n\tau x})+\mathscr{H}_n(\tau,x)\Delta_{n\tau x}-\mathscr{A}_n(\tau,x)=o_P(\kappa_n)\text{ uniformly in }(\tau,x)\in\mathscr{T}\times\mathscr{X}.$$

It follows that $\mathscr{H}_n(\tau,x)\Delta_{n\tau x}=\mathscr{A}_n(\tau,x)+o_P(\kappa_n)$ uniformly in (τ,x) as $\sup_{(\tau,x)\in\mathscr{T}\times\mathscr{X}}\|\mathscr{V}_n(\tau,x;\Delta_{n\tau x})\|=o_P(\kappa_n)$. The result then follows. ■

Proof of Lemma A.2. Let $\mathbb{V}(\tau,x)\equiv-[V_n(\tau,x;0)-\bar{V}_n(\tau,x;0)]$. Then by the Minkowski inequality, $\|V_n(\tau,x;0)\|\leq\|\mathbb{V}(\tau,x)\|+\|\bar{V}_n(\tau,x;0)\|\equiv V_{1n}+V_{2n}$, where we suppress the dependence of V_{1n} and V_{2n} on (τ,x). Let $R_i(\tau,x)\equiv m(\tau,X_i)-\boldsymbol{\beta}_{0\tau x}^T\mu_{ix}$. Then

$$R_i(\tau,x)=(p+1)\sum_{|k|=p+1}\frac{1}{k!}(X_i-x)^k\int_0^1 D^k m(\tau,x+s(X_i-x))(1-s)^p\,ds. \tag{A.6}$$

Following Masry (1996), we can show that $R_i(\tau,x)=O_P(h^{p+1})$ uniformly in (τ,x) on the set $\{i:\|X_i-x\|\leq Ch\}$. By the mean value expansion, Assumptions 2(ii), 3(i), 5, and 6 we have

$$\begin{aligned}V_{2n}&=\|a_n^{-1}\sum_{i=1}^n[F_i(m_i(\tau,X_i)|X_i)-F_i(\boldsymbol{\beta}_{0\tau x}^T\mu_{ix}|X_i)]\mu_{ix}K_{ix}\|\\&\leq Ca_n^{-1}\sum_{i=1}^n\|[n^{-1/2}c(\tau,X_i,i/n)+R_i(\tau,x)]\mu_{ix}K_{ix}\|\\&\leq Ca_n^{-1}(n^{-1/2}+h^{p+1})\sum_{i=1}^n\|\mu_{ix}K_{ix}\|\\&=O_P(h^{d/2}+n^{1/2}h^{d/2+p+1})=O_P(1).\end{aligned}$$

Now let $\xi_{ik}=[1(Y_i\leq\boldsymbol{\beta}_{0\tau x}^T\mu_{ix})-F_i(\boldsymbol{\beta}_{0\tau x}^T\mu_{ix}|X_i)]\mu_{ix,k}K_{ix}$, where $\mu_{ix,k}$ denotes the kth element of the N-vector μ_{ix}, $k=1,2,\ldots,N$. Let $\mathbb{V}_k(\tau,x)$ denote the kth element of the N-vector $\mathbb{V}(\tau,x)$. Then $E_i[\xi_{ik}]=0,\mathbb{V}_k(\tau,x)=a_n^{-1}\sum_{i=1}^n\xi_{ik}$, and $E[\mathbb{V}_k(\tau, x)] = 0$. By Assumption 1 and the Davydov inequality (e.g., Bosq, 1996, p. 19), we have

$$\begin{aligned}\mathrm{Var}(\mathbb{V}_k(\tau, x)) &= a_n^{-2}\sum_{i=1}^{n} E(\xi_{ik}^2) + 2a_n^{-2}\sum_{1\le i<j\le n}^{n} \mathrm{Cov}(\xi_{ik}, \xi_{jk}) \\ &\le a_n^{-2}\sum_{i=1}^{n} E(\xi_{ik}^2) + 2c_2 n^{-1}\sum_{1\le i<j\le n}^{n} \alpha(j-i)^{\eta/(2+\eta)} \\ &\le n^{-1}h^{-d}\sum_{i=1}^{n} E(\mu_{ix,k}^2 K_{ix}^2) + 2c_2\sum_{s=1}^{\infty}\alpha(s)^{\eta/(2+\eta)} = O(1),\end{aligned}$$

where $\sup_{n\ge 1}\max_{1\le i\le n} E\left(h^{-d}\|\mu_{ix,k}K_{ix}\|_{2+\eta}^2\right) \le c_2 < \infty$ by the compactness of $K(\cdot)$. Thus $\mathbb{V}_k(\tau, x) = O_P(1)$ by the Chebyshev inequality. It follows that $\mathbb{V}(\tau, x) = O_P(1)$. ■

Proof of Lemma A.3. Let $\mu_{ix,k}$ denote the k th element of the N-vector μ_{ix}, $k = 1, 2, \ldots, N$. Let

$$\mathbb{S}_{nk}(\tau, x; \Delta) = a_n^{-1}\sum_{i=1}^{n}\{s_{ni,k}(\tau, x; \Delta) - E_i[s_{ni,k}(\tau, x; \Delta)]\},$$

where $s_{ni,k}(\tau, x; \Delta) = [1(Y_i \le (\boldsymbol{\beta}_{0\tau x} + a_n^{-1}\Delta)^T \mu_{ix}) - 1(Y_i \le \boldsymbol{\beta}_{0\tau x}^T \mu_{ix})]\mu_{ix,k}K_{ix}$. Note that $\mathbb{S}_{nk}(\tau, x; \Delta)$ is the kth element of $-\{V_n(\tau, x; \Delta) - V_n(\tau, x; 0) - [\bar{V}_n(\tau, x; \Delta) - \bar{V}_n(\tau, x; 0)]$. It suffices to show that for each $k = 1, 2, \ldots, N$,

$$\sup_{x\in\mathscr{X}}\sup_{\tau\in\mathscr{T}}\sup_{\|\Delta\|\le M}\left|\mathbb{S}_{nk}(\tau, x; \Delta)\right| = o_P(\kappa_n). \tag{A.7}$$

By the Minkowski inequality, Eq. (A.7) will hold if

$$\sup_{x\in\mathscr{X}}\sup_{\tau\in\mathscr{T}}\sup_{\|\Delta\|\le M}\left|\mathbb{S}_{nk}^{+}(\tau, x; \Delta)\right| = o_P(\kappa_n) \text{ and } \sup_{x\in\mathscr{X}}\sup_{\tau\in\mathscr{T}}\sup_{\|\Delta\|\le M}\left|\mathbb{S}_{nk}^{-}(\tau, x; \Delta)\right| = o_P(\kappa_n), \tag{A.8}$$

where $\mathbb{S}_{nk}^{+}$ and $\mathbb{S}_{nk}^{-}$ are analogous to $\mathbb{S}_{nk}$ but with $\mu_{ix,k}$ replaced by $\mu_{ix,k}^{+} \equiv \max(\mu_{ix,k}, 0)$ and $\mu_{ix,k}^{-} \equiv \max(-\mu_{ix,k}, 0)$, respectively. We only show the first part of Eq. (A.8), as the other case is similar.

Let $\mathbf{D} \equiv \{\Delta : \|\Delta \le M\|\}$. By selecting $n_0 = O(d_{0n}^{-N})$ grid points, $\Delta_1, \ldots, \Delta_{n_0}$, we can cover $\mathbf{D}$ by $\mathbf{D}_s = \{\Delta : \|\Delta - \Delta_s\| \le d_{0n}\}$ where $d_{0n} = \kappa_n/\log\log n$. Let $d_{1n} = n^{-1/2}/\log\ \log n$, and $d_{2n} = n^{-1/2}/\log\ \log n$. By selecting $n_1 = O(d_{1n}^{-1})$ grid points, $\tau_1, \tau_2, \ldots, \tau_{n_1}$ we cover the compact set $\mathscr{T}$ by $\mathscr{T}_j = \{\tau : |\tau - \tau_j| \le d_{1n}\}$ for $j = 1, \ldots, n_1$. Similarly, we select $n_2 =$

$O(h^{-d}d_{2n}^{-d})$ grid points $x_1, ..., x_{n_2}$ to cover the compact set $\mathscr{X}$ by $\mathscr{X}_l = \{x : \|x - x_l\| \le d_{2n}h\}$, $l = 1, ..., n_2$.

Let $\varphi_{ix}(\tau, \Delta) = (\boldsymbol{\beta}_{0\tau x} + a_n^{-1}\Delta)^T \mu_{ix}$. By the definition above (Eq. (A.6)), $\boldsymbol{\beta}_{0\tau x}^T \mu_{ix} = m(\tau, x) + R_i(\tau, x)$. Then by Assumptions 3 (ii)–(iii), we can quantify several objects that are used subsequently:

$$\begin{aligned}
\bar{d}_{1n} &\equiv \sup_{|\tau-\tau^*|\le d_{1n}||\Delta-\Delta^*||\le d_{0n}} \sup_{x\in\mathscr{X},\{K_{ix}>0\}} \left|\varphi_{ix}(\tau, \Delta) - \varphi_{ix}(\tau^*, \Delta^*)\right| \\
&\le C(d_{1n} + h^{p+1}d_{1n}^{\gamma_0} + a_n^{-1}d_{0n}), \\
\bar{d}_{2n} &\equiv \sup_{|\tau-\tau^*|\le d_{1n}} \sup_{x\in\mathscr{X},\{K_{ix}>0\}} \left|\boldsymbol{\beta}_{0\tau x}^T\mu_{ix} - \boldsymbol{\beta}_{0\tau^* x}^T\mu_{ix}\right| \le C(d_{1n} + h^{p+1}d_{1n}^{\gamma_0}), \\
\bar{d}_{3n} &\equiv \sup_{(\tau,\Delta)\in\mathscr{T}\times D} \sup_{||x-x^*||\le hd_{2n},\{K_{ix}>0\}} \left|\varphi_{ix}(\tau, \Delta) - \varphi_{ix^*}(\tau, \Delta)\right| \\
&\le C(hd_{2n} + h^{p+1}(hd_{2n})^{\gamma_0} + a_n^{-1}d_{2n}).
\end{aligned}$$

For brevity, let

$$\begin{aligned}
\alpha_i^0(\tau, x, \Delta, \lambda_1) &\equiv 1(Y_i \le \varphi_{ix}(\tau, \Delta) + \lambda_1\bar{d}_{1n}) - F_i(\varphi_{ix}(\tau, \Delta) + \lambda_1\bar{d}_{1n}|X_i), \\
\alpha_i(\tau, x, \Delta) &\equiv 1\left(Y_i \le \varphi_{ix}(\tau, \Delta)\right) - F_i(\varphi_{ix}(\tau, \Delta)|X_i), \\
\beta_i^0(\tau, x, \lambda_2) &\equiv 1(Y_i \le \boldsymbol{\beta}_{0\tau x}^T\mu_{ix} + \lambda_2\bar{d}_{2n}) - F_i(\boldsymbol{\beta}_{0\tau x}^T\mu_{ix} + \lambda_2\bar{d}_{2n}|X_i), \\
\beta_i(\tau, x) &\equiv 1(Y_i \le \boldsymbol{\beta}_{0\tau x}^T\mu_{ix}) - F_i(\boldsymbol{\beta}_{0\tau x}^T\mu_{ix}|X_i).
\end{aligned}$$

Clearly, $\alpha_i^0(\tau, x, \Delta, 0) = \alpha_i(\tau, x, \Delta)$, and $\beta_i^0(\tau, x, 0) = \beta_i(\tau, x)$. Let

$$\mathbb{W}(\tau, x, \Delta) \equiv a_n^{-1}\sum_{i=1}^n \alpha_i(\tau, x, \Delta)\mu_{ix,k}^+ K_{ix}, \text{ and } \mathbb{W}^*(\tau, x) \equiv a_n^{-1}\sum_{i=1}^n \beta_i(\tau, x)\mu_{ix,k}^+ K_{ix}.$$

Then $\mathbb{S}_{nk}^+(\tau, x; \Delta) = \mathbb{W}(\tau, x, \Delta) - \mathbb{W}^*(\tau, x)$. Fix $x_l \in \mathscr{X}_l$. Then

$$\begin{aligned}
\sup_{x\in\mathscr{X}} \sup_{\tau\in\mathscr{T}} \sup_{\|\Delta\|\le M} \mathbb{S}_{nk}^+(\tau, x; \Delta) &\le \max_{1\le l\le n_2} \sup_{\tau\in\mathscr{T}} \sup_{\|\Delta\|\le M} \left|\mathbb{W}(\tau, x_l, \Delta) - \mathbb{W}^*(\tau, x_l)\right| \\
&\quad + \max_{1\le l\le n_2} \sup_{x\in\mathscr{X}_l} \sup_{\tau\in\mathscr{T}} \sup_{\|\Delta\|\le M} \left|\mathbb{D}(\tau, x, \Delta) - \mathbb{D}(\tau, x_l, \Delta)\right| \\
&\equiv W_{n1} + W_{n2},
\end{aligned}$$

where $\mathbb{D}(\tau, x, \Delta) \equiv \mathbb{W}(\tau, x, \Delta) - \mathbb{W}^*(\tau, x)$. It suffices to show $W_{na} = o_P(\kappa_n)$ for $a = 1, 2$.

Step 1. We show $W_{n1} = o_P(1)$. Fix $(\tau_j, \Delta_s) \in \mathscr{T}_j \times \mathbf{D}_s$. Then

$$\begin{aligned} W_{n1} &= \max_{1\le l\le n_2} \max_{1\le j\le n_1} \sup_{\tau\in\mathscr{T}_j} \max_{1\le s\le n_0} \sup_{\Delta\in D_s} |\mathbb{W}(\tau, x_l, \Delta) - \mathbb{W}^*(\tau, x_l)| \\ &\le \max_{1\le l\le n_2} \max_{1\le j\le n_1} \max_{1\le s\le n_0} |\mathbb{W}(\tau_j, x_l, \Delta_s) - \mathbb{W}^*(\tau_j, x_l)| \\ &\quad + \max_{1\le l\le n_2} \max_{1\le j\le n_1} \sup_{\tau\in\mathscr{T}_j} \max_{1\le s\le n_0} \sup_{\Delta\in D_s} |\mathbb{D}_s(\tau, x_l, \Delta) - \mathbb{D}_s(\tau_j, x_l, \Delta_s)| \\ &\equiv W_{n11} + W_{n12}. \end{aligned} \tag{A.9}$$

It suffices to show that $W_{n1a} = o_P(1)$ for $a = 1, 2$.

Let $\varepsilon > 0$. Let $\xi_{ni}(\tau, x, \Delta) \equiv 1(Y_i \le \varphi_{ix}(\tau, \Delta)) - 1(Y_i \le \beta_{0\tau x}^T \mu_{ix})]\mu_{ix,k}^+ K_{ix}$, and $\bar{\xi}_{ni}(\tau, x, \Delta) \equiv \xi_{ni}(\tau, x, \Delta) - E_i[\xi_{ni}(\tau, x, \Delta)]$. By Assumptions 1, 2(ii), and 5, one can readily show that there exist some positive constants c_{ξ_1} and c_{ξ_2} such that

$$\left|\bar{\xi}_{ni}(\tau, x, \Delta)\right| \le c_{\xi_1} \quad \text{and} \quad E\left[\sum_{i=a+1}^{a+p_n} \bar{\xi}_{ni}(\tau, x, \Delta)\right]^2 \le c_{\xi_2} a_n^{-1} p_n h^d$$

for any $a = 1, \ldots, p_n$ and $1 \le p_n \le n/2$. Let $\upsilon \in (\varsigma_\kappa, (1 - d/\varsigma_1)/2)$. We can apply Lemma C.3 with $M_n = c_{\xi_1}$, $p_n = n^{1/2-\upsilon} h^{d/2}$, $\varepsilon^* = n^{-1/2} h^{d/2} \kappa_n \varepsilon$ and $\sigma^2(p_n) = c_{\xi_2} a_n^{-1} p_n h^d$ to obtain

$$\begin{aligned} P(W_{n11} > \kappa_n\varepsilon) &\le n_0 n_1 n_2 \max_{1\le l\le n_2} \max_{1\le j\le n_1} \max_{1\le s\le n_0} P\left(\left|\mathbb{W}(\tau_j, x_l, \Delta_s) - \mathbb{W}^*(\tau_j, x_l)\right| > \kappa_n\varepsilon\right) \\ &= n_0 n_1 n_2 \max_{1\le l\le n_2} \max_{1\le j\le n_1} \max_{1\le s\le n_0} P\left(\left|n^{-1}\sum_{i=1}^{n} \bar{\xi}_{ni}(\tau_j, x_l, \Delta_s)\right| > n^{-1/2} h^{d/2} \kappa_n \varepsilon\right) \\ &\le n_0 n_1 n_2 C_0 \exp\left(-\frac{\kappa_n^2 h^d \varepsilon^2}{C_1 c_{\xi_2} a_n^{-1} h^d + 2C_2 c_{\xi_1} n^{-\upsilon} h^d \kappa_n \varepsilon}\right) \\ &\quad + n_0 n_1 n_2 C_3 \sqrt{\frac{c_{\xi_1}}{n^{-1/2} h^{d/2} \kappa_n \varepsilon}} n^{1/2+\upsilon} h^{-d/2} \alpha(p_n + 1) \\ &= n_0 n_1 n_2 C_0 \exp\left(-\frac{\varepsilon^2}{C_1 c_{\xi_2} n^{-1/2} h^{-d/2} \kappa_n^{-2} + 2C_2 c_{\xi_1} n^{-\upsilon} \kappa_n^{-1} \varepsilon}\right) \\ &\quad + n_0 n_1 n_2 O\left(n^{3/4+\upsilon} h^{-3d/4} \kappa_n^{-1/2}\right) \alpha(n^{1/2-\upsilon} h^{d/2}) \\ &= n_0 n_1 n_2 C_0 \exp\left(-\frac{\varepsilon^2}{C_1 c_{\xi_2} n^{-1/2} h^{-d/2} \kappa_n^{-2} + 2C_2 c_{\xi_1} n^{-\upsilon} \kappa_n^{-1} \varepsilon}\right) \\ &\quad + o(n^{3/4+\upsilon} \kappa_n^{-1/2} d_{0n}^{-N} d_{1n}^{-1} d_{2n}^{-d} h^{-3d/4} (n^{1/2-\upsilon} h^{d/2})^{-\beta_0}) \\ &\equiv p_{n1} + p_{n2}, \end{aligned}$$

where $\beta_0 = 1 + 16/\eta$. Clearly, by Assumption 6 the first term p_{n1} is $o(1)$ provided $\upsilon > \varsigma_\kappa$. Noting that $d_{0n} = \kappa_n / \log\ \log n$, $d_{1n} = d_{2n} = n^{-1/2}/\log \times \log n$, and $h = n^{-1/\varsigma_1}$, we have

$$\begin{aligned}
p_{n2} &= o(n^{3/4+\upsilon}\kappa_n^{-1/2} d_{0n}^{-N} d_{1n}^{-1} d_{2n}^{-d} h^{-3d/4}(n^{1/2-\upsilon}h^{d/2})^{-\beta_0}) \\
&= o(n^{3/4+\upsilon}\kappa_n^{-N-1/2} n^{(d+1)/2} h^{-3d/4}(n^{1/2-\upsilon}h^{d/2})^{-\beta_0}(\log\log n)^{N+d+1}) \\
&= o((n^{3/4+\upsilon} n^{(d+1)/2} n^{-(1/2-\upsilon)\beta_0} h^{-(3+2\beta_0)d/4}\kappa_n^{-N-1/2})(\log\log n)^{N+d+1}) \\
&= o(n^{5/4+d/2+\upsilon-(1/2-\upsilon)\beta_0} h^{-(3d+2\beta_0)/4}\kappa_n^{-N-1/2}(\log\log n)^{N+d+1}) \\
&= o(n^{5/4+d/2+\upsilon+3d/(4\varsigma_1)+(N+1/2)\varsigma_\kappa-(1/2-\upsilon-d/(2\varsigma_1))\beta_0}(\log\log n)^{N+d+1}).
\end{aligned}$$

Then $p_{n2} = o(1)$ because $\beta_0 > [5/2 + d + 2\upsilon + 3d/(2\varsigma_1) + (2N+1)\varsigma_\kappa]/(1 - 2\upsilon - d/\varsigma_1)$ and $\upsilon < (1 - d/\varsigma_1)/2$ by Assumption 6(iii). It follows that

$$W_{n11} = o_P(\kappa_n). \tag{A.10}$$

Now consider W_{n12}. By the monotonicity of the indicator function and the nonnegativity of $\mu_{ix,k}^+ K_{ix}$, we have that for any $(\tau, \Delta) \in \mathscr{T}_j \times \mathbf{D}_s$,

$$\begin{aligned}
\mathbb{D}(\tau, x, \Delta) - \mathbb{D}(\tau_j, x, \Delta_s) &= a_n^{-1}\sum_{i=1}^{n}\{[\alpha_i(\tau, x, \Delta) - \alpha_i(\tau_j, x, \Delta_s)] \\
&\quad - [\beta_i(\tau, x) - \beta_i(\tau_j, x)]\}\mu_{ix,k}^+ K_{ix} \\
&\geq a_n^{-1}\sum_{i=1}^{n}\{[\alpha_i^0(\tau_j, x, \Delta_s, 1) - \alpha_i(\tau_j, x, \Delta_s)] \\
&\quad - [\beta_i^0(\tau_j, x, -1) - \beta_i(\tau_j, x)]\}\mu_{ix,k}^+ K_{ix} \\
&\quad + a_n^{-1}\sum_{i=1}^{n}[F_i(\varphi_{ix}(\tau_j, \Delta_s) + \bar{d}_{1n}|X_i) \\
&\quad - F_i(\varphi_{ix}(\tau, \Delta)|X_i)]\mu_{ix,k}^+ K_{ix} \\
&\quad + a_n^{-1}\sum_{i=1}^{n}[F_i(\boldsymbol{\beta}_{0\tau x}^T \mu_{ix}|X_i) \\
&\quad - F_i(\boldsymbol{\beta}_{0\tau_j x}^T \mu_{ix} - \bar{d}_{2n}|X_i)]\}\mu_{ix,k}^+ K_{ix}.
\end{aligned}$$

Similarly,

$$\begin{aligned}
\mathbb{D}(\tau, x, \Delta) - \mathbb{D}(\tau_j, x, \Delta_s) &\leq a_n^{-1}\sum_{i=1}^{n}\{[\alpha_i^0(\tau_j, x, \Delta_s, -1) - \alpha_i(\tau_j, x, \Delta_s)] \\
&\quad - [\beta_i^0(\tau_j, x, 1) - \beta_i(\tau_j, x)]\}\mu_{ix,k}^+ K_{ix}
\end{aligned}$$

$$+ a_n^{-1} \sum_{i=1}^{n} [F_i(\varphi_{ix}(\tau_j, \Delta_s) - \bar{d}_{01n}|X_i)$$
$$- F_i(\varphi_{ix}(\tau, \Delta)|X_i)]\mu_{ix,k}^{+} K_{ix}$$
$$+ a_n^{-1} \sum_{i=1}^{n} [F_i(\boldsymbol{\beta}_{0\tau x}^T \mu_{ix}|X_i)$$
$$- F_i(\boldsymbol{\beta}_{0\tau_j x}^T \mu_{ix} + \bar{d}_{1n}|X_i)]\mu_{ix,k}^{+} K_{ix}.$$

It follows that

$$\max_{1 \le j \le n_1} \sup_{\tau \in \mathcal{T}_j} \max_{1 \le s \le n_0} \sup_{\Delta \in D_s} \left| \mathbb{D}(\tau, x, \Delta) - \mathbb{D}(\tau_j, x, \Delta_s) \right|$$
$$\le \max_{1 \le j \le n_1} \max_{1 \le s \le n_0} \left| a_n^{-1} \sum_{i=1}^{n} [\alpha_i^0(\tau_j, x, \Delta_s, \pm 1) - \alpha_i(\tau_j, x, \Delta_s)]\mu_{ix,k}^{+} K_{ix} \right|$$
$$+ \max_{1 \le j \le n_1} \max_{1 \le s \le n_0} \left| a_n^{-1} \sum_{i=1}^{n} [\boldsymbol{\beta}_i^0(\tau_j, x, \mp 1) - \boldsymbol{\beta}_i(\tau_j, x)]\mu_{ix,k}^{+} K_{ix} \right|$$
$$+ \max_{1 \le j \le n_1} \max_{1 \le s \le n_0} \left| a_n^{-1} \sum_{i=1}^{n} [F_i(\varphi_{ix}(\tau_j, \Delta_s) + \bar{d}_{1n}|X_i) \right.$$
$$\left. - F_i(\varphi_{ix}(\tau_j, \Delta_s) - \bar{d}_{1n}|X_i)]\mu_{ix,k}^{+} K_{ix} \right|$$
$$+ \max_{1 \le j \le n_1} \max_{1 \le s \le n_0} \left| a_n^{-1} \sum_{i=1}^{n} [F_i(\boldsymbol{\beta}_{0\tau_j x}^T \mu_{ix} + \bar{d}_{2n}|X_i) \right.$$
$$\left. - F_i(\boldsymbol{\beta}_{0\tau_j x}^T \mu_{ix} - \bar{d}_{2n}|X_i)]\mu_{ix,k}^{+} K_{ix} \right|$$
$$\equiv D_{n1}(x) + D_{n2}(x) + D_{n3}(x) + D_{n4}(x). \tag{A.11}$$

Let $\alpha_{i,js}(x) = [\alpha_i^0(\tau_j, x, \Delta_s, \pm 1) - \alpha_i(\tau_j, x, \Delta_s)]\mu_{ix,k}^{+} K_{ix}$. Then one can readily show that there exist some positive constants c_{α_1} and c_{α_2} such that $|\alpha_{i,js}(x)| \le c_{\alpha_1}$ and $E\left[\sum_{i=a+1}^{a+p_n} \alpha_{i,js}(x)\right]^2 \le c_{\alpha_2} a_n^{-1} p_n h^d$ for any $a = 1, \ldots, p_n$ and $1 \le p_n \le n/2$. Following the proof for W_{n11}, we can readily show that

$$P\left(\max_{1 \le l \le n_2} D_{n1}(x_l) \ge \kappa_n \varepsilon \right) \le n_0 n_1 n_2 \max_{1 \le l \le n_2} \max_{1 \le j \le n_1} \max_{1 \le s \le n_0}$$
$$\times P\left(\left| n^{-1} \sum_{i=1}^{n} \alpha_{i,js}(x_l) \right| \ge n^{-1} a_n \kappa_n \varepsilon \right) = o(1).$$

Similarly, one can show that $P(\max_{1\le l\le n_2} D_{n2}(x_l) \ge \kappa_n \varepsilon) = o(1)$. Next, by the mean value expansion and Assumptions 2, 5, and 6,

$$\max_{1\le l\le n_2} D_{n3}(x_l) \le C\bar{d}_{1n} \max_{1\le l\le n_2} \left| a_n^{-1} \sum_{i=1}^{n} \mu_{ix_l,k}^{+} K_{ix_l} \right| = O_P(n^{1/2}h^{d/2}\bar{d}_{1n})$$
$$= O_P(n^{1/2}h^{d/2}(d_{1n} + h^{p+1}d_{1n}^{\gamma_0} + a_n^{-1}d_{0n})) = o_P(\kappa_n).$$

Similarly $\max_{1\le l\le n_2} D_{n4}(x_l) = O_P(n^{1/2}h^{d/2}\bar{d}_{2n}) = o_P(\kappa_n)$. These results, together with (A.11), imply that

$$W_{n12} = o_P(\kappa_n). \tag{A.12}$$

Combining (A.9), (A.10), and (A.12) yields $W_{n1} = o_P(\kappa_n)$.

Step 2. We show $W_{n2} = o_P(1)$. Write

$$\begin{aligned}\mathbb{D}(\tau, x, \Delta) - \mathbb{D}(\tau, x_l, \Delta) &= a_n^{-1} \sum_{i=1}^{n} \{\alpha_i(\tau, x, \Delta) - \beta_i(\tau, x)\} \left(\mu_{ix,k}^{+} K_{ix} - \mu_{ix_l,k}^{+} K_{ix_l} \right) \\ &\quad + a_n^{-1} \sum_{i=1}^{n} [\alpha_i(\tau, x, \Delta) - \alpha_i(\tau, x_l, \Delta)] \mu_{ix_l,k}^{+} K_{ix_l} \\ &\quad + a_n^{-1} \sum_{i=1}^{n} [\beta_i(\tau, x_l) - \beta_i(\tau, x)] \mu_{ix_l,k}^{+} K_{ix_l} \\ &\equiv D_{n1}(\tau, x, x_l, \Delta) + D_{n2}(\tau, x, x_l, \Delta) \\ &\quad + D_{n3}(\tau, x, x_l), \text{ say.}\end{aligned} \tag{A.13}$$

It suffices to show that each of the three terms on the r.h.s. of Eq. (A.13) is $o_P(\kappa_n)$ uniformly.

First, we consider $D_{n1}(\tau, x, x_l, \Delta)$. Assumption 5 implies that for all $\|x_1 - x_2\| \le \delta \le c_k$,

$$\left| K(x_2) - K(x_1) \right| \le \delta K^*(x_1), \tag{A.14}$$

where $K^*(x) = \bar{C}1(\|x\| \le 2dc_k)$ for some constant $\bar{C}$ that depends on $\bar{c}_1$ and $\bar{c}_2$ in the assumption. For any $x \in \mathcal{X}_l$, $\|x - x_l\|/h \le d_{2n}$. It follows from Eq. (A.14) that $\left| K_{ix} - K_{ix_l} \right| \le d_{2n} K_{ix_l}^*$ with $K_{ix_l}^* \equiv K^*((x_l - X_i)/h)$, and

$$\left|\left(\frac{X_i-x}{h}\right)^k K_{ix}-\left(\frac{X_i-x_l}{h}\right)^k K_{ix_l}\right| \leq \left|\left(\frac{X_i-x}{h}\right)^k\right| |K_{ix}-K_{ix_l}| + \left|\left(\frac{X_i-x}{h}\right)^k-\left(\frac{X_i-x_l}{h}\right)^k\right| K_{ix_l}$$
$$\leq (2c_k)^{|k|} d_{2n} K^*_{ix_l} + (2c_k)^{|k|-1} d_{2n} K_{ix_l} 1(|k|>0)$$
$$\leq C d_{2n}(K^*_{ix_l}+K_{ix_l}).$$

With this, we can show that for any $x \in \mathscr{X}_l$ such that $\|x-x_l\|/h \leq d_{2n}$, $\|\mu^+_{ix,k}K_{ix} - \mu^+_{ix_l,k}K_{ix_l}\| \leq Cd_{2n}(K^*_{ix_l} + K_{ix_l})$. It follows that

$$\max_{1\leq l\leq n_2} \sup_{x\in\mathscr{X}_l} \sup_{\tau\in\mathscr{T}} \sup_{\|\Delta\|\leq M} |D_{n1}(\tau,x,x_l,\Delta)|$$
$$\leq \max_{1\leq l\leq n_2} \sup_{x\in\mathscr{X}_l} \sup_{\tau\in\mathscr{T}} \sup_{\|\Delta\|\leq M} a_n^{-1}\sum_{i=1}^n |\alpha_i(\tau,x,\Delta)-\beta_i(\tau,x)| \left|\mu^+_{ix,k}K_{ix}-\mu^+_{ix_l,k}K_{ix_l}\right|$$
$$\leq \max_{1\leq l\leq n_2} \sup_{x\in\mathscr{X}_l} a_n^{-1}\sum_{i=1}^n \left|\mu^+_{ixk}K_{ix}-\mu^+_{ix_l,k}K_{ix_l}\right|$$
$$\leq C \max_{1\leq l\leq n_2} a_n^{-1} d_{2n}\sum_{i=1}^n (K^*_{ix_l}+K_{ix_l})$$
$$= O_P(nh^d a_n^{-1} d_{2n}) = o_P(\kappa_n). \qquad \text{(A.15)}$$

Now we consider $D_{n2}(\tau,x,x_l,\Delta)$ defined in Eq. (A.13). Let $\lambda_3 \in \mathbb{R}$. Define

$$\mathscr{D}_{n2}(\tau,x_l,\Delta,\lambda_3) = a_n^{-1}\sum_{i=1}^n [1(Y_i \leq \varphi_{ix_l}(\tau,\Delta)+\lambda_3\bar{d}_{3n}) - F_i(\varphi_{ix_l}(\tau,\Delta)+\lambda_3\bar{d}_{3n}|X_i)]\mu^+_{ix_l,k}K_{ix_l}.$$

Note that $\max_{1\leq l\leq n_2}\sup_{\tau\in\mathscr{T}}\sup_{\|\Delta\|\leq M}\left|\mathscr{D}_{n2}(\tau,x_l,\Delta,\lambda_3)-\mathscr{D}_{n2}(\tau,x_l,\Delta,0)\right|$ is exactly like the object W_{n11} defined in Eq. (A.9). Following the proof of the probability order of W_{n11}, we can also show that

$$P\left(\max_{1\leq l\leq n_2}\sup_{\tau\in\mathscr{T}}\sup_{\|\Delta\|\leq M}\left|\mathscr{D}_{n2}(\tau,x_l,\Delta,\lambda_3)-\mathscr{D}_{n2}(\tau,x_l,\Delta,0)\right| \geq \kappa_n\varepsilon\right) = o(1) \text{ foreach } \lambda_3. \qquad \text{(A.16)}$$

Again, by the monotonicity of the indicator function and the CDF F_i, we have

$$\max_{1\le l\le n_2}\sup_{x\in\mathscr{X}_l}\sup_{\tau\in\mathscr{T}}\sup_{\|\Delta\|\le M}|D_{n2}(\tau,x,x_l,\Delta)|$$

$$= \max_{1\le l\le n_2}\sup_{x\in\mathscr{X}_l}\sup_{\tau\in\mathscr{T}}\sup_{\|\Delta\|\le M}\left|a_n^{-1}\sum_{i=1}^{n}[\alpha_i(\tau,x,\Delta)-\alpha_i(\tau,x_l,\Delta)]\mu_{ix_l,k}^{+}K_{ix_l}\right|$$

$$\le \max_{1\le l\le n_2}\sup_{\tau\in\mathscr{T}}\sup_{\|\Delta\|\le M}\left|\mathscr{D}_{n2}(\tau,x_l,\Delta,1)-\mathscr{D}_{n2}(\tau,x_l,\Delta,0)\right|$$

$$+ \max_{1\le l\le n_2}\sup_{\tau\in\mathscr{T}}\sup_{\|\Delta\|\le M}\left|\mathscr{D}_{n2}(\tau,x_l,\Delta,-1)-\mathscr{D}_{n2}(\tau,x_l,\Delta,0)\right|$$

$$+ \max_{1\le l\le n_2}\sup_{\tau\in\mathscr{T}}\sup_{\|\Delta\|\le M}\left|a_n^{-1}\sum_{i=1}^{n}[F_i(\varphi_{ix_l}(\tau,\Delta)+\bar{d}_{3n}|X_i)\right.$$

$$\left.- F_i(\varphi_{ix_l}(\tau,\Delta)-\bar{d}_{3n}|X_i)]\mu_{ix_l,k}^{+}K_{ix_l}\right|.$$

The first two terms are $o_P(1)$ by Eq. (A.16). For the last term, a mean value expansion implies that it is no bigger than

$$2C_1\bar{d}_{3n}a_n^{-1}\sup_{1\le l\le n_2}\sum_{i=1}^{n}\mu_{ix_l,k}^{+}K_{ix_l} = O_P(nh^d\bar{d}_{3n}a_n^{-1}) = o_P(\kappa_n).$$

It follows that

$$\max_{1\le l\le n_2}\sup_{x\in\mathscr{X}_l}\sup_{\tau\in\mathscr{T}}\sup_{\|\Delta\|\le M}|D_{n2}(\tau,x,x_l,\Delta)| = o_P(\kappa_n). \tag{A.17}$$

Analogously, one can show that $\max_{1\le l\le n_2}\sup_{x\in\mathscr{X}_l}\sup_{\tau\in\mathscr{T}}|D_{n3}(\tau,x,x_l)| = o_P(1)$. This, together with (A.13), (A.16), and (A.17), implies that $W_{n2} = o_P(1)$.

Proof of Lemma A.4. Let $\bar{H}_n(\tau,x)\equiv n^{-1}\sum_{i=1}^{n}f_i(\boldsymbol{\beta}_{0\tau x}^T\mu_{ix}|X_i)\,\mu_{ix}\mu_{ix}^TK_{ix}$. Noting that $m(\tau,X_i)-\beta_{0\tau x}^T\mu_{ix}=O_P(h^{p+1})$ uniformly in (τ,x) on the set $\{i: K_{ix}>0\}$, it is easy to show that uniformly in (τ,x), $\bar{H}_n(\tau,x)= n^{-1}h^{-d}\sum_{i=1}^{n}f_i(m(\tau,X_i)|X_i)\mu_{ix}\mu_{ix}^TK_{ix}+O_P(h^{p+1}) = H_n(\tau,x)+o_P(\kappa_n)$. Then by the Minkowski inequality, we have that

$$\sup_{\tau\in\mathscr{T}}\sup_{x\in\mathscr{X}}\sup_{\|\Delta\|\le M}\|\bar{V}_n(\tau,x;\Delta)-\bar{V}_n(\tau,x;0)+H_n(\tau,x)\Delta\|$$

$$\le \sup_{\tau\in\mathscr{T}}\sup_{x\in\mathscr{X}}\sup_{\|\Delta\|\le M}\|\bar{V}_n(\tau,x;\Delta)-\bar{V}_n(\tau,x;0)+\bar{H}_n(\tau,x)\Delta\|+o_P(\kappa_n).$$

By Assumptions 2, 5, and 6,

$$\sup_{\tau\in\mathcal{T}}\sup_{x\in\mathcal{X}}\sup_{\|\Delta\|\le M}\|\bar{V}_n(\tau,x;\Delta)-\bar{V}_n(\tau,x;0)+\bar{H}_n(\tau,x)\Delta\|$$

$$=\sup_{\tau\in\mathcal{T}}\sup_{x\in\mathcal{X}}\sup_{\|\Delta\|\le M}\left\|a_n^{-1}\sum_{i=1}^{n}[F_i((\boldsymbol{\beta}_{0\tau x}+a_n^{-1}\Delta)^T\mu_{ix}|X_i)\right.$$

$$\left.-F_i(\boldsymbol{\beta}_{0\tau x}^T\mu_{ix}|X_i)]\mu_{ix}K_{ix}-\bar{H}_n(\tau,x)\Delta\right\|$$

$$=\sup_{\tau\in\mathcal{T}}\sup_{x\in\mathcal{X}}\sup_{\|\Delta\|\le M}\left\|a_n^{-2}\sum_{i=1}^{n}\int_0^1\left[f_i((\boldsymbol{\beta}_{0\tau x}+sa_n^{-1}\Delta)^T\mu_{ix}|X_i)\right.\right.$$

$$\left.\left.-f_i(\boldsymbol{\beta}_{0\tau x}^T\mu_{ix}|X_i)\right]ds\mu_{ix}\mu_{ix}^TK_{ix}\Delta\right\|$$

$$\le\sup_{x\in\mathcal{X}}\sup_{\|\Delta\|\le M}a_n^{-3}\sum_{i=1}^{n}\|C_2(X_i)\Delta^T\mu_{ix}\mu_{ix}\mu_{ix}^TK_{ix}\Delta\|\le CM^2\sup_{x\in\mathcal{X}}a_n^{-3}\sum_{i=1}^{n}\|\mu_{ix}\|^3K_{ix}$$

$$=O_P(nh^da_n^{-3})=o_P(\kappa_n).$$

Proof of Lemma A.5. By the proof of Lemma A2 in Ruppert and Carroll (1980) and Assumptions 5 and 6,

$$\begin{aligned}\sup_{\tau\in\mathcal{T}}\sup_{x\in\mathcal{X}}\|V_n(\tau,x;\hat{\Delta}_{\tau x})\| &= \sup_{\tau\in\mathcal{T}}\sup_{x\in\mathcal{X}}\|n^{-1/2}\sum_{i=1}^{n}\psi_\tau(Y_i-\hat{\boldsymbol{\beta}}_{\tau x}^T\mu_{ix})\mu_{ix}K_{ix}\|\\ &\le \sup_{\tau\in\mathcal{T}}\sup_{x\in\mathcal{X}}n^{-1/2}\sum_{i=1}^{n}1(Y_i-\hat{\boldsymbol{\beta}}_{\tau x}^T\mu_{ix}=0)\|\mu_{ix}K_{ix}\|\\ &\le 2Nn^{-1/2}\max_{1\le i\le n}\sup_{x\in\mathcal{X}}\|\mu_{ix}K_{ix}\|=o_P(\kappa_n).\end{aligned}$$

Notation: To prove the main results in Section "Testing conditional independence", we apply some propositions in the next appendix. For notational simplicity, let $m_{i\tau}\equiv m(\tau,W_i)$, $\varepsilon_{i\tau}\equiv Y_i-m_{i\tau}$, $u_{i\tau}\equiv Y_i-m(\tau,X_i)$, and $\hat{u}_{i\tau}\equiv Y_i-\hat{m}(\tau,X_i)$. Then by Corollary 1, it is standard to show that $\max_{1\le i\le n}\sup_{\tau\in\mathcal{T}}|\hat{u}_{i\tau}-u_{i\tau}|=o_P(n^{-1/2}h_X^{-d_X/2}\sqrt{\log n})$. Clearly, $u_{i\tau}=\varepsilon_{i\tau}$ under H_0 and $u_{i\tau}=\varepsilon_{i\tau}+n^{-1/2}\delta(\tau,W_i)$ under H_{1n}. Let $\varphi_{i\gamma}=\varphi(W_i,\gamma)$. We use $F(\cdot|W_i)$, $F(\cdot|X_i)$,$f(\cdot|W_i)$, and $f(\cdot|X_i)$ to denote $F_{Y|W}(\cdot|W_i)$,$F_{Y|X}(\cdot|X_i)$, $f_{Y|W}(\cdot|W_i)$, and $f_{Y|X}(\cdot|X_i)$, respectively. Recall that S^c denotes the complex conjugate of S.

Proof of Theorem 2. The proof is a special case of that of Theorem 4, so we omit it.

Proof of Theorem 3. Following the proof of Theorem 4, we can show that $n^{-1/2}S_n(\tau,\gamma) = n^{-1/2}S_{n3}(\tau,\gamma) + o_P(1)$, where $S_{n3}(\tau,\gamma) \equiv n^{-1/2}\sum_{i=1}^n \times \{G(-\varepsilon_{i\tau}/\lambda_n) - G(-\hat{u}_{i\tau}/\lambda_n)\}\varphi_{i\gamma}$. It follows that

$$\begin{aligned}
n^{-1/2}S_n(\tau,\gamma) &= n^{-1}\sum_{i=1}^n \{G(-\varepsilon_{i\tau}/\lambda_n) - G(-\hat{u}_{i\tau}/\lambda_n)\}\varphi_{i\gamma} + o_P(1) \\
&= \lambda_n^{-1}n^{-1}\sum_{i=1}^n \{G^{(1)}(-\varepsilon_{i\tau}/\lambda_n)(\hat{u}_{i\tau} - \varepsilon_{i\tau})\}\varphi_{i\gamma} + o_P(1) \\
&= \lambda_n^{-1}n^{-1}\sum_{i=1}^n G^{(1)}(-\varepsilon_{i\tau}/\lambda_n)[m(\tau, W_i) - m(\tau, X_i)]\varphi_{i\gamma} \\
&\quad - \lambda_n^{-1}n^{-1}\sum_{i=1}^n G^{(1)}(-\varepsilon_{i\tau}/\lambda_n)[m(\tau, X_i) - \hat{m}(\tau, X_i)]\varphi_{i\gamma} + o_P(1) \\
&= \lambda_n^{-1}n^{-1}\sum_{i=1}^n G^{(1)}(-\varepsilon_{i\tau}/\lambda_n)[m(\tau, W_i) - m(\tau, X_i)]\varphi_{i\gamma} + o_P(1) \\
&= n^{-1}\sum_{i=1}^n f(m_{i\tau}|W_i)[m(\tau, W_i) - m(\tau, X_i)]\varphi_{i\gamma} + o_P(1) \\
&= D_\delta(\tau,\gamma) + o_P(1),
\end{aligned}$$

where $\Delta_\delta(\tau,\gamma) \equiv E\{f(m_{i\tau}|W_i)[m(\tau, W_i) - m(\tau, X_i)]\varphi_{i\gamma}\}$. When φ is (G)CR, $\Delta_\delta(\tau,\gamma) \neq 0$ in a set of positive Lebesgue measure. The test statistic thus diverges to ∞ under the alternative.

Proof of Theorem 4. Decompose $S_n(\tau,\gamma) = n^{-1/2}\sum_{i=1}^n[\tau - G(-\hat{u}_{i\tau}/\lambda_n)]\varphi_{i\gamma}$ as follows:

$$\begin{aligned}
S_n(\tau,\gamma) &= n^{-1/2}\sum_{i=1}^n[\tau - 1(\varepsilon_{i\tau} < 0)]\varphi_{i\gamma} + n^{-1/2}\sum_{i=1}^n[1(\varepsilon_{i\tau} < 0) - G(-\varepsilon_{i\tau}/\lambda_n)]\varphi_{i\gamma} \\
&\quad + n^{-1/2}\sum_{i=1}^n[G(-\varepsilon_{i\tau}/\lambda_n) - G(-\hat{u}_{i\tau}/\lambda_n)]\varphi_{i\gamma} \\
&\equiv S_{n1}(\tau,\gamma) + S_{n2}(\tau,\gamma) + S_{n3}(\tau,\gamma), \text{ say.}
\end{aligned}$$

By Propositions B.4 and B.7, we have that, uniformly in (τ,γ), $S_{n2}(\tau,\gamma) = o_P(1)$, and that

$$S_{n3}(\tau,\gamma) = -c_0 n^{-1/2}\sum_{i=1}^n b(X_i,\gamma)\psi_\tau(\varepsilon_{i\tau}) + \Delta(\tau,\gamma) + o_P(1),$$

where $c_0 = e_1^T \mathbb{H}^{-1}\mathbb{B}, \mathbb{B} = \int \mu(v)K(v)dv$, and $b(X_j, \gamma) = E[\varphi(W_j, \gamma)|X_j]$. It follows that $S_n(\tau, \gamma) \equiv \bar{S}_n(\tau, \gamma) + D(\tau, \gamma) + o_P(1)$, where

$$\bar{S}_n(\tau, \gamma) \equiv n^{-1/2} \sum_{i=1}^{n} [\varphi_{i\gamma} - c_0 b(X_i, \gamma)]\psi_\tau(\varepsilon_{i\tau}).$$

It suffices to show that $\bar{S}_n(\cdot, \cdot) \Rightarrow S_\infty(\cdot, \cdot)$, where $S_\infty(\cdot, \cdot)$ is defined in Theorem 2. Define the pseudometric ρ_d on $(\mathscr{T}, \Gamma)$:

$$\rho_d((\tau, \gamma), (\tau', \gamma')) \equiv \{E|\eta_i(\gamma, \tau) - \eta_i(\gamma', \tau')|^r\}^{1/r},$$

where $r \geq 2$ and $\eta_i(\gamma, \tau) \equiv [\varphi(W_i, \gamma) - c_0 b(X_i, \gamma)]\psi_\tau(\varepsilon_{i\tau})$. By Theorem 10.2 of Pollard (1990), this follows if we have (i) total boundedness of a pseudometric space $((\mathscr{T}, \Gamma), \rho_d)$, (ii) stochastic equicontinuity of $\{\bar{S}_n(\tau, \gamma) : n \geq 1\}$, and (iii) finite dimensional (fidi) convergence.

Consider the class of functions

$$\mathscr{F}_1 \equiv \{f_{(\tau,\gamma)} : (\tau, \gamma) \in \mathscr{T} \times \Gamma\},$$

where $f_{(\tau,\gamma)} : [0, 1] \times W \to \mathbb{R}$ is defined by

$$f_{(\tau,\gamma)}(U_i, W_i) \equiv [\varphi(W_i, \gamma) - c_0 b(X_i, \gamma)][\tau - 1(U_i \leq \tau)],$$

and $U_i \equiv F(Y_i|W_i)$. Let $\delta < 1$ and (τ', γ') be generic element in $\mathscr{T} \times \Gamma$. Noting that

$$\begin{aligned}
\eta_i(\tau, \gamma) - \eta_i(\tau', \gamma') &= [\varphi(W_i, \gamma) - c_0 b(X_i, \gamma)][\tau - 1(U_i \leq \tau) - \tau' + 1(U_i \leq \tau')] \\
&\quad + [\varphi(W_i, \gamma) - c_0 b(X_i, \gamma) - \varphi(W_i, \gamma') \\
&\quad + c_0 b(X_i, \gamma')][\tau' - 1(U_i \leq \tau')] \\
&\equiv \eta_{i1}(\tau, \tau', \gamma) + \eta_{i2}(\tau', \gamma, \gamma'), \text{ say,}
\end{aligned}$$

by the repeated use of C_r-inequality, the uniform boundedness of $\varphi(\cdot, \cdot)$ and Assumption 10, we have

$$\begin{aligned}
&E \sup_{|\tau-\tau'| \leq \delta_1, \|\gamma-\gamma'\| \leq \delta_2, \sqrt{\delta_1^2+\delta_2^2} \leq \delta} |\eta_i(\tau, \gamma) - \eta_i(\tau', \gamma')|^r \\
&\quad \leq 2^{r-1} E \sup_{|\tau-\tau'| \leq \delta_1, \|\gamma-\gamma'\| \leq \delta_2, \sqrt{\delta_1^2+\delta_2^2} \leq \delta} |\eta_{i1}(\tau, \tau', \gamma)|^r \\
&\quad + 2^{r-1} E \sup_{|\tau-\tau'| \leq \delta_1, \|\gamma-\gamma'\| \leq \delta_2, \sqrt{\delta_1^2+\delta_2^2} \leq \delta} |\eta_{i2}(\tau', \gamma, \gamma')|^r
\end{aligned}$$

$$\leq CE \sup_{|\tau-\tau'|\leq\delta_1} |\tau-\tau'|^r + CE \sup_{|\tau-\tau'|\leq\delta_1} \left|1(U_i \leq \tau) - 1(U_i \leq \tau')\right|^r$$
$$+ CE \sup_{\|\gamma-\gamma'\|\leq\delta_2} \left|\varphi(W_i,\gamma) - \varphi(W_i,\gamma')\right|^r + CE \sup_{\|\gamma-\gamma'\|\leq\delta_2} \left|b(X_i,\gamma) - b(X_i,\gamma')\right|^r$$
$$\leq C\delta_1^r + CP(|U_i - \tau| \leq \delta_1) + C\delta_2^{rv} + C\delta_2^{rv}$$
$$\leq C\delta_1^r + C\delta_1 + 2C\delta_2^{rv} \leq 2C\delta^{1\wedge(rv)} = 2C\delta^{\bar{v}},$$

where $\bar{v} = \min(1, rv)$. That is, $\mathscr{F}_1$ is a class of uniformly bounded functions satisfying L_r-continuity. L_r-continuity implies that the bracketing number satisfies

$$N(\varepsilon, \mathscr{F}_1, \|\cdot\|_{L_r(P)}) \leq C\left(\frac{1}{\varepsilon}\right)^{(1+d_\Gamma)/\bar{v}},$$

which in conjunction with Assumption 8(i) implies that

$$\int_0^1 \varepsilon^{-\frac{\eta}{2+\eta}} N\left(\varepsilon, \mathscr{F}_1, \|\cdot\|_{L_r(P)}\right)^{\frac{1}{6}} d\varepsilon \leq C\int_0^1 \varepsilon^{-\frac{\eta}{2+\eta}-\frac{1+d_\Gamma}{6\bar{v}}} d\varepsilon < \infty.$$

If follows that conditions (i) and (ii) are satisfied by Theorem 2.2 of Andrews and Pollard (1994). The fidi convergence holds by the Cramér-Wold device and a central limit theorem for bounded random variables under strong mixing conditions. See Corollary 5.1 in Hall and Heyde (1980, p. 132). We are left to demonstrate that the sample covariance kernel converges to that of the limiting Gaussian process $S_\infty(\cdot,\cdot)$. By the Davydov inequality,

$$\left|E[\bar{S}_n(\tau,\gamma)\bar{S}_n^c(\tau',\gamma')]\right| = \left|\frac{1}{n}\sum_{i=1}^n\sum_{j=1}^n E[\eta_i(\gamma,\tau)\eta_i^c(\gamma',\tau')]\right|$$
$$\leq \frac{4c_\varphi^2}{n}\sum_{i=1}^n\sum_{j=1}^n \alpha(|i-j|) \leq 4c_\varphi^2 \sum_{s=0}^\infty \alpha(s) < \infty.$$

It follows that $E[\bar{S}_n(\tau,\gamma)\bar{S}_n^c(\tau',\gamma')]$ is absolutely convergent, and $E[\bar{S}_n(\tau,\gamma)\times \bar{S}_n^c(\tau',\gamma')] \to E[\eta_1(\gamma,\tau)\eta_1^c(\gamma',\tau')] + \sum_{i=1}^\infty E[\eta_1(\gamma,\tau)\eta_{1+i}^c(\gamma',\tau')] + E[\eta_{1+i}(\gamma,\tau)\times \eta_1^c(\gamma',\tau')]$. This completes the proof of the theorem.

Proof of Theorem 5. Let P^* denote the probability conditional on the original sample $\mathfrak{D}_n \equiv \{(Y_t, W_t)\}_{t=1}^n$. Let E^* denote the expectation with respect to P^*. Rewrite $S_n^*(\tau,\gamma) = \sum_{i=1}^{n-L+1} s_{ni}(\zeta_i;\tau,\gamma)$, where

$$s_{ni}(\zeta_i;\tau,\gamma) \equiv n^{-1/2}\zeta_i \sum_{j=i}^{i+L-1}[\tau - G(-\hat{u}_{j\tau}/\lambda_n)][\varphi_{jw} - c_0\hat{b}(X_j,\gamma)] \tag{A.18}$$

and $\hat{u}_{j\tau} \equiv Y_j - \hat{m}(\tau, X_j)$. Define the envelope function of s_{ni} as

$$\bar{s}_{ni}(\zeta_i) \equiv |\zeta_i| n^{-1/2} \sup_{\gamma\in\Gamma}\sup_{\tau\in\mathscr{T}}\left|\sum_{j=i}^{i+L-1}[\tau - G(-\hat{u}_{j\tau}/\lambda_n)][\varphi_{jw} - c_0\hat{b}(X_j,\gamma)]\right|. \tag{A.19}$$

Conditional on $\mathfrak{D}_n$, the triangular array $\{s_{ni}(\zeta_i;\tau,\gamma)\}$ is independent within rows, so we can apply Theorem 10.6 of Pollard (1990) to show the weak convergence of $S_n^*(\cdot,\cdot)$ to $S_\infty(\cdot,\cdot)$. Recall that Pollard's theorem allows the function $s_{ni}(\cdot;\cdot,\cdot)$ to depend on both n and i.

Define the pseudo-metric

$$\rho_n(\tau,\tau';\gamma,\gamma') \equiv \left\{\sum_{i=1}^{n} E^*[|s_{ni}(\zeta_i;\tau',\gamma') - s_{ni}(\zeta_i;\tau,\gamma)|^2]\right\}^{1/2}. \tag{A.20}$$

By Theorem 10.6 of Pollard (1990), it suffices to verify the following five conditions:

(i) $\{s_{ni}\}$ is manageable in the sense of Definition 7.9 of Pollard (1990);
(ii) $E^*[S_n^*(\tau,\gamma)S_n^{*c}(\tau',\gamma)] \xrightarrow{P} \Upsilon(\tau,\tau';\gamma,\gamma')$ for every (τ,γ),(τ',γ') in $\mathscr{T}\times\Gamma$;
(iii) $\overline{\lim}_{n\to\infty}\sum_{i=1}^{n} E^*(\bar{s}_{ni}^2(z_i))$ is stochastically bounded;
(iv) $\sum_{i=1}^{n} E^*(\bar{s}_{ni}^2(z_i)1(\bar{s}_{ni}(z_i)>\varepsilon)) \xrightarrow{P} 0$ for each $\varepsilon>0$;
(v) $\rho(\tau,\tau';\gamma,\gamma') \equiv \text{plim}_{n\to\infty}\rho_n(\tau,\tau';\gamma,\gamma')$ is well defined and, for all deterministic sequences $\{\tau'_n,\gamma'_n\}$ and $\{\tau_n,\gamma_n\}$, if $\rho(\tau_n,\tau'_n;\gamma_n,\gamma'_n)\to 0$ then $\rho_n(\tau_n,\tau'_n;\gamma_n,\gamma'_n)\xrightarrow{P} 0$.

Step 1. We verify condition (i). In order for the triangular array of process $\{s_{ni}(\zeta_i;\tau,\gamma)\}$ to be manageable with respect to the envelope $\bar{s}_{ni}(\zeta_i)$, we need to find a deterministic function $\lambda(\varepsilon_0)$ that bounds the the covering number of $\alpha\odot S_n \equiv \{\alpha_i s_{ni}(\zeta_i;\tau,\gamma) : (\tau,\gamma)\in\mathscr{T}\times\Gamma$, are nonnegative finite constants for all $i = 1, \ldots, n\}$ with $\sqrt{\log\lambda(\varepsilon_0)}$ integrable. Here, the covering number refers to the smallest number of closed balls with radius $(\varepsilon_0/2)\sqrt{\sum_{i=1}^{n}\alpha_i^2|\bar{s}_{ni}(\zeta_i)|^2}$ whose unions cover $\mathbf{a}\odot\mathbf{S}_n$. It follows that within each closed ball

$$\sum_{i=1}^{n}\alpha_i^2 E^*|s_{ni}(\zeta_i;\tau,\gamma) - s_{ni}(\zeta_i;\tau',\gamma')|^2 \le \frac{\varepsilon_0^2}{4}\sum_{i=1}^{n}\alpha_i^2 E^*|\bar{s}_{ni}(\zeta_i)|^2 \forall\varepsilon_0\in(0,1]. \tag{A.21}$$

First, we study the term on the left-hand side (l.h.s.) of (A.21). Let $\tilde{\varphi}_{j\gamma} = \varphi_{j\gamma} - c_0\hat{b}(X_j,\gamma)$ and $\bar{\varphi}_{j\gamma} = \varphi_{j\gamma} - c_0 b(X_j,\gamma)$. By Propositions B.9 and B.10, we have that uniformly in (τ,γ),

$$L^{-1/2}\sum_{j=i}^{i+L-1}[\tau - G(-\hat{u}_{j\tau}/\lambda_n)]\tilde{\varphi}_{j\gamma} = L^{-1/2}\sum_{j=i}^{i+L-1}\psi_\tau(\varepsilon_{j\tau})\bar{\varphi}_{j\gamma} + o_P(1). \qquad \text{(A.22)}$$

Note that the local alternative does not contribute to the above equation because $L^{-1/2}\lambda_n^{-1}\sum_{j=i}^{i+L-1}G^{(1)}(-\varepsilon_{j\tau}/\lambda_n)\,n^{-1/2}\,\delta(\tau,W_j)\tilde{\varphi}_{j\gamma} = O_P(\sqrt{L/n}) = o_P(1)G^{(1)}(-\varepsilon_{j\tau}/\lambda_n)n^{-1/2}\delta(\tau,W_j)\tilde{\varphi}_{j\gamma} = O_P(\sqrt{L/n}) = o_P(1)$ by Proposition B.3(i) and the boundedness of $\delta(\cdot,\cdot)$ and φ. It follows that

$$\begin{aligned}
&\sum_{i=1}^{n}\alpha_i^2 E^*\left|s_{ni}(\zeta_i;\tau,\gamma) - s_{ni}(\zeta_i;\tau',\gamma')\right|^2 \\
&= \frac{1}{n}\sum_{i=1}^{n-L+1}\alpha_i^2\frac{1}{L}\left|\sum_{j=i}^{i+L-1}[\tau - G(-\hat{u}_{j\tau}/\lambda_n)]\tilde{\varphi}_{j\gamma} - \sum_{j=i}^{i+L-1}[\tau' + G(-\hat{u}_{j\tau'}/\lambda_n)]\tilde{\varphi}_{j\gamma'}\right|^2 \\
&= \frac{1}{n}\sum_{i=1}^{n-L+1}\alpha_i^2\frac{1}{L}\left|\sum_{j=i}^{i+L-1}\bar{\varphi}_{j\gamma}\psi_\tau(\varepsilon_{j\tau}) - \sum_{j=i}^{i+L-1}\bar{\varphi}_{j\gamma'}\psi_{\tau'}(\varepsilon_{j\tau'})\right|^2 + o_P(1) \qquad \text{(A.23)} \\
&\xrightarrow{P}\sum_{i=1}^{\infty}\alpha_i^2[\Upsilon(\tau,\tau;\gamma,\gamma) - 2\Upsilon(\tau,\tau';\gamma,\gamma') + \Upsilon(\tau',\tau';\gamma',\gamma')] \\
&\equiv \sum_{i=1}^{\infty}\alpha_i^2\rho^2(\tau,\tau';\gamma,\gamma'), \text{ say.}
\end{aligned}$$

Next, we study the term on the right-hand side (r.h.s.) of (A.21). By Propositions B.9 and B.10

$$\begin{aligned}
\sum_{i=1}^{n}\alpha_i^2 E^*\left|\bar{s}_{ni}(\zeta_i)\right|^2 &= \frac{1}{n}\sum_{i=1}^{n}\alpha_i^2\sup_{\gamma\in\Gamma}\sup_{\tau\in\mathscr{T}}\left|L^{-1/2}\sum_{j=i}^{i+L-1}\left[\tau - G(-\hat{u}_{j\tau}/\lambda_n)\right]\tilde{\varphi}_{j\gamma}\right|^2 \\
&\le \frac{1}{n}\sum_{i=1}^{n}\alpha_i^2\sup_{\gamma\in\Gamma}\sup_{\tau\in\mathscr{T}}\left|L^{-1/2}\sum_{j=i}^{i+L-1}\psi_\tau(\varepsilon_{j\tau})\bar{\varphi}_{j\gamma} + o_P(1)\right|^2 = O_P(1),
\end{aligned}$$

where the last equality follows because $\{L^{-1/2}\sum_{j=i}^{i+L-1}\psi_\tau(\varepsilon_{j\tau})\bar{\varphi}_{j\gamma}\}$ is an empirical process indexed by (τ,γ) by the proof of Theorem 4. It follows that $\sum_{i=1}^{n}\alpha_i^2 E^*\left|\bar{s}_{ni}(\zeta_i)\right|^2 = O_P(1)$. This, together with Eqs. (A.21) and (A.23), implies that for any small $\varepsilon_1 > 0$, there exists a large constant $M_1 \equiv M_1(\varepsilon_1)$ such that the following holds

$$\sum_{i=1}^{\infty} \alpha_i^2 \rho^2(\pi, \pi'; \tau, \tau') \leq \frac{\varepsilon_0^2}{4} M_1 \quad \text{for sufficiently large } n \tag{A.24}$$

on a set with probability $1 - \varepsilon_1$.

Now, partition the compact set $\mathcal{T}$ by finite points $\underline{\tau} = \tau_0 < \tau_1 < \cdots < \tau_{N1-1} < \tau_{N1} = \bar{\tau}$ such that $|\tau_j - \tau_{j-1}| = \delta_1$. By selecting grid points $\gamma_1, \ldots, \gamma_{N2}$, we can cover the compact set Γ by $\Gamma_k = \{\gamma : ||\gamma - \gamma_k|| \leq \delta_2\}$. Let $(\tau, \gamma) \in [\tau_{j-1}, \tau_j] \times \Gamma_k$ $(j, k = 1, 2, \ldots)$. Note that $\|\psi_\tau(\varepsilon_{i\tau})\bar{\varphi}_{i\gamma} - \psi_{\tau_j}(\varepsilon_{i\tau_j})\bar{\varphi}_{i\gamma}\|_{2+\eta}^{2+\eta} \leq C\delta_1$ and $\|[\bar{\varphi}_{i\gamma} - \bar{\varphi}_{i\gamma_k}]\psi_\tau(\varepsilon_{i\tau_j})\|_{2+\eta}^{2+\eta} \leq C\delta_2$. Denote $\varphi_n(\tau, \gamma) = \sum_{i=1}^n \bar{\varphi}_{i\gamma}\psi_\tau(\varepsilon_{i\tau})$. Let $\delta \equiv \sqrt{\delta_1^2 + \delta_2^2} < 1$. Then by the Cauchy-Schwarz and Davydov inequalities, we have

$$\begin{aligned}
\Upsilon(\tau_j, \tau; \gamma_k, \gamma) &= \lim_{n\to\infty} \frac{1}{n} E\left|\varphi_n(\tau, \gamma) - \varphi_n(\tau_j, \gamma_k)\right|^2 \\
&\leq 2 \lim_{n\to\infty} \frac{1}{n} E\left|\sum_{i=1}^{n} \bar{\varphi}_{i\gamma}\left[\psi_\tau(\varepsilon_{i\tau}) - \psi_{\tau_j}\left(\varepsilon_{i\tau_j}\right)\right]\right|^2 \\
&\quad + 2 \lim_{n\to\infty} \frac{1}{n} E\left|\sum_{i=1}^{n} \left[\bar{\varphi}_{i\gamma} - \bar{\varphi}_{i\gamma_k}\right]\psi_{\tau_j}\left(\varepsilon_{i\tau_j}\right)\right|^2 \\
&\leq C\left[O(\delta_1 + \delta_2) + \delta_1^{2/(2+\eta)} \sum_{s=1}^{\infty} \alpha(s)^{1/(2+\eta)} + \delta_2^{2/(2+\eta)} \sum_{s=1}^{\infty} \alpha(s)^{1/(2+\eta)}\right] \\
&\leq C\delta^{2/(2+\eta)},
\end{aligned}$$

where the exact values of C vary across lines. This implies that

$$\rho^2(\tau_j, \tau; \gamma_k, \gamma) = \Upsilon(\tau, \tau; \gamma, \gamma) - 2\Upsilon(\tau_j, \tau; \gamma_k, \gamma) + \Upsilon(\tau_j, \tau_j; \gamma_k, \gamma_k) \leq C_1\delta^{2/(2+\eta)}$$

for large enough C_1. Consequently, if we choose $\delta = \varepsilon_0^{2+\eta}$, then $\sum_{i=1}^{\infty}\alpha_i^2\rho^2 \times (\pi_j, \pi; \tau_k, \tau) \leq C_1\varepsilon_0^2\sum_{i=1}^{\infty}\alpha_i^2$, so that Eq. (A.24) can be satisfied for sufficiently large n and M_1. It follows that the capacity bound is $O(\delta^{-2}) = O(\varepsilon_0^{-2(2+\eta)})$ and the integrability condition is satisfied.

Step 2. We verify condition (ii). Recall $\tilde{\varphi}_{j\gamma} = \varphi_{j\gamma} - c_0\hat{b}(X_j, \gamma)$ and $\hat{\varphi}_{j\gamma} = \varphi_{j\gamma} - c_0 b(X_j, \gamma)$. By Propositions B.9 and B.10, $L^{-1/2}\sum_{j=i}^{i+L-1}[\tau - G(-\hat{u}_{j\tau}/\lambda_n)]\tilde{\varphi}_{j\gamma} = L^{-1/2}\sum_{j=i}^{i+L-1}\psi_\tau(\varepsilon_{j\tau})\bar{\varphi}_{j\gamma} + o_P(1)$ uniformly in (τ, γ). It follows that

$$E^*\left[S_n^*(\tau,\gamma)S_n^{*c}(\tau',\gamma')\right] = n^{-1}\sum_{i=1}^{n-L+1}\frac{1}{L}\sum_{j_1=i}^{i+L-1}\sum_{j_2=i}^{i+L-1}[\tau - G(-\hat{u}_{j_1\tau}/\lambda_n)]\tilde{\varphi}_{j_1\gamma} \times [\tau' - G(-\hat{u}_{j_2\tau'}/\lambda_n)]\tilde{\varphi}^c_{j_2\gamma'}$$
$$= n^{-1}\sum_{i=1}^{n-L+1}\frac{1}{L}\sum_{j_1=i}^{i+L-1}\sum_{j_2=i}^{i+L-1}\psi_\tau(\varepsilon_{j_1\tau})\bar{\varphi}_{j_1\gamma}\psi_\tau(\varepsilon_{j_2\tau'})\bar{\varphi}^c_{j_2\gamma'} + o_P(1)$$
$$\equiv \bar{S}_n^* + o_P(1),$$

where we suppress the dependence of $\bar{S}_n^* \equiv \bar{S}_n^*(\tau,\gamma,\tau',\gamma')$ on $(\tau,\gamma,\tau',\gamma')$. First,

$$E(\bar{S}_n^*) = \frac{1}{n}\sum_{i=1}^{n-L+1}\frac{1}{L}\sum_{j_1=i}^{i+L-1}\sum_{j_2=i}^{i+L-1}E[\psi_\tau(\varepsilon_{j_1\tau})\psi_\tau(\varepsilon_{j_2\tau'})\bar{\varphi}_{j_1\gamma}\bar{\varphi}^c_{j_2\gamma'} \to \Upsilon(\tau,\tau';\gamma,\gamma').$$

To show $\mathrm{Var}(\bar{S}_n^*) = o(1)$, let $\xi_{ni}^* \equiv \xi_{ni}^*(\tau,\tau';\gamma,\gamma') = L^{-2}\sum_{j_1=i}^{i+L-1}\sum_{j_2=i}^{i+L-1}\times \psi_\tau(\varepsilon_{j_1\tau})\psi_\tau(\varepsilon_{j_2\tau'})\bar{\varphi}_{j_1\gamma}\bar{\varphi}^c_{j_2\gamma'}$, and let $\xi_{ni}(\tau,\gamma) \equiv L^{-1}\sum_{j=i}^{i+L-1}\psi_\tau(\varepsilon_{j\tau})\bar{\varphi}_{j\gamma}$. Then by the Cauchy inequality,

$$\|\xi_{ni}^*\|_8 = \|\xi_{ni}(\tau,\gamma)\xi_{ni}(\tau',\gamma')\|_8 \le \|\xi_{ni}(\tau,\gamma)\|_{16}\|\xi_{ni}(\tau',\gamma')\|_{16}.$$

By Lemma 3.1 of Andrews and Pollard (1994) with $Q = 16, \|\xi_{ni}(\tau,\gamma)\|_{16}^{16} = E|\frac{1}{L}\sum_{j=i}^{i+L-1}\psi_\tau(\varepsilon_{j\tau})\varphi_{j\gamma}|^{16} = O(L^{-8})$. Consequently, $E|\xi_{ni}^*|^8 = O(L^{-8})$. Let $\kappa_{4n} = \sup_{i\le n}\sup_{\tau,\tau';\gamma,\gamma'}E|\xi_{ni}^*|^8 = O(L^{-8})$ and $\kappa_{2n} = \sup_{i\le n}\sup_{\tau,\tau';\gamma,\gamma'}E\left|\xi_{ni}^*\right|^4 = O(L^{-4})$. By Lemma A.1(b) of Inoue (2001) with $\delta = 2$ (see also Lemma 9 of Bühlmann (1994)),

$$E\left|\frac{L}{n}\sum_{i=1}^{n-L+1}\xi_{ni}^*\right|^4 = O(L^4n^{-4}L^2(n^2\kappa_{4n}^{1/2} + n\kappa_{2n})) = O(n^{-2}L^2) = o(1).$$

Hence $\bar{S}_n^* = \Upsilon(\tau,\tau;\gamma,\gamma) + o_P(1)$ by the Chebyshev inequality.

Step 3. We verify condition (iii). This follows from the proof in Step 1 by taking $\alpha_i = 1 \forall i$.

Step 4. We verify condition (iv). By the conditional Chebyshev inequality and Propositions B.9 and B.10,

$$P^*(\bar{s}_{ni}(\zeta_i) > \varepsilon) \leq \frac{L}{n\varepsilon^2}\left\{\sup_{\gamma\in\Gamma}\sup_{\tau\in\mathscr{T}}\left|\frac{1}{\sqrt{L}}\sum_{j=i}^{i+L-1}(\tau - G(-\hat{u}_{j\tau}/\lambda_n))\tilde{\varphi}_{j\gamma}\right|\right\}^2$$
$$= \frac{L}{n\varepsilon^2}\left\{\sup_{\gamma\in\Gamma}\sup_{\tau\in\mathscr{T}}\left|\frac{1}{\sqrt{L}}\sum_{j=i}^{i+L-1}\psi_\tau(\varepsilon_{j\tau})\bar{\varphi}_{j\gamma}\right|^2 + o_P(1)\right\} = O_P\left(\frac{L}{n}\right).$$

By the Cauchy-Schwarz inequality,

$$\sum_{i=1}^{n} E^*(|\bar{s}_{ni}(\zeta_i)|^2 1(\bar{s}_{ni}(\zeta_i) > \varepsilon))$$
$$= \frac{1}{n}\sum_{i=1}^{n} E^*\left\{\zeta_i^2 \sup_{\gamma\in\Gamma-}\sup_{\tau\in\mathscr{T}}\left|\sum_{j=i}^{i+L-1}[\tau - G(-\hat{u}_{j\tau}/\lambda_n)]\tilde{\varphi}_{j\gamma}\right|^2 1(\bar{s}_{ni}(\zeta_i) > \varepsilon)\right\}$$
$$\leq \frac{1}{n}\sum_{i=1}^{n}\left\{\frac{1}{L^2}\sup_{\gamma\in\Gamma-}\sup_{\tau\in\mathscr{T}}\left|\sum_{j=i}^{i+L-1}[\tau - G(-\hat{u}_{j\tau}/\lambda_n)]\tilde{\varphi}_{j\gamma}\right|^4 P^*(\bar{s}_{ni}(\zeta_i) > \varepsilon)\right\}^{1/2}$$
$$= O_P(\sqrt{L/n}) = o_P(1).$$

The result follows.

Step 5. We verify condition (v). From the verification of condition (i), we know that $\rho^2(\tau, \tau'; \gamma, \gamma') = \text{plim}_{n\to\infty}\rho_n^2(\tau, \tau'; \gamma, \gamma')$ is well defined. If $\rho(\tau_n, \gamma'; \gamma_n, \gamma'_n) \to 0$, then $\rho_n(\tau_n, \tau'_n; \gamma_n, \tau'_n) \leq |\rho_n(\tau_n, \tau'_n; \gamma_n, \tau'_n) - \rho(\tau_n, \tau'_n; \gamma_n, \tau'_n)| + \rho(\tau_n, \tau'_n; \gamma_n, \tau'_n) \xrightarrow{P} 0$.

APPENDIX B: PROPOSITIONS

In this appendix, we prove some propositions used in the proof of Theorems 2–5 and that apply some technical lemmas in the next appendix. Recall $\varphi_{i\gamma} \equiv \varphi(W_i, \gamma)$, $m_{i\tau} \equiv m(\tau, W_i)$, $g(\cdot) \equiv G^{(1)}(\cdot)$, and $\mu_{ix} \equiv \mu((X_i - x)/h)$. Let $K_{ij} \equiv K((X_i - X_j)/h)$, $\mu_{i,j} \equiv \mu((X_i - X_j)/h)$, and $g^{(s-1)}(\cdot) \equiv G^{(s)}(\cdot)$ for $s = 2, 3$. Here we use $E_i(\cdot)$ to denote expectation conditional on $W_i \equiv (X_i^T, Z_i^T)^T$ instead of X_i.

Proposition B.1.

(i) $E[G(-\varepsilon_{i\tau}/\lambda_n)] - \tau = O(\lambda_n^q)$;

(ii) $E[G(-\varepsilon_{i\tau}/\lambda_n) - \mathbf{1}(\varepsilon_{i\tau} \le 0)]^2 = O(\lambda_n)$;

(iii) $\lambda_n^{-1} E[G^{(1)}(-\varepsilon_{i\tau}/\lambda_n)] = E[f(m_{i\tau}|W_i)] + O(\lambda_n^q)$.

Proof. Under Assumptions 9(i) and 11(i)–(iii), using change of variables, integration by parts, and a qth order Taylor expansion yields

$$
\begin{aligned}
E[G(-\varepsilon_{i\tau}/\lambda_n)|W_i] &= E[G(-(Y_i - m_{i\tau})/\lambda_n)|W_i] \\
&= \int_{-\infty}^{\infty} G(-(y - m_{i\tau})/\lambda_n)dF(y|W_i) \\
&= -\int_{-\infty}^{\infty} F(y|W_i)dG(-(y - m_{i\tau})/\lambda_n) \\
&= \int_{-\infty}^{\infty} F(m_{i\tau} + v\lambda_n|W_i)g(-v)dv \\
&= \tau + \int_{-\infty}^{\infty} \sum_{s=1}^{q} \frac{1}{s!} F^{(s)}(m_{i\tau}|W_i)v^s \lambda_n^s g(v)dv + r_{ni} \\
&= \tau + \frac{\lambda_n^q \kappa_q}{q!} F^{(q)}(m_{i\tau}|W_i) + r_{ni},
\end{aligned}
$$

where $\kappa_q \equiv \int_{-\infty}^{\infty} v^q g(v)dv$, $r_{ni} \equiv (\lambda_n^q/(q-1)!) \int_{-\infty}^{\infty} \int_0^1 [F^{(q)}(m_{i\tau} + sv\lambda_n|W_i) - F_i^{(q)}(m_{i\tau}|W_i)]v^q g(v)(1-s)^{q-1} ds dv$. By Assumption 9(i), the dominated convergence theorem, and the law of iterated expectations, $E|r_{ni}| = o(\lambda_n^q)$, and $E[G(-\varepsilon_{i\tau}/\lambda_n)] = \tau + \frac{\lambda_n^q \kappa_q}{q!} E[F^{(q)}(m_{i\tau}|W_i)] + o(\lambda_n^q)$. This proves (i). For (ii), using Assumptions 7, 11(i) and (iii), we have $G(0) \equiv \int_{-\infty}^{0} g(v)dv = 0.5$, and

$$
\begin{aligned}
&E[G(-\varepsilon_{i\tau}/\lambda_n) - \mathbf{1}(\varepsilon_{i\tau} \le 0)]^2 \\
&\quad = E[G^2(-\varepsilon_{i\tau}/\lambda_n)] + E[\mathbf{1}(\varepsilon_{i\tau} \le 0)] - 2E[G(-\varepsilon_{i\tau}/\lambda_n)\mathbf{1}(\varepsilon_{i\tau} \le 0)] \\
&\quad = E\left[\int_{-\infty}^{\infty} G^2(-(y - m_{i\tau})/\lambda_n)dF(y|W_i)\right]
\end{aligned}
$$

$$
\begin{aligned}
&+\tau - 2E\left[\int_{-\infty}^{m_{i\tau}} G(-(y-m_{i\tau})/\lambda_n)dF(y|W_i)\right] \\
&= -E\left[\int_{-\infty}^{\infty} F(m_{i\tau}+\lambda_n v|W_i)dG^2(-v)\right] \\
&\quad + \tau - 2\left\{G(0)\tau + E\left[\int_{-\infty}^{0} F(m_{i\tau}+\lambda_n v|W_i)g(-v)dv\right]\right\} \\
&= -\tau\int_{-\infty}^{\infty} dG^2(-v) + \tau - 2\tau + O(\lambda_n) = O(\lambda_n).
\end{aligned}
$$

By Assumptions 9(i) and 15(ii) and (iii),

$$
\begin{aligned}
\lambda_n^{-1}E[G^{(1)}(-\varepsilon_{i\tau}/\lambda_n)] &= E\left[\lambda_n^{-1}\int_{-\infty}^{\infty} G^{(1)}(-(y-m_{i\tau})/\lambda_n)f(y|W_i)dy\right] \\
&= E\left[\int_{-\infty}^{\infty} f(m_{i\tau}+\lambda_n v|W_i)g(v)dv\right] \\
&= E\left[f(m_{i\tau}|W_i) + \int_{-\infty}^{\infty}\sum_{s=1}^{q}\frac{1}{s!}f_i^{(s)}(m_{i\tau}|W_i)\lambda_n^s v^s g(v)dv\right] \\
&\quad + o(\lambda_n^q) \\
&= E[f(m_{i\tau}|W_i)] + \frac{\lambda_n^q\kappa_q}{q!}E[f^{(q)}(m_{i\tau}|W_i)] + o(\lambda_n^q) \\
&= E[f(m_{i\tau}|W_i)] + O(\lambda_n^q)
\end{aligned}
$$

Proposition B.2.

(i) $\sup_{\tau\in\mathscr{T}}\frac{1}{n\lambda_n}\sum_{i=1}^{n}E\left|G^{(1)}(-\varepsilon_{i\tau}/\lambda_n)\right| = O(1)$;
(ii) $\sup_{\tau\in\mathscr{T}}\frac{1}{n\lambda_n^2}\sum_{i=1}^{n}E\left|G^{(2)}(-\varepsilon_{i\tau}/\lambda_n)\right| = O(1)$;
(iii) $\sup_{\tau\in\mathscr{T}}\frac{1}{n\lambda_n^3}\sum_{i=1}^{n}E\left|G^{(3)}(-\varepsilon_{i\tau}/\lambda_n)\right| = O(1)$.

Proof. By Assumptions 3(i), 9(i), and 11(ii) and (iii), we have, uniformly in τ,

$$
\begin{aligned}
\lambda_n^{-1}E\left|G^{(1)}(-\varepsilon_{i\tau}/\lambda_n)\right| &= E\left[\lambda_n^{-1}\int_{-\infty}^{\infty}\left|g(-(y-m_{i\tau})/\lambda_n)\right|f(y|W_i)dy\right] \\
&= -E\left[\int_{-\infty}^{\infty} f(m_{i\tau}+\lambda_n v|W_i)\left|g(v)\right|dv\right] \\
&= E\left[\int_{-\infty}^{\infty}(f(m_{i\tau}|W_i) + \sum_{s=1}^{q}\frac{1}{s!}f^{(s)}(m_{i\tau}|W_i)\lambda_n^s v^s)\left|g(v)\right|dv\right] \\
&\quad + o(\lambda_n^q) \\
&= E[f(m_{i\tau}|W_i)]\int_{-\infty}^{\infty}\left|g(v)\right|dv + O(\lambda_n) = O(1).
\end{aligned}
$$

Similarly, uniformly in τ,

$$\lambda_n^{-2}E|G^{(2)}(-\varepsilon_{i\tau}/\lambda_n)| = E\left[\lambda_n^{-2}\int_{-\infty}^{\infty}\left|g^{(1)}(-y-m_{i\tau})/\lambda_n)\right|f(y|W_i)dy\right]$$

$$= -\lambda_n^{-1}E\left[\int_{-\infty}^{\infty}f(m_{i\tau}+\lambda_n v|W_i)\left|g^{(1)}(v)\right|dv\right]$$

$$= E\left[\int_{-\infty}^{\infty}(f(m_{i\tau}|W_i)+\sum_{s=1}^{q}\frac{1}{s!}f^{(s)}(m_{i\tau}|\,W_i)\lambda_n^s v^s)\mathrm{sgn}(g^{(1)}(v))dg(v)\right]+o(\lambda_n^{q-1})$$

$$= E[f^{(1)}(m_{i\tau}|W_i)]\int_{-\infty}^{\infty}\left|g^{(1)}(v)\right|dv+O(\lambda_n)=O(1).$$

The proof of (iii) is similar and thus omitted.

Proposition B.3.

(i) $\sup_{\tau\in\mathscr{T}}\frac{1}{n\lambda_n}\sum_{i=1}^n\left|G^{(1)}(-\varepsilon_{i\tau}/\lambda_n)\right| = O_P(1)$;
(ii) $\sup_{\tau\in\mathscr{T}}\frac{1}{n\lambda_n^2}\sum_{i=1}^n\left|G^{(2)}(-\varepsilon_{i\tau}/\lambda_n)\right| = O_P(1+n^{-1/2}\lambda_n^{-3/2}\sqrt{\log n})$;
(iii) $\sup_{\tau\in\mathscr{T}}\frac{1}{n\lambda_n^3}\sum_{i=1}^n\left|G^{(3)}(-\varepsilon_{i\tau}/\lambda_n)\right| = O_P(1+n^{-1/2}\lambda_n^{-5/2}\sqrt{\log n})$.

Proof. We only show (i) since the other cases are similar. By Proposition B.2(i), it suffices to show that $\sup_{\tau\in\mathscr{T}}\frac{1}{n}\sum_{i=1}^n b_{ni}(\tau) = O_P(1)$, where $b_{ni}(\tau)\equiv \lambda_n^{-1}[|G^{(1)}(-\varepsilon_{i\tau}/\lambda_n)| - E|G^{(1)}(-\varepsilon_{i\tau}/\lambda_n)|]$. Let $b_n(\tau)\equiv\frac{1}{n}\sum_{i=1}^n b_{ni}(\tau)$. Noting that $||\lambda_n^{-1}g(-\varepsilon_{i\tau}/\lambda_n)||_{2+\eta} = O(\lambda_n^{-(1+\eta)/(2+\eta)})$, we have by the Davydov inequality that

$$\mathrm{Var}(b_n(\tau)) = \frac{1}{n^2}\sum_{i=1}^n\mathrm{Var}(b_{ni}(\tau))+\frac{2}{n^2}\sum_{1\le i<j\le n}^{n}E[b_{ni}(\tau)b_{nj}(\tau)]$$

$$\le O(n^{-1}\lambda_n^{-1})+C\max_{1\le i\le n}||b_{ni}(\tau)||_{2+\eta}^2\sum_{i=1}^n\sum_{s=1}^\infty\alpha(s)^{\eta/(2+\eta)}$$

$$= O(n^{-1}\lambda_n^{-1}+n^{-1}\lambda_n^{-2(1+\eta)/(2+\eta)}) = o(1).$$

It follows that $b_n(\tau)=o_P(1)$ for each τ. Following exactly the same argument as used in the proof of the uniform consistency of kernel density estimators, we can show that $\sup_{\tau\in\mathscr{T}}\left|b_n(\tau)\right| = O_P(n^{-1/2}\lambda_n^{-1/2}\sqrt{\log n})$. It follows that $\sup_{\tau\in\mathscr{T}}n^{-1}\lambda_n^{-1}\sum_{i=1}^n\left|G^{(1)}(-\varepsilon_{i\tau}/\lambda_n)\right| = O(1)+O_P(n^{-1/2}\lambda_n^{-1/2}\sqrt{\log n}) = O_P(1)$.

Proposition B.4. $\mathbb{V}_{n1}(\tau,\gamma)\equiv n^{-1/2}\sum_{i=1}^n[1(\varepsilon_{i\tau}<0)-G(-\varepsilon_{i\tau}/\lambda_n)]\varphi_{i\gamma} = o_P(1)$ uniformly in $(\tau,\gamma)\in\mathscr{T}\times\Gamma$.

Proof. Let $\mathbb{V}_{n1,1}(\tau,\gamma) \equiv n^{-1/2}\sum_{i=1}^{n}\{1(\varepsilon_{i\tau}<0) - G(-\varepsilon_{i\tau}/\lambda_n) - \tau + E_i[G(-\varepsilon_{i\tau}/\lambda_n)]\}\varphi_{i\gamma}$ and $\mathbb{V}_{n1,2}(\tau,\gamma) \equiv n^{-1/2}\sum_{i=1}^{n}\{\tau - E_i[G(-\varepsilon_{i\tau}/\lambda_n)]\}\varphi_{i\gamma}$. Then $\mathbb{V}_{n1}(\tau,\gamma) = \mathbb{V}_{n1,1}(\tau,\gamma) + \mathbb{V}_{n1,2}(\tau,\gamma)$. By Proposition B.1(i) and the uniform boundedness of φ, $\sup_{\gamma\in\Gamma}\sup_{\tau\in\mathscr{T}}|\mathbb{V}_{n1,2}(\tau,\gamma)| = O(n^{1/2}\lambda_n^q) = o_P(1)$. We partition the compact set $\mathscr{T}$ by $\bar{n}_1$ points $\underline{\tau} = \tau_0 < \tau_1 < \tau_2 < \cdots < \tau_{\bar{n}_1} = \bar{\tau}$ such that $|\tau_j - \tau_{j-1}| = \delta_{1n} = 1/\log\log n$. Let $\mathscr{T}_1 = [\tau_0, \tau_1]$ and $\mathscr{T}_j = (\tau_{j-1}, \tau_j]$ for $j = 2, \ldots, \bar{n}_1$. Let $\tau \in (\tau_j, \tau_{j+1}]$. We cover the compact set Γ by $\Gamma_k = \{\gamma : ||\gamma - \gamma_k|| \le \delta_{2n}\}$ for $k = 1, \ldots, \bar{n}_2$, where $\delta_{2n} = 1/(\log\log n)^{d_\Gamma}$, d_Γ is the dimension of $\gamma \in \Gamma$, and $\bar{n}_2 = O(\log\log n)$.

Note that

$$
\begin{aligned}
\sup_{\gamma\in\Gamma}\sup_{\tau\in\mathscr{T}}\left|\mathbb{V}_{n1,1}(\tau,\gamma)\right| &\le \max_{1\le l\le\bar{n}_2}\max_{1\le j\le\bar{n}_1}\left|\mathbb{V}_{n1,1}(\tau_j,\gamma_l)\right| \\
&\quad + \max_{1\le l\le\bar{n}_2}\max_{1\le j\le\bar{n}_1}\sup_{\gamma\in\Gamma_l}\sup_{\tau\in\mathscr{T}_j}\left|\mathbb{V}_{n1,1}(\tau,\gamma) - \mathbb{V}_{n1,1}(\tau_j,\gamma_l)\right| \\
&\equiv V_{n11} + V_{n12}.
\end{aligned}
$$

Fix $\varepsilon > 0$. Let $\xi_{i,jl} \equiv \{\mathbf{1}(\varepsilon_{i\tau_j} < 0) - G(-\varepsilon_{i\tau_j}/\lambda_n) - \tau_j + E_i[G(-\varepsilon_{i\tau_j}/\lambda_n)]\}\varphi_{i\gamma_l}$. Then $|\xi_{i,jl}| \le 2\bar{c}_G c_\varphi, E(\xi_{i,jl}) = 0$ and $E(\xi_{i,jl}^2) \le C\bar{\lambda}_n$ by Propositions B.1(i) and (ii) where $\bar{\lambda}_n \equiv \lambda_n + \lambda_n^q$. By the Davydov inequality, one can show that there exists some positive constant c_ξ such that $E[\sum_{i=s+1}^{s+p_n}\xi_{i,jl}]^2 \le c_\xi p_n\bar{\lambda}_n$ for any $s = 1, \ldots, p_n$ and $1 \le p_n \le n/2$. We can apply Lemma C.3 with $M_n = 2c_\varphi$, $p_n = n^{1/2-\upsilon}$ for some $\upsilon > 0$, $\varepsilon^* = n^{-1/2}\varepsilon$, and $\sigma^2(p_n) = c_\xi p_n\bar{\lambda}_n$ to obtain

$$
\begin{aligned}
P(V_{n11} > \varepsilon) &\le \bar{n}_1\bar{n}_2\max_{1\le l\le\bar{n}_2}\max_{1\le j\le\bar{n}_1} P\left(\left|n^{-1}\sum_{i=1}^{n}\xi_{i,jl}\right| > n^{-1/2}\varepsilon\right) \\
&\le \bar{n}_1\bar{n}_2 C_0\exp\left(-\frac{\varepsilon^2}{C_1c_\xi\bar{\lambda}_n + 4c_\varphi C_2 n^{-\upsilon}\varepsilon}\right) \\
&\quad + \bar{n}_1\bar{n}_2 C_3\sqrt{\frac{2}{n^{-1/2}c_\varphi\varepsilon}}\,n^{1/2+\upsilon}\alpha(n^{1/2-\upsilon}+1) \qquad \text{(B.1)} \\
&= \bar{n}_1\bar{n}_2\exp\left(-\frac{\varepsilon^2}{C_1c_\xi\bar{\lambda}_n + 4c_\varphi C_2 n^{-\upsilon}\varepsilon}\right) \\
&\quad + o(n^{3/4+\upsilon}(n^{1/2-\upsilon})^{-\beta_0}(\log\log n)^2) \\
&\equiv p_{n1} + p_{n2},
\end{aligned}
$$

where $\beta_0 = 1 + 16/\eta$. Clearly, the first term p_{n1} is $o(1)$ provided $\upsilon > 0$. $p_{n2} = o(n^{3/4+\upsilon-(1/2-\upsilon)\beta_0}(\log\log n)^2) = o(1)$ provided $\beta_0 > (3/4+\upsilon)/(1/2-\upsilon)$ and $v \in (0, 1/2)$.

Now consider the class of functions

$$\mathscr{F}_2 \equiv \{b_{(\tau,\gamma)} : (\tau,\gamma) \in \mathscr{T} \times \Gamma\}$$

where $b_{(\tau,\gamma)} : \mathbb{R} \times \mathbb{R}^{d_X+d_Z} \to \mathbb{R}$ is defined by

$$b_{(\tau,\gamma)}(Y_i, W_i) \equiv \left\{ G\left(\frac{-Y_i + m(\tau, W_i)}{\lambda_n}\right) - E_i\left[G\left(\frac{-Y_i + m(\tau, W_i)}{\lambda_n}\right)\right]\right\}\varphi(W_i,\gamma).$$

Let $\bar{G}(-\varepsilon_{i\tau}/\lambda_n) \equiv G(-\varepsilon_{i\tau}/\lambda_n) - E_i[G(-\varepsilon_{i\tau}/\lambda_n)$ and $\varsigma_i(\tau,\gamma) \equiv \bar{G}(-\varepsilon_{i\tau}/\lambda_n)\varphi_{i\gamma}$. Then

$$\begin{aligned}\varsigma_i(\tau,\gamma) - \varsigma_i(\tau',\gamma') &= [\bar{G}(-\varepsilon_{i\tau}/\lambda_n) - \bar{G}(-\varepsilon_{i\tau'}/\lambda_n)]\varphi_{i\gamma} + \bar{G}(-\varepsilon_{i\tau'}/\lambda_n)[\varphi_{i\gamma} - \varphi_{i\gamma'}] \\ &\equiv \varsigma_{i1}(\tau,\tau',\gamma) + \varsigma_{i2}(\tau',\gamma,\gamma'), \text{ say.}\end{aligned}$$

Following the arguments in the proof of Theorem **4** and Proposition B.7, by the C_r inequality and Assumptions 10, and 11 we have

$$\begin{aligned}
&E \sup_{|\tau-\tau'|\le\delta_1, ||\gamma-\gamma'||\le\delta_2, \sqrt{\delta_1^2+\delta_2^2}\le\delta} \left|\varsigma_i(\tau,\gamma) - \varsigma_i(\tau',\gamma')\right|^r \\
&\le 2^{r-1} E \sup_{|\tau-\tau'|\le\delta_1, ||\gamma-\gamma'||\le\delta_2, \sqrt{\delta_1^2+\delta_2^2}\le\delta} \left|\varsigma_{i1}(\tau,\tau',\gamma)\right|^r \\
&\quad + 2^{r-1} E \sup_{|\tau-\tau'|\le\delta_1, ||\gamma-\gamma'||\le\delta_2, \sqrt{\delta_1^2+\delta_2^2}\le\delta} \left|\varsigma_{i2}(\tau',\gamma,\gamma')\right|^r \\
&\le CE \sup_{|\tau-\tau'|\le\delta_1} \left|G(-\varepsilon_{i\tau}/\lambda_n) - G(-\varepsilon_{i\tau'}/\lambda_n)\right| + CE \sup_{||\gamma-\gamma'||\le\delta_2} \left|\varphi(W_i,\gamma) - \varphi(W_i,\gamma')\right|^r \\
&\le CE \left|\sum_{j=1}^{3} \lambda_n^{-j} G^{(j)}\left(\frac{-Y_i + m(\tau, W_i)}{\lambda_n}\right)\right| \sup_{|\tau-\tau'|\le\delta_1} \left|m(\tau, W_i) - m(\tau', W_i)\right|^j \\
&\quad + CE\left\{\left|\lambda_n^{-3} G^*\left(\frac{-Y_i + m(\tau, W_i)}{\lambda_n}\right)\right| \sup_{|\tau-\tau'|\le\delta_1} \left|m(\tau, W_i) - m(\tau', W_i)\right|^3\right\} + C\delta_2^{rv} \\
&\le C\delta_1 + C\delta_1^3 + C\delta_2^{rv} \le 2C\delta^{1\wedge(rs_\gamma)} = 2C\delta^{\bar{v}},
\end{aligned}$$

where $\delta \le 1, \bar{v} = \min(1, rv)$, and $G^*(\cdot)$ is defined in the proof of Proposition B.7. That is, $\mathscr{F}_2$ is a class of uniformly bounded functions satisfying L_r-continuity. The L_r-continuity implies that the bracketing number satisfies

$$N(\varepsilon, \mathscr{F}_2, ||\cdot||_{L_r(P)}) \le C_2\left(\frac{1}{\varepsilon}\right)^{(1+d_\Gamma)/\bar{v}}.$$

By Theorem 2.2 of Andrews and Pollard (1994), this, together with Assumption 8(i) and the result in the proof of Theorem 4, implies that $\{\mathbb{V}_{n12}(\tau,\gamma):(\tau,\gamma)\in\mathscr{T}\times\Gamma\}$ is stochastically equicontinuous. It follows that

$$V_{n12}=\max_{1\le l\le\bar{n}_2}\max_{1\le j\le\bar{n}_1}\sup_{\gamma\in\Gamma_l}\sup_{\tau\in\mathscr{T}_j}\left|\mathbb{V}_{1n}(\tau,\gamma)-\mathbb{V}_{1n}(\tau_j,\gamma_l)\right|=o_P(1).$$

This completes the proof of the proposition.

Proposition B.5. Under H_{1n}, $\mathbb{V}_{n2}(\tau,\gamma)\equiv n^{-1/2}h^{-d_X}\sum_{i=1}^n[1(\varepsilon_{i\tau}\le 0)-1(u_{i\tau}\le 0)]\varphi_{i\gamma}\mu_{ix}K_{ix}=n^{-1}h^{-d_X}\sum_{i=1}^n f(m_{i\tau}|W_i)\delta(\tau,W_i)\mu_{ix}K_{ix}+o_P(1)$ uniformly in $(\tau,\gamma)\in\mathscr{T}\times\Gamma$ for each $x\in\mathscr{X}$.

Proof. Let $\mathbb{V}_{n2,1}(\tau,x)\equiv n^{-1/2}h^{-d_X}\sum_{i=1}^n\{\mathbf{1}(\varepsilon_{i\tau}\le 0)-\mathbf{1}(u_{i\tau}\le 0)-\tau+E_i[\mathbf{1}(u_{i\tau}\le 0)]\}\varphi_{i\gamma}\mu_{ix}K_{ix}$, and $\mathbb{V}_{n2,2}(\tau,x)\equiv n^{-1/2}h^{-d_X}\sum_{i=1}^n\{\tau-E_i[\mathbf{1}(u_{i\tau}\le 0)]\}\varphi_{i\gamma}\mu_{ix}K_{ix}$. Then $\mathbb{V}_{n2}(\tau,\gamma)=\mathbb{V}_{n2,1}(\tau,\gamma)+\mathbb{V}_{n2,2}(\tau,\gamma)$. By the proof of Theorem 3.1 (Lemma A.3 in particular), one can readily show that $\mathbb{V}_{n2,1}(\tau,\gamma)=o_P(1)$ uniformly in $(\tau,\gamma)\in\mathscr{T}\times\Gamma$. Let $\Delta_n(\tau,\gamma)\equiv n^{-1}h^{-d_X}\sum_{i=1}^n f(m_{i\tau}|W_i)\times\delta(\tau,W_i)\varphi_{i\gamma}\mu_{ix}\times K_{ix}$. By the Taylor expansion

$$\begin{aligned}
&\sup_{(\tau,\gamma)\in\mathscr{T}\times\Gamma}||\mathbb{V}_{n2,2}(\tau,\gamma)-\Delta_n(\tau,\gamma)||\\
&=\sup_{(\tau,\gamma)\in\mathscr{T}\times\Gamma}||n^{-1/2}h^{-d_X}\sum_{i=1}^n[F(m_{i\tau}|W_i)-F(m(\tau,X_i)|W_i)]\varphi_{i\gamma}\mu_{ix}K_{ix}-\Delta_n(\tau,\gamma)||\\
&=\sup_{(\tau,\gamma)\in\mathscr{T}\times\Gamma}||n^{-1}h^{-d_X}\sum_{i=1}^n\left[f(m^*_{i\tau}|W_i)-f(m_{i\tau}|W_i)\right]\delta(\tau,W_i)\varphi_{i\gamma}\mu_{ix}K_{ix}||\\
&\le\sup_{(\tau,\gamma)\in\mathscr{T}\times\Gamma}n^{-3/2}h^{-d_X}\sum_{i=1}^n C_2(W_i)\delta^2(\tau,W_i)\varphi_{i\gamma}||\mu_{ix}||K_{ix}\\
&\le Cn^{-3/2}h^{-d_X}\sum_{i=1}^n||\mu_{ix}||K_{ix}=o_P(1),
\end{aligned}$$

where $m^*_{i\tau}$ lies between $m_{i\tau}$ and $m(\tau,X_i)$.

Proposition B.6. Under H_{1n}, $\mathbb{V}_{n3}(\tau,\gamma)\equiv n^{-1/2}\lambda_n^{-1}\sum_{i=1}^n G^{(1)}(-\varepsilon_{i\tau}/\lambda_n)\times(\hat{u}_{i\tau}-\varepsilon_{i\tau})\varphi_{i\gamma}=-c_0n^{-1/2}\times\sum_{i=1}^n b(X_i,\gamma)\psi_\tau(\varepsilon_{i\tau})+\mathbf{\Delta}(\tau,\gamma)+o_P(1)$ uniformly in (τ,γ).

Proof. Let $g_{ni\tau}\equiv\lambda_n^{-1}G^{(1)}(-\varepsilon_{i\tau}/\lambda_n)$. Using Proposition B.1(iii) and $u_{i\tau}=\varepsilon_{i\tau}+n^{-1/2}\delta(\tau,W_i)$ yields

$$\begin{aligned}\mathbb{V}_{n3}(\tau,\gamma) &= n^{-1/2}\sum_{i=1}^{n} g_{ni\tau}(\hat{u}_{i\tau}-u_{i\tau})\varphi_{i\gamma} + n^{-1/2}\sum_{i=1}^{n} g_{ni\tau}\delta(\tau,W_i)\varphi_{i\gamma}\\ &= \frac{1}{\sqrt{n}}\sum_{i=1}^{n} f(m_{i\tau}|W_i)(\hat{u}_{i\tau}-u_{i\tau})\varphi_{i\gamma}\\ &\quad+\frac{1}{\sqrt{n}}\sum_{i=1}^{n}[g_{ni\tau}-E(g_{ni\tau}|W_i)](\hat{u}_{i\tau}-u_{i\tau})\varphi_{i\gamma}\\ &\quad+\frac{1}{n}\sum_{i=1}^{n} g_{ni\tau}\delta(\tau,W_i)\varphi_{i\gamma}+o_P(1)\\ &\equiv \mathbb{V}_{n3,1}(\tau,\gamma)+\mathbb{V}_{n3,2}(\tau,\gamma)+\mathbb{V}_{n3,3}(\tau,\gamma)+o_P(1) \text{ uniformly in}(\tau,\gamma).\end{aligned} \tag{B.2}$$

By Corollary 1, we have

$$\begin{aligned}\hat{u}_{i\tau}-u_{i\tau} &= -e_1^T H(\tau,X_i)^{-1}\frac{1}{nh^{d_X}}\sum_{j=1}^{n}\psi_\tau(u_{j\tau})\mu_{j,i}K_{ij}[1+o_P(1)]+o_P(n^{-1/2})\\ &= [-\alpha_{1i}(\tau)-\alpha_{2i}(\tau)][1+o_P(1)]+o_P(n^{-1/2}),\end{aligned}$$

where both $o_P(1)$ and $o_P(n^{-1/2})$ hold uniformly in i and τ,$H(\tau,x)=f(m(\tau,x)|x)f(x)\mathbb{H}$, $\alpha_{1i}(\tau)=e_1^T H(\tau,X_i)^{-1}\frac{1}{nh^{d_X}}\sum_{j=1}^{n}\psi_\tau(\varepsilon_{j\tau})\mu_{j,i}K_{ij}$, and $\alpha_{2i}(\tau)=e_1^T H(\tau,X_i)^{-1}\frac{1}{nh^{d_X}}\sum_{j=1}^{n}[1(\varepsilon_{j\tau}\le 0)-1(u_{j\tau}\le 0)]\mu_{j,i}K_{ij}$. It follows that

$$\begin{aligned}\mathbb{V}_{n3,1}(\tau,\gamma) &\simeq -\frac{1}{\sqrt{n}}\sum_{i=1}^{n} f(m_{i\tau}|W_i)\varphi_{i\gamma}\alpha_{1i}(\tau)\\ &\quad-\frac{1}{\sqrt{n}}\sum_{i=1}^{n} f(m_{i\tau}|W_i)\varphi_{i\gamma}\alpha_{2i}(\tau)+o_P(1)\\ &\equiv -\mathbb{V}_{n3,1}^{(1)}(\tau,\gamma)-\mathbb{V}_{n3,1}^{(2)}(\tau,\gamma)+o_P(1).\end{aligned} \tag{B.3}$$

We first study $\mathbb{V}_{n3,1}^{(1)}(\tau,\gamma)$. As before, partition $\mathscr{T}$ as before by n_1 points $\underline{\tau}=\tau_0<\tau_1<\cdots<\tau_{n_1}=\bar{\tau}$ and cover the compact set Γ by $\Gamma_k\equiv\{\gamma:||\gamma-\gamma_k||\le\delta_{2n}\}$, but we now require $\tau_{s+1}-\tau_s=h^{d_X/2}/\log n$ and $\delta_{2n}=n^{-1/2}/\log n$. Fix $\gamma_l\in\Gamma_l$. Let $\mathscr{T}_s=[\tau_s,\tau_{s+1}]$ for $s=1,\ldots,n_1$ and let $(\tau,\gamma)\in\mathscr{T}_s\times\Gamma_l$. Then

$$\begin{aligned}\sup_{\gamma\in\Gamma}\sup_{\tau\in\mathscr{T}}\left|\mathbb{V}_{n3,1}^{(1)}(\tau,\gamma)\right| &\le \max_{1\le l\le n_2}\max_{1\le s\le n_1}\left|\mathbb{V}_{n3,1}^{(1)}(\tau_s,\gamma_l)\right|\\ &\quad+\max_{1\le l\le n_2}\sup_{\gamma\in\Gamma_l}\max_{1\le s\le n_1}\sup_{\tau\in\mathscr{T}_s}\left|\mathbb{V}_{n3,1}^{(1)}(\tau,\gamma)-\mathbb{V}_{n3,1}^{(1)}(\tau_s,\gamma_l)\right|.\end{aligned} \tag{B.4}$$

Let $V_i \equiv (W_i^T, Y_i)^T$ and $\varsigma_{ij}(\tau,\gamma) \equiv h^{-d_X} f(m_{i\tau}|X_i)\varphi_{i\gamma} e_1^T H(\tau, X_i)^{-1}\mu_{j,i}K_{ij}$. Introducing $\Phi_{1\tau\gamma}(V_i, V_j) \equiv \varsigma_{ij}(\tau,\gamma)\psi_\tau(\varepsilon_{j\tau}) + \varsigma_{ji}(\tau,\gamma)\psi_\tau(\varepsilon_{i\tau})]$, we can write $\mathbb{V}_{n3,1}^{(1)}(\tau,\gamma)$ as $n^{-3/2}\sum_{i=1}^n \Phi_{1\tau\gamma}(V_i, V_i)$ plus the U-statistic

$$\mathbb{U}_n(\tau,\gamma) \equiv \frac{1}{n^{3/2}} \sum_{1\le i<j\le n} \Phi_{1\tau\gamma}(V_i, V_j).$$

It is straightforward to show that $n^{-3/2}\sum_{i=1}^n \Phi_{1\tau\gamma}(V_i, V_i) = O_P(n^{-1/2}h^{-d_X}) = o_P(1)$ uniformly in (τ,γ). By the Hoeffding decomposition we have

$$\mathbb{U}_n(\tau,\gamma) = \frac{n-1}{n}\{\mathbb{U}_n^{(1)}(\tau,\gamma) + \mathbb{U}_n^{(2)}(\tau,\gamma)\}, \tag{B.5}$$

where

$$\mathbb{U}_n^{(1)}(\tau,\gamma) = \frac{1}{n^{1/2}}\sum_{j=1}^n \int \Phi_{1\tau\gamma}(V_i, V_j)dP(V_i),$$

$$\mathbb{U}_n^{(2)}(\tau,\gamma) = \frac{1}{n^{1/2}(n-1)}\sum_{1\le i<j\le n}\Bigg[\Phi_{1\tau\gamma}(V_i, V_j) - \int \Phi_{1\tau\gamma}(V_i, V_j)dP(V_i) - \int \Phi_{1\tau\gamma}(V_i, V_j)dP(V_j)\Bigg],$$

and $P(V_i)$ denotes the distribution of V_i. Noting that $\int \Phi_{1\tau\gamma}(V_i, V_j)\,dP(V_i) = h^{-d_X} E_i[f(m_{i\tau}|W_i)e_1^T H(\tau, X_i)^{-1}\mu_{j,i}K_{ij}\varphi_{i\gamma}]\psi_\tau(\varepsilon_{j\tau})$, it is straightforward to show that

$$\begin{aligned}
\mathbb{U}_n^{(1)}(\tau,\gamma) &= \frac{1}{n^{1/2}h^{d_X}}\sum_{j=1}^n \int f(m_{i\tau}|W_i)e_1^T H(\tau, X_i)^{-1}\mu_{j,i}K_{ij}\varphi_{i\gamma}dP(V_i)\psi_\tau(\varepsilon_{j\tau}) \\
&= \frac{1}{n^{1/2}}\sum_{j=1}^n \int\int f(m(\tau,(X_j+hv,z'))|X_j+hv,z') \\
&\quad \times e_1^T H(\tau, X_j+hv)^{-1}\mu(v)K(v) \\
&\quad \times \varphi((X_j+hv,z'),\gamma)f(X_j+hv,z')dvdz'\psi_\tau(\varepsilon_{j\tau}) \\
&\simeq \frac{1}{n^{1/2}}\sum_{j=1}^n \int f(m(\tau,(X_j,z'))|X_j,z')f(X_j,z')e_1^T H(\tau,X_j)^{-1} \\
&\quad \times \mathbb{B}_0\varphi((X_j,z'),\gamma)dz'\psi_\tau(\varepsilon_{j\tau}) \\
&\simeq \frac{c_0}{n^{1/2}}\sum_{j=1}^n \int f(X_j,z')f(X_j)^{-1}\varphi((X_j,z'),\gamma)dz'\psi_\tau(\varepsilon_{j\tau}) \\
&= \frac{c_0}{n^{1/2}}\sum_{j=1}^n b(X_j,\gamma)\psi_\tau(\varepsilon_{j\tau}),
\end{aligned} \tag{B.6}$$

where we use the fact that $H(\tau, X_j) = f(m(\tau, X_j)|X_j)f(X_j)\mathbb{H}$ and that $m(\tau, W_j) = m(\tau, X_j) + n^{-1/2}\delta(\tau, W_j)$. For $\Phi_{1\tau w}(V_i, V_j)$ define $M_{n1s}(s = 1, 2, 3, 4)$ and $M_{n2s}(s = 1, 2, 3)$ as in Lemma C.2. It is easy to verify that

$$M_{n11} = M_{n12} = O(h^{-d_X\eta}), M_{n13} = M_{n14} = O(h^{-d_X(1+\eta)}),$$
$$M_{n21} = O(h^{-2d_X}), M_{n22} = O(h^{-2d_X}), \text{ and } M_{n23} = O(h^{-3d_X}),$$

which implies that $E[\mathbb{U}_n^{(2)}(\tau_s, \gamma_l)]^4 = O(n^{-2}(h^{-4d_X\eta/(4+\eta)} + h^{-2d_X}))$. Fix $\varepsilon > 0$. By Lemma C.2(i) and the Markov inequality,

$$\begin{aligned} P\left(\max_{1\le l\le n_2}\max_{1\le s\le n_1}\left|\mathbb{U}_n^{(2)}(\tau_s, \gamma_l)\right| \ge \varepsilon\right) &\le n_1 n_2 \max_{1\le l\le n_2}\max_{1\le s\le n_1} P(\mathbb{U}_n^{(2)}(\tau_s, \gamma_l) \ge n^{3/2}\varepsilon) \\ &\le n_1 n_2 O(n^{-2}(h^{-4d_X\eta/(4+\eta)} + h^{-2d_X})) \\ &= O(n^{-1}(h^{-4d_X\eta/(4+\eta)} + h^{-2d_X}) \\ &\quad \times h^{-d_X/2}\log n) = o(1). \end{aligned}$$

Thus

$$\max_{1\le l\le n_2}\max_{1\le s\le n_1}\left|\mathbb{U}_n^{(2)}(\tau_s, \gamma_l)\right| = o_P(1). \tag{B.7}$$

Next, write

$$\begin{aligned} &\left|\mathbb{V}_{n3,1}^{(1)}(\tau, \gamma) - \mathbb{V}_{n3,1}^{(1)}(\tau_s, \gamma_l)\right| \\ &= \frac{1}{n^{3/2}h^{d_X}}\sum_{j=1}^{n}[\psi_\tau(\varepsilon_{j\tau}) - \psi_{\tau_s}(\varepsilon_{j\tau_s})]\sum_{i=1}^{n} f(m_{i\tau_s}|X_i)e_1^T H(\tau_s, X_i)^{-1}\mu_{j,i}K_{ij}\varphi_{i\gamma} \\ &\quad + \frac{1}{n^{3/2}h^{d_X}}\sum_{i=1}^{n}[f(m_{i\tau}|X_i)e_1^T H(\tau, X_i)^{-1} \\ &\quad - f(m_{i\tau_s}|X_i)e_1^T H(\tau_s, X_i)^{-1}]\sum_{j=1}^{n}\psi_\tau(\varepsilon_{j\tau})\mu_{j,i}K_{ij}\varphi_{i\gamma} \\ &\quad + \frac{1}{n^{3/2}h^{d_X}}\sum_{i=1}^{n}\sum_{j=1}^{n}\psi_{\tau_s}(\varepsilon_{j\tau_s})f(m_{i\tau_s}|X_i)e_1^T H(\tau_s, X_i)^{-1}\mu_{j,i}K_{ij}(\varphi_{i\gamma} - \varphi_{i\gamma_l}) \\ &\equiv V_{n31}(\tau, \tau_s; \gamma, \gamma_l) + V_{n32}(\tau, \tau_s; \gamma, \gamma_l) + V_{n33}(\tau, \tau_s; \gamma, \gamma_l). \end{aligned}$$

First, by the boundedness of φ, the absolute value of $V_{n31}(\tau, \tau_s; \gamma, \gamma_l)$ is no bigger than

$$\frac{c_\varphi}{n^{1/2}}\sum_{j=1}^{n}\left|\psi_\tau(\varepsilon_{j\tau})-\psi_{\tau_s}(\varepsilon_{j\tau_s})\right|\times\frac{1}{nh^{d_X}}\sum_{i=1}^{n}\left|f(m_{i\tau_s}|X_i)e_1^T H(\tau_s,X_i)^{-1}\mu_{j,i}K_{ij}\right|.$$

The second term in the last expression is $O_P(1)$ uniformly in j, whereas the first term is $o_P(1)$ uniformly in τ such that $|\tau-\tau_s|=o(n^{-1/2})$ by the stochastic equicontinuity of $\{n^{-1/2}\sum_{j=1}^{n}\psi_\tau(\varepsilon_{j\tau}):\tau\in\mathscr{T}\}$ (cf. the proof of Theorem **5**). It follows that $\max_{1\le l\le n_2}\sup_{\gamma\in\Gamma_l}\max_{1\le s\le n_1}\sup_{\tau\in\mathscr{T}_s}|V_{n31}(\tau,\tau_s;\gamma,\gamma_l)| = o_P(1)$. Similarly, by the fact that that $H(\tau,X_i)=f(m(\tau,X_i)|X_i)f(X_i)\mathbb{H}$ and $m(\tau,W_i)=m(\tau,X_i)+n^{-1/2}\delta(\tau,W_i)$ under H_{1n}, we can readily show that $\max_{1\le l\le n_2}\sup_{\gamma\in\Gamma_l}\max_{1\le s\le n_1}\sup_{\tau\in\mathscr{T}_s}|V_{n32}(\tau,\tau_s;\gamma,\gamma_l)|=o_P(1)$. By the boundedness of the conditional and marginal densities, we have

$$\left|V_{n33}(\tau,\tau_s;\gamma,\gamma_l)\right|\le\frac{C}{n^{1/2}}\sum_{i=1}^{n}\left|\varphi_{i\gamma}-\varphi_{i\gamma_l}\right|\times\frac{1}{nh^{d_X}}\sum_{j=1}^{n}e_1^T\mathbb{H}\mu_{j,i}K_{ij}.$$

The second term is $O_P(1)$ uniformly in j, whereas the first term is $o_P(1)$ uniformly in γ such that $\left|\gamma-\gamma_l\right|=o(n^{-1/2})$. Hence $\max_{1\le l\le n_2}\sup_{\gamma\in\Gamma_l}\max_{1\le s\le n_1}\sup_{\tau\in\mathscr{T}_s}|V_{n33}(\tau,\tau_s;\gamma,\gamma_l)| = o_P(1)$. These results, together with Eq. (B.4) and the analysis of $\mathbb{U}_n(\tau,\gamma)$ (esp. (B.5)–(B.7)), imply that uniformly in (τ,γ)

$$\mathbb{V}_{n3,1}^{(1)}(\tau,\gamma)=-\frac{c_0}{n^{1/2}}\sum_{j=1}^{n}b(X_j,\gamma)\psi_\tau(\varepsilon_{j\tau})+o_P(1). \tag{B.8}$$

Now we study $\mathbb{V}_{n3,1}^{(2)}(\tau,\gamma)$ defined in (B.3). By Proposition **16**, uniformly in (τ,γ)

$$\begin{aligned}\mathbb{V}_{n3,1}^{(2)}(\tau,\gamma)&=\frac{1}{n^2h^{d_X}}\sum_{i=1}^{n}\sum_{j=1}^{n}f(m_{i\tau}|W_i)\varphi_{i\gamma}e_1^T H(\tau,X_i)^{-1}f(m_{j\tau}|W_j)\\&\quad\times\delta(\tau,W_j)\mu_{j,i}K_{ij}+o_P(1)\\&\simeq\frac{1}{n^2h^{d_X}}\sum_{i=1}^{n}\sum_{j=1}^{n}E_i[f(m_{i\tau}|W_i)\varphi_{i\gamma}e_1^T H(\tau,X_i)^{-1}\mu_{j,i}K_{ij}]\\&\quad(m_{j\tau}|W_j)\delta(\tau,W_j)+o_P(1)\\&=\frac{c_0}{n}\sum_{j=1}^{n}f(m_{j\tau}|W_j)\delta(\tau,W_j)b(X_j,\gamma)+o_P(1),\end{aligned} \tag{B.9}$$

where we have used the fact that $f(m_{i\tau}|W_i)=f(m(\tau,X_i)|X_i)+O_P(n^{-1/2})$ under H_{1n}. Combining (B.3), (B.8), and (B.9) yields

$$\begin{aligned}\mathbb{V}_{n3,1}(\tau,\gamma) &= -\frac{c_0}{n^{1/2}}\sum_{i=1}^{n} b(X_i,\gamma)\psi_\tau(\varepsilon_{i\tau}) \\ &\quad -\frac{c_0}{n}\sum_{j=1}^{n} f(m_{j\tau}|W_j)\delta(\tau,W_j)b(X_j,\gamma)+o_P(1),\end{aligned} \tag{B.10}$$

where $o_P(1)$ holds uniformly in (τ,γ).

Analogously to the proof of $\mathbb{V}_{n3,1}^{(1)}(\tau,\gamma)$ but with the application of Lemma C.2(ii) in place of Lemma C.2(i), we can show that

$$\begin{aligned}\sup_{\gamma\in\Gamma}\sup_{\tau\in\mathscr{T}}\left|\mathbb{V}_{n3,2}(\tau,\gamma)\right| &= O_P(n^{-2}(\lambda_n h^{d_X})^{-6\eta/(\eta+6)} \\ &\quad + n^{-2}(\lambda_n h^{d_X})^{-3})h^{-d_X/2}\log n) = o_P(1).\end{aligned} \tag{B.11}$$

Now, by Proposition B.1 and Assumption 12, uniformly in (τ,γ)

$$\mathbb{V}_{n3,3}(\tau,\gamma) = \frac{1}{n}\sum_{i=1}^{n} f(m_{i\tau}|W_i)\delta(\tau,W_i)\varphi_{i\gamma} + O_P(\lambda_n^q). \tag{B.12}$$

Combining (B.2) and (B.10)–(B.12) yields the desired result.

Proposition B.7. Under H_{1n}, $\mathbb{V}_{n4}(\tau,\gamma) \equiv n^{-1/2}\sum_{i=1}^{n}[G(-\varepsilon_{i\tau}/\lambda_n)-G(-\hat{u}_{i\tau}/\lambda_n)]\varphi_{i\gamma} = -c_0 n^{-1/2}\sum_{i=1}^{n} b(X_i,\gamma)\psi_\tau(\varepsilon_{i\tau}) + \boldsymbol{\Delta}(\tau,\gamma) + o_P(1)$ uniformly in (τ,γ).

Proof. By the Taylor expansion

$$\begin{aligned}\mathbb{V}_{n4}(\tau,\gamma) &= \frac{1}{\sqrt{n}\lambda_n}\sum_{i=1}^{n} G^{(1)}(-\varepsilon_{i\tau}/\lambda_n)(\hat{u}_{i\tau}-\varepsilon_{i\tau})\varphi_{i\gamma} \\ &\quad + \frac{1}{2\sqrt{n}\lambda_n^2}\sum_{i=1}^{n} G^{(2)}(-\varepsilon_{i\tau}/\lambda_n)(\hat{u}_{i\tau}-\varepsilon_{i\tau})^2\varphi_{i\gamma} \\ &\quad + \frac{1}{6\sqrt{n}\lambda_n^3}\sum_{i=1}^{n} G^{(3)}(-\varepsilon_{i\tau}/\lambda_n)(\hat{u}_{i\tau}-\varepsilon_{i\tau})^3\varphi_{i\gamma} + R_{n1}(\tau,\gamma) \\ &\equiv V_{n41}(\tau,\gamma)+V_{n42}(\tau,\gamma)+V_{n43}(\tau,\gamma)+R_{n1}(\tau,\gamma),\end{aligned} \tag{B.13}$$

where $R_{n1}(\tau,\gamma) \equiv (1/6)n^{-1/2}\lambda_n^{-3}\sum_{i=1}^{n}[G^{(3)}(-\bar{u}_{i\tau}/\lambda_n)-G^{(3)}(-u_{i\tau}/\lambda_n)]\times(\hat{u}_{i\tau}-\varepsilon_{i\tau})^3\varphi_{i\gamma}$ with $\bar{u}_{i\tau}$ lying between $\hat{u}_{i\tau}$ and $\varepsilon_{i\tau}$. By Proposition B.6, it suffices to show the last three terms in Eq. (B.13) are uniformly $o_P(1)$.

By Proposition B.3(ii) and the boundedness of φ,

$$\sup_{\gamma\in\Gamma}\sup_{\tau\in\mathcal{T}}\left|V_{n42}(\tau,\gamma)\right| \le Cn^{1/2}\max_{1\le i\le n}\sup_{\tau\in\mathcal{T}}|\hat{u}_{i\tau}-\varepsilon_{i\tau}|^2\sup_{\tau\in\mathcal{T}}\left\{\frac{1}{2n\lambda_n^2}\sum_{i=1}^{n}\left|G^{(2)}(-\varepsilon_{i\tau}/\lambda_n)\right|\right\}$$
$$= O_P(n^{-1/2}h^{-d_X}\log n)O_P(1+n^{-1/2}\lambda_n^{-3/2}\sqrt{\log n}) = o_P(1).$$

Similarly, we have $\sup_{\gamma\in\Gamma}\sup_{\tau\in\mathcal{T}}\left|V_{n43}(\tau,\gamma)\right| = O_P(n^{-1}h^{-3d_X/2}(\log n)^{3/2})$ $O_P(1+n^{-1/2}\lambda_n^{-5/2}(\log n)^{1/2}) = o_P(1)$. Assumption 11 implies that for all $|\varepsilon-\varepsilon^*| \le \delta \le A_G, |G^{(3)}(\varepsilon^*)-G^{(3)}(\varepsilon)| \le \delta G^*(\varepsilon)$. In fact, one chooses $G^*(\varepsilon) = c_G\mathbf{1}(|\varepsilon| \le 2A_G)$ if $G^{(3)}(\varepsilon)$ has compact support and is Lipschitz continuous, and chooses $G^*(\varepsilon) = c_G\mathbf{1}(|\varepsilon| \le 2A_G) + |\varepsilon - A_G|^{-\gamma_0}\mathbf{1}(|\varepsilon|>2A_G)$. In each case, $G^*(\varepsilon)$ is bounded and integrable and behaves like the kernel function $K(\cdot)$. Let $\vartheta_n \equiv \max_{1\le i\le n}\sup_{\tau\in\mathcal{T}}|\hat{u}_{i\tau}-\varepsilon_{i\tau}|$. Then $\vartheta_n = O_P(n^{-1/2}h^{-d_X/2}\sqrt{\log n} + n^{-1/2}) = o(\lambda_n)$ so that $\vartheta_n/\lambda_n \le A_G$ with probability approaching one (w.p.a. 1). It follows that w.p.a. 1 $\left|G^{(3)}(-\bar{u}_{i\tau}/\lambda_n) - G^{(3)}(-\varepsilon_{i\tau}/\lambda_n)\right| \le \vartheta_n\lambda_n^{-1}G^*(-\varepsilon_{i\tau}/\lambda_n)$ and

$$\sup_{\gamma\in\Gamma}\sup_{\tau\in\mathcal{T}}\left|R_{n1}(\tau,\gamma)\right| \le Cn^{1/2}\vartheta_n^4\lambda_n^{-3}\sup_{\tau\in\mathcal{T}}\frac{1}{n\lambda_n}\sum_{i=1}^{n}G^*(-\varepsilon_{i\tau}/\lambda_n)$$
$$= O_P(n^{-3/2}\lambda_n^{-3}h^{-2d_X}(\log n)^2) = o_P(1)$$

because $\sup_{\tau\in\mathcal{T}}\frac{1}{n\lambda_n}\sum_{i=1}^{n}G^*(-\varepsilon_{i\tau}/\lambda_n) = O_P(1)$ following the proof of Proposition B.3(i).

Proposition B.8. $\max_{1\le j\le n}\sup_{\gamma\in\Gamma}|\hat{b}(X_j,\gamma) - b(X_j,\gamma)| = O_P(n^{-1/2}h_b^{-d_X/2}\sqrt{\log n} + h_b^{p_b+1})$.

Proof. Masry (1996) proved that the almost sure uniform convergence result holds (uniformly in X_j) for general local polynomial estimates under strong mixing conditions. It is straightforward to extend his result to allow the result also to hold uniformly in γ by the standard chaining argument. Note here we only need convergence in probability. See also Hansen (2008).

Proposition B.9. $L^{-1/2}\sum_{j=i}^{i+L-1}[\tau - G(-\varepsilon_{i\tau}/\lambda_n)]\tilde{\varphi}_{i\gamma} = L^{-1/2}\sum_{j=i}^{i+L-1}[\tau - \mathbf{1}(\varepsilon_{i\tau} \le 0)]\bar{\varphi}_{i\gamma} + o_P(1)$ uniformly in $(\tau,\gamma) \in \mathcal{T}\times\Gamma$, where we recall that $\tilde{\varphi}_{i\gamma} \equiv \varphi(W_i,\gamma) - c_0\hat{b}(X_i,\gamma)$ and $\bar{\varphi}_{i\gamma} \equiv \varphi(W_i,\gamma) - c_0 b(X_i,\gamma)$.

Proof. Write $L^{-1/2}\sum_{j=i}^{i+L-1}[\tau - G(-\varepsilon_{j\tau}/\lambda_n)]\tilde{\varphi}_{j\gamma}$ as

$$L^{-1/2}\sum_{j=i}^{i+L-1}[\tau - 1(\varepsilon_{j\tau} \leq 0)]\bar{\varphi}_{j\gamma} + L^{-1/2}\sum_{j=i}^{i+L-1}[1(\varepsilon_{j\tau} \leq 0) - G(-\varepsilon_{j\tau}/\lambda_n)]\bar{\varphi}_{j\gamma}$$
$$+ c_0 L^{-1/2}\sum_{j=i}^{i+L-1}[\tau - G(-\varepsilon_{i\tau}/\lambda_n)][\hat{b}(X_j,\gamma) - b(X_j,\gamma)]. \tag{B.14}$$

It suffices to show that the last two terms are $o_P(1)$ uniformly in $(\tau,\gamma) \in \mathscr{T} \times \Gamma$. The last term is no bigger than

$$c_0 L^{-1/2}\sum_{j=i}^{i+L-1}\left|\hat{b}(X_j,\gamma) - b(X_j,\gamma)\right| = L^{1/2}O_P(n^{-1/2}h_b^{-d_X/2}\sqrt{\log n} + h_b^{p_b+1}) = o_P(1).$$

Now, write the second term in (B.14) as

$$L^{-1/2}\sum_{j=i}^{i+L-1}\{\mathbf{1}(\varepsilon_{j\tau} \leq 0) - \tau - G(-\varepsilon_{j\tau}/\lambda_n) + E_j[G(-\varepsilon_{j\tau}/\lambda_n)]\}\bar{\varphi}_{j\gamma}$$
$$+L^{-1/2}\sum_{j=i}^{i+L-1}\{\tau - E_j\left[G(-\varepsilon_{j\tau}/\lambda_n)\right]\}\bar{\varphi}_{j\gamma}.$$

The second term is $O_P(L^{1/2}\lambda_n^q) = o_P(1)$ uniformly in (τ,γ) by Proposition B.1(i). Partition $(\mathscr{T} \times \Gamma)$ as in the proof of Proposition B.4. By the stochastic equicontinuity of $L^{-1/2}\sum_{j=i}^{i+L-1}[\mathbf{1}(\varepsilon_{j\tau} \leq 0) - \tau]\bar{\varphi}_{j\gamma}$ and $L^{-1/2}\sum_{j=i}^{i+L-1}\{G(-\varepsilon_{j\tau}/\lambda_n) - E_j[G(-\varepsilon_{j\tau}/\lambda_n)]\}\bar{\varphi}_{j\gamma}$ as proved in Theorem 4. and Proposition B.4, we have

$$\sup_{\gamma\in\Gamma}\sup_{\tau\in\mathscr{T}}\left|L^{-1/2}\sum_{j=i}^{i+L-1}\{\mathbf{1}(\varepsilon_{j\tau} \leq 0) - \tau - G(-\varepsilon_{j\tau}/\lambda_n) + E_j[G(-\varepsilon_{j\tau}/\lambda_n)]\}\bar{\varphi}_{j\gamma}\right|$$
$$\leq \max_{1\leq l\leq n_2}\max_{1\leq k\leq n_1}\left|L^{-1/2}\sum_{j=i}^{i+L-1}\{\mathbf{1}(\varepsilon_{j\tau_k} \leq 0) - \tau_k - G(-\varepsilon_{i\tau_k}/\lambda_n)\right.$$
$$\left.+ E_i[G(-\varepsilon_{j\tau_k}/\lambda_n)]\}\bar{\varphi}_{i\gamma_l}\right| + o_P(1).$$

Analogously to the proof of Proposition B.4, it is straightforward to show that the dominating term in the last expression is $o_P(1)$ by another application of Lemma C.3.

Proposition B.10. $L^{-1/2}\sum_{j=i}^{i+L-1}[G(-\varepsilon_{i\tau}/\lambda_n) - G(-\hat{u}_{i\tau}/\lambda_n)]\tilde{\varphi}_{i\gamma} = o_P(1)$ uniformly in $(\tau, \gamma) \in \mathscr{T} \times \Gamma$.

Proof. The proof is analogous to that of Proposition **18**. The difference is that one now needs to apply Proposition B.8 and the fact that $L = o(n^{1/2})$.

APPENDIX C: SOME TECHNICAL LEMMAS

This appendix presents some technical lemmas that are used in proving the main results.

Lemma C.1. Let $\{V_i, i \geq 1\}$ be a ν-dimensional strong mixing process with mixing coefficient $\alpha(\cdot)$. Let $F_{i_1,\ldots,i_m}$, denote the distribution function of $(V_{i_1},\ldots,V_{i_m})$. For any integer $m>1$ and integers $(i_1,\ldots,i_m)$ such that $1 \leq i_1 < i_2 < \cdots < i_m$, let θ be a Borel measurable function such that $\max\{\int |\theta(v_1,\ldots,v_m)|^{1+\tilde{\eta}} dF_{i_1,\ldots,i_j}(v_1,\ldots,v_j)dF_{i_{j+1},\ldots,i_m}(v_{j+1},\ldots,v_m), \int |\theta(v_1,\ldots,v_m)|^{1+\tilde{\eta}} dF_{i_1,\ldots,i_m}\} \leq M_n$ for some $\tilde{\eta}>0$. *Then* $|\int \theta(v_1,\ldots,v_m)\times dF_{i_1,\ldots,i_m}(v_1,\ldots,v_m) - \int \theta(v_1,\ldots,v_m)\, dF_{i_1,\ldots,i_j}(v_1,\ldots,v_j)\, dF_{i_{j+1},\ldots,i_m}(v_{j+1},\ldots,v_m)| \leq 4M_n^{1/(1+\tilde{\eta})}\alpha(i_{j+1}-i_j)^{\tilde{\eta}/(1+\tilde{\eta})}$.

Proof. See Lemma 2.1 of Sun and Chiang (1997).

Let $P(V_i)$ denote the probability law of a random variable V_i. Let $1 \leq i_1, i_2, \ldots, i_k \leq n$ be arbitrary positive integers. For any $j (1 \leq j \leq k)$, define a collection of probability measures $\mathscr{P}_j^k$ by

$$\mathscr{P}_j^k(V_{i_1},\ldots,V_{i_k}) \equiv \Big\{P_j^k(V_{i_1},\ldots,V_{i_k}) \equiv \Pi_{s=1}^j P(\underline{V}_s) : \underline{V}_s \text{ is a subset of } \{V_{i_1},\ldots,V_{i_k}\}, \cup_{s=1}^j \underline{V}_s = \{V_{i_1},\ldots,V_{i_k}\}, \text{ and } \underline{V}_t \cap \underline{V}_s = \emptyset \text{ for all } 1 \leq t \neq s \leq j\Big\}.$$

In the following, we frequently suppress the arguments of P_j^k and $\mathscr{P}_j^k$ when no confusion can arise. For example, when $k=2$, we use $\max_{1\leq i_1,i_2\leq n}\max_{1\leq j\leq 2}\max_{P_j^2\in\mathscr{P}_j^2}\int_{\mathbb{R}^{3\nu}} |\varphi(v_{i_1},v_{i_2})|dP_j^2$ to denote

$$\max_{1\leq i_1,i_2\leq n} \max\left\{\int_{\mathbb{R}^{2\nu}} \{|\varphi(v_1,v_2)|dF_{i_1 i_2}(v_1,v_2), \int_{\mathbb{R}^{2\nu}} |\varphi(v_1,v_2)|dF_{i_1}(v_1)dF_{i_2}(v_2)\right\}.$$

Let $\mathbb{U}_n = n^{-2}\sum_{1\leq i_1<i_2\leq n}\phi(v_{i_1},v_{i_2})$, where $\int \phi(v_1,v)dF_{v_i}(v) = \int \phi(v,v_2)\times dF_{v_i}(v) = 0$ for all i. Let $M(i_1,\ldots,i_8) \equiv \Pi_{j=1}^4 \phi(v_{i_{2j-1}},v_{i_{2j}})$ and $N(i_1,\ldots,i_{12}) \equiv \Pi_{j=1}^6 \phi(v_{i_{2j-1}},v_{i_{2j}})$. Let $I_1 = \{i_1,\ldots,i_8\}$ and $I_2 = \{i_1,\ldots,i_{12}\}$. Define

$$M_{n1s} \equiv \max_{\substack{1\leq i_{2k-1}<i_{2k}\leq n, 1\leq k\leq 4 \\ \text{exactly } 9-s \text{ indicesin } \mathrm{I}_1 \text{ are distinct}}} \max_{1\leq j\leq 9-s} \max_{P_j^{9-s}\in\mathscr{P}_j^{9-s}} \times \int |M(i_1,\ldots,i_8)|^{1+\eta/4} dP_j^{9-s}, s=1,2,3,4,$$

$$M_{n2s} \equiv \max_{\substack{1\leq i_{2k-1}<i_{2k}\leq n, 1\leq k\leq 4 \\ \text{exactly } 5-s \text{ indices in } I_1 \text{ are distinct}}} \max_{1\leq j\leq 5-s} \max_{P_j^{5-s}\in\mathscr{P}_j^{5-s}} \times \left|\int M(i_1,\ldots,i_8)dP_j^{5-s}\right|, s=1,2,3,$$

$$N_{n1s} \equiv \max_{\substack{1 \le i_{2k-1} < i_{2k} \le n, 1 \le k \le 6 \\ \text{exactly } 13-s \text{ indices in } I_2 \text{ are distinct}}} \max_{1 \le j \le 13-s} \max_{P_j^{13-s} \in \mathscr{P}_j^{13-s}} \times \int |N(i_1, \ldots, i_{12})|^{1+\eta/6} dP_j^{13-s}, s = 1, \ldots, 6,$$

$$N_{n2s} \equiv \max_{\substack{1 \le i_{2k-1} < i_{2k} \le n, 1 \le k \le 6 \\ \text{exactly } 7-s \text{ indices in } I_2 \text{ are distinct}}} \max_{1 \le j \le 7-s} \max_{P_j^{7-s} \in \mathscr{P}_j^{7-s}} \times \left| \int N(i_1, \ldots, i_{12}) dP_j^{13-s} \right|, s = 1, \cdots, 5.$$

Lemma C.2. Using the notation defined above,

(i) if $\sum_{s=1}^{\infty} s^3 \alpha(s)^{\eta/(4+\eta)} < \infty$ for some $\eta > 0$, then $E[\mathbb{U}_n^4] = O\Big(\sum_{s=1}^{4} n^{-3-s} \times M_{n1s}^{4/(4+\eta)} + \sum_{s=1}^{3} n^{-3-s} M_{n2s});$

(ii) if $\sum_{s=1}^{\infty} s^5 \alpha(s)^{\eta/(4+\eta)} < \infty$ for some $\eta > 0$, then $E[\mathbb{U}_n^6] = O\Big(\sum_{s=1}^{4} n^{-5-s} \times N_{n1s}^{6/(6+\eta)} + \sum_{s=1}^{3} n^{-5-s} N_{n2s}).$

Proof. Write

$$E[\mathbb{U}_n^4] = n^{-8} \sum_{1 \le i_1 < i_2 \le n} \sum_{1 \le i_3 < i_4 \le n} \sum_{1 \le i_5 < i_6 \le n} \sum_{1 \le i_7 < i_8 \le n} \phi(v_{i_1}, v_{i_2}) \phi(v_{i_3}, v_{i_4}) \times \phi(v_{i_5}, v_{i_6}) \phi(v_{i_7}, v_{i_8}). \tag{C.1}$$

It is easy to show that the terms in the above summation constitute seven cases: for $s = 1, 2, \ldots, 7$, in case (s) there are exactly $9 - s$ distinct indices among $i_1, \ldots, i_8$. We will use $EU_{n(s)}$ to denote these cases $(s = 1, 2, \ldots, 7)$. For case (1), following Yoshihara (1976), let $i_1, \ldots, i_8$ be distinct integers with $1 \le i_j \le n$. Let $1 \le k_1 < \cdots < k_8 \le n$ be the permutation of $i_1, \ldots, i_8$ in ascending order and let d_c be the c-th largest difference among $k_{j+1} - k_j, j = 1, \ldots, 7$. Define

$$H(k_1, \ldots, k_8) = \phi(v_{i_1}, v_{i_2}) \phi(v_{i_3}, v_{i_4}) \phi(v_{i_5}, v_{i_6}) \phi(v_{i_7}, v_{i_8}).$$

For any $1 \le j \le 7$, put $P_0^{(8)}(E^{(8)}) = P((v_{i_1}, \ldots, v_{i_8}) \in E^{(8)})$, and

$$P_j^{(8)}(E^{(j)} \times E^{(8-j)}) = P((v_{i_1}, \ldots, v_{i_j}) \in E^{(j)}) P((v_{i_{j+1}}, \ldots, v_{i_8}) \in E^{(8-j)}),$$

where $E^{(j)}$ is a Borel set in $\mathbb{R}^{j\upsilon}$ and υ is the dimension of v_i. Since $\int H(i_1, \ldots, i_8) dP_j^{(8)} = 0$ for $j = 1, 7$, we have, by Lemma C.1 with $\tilde{\eta} = \eta/4$,

$$\sum_{1\le k_1<\ldots<k_8\le n k_2-k_1=d_1} \left|E[H(k_1,\ldots,k_8)]\right|$$

$$\le 4M_{n11}^{4/(4+\eta)} \sum_{k_1=1}^{n-7} \sum_{k_2=k_1+\max_{j\ge 3}\{k_j-k_{j-1}\}}^{n-6} \sum_{k_3=k_2+1}^{n-5} \cdots \sum_{k_8=k_7+1}^{n} \alpha^{\frac{\eta}{4+\eta}}(k_2-k_1)$$

$$\le 4M_{n11}^{4/(4+\eta)} \sum_{k_1=1}^{n-7} \sum_{k_2=k_1+1}^{n-6} (k_2-k_1)^6 \alpha^{\frac{\eta}{4+\eta}}(k_2-k_1)$$

$$\le 4n^4 M_{n11}^{4/(4+\eta)} \sum_{j=1}^{n} j^3 \alpha^{\frac{\eta}{4+\eta}}(j),$$

and similarly $\sum_{1\le k_1<\ldots<k_8\le n k_8-k_7=d_1}\left|E[H(k_1,\ldots,k_8)]\right| \le 4n^4 M_{n11}^{4/(4+\eta)}\sum_{j=1}^{n}\times j^3\alpha^{\frac{\eta}{4+\eta}}(j)$. If for some $j_\alpha(2\le j_\alpha\le 6, 1\le\alpha\le 4)$, $k_{j_\alpha+1}-k_{j_\alpha}=d_\alpha$, then

$$\sum_{1\le k_1<\cdots<k_8\le n k_{j_\alpha+1}-k_{j_\alpha}=d_\alpha(1\le\alpha\le 4)} \left|E[H(k_1,\ldots,k_8)]\right| \le 4n^4 M_{n11}^{4/(4+\eta)} \sum_{j=1}^{n} j^3 \alpha^{\frac{\eta}{4+\eta}}(j).$$

It follows that $EU_{n(1)} \le \sum_{1\le k_1<\cdots<k_8\le n}\left|E[H(k_1,\ldots,k_8)]\right| = O(n^4 M_{n11}^{4/(4+\eta)})$. For cases (2)–(4), by using Lemma **22** repeatedly, we can show that

$$EU_{n(2)} = O(n^3 M_{n12}^{4/(4+\eta)}), EU_{n(3)} = O(n^2 M_{n13}^{4/(4+\eta)}), \text{ and } EU_{n(4)} = O(nM_{n14}^{4/(4+\eta)}).$$

For all other cases, we can calculate the expectations directly to obtain

$$EU_{n(5)} = O(n^4 M_{n21}), EU_{n(6)} = O(n^3 M_{n22}), \quad \text{and} \quad EU_{n(7)} = O(n^2 M_{n23}).$$

The result in (i) follows. The proof of (ii) is analogous and thus is omitted.

Lemma C.3. Let $\{\xi_t \in \mathbb{R}^q, t=1,2,\ldots\}$ be a strong mixing process, not necessarily stationary, with the mixing coefficients $\alpha(t)$ satisfying $\sum_{t=1}^{\infty}\alpha(t)<\infty$. Suppose that $\varsigma_n : \mathbb{R}^q \to \mathbb{R}$ is a measurable function such that $E[\varsigma_n(\xi_t)]=0$, and $\left|\varsigma_n(\xi_t)\right| \le M_n$ for every $t=1,2,\ldots$ Then for any $\varepsilon^*>0$,

$$P\left(\left|n^{-1}\sum_{i=1}^{n}\varsigma_n(\xi_t)\right|>\varepsilon\right) \le C_0 \exp\left(-\frac{np_n\varepsilon^{*2}}{C_1\sigma^2(p_n)+C_2M_np_n(p_n+1)\varepsilon^*}\right) + C_3\sqrt{\frac{M_n}{\varepsilon}}\frac{n}{p_n}\alpha(p_n+1),$$

where $1\le p_n\le n/2$, $\sigma^2(p_n)=\sup_{1\le j\le 2p_n}\max\{\sigma^2_{j,p_n},\sigma^2_{j,p_n+1}\}$, $\sigma^2_{j,p_n}=E\left[\sum_{t=1}^{p_n}\varsigma_n\times(\xi_{j+t})\right]^2$, and $C'_i s$, $i=0,1,2,3$, are constants that do not depend on n, ε, M_n, and p_n.

Proof. See Lemma 5.2 in Shen and Huang (1998).

EXTENDING THE HAUSMAN TEST TO CHECK FOR THE PRESENCE OF OUTLIERS

Catherine Dehon, Marjorie Gassner and Vincenzo Verardi

ABSTRACT

In this paper, we follow the same logic as in Hausman (1978) to create a testing procedure that checks for the presence of outliers by comparing a regression estimator that is robust to outliers (S-estimator), with another that is more efficient but affected by them. Some simulations are presented to illustrate the good behavior of the test for both its size and its power.

Keywords: S-estimators; MM-estimators; outliers; linear regression; generalized method of moments; robustness

JEL classification: C12; C21; H11

Essays in Honor of Jerry Hausman
Advances in Econometrics, Volume 29, 435–453

ISSN: 0731-9053/doi:10.1108/S0731-9053(2012)0000029019

INTRODUCTION

In a seminal paper, Hausman (1978) introduced a testing procedure that, under some assumptions, provides a way to balance consistency and efficiency when comparing two estimators. Hausman's testing procedure is used extensively in econometrics: in the context of panel data, for example, it is called on to check whether the assumptions underlying the random-effects model are satisfied. This is done by comparing the fixed-effects model (consistent, but inefficient) with the random-effects model (more efficient, but potentially inconsistent if a set of assumptions is not fulfilled). If the differences between the corresponding coefficients of the two models is not systematic, the test indicates that it is preferable to use a random-effects model given its higher efficiency. In this paper, we follow the same logic as in Hausman (1978) to create a testing procedure for checking if the presence of outliers influences the estimation of the regression parameters in a linear model. To do so, we extend the testing procedure proposed in Dehon, Gassner, and Verardi (2009a) in order to relax the classical strong assumptions (normality, symmetry and homoskedasticity of the error term). The idea is to compare a regression estimator that is robust (S), with an estimator that has higher efficiency but is more influenced by outliers (hereafter called MM, not to be mistaken for the exactly identified Generalized Method of Moments estimator that will be denoted by GMM). More precisely, consider the regression model

$$Y_i = X_i^t\theta + \varepsilon_i$$

where Y_i is the dependent variable and X_i is the $((p+1)\times 1)$ vector of covariates (plus the constant) observed for $i = 1,...N$. The null hypothesis here is that the model is valid for the entire population. Thus, at the sample level, under the null, no outliers are present and LS, S, and MM have the same limit in probability (plim). The alternative hypothesis is that the model is misspecified for a minority of the population, implying a possible significant difference between classical and robust estimators. Indeed, it is well-known that the classical LS-estimator is distorted by outliers, leading to a different plim than robust estimators. Concerning the consistency of S- and MM-estimators, some theoretical results (see Omelka & Salibian-Barrera, 2010) exist over contaminated neighborhoods (i.e., H_1) under some assumptions. Our testing procedure consists of comparing the regression coefficients respectively estimated by the S- and MM-estimators to check if they are statistically different (as will be explained later, the constant is disregarded). The above-mentioned comparison of the regression coefficients is carried out by calling on the Generalized Hausman test statistic defined as

$$H = (\hat{\theta}^{S} - \hat{\theta}^{MM})^{t} [Var(\hat{\theta}^{S} - \hat{\theta}^{MM})]^{-1} (\hat{\theta}^{S} - \hat{\theta}^{MM}) \quad (1)$$

where $\hat{\theta}^{S}$ and $\hat{\theta}^{MM}$ represent respectively the S- and MM-estimators of θ (with a given Gaussian efficiency). Since the Generalized Hausman statistic is asymptotically distributed as a χ_p^2 under the null, where p is the number of covariates, it is possible to set an upper bound above which the estimated parameters can be considered as statistically different: if the value of H is above $\chi^2_{p,(1-\alpha)}$ (where α is the given significance level), the difference between $\hat{\theta}^{S}$ and $\hat{\theta}^{MM}$ (and hence the lack of robustness of MM) is too large with respect to the gain in efficiency.

For this testing procedure to be robust, we need an estimate of the variance of the difference $(\hat{\theta}^{S} - \hat{\theta}^{MM})$ that remains consistent under heteroskedasticity and/or asymmetry. This paper develops a modified Hausman testing procedure that can be used not only to compare S-estimators with MM-estimators (with a given efficiency level), but also to detect the presence of outliers by comparing S-estimators with non-robust LS-estimators (a limit case of MM). The structure of the paper is the following: after the first introductory section, in the second section we develop the robustness test. In the third section we run some simulations to observe its behavior in finite samples and in the fourth section we conclude.

GENERAL TESTING PROCEDURE

Consider the regression model

$$Y_i = X_i^t \theta + \varepsilon_i$$

where Y_i is the dependent variable, X_i is the $((p+1) \times 1)$ vector of covariates observed for $i = 1, \ldots, N$ and σ is the dispersion of the error ε. To estimate parameter column vector θ, a measure s of the dispersion of the residuals $r_i(\theta) = Y_i - X_i^t \theta$ for $1 \leq i \leq n$ is minimized. The regression estimate $\hat{\theta}_0$ can then be defined by

$$\hat{\theta}_0 = \arg\min_{\theta} s(r_1(\theta), \ldots, r_n(\theta)) \quad (2)$$

In the case of LS, the measure of dispersion that is minimized is the (square root of the) variance. The problem with LS is that an excessive importance is awarded to observations with very large residuals and, consequently, the estimated parameters are distorted if outliers are present. To take this into account, Rousseeuw and Yohai (1984) propose to minimize another measure of dispersion s of the residuals, an M-estimator of scale $\hat{\sigma}$, defined as the solution in s to

$$\frac{1}{n}\sum_{i=1}^{n}\rho_0\left(\frac{r_i(\theta)}{s}\right) = \delta \tag{3}$$

where $\delta = E[\rho_0(Z)]$ with $Z \sim N(0,1)$ where function $\rho_0(\cdot)$ is even, non-decreasing for positive values and less increasing than the square. This is equivalent to solving

$$\begin{cases} \min\limits_{\theta} s(r_1(\theta), ..., r_n(\theta)) \\ \text{s.t.} \frac{1}{n}\sum\limits_{i=1}^{n}\rho_0\left(\frac{Y_i - X_i^t\theta}{s}\right) = \delta \end{cases} \tag{4}$$

yielding solutions $\hat{\theta}_0$ and $\hat{\sigma}$ such that

$$\begin{cases} \frac{1}{n}\sum\limits_{i=1}^{n}\rho'_0\left(\frac{Y_i - X_i^t\hat{\theta}_0}{\hat{\sigma}}\right)X_i^t = 0 \\ \frac{1}{n}\sum\limits_{i=1}^{n}\rho_0\left(\frac{Y_i - X_i^t\hat{\theta}_0}{\hat{\sigma}}\right) = \delta \end{cases} \tag{5}$$

where ρ'_0 is the first derivative of ρ_0. If ρ_0 is the square function (and $\delta = 1$), this becomes a standard LS optimization problem. The practical implementation of an S-estimator is based on an iterative subsampling algorithm such as the one described by Salibian-Barrera and Yohai (2006). Obviously, this does not yield an exact solution, but the authors showed that if a sufficient number of subsamples are drawn, the solution obtained will be close to the global optimum.

The choice of $\rho_0(\cdot)$ is crucial to guarantee robustness and high Gaussian efficiency. The function ρ_0 usually used in Eq. (3) is the Tukey Biweight function defined as

$$\rho_0(u) = \begin{cases} \frac{k^2}{6}\left(1 - \left[1 - \left(\frac{u}{k}\right)^2\right]^3\right) & \text{if} \quad |u| \le k \\ \frac{k^2}{6} \quad \text{if} \quad |u| > k \end{cases} \tag{6}$$

If the tuning parameter k is set at 1.547, it can be shown that the breakdown point (i.e., the maximal contamination an estimator can withstand before breaking) reaches 50%. The Gaussian efficiency is however rather low (28%). To increase the efficiency, Rousseeuw and Yohai (1984) and Yohai (1987) introduced MM-estimators that combine a high-breakdown point and high efficiency. These estimates result from minimizing a loss function of the residuals $\sum_{i=1}^{n}\rho\left(\frac{r_i(\theta)}{\hat{\sigma}}\right)$ where the parameter σ is set at the value estimated by the S-estimator ($\hat{\sigma}$) and, as $\rho_0(\cdot)$, the function $\rho(\cdot)$ is even, non-decreasing for positive values and less increasing than the square with $\rho(\cdot) \leq \rho_0(\cdot)$. The estimate $\hat{\theta}$ is defined by:

$$\hat{\theta} = \arg\min_{\theta} \sum_{i=1}^{n} \rho\left(\frac{r_i(\theta)}{\hat{\sigma}}\right)$$

Values $\hat{\theta}$, $\hat{\theta}_0$ and $\hat{\sigma}$ are such that

$$\begin{cases} \frac{1}{n}\sum_{i=1}^{n} \psi\left(\frac{Y_i - X_i^t\hat{\theta}}{\hat{\sigma}}\right)X_i^t = 0 \\ \frac{1}{n}\sum_{i=1}^{n} \rho'_0\left(\frac{Y_i - X_i^t\hat{\theta}_0}{\hat{\sigma}}\right)X_i^t = 0 \\ \frac{1}{n}\sum_{i=1}^{n} \rho_0\left(\frac{Y_i - X_i^t\hat{\theta}_0}{\hat{\sigma}}\right) = \delta \end{cases} \tag{7}$$

where ψ is ρ', the first derivative of ρ. The consistency and asymptotic distribution of S- and MM-estimators have been proven (Maronna, Martin, & Yohai 2006) under an uncontaminated scenario.

It is common to also use a Tukey Biweight $\rho(\cdot)$ function for the final MM-estimator where the tuning constant can be modified to attain a Gaussian efficiency much higher than 28%. For example, if $k = 4.685$, the Gaussian efficiency is 95% and if $k = 6.256$ it is 99%. For the sake of clarity, we denote by ρ_0 (and ρ'_0) the Tukey Biweight function (and its first derivative) in which the tuning parameter is set to 1.547, the function used for the preliminary S-estimator. On the other hand, we use the general notation of ρ (and ψ) for the Tukey Biweight function (and its first derivative) used in the final MM-estimator where the tuning parameter is set according to the desired Gaussian efficiency. It might thus be tempting to only consider highly efficient MM-estimators. This is not advised since the associated bias might be large even if the estimator does not break (see Maronna et al., 2006). As a consequence, it is of the utmost importance to find the highest efficiency without paying the price of an excessive bias. As an extension, the test we propose hereunder could be used in a procedure aimed at determining the "optimal" efficiency of an MM-estimator. The computation of an MM-estimator is quite simple once the S-estimator is computed since it calls on an iteratively reweighted least-squares algorithm. Consequently, having estimated the MM, our test will come at no additional computational cost.

From Eq. (7) and as shown by Croux, Dhaene, and Hoorelbeke (2003), MM-estimators are first-order equivalent with exactly identified GMM-estimators for $\vartheta = (\theta^t, \theta_0^t, \sigma)^t$ with moment function m_i (for observation i)

$$m_i(\vartheta) = \begin{pmatrix} \psi(\varepsilon_i)X_i \\ \rho'_0(\varepsilon_{0i})X_i \\ \rho_0(\varepsilon_{0i}) - \delta \end{pmatrix}, \text{ from here on abbreviated by } \begin{pmatrix} \psi_i X_i \\ \rho'_{0i} X_i \\ \rho_{0i} - \delta \end{pmatrix}$$

where $\varepsilon_i = \frac{Y_i - X_i^t\theta}{\sigma}$ and $\varepsilon_{0i} = \frac{Y_i - X_i^t\theta_0}{\sigma}$. To clarify notations, we denote by θ_0 the regression parameter that is estimated by the S-estimator and by θ, the parameter estimated by MM. Nevertheless $\theta = \theta_0$ under the null. This means (under the null) that S and MM (that are Fisher consistent) estimate the same unknown regression parameters.

Following Hansen (1982), Croux et al. (2003) show that $\hat{\vartheta}$ has a limiting normal distribution given by

$$\sqrt{N}(\hat{\vartheta} - \vartheta) \to N(0, V)$$

where, defining $G = E\left[\frac{\partial m_i(\vartheta)}{\partial \vartheta^t}\right]$ and $\Omega = E[m_i(\vartheta)m_i^t(\vartheta)]$, the asymptotic variance V is

$$V = G^{-1}\Omega(G^t)^{-1} \tag{8}$$

$$\text{Since } \Omega = E\begin{pmatrix} \psi_i^2 X_i X_i^t & \psi_i \rho'_{0i} X_i X_i^t & \psi_i \rho_{0i} X_i \\ \rho'_{0i}\psi_i X_i X_i^t & (\rho'_{0i})^2 X_i X_i^t & \rho'_{0i}\rho_{0i} X_i \\ \rho_{0i}\psi_i X_i^t & \rho_{0i}\rho'_{0i} X_i^t & (\rho_{0i})^2 - \delta^2 \end{pmatrix}$$

and

$$G^{-1} = -\begin{pmatrix} \sigma\,[E(\psi'_i X_i X_i^t)]^{-1} & 0 & -\sigma\,[E(\psi'_i X_i X_i^t)]^{-1} E(\psi'_i X_i \varepsilon_i)[E(\rho'_{0i}\varepsilon_{0i})]^{-1} \\ 0 & \sigma\,[E(\rho''_{0i} X_i X_i^t)]^{-1} & -\sigma\,[E(\rho''_{0i} X_i X_i^t)]^{-1} E(\rho''_{0i} X_i \varepsilon_{0i})[E(\rho'_{0i}\varepsilon_{0i})]^{-1} \\ 0 & 0 & \sigma\,[E(\rho'_{0i}\varepsilon_{0i})]^{-1} \end{pmatrix}$$

defining

$$A = \sigma\,[E(\psi'_i X_i X_i^t)]^{-1}$$

$$a = AE(\psi'_i X_i \varepsilon_i)[E(\rho'_{0i}\varepsilon_{0i})]^{-1}$$

$$B = \sigma\ [E(\rho''_{0i} X_i X_i^t)]^{-1} \text{ and}$$

$$b = BE(\rho''_{0i} X_i \varepsilon_{0i})[E(\rho'_{0i}\varepsilon_{0i})]^{-1}$$

Eq. (8) yields the asymptotic variances and covariances, that is,

$$Var(\hat{\theta}^{MM}) = AE(\psi_i^2 X_i X_i^t)A - aE(\psi_i \rho_{0i} X_i^t)A - AE(\psi_i X_i \rho_{0i})a^t + aE((\rho_{0i})^2 - b^2)a^t$$

$$Var(\hat{\theta}^{S}) = BE((\rho'_{0i})^2 X_i X_i^t)B - bE(\rho'_{0i}\rho_{0i} X_i^t)B - BE(\rho'_{0i}\rho_{0i} X_i)b^t + bE((\rho_{0i})^2 - b^2)b^t$$

$$Cov(\hat{\theta}^{S}, \hat{\theta}^{MM}) = AE(\psi_i \rho'_{0i} X_i X_i^t)B - aE(\rho'_{0i}\rho_{0i} X_i^t)B - AE(\psi_i X_i \rho_{0i})b^t + aE((\rho_{0i})^2 - b^2)b^t$$

System (7) enables to estimate the unknown parameters of the covariance matrix, yielding estimates $\widehat{Var}(\hat{\theta}^{MM}), \widehat{Var}(\hat{\theta}^{S})$ and $\widehat{Cov}(\hat{\theta}^{S}, \hat{\theta}^{MM})$. It is then straightforward to compare the S-estimator with the MM-estimator by using the Generalized Hausman statistic defined by Eq. (1) with $Var(\hat{\theta}^{S} - \hat{\theta}^{MM}) = Var(\hat{\theta}^{S}) + Var(\hat{\theta}^{MM}) - 2Cov(\hat{\theta}^{S}, \hat{\theta}^{MM})$, that is,

$$H = (\hat{\theta}^{S} - \hat{\theta}^{MM})^t \left[\widehat{Var}(\hat{\theta}^{S}) + \widehat{Var}(\hat{\theta}^{MM}) - 2\widehat{Cov}(\hat{\theta}^{S}, \hat{\theta}^{MM})\right]^{-1} (\hat{\theta}^{S} - \hat{\theta}^{MM}) \quad (9)$$

In this way, we test the null hypothesis that an MM-estimator with a given level of efficiency is not statistically different from an S-estimator and hence should be preferred due to its higher efficiency.

Since Gervini and Yohai (2002) showed that, in the presence of outliers, only slopes can be satisfactorily estimated when the error distribution is asymmetric, the test will be based on the comparison of the slope estimated parameters and the constant will be disregarded.

Outlier Identification Test

Since LS is the special case of the MM-estimator, where, in the corresponding Tukey biweight function, $k \to \infty$, $\rho(\varepsilon) = \frac{\varepsilon^2}{2}$, thus $\psi(\varepsilon) = \varepsilon$ and $\psi'(\varepsilon) = 1$, Eq. (9) can be directly used to test if outliers have distorted classical regression parameters. The values of A and a become $A = \sigma\ [E(X_i X_i^t)]^{-1}$ and $a = AE(X_i \varepsilon_i)[E(\rho'_{0i}\varepsilon_{0i})]^{-1}$ while those of B and b remain unchanged. As a consequence,

$$Var(\hat{\theta}^{LS}) = AE(\varepsilon_i^2 X_i X_i^t)A - aE(\varepsilon_i \rho_{0i} X_i^t)A - AE(\varepsilon_i X_i \rho_{0i})a^t + aE((\rho_{0i})^2 - b^2)a^t$$

$$Cov(\hat{\theta}^S, \hat{\theta}^{LS}) = AE(\varepsilon_i \rho'_{0i} X_i X_i^t)B - aE(\rho'_{0i}\rho_{0i} X_i^t)B - AE(\varepsilon_i X_i \rho_{0i})b^t + aE((\rho_{0i})^2 - b^2)b^t$$

while $Var(\hat{\theta}^S)$ remains unchanged. By replacing $\widehat{Var}(\hat{\theta}^{MM})$ by $\widehat{Var}(\hat{\theta}^{LS})$ and $\widehat{Cov}(\hat{\theta}^S, \hat{\theta}^{MM})$ by $\widehat{Cov}(\hat{\theta}^S, \hat{\theta}^{LS})$ in Eq. (9) we can check whether the difference between the coefficients in the S- and LS-estimators is systematic or not. If the null is rejected, the influence of the outliers is such that the gained efficiency associated with a classical estimator is not sufficient to balance the corresponding bias (due to outliers). In such a case, a robust estimator should be preferred. On the other hand, if it is not rejected, the influence of the outliers is clearly rather limited, implying that a classical estimator will be only mildly biased and should be preferred to a robust one given its higher statistical precision.

In the particular case of symmetric errors and homoskedasticity, this test simplifies to the test proposed by Dehon *et al.* (2009a), that is,

Proposition 1. If the error term is symmetric and homoskedastic and $k \to \infty$, then $Cov(\hat{\theta}^S, \hat{\theta}^{LS}) = Var(\hat{\theta}^{LS})$.

Proof. When $k \to \infty$, $\rho(\varepsilon) = \frac{\varepsilon^2}{2}$, thus $\psi(\varepsilon) = \varepsilon$ and $\psi'(\varepsilon) = 1$.

From the symmetry and homoskedasticity hypotheses, $a = b = 0$, thus $A = \sigma\ [E(\psi'_i X_i X_i^t)]^{-1} = \sigma\ [X_i X_i^t]^{-1}$ and $B = \sigma\ [E(\rho''_{0i} X_i X_i^t)]^{-1} = \sigma E(\rho''_{0i})^{-1}$ $[X_i X_i^t]^{-1}$ and

$$\begin{aligned} Cov(\hat{\theta}^S, \hat{\theta}^{MM}) &= AE(\psi_i \rho'_{0i} X_i X_i^t)B = \sigma [X_i X_i^t]^{-1} E(\psi_i \rho'_{0i} X_i X_i^t)\sigma E(\rho''_{0i})^{-1} [X_i X_i^t]^{-1} \\ &= \sigma [X_i X_i^t]^{-1} E\left(\varepsilon\left(\frac{\varepsilon^5}{k^4} - \frac{2\varepsilon^3}{k^2} + \varepsilon\right)\right) X_i X_i^t . \sigma \left\{E\left(\frac{5\varepsilon^4}{k^4} - \frac{6\varepsilon^2}{k^2} + 1\right)\right\}^{-1} [X_i X_i^t]^{-1} \\ &= \sigma^2 [X_i X_i^t]^{-1} \left(\frac{1}{k^4} E(\varepsilon^6) - \frac{2}{k^2} E(\varepsilon^4) + E(\varepsilon^2)\right) X_i X_i^t \\ &\times \left(\frac{5}{k^4} E(\varepsilon^4) - \frac{6}{k^2} E(\varepsilon^2) + 1\right)^{-1} [X_i X_i^t]^{-1} \\ &= \sigma^2 [X_i X_i^t]^{-1} \left(\frac{15}{k^4} - \frac{6}{k^2} + 1\right) \left(\frac{15}{k^4} - \frac{6}{k^2} + 1\right)^{-1} X_i X_i^t [X_i X_i^t]^{-1} \\ &= \sigma^2 [X_i X_i^t]^{-1} = Var(\hat{\theta}^{LS}). \end{aligned}$$

From there, $H = (\hat{\theta}^S - \hat{\theta}^{LS})^t \left[Var(\hat{\theta}^S) - Var(\hat{\theta}^{LS})\right]^{-1} (\hat{\theta}^S - \hat{\theta}^{LS})$ which is the test statistic proposed by Dehon et al. (2009a).

In the following section, we run some simulations to check how the test behaves in finite samples. Before that, we briefly present a robust alternative test that is available in the literature (see Yohai, Stahel, & Zamar, 1991). It will serve as the comparison benchmark for the simulations. The test proposed by Dehon et al. (2009a) is not considered in the simulations since it is nothing else than a specific case of the one we propose here.

SIMULATIONS

The Yohai et al. *(1991) test*

In 1991, Yohai, Stahel, and Zamar developed a test (YSZ) to compare the behavior of an S-estimator with that of an MM-estimator (with a given efficiency), based on the scale of the residuals. The test statistic they propose is

$$T = \frac{2n(\hat{\sigma}_{MM} - \hat{\sigma})}{\upsilon_0 d^2 (\hat{\sigma})^2} \tag{10}$$

where n is the number of observations, $\hat{\sigma}_{MM}$ is the M-estimator of scale of the residuals (defined in Eq. 3) fitted by the MM-estimator, $\hat{\sigma}$ is the M-estimator of scale of the residuals fitted by the S-estimator, $\tilde{r}_i$ are the robust standardized residuals fitted by the S-estimator, $\upsilon_0 = (\Sigma \rho''_0(\tilde{r}_i))/\ (\hat{\sigma}_{MM} \Sigma \rho'_0(\tilde{r}_i)\tilde{r}_i)$ and $d^2 = \frac{1}{n}\Sigma\big((\rho'(\tilde{r}_i))\ /\ ((1/n)\Sigma\rho''(\tilde{r}_i)) - (\rho'_0(\tilde{r}_i))/((1/n)\Sigma\rho''_0(\tilde{r}_i))\big)^2$.

Using standard asymptotic theory, they show that T is asymptotically distributed as a χ^2_{p+1}. However, examining Eq. (10), two drawbacks of the test emerge: First, the test focuses on the bias of the MM-estimator. Second, it is based on the assumption of a single scale of the residuals and is thus not appropriate in case of heteroskedasticity and/or asymmetry in the error term. This test will serve as the benchmark in the simulations since it is the one commonly used to test whether an MM-estimator (with a given level of efficiency) can be safely used.

Size and power of the test

In this section, we consider two aspects of the behavior of the test we propose. First, we study its finite-sample behavior (under the null hypothesis of no outlier contamination) by comparing: (i) an MM- to an S-estimator and (ii) an LS- to an S-estimator. The loss function (ρ_0) used to compute the S-estimator (with a breakdown point of 50%) and the MM-estimator with a Gaussian efficiency set to 95% where ρ is Tukey's biweight function given in Eq. (6) with the tuning parameter set respectively to $k = 1.546$ and $k = 4.685$. We check the size of the test under three assumptions on the error term: (i) homoskedastic normality, (ii) heteroskedastic normality, and (iii) homoskedastic asymmetry.

Second, we investigate the behavior of the test under contamination. The power is computed considering the most influential type of outliers (i.e., bad leverage points), but also vertical outliers (outlying in the y-dimension but not in the x-dimension) that obviously affect the estimation of the intercept but only mildly the slope estimates.

For the size of the test we simulate the data under three different sampling schemes for the error terms (homoskedastic normality, heteroskedastic normality and asymmetry) and three different sample sizes ($n = 500$, $n = 1,000$, and $n = 2,000$). More precisely, the data generating process is

$$y_i = \theta_0 + \theta_1 x_{i1} + \theta_2 x_{i2} + \varepsilon_i \tag{11}$$

for $i = 1, \ldots, n$. The regression parameters $\theta_0, \theta_1, \theta_2$ are set to 1. The explanatory variables x_1 and x_2 are generated as *i.i.d.* standard normal random variables. The error term ε is generated according to three different designs:

(i) Homoskedastic Normal errors: ε_i is generated from a standard normal distribution for $i = 1, \ldots, n$;
(ii) Heteroskedastic Normal errors: $\varepsilon_i = |x_{i1}| u_i$ for $i = 1, \ldots, n$ where u is generated from a standard normal distribution;
(iii) Homoskedastic Asymmetric errors: ε_i is generated from a log-normal with mean zero and variance $e(e-1)$ for $i = 1, \ldots, n$.

For each case, we generate $m = 5,000$ samples of n observations. The size of the test we propose and of that of Yohai et al. (1991), are reported in Table 1. These sizes are measured by counting the percentage of times (over repeated samples) that the test statistic is larger than a given percentile (95th in our case) of a χ^2 distribution with respectively p and $(p + 1)$ degrees of freedom. Ideally they should therefore be close to 5%. The QQ-plots comparing empirical and theoretical quantiles of the χ^2 in each situation can be found at "http://homepages.ulb.ac.be/126vverardi/graphs/QQplots.pdf". From Table 1, it is clear that under Gaussian and asymmetric assumptions

Table 1. Percentage of Rejections Without Contamination at $\alpha = 5\%$.

		LS vs. S		MM95 vs. S	
Size of the test with $\alpha = 5\%$		H	YSZ	H	YSZ
i.i.d. normal errors	$n = 500$	6.08	3.12	8.86	6.60
	$n = 1{,}000$	4.38	2.66	6.72	5.88
	$n = 2{,}000$	5.74	5.38	5.64	5.54
Heteroskedastic errors	$n = 500$	5.30	0.12	11.80	21.30
	$n = 1{,}000$	4.46	0.80	11.06	23.50
	$n = 2{,}000$	8.22	8.48	7.84	21.64
Asymmetric errors	$n = 500$	4.90	99.98	4.04	100
	$n = 1{,}000$	4.62	100	4.30	100
	$n = 2{,}000$	4.68	100	4.40	100

for the error term, the empirical level of the two versions of our test (LS vs. S and MM vs. S) is very close to the theoretical value of 5%. The same conclusion holds for the Yohai, Stahel, and Zamar test under the assumption of normality but not in the case of asymmetry. The situation is not as good under the specification of heteroskedastic errors that we used in the simulations since the level of our test is adequate for the comparison between the LS- and S-estimators but is slightly higher than 5% for the comparison with the MM-estimator. However, the YSZ test yields an even higher difference between empirical and theoretical levels. These results also show that since the test is asymptotic, its behavior improves when the sample size increases.

The second part of this section is devoted to the study of the power of the test under contamination. It is well-known that points outlying in the x-dimension (design space) and that lie far away from the regression line, called leverage points, are the most "dangerous" outliers (see Dehon, Gassner & Verardi 2009b). We therefore focus on this type of outliers in the simulations. For the simulations, observations were generated according to model

$$y_i = \theta_0 + \theta_1 x_i + \varepsilon_i \qquad (12)$$

for $i = 1, \ldots, n$ where both parameters θ_0 and θ_1 are equal to one. For each case, we generate $m = 1{,}000$ samples of n observations. The sample sizes used are $n = 500, 1{,}000$, and $2{,}000$ and the specifications for the error term are the same as for previous simulations. For all of the replications we

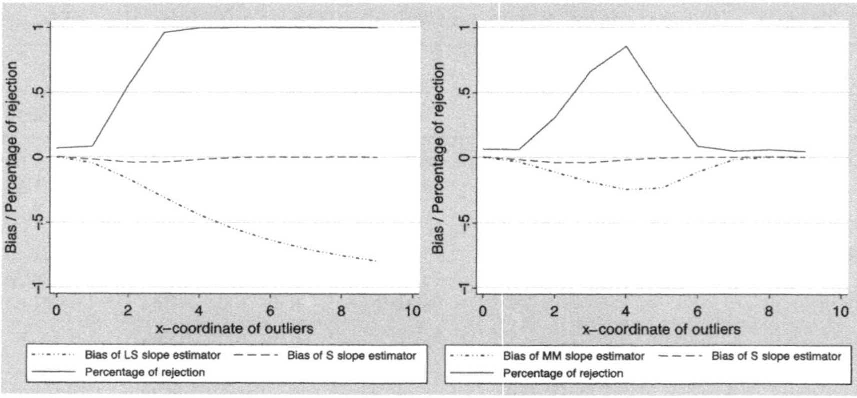

Fig. 1. Bias of the Estimators.

introduced a small percentage of contamination (5%). To generate the contamination, we replaced 5% of the x-values by an integer constant C that increases in succession from 0 to 9. The biases of the LS-, MM- and S-slope estimators are computed for all types of bad leverage outliers and presented in Figure 1 (where $n = 1,000$ and the error term is assumed symmetric and homoskedastic). On the left panel, the bias of LS (dotted line) is compared to that of S (dashed line) while on the right one it is the bias of MM (dotted line) that is compared to that of S (dashed line). The percentage of rejection of the null is represented by the plain line.

The left panel of Figure 1 shows that the bias of the LS-estimator increases rapidly when the leverage effect becomes substantial (i.e., for x-coordinates ranging from 2 to 9). On the other hand, the bias of the S-estimator remains very small, which is not surprising as the S-estimator is very robust. The percentage of rejection of the null of no contamination increases quickly to reach 100% for an x-coordinate of 3. Though we only present the homoskedastic case here, whatever the scenario (normality, heteroskedasticity, or asymmetry) the test behaves comparably well. When the x-coordinate of the contamination is smaller than 1, the percentage of rejection (hence the size of the test) is close to 5%. The right panel of Figure 1 shows that the bias of the MM-estimator starts increasing proportionally to the leverage effect. However, from a certain point on, it decreases. The reason for this is that the MM is a redescending estimator: the importance awarded to residuals increases up to a point and then starts decreasing toward zero. The influence of outliers is therefore significant only if they are located in the neighborhood of this point which is at 4 in this case.

To get a clearer idea of the power of the test, we generated 1,000 samples for each type of contamination, and for each of them computed the percentage of rejection of the null. Results are presented in Figure 2 and Tables 2 and 3. The biases of the three estimators are given in Table 3. Obviously, the bias of the LS-estimator increases with the x-coordinate of the outliers. In most situations, such as the one presented here, the bias of the S-estimator remains rather small while the bias of the MM-estimator increases for mild outliers but decreases when the x-coordinates of the outliers become larger. On the left panel of Figure 2, the test compares S to LS, while on the right it compares S to MM.

The percentage of rejection for two different sample sizes ($n = 500$ and $n = 2,000$) and the three scenarios for the error term are plotted in Figure 2. On the left, we compare the LS-estimator to the S-estimator and on the right, MM is compared to S. As expected, the test obtained by comparing the LS- and S-estimators rejects the null hypothesis more rapidly when the sample size is larger (for all scenarios). The heteroskedastic case seems to yield the least powerful result. Concerning the comparison between the MM- and the S-estimators, again the null hypothesis is more rapidly rejected when the sample size is larger. The test behaves very well under normality or asymmetry, but it seems that the detection of outliers is more difficult with heteroskedastic errors (see Table 3).

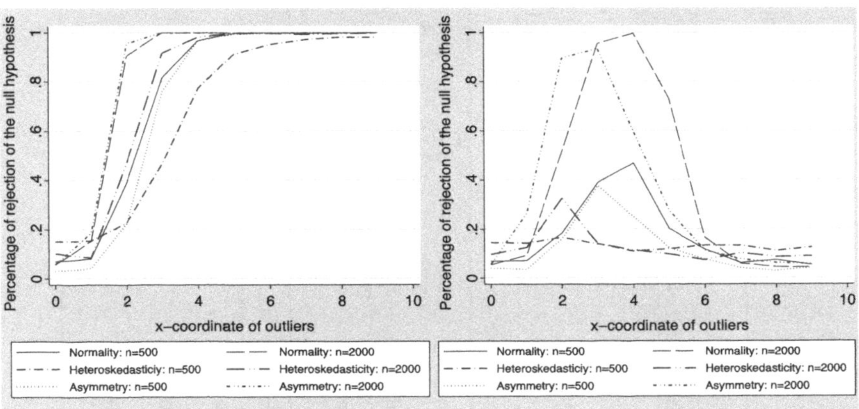

Fig. 2. Power of the Test.

Table 2. Percentage of Rejection with 5% of Bad Leverage Points.

Normality		$C=0$	$C=1$	$C=2$	$C=3$	$C=4$	$C=5$	$C=6$	$C=7$	$C=8$	$C=9$
$n=500$	LS	6.9	8.0	39.2	81.6	96.7	99.8	100	99.8	100	100
	MM	6.8	7.0	18.4	38.9	46.9	20.2	11.6	6.1	7.3	5.3
$n=1{,}000$	LS	6.9	8.3	55.7	96.1	99.7	99.9	100	100	100	100
	MM	6.3	6.1	30.8	66.5	85.6	44.0	8.4	4.7	5.6	4.4
$n=2{,}000$	LS	5.6	15.2	90.5	100	100	100	100	100	100	100
	MM	5.3	9.2	51.6	95.5	99.8	73.0	16.5	5.8	4.4	4.3
Heteroskedastic errors		$C=0$	$C=1$	$C=2$	$C=3$	$C=4$	$C=5$	$C=6$	$C=7$	$C=8$	$C=9$
$n=500$	LS	15.0	15.3	22.8	46.8	77.3	91.3	95.2	97.2	98.2	98.1
	MM	14.4	14.2	16.5	13.8	10.9	11.8	13.3	13.2	11.1	12.5
$n=1{,}000$	LS	11.1	10.9	41.6	79.8	95.8	97.8	98.9	99.0	99.7	100
	MM	11.2	12.7	31.8	7.3	9.3	11.3	9.7	11.9	10.0	9.2
$n=2{,}000$	LS	10.1	8.4	47.3	91.7	98.2	99.8	99.8	99.4	99.8	99.9
	MM	9.6	12.4	32.6	13.9	11.3	9.6	7.3	10.1	8.6	8.9
Asymmetry errors		$C=0$	$C=1$	$C=2$	$C=3$	$C=4$	$C=5$	$C=6$	$C=7$	$C=8$	$C=9$
$n=500$	LS	3.0	4.0	22.6	76.1	96.8	99.4	99.9	99.9	99.9	100
	MM	3.9	3.4	15.9	37.6	25.1	12.2	7.5	4.0	2.8	4.2
$n=1{,}000$	LS	4.8	10.5	68.0	98.7	99.8	100	100	100	100	100
	MM	4.5	15.8	57.5	61.4	32.3	15.2	7.8	5.3	4.8	5.9
$n=2{,}000$	LS	5.7	18.5	95.6	99.9	100	100	99.9	100	100	100
	MM	5.5	26.4	89.5	93.5	59.7	27.7	11.2	7.6	6.1	5.7

Table 3. Bias of the LS-, MM- and S-Slope Estimator with 5% of Bad Leverage Points.

Normality		$C=0$	$C=1$	$C=2$	$C=3$	$C=4$	$C=5$	$C=6$	$C=7$	$C=8$	$C=9$
$n=500$	LS	−0.01	−0.06	−0.20	−0.35	−0.49	−0.60	−0.68	−0.74	−0.80	−0.83
	MM	−0.01	−0.05	−0.13	−0.20	−0.25	−0.24	−0.14	−0.03	−0.01	−0.01
	S	0.00	−0.03	−0.05	−0.04	−0.02	−0.01	0.00	0.00	−0.01	0.00
$n=1,000$	LS	0.00	−0.05	−0.17	−0.31	−0.44	−0.56	−0.64	−0.71	−0.76	−0.80
	MM	0.00	−0.04	−0.12	−0.19	−0.25	−0.23	−0.12	−0.02	0.00	0.00
	S	0.00	−0.02	−0.04	−0.04	−0.02	−0.01	0	−0.01	0.00	0.00
$n=2,000$	LS	0.00	−0.05	−0.17	−0.31	−0.45	−0.56	−0.65	−0.71	−0.77	−0.81
	MM	0.00	−0.04	−0.11	−0.18	−0.22	−0.18	−0.06	−0.01	−0.01	0.00
	S	0.00	−0.02	−0.04	−0.04	−0.01	0.00	0.00	−0.01	0.00	−0.01
Heteroskedastic errors		$C=0$	$C=1$	$C=2$	$C=3$	$C=4$	$C=5$	$C=6$	$C=7$	$C=8$	$C=9$
$n=500$	LS	0.00	−0.03	−0.13	−0.27	−0.40	−0.51	−0.60	−0.67	−0.72	−0.77
	MM	0.00	−0.05	−0.12	−0.12	−0.09	−0.06	−0.04	−0.02	−0.01	0.00
	S	0.00	−0.03	−0.03	−0.03	−0.03	−0.02	−0.02	−0.01	−0.01	−0.01
$n=1,000$	LS	−0.01	−0.06	−0.19	−0.34	−0.48	−0.59	−0.67	−0.74	−0.79	−0.83
	MM	−0.01	−0.08	−0.16	−0.10	−0.04	−0.02	−0.01	−0.01	−0.01	−0.01
	S	0.00	−0.05	−0.02	−0.02	−0.01	−0.01	−0.01	0.00	0.00	−0.01
$n=2,000$	LS	−0.01	−0.06	−0.17	−0.32	−0.45	−0.56	−0.65	−0.72	−0.77	−0.81
	MM	−0.01	−0.07	−0.13	−0.08	−0.04	−0.03	−0.01	−0.01	−0.01	−0.01
	S	−0.01	−0.03	−0.02	−0.02	−0.01	−0.01	−0.01	−0.01	−0.01	−0.01
Asymmetry errors		$C=0$	$C=1$	$C=2$	$C=3$	$C=4$	$C=5$	$C=6$	$C=7$	$C=8$	$C=9$
$n=500$	LS	−0.01	−0.03	−0.12	−0.26	−0.39	−0.50	−0.59	−0.66	−0.72	−0.76
	MM	0.00	−0.01	−0.07	−0.11	−0.13	−0.12	−0.09	−0.05	−0.03	−0.02
	S	0.00	−0.01	−0.02	−0.01	−0.02	−0.01	−0.01	−0.01	−0.01	−0.01
$n=1,000$	LS	−0.01	−0.05	−0.17	−0.30	−0.44	−0.55	−0.64	−0.71	−0.76	−0.80
	MM	0.00	−0.03	−0.08	−0.10	−0.08	−0.05	−0.03	−0.02	−0.02	−0.01
	S	0.00	−0.01	−0.01	−0.01	−0.01	−0.01	−0.01	−0.01	−0.01	−0.01
$n=2,000$	LS	0.00	−0.06	−0.19	−0.34	−0.47	−0.58	−0.67	−0.74	−0.79	−0.83
	MM	−0.01	−0.03	−0.08	−0.10	−0.08	−0.05	−0.03	−0.02	−0.01	−0.01
	S	−0.01	−0.01	−0.01	−0.01	−0.01	−0.01	−0.01	−0.01	−0.01	−0.01

Table 4. Percentage of Rejection with 5% of Vertical Outliers.

Normality		$C=0$	$C=1$	$C=2$	$C=3$	$C=4$	$C=5$	$C=6$	$C=7$	$C=8$	$C=9$
$n=500$	LS	6.8	7.3	7.6	5.5	6.7	7.0	6.9	6.1	7.0	5.2
	MM	7.0	6.9	8.0	5.9	6.4	5.7	6.2	4.4	6.4	5.6
$n=1,000$	LS	7.1	5.3	6.7	6.5	6.0	5.7	5.1	5.2	3.8	4.1
	MM	6.6	4.9	6.3	6.9	6.7	6.1	5.6	6.1	5.2	5.9
$n=2,000$	LS	6.6	5.8	5.0	6.0	5.9	6.4	7.2	7.7	6.5	6.0
	MM	7.0	5.5	4.7	5.7	6.1	6.2	7.0	5.9	6.2	5.4
Heteroskedastic errors		$C=0$	$C=1$	$C=2$	$C=3$	$C=4$	$C=5$	$C=6$	$C=7$	$C=8$	$C=9$
$n=500$	LS	17.5	12.7	12.0	13.6	12.3	12.3	9.9	11.3	13.0	12.4
	MM	14.9	12.3	10.9	11.4	11.8	10.8	10.1	11.3	12.3	9.7
$n=1,000$	LS	14.0	11.6	9.6	10.2	11.8	12.0	10.2	9.5	9.7	10.3
	MM	14.6	11.3	9.6	10.5	12.0	11.9	9.2	9.8	8.6	9.0
$n=2,000$	LS	11.9	7.4	8.7	6.7	6.1	7.8	9.0	8.1	7.1	8.3
	MM	11.6	8.5	7.5	7.8	7.7	8.2	8.7	9.5	6.0	7.7
Asymmetry errors		$C=0$	$C=1$	$C=2$	$C=3$	$C=4$	$C=5$	$C=6$	$C=7$	$C=8$	$C=9$
$n=500$	LS	3.5	3.1	6.5	4.0	5.1	5.1	5.0	6.2	5.0	4.2
	MM	3.8	4.2	5.1	4.1	4.4	4.4	3.5	4.8	4.6	3.9
$n=1,000$	LS	4.8	4.9	4.2	5.8	4.7	4.5	4.8	4.3	3.8	4.1
	MM	4.0	5.7	3.7	3.8	3.9	4.5	4.0	4.4	4.8	5.6
$n=2,000$	LS	5.4	6.4	6.2	4.9	5.2	5.1	4.6	5.2	6.4	5.6
	MM	5.7	7.2	5.5	4.9	4.5	4.2	5.7	3.8	4.9	4.6

Table 5. Bias of the LS-, MM-, and S-Slope Estimator with 5% Of Vertical Outliers.

Normality		$C=0$	$C=1$	$C=2$	$C=3$	$C=4$	$C=5$	$C=6$	$C=7$	$C=8$	$C=9$
$n=500$	LS	0.000	0.002	0.006	0.011	0.013	0.015	0.019	0.022	0.022	0.026
	MM	0.001	0.003	0.005	0.007	0.003	0.000	0.001	0.001	−0.001	−0.001
	S	0.002	0.011	−0.005	0.001	0.000	−0.001	0.002	−0.003	−0.002	0.001
$n=1{,}000$	LS	−0.001	0.001	0.000	−0.002	−0.003	−0.003	−0.002	−0.002	−0.003	−0.002
	MM	−0.001	0.001	0.000	−0.002	−0.002	−0.002	−0.001	−0.001	−0.001	0.000
	S	−0.003	−0.002	−0.002	−0.002	−0.003	−0.001	−0.001	0.000	−0.001	0.000
$n=2{,}000$	LS	−0.003	0.002	0.002	0.005	0.004	0.008	0.009	0.012	0.013	0.014
	MM	−0.003	0.003	0.002	0.003	−0.001	0.000	−0.001	0.001	0.000	0.000
	S	−0.005	0.004	−0.002	−0.001	−0.001	−0.001	−0.002	−0.001	0.003	0.000
Heteroskedastic errors		$C=0$	$C=1$	$C=2$	$C=3$	$C=4$	$C=5$	$C=6$	$C=7$	$C=8$	$C=9$
$n=500$	LS	−0.002	0.002	0.006	0.010	0.014	0.020	0.021	0.028	0.030	0.028
	MM	0.002	0.000	0.002	0.002	−0.001	0.002	0.002	0.003	0.006	−0.003
	S	0.001	0.000	−0.001	0.001	0.003	0.003	0.005	0.004	0.007	−0.006
$n=1{,}000$	LS	−0.001	0.001	0.001	0.004	0.005	0.001	0.003	0.004	0.005	0.002
	MM	0.001	0.006	0.005	0.002	0.002	−0.002	0.001	−0.001	0.000	0.001
	S	−0.002	0.004	−0.004	0.005	−0.001	−0.006	−0.007	−0.001	−0.002	0.004
$n=2{,}000$	LS	0.002	0.001	0.001	0.002	0.004	0.004	0.007	0.004	0.008	0.008
	MM	−0.001	0.002	0.000	−0.001	0.000	−0.002	−0.001	−0.001	0.000	0.000
	S	0.002	0.002	−0.001	−0.002	0.002	−0.006	−0.002	−0.005	0.000	0.000
Asymmetry errors		$C=0$	$C=1$	$C=2$	$C=3$	$C=4$	$C=5$	$C=6$	$C=7$	$C=8$	$C=9$
$n=500$	LS	−0.005	0.000	0.009	0.012	0.014	0.014	0.021	0.025	0.021	0.021
	MM	0.004	0.006	0.002	0.002	0.000	0.000	0.000	−0.001	−0.001	0.001
	S	0.004	0.000	−0.001	0.000	0.001	−0.001	0.000	0.000	−0.001	−0.001
$n=1{,}000$	LS	−0.001	0.002	−0.000	0.007	0.004	0.001	0.003	0.005	0.006	0.001
	MM	0.002	0.002	0.001	0.001	0.001	−0.001	0.000	0.000	0.001	−0.000
	S	0.001	0.001	−0.000	0.001	0.001	−0.001	0.000	0.000	−0.000	0.000
$n=2{,}000$	LS	0.001	−0.002	−0.007	−0.005	−0.008	−0.009	−0.010	−0.013	−0.013	−0.0162
	MM	−0.003	−0.003	−0.004	−0.000	−0.000	−0.000	0.001	−0.001	0.001	0.001
	S	−0.002	0.000	0.000	0.000	−0.000	−0.000	−0.000	−0.001	0.000	−0.000

To generate the contamination with vertical outliers, we replaced 5% of the y-values by an integer constant that increases in succession from 0 to 9. With this type of outliers, the percentage of rejection of our test in all situations is very close to 5% (Table 4). These results are not surprising since vertical outliers mainly affect the intercept (Table 5) and the test is based on the comparison of the estimated slope parameter (remember the constant is disregarded). The results of the simulations for good leverage points are not reported here because they only marginally influence the estimation of the regression coefficients leading to very small biases for LS, MM and S-estimators in all the simulated situations.

CONCLUSION

The objective of the paper is to extend Hausman's (1978) specification test to outlier detection. More precisely, we adopt a similar approach to compare an estimator (S) that withstands outlier contamination (and is rather inefficient) with a more efficient but potentially inconsistent one (MM). We believe that the trade-off between consistency and efficiency will enable to make an informed decision as to which estimator should be preferred. From a practical point of view, what we suggest is to start by testing if regression coefficients estimated by least squares (a limit case of MM), have not been excessively influenced by the presence of outliers. If they have not, least squares is the preferable method. Otherwise, we suggest to compare an S with several MMs with different efficiencies. The estimator that will ultimately be retained is the one that, while not rejecting the null, has the highest efficiency.

ACKNOWLEDGMENTS

The authors would like to thank Christophe Croux for his insightful comments. Catherine Dehon gratefully acknowledges research support from FRFC (Fonds de Recherche Fondamentale Collective) and from the ARC contract of the Communauté Française de Belgique. Catherine Dehon is also member of ECORE, the association between CORE and ECARES. Vincenzo Verardi is Associated Researcher of the FNRS and gratefully acknowledges their financial support.

REFERENCES

Croux, C., Dhaene, G., Hoorelbeke, D. (2003). *Robust standard errors for robust estimators*. Discussions Paper Series (DPS) 03.16. Center for Economic Studies, KULeuven.

Dehon, C., Gassner, M., & Verardi, V. (2009a). A new hausman type test to detect the presence of in uential outliers. *Economics Letters*, *105*, 64–67.

Dehon, C., Gassner, M., & Verardi, V. (2009b). Beware of good outliers and overoptimistic conclusions. *Oxford Bulletin of Economics and Statistics*, *71*, 437–452.

Gervini, D., & Yohai, V. J. (2002). A class of robust and fully e cient regression estimators. *Annals of Statistics*, *30*, 583–616.

Hansen, L. P. (1982). Large sample properties of generalized method of moments estimators. *Econometrica*, *50*(4), 1029–1054.

Hausman, J. A. (1978). Speci cation tests in econometrics. *Econometrica*, *46*(6), 1251–1271.

Maronna, R., Martin, D., & Yohai, V. J. (2006). *Robust statistics: Theory and methods*. John Wiley & Sons, Chichester.

Omelka, M., & Salibian-Barrera, M. (2010). Uniform asymptotics for S- and MM- regression esti-mators. *Annals of the Institute of Statistical Mathematics*, *62*(5), 897–927.

Rousseeuw, P. J., & Yohai, V. J. (1984). Robust regression by means of S-estimators. In J. Franke, W. Härdle & R. D. Martin (Eds.), *Robust and nonlinear time series analysis. Lecture notes in statistics* (p. 26). New York, NY: Springer Verlag.

Salibian-Barrera, M., & Yohai, V. J. (2006). A fast algorithm for S-regression estimates. *Journal of Computational and Graphical Statistics*, *15*, 414–427.

Yohai, V. J., Stahel, W., & Zamar, R. H. (1991). A procedure for robust estimation and inference in regression. In W. Stahel & S. Weisberg (Eds.), *Directions in robust statistics and diagnosis Part II, IMA volumes in mathematics and its applications*, (Vol. 34, pp. 365–374).

Yohai, V. J. (1987). High breakdown-point and high e ciency M-estimates for regression. *The Annals of Statistics*, *15*, 642–656.

A SIMPLE TEST FOR IDENTIFICATION IN GMM UNDER CONDITIONAL MOMENT RESTRICTIONS

Francesco Bravo, Juan Carlos Escanciano and Taisuke Otsu

ABSTRACT

This chapter proposes a simple, fairly general, test for global identification of unconditional moment restrictions implied from point-identified conditional moment restrictions. The test is a Hausman-type test based on the Hausdorff distance between an estimator that is consistent even under global identification failure of the unconditional moment restrictions, and an estimator of the identified set of the unconditional moment restrictions. The proposed test has a χ^2 *limiting distribution and is also able to detect weak identification. Some Monte Carlo experiments show that the proposed test has competitive finite sample properties already for moderate sample sizes.*

Essays in Honor of Jerry Hausman
Advances in Econometrics, Volume 29, 455–477

ISSN: 0731-9053/doi:10.1108/S0731-9053(2012)0000029020

Keywords: Conditional moment restrictions; generalized method of moments; global identification; Hausman test; asset pricing

JEL classification: C12; C13; C32

INTRODUCTION

Economic models can often be characterized by conditional moment restrictions in the underlying economic variables. For example, rational expectations and dynamic asset pricing models used in macroeconomics and international finance give rise to conditional moment restrictions in the form of stochastic Euler conditions. Alternatively, exogeneity or other statistical assumptions can also lead to conditional moment restrictions. The typical approach to estimate these models is to find a set of unconditional moment restrictions implied from the conditional ones, and use Hansen's (1982) generalized method of moments (GMM) estimator, as for example Hansen and Singleton (1982) did in their seminal paper on estimating a consumption based capital asset pricing model.[1] The key assumption in this unconditional GMM-based approach is that the parameters identified in the conditional moment restrictions can be globally identified by the implied unconditional moment restrictions. However, as recently emphasized by Dominguez and Lobato (2004, henceforth DL), this needs not be the case. These authors showed that the global identification condition of GMM can fail in nonlinear models, regardless of whether the instruments are optimally chosen. Moreover, since the seminal theoretical works by Staiger and Stock (1997) and Stock and Wright (2000), there is growing empirical evidence indicating potential (weak) identification problems in commonly used macroeconomic models: Canova and Sala (2006) in dynamic stochastic general equilibrium models, Nason and Smith (2008) in the new Keynesian Phillips curve or Yogo (2004) in consumption Euler equations, to name just a few. Given the popularity among applied economists of the unconditional GMM-based approach and its potential identification problem, it seems important to investigate the possibility of testing for global identification in unconditional moment restrictions models, and whether any such procedure can be easily implemented, making it therefore appealing from a practical point of view.

This chapter proposes a simple yet general test for the hypothesis that the unconditional moment restrictions globally identify the true parameter identified in the conditional moment restrictions. The test is in the same spirit as that originally proposed in the seminal paper by Hausman (1978), and it is based on the Hausdorff distance between an estimator that is always consistent for the true parameter, namely DL's consistent estimator, and a GMM-based estimator of the identified set of the unconditional moments. It is important to note that the test is valid for any other always-consistent estimator for the true parameter, as, for example, those proposed by Carrasco and Florens (2000), Donald, Imbens, and Newey (2003), or Kitamura, Tripathi, and Ahn (2004). Likewise the test is valid for other estimators different from GMM such as the continuous updating estimator (Hansen, Heaton, & Yaron, 1996) or any of the members of the generalized empirical likelihood family (Newey & Smith, 2004). We chose DL and the standard GMM estimator because of their simple implementation compared to any of the above mentioned alternatives; in particular no tuning parameters, such as the bandwidth or the rate of growth of the approximating functions, have to be selected for the conditional model and no saddlepoint estimation typical of GEL estimators has to be carried out. We also note that the proposed test is valid with weakly dependent observations as well as with the same type of misspecified conditional moment restrictions as those considered, for example, by Ai and Chen (2007).

The intuition behind the proposed test is that under the null hypothesis of global identification any GMM estimator of the identified set is consistent and asymptotically normal under some regularity conditions. Therefore the test has, as the classical Hausman specification test, a simple χ^2 limiting distribution. On the other hand under the alternative hypothesis of identification failure, the Hausdorff distance is expected to be non-zero, leading to a powerful test. It is important to note that the proposed test can also be used in the context of weakly identified unconditional moment restriction models (Stock & Wright, 2000), where the unconditional moments may be close to zero in finite samples for possibly a large set of parameter values. Under weak identification, GMM estimators have nonstandard limiting distributions and traditional approaches to inference are not valid; see Stock, Wright, and Yogo (2005) for a review. The test of this chapter is able to detect weak identification alternatives with probability tending to one as the sample size increases, and with high probability in finite samples for the data generating processes used in the simulations.

Practitioners of the GMM methodology can use our test as follows: if the null hypothesis of global identification is rejected one should change the instruments until identification is achieved. Alternatively, one could use our test to propose the following pre-testing estimator: if the null hypothesis of global identification is rejected one should use DL, otherwise use GMM. A Monte Carlo experiment below provides some finite sample evidence on the benefits of this pre-testing procedure, but theoretical results in Guggenberger (2010) suggest potential problems of related pre-testing strategies for inference. In any case, an important motivation for using GMM estimates rather than directly the DL's estimator, in addition to the GMM's popularity mentioned above, is the difficult interpretation of the latter relative to the former, as discussed further in the second section.

It is important to note that most of the existing tests for identification have been confined to linear models; see earlier contributions by Koopmans and Hood (1953) and Sargan (1958), and more recent ones by Cragg and Donald (1993), Hahn and Hausman (2002), and Stock and Yogo (2005). In linear models, global identification reduces to a rank condition. Although this rank condition can also be applied to nonlinear models, as in Wright (2003), it is in general neither necessary nor sufficient for global identification, see Sargan (1983) and an example below illustrating this point. In addition to Wright's (2003) test, the only available tests for identification in nonlinear models we are aware of are those of Arellano, Hansen, and Sentana (2012), Inoue and Rossi (2011), and Wright (2010). Arellanoet et al.'s (2012) test is an overidentification test (similar to that of Carrasco & Florens, 2000) in which the parameter of interest is a continuous reparametrization of the original (not identified) one. Inoue and Rossi's (2012) test is based on comparing two different GMM estimators which converge to the same probability limit when the model is identified but have different probability limits when the model is not identified. Wright's (2010) test compares the volume of a Wald confidence set with that of Stock and Wright's (2000) S-confidence set in overidentified unconditional moment restrictions. The proposed test is a useful complement to those proposed by Arellano et al. (2012) and Wright (2010) because it is does not require the specification of the identified set or of the lack of identification structure, and it can be applied to both just-identified and overidentified models. The proposed test complements also that of Inoue and Rossi (2011), which is its closest in terms of generality and applicability. Like the one proposed here, Inoue and Rossi's (2011) test can detect departures from the null hypotheses of no or weak identification and it is characterized by an asymptotic chi-squared distribution. However their test depends crucially on the choice of two different GMM objective functions and that might result in misleading inferences, as we illustrate with a simple example in the fourth section.

Summarizing, this chapter takes the original and fundamental idea of Hausman (1978) and extends it to the case where the estimator that is inconsistent under the alternative is a set rather than a point estimator, so that the test statistic is well-defined under lack of identification. The resulting procedure is a test that can be used to check the validity of a finite number of instrument in standard GMM estimation.

The rest of this chapter is organized as follows: next section briefly reviews standard GMM estimation and illustrates the associated potential identification problem. This section also makes explicit the null and alternative hypotheses and introduces the Hausman-type test statistic for global identification. Section 3 develops the asymptotic theory, whereas the fourth section reports a Monte Carlo experiment showing that the new test possesses satisfactory finite-sample properties. The fifth section concludes. Finally an Appendix contains formulae for the variances and the proof of the main theorem.

GMM AND GLOBAL IDENTIFICATION FAILURE

The model we consider is defined by a set of conditional moment restrictions

$$E[h(Y_t, \theta_0)|X_t] = 0 \text{ almost surely } (a.\text{s.}), \text{ at some unique } \theta_0 \in \Theta \subset \mathbb{R}^p \quad (1)$$

for a measurable moment function $h : \mathbb{R}^{d_y} \times \Theta \to \mathbb{R}^{d_h}$ that is assumed to be known up to the finite-dimensional parameter θ_0. For the sake of exposition we only consider the case $d_h = 1$, the extension of our methods to the case $d_h > 1$ being straightforward. The vector-valued stochastic process $\{Z_t \equiv (Y'_t, X'_t)'\}_{t \in \mathbb{Z}}$ is a strictly stationary and ergodic time series. Henceforth, $tr(A)$, $|A|$ and A' denote the trace, Euclidean norm $|A| \equiv (tr(A'A))^{1/2}$ and the transpose of a matrix A, respectively. The conditioning variable X_t takes values in $\mathbb{R}^{d_x}$ and can contain lagged values of Y_t and other exogenous variables. Throughout the chapter we shall assume that the conditional moment Eq. (1) uniquely identifies the parameter θ_0. The standard unconditional GMM estimator for θ_0 is constructed as follows. Given an $r \times 1$ vector of " instruments" $a(X_t)$ with $r \geq p$, possibly depending on θ_0, the unconditional GMM estimator $\hat{\theta}_{GMM}$ is defined as any solution of the optimization problem

$$\min_{\theta \in \Theta} Q_n(\theta) \equiv \left(\frac{1}{n} \sum_{t=1}^{n} f(Z_t, \theta) \right)' W_n \left(\frac{1}{n} \sum_{t=1}^{n} f(Z_t, \theta) \right) \quad (2)$$

where $f(Z_t, \theta) \equiv a(X_t) h(Y_t, \theta)$ and W_n is a possibly stochastic matrix satisfying some mild conditions; see Assumption A3 below. The critical assumption in the unconditional GMM is that the identified set $\Theta_I \equiv \{\theta \in \Theta : \{E[f(Z_t, \theta)] = 0\}$ defined by the unconditional moment restrictions is a singleton $\Theta_I = \{\theta_0\}$, that is,

$$E[f(Z_t, \theta)] = 0 \Rightarrow \theta = \theta_0. \tag{3}$$

This is the global identification assumption of GMM. This assumption was questioned by DL. They provided some examples where Eq. (3) is not satisfied. The following example generalizes in an important way one of the examples of DL.

Example 1. (DL's Example 2): Assume that (Y, X) satisfies $E[Y|X] = \theta_0^2 X + \theta_0 X^2$ at $\theta_0 = 5/4$. For the unconditional moment restriction $E[a(X)(Y - \theta^2 X - \theta X^2)] = 0$ with a scalar instrument $a(X)$, it can be shown that, provided $E[Xa(X)]$ is non-zero, $\Theta_I = \{\theta_0, \theta_1\}$, where $\theta_1 = (-E[X^2 a(X)]/E[Xa(X)]) - \theta_0$. So, global identification of θ_0 holds if and only if $E[a(X)a^*(X)] = 0$, where $a^*(X) = 2\theta_0 X + X^2$. This example contains three important features. (i) Note that $a^*(X)$ is the optimal instrument of Eq. (1) provided $Var[Y|X] = 1$. Hence, the use of the optimal instrument (i.e., $a(X) = a^*(X)$) leads to global identification failure, *regardless of the distribution of X*. (ii) The identification failure for the instrument $a(X) = a^*(X)$ occurs even if the rank condition $E[a^*(X)^2] > 0$ is satisfied. The full rank condition in GMM does not imply nor is implied by global identification. (iii) When the feasible optimal instrument $a(X) = 2\theta X + X^2$ is employed, the moment condition becomes $E[(2\theta X + X^2)(Y - \theta^2 X - \theta X^2)] = 0$. In this case, it can be proved that the parameter is not identified when $X \sim N(1, \sigma^2)$, provided $\sigma^2 < 2.0163$. In particular, if $\sigma^2 = 1$, the identified set is $\Theta_I = \{5/4, -5/4, -3\}$.

To circumvent the identification problem of the unconditional GMM, DL proposed a consistent estimator based on a continuum number of unconditional moment restrictions that are equivalent to the original conditional moment restrictions Eq. (1), and hence preserve the identification of θ_0. This DL estimator plays a crucial role in our arguments and is discussed below. We introduce our null and alternative hypotheses and the test statistic for global identification of the unconditional moment restrictions implied from the conditional ones. Let P_0 be the true unknown (joint) probability measure of Z_t, and $\mathcal{M}$ be the set of all possible measures for Z_t consistent with Assumptions A2 and A3 below. Define the subset of measures which are compatible with the conditional moment restrictions Eq. (1) as

$$\mathscr{P}_c = \left\{ P \in \mathcal{M} : \int h(y, \theta_0) dP_{Y|X=x} = 0 \text{ a.s at some unique } \theta_0 \in \Theta \right\}$$

where $P_{Y|X=x}$ is the conditional probability measure of Y_t given $X_t = x$. On the other hand, the subset of measures where the parameter value θ_0, identified from Eq. (1), is also globally identified from the unconditional moments is defined as

$$\mathscr{P}_u = \left\{ P \in \mathscr{P}_c : \int f(z, \theta) dP = 0 \text{ only at } \theta = \theta_0 \right\}$$

Based on the above notation, our testing problem is written as

$$H_0 : P_0 \in \mathscr{P}_u, \quad H_A : P_0 \in \mathscr{P}_c \backslash \mathscr{P}_u \tag{4}$$

Note that the correct specification of the conditional moment restriction Eq. (1) is always maintained in our testing problem.[2] Several test statistics are available in the liteature for the correct specification hypothesis, that is $P_0 \in \mathscr{P}_c$, such as Bierens (1982). We now introduce our identification test based on the following intuition. Under the null hypothesis H_0, it holds that $\Theta_I = \{\theta_0\}$ and the unconditional GMM estimator $\hat{\theta}_{GMM}$ is consistent for θ_0 under some regularity conditions; under the alternative hypothesis H_1, the identified set Θ_I contains elements different from θ_0 and $\hat{\theta}_{GMM}$ is typically inconsistent. On the other hand there are estimators that are consistent for θ_0 under both the null and alternative hypotheses, which can provide a basis for a Hausman-type test statistic. To construct such an estimator there are at least two available possibilities: one based on unknown instruments that lead to unique identification, for instance $a(X) = E[h(Y, \theta)|X]$, and another based on the characterization of the conditional moment Eq. (1) by an infinite number of unconditional moments,[3]

$$E[h(Y_t, \theta_0)|X_t] = 0 \; a.s. \Leftrightarrow H(x, \theta_0) \equiv E[h(Y_t, \theta_0) 1(X_t \leq x)] = 0 \; a.s. \; x \in \mathbb{R}^{d_x}$$

To see the equivalence, define $m(X_t, \theta) = E[h(Y_t, \theta)|X_t]$ and write, by the law of iterated expectations,

$$H(x, \theta_0) = \int_{(-\infty, x]} m(y, \theta) dF_X(y)$$

where F_X is the cumulative distribution function of X_t. Since $dF_X(y) > 0$ a.s, it follows by standard arguments in calculus that $H(x, \theta_0) \equiv 0$ if and only if $m(x, \theta_0) \equiv 0$ (modulo sets of probability zero). In other words, θ_0 is the unique solution of the minimization problem

$$\min_{\theta \in \Theta} \int_{\mathbb{R}^{d_x}} |H(x, \theta)|^2 dF_X(x).$$

This suggests the following minimum-distance estimator proposed in DL

$$\hat{\theta}_C = \arg\min_{\theta \in \Theta} \int_{\mathbb{R}^{d_x}} |H_n(x, \theta)|^2 dF_{n,X}(x)$$

where $H_n(x, \theta) = n^{-1/2} \sum_{t=1}^{n} h(Y_t, \theta) 1(X_t \leq x)$, and $F_{n,X}$ is the empirical distribution function of $\{X_t\}_{t=1}^{n}$, i.e., $F_{n,X}(x) = n^{-1} \sum_{t=1}^{n} 1(X_t \leq x)$. For computational purposes it is better to write the above objective function as a quadratic form of " errors" . If we denote $h(\theta) \equiv (h(Y_1, \theta), \ldots, h(Y_n, \theta))'$ and $P \equiv (1(X_t \leq X_s))_{t,s})$, then DL's estimator can be simply computed as

$$\hat{\theta}_C = \arg\min_{\theta \in \Theta} h(\theta)'(P'P)h(\theta)$$

Under certain regularity conditions, DL's estimator $\hat{\theta}_C$ is strongly consistent and asymptotically normal under both the null and alternative hypotheses in Eq. (4), which shows the robustness of $\hat{\theta}_C$. The estimator is, however, difficult to interpret. Let $\{\varphi_j(\cdot)\}_{j=1}^{\infty}$ be an orthonormal basis for the Hilbert space of square-integrable functions of X_t. Then, Parserval's identity[4] and Fubini's theorem imply that

$$\int_{\mathbb{R}^{d_x}} |H(x, \theta)|^2 dF_X(x) = \sum_{j=1}^{\infty} (E[h(Y_t, \theta)\psi_j(X_t)])^2$$

for suitable instruments $\{\psi_j(\cdot)\}_{j=1}^{\infty}$ related to $\{\varphi_j(\cdot)\}_{j=1}^{\infty}$ through the equations, for all $j \in \mathbb{N}$,

$$\psi_j(x) = E[\varphi_j(X_t) 1(x \leq X_t)]$$

See Escanciano (2009) for related expansions. Hence, DL's estimator can be seen as a GMM estimator using an infinite number of instruments that depend in a complicated way on the data generating process and have difficult interpretation.

The unconditional GMM estimator $\hat{\theta}_{GMM}$ is easy to interpret, but is consistent and asymptotically normal only under the null hypothesis H_0. This suggests to construct a Hausman-type test statistic for H_0 based on the contrast between $\hat{\theta}_C$ and $\hat{\theta}_{GMM}$, that is,

$$T_n(\hat{\theta}_{GMM}) \equiv n(\hat{\theta}_C - \hat{\theta}_{GMM})'\Sigma_n^{-1}(\hat{\theta}_C - \hat{\theta}_{GMM}) \tag{5}$$

where Σ_n is a consistent estimator for the asymptotic variance-covariance matrix Σ of $\sqrt{n}(\hat{\theta}_C - \hat{\theta}_{GMM})$, and Σ_n and Σ are both defined in Appendix A. However, since under the alternative H_A we may expect many solutions to the optimization problem Eq. (2), the test statistic $T_n(\hat{\theta}_{GMM})$ may not be uniquely defined even in finite samples. Example 1 illustrates this issue.

Example 1. (Cont.): In this example there are two GMM estimators, that is, solutions to the estimating equation $n^{-1}\sum_{t=1}^{n} a(X_t)(Y_t - \theta^2 X_t - \theta X_t^2) = 0$, namely

$$\frac{-n^{-1}\sum_{t=1}^{n} X_t^2 a(X_t) \pm \sqrt{\left(-n^{-1}\sum_{t=1}^{n} X_t^2 a(X_t)\right)^2 + 4\left(n^{-1}\sum_{t=1}^{n} X_t a(X_t)\right)\left(n^{-1}\sum_{t=1}^{n} Y_t a(X_t)\right)}}{2n^{-1}\sum_{t=1}^{n} X_t a(X_t)}$$

Denote by $\hat{\theta}_{GMM,+}$ and $\hat{\theta}_{GMM,-}$ these two solutions, according to the operation used. Associated to these two solutions we have two possible values for the test statistic Eq. (5), that is, $T_n(\hat{\theta}_{GMM,+})$ and $T_n(\hat{\theta}_{GMM,-})$.

To solve the difficulty of defining the test statistic when there is more than one global minimum in Eq. (2), we propose a modified test statistic based on the Hausdorff distance

$$T_n \equiv \max_{\theta \in \hat{\Theta}_{GMM}} T_n(\theta) = \max_{\theta \in \hat{\Theta}_{GMM}} n(\hat{\theta}_C - \theta)'\Sigma_n^{-1}(\hat{\theta}_C - \theta)$$

where $\hat{\Theta}_{GMM}$ is a suitable estimator of the identified set Θ_I. In particular cases such as Example 1, there is a natural choice for $\hat{\Theta}_{GMM}$, namely $\hat{\Theta}_{GMM} = \{\hat{\theta}_{GMM,+}, \hat{\theta}_{GMM,-}\}$. In general, we suggest to construct $\hat{\Theta}_{GMM}$ using the following algorithm; see Veall (1990) for a related method. First we generate $m \in \mathbb{N}$ random independent initial conditions from a random variable taking values in Θ and compute the resulting m minima $Q_n(\hat{\theta}_{GMM}^{(j)})$ for $j = 1, \ldots, m$, where $Q_n(\theta)$ is the GMM objective function in Eq. (2). We define $\hat{\Theta}_{GMM}$ as the set of values $\hat{\theta}_{GMM}^{(j)}$ satisfying

$$\hat{\Theta}_{GMM} = \left\{ \hat{\theta}_{GMM}^{(j)} : Q_n(\hat{\theta}_{GMM}^{(j)}) \leq \min_{1 \leq j \leq m} Q_n(\hat{\theta}_{GMM}^{(j)}) + a_n \right\} \tag{6}$$

where $a_n = 1/(n\log(n))$. For this choice of a_n (or indeed any other one satisfying $a_n = o(1/n)$) any member of $\hat{\Theta}_{GMM}$ is characterized by the same pointwise asymptotic distribution under the null hypothesis H_0; see Theorem 5.23 in van der Vaart (1998). This implies that under H_0 the asymptotic behavior of the statistic T_n can be studied using standard methods. Note that the choice of m under the null is irrelevant.

On the other hand, under the alternative hypothesis H_A, no general point-wise asymptotic theory is available for GMM estimation; $\hat{\theta}_{GMM}$ is not necessarily a consistent estimator for θ_0 and standard methods cannot be applied (see, e.g., Chernozhukov, Hong, & Tamer, 2007). Despite the lack of point-wise asymptotic theory for GMM estimates under lack of identification we are able to show the consistency of our test under a general class of unidentified models that includes weak identification alternatives. This is because in this case the asymptotic properties of the GMM estimators (and hence those of $\hat{\Theta}_{GMM}$) are well known; see Stock and Wright (2000). The choice of m should be such that under the alternative $\hat{\Theta}_{GMM}$ contains distinct points from θ_0 with high probability asymptotically, so that the test is consistent. See next section for a formalization of a sufficient condition for consistency. The simulations of the fourth section below suggest that the finite sample power of the proposed test is high for small and moderate sample sizes.

ASYMPTOTIC THEORY

Asymptotic Null Distribution

This section investigates the asymptotic null distribution of the test statistic T_n. Let $\mathcal{F}_t \equiv \sigma(Y_{t-1}, X_t, ...)$ be the σ-field generated by the information set obtained up to time t, and $G_t(x) \equiv E[E[h(Y_t, \theta_0)^2 | X_t] 1(X_t \leq x) | \mathcal{F}_{t-1}]$. We impose the following assumptions:

Assumption A1. There exists a unique $\theta_0 \in \Theta$ such that $E[h(Y_t, \theta_0)|X_t] = 0$ a.s.

Assumption A2. (i) $\{(Y'_t, X'_t)'\}_{t \in \mathbb{Z}}$ is a strictly stationary and ergodic process with an absolutely continuous distribution function F_X for X_t; (ii) $E[h(Y_t, \theta_0)|\mathcal{F}_t] = E[h(Y_t, \theta_0)|X_t]$ a.s.; (iii) $h : \mathbb{R}^{d_y} \times \Theta \to \mathbb{R}$ is continuous in Θ a.s. and is continuously differentiable in a neighborhood $\mathcal{N}$ of θ_0, $E[sup_{\theta \in \Theta} |h(Y_t, \theta)|] < \infty$, and $E[sup_{\theta \in \mathcal{N}} |(\partial / \partial \theta') h(Y_t, \theta)|] < \infty$; (iv) Θ is compact and θ_0 belongs to the interior of Θ; (v) the matrix $\Sigma_{GG'}$, given in Appendix A, is nonsingular; (vi) there exist a constant $s > 0$ and stationary sequence $\{C_t\}_{t \in \mathbb{Z}}$ with $E|C_t| < \infty$ such that $|G_t(x_1) - G_t(x_2)| \leq C_t |x_1 - x_2|^s$ for each $x_1, x_2 \in \mathbb{R}^{d_x}$.

Assumption A3. $f : \mathbb{R}^{d_y+d_x} \times \Theta \rightarrow \mathbb{R}^r$ is continuous in Θ a.s. and is continuously differentiable in $\mathcal{N}$, $E[\sup_{\theta\in\Theta}|f(Z_t,\theta)|]<\infty$, and $E[\sup_{\theta\in\mathcal{N}}|(\partial/\partial\theta')f(Z_t,\theta)|]<\infty$. $W_n \rightarrow_P W$, with a symmetric positive definite matrix W. The matrix $\Xi' W \Xi$, given in Appendix A, is nonsingular.

Assumption A4. The matrix Σ is positive definite and the estimator $\Sigma_n \rightarrow_P \Sigma$.

Assumption A1 imposes identification of θ_0 in the conditional moment restrictions. Assumption A2 guarantees consistency and asymptotic normality of the DL estimator $\hat{\theta}_C$. Our Assumption A2 is in general weaker than conditions assumed in DL and related literature. For example, DL assumed $E[|h(Y_t,\theta_0)|^4|X|^{1+\delta}]<\infty$, whereas we only require bounded second-order moments. Also, DL required the density of X_t conditioning on $\mathcal{F}_{t-1}$ to be bounded and continuous. By Hölder's inequality, this latter assumption implies our Assumption A2(c) with $s_1 = \delta/(1+\delta)$ for some $\delta>0$, provided $E[|h(Y_t,\theta_0)|^{2(1+\delta)}]<\infty$. Finally the smoothness condition for h can be relaxed at the cost of longer proofs. Assumption A3 is standard in the literature of GMM. Assumption A4 involves the variance matrix Σ used in the construction of the test. Its expression and a consistent estimator can be found in Appendix A. Under these assumptions, we obtain the asymptotic null distribution of our global identification test statistic T_n.

Theorem 1. *Suppose Assumptions A1-A4 hold. Under*H_0 , the test statistic T_n with $\hat{\Theta}_{GMM}$ in Eq. (6) satisfies

$$T_n \rightarrow_d \chi_p^2.$$

The proof of Theorem 1 can be found in Appendix B.

Power Properties

This section shows that the proposed test is consistent under a high-level condition that is satisfied for a general class of unidentified or weakly identified unconditional moment restriction models, including weak identified alternatives as defined by Stock and Wright (2000).

Assumption A5. For $\hat{\Theta}_{GMM}$ defined in Eq. (6), it holds $\lim_{n\rightarrow\infty} \max_{\theta\in\hat{\Theta}_{GMM}} \sqrt{n}|\theta-\theta_0| = \infty$ a.s.

Theorem 2. Suppose Assumptions A1-A5 hold. Then $T_n \to_P \infty$.

The proof of Theorem 2 is straightforward, and hence it is omitted. We now verify that Assumption A5 holds for weakly identified unconditional moment restriction models. Assume that there exists a measurable function m satisfying $m(\theta_0) = 0$ and

$$E\left[\frac{1}{n}\sum_{t=1}^{n} f(Z_t, \theta)\right] = \frac{m(\theta)}{\sqrt{n}}$$

for each $n \in \mathbb{N}$ and $\theta \in \Theta$. In this case the asymptotic distribution of the DL estimator $\hat{\theta}_C$ does not change under Assumptions A1 and A2, whereas the results in Stock and Wright (2000, Theorem 1) yield that any member of $\hat{\Theta}_{GMM}$ converges in distribution to a stochastic limit that is different from θ_0 with probability one. Hence, under the conditions in Stock and Wright (2000) we conclude that Assumption A5 holds, and our test is consistent against weak identification. Formally, Stock and Wright (2000) showed that $\hat{\theta}_{GMM} \to_{a.s} \theta_1 \neq \theta_0$, then

$$\lim_{n\to\infty} \max_{\theta\in\hat{\Theta}_{GMM}} \sqrt{n}|\theta - \theta_0| \geq \lim_{n\to\infty} \sqrt{n}|\hat{\theta}_{GMM} - \theta_0| = \infty \text{ a.s.}$$

For other alternatives, the power of our test has to be analyzed on a case-by-case basis, given that there is no general point-wise limit distribution theory for estimation under lack of identification. For instance, in Example 1 we can prove Assumption A5 by simple arguments.

Example 1. (Cont.): Suppose that $a(X)$ is such that $E[a(X)a^*(X)] \neq 0$, so the unconditional moment restriction $E[a(X)(Y - \theta^2 X - \theta X^2)] = 0$ does not identify θ_0. It can be shown that $\hat{\theta}_{GMM,+}$ and $\hat{\theta}_{GMM,-}$ are consistent and asymptotically normal for θ_1 and θ_0, respectively. If we define $\hat{\Theta}_{GMM} \equiv \{\hat{\theta}_{GMM,-}, \hat{\theta}_{GMM,+}\}$, then by $\theta_1 \neq \theta_0$, we obtain

$$\lim_{n\to\infty} \max_{\theta\in\hat{\Theta}_{GMM}} \sqrt{n}|\theta - \theta_0| = \lim_{n\to\infty} \max\left\{\sqrt{n}|\hat{\theta}_{GMM,-} - \theta_0|, \sqrt{n}|\hat{\theta}_{GMM,+} - \theta_0|\right\} = \infty \text{ a.s.}$$

Thus, our test is consistent for this example. Note that in this example, there exists a consistent and asymptotically normal estimator for θ_0 even under identification failure, namely $\hat{\theta}_{GMM,-}$. Hence, this example illustrates that taking the Hausdorff distance is crucial to make our test consistent.

MONTE CARLO SIMULATIONS

In this section we investigate the finite-sample performance of the proposed test using some Monte Carlo experiments. First, we consider Example 1 using feasible instruments and several marginal distributions for the conditioning variable X. This example is useful because it illustrates a simple situation in which existing tests for identification either cannot be used or could potentially lead to misleading conclusions. The model is

$$Y = \theta_0^2 X + \theta_0 X^2 + \varepsilon$$

where ε is distributed as $N(0,1)$ independently of X, and $\theta_0 = 5/4$. For the unconditional GMM, we consider the unconditional moment restriction using the optimal instrument $a^*(X,\theta) = 2\theta X + X^2$, that is,

$$E[(2\theta X + X^2)(Y - \theta^2 X - \theta X^2)] = 0 \quad (7)$$

As in DL we consider four possible distributions for X, namely $X \sim N(0,1)$, $X \sim N(1,3)$, $X \sim N(1,1)$, and $X \sim N(1,2)$. In the first two cases, the parameter θ_0 is identified and GMM provides consistent estimates. In the third and fourth cases there are, respectively, three and two solutions to the unconditional moments so that Eq. (7) does not globally identify θ_0 and GMM is inconsistent.

To approximate $\hat{\Theta}_{GMM}$ as given in Eq. (6) we generate $m = 20$ random independent initial conditions from $N(0,1)$. Table 1 reports the rejection probabilities (RP) for the sample sizes $n = 50$, 100, 200, and 500 at the 0.01, 0.05, and 0.10 nominal level using 1000 Monte Carlo replications.

Table 1. RP for DL's Example 2.

		Size				Power		
n	X	0.01	0.05	0.10	X	0.01	0.05	0.10
50		0.032	0.049	0.081		0.642	0.644	0.662
100	$N(0, 1)$	0.016	0.038	0.077	$N(1, 2)$	0.631	0.637	0.662
200		0.013	0.043	0.087		0.573	0.589	0.614
500		0.006	0.045	0.105		0.577	0.591	0.609
50		0.178	0.194	0.221		0.978	0.979	0.980
100	$N(1, 3)$	0.088	0.105	0.148	$N(1, 1)$	0.978	0.998	0.998
200		0.039	0.071	0.121		0.999	0.999	0.999
500		0.009	0.048	0.101		1.000	1.000	1.000

The size performance of our test is satisfactory for both DGPs in the null hypothesis, although there are some size distortions when $X \sim N(1,3)$ for $n=50$ and $n=100$. Table 1 also shows that the power performance of our test is satisfactory. The finite sample power against the alternative with $X \sim N(1,1)$ is high already for $n=50$. For the alternative with $X \sim N(1,2)$ the test has a satisfactory power, but it is lower than for $X \sim N(1,1)$, and it does not increase with the sample size. This result is consistent with the fact that the alternative corresponding to $X \sim N(1,2)$ is very close to the identification region $\sigma^2 < 2.0163$.

It is important to note that neither of Wright's (2003) and Wright's (2010) tests can be used in this example because the full rank condition holds regardless of the identification and because the original model is not overidentified. Also Inoue and Rossi's (2011) test could lead to a misleading conclusion as the following example suggests. Suppose that $X \sim N(1,3)$ and that a researcher applying their test chooses the GMM estimator with the optimal instrument assuming homoskedasticity and the GMM estimator with a constant instrument. The former identifies the true parameter, however the latter does not by the results of the example. Indeed unreported simulations show that in this case their test rejects the null hypothesis of identification with probability one when $n=200$. Interestingly, the proposed test would also be useful in this context because it would allow to find out which estimator is causing the rejection of Inoue and Rossi's null hypothesis.

Before we consider the second experiment, we provide some Monte Carlo evidence on the finite sample properties of the pre-test estimator defined as

$$\hat{\theta}_{PT} = \begin{cases} \hat{\theta}_{GMM} & \text{if } T_n \leq c_{.95}^{\chi_1^2} \\ \hat{\theta}_C & \text{if } T_n > c_{.95}^{\chi_1^2} \end{cases}$$

where T_n is the sample value of the test statistic of Example 1, and $c_{.95}^{\chi_1^2}$ is the upper 0.05 critical value of a χ^2 random variable with one degree of freedom. Table 2 reports the finite sample bias, standard deviation (Std.

Table 2. Finite sample properties of $\hat{\theta}_{GMM}$, $\hat{\theta}_C$ and $\hat{\theta}_{PT}$.

	$X \sim N(0, 1)$			$X \sim N(1, 3)$		
	$\hat{\theta}_{GMM}$	$\hat{\theta}_C$	$\hat{\theta}_{PT}$	$\hat{\theta}_{GMM}$	$\hat{\theta}_C$	$\hat{\theta}_{PT}$
Bias	−0.0020	0.0010	0.0090	−0.0006	−0.0008	−0.0008
Std. Dev.	0.0509	0.0921	0.0649	0.0143	0.0197	0.0158
IQR	0.0641	0.1215	0.0692	0.0179	0.0239	0.0191

Dev.) and interquartile range (IQR) for the efficient GMM $\hat{\theta}_{GMM}$, the DL estimator $\hat{\theta}_C$ and the pre-test estimator $\hat{\theta}_{PT}$ for the cases when $X \sim N(0, 1)$ and $X \sim N(1, 3)$ with sample size $n = 50$. Results for the other sample sizes are similar and hence not reported.

Table 2 seems to suggest that the pre-test estimator $\hat{\theta}_{PT}$ is "in between" the DL and efficient GMM estimator in terms of its finite sample properties, which is further confirmed by Figs. 1 and 2 showing the density of the three estimators.

Table 2 and Figs. 1 and 2 are useful because they indicate that the finite sample distribution of the pre-test estimator $\hat{\theta}_{PT}$ does not seem to be affected by the pretesting procedure. This is important, in particular, in view of some recent results of Guggenberger (2010) that show the potential negative effect of using a Hausman pretest on a t-statistic in linear IV models.

In the second experiment, we investigate the finite-sample performance of our test in a consumption capital asset pricing model (CCAPM) with a

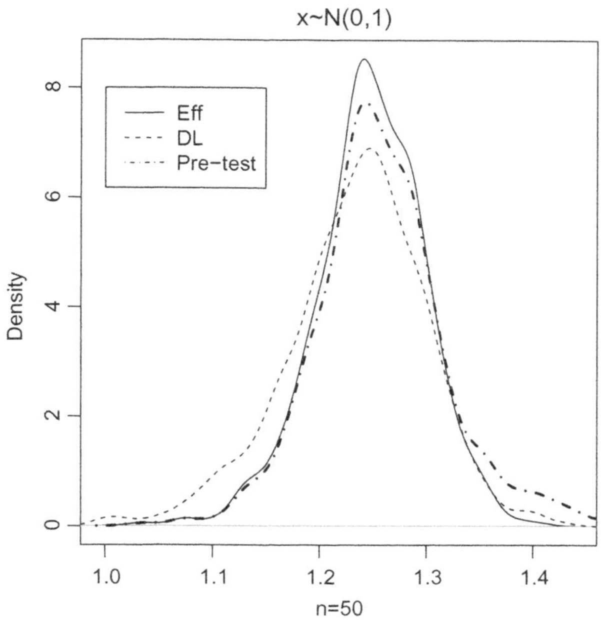

Fig. 1. Density of the efficient GMM estimator $\hat{\theta}_{GMM}$ ("Eff", solid line), the DL estimator ("DL", dotted line) and the pre-test estimator $\hat{\theta}_{PT}$ ("Pretest" dashed line).

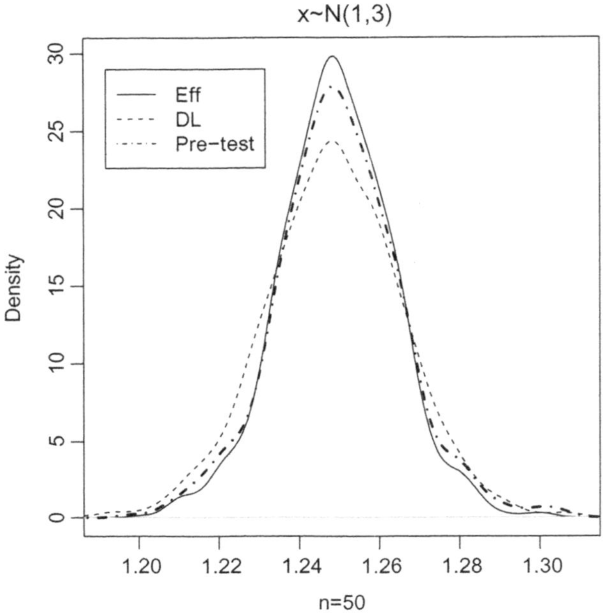

Fig. 2. Density of the efficient GMM estimator $\hat{\theta}_{GMM}$ ("Eff", solid line), the DL estimator ("DL", dotted line) and the pre-test estimator $\hat{\theta}_{PT}$ ("Pre-test" dashed line).

constant relative risk aversion preferences model that has been used in much of the literature on GMM identification; see, for example, Stock and Wright (2000), Wright (2003), Wright (2010), and Inoue and Rossi (2011). The CCAPM data are generated using Tauchen and Hussey's (1991) method which involves fitting a 16-state Markov chain to consumption and dividend growth calibrated so as to approximate the first-order vector autoregression

$$\begin{bmatrix} \log\left(\frac{C_t}{C_{t-1}}\right) \\ \log\left(\frac{D_t}{D_{t-1}}\right) \end{bmatrix} = \mu + \Phi \begin{bmatrix} \log\left(\frac{C_{t-1}}{C_{t-2}}\right) \\ \log\left(\frac{D_{t-1}}{D_{t-2}}\right) \end{bmatrix} + \begin{bmatrix} u_{ct} \\ u_{dt} \end{bmatrix}$$

where C_t is the consumption, D_t is the dividend, μ is a 2×1 vector, Φ is a 2×2 matrix of constants, and $(u_{ct}, u_{dt})' \sim N(0, \Lambda)$. Assets prices are then generated so that they satisfy the stochastic Euler equation

$$E\left[\delta R_{t+1}\left(\frac{C_{t+1}}{C_t}\right)^{-\gamma}-1|\mathcal{F}_t\right]=0\ a.s.$$

where δ is the discount factor, R_t is the gross stock return, and γ is the coefficient of relative risk aversion. Following Inoue and Rossi (2011), we use the instruments $X_t=(1,R_t,C_t/C_{t-1})'$, and consider five different combinations of the parameters $\theta=(\delta,\gamma)'$, μ, Φ, and Λ, as listed in Table 3.

The first one (SI) is for the strongly identified case; the second and third ones (PI1 and PI2) are for two partially identified cases where the instruments are independent of $R_{t+1}, C_{t+1}/C_t$; the last two ones (WI1 and WI2) are for two weakly identified cases; see Inoue and Rossi (2011) for further details. Table 4 reports the rejection probabilities of the proposed test and those of Wright's (2003) test for his null of lack of identification.

In the SI case both tests perform well. The proposed test is slightly oversized for $n=50$ but its accuracy improves as the sample size increases. In the two PI cases the proposed test has some power for $n=50$, but it increases with the sample size. On the other hand Wright's (2003) test performs rather differently for the two cases: it is slightly oversized for PI1 but it is very oversized for the second case. Finally the proposed test has good power in both WI cases even for $n=50$.

Table 3. Parameter Values for CCAPM.

Model	μ	Φ	Λ	δ	γ
SI	$\begin{bmatrix}0\\0\end{bmatrix}$	$\begin{bmatrix}-0.5 & 0.1\\0.1 & -0.5\end{bmatrix}$	$\begin{bmatrix}0.01 & 0.005\\0.005 & 0.01\end{bmatrix}$	0.97	1.3
PI1	$\begin{bmatrix}0.018\\0.013\end{bmatrix}$	$\begin{bmatrix}0 & 0\\0 & 0\end{bmatrix}$	$\begin{bmatrix}0.0012 & 0.0017\\0.0017 & 0.0146\end{bmatrix}$	1.139	13.7
PI2	$\begin{bmatrix}0.018\\0.013\end{bmatrix}$	$\begin{bmatrix}0 & 0\\0 & 0\end{bmatrix}$	$\begin{bmatrix}0.0012 & 0.0017\\0.0017 & 0.0146\end{bmatrix}$	1.139	13.7
WI1	$\begin{bmatrix}0.021\\0.004\end{bmatrix}$	$\left(\frac{90}{n}\right)^{1/2}\begin{bmatrix}-0.162 & 0.017\\0.017 & 0.117\end{bmatrix}$	$\begin{bmatrix}0.0012 & 0.0017\\0.0017 & 0.0146\end{bmatrix}$	0.97	1.3
WI2	$\begin{bmatrix}0.021\\0.004\end{bmatrix}$	$\left(\frac{90}{n}\right)^{1/2}\begin{bmatrix}-0.162 & 0.017\\0.017 & 0.117\end{bmatrix}$	$\begin{bmatrix}0.0012 & 0.0017\\0.0017 & 0.0146\end{bmatrix}$	1.139	13.7

Table 4. RP of Wright's (2003) and the Proposed Test.

		$\alpha = 0.01$		$\alpha = 0.05$		$\alpha = 0.10$	
Model	n	Wright	Proposed	Wright	Proposed	Wright	Proposed
SI	50	0.660	0.051	0.748	0.101	0.795	0.171
	200	0.983	0.016	0.987	0.061	0.988	0.116
PI1	50	0.075	0.186	0.142	0.224	0.202	0.284
	200	0.036	0.292	0.097	0.334	0.141	0.374
PI2	50	0.702	0.203	0.751	0.240	0.778	0.282
	200	0.702	0.303	0.606	0.352	0.667	0.394
WI1	50	0.220	0.538	0.330	0.729	0.407	0.810
	200	0.219	0.781	0.337	0.869	0.407	0.914
WI2	50	0.220	0.756	0.511	0.804	0.533	0.892
	200	0.219	0.826	0.281	0.874	0.322	0.892

CONCLUSIONS

There is growing evidence that many unconditional moment restriction models used in empirical economics are potentially not (or weakly) identified. In this chapter we propose a Hausman-type test statistic that can be used to test the null hypothesis of identification for the unconditional moment restrictions. Our test has a number of appealing properties that we summarize as follows: it is computationally simple, does not require any choice of regularization parameters (such as bandwidths) and has a simple χ^2 limiting distribution. Furthermore, it can be applied to dependent data and to just identified models as well. The test is consistent against weak identification. Monte Carlo simulations suggest that the proposed test has good finite sample size and power properties under both the alternative of lack of identification and weak identification. These results illustrate the general applicability and usefulness of the proposed test.

ACKNOWLEDGMENT

We thank two referees for their careful reading of the chapter and for some useful suggestions. We also thank David Jacho-Chavez for a useful initial discussion and Lin Zhu for excellent research assistance. We are grateful to Barbara Rossi, Atsushi Inoue and Jonathan Wright for providing us with their Matlab codes. Finally we thank participants at various seminars and conferences for useful comments. All errors are our own.

NOTES

1. Further examples of applications of GMM abound in the economics and financial literature; see, for example, the monograph by Hall (2005) and the anniversary issue on GMM of the *Journal of Business and Economics Statistics* in 2002.

2. If the conditional model is misspecified but DL's population objective function is uniquely minimized, say at θ_*, then it can be shown that all our theory goes through provided we replace θ_0 with θ_* and use some adequate asymptotic variance estimator, see for example Ai and Chen (2007). Details are omitted to save space.

3. This characterization generally holds for the unconditional moments in the form of $E[h(Y_t,\theta_0)w(X_t,x)] = 0$ a.s. $x \in \Pi \subseteq \mathbb{R}^q$, where $w(\cdot,x)$ is a suitable parametric family of functions; see Stinchcombe and White (1998), Bierens and Ploberger (1997), and Escanciano (2006b) for examples of Π and w. To simplify the exposition, we follow DL and choose $w(X_t,x) = 1(X_t \leq x)$, but it must be stressed that all the theory that follows holds with other choices of $w(X_t,x)$ as well. For practical reasons, when d_x is moderate or large (say >3 for commonly used sample sizes) it is better to use other weighting functions different from $w(X_t,x) = 1(X_t \leq x)$. The reason is that in a given sample it could be the case that most of the indicators $1(X_t \leq x)$ are zero when x is evaluated at the sample. Alternative weighting functions such as those proposed in Bierens (1982) and Escanciano (2006a) solve this practical deficiency.

4. This is the infinite-dimensional extension of the well-known formula that for a vector $a = (a_1, ..., a_p), |a|^2 = \sum_{j=1}^{p} a_j^2$.

REFERENCES

Ai, C., & Chen, X. (2007). Estimation of possibly misspecified semiparametric condi-tional moment restrictions models with different conditioning variables. *Journal of Econo-Metrics, 141*, 5–43.

Arellano, M., Hansen, L. P., & Sentana, E. (2012). Underidentification? *Journal of Econometrics, 170*, 256–280.

Bierens, H. J. (1982). Consistent model specification tests. *Journal of Econometrics, 20*, 105–134.

Bierens, H. J., & Ploberger, W. (1997). Asymptotic theory of integrated conditional moment tests. *Econometrica, 65*, 1129–1151.

Billingsley, P. (1961). The lindeberg-levy theorem for martingales. *Proceedings of the American Mathematical Society, 12*, 788–792.

Canova, F., Sala, L. (2006). Back to square one: Identification issues in DSGE models. Unpublished manuscript.

Carrasco, M., & Florens, J. P. (2000). Generalization of GMM to a continuum of moment conditions. *Econometric Theory, 16*, 797–834.

Chang, N. M. (1990). Weak convergence of a self-consistent estimator of a survival function with doubly censored data. *Annals of Statistics*, *18*, 391–404.

Chernozhukov, V., Hong, H., & Tamer, E. (2007). Estimation and confidence regions for parameter sets in econometric models. *Econometrica*, *75*, 1243–1284.

Cragg, J. G., & Donald, S. G. (1993). Testing identi…ability and specification in instrumental variables models. *Econometric Theory*, *9*, 222–240.

Delgado, M. A., & Escanciano, J. C. (2007). Nonparametric tests for conditional symmetry in dynamic models. *Journal of Econometrics*, *141*, 652–682.

Dominguez, M. A., & Lobato, I. N. (2004). Consistent estimation of models defined by conditional moment restrictions. *Econometrica*, *72*, 1601–1615.

Donald, S. G., Imbens, G. W., & Newey, W. K. (2003). Empirical likelihood es-timation and consistent tests with conditional moment restrictions. *Journal of Econometrics*, *117*, 55–93.

Escanciano, J. C. (2006a). Consistent diagnostic test for regression models using projections. *Econometric Theory*, *22*, 1030–1051.

Escanciano, J. C. (2006b). Goodness-of-fit tests for linear and non-linear time series models. *Journal of the American Statistical Association*, *101*, 531–541.

Escanciano, J. C. (2007). Weak convergence of non-stationary multivariate marked processes with applications to martingale testing. *Journal of Multivariate Analysis*, *98*, 1321–1336.

Escanciano, J. C. (2009). On the lack of power of omnibus specification tests. *Econometric Theory*, *25*, 162–194.

Guggenberger, P. (2010). The impact of a Hausman pre test on the asymptotic size of a a hypothesis test. *Econometric Theory*, *26*, 369–382.

Hahn, J., & Hausman, J. (2002). A new specification test for the validity of instru-mental variables. *Econometrica*, *70*, 163–189.

Hall, A. R. (2005). *Generalized method of moments*. Oxford: Oxford University Press.

Hansen, L. P. (1982). Large sample properties of generalized method of moment es-timators. *Econometrica*, *50*, 1029–1054.

Hansen, L. P., & Singleton, K. J. (1982). Generalized instrumental variables estimation of nonlinear rational expectations models. *Econometrica*, *50*, 1269–1286.

Hansen, L. P., Heaton, J., & Yaron, A. (1996). Finite sample properties of some alternative GMM estimators. *Journal of Business and Economic Statistics*, *14*, 262–280.

Hausman, J. (1978). Specification tests in econometrics. *Econometrica*, *46*, 1251–1272.

Inoue, A., & Rossi, B. (2011). Testing for identifcation in possibly nonlinear models. *Journal of Econometrics*, *161*, 246–261.

Kitamura, Y., Tripathi, G., & Ahn, H. (2004). Empirical likelihood-based infer-ence for conditional moment restriction models. *Econometrica*, *72*, 1667–1714.

Koopmans, T. C., & Hood, W. C. (1953, Chap. 6). The estimation of simultaneous lin-ear economic relationships. In W. C. Hood & T. C. Koopmans (Eds.), *Studies in econometric methods*. WileyCowles Commission Monograph No. 14.

Nason, J. M., & Smith, G. W. (2008). Identifying the new keynesian curve. *Journal of Applied Econometrics*, *23*, 525–551.

Newey, W. K., & Smith, R. J. (2004). Higher order properties of GMM and gen-eralized empirical likelihood estimators. *Econometrica*, *72*, 219–255.

Ranga Rao, R. (1962). Relations between weak and uniform convergence of measures with applications. *Annals of Mathematical Statistics*, *33*, 659–680.

Sargan, J. D. (1958). The estimation of economic relationships using instrumental variables. *Econometrica*, *26*, 393–415.

Sargan, J. D. (1983). Identification and lack of identi…cation. *Econometrica*, *51*, 1605–1634.

Staiger, D., & Stock, J. H. (1997). Instrumental variables regression with weak instruments. *Econometrica*, *65*, 557–586.

Stinchcombe, M., & White, H. (1998). Consistent speci…cation testing with nui-sance parameters present only under the alternative. *Econometric Theory*, *14*, 295–325.

Stock, J. H., & Wright, J. H. (2000). GMM with weak identi…cation. *Economet-Rica*, *68*, 1055–1096.

Stock, J., & Yogo, M. (2005). Testing for weak instruments in linear IV regression. In *Identification and inference for econometric models: Essays in Honor of Thomas J. Rothenberg*. Cambridge: Cambridge University Press.

Stock, J. H., Wright, J. H., & Yogo, M. (2005). A survey of weak instruments and weak identi…cation in generalized method of moments. *Journal of Business and Economic Statistics*, *20*, 518–529.

Tauchen, G., & Hussey, R. (1991). Quadrature-based methods for obtaining approximate solutions to nonlinear asset pricing models. *Econometrica*, *59*, 371–396.

van der Vaart, A. W. (1998). *Asymptotic statistics*. Cam-bridge, UK: Cambridge University Press.

Wright, J. (2003). Detecting lack of identification in GMM. *Econometric Theory*, *19*, 322–330.

Wright, J. (2010). Testing the adequacy of conventional asymptotics in GMM. *Econometrics Journal*, *13*, 205–217.

Yogo, M. (2004). Estimating the elasticity of intertemporal substitution when instruments are weak. *Review of Economics and Statistics*, *86*, 797–810.

APPENDIX

Appendix A: Asymptotic Variance and Its Estimator

Define the quantities $h_\theta(Y_t, \theta) \equiv (\partial/\partial\theta')h(Y_t, \theta)$, $f_\theta(Z_t, \theta) \equiv (\partial/\partial\theta')f(Z_t, \theta)$, $\Xi \equiv E[f_\theta(Z_t, \theta_0)]$, $S \equiv E[f(Z_t, \theta_0)f(Z_t, \theta_0)']$, $G(x, \theta) \equiv E[h_\theta(Y_t, \theta)1(X_t \leq x)]$, $J(x) \equiv E[G(X_t, \theta)1(x \leq X_t)]$, and $\Sigma_{GG'} \equiv E_X\left[G(x, \theta_0)G(x, \theta_0)'\right]$, where E_X denotes expectation with respect to the distribution of X. Let I_p be the $p \times p$ identity matrix and $\tilde{I} \equiv [I, -I]$ be a $p \times 2p$ matrix. Then, the variance Σ is defined as

$$\Sigma \equiv \tilde{I}VAV'\tilde{I}'$$

where

$$V \equiv \begin{bmatrix} \Sigma_{GG'}^{-1} & 0 \\ 0 & (\Xi' W \Xi)^{-1} \end{bmatrix} \text{and}$$

$$A \equiv \begin{bmatrix} E[h^2(Y_t, \theta_0)J(X_t)J(X_t)'] & E[J(X_t)h(Y_t, \theta_0)f(Z_t, \theta_0)']W\Xi \\ (E[J(X_t)h(Y_t, \theta_0)f(Z_t, \theta_0)']W\Xi)' & \Xi' WSW\Xi \end{bmatrix}$$

Let $\Xi_n \equiv n^{-1}\sum_{t=1}^n f_\theta(Z_t, \hat{\theta}_C)$, $S_n \equiv n^{-1}\sum_{t=1}^n f(Z_t, \hat{\theta}_C)\, f(Z_t, \hat{\theta}_C)'$, $G_n(x, \hat{\theta}_C) \equiv n^{-1}\sum_{t=1}^n h_\theta(Y_t, \hat{\theta}_C)1(X_t \leq x)$, $J_n(x) \equiv n^{-1}\sum_{t=1}^n G_n(X_t, \hat{\theta}_C)1(x \leq X_t)$, and $\Sigma_{GG,n} \equiv n^{-1}\sum_{t=1}^n G_n(X_t, \hat{\theta}_C)G_n(X_t, \hat{\theta}_C)'$. A consistent estimator of Σ is defined as

$$\Sigma_n \equiv \tilde{I}V_nA_nV'_n\tilde{I}' \tag{A.1}$$

where V_n and A_n replace population expectations with sample counterparts and make use of the previous quantities in a routine fashion. The consistency of Σ_n follows easily under Assumptions A1–A3. Further simplications in Σ and its estimators Σ_n are obtained if an efficient GMM estimator is used, following the original idea of Hausman (1978).

Appendix B: Proof of Theorem 1

By standard arguments, see e.g. Theorem 1 in DL, Assumptions A1 and A2 imply that $\hat{\theta}_C \to_P \theta_0$, and likewise Assumption A3 implies $\hat{\theta}_{GMM} \to_P \theta_0$ under H_0. By the definition of $\hat{\Theta}_{GMM}$, we can apply Theorem 5.23 of van der Vaart

(1998) to $\hat{\theta}_{GMM}$, and hence the first-order conditions of the estimators imply that for sufficiently large n,

$$\begin{bmatrix} \sqrt{n}(\hat{\theta}_C - \theta_0) \\ \sqrt{n}(\hat{\theta}_{GMM} - \theta_0) \end{bmatrix} = -\begin{bmatrix} \Sigma_{1n}^{-1} & 0 \\ 0 & \Sigma_{2n}^{-1} \end{bmatrix} \begin{bmatrix} \frac{1}{\sqrt{n}} \sum_{t=1}^{n} G_n(X_t, \hat{\theta}_C) H_n(X_t, \theta_0) \\ \bar{\Xi}'_n W_n \frac{1}{\sqrt{n}} \sum_{t=1}^{n} f(Z_t, \theta_0) \end{bmatrix}$$

where $\Sigma_{1n} \equiv n^{-1/2} \sum_{t=1}^{n} G_n(X_t, \hat{\theta}_C) G_n(X_t, \theta_c)$, $\Sigma_{2n} \equiv \tilde{\Xi}'_n W_n \Xi_n$, $\tilde{\Xi}_n \equiv n^{-1} \sum_{t=1}^{n} f_\theta(Z_t, \hat{\theta}_{GMM})$, $\Xi_n \equiv n^{-1} \sum_{t=1}^{n} f_\theta(Z_t, \theta_{GMM})$, and θ_c and θ_{GMM} are mean values. The uniform law of large numbers of Ranga Rao (1962) and standard arguments imply that $\overline{\Xi}_n, \Xi_n \to_P \Xi$,

$$G_n(x, \theta) \to_{a.s.} G(x, \theta), \qquad \text{uniformly in } (x, \theta)$$

and $V_n \to_P V$.

By Theorem A1 in Delgado and Escanciano (2007), see also Theorem 1 in Escanciano (2007), it follows that $H_n(x, \theta_0)$ is asymptotically stochastic equicontinuous in x with respect to the pseudo-metric $d(x_1, x_2) \equiv |F_X(x_1) - F_X(x_2)|$. Hence, from Lemma 3.1 in Chang (1990) we conclude that

$$\frac{1}{\sqrt{n}} \sum_{t=1}^{n} G_n(X_t, \hat{\theta}_C) H_n(X_t, \theta_0) = \frac{1}{\sqrt{n}} \sum_{t=1}^{n} h(Y_t, \theta_0) J(X_t) + o_P(1).$$

Hence, the theorem follows from a straightforward application of a multivariate central limit theorem of strictly stationary and ergodic martingales, see e.g. Billingsley (1961), applied to the vector

$$\begin{bmatrix} \frac{1}{\sqrt{n}} \sum_{t=1}^{n} h(Y_t, \theta_0) J(X_t) \\ \frac{1}{\sqrt{n}} \sum_{t=1}^{n} f(Z_t, \theta_0) \end{bmatrix}$$

The conclusion follows by the continuous mapping theorem.

FIXED VS RANDOM: THE HAUSMAN TEST FOUR DECADES LATER

Shahram Amini, Michael S. Delgado,
Daniel J. Henderson and Christopher F. Parmeter

ABSTRACT

Hausman (1978) represented a tectonic shift in inference related to the specification of econometric models. The seminal insight that one could compare two models which were both consistent under the null spawned a test which was both simple and powerful. The so-called 'Hausman test' has been applied and extended theoretically in a variety of econometric domains. This paper discusses the basic Hausman test and its development within econometric panel data settings since its publication. We focus on the construction of the Hausman test in a variety of panel data settings, and in particular, the recent adaptation of the Hausman test to semiparametric and nonparametric panel data models. We present simulation experiments which show the value of the Hausman test in a nonparametric setting, focusing primarily on the consequences of parametric model misspecification for the Hausman test procedure. A formal application of the Hausman test is also given focusing on testing between fixed and random effects within a panel data model of gasoline demand.

Essays in Honor of Jerry Hausman
Advances in Econometrics, Volume 29, 479–513

ISSN: 0731-9053/doi:10.1108/S0731-9053(2012)0000029021

Keywords: Hausman test; Model misspecification; Nonparametric; Monte Carlo

JEL classifications: C12; C14; C15

INTRODUCTION

The model specification test proposed by Hausman (1978) spawned a vast literature on model specification tests of the conditional mean in regression function estimation. As of this writing, the original 1978 paper published in *Econometrica* by Jerry Hausman has been cited 3087 times, and remains one of the most influential papers in applied economics and econometrics.[1] The generality and applicability of the test lies in its simplicity: all the test requires is that one of the competing econometric models be consistent and efficient only under the null hypothesis, and the other model be consistent under both the null and alternative hypotheses. Such simplicity and generality give rise to a host of arenas in which the test can be applied.

One area in particular in which the test is often applied is in testing between fixed or random individual effects in the panel data literature. Often referred to as a test of the exogeneity assumption, the Hausman test provides a formal statistical assessment of whether or not the unobserved individual effect is correlated with the conditioning regressors in the model. Failing to reject the exogeneity of the unobserved individual effect provides statistical evidence in favor of a random effects model, while a rejection of the exogeneity assumption provides support for a fixed effects specification. Selection of the appropriate econometric framework is crucial for accurate estimation of the relationship of interest. If, for example, a correlation exists between the unobserved individual effect and the conditioning regressors, estimation of a random effects specification that does not address the endogeneity of the conditioning regressors will yield biased and inconsistent estimates of the conditional mean. Conversely, if the unobserved individual effect is drawn randomly from a given population and is uncorrelated with the other conditioning regressors, a fixed effects model will yield consistent, yet inefficient estimates.

In addition to issues of econometric efficiency, the choice of error specification can dramatically influence the magnitude of the estimated slope coefficients – even under the null hypothesis in which both fixed effects and random effects estimators yield consistent parameter estimates.[2] Hausman (1978), for example, finds the fixed and random effects specifications produce significantly different estimates of (some of) the parameters of interest in a wage equation for a sample of 629 high school graduates. The difference in estimates comes primarily from fundamental differences in specification between the fixed and random effects model (Hsiao, 2003). The fixed effects model allows for the unobserved individual effect to be correlated with the conditioning regressors. The random effects specification, on the other hand, treats the regressors as exogenous by assuming that the individual error component is drawn randomly from a single population.

Clearly, the assumptions regarding the nature of the unobserved individual effects are crucial for correctly specifying the regression function, and in general, selection between the fixed or random effects models is not clear-cut (see, e.g., Baltagi, 2008; Hsiao, 2003). As a result, it is especially important for applied researchers to develop both a theoretical and statistical basis for the chosen econometric specification – the theoretical basis coming from the econometrician's beliefs about the nature of the unobserved individual error component, and the statistical basis being derived from a test such as that proposed by Hausman (1978).

One goal of this paper is to provide a detailed overview of the original specification test proposed in Hausman (1978), specifically focusing on the generality and applicability of the test within a panel data context. In this vain, we will discuss theoretical developments and extensions of the original Hausman test, with the ultimate goal of demonstrating how the test can complement recent theoretical developments in the nonparametric panel data literature. Indeed, one of the many advantages of the Hausman test is that the test does not require a parametric specification of the conditional mean (Holly, 1982). Given that the Hausman test is designed to test for correct specification of the unobserved individual effects in a panel data context, it is only natural that the test be adapted toward nonparametric techniques that do not require specification of the functional form of the regression function and are often called into action when the underlying functional form assumptions inherent in parametric models yield conflicting results.

An issue that is often overlooked in the empirical literature is the dependence of the Hausman test on correct parametric specification of the regression function as a whole (instead of just testing for a correlation between the regressors and the error component) *if a parametric modeling approach is employed.* As is widely known, but often receives little attention in practice, parametric model misspecification renders inconsistent standard (parametric) estimators in the panel data literature, for example, the generalized least squares estimator and the within estimator. Since the Hausman test assumes that the underlying parametric regression model(s) is consistent and is hence correctly specified (at least up to the unobserved individual error component), it is not necessarily clear how the test will perform under parametric model misspecification. Likely, the size and power of the test will suffer.

Hence, a second goal of this paper is to explore the effect of parametric model misspecification on the standard Hausman test using a Monte Carlo analysis. Specifically, we focus on the size and power of a standard parametric Hausman test under parametric misspecification of the conditional mean. As expected, our analysis shows that the performance of the Hausman test suffers if the model is not correctly specified. We then compare the performance of the traditional parametric Hausman test under parametric model misspecification to a recently developed nonparametric Hausman test (Henderson, Carroll & Li, 2008) that does not depend on a priori (correct) parametric specification of the model. Our analysis shows that because the nonparametric estimator does not require a priori specification of the conditional mean, the nonparametric Hausman test is robust to model misspecification.

We then focus on applying the nonparametric Hausman test to an empirical model of gasoline demand. A traditional parametric setup using a static model of demand rejects the random effects model in favor of a fixed effects approach. However, migrating to a more robust setting, we see that once neglected nonlinearities are allowed in the model, a nonparametric Hausman test fails to reject the random effects model as the appropriate specification. Both models also offer additional insights into the elasticity of demand for gasoline beyond the simple parametric model. These results directly relate to the work of Baltagi and Griffin (1983) who uncovered the same phenomena but focused on neglected dynamics of the model. In either case, when model misspecification is of concern, the outcome of the Hausman test may be misleading.

The outline for this paper is as follows. The next section provides a detailed overview of the basic Hausman test in a standard parametric panel data setting, paying careful attention to developments and extensions of the original test that are relevant within this context. The third section discusses more recent extensions of the Hausman test to a nonparametric setting, while the fourth section provides Monte Carlo simulations of a Hausman test in a fully nonparametric setting. The fifth section provides a formal application of a nonparametric Hausman test to an empirical model of gasoline demand, and the last section contains concluding remarks as well as several suggestions for which future research may be directed.

THE HAUSMAN TEST AND HISTORICAL DEVELOPMENTS

The test

Consider the following standard linear in parameter's one-way error component model:

$$y_{it} = x_{it}\beta + v_i + \varepsilon_{it}, \quad i = 1, 2, \ldots, n, \quad t = 1, 2, \ldots T \tag{1}$$

in which y is the outcome variable, x is a $p \times 1$ vector of conditioning variables, β is a vector of parameters of interest to be estimated, v is an unobserved time-invariant individual effect, ε is a random error term, and i and t denote individual and time, respectively. The individual effect, v, is unobserved, and estimation of Eq. (1) using ordinary least squares will yield biased and inconsistent estimates of β if v is not accounted for and is correlated with x. Taking v into account requires explicit assumptions on the nature of the unobserved individual effect, v. If one assumes that v is correlated with the regressors in x, then the appropriate econometric model is the fixed effects specification, to be estimated consistently with a standard fixed effects (i.e., within or LSDV) model. Conversely, if v is assumed to be uncorrelated with the regressors in x, yet drawn randomly from some independently and identically distributed distribution (i.e., $v \sim IID(0, \sigma_v^2)$) and is independent from the error term ε, then the random effects model is appropriate and can be estimated consistently and efficiently using generalized least squares.

The test proposed by Hausman provides a formal statistical assessment of whether the fixed or random effects model is supported by the data. The general intuition for the test, as given by Hausman, is the following. Assuming that the null hypothesis is of no misspecification, then there must exist a consistent and fully efficient estimator of the proposed econometric specification. Under the alternative hypothesis that the model is misspecified, this estimator will be inconsistent. If we can identify another estimator that is consistent under both the null and alternative hypotheses, albeit not efficient under the null hypothesis, then we can formulate a statistical test using estimates from both specifications. In the panel data context, because the fixed effects estimator yields consistent estimates regardless of whether or not v is correlated with x, and the random effects estimator is inconsistent if v is correlated with x, the appropriate null hypothesis is that v is uncorrelated with x, so that the alternative hypothesis is that v is correlated with x.

More formally, let $\hat{\beta}_{GLS}$ be the generalized least squares estimator of β under the null hypothesis that v is uncorrelated with x, and let $\hat{\beta}_W$ be the fixed effects estimator under the alternative hypothesis. Define $\hat{q} = \hat{\beta}_W - \hat{\beta}_{GLS}$ to be the difference between the fixed and random effects estimators. In the case of no misspecification, since both $\hat{\beta}_{GLS}$ and $\hat{\beta}_W$ are consistent, the probability limit of $\hat{q}$ is zero: $\hat{q} = 0$. Because $\hat{\beta}_{GLS}$ is inconsistent under the alternative hypothesis, we can expect the probability limit of $\hat{q}$ to differ from zero under the alternative hypothesis: $\hat{q} \neq 0$. Define the asymptotic variance of $\hat{q}$ to be $V(\hat{q}) = V(\hat{\beta}_W) - V(\hat{\beta}_{GLS})$, noting that under the null hypothesis the covariance between $\hat{\beta}_{GLS}$ and $\hat{q}$ must equal zero.[3] Letting $\hat{V}(\hat{q})$ be a consistent estimator of $V(\hat{q})$, the test statistic can be defined as

$$m = nT\hat{q}' V(\hat{q})^{-1}\hat{q}. \tag{2}$$

Theorem 2.1 in Hausman (1978) establishes that m is asymptotically distributed as a χ^2 distribution with K degrees of freedom, in which K is defined as the number of parameters under the null hypothesis: $m \sim \chi^2_K$.[4]

Hausman (1978) shows that an alternative and equivalent test is a significance test of the coefficient α in the augmented regression

$$\tilde{y} = \tilde{x}\tilde{\beta} + \overline{x}\alpha + \tilde{\varepsilon} \tag{3}$$

in which $\tilde{y}$ and $\tilde{x}$ are the transforms of y and x under the random effects transformation $\tilde{y}_{it} = y_{it} - \gamma\overline{y}_i$ and $\tilde{x}_{it} = x_{it} - \gamma\overline{x}_i$ in which $\gamma = 1 - [\sigma^2_\varepsilon/(\sigma^2_\varepsilon + T\sigma^2_v)]^{\frac{1}{2}}$, σ^2_ε and σ^2_v are the variances of ε and v, and $\overline{y}_i$ and $\overline{x}_i$ are the time means of y_{it} and x_{it}. The intuition here is that under the transform, ordinary least squares can be used to regress $\tilde{x}$ on $\tilde{y}$ to obtain the random effects estimate, $\tilde{\beta}$. Hence, testing the null hypothesis $\alpha = 0$ in the augmented regression model given by Eq. (3) is a test for an omitted variable from the random effects specification.

The strength of Hausman's (1978) test is demonstrated empirically by Baltagi (1981) through a series of Monte Carlo analyses. His analysis focuses on the performance of the Hausman test under a correctly specified null hypothesis, and shows a very low probability of a Type I error (and is perhaps undersized). The empirical simulations conducted by Baltagi (1981) provide early evidence that the test performs well in practice.

Developments

Perhaps the greatest strength of the basic Hausman test is its simplicity and generality, which, as noted previously, makes the test applicable in a wide variety of econometric domains. Within the panel data literature, the primary developments of the Hausman test, following the original Hausman (1978) paper, have been to focus on generalizations of the test. Such generalizations include alternative and equivalent tests based, for example, on augmented or artificial regressions, extensions of the Hausman test to dynamic panel data models, and the finite sample performance of the test in a variety of panel data settings based on Monte Carlo simulations. It is these developments that we focus on in this section.

A Critique, a Generalization, and a Clarification

Shortly after the publication of the test in 1978, Holly (1982) raised two insightful critiques of the Hausman (1978) test by comparing the test to classical tests, i.e., the likelihood ratio, Wald and Lagrange multiplier tests. First, Holly (1982) shows that the Hausman procedure is only valid if $V(\hat{q})$ is a positive definite matrix (which may not always be true). Hausman and Taylor (1980, 1981a) generalize the Hausman (1978) test to allow $V(\hat{q})$ to be a singular matrix by modifying the test statistic to be (following the notation in the previous section) $m = nT\hat{q}'V(\hat{q})^{+}\hat{q}$, in which $[\cdot]^{+}$ denotes the Moore–Penrose generalized inverse of $[\cdot]$.

The second critique raised by Holly (1982) is on the equivalence of the Hausman (1978) specification test with the classical tests. He shows that only under certain conditions are the tests equivalent, and if the tests are not equivalent, he shows that the Hausman (1978) test is potentially inconsistent. As Hausman and Taylor (1980) point out, the relevance of this critique depends crucially on the hypothesis being tested.

To understand this discussion, consider the following simple linear model

$$y = x_1\beta_1 + x_2\beta_2 + \varepsilon, \tag{4}$$

in which β_1 is a vector of parameters of interest, β_2 is a vector of nuisance parameters, and x_2 is included in the model only to avoid biases when estimating β_1. Holly (1982) shows that asymptotically, the Hausman specification test is a test of the null hypothesis, $H_0^{\star} : (x'_1x_1)^{-1}x'_1x_2\beta_2 = 0$, whereas the classical tests consider the null hypothesis, $H_0 : \beta_2 = 0$. He shows that (i) $H_0^{\star}$ and H_0 are equivalent tests only if the dimension of x_1 is greater than or equal to the dimension of x_2, and (ii) if the dimension of x_1 is smaller than that of x_2 (so that the Hausman and classical tests are not equivalent), the Hausman test may not be a consistent test of H_0.

Hausman and Taylor (1980) argue that, in fact, $H_0^{\star}$ is the appropriate null hypothesis *for the specification tests* proposed by Hausman (1978). Viewed in this light, the inconsistency of the Hausman (1978) test for $H_0 : \beta_2 = 0$ is irrelevant. To understand this reasoning, it is important to make a careful distinction between a test of specification (i.e., the Hausman (1978) test) and a test of parameter restrictions (i.e., the classical tests). Hausman (1978) proposed a test of misspecification for β_1, testing the hypothesis that the bias in the estimates of β_1 from omission of x_2 is zero. Viewed from this standpoint, the appropriate test is of the null hypothesis, $H_0^{\star}$: $(x'_1x_1)^{-1}x'_1x_2\beta_2 = 0$. Furthermore, Hausman and Taylor (1980) show that the classical tests of H_0 are of the wrong size when testing $H_0^{\star}$. Therefore, while the Hausman (1978) test is not always an equivalent test to the classical tests in terms of testing H_0, it is the most powerful test, and is therefore preferred to the classical tests, when testing $H_0^{\star}$.

Three Equivalent Specifications of the Hausman Test

The original test in Hausman (1978) proposed comparing a generalized least squares (i.e., random effects) estimator with the within (i.e., fixed effects) estimator to test for the exogeneity of the unobserved individual effect. Hausman and Taylor (1981b) provide an important generalization of the original test by proving the equivalence of three different tests of exogeneity based on three classic panel data estimators: the generalized least squares estimator, the within estimator, and the between estimator. Specifically, Hausman and Taylor (1981b) propose that the following specification tests are equivalent: (i) generalized least squares vs within; (ii) generalized least squares vs between; and (iii) within vs between.

The first test, generalized least squares vs within, is the original test proposed by Hausman (1978). Letting $\hat{\beta}_{GLS}$ be the estimator of β from the generalized least squares model and $\hat{\beta}_W$ be the estimator from the within model, define $\hat{q}_1 = \hat{\beta}_{GLS} - \hat{\beta}_W$. Assuming H_0, plim $\hat{q}_1 = 0$, but under the alternative hypothesis, H_1, plim $\hat{q}_1 \neq 0$. Following Hausman (1978), and denoting the asymptotic variance with $V(\cdot)$, $V(\hat{q}_1) = V(\hat{\beta}_W) - V(\hat{\beta}_{GLS})$, and we can construct the χ^2 test statistic.

In the second test, $\hat{q}_2 = \hat{\beta}_{GLS} - \hat{\beta}_B$, in which $\hat{\beta}_B$ is the estimator of β from the between estimator. Assuming H_0, plim $\hat{q}_2 = 0$, and under H_1, plim $\hat{q}_2 = (I - \Delta)$ plim$(\hat{\beta}_B - \beta)$, in which $\Delta = [V(\hat{\beta}_B) + V(\hat{\beta}_W)]^{-1} V(\hat{\beta}_W)$. Since, $V(\hat{q}_2) = V(\hat{\beta}_B) - V(\hat{\beta}_{GLS})$, we obtain another χ^2 test statistic.

Following the same procedure for the third test, we obtain $\hat{q}_3 = \hat{\beta}_W - \hat{\beta}_B$, and as before, under H_0, plim $\hat{q}_3 = 0$ and under H_1, plim $\hat{q}_3 = \beta -$plim $\hat{\beta}_B \neq 0$. Since $V(\hat{q}_3) = V(\hat{\beta}_W) + V(\hat{\beta}_B)$, we obtain a χ^2 statistic for $\hat{q}_3$.

Hausman and Taylor (1981b) prove that these three tests are equivalent using the following argument. It is well known that $\hat{\beta}_{GLS} = \Delta\hat{\beta}_B + (I - \Delta)\hat{\beta}_W$. Hence, it is simple to verify that $\hat{q}_1 = -\Delta\hat{q}_3$ and $\hat{q}_2 = (I - \Delta)\hat{q}_3$. Then, we can show that $\hat{q}'_1 V(\hat{q}_1)^{-1}\hat{q}_1 = \hat{q}'_3\Delta'[\Delta V(\hat{q}_3)\Delta']^{-1}\Delta\hat{q}_3 = \hat{q}'_3 V(\hat{q}_3)^{-1}\hat{q}_3$ and $\hat{q}'_2 V(\hat{q}_2)^{-1}\hat{q}_2 = \hat{q}'_3(I - \Delta)'[(I - \Delta)V(\hat{q}_3)(I - \Delta)']^{-1}(I - \Delta)\hat{q}_3 = \hat{q}'_3 V(\hat{q}_3)^{-1}\hat{q}_3$. This establishes the equivalence of each of the three specification tests. The intuition for the proof is that any two tests will be equivalent so long as it can be shown that they differ by a non-singular transformation.

The Hausman Test in a Two-Way Error Component Model

In light of the generalization of the Hausman (1978) test provided by Hausman and Taylor (1981b), it is natural to ask whether such generalizations also hold in a two-way error component specification. Kang (1985) shows that the equivalence identified by Hausman and Taylor (1981b) no longer holds in the two-factor specification, because the presence of one additional factor gives rise to a larger set of possible assumptions regarding the exogeneity of the unobserved error components. Instead, Kang (1985) derives a set of equivalent tests for the two-factor specification.

Kang (1985) considers the following two-factor specification:

$$y_{it} = x_{it}\beta + v_i + u_t + \varepsilon_{it}, \quad i = 1, 2, \ldots, n, \quad t = 1, 2, \ldots, T \tag{5}$$

in which v_i is a time-invariant error component that varies across individuals and u_t is a time-varying error component that does not vary across individuals. In the two-factor model, Kang (1985) shows that the generalized least squares estimator, $\hat{\beta}_{GLS}$, is a weighted average of three different estimators: the between individual estimator, the between time estimator, and the within individual and time estimator. Kang (1985) shows that three separate tests comparing the generalized least squares estimator with each of the above three estimators does not yield three equivalent specification tests, as shown in the one factor model by Hausman and Taylor (1981b).

Kang (1985) proposes the following five tests: (i) assume v_i is correlated with x_{it} and test for a correlation between u_t and x_{it}; (ii) assume v_i is uncorrelated with x_{it} and test for a correlation between u_t and x_{it}; (iii) assume u_t is correlated with x_{it} and test for a correlation between v_i and x_{it}; (iv) assume u_t is uncorrelated with x_{it} and test for a correlation between v_i and x_{it}; (v) test whether or not both v_i and u_t are uncorrelated with x_{it} (i.e., H_1 is that both v_i and u_t are correlated with x_{it}).

Kang (1985) defines the following five estimators necessary for conducting the five tests proposed above. Define $\hat{\beta}_W$ to be the estimator of β from the within individual and time model, $\hat{\beta}_{BT}$ the between time estimator, and $\hat{\beta}_{BI}$ the between individual estimator. Next, define $\hat{\beta}_{PGLS1}$ to be the partial generalized least squares estimator that treats v_i as correlated with x_{it} and u_t as uncorrelated with x_{it}, and $\hat{\beta}_{PGLS2}$ to be the partial generalized least squares estimator that treats u_t as correlated with x_{it} and v_i as uncorrelated with x_{it}. The last two estimators are partial in the sense that they apply generalized least squares to only the error component that is assumed to be uncorrelated with x_{it}. Kang (1985) further defines $\hat{\beta}_{PGLS3}$ to be the partial generalized least squares estimator that treats both v_i and u_t as correlated with x_{it}, and is a weighted average of $\hat{\beta}_{BT}$ and $\hat{\beta}_{BI}$. See Kang (1985) for a more detailed description of each estimator.

Table 1 provides a summary of the results proved in Kang (1985). The proofs given in Kang (1985) follow from the original equivalence proofs given in Hausman and Taylor (1981b): any pair of tests will be equivalent as long as the tests can be written as non-singular transformations of each other. Note that the specification test column describes, for each of the five tests, the estimator that is efficient under H_0 and the estimator that is consistent under both H_0 and H_1, thereby defining the appropriate Hausman test. The table then lists two corresponding tests for each of the five proposed tests that are equivalent to the standard test.

A Generalized Method of Moments Framework

Both Arellano (1993) and Ahn and Low (1996) consider an adaptation of the Hausman (1978) test to generalized method of moments estimation.

Table 1. Summary of Equivalent Tests for the Two-factor Model as Proved by Kang (1985).

Test	Correlation Between x_{it} and	Specification Test	Equivalent Tests
(i)	time effect: u_t	$\hat{\beta}_{PGLS1}$ vs $\hat{\beta}_W$	$\hat{\beta}_W$ vs $\hat{\beta}_{BT}$ & $\hat{\beta}_{PGLS1}$ vs $\hat{\beta}_{BT}$
(ii)	time effect: u_t	$\hat{\beta}_{GLS}$ vs $\hat{\beta}_{PGLS2}$	$\hat{\beta}_{GLS}$ vs $\hat{\beta}_{BT}$ & $\hat{\beta}_{PGLS2}$ vs $\hat{\beta}_{BT}$
(iii)	individual effect: v_i	$\hat{\beta}_{PGLS2}$ vs $\hat{\beta}_W$	$\hat{\beta}_W$ vs $\hat{\beta}_{BI}$ & $\hat{\beta}_{PGLS2}$ vs $\hat{\beta}_{BI}\hat{\beta}_{GLS}$
(iv)	individual effect: v_i	$\hat{\beta}_{GLS}$ vs $\hat{\beta}_{PGLS1}$	$\hat{\beta}_{GLS}$ vs $\hat{\beta}_{BI}$ & $\hat{\beta}_{PGLS1}$ vs $\hat{\beta}_{BI}$
(v)	individual/time effects: v_i, u_t	$\hat{\beta}_{GLS}$ vs $\hat{\beta}_W$	$\hat{\beta}_{PGLS3}$ vs $\hat{\beta}_W$ & $\hat{\beta}_{GLS}$ vs $\hat{\beta}_{PGLS3}$

Arellano (1993) considers the model in Eq. (1), assuming the null hypothesis $H_0 : E[v_i|x_i] = 0$ with the corresponding alternative hypothesis given by $H_1 : E[v_i|x_i] = \overline{x}'_i\gamma$, in which $\overline{x}_i$ denotes the time mean of x_i. Letting starred variables refer to variables transformed using a forward orthogonal deviations operator, Arellano (1993) defined the following artificial regression model

$$\begin{bmatrix} y_i^* \\ \overline{y}_i \end{bmatrix} = \begin{bmatrix} x_i^* & 0 \\ \overline{x}_{i'} & \overline{x}_{i'} \end{bmatrix} \begin{bmatrix} \beta \\ \gamma \end{bmatrix} + \begin{bmatrix} \varepsilon_i^* \\ \overline{\varepsilon}_i \end{bmatrix} \tag{6}$$

in which ordinary least squares applied to the first $(T-1)$ equations yields the within estimator and ordinary least squares applied to the last (T^{th}) equation yields the between groups estimator. Using the equivalence results identified by Hausman and Taylor (1981b), Arellano (1993) shows that the standard Hausman (1978) test statistic is equivalent to a Wald test of $\gamma = 0$ in the above artificial regression. Arellano (1993) further shows that the Hausman test is a special case of the specification tests proposed by Chamberlain (1982) in that the Hausman test is a test of time means across individuals. Arellano (1993) shows that the artificial regression model can be adapted to test the $\gamma = 0$ hypothesis in a dynamic panel model as well, assuming the existence of an instrumental variable, z.

Ahn and Low (1996) consider the result identified by Arellano (1993) that in a generalized method of moments framework the Hausman test is a test of the exogeneity of the time means across individuals. Ahn and Low (1996) show that the Hausman test is a special case of the J statistic proposed by Hansen (1982). Using Monte Carlo simulations, Ahn and Low (1996) show that the Hausman test performs well in practice at detecting a correlation between the unobserved individual effect and the time varying regressors in the model.[5]

An interesting extension to the dynamic panel framework arises when (at least some of) the instrumental variables are predetermined. In this case, Keane and Runkle (1992) propose testing the null hypothesis that the individual effect is uncorrelated with the matrix of instrumental variables using a Hausman test based on the difference between the first differenced two-stage least squares and standard two-stage least squares estimators. In this setup, the first difference estimator is consistent under both the null and alternative hypothesis, while the two-stage least squares estimator is only consistent under the null. See Keane and Runkle (1992) and Baltagi (2008) for a derivation and explanation for the variance between these two estimators to be used when constructing the Hausman test statistic.

A Hausman Test for Interactive Fixed Effects

A recent development in the panel data literature is a general model of interactive fixed effects proposed by Bai (2009). Specifically, Bai (2009) considers the model

$$y_{it} = x_{it}\beta + V'_i U_t + \varepsilon_{it}, \quad i = 1, 2, \ldots, n, \quad t = 1, 2, \ldots, T \tag{7}$$

in which V_i and U_t are matrices containing individual and time fixed effects v_i and u_t. In this framework, V_i and U_t are allowed to interact with each other, and be correlated with x_{it}. Specifically, Bai (2009) considers the case of large n and large T, and does not impose any a priori structure on the nature of $V'_i U_t$, noting that the standard two-way error component model with additive fixed effects is a special case by setting $V'_i = [v_i, 1]$ and $U_t = [1, u_t]$. We refer the interested reader to Bai (2009) for a more in-depth discussion.

In order to estimate the interactive fixed effects model, Bai (2009) proposes the interactive effects estimator, with $\hat{\beta}_{IE}$ being the interactive effects estimator of β. Note that when the fixed effects interact, standard fixed effects estimators are incapable of eliminating the fixed effects, and hence yield inconsistent estimates of β. Since the standard additive effects model is shown to be a special case of the interactive effects model, $\hat{\beta}_{IE}$ is a consistent estimator of β regardless of whether or not the fixed effects are additive or interactive, but inefficient in the case of additive effects. The standard fixed effects estimator, $\hat{\beta}_{FE}$, is both consistent and efficient in the special case that the fixed effects are additive (and inconsistent otherwise).

Hence, the proposed structure and nesting of the standard additive model as a special case of the interactive effects model, suggests that a Hausman test is applicable for testing between the additive and interactive fixed effects models. Bai (2009) proposes the following test procedure. Let the null hypothesis be of additive fixed effects, and the alternative hypothesis be of interactive fixed effects. Bai (2009) shows that the standard Hausman test between $\hat{\beta}_{IE}$ and $\hat{\beta}_{FE}$ applies and follows a χ^2 distribution with degrees of freedom equal to the dimension of x_{it}. Bai (2009) shows that a similar Hausman test can be applied to special cases of the interactive effects model, such as the case in which there are no individual effects, or no time effects.

DISCUSSION

So far, our discussion of developments in the Hausman test since the original publication have focused on results identified within a panel data context. Indeed, one of the strengths of the Hausman (1978) specification test is its generality and simplicity, making the test applicable in a variety of econometric domains. In addition to the panel data literature discussed previously, the Hausman test has also been proposed as a test of the independence of irrelevant alternatives assumption in a multinomial logit framework (Hausman & McFadden, 1984; Wills, 1987), a test of distributional assumptions in Tobit models (Newey, 1987), a test of model specification in nonlinear parametric models (White, 1981), a test of spatial dependence in spatial econometric models (Pace & LeSage, 2008), and a test of model specification in semiparametric partial linear models (Li & Stengos, 1992; Robinson, 1988). Hausman and Pesaran (1983) establish the equivalence of the Hausman (1978) test to a specification test between non-nested regression models, while the Hausman methodology has also been used to construct a test for specification between models of misclassification of discrete dependent variables (Hausman, Abrevaya & Scott-Morton, 1998), and as a test for exogeneity of the treatment variable in a quantile treatment effects model (Chernozhukov & Hansen, 2006).

In addition to the theoretical developments related to the Hausman (1978) test discussed above, the generality and simplicity of the test have made the test a standard test of specification by applied researchers. Indeed, the Hausman test generally is shown to perform well in finite sample simulations (e.g., Ahn & Low, 1996; Arellano & Bond, 1991; Baltagi, 1981), which provides reassurance on the reliability of the test in practice.[6] The Hausman (1978) test has been implemented to test for a correlation between the unobserved individual effect and the included regressors by numerous researchers. Baltagi and Griffin (1983), Blonigan (1997), Cardellichio (1990), Cornwell and Rupert (1997), Egger (2000), and Hastings (2004) all test for a correlation between the unobserved individual effect and the regressors and reject the null hypothesis of no correlation. Conversely, Hausman, Hall and Griliches (1984) and Baltagi (2006) fail to reject the null hypothesis of no correlation based on the standard Hausman (1978) test.[7]

SEMIPARAMETRIC AND NONPARAMETRIC HAUSMAN TESTS

More recent developments in the panel data literature have focused on semiparametric and nonparametric random effects (e.g., Henderson & Ullah, 2005; Lin & Carroll, 2000, 2001, 2006; Sun, Carroll, & Li, 2009) and fixed effects (Henderson et al., 2008; Sun et al., 2009; Su & Lu, 2012) panel data models.[8] Naturally, the development of both random and fixed effects estimators in the nonparametric literature, in addition to the fundamental empirical problem of deciding whether or not the unobserved individual effects are correlated with the observed regressors, has led to the emergence of semiparametric and nonparametric versions of the test of the exogeneity assumption. Indeed, as noted by Holly (1982), one of the advantages of the Hausman (1978) test is its lack of dependence on functional form assumptions, which ensures that the standard Hausman test is applicable under more general econometric assumptions about the conditional mean. In this section, we outline several recently developed semiparametric and nonparametric Hausman tests of the exogeneity of the unobserved individual effects.

A Smooth Coefficient Hausman Test

Sun et al. (2009) consider the following semiparametric smooth coefficient one-way error component panel data specification:

$$y_{it} = x_{it}{}' \beta(z_{it}) + v_i + \varepsilon_{it}, \quad i = 1, 2, \ldots, n, \quad t = 1, 2, \ldots, T \tag{8}$$

in which $\beta(z_{it})$ is a vector of smooth coefficient functions of unknown form. Sun et al. (2009) propose estimators of (8) depending on whether or not v_i is assumed to be correlated or uncorrelated with x_{it}. The random effects estimator discussed in Sun et al. (2009) is a standard smooth coefficient estimator that ignores v_i; denote the random effects estimator of $\beta(z_{it})$ by $\hat{\beta}_{RE}(z) = (x'K(z)x)^{-1}x'K(z)y$ in which $K(z)$ is a matrix of product kernel functions of the variables in z.[9] The fixed effects estimator proposed by Sun et al. (2009) eliminates v_i by altering the kernel weighting matrix; denote the fixed effects estimator by $\hat{\beta}_{FE}(z) = (x'\tilde{K}(z)x)^{-1}x'\tilde{K}(z)y$, in which $\tilde{K}(z)$ is the modified matrix of kernel weights that removes v_i. We refer the interested reader to Sun et al. (2009) for further information regarding the proposed fixed effects estimator and the modified kernel weighting scheme that removes v_i.

We now follow Sun et al. (2009) and construct a semiparametric smooth coefficient version of the standard Hausman test based on $\hat{\beta}_{RE}(z)$ and $\hat{\beta}_{FE}(z)$. The null hypothesis proposed by Sun et al. (2009) is $H_0 : P\{E[v_i|z_{i1}, z_{i2}, \ldots, z_{iT}, x_{i1}, x_{i2}, \ldots, x_{iT}] = 0\} = 1$, for all i in which $P\{\cdot\}$ denotes a probability. The corresponding alternative hypothesis is given by $H_1 : P\{E[v_i|z_{i1}, z_{i2}, \ldots, z_{iT}, x_{i1}, x_{i2}, \ldots, x_{iT}] \neq 0\} > 0$, for some i.

The test statistic proposed by Sun et al. (2009) is constructed from the square of the difference between $\hat{\beta}_{RE}(z)$ and $\hat{\beta}_{FE}(z)$, noting that under H_0 such a statistic will equal zero and under H_1 the statistic will be some positive (nonzero) value. After multiplying the difference between $\hat{\beta}_{RE}(z)$ and $\hat{\beta}_{FE}(z)$ by $x'\tilde{K}(z)x$ to remove the random denominator, Sun et al. (2009) propose the following test statistic:

$$J = \int [\hat{\beta}_{FE}(z) - \hat{\beta}_{RE}(z)]'[x'\tilde{K}(z)x]'[x'\tilde{K}(z)x][\hat{\beta}_{FE}(z) - \hat{\beta}_{RE}(z)]dz. \quad (9)$$

Letting I_T be an identity matrix of dimension T and e_T be a column of ones of length T, Sun et al. (2009) show that the feasible test statistic can be written as

$$\hat{J} = \frac{1}{n^2 h} \sum_{i=1}^{n} \sum_{j \neq i}^{n} \hat{\varepsilon}_i' Q_T A_{ij} Q_T \hat{\varepsilon}_j \quad (10)$$

in which h is a product of bandwidths $\hat{\varepsilon}_i$ contains the residuals from the random effects model, $Q_T = I_T - T^{-1} e_T e'_T$, and A_{ij} is a $(T \times T)$ matrix containing $K(z_{it}, z_{js})x'_{it}x_{js}$. Note that Sun et al. (2009) use a leave-one-out random effects estimator when calculating $\hat{J}$ to asymptotically center the statistic around zero. Sun et al. (2009) recommend using a bootstrap procedure to approximate the distribution of the test statistic, and show that the proposed semiparametric Hausman test performs well in Monte Carlo simulations.

A Nonparametric Hausman Test

We now consider a class of nonparametric panel data models with additive individual effects given by

$$y_{it} = g(x_{it}) + v_i + \varepsilon_{it}, \quad i = 1, 2, \ldots, n, \quad t = 1, 2, \ldots, T \quad (11)$$

in which the function $g(x_{it})$ is assumed to be a smooth function of unknown form and x_{it} is a $q-$dimensioned vector of conditioning variables. The basic nonparametric structure of additively separable individual effects has been considered previously by, for example, Wang (2003), Henderson and

Ullah (2005), and Henderson et al. (2008). A special case of the fully nonparametric panel structure with additive individual effects is a panel data version of the semiparametric partial linear model first proposed by Robinson (1988). Such a specification would take the form

$$y_{it} = g(x_{1it}) + x'_{2it}\beta + v_i + \varepsilon_{it}, \quad i = 1, 2, \ldots, n, \quad t = 1, 2, \ldots, T \tag{12}$$

in which the q_1 regressors in x_1 enter nonparametrically into the regression function and the q_2 regressors in x_2 enter linearly with coefficients β. See, for example, Henderson et al. (2008) and Lin and Carroll (2006) for fixed and random effects estimators of the partial linear panel data model, respectively. In the present case, we focus primarily on the fully nonparametric specification given by Eq. (11) but acknowledge that the Hausman test proposed by Henderson et al. (2008) applies to the partial linear model in Eq. (12) as well.

We now define a fully nonparametric Hausman test to test for the correlation of the individual effect, v_i, with the regressors in x_{it} based on the model in Eq. (11). The null hypothesis, of course, is that v_i is not correlated with x_{it}, which implies that the alternative hypothesis is that v_i is correlated with x_{it}. Formally, we write the null and alternative hypotheses as

$$H_0 : E[v_i|x_{i1}, \ldots, x_{iT}] = 0 \quad \text{almost everywhere} \tag{13}$$

and

$$H_1 : E[v_i|x_{i1}, \ldots, x_{iT}] \neq 0 \quad \text{on a set with positive measure.} \tag{14}$$

Letting $u_{it} = v_i + \varepsilon_{it}$ and assuming $E[\varepsilon_{it}|x_{i1}, \ldots, x_{iT}] = 0$ under both H_0 and H_1, the null hypothesis can be written as $H_0 : E[u_{it}|x_{i1}, \ldots, x_{iT}] = 0$, almost everywhere, and the alternative hypothesis can be analogously written as $H_1 : E[u_{it}|x_{i1}, \ldots, x_{iT}] \neq 0$ on a set with positive measure.

The nonparametric Hausman test proposed by Henderson et al. (2008) comes from the sample analogue of the statistic $J = E[u_{it}E(u_{it}|x_{it})f(x_{it})]$. Since $J = 0$ under the null hypothesis and $J = E\{[E(u_{it}|x_{it})]^2 f(x_{it})\}$ when the null hypothesis is false, J serves as a proper test statistic to test for a correlation between the v_i and x_{it}.

Assuming, for notational simplicity, that $f_t(\cdot) = f(\cdot)$ for all T, and defining $\hat{g}(x)$ to be a consistent estimator of $g(x)$ under the alternative hypothesis, we can obtain a consistent estimate of u_{it} defining $\hat{u}_{it} = y_{it} - \hat{g}(x_{it})$. Hence, the feasible test statistic is

$$\hat{J} = (nT)^{-1} \sum_{i=1}^{n} \sum_{t=1}^{T} \hat{u}_{it} \hat{E}_{-it}[\hat{u}_{it}|x_{it}] \hat{f}_{-it}(x_{it}). \tag{15}$$

Let $E_{-it}[\hat{u}_{it}|x_{it}] = [n(T-1)]^{-1} \sum_{j=1}^{n} \sum_{s=1,[js]\neq[it]}^{T} \hat{u}_{js} K_{h,it,js} / \hat{f}_{-it}(x_{it})$ and $\hat{f}_{-it}(x_{it}) = [n(T-1)]^{-1} \sum_{j=1}^{n} \sum_{s=1,js,[js]\neq[it]}^{T} K_{h,it,js}$ be leave-one-out kernel estimators of $E[u_{it}|x_{it}]$ and $f(x_{it})$ in which $K_{h,it,js} = K_h(x_{it} - x_{js})$ and $K_h(v)$ and $k(\cdot)$ are defined as before, we can rewrite the test statistic as

$$\hat{J} = [nT(nT-1)]^{-1} \sum_{i=1}^{n} \sum_{t=1}^{T} \sum_{j=1}^{n} \sum_{s=1,[j,s]\neq[i,t]}^{T} \hat{u}_{it} \hat{u}_{js} K_{h,it,js}. \tag{16}$$

Since $\hat{J}$ is a consistent estimator of J, plim $\hat{J} = 0$ under H_0 and plim $g(\cdot)$ if H_0 is false for some positive constant C. For large values of $\hat{J}$, we can reject the null hypothesis that v_i is not correlated with x_{it}.

Henderson et al. (2008) propose the following bootstrap procedure for implementing the nonparametric Hausman test. Define the nonparametric random effects estimator of $g(x)$ to be $\tilde{g}(x)$, so that $\hat{u}_i = (\hat{u}_{i1}, \ldots, \hat{u}_{iT})'$ comes from the residual from the random effects model $\hat{u}_{it} = y_{it} - \tilde{g}(x_{it})$. Then, use a wild bootstrap to generate the two-point residuals $\hat{u}_i^\star = [(1-\sqrt{5})/2]\hat{u}_i$ with probability $p = (1+\sqrt{5})/(2\sqrt{5})$, and $\hat{u}_i^\star = [(1+\sqrt{5})/2]\hat{u}_i$ with probability $(1-p)$. Generate the bootstrap sample $\{x_{it}, y_{it}^\star\}$ from $y_{it}^\star = \tilde{g}(x_{it}) + u_{it}^\star$. Then, using the bootstrap sample, estimate $g^\star(x)$ using the fixed effects estimator. Obtain $\hat{u}_{it}^\star = y_{it}^\star - \hat{g}^\star(x_{it})$. Using $\hat{u}_{it}^\star$ and $\hat{u}_{js}^\star$, calculate $\hat{J}^\star$. Repeat this process B number of times to approximate the distribution of $\hat{J}$ under the null hypothesis. Henderson et al. (2008) use Monte Carlo simulations to assess the size of the nonparametric Hausman test, and show that the test performs well in cases of large n and small T.

For completeness of our discussion of the nonparametric Hausman test, the following modifications would be necessary if one wanted to implement a partial linear version of the test, following the model in Eq. (12). First, redefine the null hypotheses to include both x_{1it} and x_{2it} as $H_0: E[v_i|x_{1i1}, \ldots, x_{1iT}, x_{2i1}, \ldots, x_{2iT}] = 0$, almost everywhere, and let the alternative hypothesis be given by $E[v_i|x_{1i1}, \ldots, x_{1iT}, x_{2i1}, \ldots, x_{2iT}] \neq 0$, on a set with positive measure. Next, we modify the test statistic J and its sample analogues in Eqs. (15) and (16) by defining $x_{it} = [x_{1it}, x_{2it}]$ and $\hat{u}_{it} = y_{it} - \hat{g}(x_{1it}) - x'_{2it}\hat{\beta}$ in which $\hat{g}(x_{1it})$ and $\hat{\beta}$ are consistent estimates of $g(x_{1it})$ and β. We would then modify the bootstrap procedure by defining $\hat{u}_{it}$ under the null hypothesis to be $\hat{u}_{it} = y_{it} - \tilde{g}(x_{1it}) - x'_{2it}\tilde{\beta}$, in which $\tilde{g}(x_{1it})$ and $\tilde{\beta}$ are estimates from the semiparametric random effects estimator. After obtaining $\hat{u}_{it}^{\star}$, generate the bootstrap sample as $\{x_{it}, y_{it}^{\star}\}$ from $y_{it}^{\star} = \tilde{g}(x_{1it}) + x'_{2it}\tilde{\beta} + u_{it}^{\star}$. The rest of the bootstrap procedure follows the nonparametric procedure, albeit with the semiparametric fixed effects estimator proposed by Henderson et al. (2008).

MONTE CARLO SIMULATIONS

This section performs Monte Carlo simulations to assess the relative performance of the parametric and nonparametric Hausman tests detailed in the previous sections of this paper. In particular our analysis focuses on how the size and power of a standard parametric Hausman test are adversely affected when the conditional mean in the parametric model is not correctly specified, and how the nonparametric Hausman test avoids this potential pitfall. This analysis highlights the generality and applicability of the Hausman test in the nonparametric setting since the nonparametric models do not require the a priori specification of a parametric functional form.

To be consistent with existing studies focusing on nonparametric panel data estimators, we use the DGPs found in Wang (2003). The specific DGPs we deploy are

$$y_{it} = \sin(2x_{it}) + v_i + \varepsilon_{it} \tag{17}$$

$$y_{it} = 2x_{it} + v_i + \varepsilon_{it} \tag{18}$$

$$y_{it} = 2x_{it} - 3x_{it}^2 + v_i + \varepsilon_{it} \tag{19}$$

in which x_{it} is *iid* $\mathcal{U}[0, 2]$ and ε_{it} is *iid* $N(0, 1)$. Moving our attention to v_i, we generate μ_i as an *iid* $\mathcal{U}[-1, 1]$ sequence of random variables and construct v_i as

$$v_i = \mu_i + c_0\overline{x}_i, \tag{20}$$

in which $\overline{x}_i = T^{-1}\sum_{t=1}^{T} x_{it}$. The generation of v_i follows from Henderson et al. (2008) since Wang (2003) only focused on the random effects setting. Note that when $c_0 = 0$, the individual effects in our DGPs are uncorrelated with x so that a random effects estimator is appropriate, and for $c_0 \neq 0$ the individual effects are correlated with x so that a fixed effects estimator is appropriate. We deploy a Gaussian kernel for all nonparametric estimation with a Silverman type rule-of-thumb bandwidth, $h = \hat{\sigma}_x(nT)^{-1/5}$, where $\hat{\sigma}_x$ is the sample standard deviation of $\{x_{it}\}_{i=1,t=1}^{n,T}$.

For each of our three DGPs, we consider two versions of assessment of our Hausman test. First, we investigate the performance of both the parametric and nonparametric Hausman tests under correct specification of the DGP for $c_0 \in \{-1, -0.9, \ldots, 0, \ldots, 0.9, 1\}$, $n \in \{50, 100, 200\}$, and $T \in \{3, 6, 9\}$. For all simulations we conduct 1,000 Monte Carlos simulations with 399 bootstrap replications (for the nonparametric Hausman test) within each iteration.

We then consider the performance of the parametric Hausman test under model misspecification. In this setting we only consider the DGPs given by Eqs. (17) and (19), but we deploy a linear (in x_{it}) model. In this case we will be readily able to assess the limitations of the general Hausman test to model misspecification. This is an area that has yet to garner much focus in the applied literature.

The Hausman Test Under Correct Specification

Figs. 1–3 present power curves for each of the three DGPs under consideration. We see that even for small T, the Hausman test has correct size and power increases quickly as c_0 moves away from 0. These results are robust across DGPs as well. The power curves are presented for $\alpha = 0.05$. Qualitatively identical results were obtained for $\alpha = 0.01$ and 0.10.

The nonparametric power curves for DGP (Eq. (17)) are presented in Fig. 4.[10] As expected we see that the nonparametric version of the Hausman test has appropriate size, but the increase in power is smaller than the parametric equivalents, which is to be expected. For example, the parametric results for DGP (Eq. (17)) give power approximately 1 when $N = 50$ when $c_0 = |1|$, whereas the results here give power at 0.6 when $c_0 = |1|$. Alternatively, the parametric Hausman test has power 1 for values of c_0 as low as $|0.5|$ when $N = 200$, while the nonparametric Hausman test only has power 1 for $c_0 = |1|$ for $N = 200$. This is not to undermine the performance of the nonparametric Hausman test, only to further highlight that under correct specification parametric tests will outperform their nonparametric counterparts; a truism no less important for being bland. These results further strengthen the simulation results provided in Henderson et al. (2008)

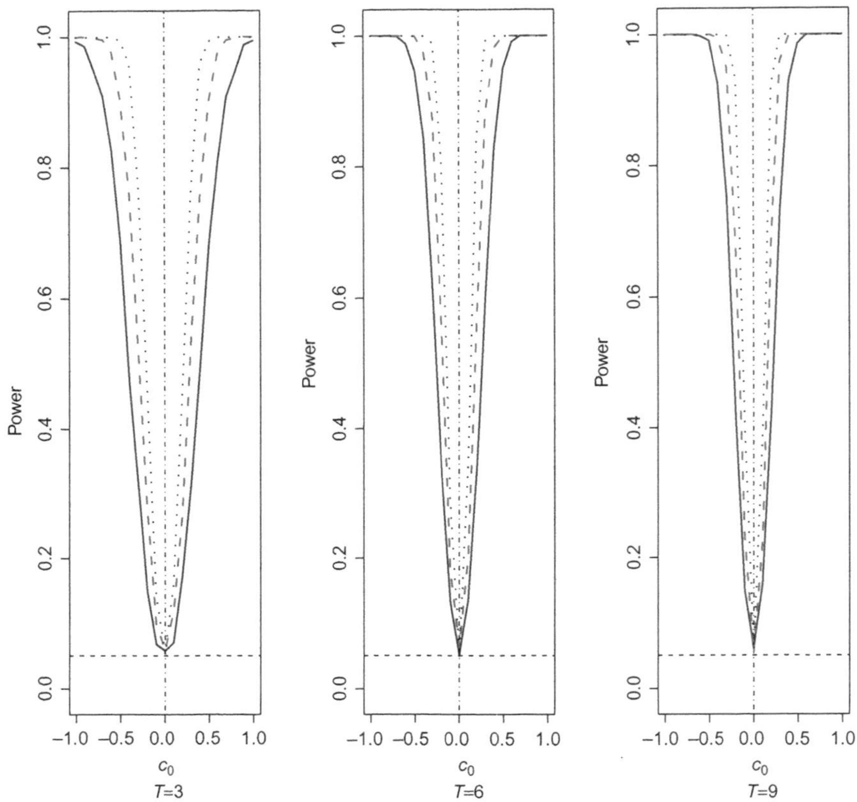

Fig. 1. Power Curves for DGP (Eq. (17)). The Solid Curve Represents $N = 50$, the Dashed Curve $N = 100$, and the Dotted Curve $N = 200$.

on the power of the nonparametric Hausman test. The fact that for $N = 50$ we still have almost exact size suggests that this test should serve as a reliable gauge to the presence of fixed effects in applied panel settings.

The Hausman Test Under Parametric Misspecification

If we deploy the Hausman test when the true DGP is either Eq. (17) or (19), but we erroneously assume it is Eq. (18), we see from the power curves in

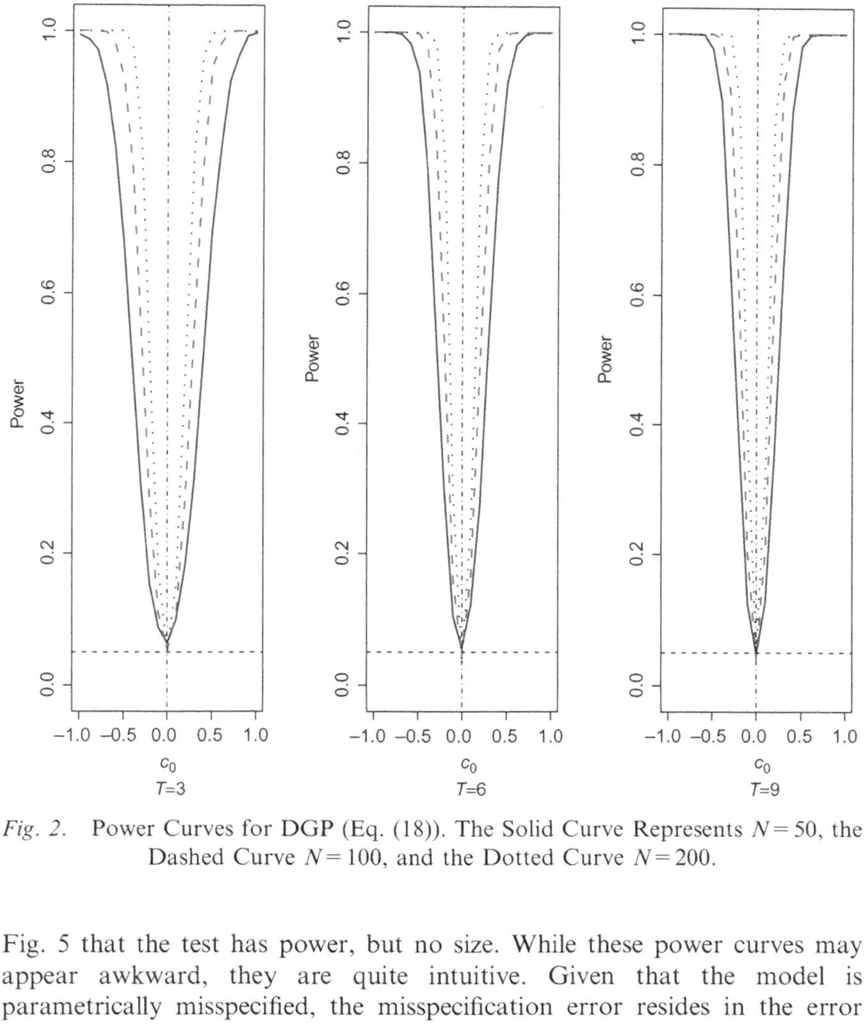

Fig. 2. Power Curves for DGP (Eq. (18)). The Solid Curve Represents $N = 50$, the Dashed Curve $N = 100$, and the Dotted Curve $N = 200$.

Fig. 5 that the test has power, but no size. While these power curves may appear awkward, they are quite intuitive. Given that the model is parametrically misspecified, the misspecification error resides in the error term. In our setting this additional error can take on a mean effect which enters the individual effect and an idiosyncratic effect (think of this as an approximation error between the linear conditional mean and the actual conditional mean) that varies over i and t. Thus, we see for the range of c_0 values we have looked over that at $c_0 \approx -0.9$, the misspecification manifests in such a way that one cannot discriminate between the fixed and random effects models for DGP (Eq. (17)). Alternatively, for DGP (Eq. (19)), there is

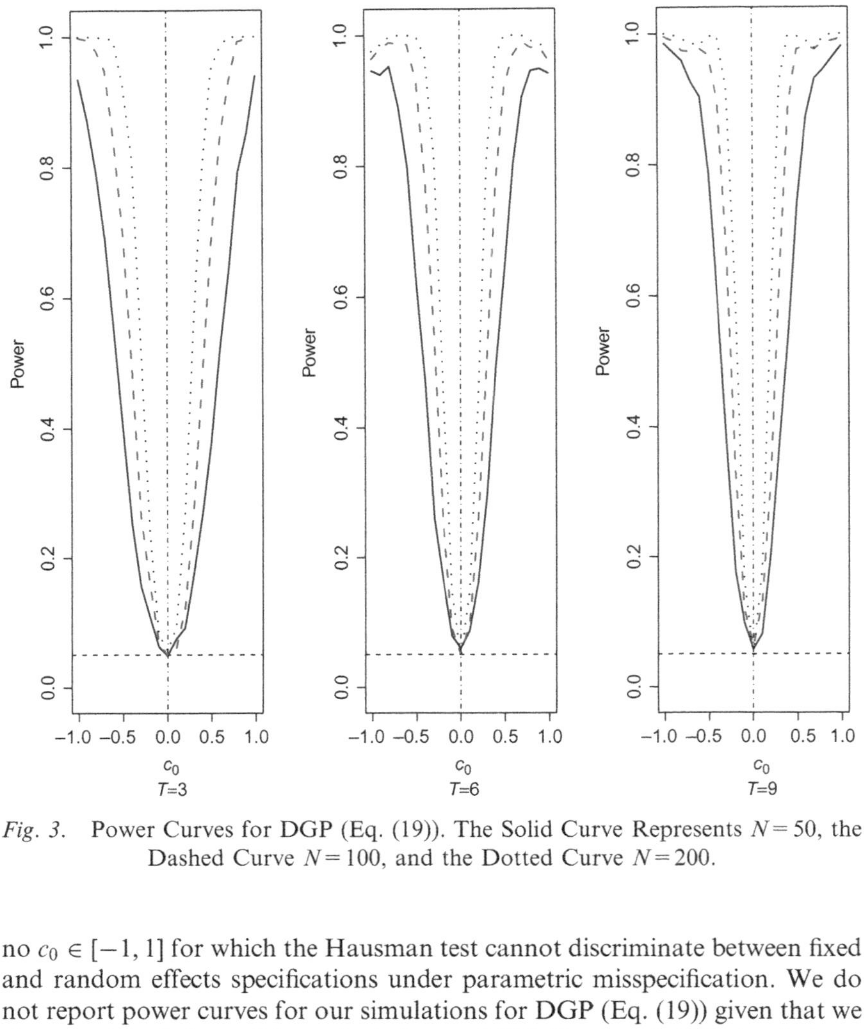

Fig. 3. Power Curves for DGP (Eq. (19)). The Solid Curve Represents $N=50$, the Dashed Curve $N=100$, and the Dotted Curve $N=200$.

no $c_0 \in [-1, 1]$ for which the Hausman test cannot discriminate between fixed and random effects specifications under parametric misspecification. We do not report power curves for our simulations for DGP (Eq. (19)) given that we always rejected the null hypothesis in our 9,000 ($3 \times 3 \times 1{,}000$) simulations.

Thus, while the Hausman test has remarkable performance under correct specification, these limited simulations suggest that one carefully scrutinize the specification of their panel data model (via a specification test) to ensure that the results of the test are discriminating between fixed and random effects and not through approximation error that resides in the error components.

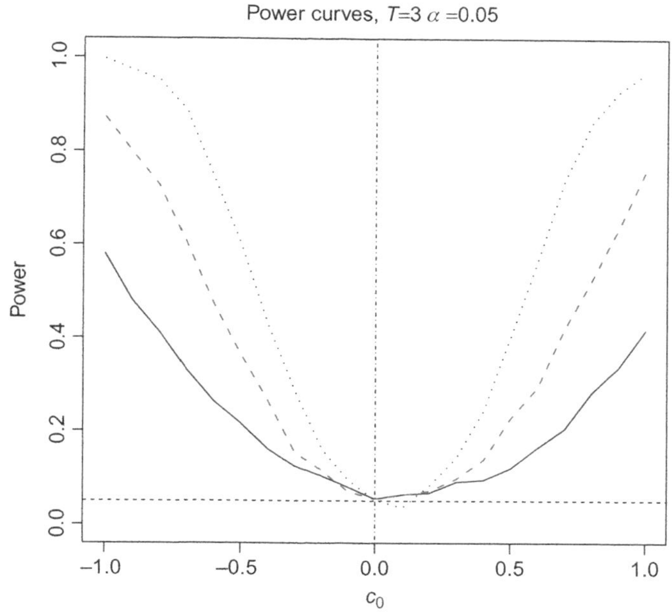

Fig. 4. Nonparametric Power Curves for DGP (Eq. (17)). The Solid Curve Represents $N = 50$, the Dashed Curve $N = 100$, and the Dotted Curve $N = 200$.

AN ILLUSTRATION MODELING GASOLINE DEMAND

This section provides an application of the nonparametric Hausman test to an empirical model of gasoline demand. The focus is less on the nonparametric estimates of the regression functions, and more on what the nonparametric Hausman test tells us in this setting. Our data stems from Baltagi and Griffin (1983).[11] The data comes from annual observations for 18 OECD countries over the period 1960–1978. One of the main findings that Baltagi and Griffin arrive at is that by pooling the data across countries, more robust and economically reasonable estimates of the price elasticity of gasoline can be had. They further investigated their demand model by deploying several different lag structures. For our expository purposes we will focus exclusively on their static demand model, Eq. (6) in Baltagi and Griffin (1983).

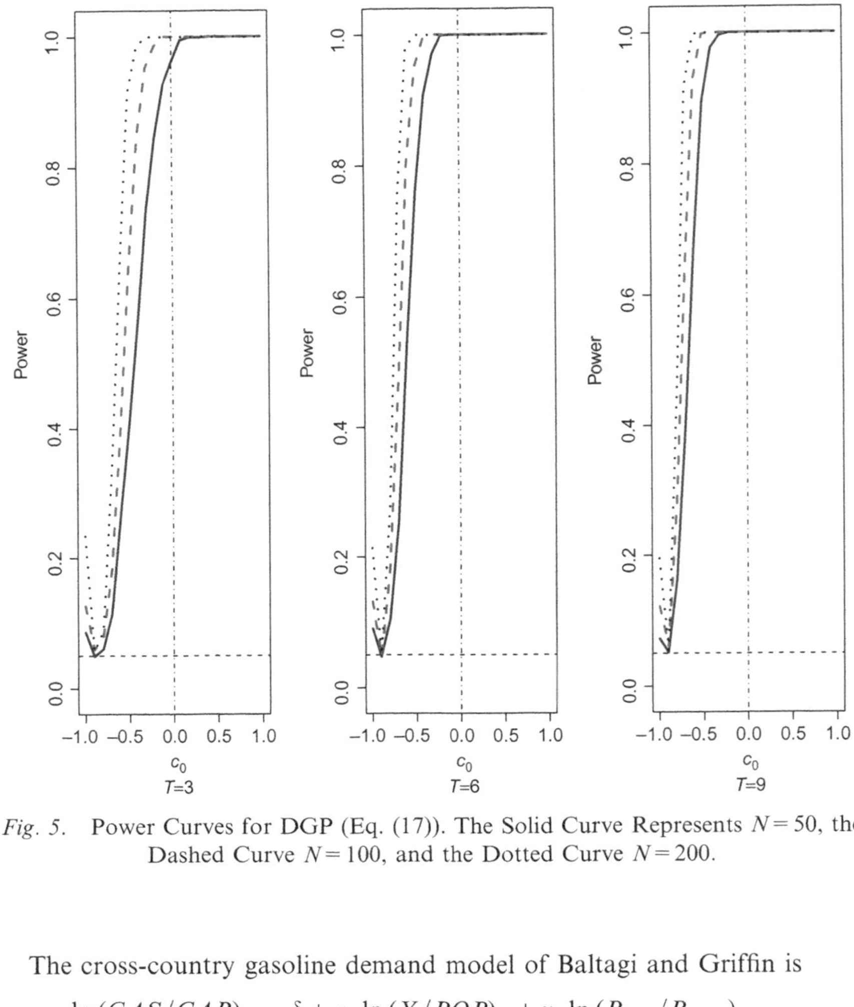

Fig. 5. Power Curves for DGP (Eq. (17)). The Solid Curve Represents $N=50$, the Dashed Curve $N=100$, and the Dotted Curve $N=200$.

The cross-country gasoline demand model of Baltagi and Griffin is

$$\begin{aligned} \ln(GAS/CAR)_{it} = \delta + \gamma_1 \ln(Y/POP)_{it} + \gamma_2 \ln(P_{MG}/P_{GDP})_{it} \\ + \gamma_3 \ln(CAR/POP)_{it} + V_i + \varepsilon_{it} \end{aligned} \tag{21}$$

where GAS/CAR represents gasoline consumption per automobile, Y/POP is per capita income, P_{MG}/P_{GDP} is the relative price of gasoline and CAR/POP represents the number of cars per capita. At issue is whether the determinants of demand are potentially correlated with unobserved, time constant effects, captured in V_i. A primary aim of the Baltagi and Griffin (1983) analysis was the price elasticity of gasoline demand, captured by β.

We first analyze the gasoline demand model in Eq. (21) treating the correlation between the covariates and α_i as both zero and nonzero. We use the standard least squares dummy variable (LSDV) (within estimator) for our fixed effects estimation as well as the common generalized least squares estimator to conduct random effects estimation. While there are a wide variety of methods for estimating the unknown variance components for the random effects estimator, we elect to use the procedure proposed by Amemiya (1971). The generic parametric results are presented in Table 2. We also present the Hausman test statistic and $p-$ value in the table. The Hausman test rejects the random effects estimator, suggesting that correlation exists between the determinants of gasoline demand and the time constant effects. The estimated price elasticity from the random effects model is almost 14 percent higher than that found by the fixed effects model. The random effects model also fits the data better as well so the results of the Hausman test are important in this context. We also mention that all three of the determinants are statistically significant at conventional levels.

To determine if our insights from the Hausman test may be induced by model misspecification, we deploy the consistent model specification test of Hsiao, Li, and Racine (2007) to the fixed effects version of model (21). This test soundly rejects that the model is correctly specified, providing a wild bootstrapped $p-$ value of 0 to more than 16 decimal places. Thus, there is

Table 2. Fixed and Random Effects Estimates of the Gasoline Demand Model in Eq. (21).

	Fixed		Random
$\ln(Y/N)$	0.6623		0.6005
	(0.1533)		(0.1346)
$\ln(P_{MG}/P_{GDP})$	−0.3217		−0.3667
	(0.1223)		(0.1204)
$\ln(CAR/N)$	−0.6405		−0.6203
	(0.0967)		(0.0922)
$\bar{R}^2$	0.788		0.825
Hausman test			
Statistic		10.3687	
$p-$ value		0.0157	

Table reports heteroskedasticity robust standard errors (Arellano 1987) in parentheses, adjusted $\bar{R}^2$, and results from a standard Hausman test.

the potential that the insights from the parametric Hausman test hinge on model misspecification.

To remedy this we deploy the nonparametric fixed effects estimator of Henderson et al. (2008) and the nonparametric random effects estimator of Wang (2003). These two estimators are then used to test for the presence of correlation among the covariates and the time constant country effects via the nonparametric Hausman test of Henderson et al. (2008). Prior to presenting the results of this test we compare the estimated price elasticities of these models to each other and to the parametric results in Table 2. We see that the estimated price elasticities are heavily skewed in the nonparametric models, suggesting that perhaps a mean elasticity is not fully representative of the underlying behavior.

Table 3 presents the quartile and extreme decile estimates (along with 399 bootstrapped standard errors) for the estimated price elasticities for further comparison. The first thing to notice is that while the elasticity estimates for the nonparametric fixed effects model of the relative price of gasoline are reasonably similar to the parametric estimates across quantiles, the estimated elasticities in the nonparametric random effects model are substantially larger in magnitude.[12] Further, the estimated elasticities across quantiles are strongly

Table 3. Nonparametric Fixed and Random Effects Estimates of the Gasoline Demand Model in Eq. (21).

	D_{10}	Q_{25}	D_{50}	Q_{75}	D_{90}	Mean
Fixed Effects						
$\ln(Y/POP)$	0.1345	0.1742	0.5730	0.9275	1.0650	0.5248
	(0.0500)	(0.0727)	(0.2406)	(0.4187)	(0.4089)	(0.1873)
$\ln(P_{MG}/P_{GDP})$	−0.4204	−0.3210	−0.2055	−0.0679	−0.0496	−0.2118
	(0.2105)	(0.1776)	(0.2157)	(0.0349)	(0.0321)	(0.0994)
$\ln(CAR/POP)$	−3.6126	−3.1720	−1.9909	−0.5972	−0.5063	−1.8797
	(0.5543)	(0.5972)	(0.3372)	(0.0916)	(0.4659)	(0.3460)
Random Effects						
$\ln(Y/POP)$	0.1451	0.4340	0.4619	0.5063	0.5512	0.3895
	(0.4145)	(0.3000)	(0.2995)	(0.4165)	(0.2626)	(0.0998)
$\ln(P_{MG}/P_{GDP})$	−1.1418	−0.9550	−0.7967	−0.6100	−0.5759	−0.8095
	(0.0421)	(0.1213)	(0.1822)	(0.0492)	(0.0584)	(0.1122)
$\ln(CAR/POP)$	−0.6356	−0.6049	−0.5856	−0.5682	−0.4595	−0.5451
	(0.3984)	(0.1046)	(0.1117)	(0.4377)	(0.6684)	(0.3649)

Table reports partial effects at the deciles (D), quartiles (Q), and mean. Wild bootstrapped standard errors are in parentheses.

statistically significant for the nonparametric random effects estimator, but are only moderately statistically significant at the lower decile and quartile, with the median estimate being statistically insignificant in the fixed effect model.

Turning our attention to the findings of the nonparametric Hausman test, we obtain a bootstrapped $p-$ value of 0.68, which suggests that after accounting for neglected nonlinearities we have successfully purged any correlation between the time constant country-specific effects and the determinants of gasoline demand. Baltagi and Griffin (1983) arrived at a similar insight regarding the findings of the Hausman test except that they allowed for dynamics in the relative price of gasoline to enter the benchmark model.

CONCLUSION

Through an historical survey of the Hausman test and several of its many theoretical advances and adaptations within a panel data context, we have emphasized the generality of the standard Hausman test and its usefulness in a variety of panel data settings. In particular, we focus on one primary strength of the test, that the test does not require specific functional form assumptions of the conditional mean. This generality is crucial in an applied nonparametric or semiparametric panel data setting in which the econometrician aims to test for the presence of a correlation between the included regressors and the individual specific error component, yet wants to impose minimal assumptions on the regression function.

Through our discussion of two existing semiparametric and nonparametric versions of the Hausman test, we illustrate the attractiveness of the Hausman test in a nonparametric setting. We show how the size and power of the test are adversely affected under parametric model misspecification, an important consideration that may often be overlooked in practice. Of course, the nonparametric Hausman test, based on nonparametric fixed and random effects estimators that do not require correct specification of the conditional mean, is able to overcome such potential pitfalls. We further demonstrate the usefulness of the nonparametric Hausman test in an empirical model of gasoline demand.

Upon further reflection of the generality and applicability of the Hausman test, we point out that there are a variety of new dimensions in which the test has yet to be adapted. For example, the semiparametric and nonparametric Hausman test models discussed in this paper have assumed that the individual specific error components are additively separable from the regression function. This assumption can, of course, be relaxed. The standard nonparametric model is also based on the assumption that the set of regressors is static. Su and Lu (2012) relax this assumption and propose a nonparametric dynamic panel data fixed effects estimator. Hausman tests developed in these nonparametric settings would be useful and welcomed.

NOTES

1. The citation count was obtained from the Web of Science Social Sciences Citation Index, accessed on July 27, 2012.
2. To be clear, this difference occurs only when the time dimension is finite, as is typically the case in applied microeconomic research. When the time dimension is large, the fixed effects estimator and generalized least squares (i.e., random effects) estimator are equivalent (Hsiao, 2003).
3. See Lemma 2.1 and the associated proof in Hausman (1978). Hausman proves that unless the covariance between $\hat{\beta}_{GLS}$ and $\hat{q}$ is zero, it is possible to construct a more efficient estimator than $\hat{\beta}_{GLS}$, which contradicts the assumption that $\hat{\beta}_{GLS}$ is fully efficient.
4. As noted by Hausman, an alternative and equivalent way of writing the test statistic is to define $M(\hat{q}) = (1/nT)V(\hat{q})$, $M_{GLS} = (1/nT)V(\hat{\beta}_{GLS})$, and $M_W = (1/nT)V(\hat{\beta}_W)$ which subsequently redefines the test statistic to be $m = \hat{q}'\hat{M}(\hat{q})^{-1}\hat{q}$.
5. See the Monte Carlo simulations in Ahn and Low (1996) for a comparison between several proposed specification tests under a variety of different scenarios.
6. It is important to acknowledge that Arellano and Bond (1991) and Ahn and Low (1996) identify empirical scenarios under which the Hausman test performs poorly; however, we note that these scenarios do not include the test for exogeneity of the unobserved individual effects in a panel data context, which is the primary focus of this paper.
7. The null hypothesis of zero correlation is supported for certain specifications estimated by Hausman et al. (1984), and rejected for others.
8. See, also, Su and Ullah (2010) for a recent overview.
9. Both random and fixed effects estimators proposed by Sun et al. (2009) can be estimated using either a local constant or local linear least squares approach.
10. For succinctness, we only present the results for DGP (Eq. (17)) when $T=3$. Power curves for other DGPs (Eqs. (18) and (19)) are available upon request.
11. This dataset is available with R in the plm package.
12. We note that Baltagi and Griffin obtain an estimated price elasticity of -0.96 when using the between estimator.

REFERENCES

Ahn, S. C., & Low, S. (1996). A reformulation of the Hausman test for regression models with pooled cross-section time-series data. *Journal of Econometrics*, *71*, 309–319.

Arellano, M., & Bond, S. (1991). Some tests of specification for panel data: Monte Carlo evidence and an application to employment equations. *Review of Economic Studies*, *58*, 277–297.
Amemiya, T. (1971). The estimation of variances in a variance-component model. *International Economic Review*, *12*, 1–13.
Bai, J. (2009). Panel data models with interactive fixed effects. *Econometrica*, *77*, 1229–1279.
Baltagi, B. (1981). Pooling: An experimental study of alternative testing and estimation procedures in a two-way error component model. *Journal of Econometrics*, *17*, 21–49.
Baltagi, B. H. (2006). Estimating an economic model of crime using panel data from North Carolina. *Journal of Applied Econometrics*, *21*, 543–547.
Baltagi, B. H. (2008). *Econometric analysis of panel data* (4th ed.). West Sussex, UK: Wiley.
Baltagi, B. H., & Griffin, J. M. (1983). Gasoline demand in the OECD: An application of pooling and testing procedures. *European Economic Review*, *22*, 117–137.
Blonigen, B. A. (1997). Firm-specific assets and the link between exchange rates and foreign direct investment. *American Economic Review*, *87*, 447–465.
Cardellichio, P. A. (1990). Estimation of production behavior using pooled microdata. *Review of Economics and Statistics*, *72*, 11–18.
Chamberlain, G. (1982). Multivariate regression models for panel data. *Journal of Econometrics*, *18*, 5–46.
Chernozhukov, V., & Hansen, C. (2006). Instrumental quantile regression inference for structural and treatment effect models. *Journal of Econometrics*, *132*, 491–525.
Cornwell, C., & Rupert, P. (1997). Unobservable individual effects, marriage and the earnings of young men. *Economic Inquiry*, *35*, 285–294.
Egger, P. (2000). A note on the proper econometric specification of the gravity equation. *Economics Letters*, *66*, 25–31.
Hansen, L. P. (1982). Large sample properties of generalized method of moments estimators. *Econometrica*, *50*, 1029–1054.
Hastings, J. S. (2004). Vertical relationships and competition in retail gasoline markets: Empirical evidence from contract changes in Southern California. *American Economic Review*, *91*, 317–328.
Hausman, J. A. (1978). Specification tests in econometrics. *Econometrica*, *46*(6), 1251–1271.
Hausman, J. A., Abrevaya, J., & Scott-Morton, F. M. (1998). Misclassification of the dependent variable in a discrete-response setting. *Journal of Econometrics*, *87*, 239–269.
Hausman, J. A., Hall, B. H., & Griliches, Z. (1984). Econometric models for count data with an application to the patents-R&D relationship. *Econometrica*, *52*, 909–938.
Hausman, J. A., & McFadden, D. (1984). Specification tests for the multinomial logit model. *Econometrica*, *52*(5), 1219–1240.
Hausman, J. A., & Pesaran, H. (1983). The *J*-test as a Hausman specification test. *Economics Letters*, *12*, 277–281.
Hausman, J.A., Taylor, W.E. (1980). *Comparing specification tests and classical tests.* Unpublished manuscript.
Hausman, J. A., & Taylor, W. E. (1981a). A generalized specification test. *Economics Letters*, *8*, 239–245.
Hausman, J. A., & Taylor, W. E. (1981b). Panel data and unobservable individual effects. *Econometrica*, *49*, 1377–1398.
Henderson, D. J., Carroll, R. J., & Li, Q. (2008). Nonparametric estimation and testing of fixed effects panel data models. *Journal of Econometrics*, *144*, 257–275.

Henderson, D. J., & Ullah, A. (2005). A nonparametric random effects estimator. *Economics Letters*, *88*, 403–407.

Holly, A. (1982). A remark on Hausman's specification test. *Econometrica*, *50*, 749–759.

Hsiao, C. (2003). *Analysis of panel data* (2nd ed.). New York, NY: Cambridge University Press.

Hsiao, C., Li, Q., & Racine, J. S. (2007). A consistent model specification test with mixed discrete and continuous data. *Journal of Econometrics*, *140*, 802–826.

Kang, S. (1985). A note on the equivalence of specification tests in the two-factor multivariate variance components model. *Journal of Econometrics*, *28*, 193–203.

Keane, M. P., & Runkle, D. E. (1992). On the estimation of panel-data models with serial correlation when instruments are not strictly exogenous. *Journal of Business and Economic Statistics*, *10*, 1–9.

Li, Q., & Stengos, T. (1992). A Hausman specification test based on root-N-consistent semiparametric estimators. *Economics Letters*, *40*, 141–146.

Lin, X., & Carroll, R. J. (2000). Nonparametric function estimation for clustered data when the predictor is measured without/with error. *Journal of the American Statistical Association*, *95*, 520–534.

Lin, X., & Carroll, R. J. (2001). Semiparametric regression for clustered data using generalized estimation equations. *Journal of the American Statistical Association*, *96*, 1045–1056.

Lin, X., & Carroll, R. J. (2006). Semiparametric estimation in general repeated measures problems. *Journal of the Royal Statistical Society, Series B*, *68*, 68–88.

Newey, W. K. (1987). Specification tests for distributional assumptions in the tobit model. *Journal of Econometrics*, *34*, 125–145.

Pace, R. K., & LeSage, J. P. (2008). A spatial Hausman test. *Economics Letters*, *101*, 282–284.

Robinson, P. M. (1988). Root-N-consistent semiparametric regression. *Econometrica*, *56*, 931–954.

Su, L., Lu, X. (2012). *Nonparametric dynamic panel data models: Kernel estimation and specification testing*. Working Paper.

Su, L., Ullah, A. (2010). *Nonparametric and semiparametric panel econometric models: Estimation and testing*. Working Paper.

Sun, Y., Carroll, R. J., & Li, D. (2009). Semiparametric estimation of fixed-effects panel data varying coefficient models. In Q. Li & J. S. Racine (Eds.), *Nonparametric econometric methods (Advances in Econometrics)*(Vol. 25, pp. 101–129). Bingley, UK: Emerald.

Wang, N. (2003). Marginal nonparametric kernel regression accounting for within-subject correlation. *Biometrika*, *90*, 43–52.

White, H. (1981). Consequences and detection of misspecified nonlinear regression models. *Journal of the American Statistical Association*, *76*, 419–433.

Wills, H. (1987). A note on specification tests for the multinomial logit model. *Journal of Econometrics*, *34*, 263–274.

APPENDIX

This appendix details the fully nonparametric random effects (Wang, 2003) and fixed effects (Henderson et al., 2008) estimators of the model in Eq. (11) that are used throughout the Monte Carlo analyses conducted in this paper.

A Nonparametric Random Effects Estimator

Wang (2003) considers a nonparametric model in which the unobserved individual effect is uncorrelated with the regressors, i.e., a nonparametric random effects estimator. Specifically, the model takes the form

$$y_{it} = g(x_{it}) + v_i + \varepsilon_{it}. \tag{A.1}$$

The random effects estimator requires assumptions about the variance-covariance matrix of the errors. Specifically, define $V_it = V_i + \varepsilon_{it}$ and assume that if $v_i = [v_{i1}, v_{i2}, \ldots, v_{iT_i}]'$ is a $T_i \times 1$ vector, then $\Sigma_i \equiv E(v_i v'_i)$ takes the form

$$\Sigma_i = \sigma_\varepsilon^2 I_{T_i} + \sigma_v^2 i_{T_i} i'_{T_i} \tag{A.2}$$

in which I_{T_i} is an identity matrix of dimension T_i and i_{T_i} is a $T_i \times 1$ column vector of ones. Since the observations are independent over i and j, the covariance matrix for the full $nT \times 1$ disturbance vector $\mu, \Sigma = E(vv')$ is a $nT \times nT$ block diagonal matrix where the blocks are equal to $\Sigma_i, i = 1, 2, \ldots, n$. Note that this specification assumes a homoskedastic variance for all i and t. Here we allow for serial correlation over time, but only between the disturbances for the same individuals:

$$\begin{aligned} cov(\mu_{it}, \mu_{js}) &= cov(v_i + \varepsilon_{it}, v_j + \varepsilon_{js}) = E[(v_i + \varepsilon_{it})(v_j + \varepsilon_{js})] \\ &= E[v_i v_j + v_i \varepsilon_{js} + \varepsilon_{it} v_j + \varepsilon_{it}\varepsilon_{js}] = E[v_i v_j] + E[\varepsilon_{it}\varepsilon_{js}] \end{aligned} \tag{A.3}$$

Hence, the covariance equals $\sigma_v^2 + \sigma_\varepsilon^2$ when $i = j$ and $t = s$, it is equal to σ_v^2 when $i = j$ and $t \neq s$, and it is equal to zero when $i \neq j$.

Wang (2003) develops an iterative procedure with which to estimate $g(\cdot)$, and has the advantage of eliminating biases and reducing the variation compared to alternative random effects estimators (e.g., Lin & Carroll, 2000; Henderson & Ullah, 2005). The basic idea behind her estimator is that once a data point within a cluster (cross sectional unit) has a value within a bandwidth of the x value, and is used to estimate the unknown function, all points in that cluster are used. For data points which lie outside the bandwidth, the contributions of the remaining data in the local estimate are through their residuals. The residuals are calculated by subtracting the fitted values from a preliminary step from y_{it}.

Estimation in the first stage is conducted by using any consistent estimator of the conditional mean, for example, the pooled local linear least squares estimator. Denote the pooled local linear estimator $\hat{g}_{[1]}(x)$ and the residuals from this model $\hat{\varepsilon}_{it} = y_{it} - \hat{g}_{[1]}(x_{it})$, in which the subscript [1] refers to the $l = 1$ step in the iteration procedure. The estimate of the conditional mean and gradient, respectively $\hat{g}_{[l]}(x)$ and $\hat{\beta}_{[l]}(x)$, can be obtained by solving the kernel-weighted equation

$$0 = \sum_{i=1}^{n}\sum_{t=1}^{T_i} K\left(\frac{x_{it}-x}{h}\right)\begin{pmatrix} 1 \\ \frac{x_{it}-x}{h} \end{pmatrix}\left\{\begin{matrix} \sigma^{tt}\left[y_{it} - \hat{g}_{[l]}(x) - \left(\frac{x_{it}-x}{h}\right)\hat{\beta}_{[l]}(x)\right] \\ + \sum_{\substack{s=1 \\ s\neq t}}^{T_i} \sigma^{st}\left[y_{is} - \hat{g}_{[l-1]}(x_{is})\right] \end{matrix}\right\} \tag{A.4}$$

in which σ^{st} is the (t, s)th element of Σ_i^{-1}. Note that σ^{tt} and σ^{st} differ across cross-sectional units when the number of time dimensions (T_i) differ. The third summation shows that when the value of x_{is} associated with y_{is} is not within one bandwidth of x, the residual $y_{is} - \hat{g}_{[l-1]}(x_{is})$, rather than y_{is}, is taken into account in the weighted average. One can show that the lth step estimator is equal to

$$\begin{pmatrix} \hat{g}_{[l]}(x) \\ \hat{\beta}_{[l]}(x) \end{pmatrix} = \left[\sum_{i=1}^{n}\sum_{t=1}^{T_i} K\left(\frac{x_{it}-x}{h}\right)\sigma^{tt}\begin{pmatrix} 1 \\ \frac{x_{it}-x}{h} \end{pmatrix}\begin{pmatrix} 1 & \frac{x_{it}-x}{h} \end{pmatrix}\right]^{-1}$$
$$\times\left\{\sum_{i=1}^{n}\sum_{t=1}^{T_i} K\left(\frac{x_{it}-x}{h}\right)\begin{pmatrix} 1 \\ \frac{x_{it}-x}{h} \end{pmatrix}\left[\sigma^{tt}y_{it} + \sum_{\substack{s=1 \\ s\neq t}}^{T_i}\sigma^{st}(y_{is} - \hat{g}_{[l-1]}(x_{is}))\right]\right\} \tag{A.5}$$

The iterative process is continued until convergence is reached. Wang (2003) argues that the once-iterated estimator has the same asymptotic behavior as the fully iterated estimator, and uses a Monte Carlo exercise to show that it performs well for the single regressor case.

A Nonparametric Fixed Effects Estimator

Henderson et al. (2008) consider the case in which the additively separable individual effect in Eq. (11) is correlated with the regressors in x. Specifically, Henderson et al. (2008) consider the model

$$y_{it} = g(x_{it}) + v_i + \varepsilon_{it} \tag{A.6}$$

Assuming the standard case of large n and small T, Henderson et al. (2008) propose removing the individual effect by subtracting observation $t = 1$ from each t:

$$\tilde{y}_{it} \equiv y_{it} - y_{i1} = g(x_{it}) - g(x_{i1}) + \varepsilon_{it} - \varepsilon_{i1} \tag{A.7}$$

Following the above transformation, define $\tilde{\varepsilon}_{it} = \varepsilon_{it} - \varepsilon_{i1}$ and $\tilde{\varepsilon}_i = (\tilde{\varepsilon}_{i2}, \ldots, \tilde{\varepsilon}_{iT})'$. Then, the variance-covariance matrix of $\tilde{\varepsilon}_i$, defined as $\Sigma = \text{cov}(\tilde{\varepsilon}_i | x_{i1}, \ldots, x_{iT}) = \text{cov}(\tilde{\varepsilon}_i)$ is $\Sigma = \sigma_\varepsilon^2(I_{T-1} + e_{T-1}e'_{T-1})$, in which I_{T-1} is an identity matrix of dimension $(T-1)$ and e_{T-1} is a $(T-1)$-dimensioned column of ones. Hence, $\Sigma^{-1} = \sigma_\varepsilon^{-2}(I_{T-1} - e_{T-1}e'_{T-1}/T)$. We point out that this approach assumes that the structure of the variance is known. Alternatively, if the variance structure is unknown, Henderson et al. (2008) propose setting $\Sigma^{-1} = I_{T-1}$.

Henderson et al. (2008) adopt a profile likelihood approach for estimating $g(\cdot)$. Letting $y_i = (y_{i1}, \ldots, y_{iT})$, the profile likelihood criterion function for individual i is

$$L_i(\cdot) = L(y_i, g_i) = -\frac{1}{2}(\tilde{y}_i - g_i + g_{i1}e_{T-1})'\Sigma^{-1}(\tilde{y}_i - g_i + g_{i1}e_{T-1}) \tag{A.8}$$

in which $\tilde{y}_i = (\tilde{y}_{i2}, \ldots, \tilde{y}_{iT})'$, $g_{it} = g(x_{it})$, and $g_i = (g_{i2}, \ldots, g_{iT})'$. Next, let $L_{i,tg} = \partial L_i(\cdot)/\partial g_{it}$ and $L_{i,tsg} = \partial^2 L_i(\cdot)/(\partial g_{it}\partial g_{is})$. Then, from Eq. (29) we get $L_{i,1g} = -e'_{T-1}\Sigma^{-1}(\tilde{y}_i - g_i + g_{i1}e_{T-1})$ and $L_{i,tg} = c'_{t-1}\Sigma^{-1}(\tilde{y}_i - g_i + g_{i1}e_{T-1})$ with the $L_{i,tg}$ expression applying for any $t \geq 2$, in which c_{t-1} is a scalar of length $(T-1)$ that has the $t-1$ element equal to unity and zero otherwise.

Define $K_h(\varepsilon) = \Pi_{j=1}^q h_j^{-1} k(v_j/h_j)$ to be a standard product kernel function with univariate kernel $k(\cdot)$ and bandwidth h, and let $(x_{it} - x)/h = [(x_{it,1} - x_1)/h_1, \ldots, (x_{it,q} - x_q)/h_q]'$ and $G_{it}(x, h) = \{1, [(x_{it} - x)/h]'\}'$, in which

G_{it} is a scalar of length $(q+1)$. Then, letting $g^{(1)}(x) = \partial g(x)/\partial x$ be the first-order derivative of $g(\cdot)$ with respect to z, the estimate of $g(x)$ is obtained by solving the first-order condition

$$0=\sum_{i=1}^{n}\sum_{t=1}^{T}K_h(x_{it}-x)G_{it}(x,h)L_{i,tg}\{y_i,\hat{g}(x_{i1}),\ldots,\hat{g}(x)+[(x_{it}-x)/h]\hat{g}^{(1)}(x),\ldots,\hat{g}(x_{iT})\} \tag{A.9}$$

in which $L_{i,tg}$ is equal to $\hat{g}(x_{is})$ for $s\neq t$ and $\hat{g}(x)+[(x_{it}-x)/h]\hat{g}^{(1)}(x)$ when $s=t$.

Henderson et al. (2008) propose the following iterative procedure for solving the above first-order condition for $\hat{g}(\cdot)$. Denote the estimate of $g(x)$ at the $[l-1]$ step to be $\hat{g}_{[l-1]}(x)$. Then, the l-step estimate of $g(x)$ is $\hat{g}_{[l]}(x) = \hat{\alpha}_0(x)$, such that $(\hat{\alpha}_0, \hat{\alpha}_1)$ solve

$$0=\sum_{i=1}^{n}\sum_{t=1}^{T}K_h(x_{it}-x)G_{it}(x,h)L_{i,tg}\{y_i,\hat{g}_{[l-1]}(x_{i1}),\ldots,\hat{\alpha}_0+[(x_{it}-x)/h]\hat{\alpha}_1,\ldots,\hat{g}_{[l-1]}(x_{iT})\}. \tag{A.10}$$

Hence, using the restriction $\sum_{i=1}^{n}\sum_{t=1}^{T}[y_{it}-\hat{g}(x_{it})] = 0$ so that $g(\cdot)$ can be uniquely defined, the iterative procedure gives rise to the following estimation procedure. Define

$$H_{i,[l-1]} = \begin{bmatrix} y_{i2}-\hat{g}_{[l-1]}(x_{i2}) \\ \vdots \\ y_{iT}-\hat{g}_{[l-1]}(x_{iT}) \end{bmatrix} -[y_{i1}-\hat{g}_{[l-1]}(x_{i1})]e_{T-1}. \tag{A.11}$$

Then, the first-order condition becomes

$$\begin{aligned} 0 = {} & \sum_{i=1}^{n} K_h(x_{i1}-x)G_{i1}\{-e'_{T-1}\Sigma^{-1}H_{i,[l-1]} + e'_{T-1}\Sigma^{-1}e_{T-1}[\hat{g}_{[l-1]}(x_{i1}) \\ & -G'_{i1}(\alpha_0,\alpha_1)']\} + \sum_{i=1}^{n}\sum_{t=2}^{T} K_h(x_{it}-x)G_{it}\{c'_{t-1}\Sigma^{-1}H_{i,[l-1]} \\ & + c'_{t-1}\Sigma^{-1}c_{t-1}[\hat{g}_{[l-1]}(x_{it})-G'_{it}(\alpha_0,\alpha_1)']\}. \end{aligned} \tag{A.12}$$

Solving for α_0 and α_1 gives $[\hat{\alpha}_0(x), \hat{\alpha}_1(x)]' = D_1^{-1}(D_2 + D_3)$, in which D_1, D_2, and D_3 are defined as

$$D_1 = n^{-1} \sum_{i=1}^{n} \left[e'_{T-1} \Sigma^{-1} e_{T-1} K_h(x_{i1} - x) G_{i1} G'_{i1} + \sum_{t=2}^{T} c'_{t-1} \Sigma^{-1} c_{t-1} K_h(x_{it} - x) G_{it} G'_{it} \right] \tag{A.13}$$

$$D_2 = n^{-1} \sum_{i=1}^{n} \left[e'_{T-1} \Sigma^{-1} e_{T-1} K_h(x_{i1} - x) G_{i1} \hat{g}_{[l-1]}(x_{i1}) + \sum_{t=2}^{T} c'_{t-1} \Sigma^{-1} c_{t-1} K_h(x_{it} - x) G_{it} \hat{g}_{[l-1]}(x_{it}) \right] \tag{A.14}$$

and

$$D_3 = n^{-1} \sum_{i=1}^{n} \left[\sum_{t=2}^{T} K_h(x_{it} - x) G_{it} c'_{t-1} \Sigma^{-1} H_{i,[l-1]} - K_h(x_{i1} - x) G_{i1} e'_{T-1} \Sigma^{-1} H_{i,[l-1]} \right]. \tag{A.15}$$

The estimate of $g(x)$ is given by $\hat{g}_{[l]}(x) = \hat{\alpha}_0(x)$.

THE HAUSMAN TEST, AND SOME ALTERNATIVES, WITH HETEROSKEDASTIC DATA

Lee C. Adkins, Randall C. Campbell, Viera Chmelarova and R. Carter Hill

ABSTRACT

The Hausman test is used in applied economic work as a test of misspecification. It is most commonly thought of as a test of whether one or more explanatory variables in a regression model are endogenous. The usual Hausman contrast test requires one estimator to be efficient under the null hypothesis. If data are heteroskedastic, the least squares estimator is no longer efficient. The first option is to estimate the covariance matrix of the difference of the contrasted estimators, as suggested by Hahn, Ham, and Moon (2011). Other options for carrying out a Hausman-like test in this case include estimating an artificial regression and using robust standard errors. Alternatively, we might seek additional power by estimating the artificial regression using feasible generalized least squares. Finally, we might stack moment conditions leading to the two estimators and estimate the resulting system by GMM. We examine these options in a Monte Carlo experiment. We conclude that the test based on the procedure by Hahn, Ham, and Moon has good properties. The generalized least squares-based tests have higher

Essays in Honor of Jerry Hausman
Advances in Econometrics, Volume 29, 515–546

ISSN: 0731-9053/doi:10.1108/S0731-9053(2012)0000029022

size-corrected power when heteroskedasticity is detected in the DWH regression, and the heteroskedasticity is associated with a strong external IV. We do not consider the properties of the implied pretest estimator.

Keywords: Hausman test; heteroskedasticity; GMM; Monte Carlo

JEL classification: C01; C12; C15; C26

INTRODUCTION

The Hausman (1978) test is used in applied economic work as a test of misspecification. It is most commonly thought of as a test of whether one or more explanatory variables in a regression model are endogenous. The idea of testing for endogeneity was also considered by Durbin (1954) and Wu (1973), so the tests will be referred to as Durbin–Wu–Hausman, or DWH, tests. The usual DWH contrast test requires one estimator to be efficient under the null hypothesis. If data are heteroskedastic, the least squares estimator is no longer efficient. Traditional options for carrying out a Hausman-like test in this case include estimating an artificial regression (the DWH regression-based test) and using robust standard errors. A second alternative, and the one we introduce here, is using a feasible generalized least squares (FGLS) estimator for the DWH artificial regression using a multiplicative heteroskedasticity framework. A third alternative has been recently proposed by Hahn, Ham, and Moon (2011). It is a contrast test with a consistent estimator of the covariance matrix of the difference between the two estimators. A fourth alternative is to use a generalized method-of-moments (GMM) approach. Creel (2004) suggests stacking the moment conditions and implementing a Wald test of the equality of coefficients.

THE DURBIN–WU–HAUSMAN TESTS

The linear regression model is $y = X\beta + u$. Initially assume that the errors are homoscedastic with variance σ^2, thus $V(u) = \sigma^2 I_n$. Let the $n \times K$ matrix of explanatory variables X be partitioned as $X = [X_1 \;\; X_2]$, where X_1 is $n \times K_1$ and potentially endogenous, $plim(X_1'u/n) \neq 0$, and X_2 is $n \times K_2$ and assumed exogenous, $plim(X_2'u/n) = 0$. Assume that there is an $n \times L$ matrix $Z = [Z_1 \;\; X_2]$ of instruments that is uncorrelated with the error,

$plim(Z'u/n) = 0$; X_2 contains the included or "internal" instruments. The matrix Z_1 is $n \times L_1$ and comprises the excluded or "external" instruments, which do not appear in the regression equation. Valid instruments must also be correlated with the regressors so that $plim(Z'X/n) = Q_{ZX} \neq 0$ and is of full rank. The number of instruments $L = L_1 + K_2$ must be greater than or equal to the number of regressors K. So L_1, the number of external instruments, must be greater than or equal to K_1, the number of potentially endogenous variables. This is the necessary order condition.

The ordinary least squares estimator (OLS) $\hat{\beta}_{OLS} = (X'X)^{-1}X'y$ is consistent if X and u are uncorrelated, and with homoscedastic errors $V(\hat{\beta}_{OLS}) = \sigma^2(X'X)^{-1}$ with $\hat{\sigma}^2_{OLS} = (y - X\hat{\beta}_{OLS})'(y - X\hat{\beta}_{OLS})/(n - K)$. If X and u are correlated, then the least squares estimator is inconsistent. Define the matrix $P_Z = Z(Z'Z)^{-1}Z'$. A consistent estimator is the instrumental variables (two-stage least squares, 2SLS) estimator $\hat{\beta}_{IV} = (X'P_ZX)^{-1}X'P_Zy$ that has covariance matrix $V(\hat{\beta}_{IV}) = \sigma^2(X'P_ZX)^{-1}$ with $\hat{\sigma}^2_{IV} = (y - X\hat{\beta}_{IV})'(y - X\hat{\beta}_{IV})/(n - K)$. If X is uncorrelated with the error, then the $\hat{\beta}_{IV}$ estimator is inefficient relative to $\hat{\beta}_{OLS}$.

If we are not sure about the endogeneity of a subset of regressors, then we can resort to a test belonging to the DWH family. If we define $q = (\hat{\beta}_{IV} - \hat{\beta}_{OLS})$, then the DWH contrast test statistic is $H = q'[V(\hat{\beta}_{IV}) - V(\hat{\beta}_{OLS})]^+q$, where "+" denotes a generalized inverse. Under the null hypothesis that both estimators are consistent (or that X_1 is uncorrelated with the error term), then $H \overset{a}{\sim} \chi^2_{(K_1)}$. The DWH tests and some modifications are described in Baum, Schaffer, and Stillman (2003).

Using an Artificial Regression

In addition to contrast tests, there are some auxiliary regression equivalents.[1] Consider the contrast vector:

$$q = \hat{\beta}_{IV} - \hat{\beta}_{OLS} = (X'P_ZX)^{-1}\left[X'P_Z\left(I - X(X'X)^{-1}X'\right)y\right] = (X'P_ZX)^{-1}X'P_ZM_Xy \tag{1}$$

The test of whether $q \to 0$ asymptotically is equivalent to testing whether $X'P_ZM_Xy$ has zero mean asymptotically. The matrix of fitted values in the reduced form regression of X on Z is $P_ZX = Z(Z'Z)^{-1}Z'X = \hat{X} = [\hat{X}_1\ X_2]$ and $M_X\hat{X} = [M_X\hat{X}_1\ 0]$. Thus, the portion of $X'P_ZM_Xy$ that is relevant is $X_1'P_ZM_Xy$. Defining $\tilde{P} = M_XP_ZX_1$, consider the artificial regression:

$$y = X\beta + P_Z X_1 \delta + \text{error} = X\beta + \hat{X}_1 \delta + \text{error} \tag{2}$$

Applying the Frisch–Waugh–Lovell (FWL) theorem,[2] we obtain

$$M_X y = M_X P_Z X_1 \delta + \text{error} \Rightarrow \tilde{y} = \tilde{P}\delta + \text{error} \tag{3}$$

Thus, the test for $\delta = 0$ is testing for zero correlation between residuals from the regression of y on X ($M_X y$) and a transformation ($M_X P_Z X_1$) of the potentially endogenous regressors, X_1.

The least squares residuals from Eq. (3) are

$$\tilde{y} - \tilde{P}\hat{\delta} = M_X y - M_X P_Z X_1 (X_1' P_Z M_X P_Z X_1)^{-1} X_1' P_Z M_X y = M_{\tilde{P}} M_X y$$

The unrestricted sum of squared residuals (SSR_{un}) $= y' M_X M_{\tilde{P}} M_X y$ and an estimator of the error variance that is consistent under the null hypothesis that $\delta = 0$ is $\tilde{\sigma}^2 = \text{SSR}_{\text{un}}/(n - K - K_1)$. Under the null hypothesis that $\delta = 0$, the restricted model is the usual regression model with $\text{SSR}_{\text{rest}} = y' M_X y$. Taking the difference, we obtain

$$\begin{aligned} \text{SSR}_{\text{rest}} - \text{SSR}_{\text{un}} &= y' M_X y - y' M_X M_{\tilde{P}} M_X y = y' M_X (I - M_{\tilde{P}}) M_X y \\ &= y' \tilde{P} (\tilde{P}' \tilde{P})^{-1} \tilde{P}' y \end{aligned}$$

using the fact that $M_X \tilde{P} = \tilde{P}$. Therefore, a test that is asymptotically equivalent to the Hausman test is an F-test of the null hypothesis that $\delta = 0$ in the artificial regression (2), with the Wald test statistic[3] being

$$W_{\text{DWH}} = \frac{y' \tilde{P} (\tilde{P}' \tilde{P})^{-1} \tilde{P}' y}{\tilde{\sigma}^2} \overset{a}{\sim} \chi^2_{(K_1)} \tag{4}$$

An alternative version of the artificial regression is

$$y = X\beta + M_Z X_1 \eta + \text{error} = X\beta + (X_1 - \hat{X}_1)\eta + \text{error} = X\beta + \hat{V}_1 \eta + \text{error} \tag{5}$$

In this regression, instead of augmenting the original model with the predicted values of the endogenous regressors from the reduced form, we add to the original model the residuals from reduced form equations. The Wald test that results is identical to the earlier one because

$$M_X y = M_X M_Z X_1 \eta + \text{error}$$

Note that

$$M_X M_Z X_1 = M_X (I - P_Z) X_1 = M_X X_1 - M_X P_Z X_1 = -M_X P_Z X_1$$

since $M_X X_1 = 0$. So the regression

$$M_X y = M_X M_Z X_1 \eta + \text{error} = M_X P_Z X_1(-\eta) + \text{error} = M_X P_Z X_1 \delta + \text{error}$$

has the same SSR as in the earlier case, Eq. (2), and thus the test of $\eta = 0$ in Eq. (5) is identical to that for $\delta = 0$ in Eq. (2), which uses the DWH Wald statistic in Eq. (4).

HAUSMAN TESTS WITH HETEROSKEDASTICITY

A Robust Artificial Regression Test

A simple correction[4] for heteroskedasticity is to use a robust covariance matrix estimator for the augmented regression $y = X\beta + \hat{V}_1\eta + \varepsilon = \check{X}\theta + \varepsilon$, where $\check{X} = [X \quad \hat{V}_1]$ and $\theta' = [\beta' \quad \eta']$. The standard robust covariance matrices for the OLS estimator $\check{\theta}$, denoted *hccme* 0, 1, 2, or 3, are

$$V(\check{\theta}) = (\check{X}'\check{X})^{-1}\check{X}'D_{hccme}\check{X}(\check{X}'\check{X})^{-1}$$

The choice D_0 is a diagonal matrix using only the uncorrected squares of the least squares residuals $\check{\varepsilon} = y - \check{X}\check{\theta}$ on the diagonal. The other methods adjust the squared residuals in one way or another. The choice D_1 inflates the residuals by $n/(n - ncol(\check{X}))$. The alternative D_2 is derived on the basis of the fact that under homoscedasticity, the variance of the least squares residual $\check{\varepsilon}_i$ is given by

$$\text{var}(\check{\varepsilon}_i) = \sigma_\varepsilon^2(1 - \check{x}'_i(\check{X}'\check{X})^{-1}\check{x}_i)$$

where $\check{x}'_i$ is the *i*th row of the $\check{X}$ matrix. It divides the squared residual by the quantity in the outer parentheses. Option D_3 divides the squared residual by the square of the quantity in parentheses. The relative merits of these alternatives are discussed in Davidson and MacKinnon (1993, pp. 553–554) and MacKinnon and White (1985). Briefly, D_0 should not be used because the least squares residuals are too small; D_1 inflates the residuals using a degrees of freedom correction.[5] Under the null hypothesis of homoscedasticity, D_2 is "almost unbiased" (MacKinnon & White, 1985, p. 308). The option D_3 is related to "jackknife" methods for resampling and in fact is an approximation (Davidson & MacKinnon, 1993, p. 554) to a more complicated version (MacKinnon & White, 1985, p. 309), which performed well in Monte Carlo experiments exploring the finite sample properties of test statistics. The term $0 < (1 - \check{x}'_i(\check{X}'\check{X})^{-1}\check{x}_i) < 1$, and thus the option D_3, inflates the least squares residuals more than option D_2. These options are preferred by Davidson and MacKinnon to either D_0 or D_1. In matrix terms, these alternatives are

$$D_0 = \begin{bmatrix} \breve{\varepsilon}_1^2 & 0 & \cdots & 0 \\ 0 & \breve{\varepsilon}_2^2 & 0 & 0 \\ \vdots & 0 & \ddots & \vdots \\ 0 & 0 & \cdots & \breve{\varepsilon}_N^2 \end{bmatrix} = \mathrm{diag}(\breve{\varepsilon}_1^2, \breve{\varepsilon}_2^2, \ldots, \breve{\varepsilon}_N^2), \quad D_1 = \frac{n}{n - ncol(\breve{X})} \mathrm{diag}(\breve{\varepsilon}_1^2, \breve{\varepsilon}_2^2, \ldots, \breve{\varepsilon}_N^2)$$

$$D_2 = \mathrm{diag}\left(\ldots, \frac{\breve{\varepsilon}_i^2}{1 - \breve{x}'_i(\breve{X}'\breve{X})^{-1}\breve{x}_i}, \ldots \right), \quad D_3 = \mathrm{diag}\left(\ldots, \frac{\breve{\varepsilon}_i^2}{(1 - \breve{x}'_i(\breve{X}'\breve{X})^{-1}\breve{x}_i)^2}, \ldots \right)$$

A FGLS Artificial Regression Test

Applying FGLS to the augmented regression may have benefits. If the regression errors u_i are heteroskedastic then, under the null hypothesis of no endogeneity ($\eta = 0$), so are the errors ε_i. We posit that modeling the heteroskedasticity in a general way, namely, using Harvey's (1976) model of multiplicative heteroskedasticity with generally correct culprits, may lead to a test with more power. That is, suppose $\mathrm{var}(\varepsilon_i) = \exp(w_i'\gamma)$, where w_i is a vector of exogenous variables related to the variance of ε_i, including an intercept, and γ is a vector of parameters. This formulation is flexible and parsimonious. If we transform the augmented model $y_i = \breve{x}_i'\theta + \varepsilon_i$ by $[\exp(w_i'\hat{\gamma})]^{-.5}$, where $\hat{\gamma}$ is a consistent estimator, and apply least squares, this is the FGLS estimator. The estimator $\hat{\gamma}$ we employ is the least squares estimator from the regression of $\ln(\breve{\varepsilon}^2)$ on candidate variables that may be related to the heteroskedasticity.[6] If the model of heteroskedasticity is correct, then the FGLS estimator $\tilde{\theta}$ is asymptotically more efficient than the OLS estimator $\breve{\theta}$. If the model specified is not correct, the FGLS estimator is still consistent, but no longer asymptotically efficient, and the usual FGLS-estimated covariance matrix is incorrect. The latter problem is resolved by using a heteroskedasticity robust covariance estimator, *hccme* 0, 1, 2, or 3, for the FGLS estimator. The resulting Wald test of $\eta = 0$ then is asymptotically valid.

A GMM/OLS Contrast Test

Suppose we form a contrast between OLS and another linear estimator that is consistent if some regressors are endogenous. Let it take the form (MacKinnon, 1992, p. 125)

$$\hat{\beta}_A = (X'AX)^{-1}X'Ay \tag{6}$$

where A is a symmetric $n \times n$ matrix with rank no less than K. Then the contrast with the OLS estimator is

$$q = \hat{\beta}_A - \hat{\beta}_{\text{OLS}} = (X'AX)^{-1}X'AM_X y \tag{7}$$

and the question is whether $X'AM_X y$ has zero mean asymptotically. Going through the same steps as in section "Using an Artificial Regression," we can form the artificial regression:

$$y = X\beta + AX\delta + \text{error} \tag{8}$$

which leads to the estimator

$$\hat{\delta} = (X'AM_X AX)^{-1}X'AM_X y \tag{9}$$

and a robust Wald test statistic for the hypothesis $\delta = 0$ of

$$W_{\text{DM}} = y'M_X AX(X'AM_X\hat{\Omega}M_X AX)^{-1}X'AM_X y \overset{a}{\sim} \chi^2_{(\text{rank}[\cdot])} \tag{10}$$

where the degrees of freedom are the rank of the matrix inversed in the quadratic form. The rank is nominally K, but $M_X AX$ may not have rank K depending on the choice of A.[7]

One logical choice for A, since we would like to form the contrast with the most efficient consistent estimator, is $Z\hat{S}^{-1}Z'$. Then $\hat{\beta}_A = \hat{\beta}_{\text{EGMM}}$, which is the efficient two-step GMM estimator of β in the original model $y = X\beta + u$. In this case, $\hat{S} = Z'\tilde{\Omega}Z$, where $\tilde{\Omega}$ is a diagonal matrix of squared residuals based either on the OLS or IV estimator. The simplicity of this estimator is attractive. Let $\tilde{X} = M_X AX_1$ and it is easy to see that $\hat{\delta} = (\tilde{X}'\tilde{X})^{-1}\tilde{X}'y$, the robust covariance of which is $(\tilde{X}'\tilde{X})^{-1}\tilde{X}'\hat{\Omega}\tilde{X}(\tilde{X}'\tilde{X})^{-1}$.

Direct Testing in a GMM Framework

Creel (2004) suggests that we combine the sets of moment conditions that lead to OLS and IV estimators into a single estimation problem. The moment conditions leading to OLS are $E[x_i(y_i - x_i'\beta)] = 0$, and those leading to the IV estimator are $E[z_i(y_i - x_i'\beta)] = 0$. These have the sample analogues $h_1 = n^{-1}\sum h_{1i} = n^{-1}\sum x_i(y_i - x_i'\beta_1)$ and $h_2 = n^{-1}\sum h_{2i} = n^{-1}\sum z_i(y_i - x_i'\beta_2)$. Now let us assume that the "first round" estimates of $\beta' = (\beta_1' \ \beta_2')$ are $\hat{\beta}_1 = \hat{\beta}_{\text{OLS}}$(the OLS estimator of the original model $y = X\beta + u$) and $\hat{\beta}_2 = \hat{\beta}_{\text{GMM}}$(the optimal two-step estimator of the original model using instruments Z). Using these first round estimates, we can obtain $\hat{S} = n^{-1}\sum h_i(\hat{\beta})h_i(\hat{\beta})'$ and the two-step GMM estimator minimizes:

$$Q(\beta) = \left[n^{-1}\sum h_i\right]'\hat{S}^{-1}\left[n^{-1}\sum h_i\right] \tag{11}$$

The resulting estimator is

$$\hat{\beta}_{\text{GMM2}} = \left\{\begin{bmatrix} X'X & 0 \\ 0 & Z'X \end{bmatrix}'\hat{S}^{-1}\begin{bmatrix} X'X & 0 \\ 0 & Z'X \end{bmatrix}\right\}^{-1}\begin{bmatrix} X'X & 0 \\ 0 & Z'X \end{bmatrix}'\hat{S}^{-1}\begin{bmatrix} X'y \\ Z'y \end{bmatrix} \tag{12}$$

with asymptotic covariance matrix

$$V(\hat{\beta}_{\text{GMM2}}) = n\left\{\begin{bmatrix} X'X & 0 \\ 0 & Z'X \end{bmatrix}'\hat{S}^{-1}\begin{bmatrix} X'X & 0 \\ 0 & Z'X \end{bmatrix}\right\}^{-1} \tag{13}$$

A Wald test statistic for the null hypothesis that $H_0 : plim(\hat{\beta}_{\text{OLS}} - \hat{\beta}_{\text{GMM}}) = 0$ is

$$W_2 = (R\hat{\beta}_{\text{GMM2}})'[RV(\hat{\beta}_{\text{GMM2}})R']^{-1}(R\hat{\beta}_{\text{GMM2}}) \tag{14}$$

where $R = [I_K \quad -I_K]$. Under the null hypothesis, the test statistic W_2 has an asymptotic distribution with K_1 degrees of freedom.[8]

Hahn, Ham, and Moon Test

Hahn et al. (2011) (hereinafter HHM) develop a modified version of the Hausman test that is valid under heteroskedasticity. Their test compares a weak IV estimator to a strong IV estimator, but is easily modified to compare $\hat{\beta}_{\text{IV}}$ and $\hat{\beta}_{\text{OLS}}$ under heteroskedasticity. The HHM test statistic takes the form:

$$(\hat{\beta}_{\text{IV}} - \hat{\beta}_{\text{OLS}})'[V(\hat{\beta}_{\text{IV}} - \hat{\beta}_{\text{OLS}})]^{-1}(\hat{\beta}_{\text{IV}} - \hat{\beta}_{\text{OLS}})$$

where $V(\hat{\beta}_{\text{IV}} - \hat{\beta}_{\text{OLS}})$ is a consistent estimator of the asymptotic variance of $\hat{\beta}_{\text{IV}} - \hat{\beta}_{\text{OLS}}$. The HHM approach is to directly estimate the asymptotic covariance matrix of the contrast.[9] Under the null hypothesis,

$$\begin{aligned} \sqrt{n}(\hat{\beta}_{\text{IV}} - \hat{\beta}_{\text{OLS}}) &= \sqrt{n}(\hat{\beta}_{\text{IV}} - \beta) - \sqrt{n}(\hat{\beta}_{\text{OLS}} - \beta) \\ &= (n^{-1}X'P_ZX)^{-1}(n^{-1/2}X'P_Zu) - (n^{-1}X'X)^{-1}(n^{-1/2}X'u) \end{aligned}$$

and its asymptotic variance is given by

$$V(\sqrt{n}(\hat{\beta}_{\mathrm{IV}} - \hat{\beta}_{\mathrm{OLS}})) = [E(x_i z_i')(E(z_i z_i'))^{-1} E(z_i x_i')]^{-1} E(x_i z_i')(E(z_i z_i'))^{-1} E(z_i z_i' u_i^2) \times (E(z_i z_i'))^{-1} E(z_i x_i')[E(x_i z_i')(E(z_i z_i'))^{-1} E(z_i x_i')]^{-1} - [E(x_i z_i')(E(z_i z_i'))^{-1} E(z_i x_i')]^{-1} E(x_i z_i')(E(z_i z_i'))^{-1} E(z_i x_i' u_i^2)(E(x_i x_i'))^{-1} - (E(x_i x_i'))^{-1} E(x_i z_i' u_i^2)(E(z_i z_i'))^{-1} E(z_i x_i')[E(x_i z_i')(E(z_i z_i'))^{-1} E(z_i x_i')]^{-1} + (E(x_i x_i'))^{-1} E(x_i x_i' u_i^2)(E(x_i x_i'))^{-1}$$

We obtain a consistent estimator using

$$V(\sqrt{n}(\hat{\beta}_{\mathrm{IV}} - \hat{\beta}_{\mathrm{OLS}})) = \left[\left(n^{-1}\sum x_i z_i'\right)\left(n^{-1}\sum z_i z_i'\right)^{-1}\left(n^{-1}\sum z_i x_i'\right)\right]^{-1} \times \{A - B - B' + C\}\left[\left(n^{-1}\sum x_i z_i'\right)\left(n^{-1}\sum z_i z_i'\right)^{-1}\left(n^{-1}\sum z_i x_i'\right)\right]^{-1}$$

where

$$A = \left(n^{-1}\sum x_i z_i'\right)\left(n^{-1}\sum z_i z_i'\right)^{-1}\left(n^{-1}\sum z_i z_i' \hat{u}_i^2\right)\left(n^{-1}\sum z_i z_i'\right)^{-1}\left(n^{-1}\sum z_i x_i'\right)$$

$$B = \left(n^{-1}\sum x_i z_i'\right)\left(n^{-1}\sum z_i z_i'\right)^{-1}\left(n^{-1}\sum z_i x_i' \hat{u}_i^2\right)\left(n^{-1}\sum x_i x_i'\right)^{-1} \left[\left(n^{-1}\sum x_i z_i'\right)\left(n^{-1}\sum z_i z_i'\right)^{-1}\left(n^{-1}\sum z_i x_i'\right)\right]$$

$$C = \left[\left(n^{-1}\sum x_i z_i'\right)\left(n^{-1}\sum z_i z_i'\right)^{-1}\left(n^{-1}\sum z_i x_i'\right)\right]\left(n^{-1}\sum x_i x_i'\right)^{-1} \left(n^{-1}\sum x_i x_i' \hat{u}_i^2\right)\left(n^{-1}\sum x_i x_i'\right)^{-1} \times \left[\left(n^{-1}\sum x_i z_i'\right)\left(n^{-1}\sum z_i z_i'\right)^{-1}\left(n^{-1}\sum z_i x_i'\right)\right]$$

and $\hat{u}_i^2$ are the squared OLS residuals.

Finally, we note that following Hahn et al. (2011), the above results assume that included exogenous variables have been "partialled out." Thus, the variables in the regressions are the residuals when y, X_1, and Z, respectively, are regressed on X_2.

A MONTE CARLO EXPERIMENT

The model we consider is

$$y = \beta_1 + \beta_2 x_2 + \beta_3 x_3 + u = x_2 + x_3 + u \tag{15}$$

The variable x_2 is potentially endogenous with reduced form

$$x_2 = \pi_1 + \pi_2 z_2 + \pi_3 z_3 + \pi_4 x_3 + v = 0.5z_2 + 0.1z_3 + 0.5x_3 + v \tag{16}$$

The exogenous variables are jointly normal with correlation $c = 0.3$,

$$\begin{bmatrix} z_2 \\ z_3 \\ x_3 \\ z_4 \end{bmatrix} \sim N\left(\begin{bmatrix} 0 \\ 0 \\ 0 \\ 0 \end{bmatrix}, \begin{bmatrix} 1 & c & c & c \\ c & 1 & c & c \\ c & c & 1 & c \\ c & c & c & 1 \end{bmatrix} \right) \tag{17}$$

To introduce heteroskedasticity into the experiment, we set

$$\sigma_u^2 = \exp(\alpha_1 + \alpha_2 z) \tag{18}$$

where $z \sim N(0, 1)$ and will be chosen to be one of the exogenous variables in Eq. (17). Let $w = \alpha_1 + \alpha_2 z$, then

$$E(w) = \mu_w = \alpha_1 + \alpha_2 E(z) = \alpha_1 \tag{19}$$

and

$$\text{var}(w) = \sigma_w^2 = \text{var}(\alpha_1 + \alpha_2 z) = \alpha_2^2 \text{var}(z) = \alpha_2^2 \tag{20}$$

Using the properties of the log-normal distribution,

$$E(\sigma_u^2) = \exp(\mu_w + \sigma_w^2/2) = \exp(\alpha_1 + \alpha_2^2/2) \tag{21}$$

To control total error variation, we set $\alpha_1 + \alpha_2^2/2 = 2$. As α_2 is increased from 0, stronger heteroskedasticity related to z is induced, while setting $\alpha_1 = 2 - \alpha_2^2/2$ holds expected overall variation constant.

Endogeneity is controlled by inducing correlation between the structural equation error u in Eq. (15) and the reduced form error v in Eq. (16). We set

$$\begin{bmatrix} u \\ v \end{bmatrix} \sim N\left(\begin{bmatrix} \mu_1 \\ \mu_2 \end{bmatrix}, \Sigma = \begin{bmatrix} \sigma_u^2 & \rho\sigma_u\sigma_v \\ \rho\sigma_u\sigma_v & \sigma_v^2 \end{bmatrix} \right) = N\left(\begin{bmatrix} 0 \\ 0 \end{bmatrix}, \begin{bmatrix} \sigma_u^2 & \rho\sigma_u \\ \rho\sigma_u & 1 \end{bmatrix} \right) \tag{22}$$

The Cholesky decomposition of Σ is

$$\Sigma^{1/2} = \begin{bmatrix} \sigma_u & 0 \\ \rho\sigma_v & \sqrt{\sigma_v^2(1-\rho^2)} \end{bmatrix} = \begin{bmatrix} \sigma_u & 0 \\ \rho & \sqrt{(1-\rho^2)} \end{bmatrix} \tag{23}$$

Let u_1 and u_2 be independent standard normal random variables. Then the structural and reduced form errors with the desired distribution are obtained as[10]

$$\begin{bmatrix} u \\ v \end{bmatrix} = \Sigma^{1/2} \begin{bmatrix} u_1 \\ u_2 \end{bmatrix} = \begin{bmatrix} \sigma_u & 0 \\ \rho & \sqrt{(1-\rho^2)} \end{bmatrix} \begin{bmatrix} u_1 \\ u_2 \end{bmatrix} = \begin{bmatrix} \sigma_u u_1 \\ \rho u_1 + \sqrt{(1-\rho^2)} u_2 \end{bmatrix} \tag{24}$$

The key features are as follows:

- The first stage R^2 values are 0.42–0.43 over all experimental designs.
- Endogeneity is controlled by the parameter ρ (**rho**), which takes the values 0, 0.1, ..., 0.7.
- Heteroskedasticity is controlled by the parameter α_2 (**a2**) that takes values 0, 0.1, ..., 0.8. The culprit variable z is considered to be each of the exogenous variables z_2 (**Model 1**), z_3 (**Model 2**), x_3 (**Model 3**), and z_4 (**Model 4**) in turn. The variables z_2 and z_3 are external instruments, the former strong and the latter weaker. The exogenous variable x_3 is included in the structural equation and is related to the endogenous variable x_2 moderately.
- Samples of sizes $n = 100$, 200, 300, and 400 are considered.

For reference purposes, an abbreviated glossary of notation is given as follows:

n	sample size
a2	sig2(n) = exp(a1 + a2*culprit)
rho	correlation between structural and reduced form error
LM	LM = N*R^2 test for heteroskedasticity in OLS regression, IV culprit
LM_dwh	LM = N*R^2 test for heteroskedasticity in DWH regression, RHS culprit
t	DWH t-stat
rt1	DWH robust hccme = 1 t-stat
rt2	DWH robust hccme = 2 t-stat
rt3	DWH robust hccme = 3 t-stat

rt1ggls	DWH general GLS robust hccme = 1 *t*-stat
rt2ggls	DWH general GLS robust hccme = 2 *t*-stat
rt3ggls	DWH general GLS robust hccme = 3 *t*-stat
rt1sgls	DWH specific GLS robust hccme = 1 *t*-stat
rt2sgls	DWH specific GLS robust hccme = 2 *t*-stat
rt3sgls	DWH specific GLS robust hccme = 3 *t*-stat
rt1cgls	DWH correct GLS robust hccme = 1 *t*-stat
rt2cgls	DWH correct GLS robust hccme = 2 *t*-stat
rt3cgls	DWH correct GLS robust hccme = 3 *t*-stat
gmm	GMM system chi-square test with two-step estimator
dm	Davidson and MacKinnon chi-square test
hhm	Hahn, Ham, and Moon chi-square test

The augmented DWH regression for the experiment is

$$y = \beta_1 + \beta_2 x_2 + \beta_3 x_3 + \eta \hat{v} + \varepsilon \tag{25}$$

where $\hat{v}$ is the least squares residual from the first-stage Eq. (16). Heteroskedasticity is monitored using two LM tests. In the first case, the squared residuals from Eq. (15) $\hat{u}^2$ are regressed on the potential instrument set, variables z_2, z_3, and x_3. Then the first LM test statistic (**LM**) is the sample size times the squared correlation between the squared residuals and the fitted value from this regression. A second LM test (**LM_dwh**) uses the squared residuals from the augmented regression (25) regressed on x_2, x_3, and $\hat{v}$. In each case, the *p*-value is based on a $\chi^2_{(3)}$ distribution.[11]

The usual regression-based Hausman test based on Eq. (25) is a *t*-test of the null hypothesis $H_0 : \eta = 0$. If heteroskedasticity is expected, the usual advice is to employ a heteroskedasticity robust covariance matrix estimator using *hccme* 1, 2, or 3. The resulting tests are denoted **rt1**, **rt2**, and **rt3**. The simulation results below report the percentage rejections at the 5% level.

An alternative to using least squares to estimate Eq. (25) is generalized least squares. Usually one or more exogenous variables are linked to the heteroskedasticity based on some combination of diagnostics, like residual plots and the LM test, and intuition. In our experiments, we broadly define as a general model the heteroskedasticity related to the included exogenous variable, x_3, and the two external instruments, z_2 and z_3. For modeling, we choose Harvey's (1976) multiplicative heteroskedasticity. This model is easy to estimate, robust, and parsimonious. We propose the trial model:

$$\sigma^2_\varepsilon = \exp(\alpha_1 + \alpha_2 z_2 + \alpha_3 z_3 + \alpha_4 x_3) \tag{26}$$

FGLS is implemented by estimating the log-linear model in Eq. (27) using OLS:

$$\ln(\breve{\varepsilon}^2) = \alpha_1 + \alpha_2 z_2 + \alpha_3 z_3 + \alpha_4 x_3 + \text{error} \tag{27}$$

The error variance is then estimated by

$$\hat{\sigma}_\varepsilon^2 = \exp(\hat{\alpha}_1 + \hat{\alpha}_2 z_2 + \hat{\alpha}_3 z_3 + \hat{\alpha}_4 x_3) \tag{28}$$

The observations in Eq. (25) are then weighted by $\hat{\sigma}_\varepsilon$ and least squares applied to the model:

$$\frac{y}{\hat{\sigma}_\varepsilon} = y^* = \beta_1 \frac{1}{\hat{\sigma}_\varepsilon} + \beta_2 \frac{x_2}{\hat{\sigma}_\varepsilon} + \beta_{i3} \frac{x_3}{\hat{\sigma}_\varepsilon} + \eta \frac{\hat{v}}{\hat{\sigma}_\varepsilon} + \frac{\varepsilon}{\hat{\sigma}_\varepsilon} = \beta_1 x_1^* + \beta_2 x_2^* + \beta_3 x_3^* + \eta \hat{v}^* + \varepsilon_i^* \tag{29}$$

The test of $H_0: \eta = 0$ is carried out using the t-test with the robust covariance *hccme* 1, 2, and 3. The resulting test statistics are **rt1ggls**, **rt2ggls**, and **rt3ggls**. The "**ggls**" part denotes what we call a "general" generalized least squares approach, where x_3, z_2, and z_3 are all considered potential culprits in the heteroskedasticity. A second variation we call the "specific" generalized least squares approach in which the heteroskedasticity model includes only the stronger IV z_2. This choice is incorrect in all but **Model 1**; however, since z_2 is correlated with the other exogenous variables, this choice may have some power. The resulting tests are called **rt1sgls**, **rt2sgls**, and **rt3sgls**, where the **sgls** part denotes "specific" generalized least squares. The final GLS approach uses the true culprit variable, z_2, z_3, x_3, or z_4, from the data generation process (DGP) of the four models. This would correspond to the case when we happen to model the heteroskedasticity pattern exactly correctly. The resulting tests are called **rt1cgls**, **rt2cgls**, and **rt3cgls**, where the **cgls** part denotes "correct" generalized least squares. The reason for implementing a robust covariance matrix in the FGLS estimation is that the model for heteroskedasticity (26) might be incorrect. Our suspicion is that if Eq. (26) is even close to correct, the estimator of Eq. (29) will be "better" than the least squares estimator of Eq. (25). However, to guard against misspecification in Eq. (26), we can apply robust inference, and hope that the resulting tests have reasonable size and power properties.

MONTE CARLO RESULTS

Selected experimental results[12] are reported in Tables 1a–4c. These summarize 20,000 Monte Carlo simulations. Our discussion is organized

Table 1a. Model 1, Nominal Rejection Rates, rho = 0.0.

a2	LM	LM_dwh	t	rt1	rt2	rt3	rt1ggls	rt2ggls	rt3ggls	rt1sgls	rt2sgls	rt3sgls	rt1cgls	rt2cgls	rt3cgls	gmm2	dm	hhm
$n = 100$																		
0.0	0.4973	0.5019	0.0507	0.0587	0.0564	0.0490	0.0824	0.0781	0.0685	0.0691	0.0658	0.0577	0.0691	0.0658	0.0577	0.0373	0.0703	0.0529
0.1	0.4514	0.4619	0.0536	0.0603	0.0579	0.0510	0.0836	0.0791	0.0682	0.0705	0.0673	0.0586	0.0705	0.0673	0.0586	0.0399	0.0726	0.0545
0.2	0.3439	0.3578	0.0562	0.0617	0.0593	0.0527	0.0825	0.0774	0.0669	0.0724	0.0685	0.0589	0.0724	0.0685	0.0589	0.0389	0.0714	0.0553
0.3	0.2247	0.2461	0.0588	0.0595	0.0578	0.0517	0.0809	0.0765	0.0657	0.0682	0.0646	0.0567	0.0682	0.0646	0.0567	0.0396	0.0728	0.0549
0.4	0.1269	0.1477	0.0643	0.0620	0.0596	0.0526	0.0800	0.0748	0.0637	0.0698	0.0657	0.0565	0.0698	0.0657	0.0565	0.0392	0.0695	0.0542
0.5	0.0674	0.0845	0.0671	0.0572	0.0550	0.0474	0.0802	0.0740	0.0636	0.0695	0.0641	0.0532	0.0695	0.0641	0.0532	0.0382	0.0674	0.0511
0.6	0.0327	0.0453	0.0754	0.0625	0.0593	0.0514	0.0799	0.0725	0.0598	0.0691	0.0637	0.0526	0.0691	0.0637	0.0526	0.0403	0.0729	0.0528
0.7	0.0163	0.0252	0.0857	0.0616	0.0583	0.0511	0.0817	0.0749	0.0627	0.0693	0.0633	0.0520	0.0693	0.0633	0.0520	0.0407	0.0691	0.0527
0.8	0.0084	0.0146	0.0941	0.0612	0.0580	0.0498	0.0847	0.0762	0.0618	0.0739	0.0674	0.0547	0.0739	0.0674	0.0547	0.0396	0.0730	0.0507
$n = 200$																		
0.0	0.4989	0.4963	0.0488	0.0532	0.0518	0.0485	0.0635	0.0620	0.0570	0.0575	0.0567	0.0531	0.0575	0.0567	0.0531	0.0433	0.0591	0.0508
0.1	0.4107	0.4168	0.0506	0.0549	0.0538	0.0505	0.0655	0.0633	0.0587	0.0596	0.0582	0.0544	0.0596	0.0582	0.0544	0.0433	0.0574	0.0524
0.2	0.2255	0.2381	0.0546	0.0550	0.0537	0.0506	0.0668	0.0650	0.0607	0.0599	0.0583	0.0536	0.0599	0.0583	0.0536	0.0442	0.0612	0.0520
0.3	0.0893	0.1022	0.0575	0.0551	0.0537	0.0502	0.0676	0.0656	0.0608	0.0620	0.0601	0.0555	0.0620	0.0601	0.0555	0.0446	0.0592	0.0520
0.4	0.0258	0.0326	0.0602	0.0526	0.0512	0.0476	0.0641	0.0615	0.0564	0.0583	0.0564	0.0513	0.0583	0.0564	0.0513	0.0413	0.0611	0.0496
0.5	0.0065	0.0093	0.0696	0.0547	0.0534	0.0496	0.0666	0.0635	0.0578	0.0609	0.0580	0.0530	0.0609	0.0580	0.0530	0.0450	0.0574	0.0508
0.6	0.0015	0.0026	0.0751	0.0539	0.0526	0.0495	0.0659	0.0627	0.0572	0.0609	0.0582	0.0522	0.0609	0.0582	0.0522	0.0446	0.0580	0.0495
0.7	0.0003	0.0007	0.0875	0.0566	0.0546	0.0503	0.0665	0.0628	0.0566	0.0623	0.0590	0.0523	0.0623	0.0590	0.0523	0.0460	0.0595	0.0509
0.8	0.0001	0.0002	0.1009	0.0578	0.0557	0.0521	0.0690	0.0638	0.0567	0.0641	0.0589	0.0527	0.0641	0.0589	0.0527	0.0470	0.0618	0.0522
$n = 400$																		
0.0	0.4993	0.4984	0.0484	0.0492	0.0487	0.0472	0.0552	0.0545	0.0526	0.0528	0.0522	0.0503	0.0528	0.0522	0.0503	0.0436	0.0523	0.0480
0.1	0.3304	0.3365	0.0479	0.0492	0.0488	0.0471	0.0547	0.0541	0.0519	0.0513	0.0507	0.0491	0.0513	0.0507	0.0491	0.0448	0.0523	0.0479
0.2	0.0955	0.1046	0.0508	0.0510	0.0505	0.0487	0.0565	0.0556	0.0534	0.0544	0.0538	0.0518	0.0544	0.0538	0.0518	0.0457	0.0550	0.0499
0.3	0.0138	0.0169	0.0595	0.0550	0.0543	0.0524	0.0606	0.0596	0.0576	0.0562	0.0555	0.0535	0.0562	0.0555	0.0535	0.0496	0.0569	0.0529
0.4	0.0010	0.0014	0.0626	0.0517	0.0510	0.0490	0.0578	0.0564	0.0541	0.0544	0.0531	0.0506	0.0544	0.0531	0.0506	0.0466	0.0554	0.0501
0.5	0.0001	0.0001	0.0681	0.0518	0.0513	0.0499	0.0595	0.0583	0.0551	0.0559	0.0547	0.0512	0.0559	0.0547	0.0512	0.0466	0.0558	0.0498
0.6	0.0000	0.0000	0.0807	0.0549	0.0543	0.0523	0.0600	0.0578	0.0545	0.0567	0.0547	0.0513	0.0567	0.0547	0.0513	0.0497	0.0567	0.0527
0.7	0.0000	0.0000	0.0869	0.0530	0.0520	0.0504	0.0584	0.0559	0.0524	0.0563	0.0536	0.0506	0.0563	0.0536	0.0506	0.0473	0.0564	0.0500
0.8	0.0000	0.0000	0.0998	0.0524	0.0515	0.0493	0.0604	0.0580	0.0539	0.0586	0.0556	0.0513	0.0586	0.0556	0.0513	0.0472	0.0573	0.0488

Table 1b. Model 1, Size-Corrected Rejection Rates, rho = 0.3.

a2	LM	LM_dwh	t	rt1	rt2	rt3	rt1ggls	rt2ggls	rt3ggls	rt1sgls	rt2sgls	rt3sgls	rt1cgls	rt2cgls	rt3cgls	gmm2	dm	hhm
$n = 100$																		
0.0	0.4877	0.4963	0.2660	0.2584	0.2579	0.2580	0.2266	0.2281	0.2281	0.2463	0.2455	0.2443	0.2463	0.2455	0.2443	0.2435	0.2035	0.2577
0.1	0.4507	0.4576	0.2578	0.2530	0.2526	0.2520	0.2265	0.2271	0.2270	0.2364	0.2368	0.2368	0.2364	0.2368	0.2368	0.2353	0.2019	0.2491
0.2	0.3458	0.3643	0.2546	0.2447	0.2436	0.2425	0.2257	0.2253	0.2259	0.2353	0.2357	0.2366	0.2353	0.2357	0.2366	0.2345	0.1964	0.2431
0.3	0.2247	0.2461	0.2499	0.2417	0.2413	0.2407	0.2247	0.2238	0.2238	0.2394	0.2399	0.2384	0.2394	0.2399	0.2384	0.2281	0.1920	0.2401
0.4	0.1305	0.1513	0.2354	0.2319	0.2311	0.2313	0.2258	0.2277	0.2264	0.2376	0.2385	0.2386	0.2376	0.2385	0.2386	0.2184	0.1927	0.2325
0.5	0.0701	0.0859	0.2358	0.2368	0.2358	0.2357	0.2306	0.2290	0.2282	0.2452	0.2462	0.2436	0.2452	0.2462	0.2436	0.2150	0.1889	0.2329
0.6	0.0346	0.0472	0.2089	0.2049	0.2051	0.2060	0.2236	0.2255	0.2271	0.2361	0.2347	0.2341	0.2361	0.2347	0.2341	0.1920	0.1664	0.2072
0.7	0.0176	0.0267	0.2026	0.1991	0.1993	0.2005	0.2153	0.2150	0.2138	0.2255	0.2261	0.2273	0.2255	0.2261	0.2273	0.1836	0.1624	0.1983
0.8	0.0088	0.0143	0.1913	0.1933	0.1929	0.1923	0.2043	0.2061	0.2044	0.2116	0.2123	0.2118	0.2116	0.2123	0.2118	0.1744	0.1497	0.1919
$n = 200$																		
0.0	0.4994	0.5008	0.5069	0.4994	0.4996	0.4990	0.4676	0.4674	0.4669	0.4825	0.4817	0.4814	0.4825	0.4817	0.4814	0.4856	0.4064	0.4949
0.1	0.4052	0.4110	0.5033	0.4920	0.4913	0.4910	0.4623	0.4626	0.4613	0.4808	0.4801	0.4796	0.4808	0.4801	0.4796	0.4852	0.4052	0.4920
0.2	0.2278	0.2397	0.4850	0.4781	0.4779	0.4776	0.4594	0.4595	0.4575	0.4763	0.4751	0.4745	0.4763	0.4751	0.4745	0.4720	0.3877	0.4789
0.3	0.0903	0.1008	0.4679	0.4622	0.4619	0.4627	0.4502	0.4487	0.4470	0.4633	0.4623	0.4624	0.4633	0.4623	0.4624	0.4510	0.3771	0.4592
0.4	0.0271	0.0332	0.4515	0.4469	0.4469	0.4476	0.4467	0.4472	0.4476	0.4650	0.4638	0.4629	0.4650	0.4638	0.4629	0.4333	0.3519	0.4435
0.5	0.0066	0.0090	0.4229	0.4220	0.4219	0.4215	0.4340	0.4345	0.4352	0.4506	0.4496	0.4503	0.4506	0.4496	0.4503	0.4090	0.3449	0.4206
0.6	0.0016	0.0025	0.3974	0.3913	0.3914	0.3925	0.4222	0.4225	0.4219	0.4407	0.4371	0.4373	0.4407	0.4371	0.4373	0.3794	0.3157	0.3958
0.7	0.0004	0.0007	0.3552	0.3579	0.3574	0.3580	0.4107	0.4098	0.4089	0.4265	0.4236	0.4213	0.4265	0.4236	0.4213	0.3433	0.2874	0.3564
0.8	0.0001	0.0002	0.3311	0.3226	0.3228	0.3229	0.4074	0.4052	0.3982	0.4146	0.4111	0.4062	0.4146	0.4111	0.4062	0.3124	0.2607	0.3254
$n = 400$																		
0.0	0.4983	0.5002	0.8088	0.8103	0.8103	0.8099	0.7871	0.7870	0.7874	0.8004	0.8001	0.8000	0.8004	0.8001	0.8000	0.8081	0.7196	0.8103
0.1	0.3289	0.3368	0.8024	0.7974	0.7973	0.7971	0.7810	0.7808	0.7805	0.7905	0.7908	0.7905	0.7905	0.7908	0.7905	0.7920	0.7091	0.7954
0.2	0.0987	0.1066	0.7837	0.7763	0.7761	0.7759	0.7702	0.7702	0.7701	0.7772	0.7768	0.7763	0.7772	0.7768	0.7763	0.7722	0.6833	0.7752
0.3	0.0137	0.0167	0.7605	0.7501	0.7499	0.7499	0.7602	0.7608	0.7600	0.7734	0.7733	0.7732	0.7734	0.7733	0.7732	0.7479	0.6630	0.7515
0.4	0.0011	0.0015	0.7445	0.7403	0.7396	0.7394	0.7632	0.7629	0.7618	0.7730	0.7718	0.7709	0.7730	0.7718	0.7709	0.7334	0.6407	0.7396
0.5	0.0001	0.0001	0.7062	0.7014	0.7013	0.7011	0.7471	0.7453	0.7443	0.7589	0.7570	0.7560	0.7589	0.7570	0.7560	0.6996	0.6065	0.7036
0.6	0.0000	0.0000	0.6643	0.6588	0.6580	0.6577	0.7356	0.7343	0.7340	0.7475	0.7462	0.7452	0.7475	0.7462	0.7452	0.6518	0.5587	0.6601
0.7	0.0000	0.0000	0.6292	0.6283	0.6284	0.6288	0.7233	0.7229	0.7195	0.7313	0.7309	0.7287	0.7313	0.7309	0.7287	0.6228	0.5220	0.6320
0.8	0.0000	0.0000	0.5733	0.5771	0.5775	0.5770	0.7006	0.6981	0.6966	0.7092	0.7085	0.7050	0.7092	0.7085	0.7050	0.5664	0.4767	0.5795

Table 1c. Model 1, Size-Corrected Rejection Rates, rho = 0.6.

a2	LM	LM_dwh	t	rt1	rt2	rt3	rt1ggls	rt2ggls	rt3ggls	rt1sgls	rt2sgls	rt3sgls	rt1cgls	rt2cgls	rt3cgls	gmm2	dm	hhm
$n=100$																		
0.0	0.4808	0.4968	0.8867	0.8764	0.8757	0.8751	0.8238	0.8238	0.8222	0.8547	0.8532	0.8514	0.8547	0.8532	0.8514	0.8458	0.8196	0.8729
0.1	0.4403	0.4595	0.8767	0.8646	0.8641	0.8636	0.8123	0.8116	0.8110	0.8370	0.8363	0.8346	0.8370	0.8363	0.8346	0.8310	0.8056	0.8599
0.2	0.3485	0.3622	0.8749	0.8593	0.8578	0.8569	0.8154	0.8144	0.8130	0.8412	0.8405	0.8391	0.8412	0.8405	0.8391	0.8320	0.8056	0.8567
0.3	0.2286	0.2460	0.8578	0.8423	0.8406	0.8400	0.8067	0.8055	0.8021	0.8330	0.8320	0.8294	0.8330	0.8320	0.8294	0.8098	0.7739	0.8410
0.4	0.1375	0.1521	0.8278	0.8147	0.8134	0.8127	0.7963	0.7969	0.7947	0.8232	0.8228	0.8194	0.8232	0.8228	0.8194	0.7789	0.7590	0.8156
0.5	0.0750	0.0859	0.8119	0.7980	0.7964	0.7952	0.7879	0.7849	0.7814	0.8181	0.8160	0.8116	0.8181	0.8160	0.8116	0.7440	0.7236	0.7947
0.6	0.0400	0.0480	0.7657	0.7450	0.7447	0.7440	0.7695	0.7670	0.7630	0.7949	0.7914	0.7879	0.7949	0.7914	0.7879	0.6981	0.6642	0.7474
0.7	0.0216	0.0277	0.7175	0.6967	0.6960	0.6947	0.7428	0.7379	0.7297	0.7713	0.7681	0.7625	0.7713	0.7681	0.7625	0.6444	0.6260	0.6947
0.8	0.0117	0.0163	0.6758	0.6632	0.6612	0.6571	0.7143	0.7142	0.7076	0.7386	0.7328	0.7267	0.7386	0.7328	0.7267	0.6039	0.5782	0.6586
$n=200$																		
0.0	0.4831	0.4978	0.9966	0.9962	0.9962	0.9962	0.9915	0.9915	0.9914	0.9945	0.9945	0.9945	0.9945	0.9945	0.9945	0.9953	0.9899	0.9960
0.1	0.4004	0.4137	0.9956	0.9950	0.9949	0.9949	0.9912	0.9912	0.9907	0.9936	0.9935	0.9934	0.9936	0.9935	0.9934	0.9938	0.9886	0.9950
0.2	0.2328	0.2407	0.9947	0.9942	0.9941	0.9941	0.9907	0.9899	0.9895	0.9933	0.9932	0.9930	0.9933	0.9932	0.9930	0.9929	0.9864	0.9941
0.3	0.0967	0.1033	0.9918	0.9908	0.9907	0.9907	0.9894	0.9892	0.9889	0.9909	0.9908	0.9907	0.9909	0.9908	0.9907	0.9886	0.9805	0.9905
0.4	0.0317	0.0352	0.9882	0.9864	0.9863	0.9861	0.9874	0.9873	0.9867	0.9906	0.9901	0.9894	0.9906	0.9901	0.9894	0.9827	0.9715	0.9863
0.5	0.0091	0.0102	0.9816	0.9774	0.9772	0.9770	0.9828	0.9824	0.9813	0.9857	0.9850	0.9841	0.9857	0.9850	0.9841	0.9730	0.9603	0.9779
0.6	0.0024	0.0029	0.9710	0.9636	0.9633	0.9633	0.9782	0.9772	0.9751	0.9833	0.9820	0.9802	0.9833	0.9820	0.9802	0.9551	0.9389	0.9649
0.7	0.0006	0.0009	0.9554	0.9480	0.9472	0.9470	0.9711	0.9687	0.9663	0.9770	0.9746	0.9720	0.9770	0.9746	0.9720	0.9374	0.9105	0.9481
0.8	0.0002	0.0003	0.9287	0.9178	0.9171	0.9167	0.9664	0.9625	0.9579	0.9711	0.9680	0.9627	0.9711	0.9680	0.9627	0.9016	0.8711	0.9204

Table 2a. Model 2, Nominal Rejection Rates, rho = 0.0.

a2	LM	LM_dwh	t	rt1	rt2	rt3	rt1ggls	rt2ggls	rt3ggls	rt1sgls	rt2sgls	rt3sgls	rt1cgls	rt2cgls	rt3cgls	gmm2	dm	hhm
$n = 100$																		
0.0	0.4973	0.5019	0.0507	0.0587	0.0564	0.0490	0.0824	0.0781	0.0685	0.0691	0.0658	0.0577	0.0658	0.0628	0.0551	0.0373	0.0703	0.0529
0.1	0.4527	0.4920	0.0530	0.0598	0.0581	0.0513	0.0830	0.0786	0.0682	0.0695	0.0671	0.0586	0.0675	0.0646	0.0566	0.0401	0.0727	0.0552
0.2	0.3406	0.4581	0.0532	0.0603	0.0577	0.0505	0.0815	0.0769	0.0658	0.0704	0.0673	0.0594	0.0675	0.0645	0.0555	0.0380	0.0717	0.0538
0.3	0.2216	0.4133	0.0532	0.0598	0.0577	0.0507	0.0818	0.0766	0.0666	0.0668	0.0633	0.0558	0.0670	0.0643	0.0566	0.0392	0.0723	0.0535
0.4	0.1267	0.3697	0.0563	0.0598	0.0575	0.0503	0.0813	0.0756	0.0657	0.0674	0.0647	0.0568	0.0663	0.0626	0.0536	0.0365	0.0703	0.0536
0.5	0.0662	0.3277	0.0531	0.0553	0.0534	0.0468	0.0824	0.0761	0.0645	0.0631	0.0602	0.0519	0.0659	0.0619	0.0525	0.0378	0.0710	0.0499
0.6	0.0327	0.2931	0.0539	0.0550	0.0532	0.0472	0.0838	0.0777	0.0657	0.0636	0.0606	0.0531	0.0679	0.0634	0.0541	0.0354	0.0735	0.0499
0.7	0.0162	0.2591	0.0568	0.0577	0.0556	0.0486	0.0835	0.0764	0.0637	0.0664	0.0633	0.0553	0.0684	0.0630	0.0536	0.0359	0.0690	0.0522
0.8	0.0082	0.2374	0.0591	0.0576	0.0546	0.0482	0.0847	0.0757	0.0622	0.0667	0.0625	0.0534	0.0709	0.0644	0.0527	0.0351	0.0734	0.0507
$n = 200$																		
0.0	0.4989	0.4963	0.0488	0.0532	0.0518	0.0485	0.0635	0.0620	0.0570	0.0575	0.0567	0.0531	0.0560	0.0549	0.0508	0.0433	0.0591	0.0508
0.1	0.4110	0.4763	0.0504	0.0544	0.0535	0.0501	0.0642	0.0627	0.0586	0.0598	0.0584	0.0536	0.0575	0.0565	0.0530	0.0432	0.0577	0.0517
0.2	0.2287	0.4145	0.0515	0.0546	0.0533	0.0502	0.0673	0.0651	0.0603	0.0595	0.0584	0.0548	0.0579	0.0564	0.0529	0.0442	0.0617	0.0517
0.3	0.0902	0.3420	0.0514	0.0540	0.0527	0.0493	0.0657	0.0638	0.0597	0.0600	0.0585	0.0543	0.0595	0.0579	0.0540	0.0439	0.0600	0.0514
0.4	0.0273	0.2689	0.0515	0.0514	0.0505	0.0471	0.0634	0.0608	0.0563	0.0576	0.0562	0.0524	0.0571	0.0549	0.0495	0.0406	0.0633	0.0483
0.5	0.0067	0.2094	0.0515	0.0529	0.0514	0.0476	0.0666	0.0633	0.0581	0.0581	0.0563	0.0532	0.0600	0.0581	0.0537	0.0422	0.0577	0.0489
0.6	0.0016	0.1696	0.0530	0.0509	0.0496	0.0458	0.0645	0.0607	0.0550	0.0570	0.0556	0.0511	0.0576	0.0544	0.0489	0.0401	0.0587	0.0472
0.7	0.0004	0.1384	0.0542	0.0522	0.0511	0.0474	0.0659	0.0621	0.0566	0.0560	0.0544	0.0505	0.0591	0.0564	0.0511	0.0420	0.0588	0.0494
0.8	0.0001	0.1182	0.0601	0.0534	0.0521	0.0484	0.0690	0.0647	0.0577	0.0589	0.0571	0.0535	0.0605	0.0574	0.0519	0.0434	0.0593	0.0502
$n = 400$																		
0.0	0.4993	0.4984	0.0484	0.0492	0.0487	0.0472	0.0552	0.0545	0.0526	0.0528	0.0522	0.0503	0.0517	0.0512	0.0497	0.0436	0.0523	0.0480
0.1	0.3341	0.4524	0.0478	0.0494	0.0486	0.0471	0.0543	0.0535	0.0516	0.0512	0.0508	0.0490	0.0516	0.0505	0.0481	0.0452	0.0527	0.0482
0.2	0.0973	0.3406	0.0503	0.0513	0.0507	0.0490	0.0567	0.0558	0.0533	0.0538	0.0531	0.0511	0.0516	0.0510	0.0492	0.0448	0.0550	0.0501
0.3	0.0137	0.2293	0.0534	0.0548	0.0545	0.0527	0.0586	0.0576	0.0552	0.0561	0.0557	0.0538	0.0549	0.0541	0.0524	0.0495	0.0557	0.0531
0.4	0.0011	0.1405	0.0512	0.0509	0.0503	0.0488	0.0569	0.0556	0.0530	0.0532	0.0523	0.0501	0.0537	0.0526	0.0510	0.0458	0.0561	0.0501
0.5	0.0001	0.0858	0.0533	0.0520	0.0512	0.0498	0.0587	0.0573	0.0548	0.0552	0.0542	0.0519	0.0534	0.0524	0.0502	0.0468	0.0568	0.0505
0.6	0.0000	0.0537	0.0565	0.0530	0.0526	0.0507	0.0605	0.0590	0.0568	0.0549	0.0542	0.0524	0.0558	0.0541	0.0518	0.0476	0.0552	0.0516
0.7	0.0000	0.0372	0.0552	0.0499	0.0494	0.0477	0.0590	0.0569	0.0536	0.0526	0.0518	0.0495	0.0549	0.0536	0.0508	0.0452	0.0537	0.0486
0.8	0.0000	0.0285	0.0580	0.0512	0.0506	0.0485	0.0607	0.0583	0.0546	0.0518	0.0513	0.0491	0.0566	0.0546	0.0508	0.0460	0.0543	0.0492

Table 2b. Model 2, Size-Corrected Rejection Rates, rho = 0.3.

a2	LM	LM_dwh	t	rt1	rt2	rt3	rt1ggls	rt2ggls	rt3ggls	rt1sgls	rt2sgls	rt3sgls	rt1cgls	rt2cgls	rt3cgls	gmm2	dm	hhm
$n = 100$																		
0.0	0.4877	0.4963	0.2660	0.2584	0.2579	0.2580	0.2266	0.2281	0.2281	0.2463	0.2455	0.2443	0.2453	0.2456	0.2451	0.2435	0.2035	0.2577
0.1	0.4484	0.4865	0.2581	0.2550	0.2542	0.2532	0.2288	0.2293	0.2291	0.2416	0.2412	0.2420	0.2460	0.2462	0.2463	0.2378	0.2016	0.2499
0.2	0.3411	0.4606	0.2558	0.2505	0.2496	0.2490	0.2278	0.2280	0.2265	0.2324	0.2316	0.2306	0.2429	0.2417	0.2412	0.2391	0.2005	0.2473
0.3	0.2223	0.4135	0.2586	0.2517	0.2509	0.2499	0.2263	0.2246	0.2259	0.2424	0.2424	0.2408	0.2395	0.2412	0.2406	0.2373	0.1993	0.2491
0.4	0.1265	0.3713	0.2500	0.2490	0.2482	0.2488	0.2268	0.2284	0.2296	0.2423	0.2414	0.2417	0.2483	0.2484	0.2481	0.2419	0.2000	0.2495
0.5	0.0674	0.3250	0.2531	0.2515	0.2522	0.2526	0.2292	0.2307	0.2316	0.2470	0.2479	0.2495	0.2499	0.2486	0.2466	0.2391	0.1976	0.2531
0.6	0.0334	0.2881	0.2381	0.2348	0.2355	0.2347	0.2215	0.2213	0.2202	0.2340	0.2358	0.2350	0.2317	0.2309	0.2307	0.2289	0.1883	0.2349
0.7	0.0176	0.2607	0.2351	0.2329	0.2323	0.2323	0.2230	0.2217	0.2221	0.2270	0.2266	0.2270	0.2371	0.2381	0.2365	0.2284	0.1874	0.2316
0.8	0.0084	0.2398	0.2230	0.2241	0.2250	0.2253	0.2061	0.2048	0.2051	0.2192	0.2188	0.2200	0.2241	0.2232	0.2244	0.2209	0.1732	0.2257
$n = 200$																		
0.0	0.4994	0.5008	0.5069	0.4994	0.4996	0.4990	0.4676	0.4674	0.4669	0.4825	0.4817	0.4814	0.4906	0.4897	0.4899	0.4856	0.4064	0.4949
0.1	0.4040	0.4747	0.5046	0.4970	0.4963	0.4957	0.4648	0.4644	0.4646	0.4795	0.4793	0.4797	0.4857	0.4862	0.4861	0.4926	0.4075	0.4958
0.2	0.2226	0.4191	0.4921	0.4878	0.4873	0.4870	0.4526	0.4521	0.4520	0.4708	0.4715	0.4709	0.4850	0.4839	0.4829	0.4794	0.3887	0.4854
0.3	0.0887	0.3396	0.4900	0.4809	0.4801	0.4802	0.4495	0.4490	0.4495	0.4653	0.4653	0.4650	0.4713	0.4711	0.4708	0.4714	0.3887	0.4782
0.4	0.0275	0.2681	0.4793	0.4773	0.4779	0.4789	0.4536	0.4530	0.4523	0.4618	0.4614	0.4612	0.4741	0.4737	0.4729	0.4690	0.3698	0.4779
0.5	0.0068	0.2095	0.4723	0.4700	0.4688	0.4683	0.4438	0.4444	0.4451	0.4547	0.4557	0.4551	0.4574	0.4572	0.4588	0.4638	0.3815	0.4673
0.6	0.0016	0.1640	0.4526	0.4555	0.4552	0.4539	0.4436	0.4423	0.4392	0.4469	0.4465	0.4449	0.4625	0.4615	0.4608	0.4478	0.3664	0.4542
0.7	0.0004	0.1343	0.4352	0.4337	0.4336	0.4322	0.4223	0.4242	0.4235	0.4380	0.4374	0.4368	0.4410	0.4421	0.4395	0.4351	0.3528	0.4310
0.8	0.0001	0.1179	0.4071	0.4131	0.4124	0.4116	0.4091	0.4087	0.4096	0.4129	0.4130	0.4128	0.4272	0.4257	0.4239	0.4134	0.3451	0.4119
$n = 400$																		
0.0	0.4983	0.5002	0.8088	0.8103	0.8103	0.8099	0.7871	0.7870	0.7874	0.8004	0.8001	0.8000	0.8015	0.8020	0.8018	0.8081	0.7196	0.8103
0.1	0.3287	0.4529	0.8041	0.7982	0.7985	0.7989	0.7796	0.7792	0.7786	0.7911	0.7910	0.7910	0.7936	0.7933	0.7934	0.7926	0.7105	0.7976
0.2	0.0994	0.3452	0.7895	0.7863	0.7863	0.7861	0.7724	0.7725	0.7722	0.7806	0.7806	0.7799	0.7866	0.7867	0.7862	0.7855	0.6924	0.7863
0.3	0.0137	0.2269	0.7767	0.7713	0.7711	0.7714	0.7636	0.7637	0.7631	0.7688	0.7687	0.7688	0.7766	0.7762	0.7759	0.7671	0.6880	0.7718
0.4	0.0011	0.1396	0.7813	0.7780	0.7772	0.7774	0.7674	0.7671	0.7670	0.7758	0.7757	0.7762	0.7742	0.7737	0.7733	0.7731	0.6821	0.7759
0.5	0.0001	0.0853	0.7570	0.7556	0.7553	0.7555	0.7515	0.7512	0.7508	0.7560	0.7562	0.7560	0.7677	0.7684	0.7670	0.7564	0.6650	0.7550
0.6	0.0000	0.0533	0.7433	0.7391	0.7389	0.7385	0.7346	0.7343	0.7339	0.7456	0.7456	0.7455	0.7491	0.7493	0.7484	0.7410	0.6468	0.7400
0.7	0.0000	0.0379	0.7344	0.7325	0.7323	0.7323	0.7321	0.7318	0.7312	0.7430	0.7428	0.7436	0.7449	0.7448	0.7443	0.7375	0.6466	0.7328
0.8	0.0000	0.0282	0.6970	0.6954	0.6952	0.6947	0.7139	0.7131	0.7114	0.7206	0.7203	0.7203	0.7297	0.7288	0.7262	0.7061	0.6132	0.6962

Table 2c. Model 2, Size-Corrected Rejection Rates, rho = 0.6.

a2	LM	LM_dwh	t	rt1	rt2	rt3	rt1ggls	rt2ggls	rt3ggls	rt1sgls	rt2sgls	rt3sgls	rt1cgls	rt2cgls	rt3cgls	gmm2	dm	hhm
$n = 100$																		
0.0	0.4808	0.4968	0.8867	0.8764	0.8757	0.8751	0.8238	0.8238	0.8222	0.8547	0.8532	0.8514	0.8571	0.8572	0.8563	0.8458	0.8196	0.8729
0.1	0.4370	0.4870	0.8782	0.8669	0.8662	0.8654	0.8143	0.8132	0.8126	0.8420	0.8409	0.8399	0.8486	0.8490	0.8477	0.8351	0.8082	0.8612
0.2	0.3380	0.4588	0.8809	0.8681	0.8674	0.8666	0.8200	0.8188	0.8165	0.8380	0.8369	0.8354	0.8554	0.8541	0.8522	0.8425	0.8143	0.8634
0.3	0.2189	0.4144	0.8717	0.8591	0.8582	0.8569	0.8145	0.8105	0.8086	0.8394	0.8389	0.8363	0.8442	0.8435	0.8425	0.8342	0.8018	0.8569
0.4	0.1265	0.3656	0.8561	0.8496	0.8484	0.8483	0.8047	0.8052	0.8025	0.8332	0.8316	0.8312	0.8393	0.8387	0.8364	0.8289	0.7922	0.8487
0.5	0.0690	0.3202	0.8477	0.8390	0.8389	0.8385	0.8009	0.8009	0.7979	0.8249	0.8242	0.8243	0.8393	0.8377	0.8352	0.8086	0.7755	0.8374
0.6	0.0343	0.2843	0.8328	0.8247	0.8246	0.8230	0.7870	0.7846	0.7805	0.8100	0.8104	0.8082	0.8212	0.8187	0.8163	0.8031	0.7577	0.8210
0.7	0.0183	0.2533	0.8015	0.7914	0.7901	0.7892	0.7762	0.7722	0.7677	0.7827	0.7802	0.7794	0.8084	0.8069	0.8021	0.7796	0.7411	0.7877
0.8	0.0098	0.2319	0.7806	0.7699	0.7697	0.7682	0.7550	0.7507	0.7463	0.7641	0.7633	0.7638	0.7929	0.7893	0.7881	0.7605	0.7129	0.7688
$n = 200$																		
0.0	0.4831	0.4978	0.9966	0.9962	0.9962	0.9962	0.9915	0.9915	0.9914	0.9945	0.9945	0.9945	0.9952	0.9952	0.9951	0.9953	0.9899	0.9960
0.1	0.3938	0.4739	0.9958	0.9951	0.9951	0.9951	0.9912	0.9911	0.9910	0.9930	0.9930	0.9930	0.9944	0.9945	0.9945	0.9943	0.9889	0.9950
0.2	0.2224	0.4169	0.9957	0.9950	0.9949	0.9949	0.9910	0.9908	0.9906	0.9930	0.9927	0.9927	0.9943	0.9943	0.9942	0.9942	0.9878	0.9950
0.3	0.0890	0.3386	0.9942	0.9936	0.9936	0.9936	0.9889	0.9891	0.9888	0.9915	0.9914	0.9914	0.9928	0.9927	0.9927	0.9930	0.9858	0.9933
0.4	0.0272	0.2669	0.9930	0.9922	0.9922	0.9922	0.9883	0.9879	0.9875	0.9905	0.9905	0.9904	0.9919	0.9917	0.9914	0.9911	0.9825	0.9922
0.5	0.0072	0.2082	0.9916	0.9900	0.9900	0.9898	0.9864	0.9860	0.9857	0.9887	0.9887	0.9886	0.9898	0.9896	0.9893	0.9899	0.9807	0.9898
0.6	0.0017	0.1655	0.9876	0.9865	0.9864	0.9862	0.9838	0.9831	0.9821	0.9860	0.9859	0.9856	0.9883	0.9874	0.9864	0.9858	0.9746	0.9865
0.7	0.0004	0.1340	0.9827	0.9806	0.9806	0.9805	0.9804	0.9794	0.9778	0.9808	0.9807	0.9804	0.9858	0.9852	0.9841	0.9821	0.9688	0.9806
0.8	0.0001	0.1180	0.9751	0.9732	0.9725	0.9718	0.9764	0.9753	0.9740	0.9752	0.9751	0.9746	0.9806	0.9796	0.9780	0.9767	0.9603	0.9727

Table 3a. Model 3, Nominal Rejection Rates, rho = 0.0.

a2	LM	LM_dwh	t	rt1	rt2	rt3	rt1ggls	rt2ggls	rt3ggls	rt1sgls	rt2sgls	rt3sgls	rt1cgls	rt2cgls	rt3cgls	gmm2	dm	hhm
$n=100$																		
0.0	0.4973	0.5019	0.0507	0.0587	0.0564	0.0490	0.0824	0.0781	0.0685	0.0691	0.0658	0.0577	0.0656	0.0628	0.0548	0.0373	0.0703	0.0529
0.1	0.4549	0.4618	0.0524	0.0601	0.0578	0.0513	0.0830	0.0782	0.0673	0.0700	0.0673	0.0582	0.0648	0.0618	0.0557	0.0398	0.0718	0.0554
0.2	0.3487	0.3532	0.0522	0.0599	0.0578	0.0506	0.0837	0.0786	0.0683	0.0725	0.0691	0.0600	0.0659	0.0634	0.0552	0.0395	0.0724	0.0534
0.3	0.2286	0.2349	0.0515	0.0594	0.0569	0.0499	0.0827	0.0775	0.0667	0.0671	0.0643	0.0576	0.0656	0.0621	0.0548	0.0391	0.0726	0.0541
0.4	0.1280	0.1329	0.0516	0.0583	0.0562	0.0494	0.0824	0.0768	0.0645	0.0680	0.0647	0.0570	0.0668	0.0636	0.0555	0.0360	0.0661	0.0528
0.5	0.0695	0.0733	0.0515	0.0572	0.0542	0.0472	0.0821	0.0762	0.0648	0.0675	0.0628	0.0543	0.0634	0.0598	0.0507	0.0376	0.0682	0.0513
0.6	0.0342	0.0362	0.0496	0.0556	0.0534	0.0468	0.0799	0.0734	0.0635	0.0668	0.0638	0.0553	0.0638	0.0587	0.0503	0.0364	0.0689	0.0504
0.7	0.0176	0.0186	0.0518	0.0582	0.0552	0.0487	0.0854	0.0768	0.0647	0.0696	0.0649	0.0565	0.0673	0.0622	0.0519	0.0373	0.0642	0.0537
0.8	0.0092	0.0098	0.0511	0.0573	0.0550	0.0481	0.0838	0.0761	0.0634	0.0710	0.0668	0.0574	0.0693	0.0633	0.0525	0.0370	0.0685	0.0521
$n=200$																		
0.0	0.4989	0.4963	0.0488	0.0532	0.0518	0.0485	0.0635	0.0620	0.0570	0.0575	0.0567	0.0531	0.0554	0.0543	0.0499	0.0433	0.0591	0.0508
0.1	0.4100	0.4121	0.0507	0.0545	0.0530	0.0496	0.0654	0.0636	0.0598	0.0595	0.0576	0.0537	0.0575	0.0566	0.0522	0.0430	0.0575	0.0517
0.2	0.2325	0.2328	0.0499	0.0549	0.0538	0.0507	0.0660	0.0644	0.0600	0.0607	0.0591	0.0556	0.0588	0.0572	0.0530	0.0432	0.0609	0.0521
0.3	0.0914	0.0949	0.0513	0.0554	0.0540	0.0503	0.0651	0.0632	0.0587	0.0599	0.0583	0.0544	0.0575	0.0563	0.0527	0.0444	0.0610	0.0531
0.4	0.0281	0.0289	0.0505	0.0525	0.0513	0.0479	0.0631	0.0608	0.0561	0.0572	0.0556	0.0515	0.0556	0.0540	0.0495	0.0427	0.0600	0.0494
0.5	0.0068	0.0071	0.0475	0.0514	0.0504	0.0468	0.0659	0.0630	0.0581	0.0580	0.0567	0.0524	0.0575	0.0554	0.0517	0.0401	0.0540	0.0487
0.6	0.0016	0.0017	0.0487	0.0512	0.0501	0.0465	0.0663	0.0634	0.0579	0.0583	0.0571	0.0529	0.0557	0.0534	0.0490	0.0396	0.0548	0.0484
0.7	0.0004	0.0004	0.0490	0.0531	0.0516	0.0471	0.0659	0.0629	0.0577	0.0571	0.0552	0.0508	0.0598	0.0575	0.0518	0.0419	0.0557	0.0494
0.8	0.0001	0.0001	0.0503	0.0526	0.0515	0.0479	0.0702	0.0654	0.0589	0.0601	0.0583	0.0536	0.0618	0.0586	0.0523	0.0428	0.0585	0.0509
$n=400$																		
0.0	0.4993	0.4984	0.0484	0.0492	0.0487	0.0472	0.0552	0.0545	0.0526	0.0528	0.0522	0.0503	0.0512	0.0505	0.0488	0.0436	0.0523	0.0480
0.1	0.3325	0.3326	0.0472	0.0499	0.0495	0.0475	0.0545	0.0539	0.0520	0.0513	0.0507	0.0489	0.0517	0.0510	0.0491	0.0458	0.0525	0.0481
0.2	0.0981	0.0987	0.0504	0.0506	0.0500	0.0487	0.0558	0.0552	0.0532	0.0533	0.0531	0.0513	0.0517	0.0509	0.0495	0.0458	0.0551	0.0497
0.3	0.0139	0.0141	0.0520	0.0531	0.0522	0.0507	0.0589	0.0582	0.0558	0.0564	0.0554	0.0529	0.0541	0.0531	0.0515	0.0475	0.0563	0.0513
0.4	0.0011	0.0011	0.0493	0.0523	0.0513	0.0497	0.0578	0.0570	0.0549	0.0534	0.0527	0.0512	0.0557	0.0543	0.0519	0.0456	0.0549	0.0505
0.5	0.0001	0.0001	0.0498	0.0530	0.0524	0.0510	0.0576	0.0564	0.0540	0.0551	0.0543	0.0524	0.0542	0.0531	0.0511	0.0482	0.0548	0.0520
0.6	0.0000	0.0000	0.0511	0.0524	0.0519	0.0500	0.0604	0.0587	0.0557	0.0565	0.0558	0.0537	0.0565	0.0553	0.0524	0.0476	0.0553	0.0512
0.7	0.0000	0.0000	0.0479	0.0509	0.0504	0.0490	0.0583	0.0564	0.0535	0.0545	0.0535	0.0515	0.0533	0.0517	0.0489	0.0460	0.0546	0.0498
0.8	0.0000	0.0000	0.0479	0.0500	0.0493	0.0473	0.0595	0.0571	0.0541	0.0526	0.0520	0.0498	0.0554	0.0535	0.0506	0.0448	0.0551	0.0486

Table 3b. Model 3, Size-Corrected Rejection Rates, rho = 0.3.

a2	LM	LM_dwh	t	rt1	rt2	rt3	rt1ggls	rt2ggls	rt3ggls	rt1sgls	rt2sgls	rt3sgls	rt1cgls	rt2cgls	rt3cgls	gmm2	dm	hhm
$n = 100$																		
0.0	0.4877	0.4963	0.2660	0.2584	0.2579	0.2580	0.2266	0.2281	0.2281	0.2463	0.2455	0.2443	0.2448	0.2439	0.2436	0.2435	0.2035	0.2577
0.1	0.4522	0.4564	0.2606	0.2540	0.2536	0.2539	0.2272	0.2276	0.2282	0.2398	0.2394	0.2387	0.2410	0.2400	0.2393	0.2365	0.2004	0.2514
0.2	0.3437	0.3534	0.2565	0.2506	0.2504	0.2495	0.2257	0.2275	0.2275	0.2323	0.2322	0.2320	0.2431	0.2427	0.2429	0.2374	0.2002	0.2488
0.3	0.2266	0.2309	0.2593	0.2531	0.2527	0.2520	0.2268	0.2263	0.2249	0.2391	0.2389	0.2382	0.2444	0.2445	0.2428	0.2386	0.1953	0.2469
0.4	0.1290	0.1359	0.2552	0.2540	0.2546	0.2543	0.2322	0.2337	0.2333	0.2384	0.2365	0.2363	0.2418	0.2420	0.2400	0.2476	0.2056	0.2522
0.5	0.0681	0.0720	0.2550	0.2549	0.2549	0.2540	0.2328	0.2348	0.2339	0.2440	0.2435	0.2418	0.2505	0.2508	0.2501	0.2428	0.2025	0.2528
0.6	0.0347	0.0371	0.2503	0.2431	0.2445	0.2427	0.2242	0.2243	0.2235	0.2315	0.2324	0.2311	0.2444	0.2442	0.2436	0.2344	0.1920	0.2439
0.7	0.0173	0.0185	0.2430	0.2406	0.2408	0.2403	0.2197	0.2191	0.2207	0.2249	0.2260	0.2273	0.2387	0.2393	0.2394	0.2280	0.1977	0.2373
0.8	0.0087	0.0094	0.2349	0.2332	0.2330	0.2342	0.2120	0.2116	0.2113	0.2144	0.2146	0.2134	0.2255	0.2244	0.2233	0.2215	0.1797	0.2322
$n = 200$																		
0.0	0.4994	0.5008	0.5069	0.4994	0.4996	0.4990	0.4676	0.4674	0.4669	0.4825	0.4817	0.4814	0.4922	0.4922	0.4916	0.4856	0.4064	0.4949
0.1	0.4081	0.4117	0.5038	0.4989	0.4984	0.4978	0.4636	0.4633	0.4633	0.4842	0.4839	0.4839	0.4863	0.4870	0.4875	0.4908	0.4078	0.4989
0.2	0.2286	0.2343	0.5009	0.4879	0.4879	0.4884	0.4559	0.4558	0.4563	0.4702	0.4698	0.4691	0.4804	0.4807	0.4808	0.4820	0.3950	0.4895
0.3	0.0912	0.0933	0.4885	0.4815	0.4820	0.4818	0.4545	0.4552	0.4546	0.4659	0.4657	0.4654	0.4760	0.4757	0.4758	0.4728	0.3905	0.4779
0.4	0.0270	0.0279	0.4841	0.4813	0.4806	0.4810	0.4565	0.4560	0.4549	0.4675	0.4660	0.4655	0.4793	0.4783	0.4777	0.4719	0.3790	0.4826
0.5	0.0069	0.0074	0.4887	0.4840	0.4836	0.4827	0.4438	0.4434	0.4423	0.4570	0.4566	0.4577	0.4644	0.4648	0.4634	0.4760	0.3943	0.4834
0.6	0.0016	0.0016	0.4661	0.4647	0.4648	0.4651	0.4385	0.4365	0.4354	0.4407	0.4403	0.4398	0.4619	0.4617	0.4610	0.4597	0.3789	0.4645
0.7	0.0004	0.0004	0.4495	0.4498	0.4498	0.4497	0.4284	0.4293	0.4290	0.4329	0.4332	0.4335	0.4437	0.4435	0.4433	0.4400	0.3682	0.4499
0.8	0.0001	0.0001	0.4427	0.4425	0.4422	0.4416	0.4079	0.4062	0.4070	0.4190	0.4185	0.4186	0.4306	0.4289	0.4284	0.4328	0.3532	0.4395
$n = 400$																		
0.0	0.4983	0.5002	0.8088	0.8103	0.8103	0.8099	0.7871	0.7870	0.7874	0.8004	0.8001	0.8000	0.8034	0.8034	0.8038	0.8081	0.7196	0.8103
0.1	0.3293	0.3326	0.8029	0.7969	0.7967	0.7967	0.7798	0.7800	0.7795	0.7910	0.7908	0.7904	0.7921	0.7920	0.7917	0.7910	0.7131	0.7964
0.2	0.0969	0.0992	0.7912	0.7894	0.7896	0.7892	0.7716	0.7710	0.7713	0.7770	0.7774	0.7778	0.7868	0.7866	0.7862	0.7876	0.6977	0.7881
0.3	0.0135	0.0142	0.7821	0.7816	0.7815	0.7818	0.7640	0.7634	0.7631	0.7708	0.7708	0.7715	0.7777	0.7778	0.7783	0.7772	0.6899	0.7824
0.4	0.0010	0.0011	0.7889	0.7839	0.7836	0.7834	0.7637	0.7642	0.7642	0.7715	0.7711	0.7710	0.7731	0.7737	0.7734	0.7815	0.6916	0.7837
0.5	0.0001	0.0001	0.7765	0.7689	0.7692	0.7687	0.7551	0.7557	0.7560	0.7553	0.7551	0.7549	0.7668	0.7672	0.7672	0.7666	0.6788	0.7687
0.6	0.0000	0.0000	0.7583	0.7563	0.7566	0.7568	0.7400	0.7400	0.7391	0.7363	0.7364	0.7367	0.7552	0.7549	0.7532	0.7546	0.6693	0.7563
0.7	0.0000	0.0000	0.7565	0.7506	0.7506	0.7504	0.7420	0.7418	0.7411	0.7299	0.7297	0.7289	0.7557	0.7541	0.7530	0.7482	0.6559	0.7512
0.8	0.0000	0.0000	0.7361	0.7353	0.7355	0.7352	0.7175	0.7171	0.7170	0.7113	0.7108	0.7120	0.7299	0.7294	0.7291	0.7317	0.6344	0.7339

Table 3c. Model 3, Size-Corrected Rejection Rates, rho = 0.6.

a2	LM	LM_dwh	t	rt1	rt2	rt3	rt1ggls	rt2ggls	rt3ggls	rt1sgls	rt2sgls	rt3sgls	rt1cgls	rt2cgls	rt3cgls	gmm2	dm	hhm
$n = 100$																		
0.0	0.4808	0.4968	0.8867	0.8764	0.8757	0.8751	0.8238	0.8238	0.8222	0.8547	0.8532	0.8514	0.8597	0.8588	0.8569	0.8458	0.8196	0.8729
0.1	0.4395	0.4572	0.8780	0.8660	0.8655	0.8655	0.8141	0.8130	0.8117	0.8420	0.8412	0.8390	0.8485	0.8472	0.8469	0.8361	0.8077	0.8618
0.2	0.3433	0.3560	0.8828	0.8711	0.8711	0.8700	0.8193	0.8201	0.8187	0.8394	0.8392	0.8385	0.8556	0.8542	0.8530	0.8407	0.8169	0.8674
0.3	0.2190	0.2326	0.8752	0.8654	0.8651	0.8646	0.8147	0.8123	0.8085	0.8378	0.8365	0.8351	0.8513	0.8500	0.8484	0.8375	0.7983	0.8596
0.4	0.1286	0.1374	0.8664	0.8579	0.8578	0.8569	0.8124	0.8136	0.8107	0.8325	0.8303	0.8294	0.8425	0.8418	0.8401	0.8362	0.8046	0.8560
0.5	0.0691	0.0735	0.8605	0.8543	0.8535	0.8523	0.8045	0.8034	0.8011	0.8296	0.8283	0.8256	0.8441	0.8429	0.8398	0.8230	0.7879	0.8509
0.6	0.0360	0.0395	0.8499	0.8437	0.8436	0.8419	0.7974	0.7958	0.7924	0.8141	0.8138	0.8116	0.8348	0.8315	0.8291	0.8108	0.7710	0.8398
0.7	0.0180	0.0202	0.8247	0.8203	0.8196	0.8178	0.7775	0.7741	0.7718	0.7897	0.7896	0.7897	0.8182	0.8160	0.8130	0.7882	0.7630	0.8145
0.8	0.0097	0.0106	0.8096	0.8049	0.8041	0.8038	0.7716	0.7678	0.7626	0.7705	0.7692	0.7658	0.8034	0.8006	0.7957	0.7743	0.7354	0.8013
$n = 200$																		
0.0	0.4831	0.4978	0.9966	0.9962	0.9962	0.9962	0.9915	0.9915	0.9914	0.9945	0.9945	0.9945	0.9956	0.9956	0.9956	0.9953	0.9899	0.9960
0.1	0.3960	0.4107	0.9958	0.9954	0.9954	0.9953	0.9916	0.9915	0.9912	0.9934	0.9935	0.9933	0.9946	0.9946	0.9947	0.9944	0.9893	0.9954
0.2	0.2223	0.2324	0.9959	0.9955	0.9954	0.9955	0.9914	0.9914	0.9911	0.9930	0.9929	0.9927	0.9946	0.9944	0.9944	0.9943	0.9880	0.9950
0.3	0.0902	0.0948	0.9947	0.9941	0.9941	0.9940	0.9900	0.9897	0.9893	0.9921	0.9920	0.9920	0.9929	0.9928	0.9928	0.9931	0.9861	0.9939
0.4	0.0282	0.0301	0.9945	0.9935	0.9935	0.9935	0.9890	0.9891	0.9887	0.9914	0.9912	0.9909	0.9926	0.9925	0.9924	0.9920	0.9843	0.9939
0.5	0.0070	0.0080	0.9935	0.9922	0.9921	0.9920	0.9856	0.9851	0.9845	0.9890	0.9888	0.9888	0.9901	0.9898	0.9896	0.9908	0.9845	0.9918
0.6	0.0016	0.0018	0.9917	0.9911	0.9909	0.9911	0.9845	0.9838	0.9828	0.9868	0.9867	0.9860	0.9888	0.9884	0.9878	0.9897	0.9799	0.9909
0.7	0.0004	0.0005	0.9876	0.9882	0.9881	0.9881	0.9821	0.9816	0.9807	0.9833	0.9829	0.9825	0.9879	0.9872	0.9860	0.9856	0.9760	0.9878
0.8	0.0001	0.0002	0.9847	0.9839	0.9837	0.9834	0.9787	0.9776	0.9763	0.9771	0.9766	0.9763	0.9844	0.9835	0.9816	0.9807	0.9684	0.9830

Table 4a. Model 4, Nominal Rejection Rates, rho = 0.0.

a2	LM	LM_dwh	t	rt1	rt2	rt3	rt1ggls	rt2ggls	rt3ggls	rt1sgls	rt2sgls	rt3sgls	rt1cgls	rt2cgls	rt3cgls	gmm2	dm	hhm
$n=100$																		
0.0	0.4973	0.5019	0.0507	0.0587	0.0564	0.0490	0.0824	0.0781	0.0685	0.0691	0.0658	0.0577	0.0646	0.0613	0.0536	0.0373	0.0703	0.0529
0.1	0.4893	0.4969	0.0533	0.0601	0.0579	0.0512	0.0831	0.0787	0.0674	0.0703	0.0674	0.0593	0.0662	0.0637	0.0558	0.0397	0.0719	0.0548
0.2	0.4687	0.4753	0.0529	0.0595	0.0574	0.0513	0.0825	0.0776	0.0672	0.0720	0.0690	0.0609	0.0660	0.0632	0.0558	0.0389	0.0714	0.0544
0.3	0.4360	0.4482	0.0530	0.0587	0.0565	0.0501	0.0797	0.0761	0.0662	0.0659	0.0634	0.0570	0.0667	0.0630	0.0544	0.0386	0.0726	0.0541
0.4	0.3995	0.4140	0.0532	0.0588	0.0569	0.0495	0.0806	0.0753	0.0651	0.0681	0.0650	0.0559	0.0655	0.0613	0.0524	0.0371	0.0661	0.0529
0.5	0.3644	0.3841	0.0524	0.0563	0.0536	0.0469	0.0793	0.0747	0.0650	0.0660	0.0621	0.0536	0.0646	0.0612	0.0528	0.0363	0.0692	0.0514
0.6	0.3377	0.3601	0.0505	0.0565	0.0544	0.0468	0.0773	0.0725	0.0623	0.0656	0.0616	0.0533	0.0635	0.0595	0.0499	0.0348	0.0702	0.0509
0.7	0.3106	0.3327	0.0519	0.0554	0.0530	0.0466	0.0803	0.0753	0.0646	0.0668	0.0639	0.0558	0.0675	0.0622	0.0523	0.0357	0.0637	0.0509
0.8	0.2911	0.3131	0.0535	0.0556	0.0536	0.0463	0.0792	0.0736	0.0619	0.0670	0.0638	0.0555	0.0712	0.0650	0.0543	0.0363	0.0682	0.0500
$n=200$																		
0.0	0.4989	0.4963	0.0488	0.0532	0.0518	0.0485	0.0635	0.0620	0.0570	0.0575	0.0567	0.0531	0.0568	0.0553	0.0514	0.0433	0.0591	0.0508
0.1	0.4836	0.4862	0.0505	0.0543	0.0530	0.0499	0.0654	0.0635	0.0599	0.0596	0.0575	0.0535	0.0576	0.0558	0.0519	0.0434	0.0583	0.0516
0.2	0.4401	0.4446	0.0508	0.0547	0.0535	0.0506	0.0671	0.0647	0.0603	0.0604	0.0591	0.0547	0.0580	0.0566	0.0528	0.0437	0.0620	0.0523
0.3	0.3804	0.3951	0.0516	0.0552	0.0541	0.0511	0.0659	0.0642	0.0607	0.0601	0.0587	0.0548	0.0579	0.0558	0.0523	0.0447	0.0597	0.0535
0.4	0.3222	0.3405	0.0503	0.0520	0.0511	0.0472	0.0625	0.0602	0.0564	0.0554	0.0541	0.0508	0.0568	0.0548	0.0514	0.0408	0.0599	0.0492
0.5	0.2661	0.2869	0.0502	0.0520	0.0511	0.0473	0.0639	0.0620	0.0575	0.0582	0.0569	0.0526	0.0580	0.0557	0.0511	0.0413	0.0556	0.0491
0.6	0.2249	0.2478	0.0492	0.0504	0.0491	0.0454	0.0624	0.0599	0.0554	0.0556	0.0543	0.0498	0.0575	0.0548	0.0500	0.0389	0.0542	0.0475
0.7	0.1897	0.2148	0.0520	0.0521	0.0512	0.0477	0.0614	0.0588	0.0547	0.0565	0.0552	0.0523	0.0619	0.0588	0.0540	0.0420	0.0544	0.0502
0.8	0.1647	0.1903	0.0524	0.0546	0.0535	0.0490	0.0635	0.0615	0.0569	0.0580	0.0562	0.0518	0.0595	0.0566	0.0517	0.0435	0.0578	0.0513
$n=400$																		
0.0	0.4993	0.4984	0.0484	0.0492	0.0487	0.0472	0.0552	0.0545	0.0526	0.0528	0.0522	0.0503	0.0503	0.0499	0.0483	0.0436	0.0523	0.0480
0.1	0.4667	0.4691	0.0483	0.0498	0.0493	0.0482	0.0542	0.0537	0.0520	0.0514	0.0509	0.0491	0.0509	0.0503	0.0483	0.0461	0.0529	0.0490
0.2	0.3819	0.3925	0.0498	0.0511	0.0508	0.0493	0.0560	0.0550	0.0527	0.0535	0.0530	0.0513	0.0510	0.0508	0.0487	0.0449	0.0545	0.0503
0.3	0.2882	0.3061	0.0518	0.0526	0.0521	0.0506	0.0577	0.0572	0.0550	0.0549	0.0542	0.0528	0.0555	0.0546	0.0523	0.0480	0.0557	0.0511
0.4	0.1998	0.2218	0.0504	0.0514	0.0510	0.0492	0.0558	0.0552	0.0535	0.0540	0.0535	0.0517	0.0545	0.0537	0.0519	0.0465	0.0534	0.0499
0.5	0.1369	0.1594	0.0514	0.0526	0.0520	0.0504	0.0579	0.0568	0.0552	0.0543	0.0537	0.0515	0.0532	0.0525	0.0503	0.0470	0.0556	0.0514
0.6	0.0955	0.1161	0.0544	0.0543	0.0534	0.0518	0.0588	0.0580	0.0559	0.0561	0.0548	0.0523	0.0564	0.0556	0.0530	0.0490	0.0545	0.0519
0.7	0.0702	0.0879	0.0528	0.0519	0.0513	0.0499	0.0576	0.0567	0.0544	0.0545	0.0538	0.0518	0.0548	0.0535	0.0507	0.0463	0.0541	0.0505
0.8	0.0547	0.0705	0.0531	0.0504	0.0502	0.0486	0.0548	0.0539	0.0521	0.0519	0.0513	0.0493	0.0554	0.0537	0.0512	0.0459	0.0547	0.0493

Table 4b. Model 4, Size-Corrected Rejection Rates, rho = 0.3.

a2	LM	LM_dwh	t	rt1	rt2	rt3	rt1ggls	rt2ggls	rt3ggls	rt1sgls	rt2sgls	rt3sgls	rt1cgls	rt2cgls	rt3cgls	gmm2	dm	hhm
$n = 100$																		
0.0	0.4877	0.4963	0.2660	0.2584	0.2579	0.2580	0.2266	0.2281	0.2281	0.2463	0.2455	0.2443	0.2496	0.2489	0.2488	0.2435	0.2035	0.2577
0.1	0.4862	0.4910	0.2596	0.2523	0.2523	0.2530	0.2271	0.2275	0.2274	0.2395	0.2385	0.2406	0.2476	0.2466	0.2464	0.2384	0.2008	0.2514
0.2	0.4647	0.4774	0.2580	0.2491	0.2472	0.2467	0.2249	0.2253	0.2251	0.2329	0.2326	0.2324	0.2383	0.2385	0.2382	0.2400	0.2033	0.2483
0.3	0.4357	0.4456	0.2550	0.2501	0.2501	0.2503	0.2257	0.2259	0.2262	0.2414	0.2408	0.2393	0.2451	0.2444	0.2440	0.2393	0.1955	0.2460
0.4	0.4015	0.4196	0.2547	0.2510	0.2505	0.2502	0.2309	0.2309	0.2302	0.2432	0.2436	0.2441	0.2473	0.2489	0.2486	0.2393	0.2054	0.2493
0.5	0.3679	0.3825	0.2573	0.2554	0.2543	0.2545	0.2315	0.2307	0.2318	0.2480	0.2487	0.2512	0.2476	0.2483	0.2460	0.2428	0.1977	0.2519
0.6	0.3381	0.3587	0.2466	0.2405	0.2398	0.2383	0.2238	0.2257	0.2270	0.2352	0.2350	0.2359	0.2449	0.2436	0.2447	0.2328	0.1855	0.2386
0.7	0.3103	0.3313	0.2437	0.2452	0.2453	0.2463	0.2176	0.2187	0.2185	0.2292	0.2282	0.2279	0.2364	0.2373	0.2359	0.2278	0.1995	0.2398
0.8	0.2921	0.3164	0.2272	0.2293	0.2281	0.2282	0.2056	0.2056	0.2070	0.2187	0.2195	0.2195	0.2229	0.2215	0.2223	0.2174	0.1755	0.2297
$n = 200$																		
0.0	0.4994	0.5008	0.5069	0.4994	0.4996	0.4990	0.4676	0.4674	0.4669	0.4825	0.4817	0.4814	0.4859	0.4855	0.4848	0.4856	0.4064	0.4949
0.1	0.4790	0.4845	0.5059	0.4989	0.4983	0.4974	0.4623	0.4619	0.4628	0.4815	0.4817	0.4815	0.4902	0.4899	0.4890	0.4895	0.4082	0.4966
0.2	0.4363	0.4488	0.4956	0.4857	0.4862	0.4863	0.4545	0.4547	0.4548	0.4740	0.4733	0.4730	0.4797	0.4791	0.4797	0.4777	0.3912	0.4876
0.3	0.3796	0.3941	0.4895	0.4771	0.4765	0.4767	0.4446	0.4447	0.4440	0.4621	0.4621	0.4616	0.4734	0.4742	0.4738	0.4676	0.3895	0.4738
0.4	0.3178	0.3348	0.4819	0.4801	0.4802	0.4802	0.4528	0.4519	0.4519	0.4676	0.4674	0.4670	0.4730	0.4723	0.4724	0.4715	0.3794	0.4796
0.5	0.2662	0.2875	0.4800	0.4761	0.4758	0.4758	0.4424	0.4430	0.4435	0.4619	0.4617	0.4615	0.4698	0.4701	0.4705	0.4710	0.3862	0.4759
0.6	0.2262	0.2462	0.4666	0.4643	0.4641	0.4640	0.4410	0.4403	0.4408	0.4569	0.4569	0.4570	0.4568	0.4563	0.4570	0.4587	0.3751	0.4614
0.7	0.1924	0.2152	0.4439	0.4415	0.4420	0.4414	0.4292	0.4297	0.4294	0.4359	0.4358	0.4360	0.4337	0.4330	0.4316	0.4340	0.3667	0.4381
0.8	0.1685	0.1911	0.4297	0.4274	0.4278	0.4269	0.4113	0.4109	0.4104	0.4237	0.4222	0.4225	0.4296	0.4286	0.4290	0.4192	0.3465	0.4247
$n = 400$																		
0.0	0.4983	0.5002	0.8088	0.8103	0.8103	0.8099	0.7871	0.7870	0.7874	0.8004	0.8001	0.8000	0.8062	0.8062	0.8062	0.8081	0.7196	0.8103
0.1	0.4631	0.4701	0.8022	0.7965	0.7964	0.7966	0.7815	0.7812	0.7806	0.7913	0.7914	0.7912	0.7929	0.7926	0.7921	0.7923	0.7109	0.7947
0.2	0.3836	0.3968	0.7900	0.7858	0.7857	0.7857	0.7705	0.7706	0.7700	0.7788	0.7786	0.7784	0.7871	0.7872	0.7877	0.7859	0.6965	0.7850
0.3	0.2819	0.3020	0.7828	0.7824	0.7822	0.7819	0.7665	0.7667	0.7666	0.7748	0.7746	0.7746	0.7770	0.7770	0.7771	0.7771	0.6890	0.7828
0.4	0.1991	0.2216	0.7835	0.7800	0.7797	0.7795	0.7659	0.7657	0.7654	0.7751	0.7747	0.7749	0.7731	0.7726	0.7723	0.7745	0.6901	0.7807
0.5	0.1366	0.1576	0.7700	0.7639	0.7636	0.7633	0.7509	0.7503	0.7499	0.7627	0.7627	0.7627	0.7696	0.7691	0.7688	0.7604	0.6765	0.7628
0.6	0.0977	0.1167	0.7494	0.7472	0.7470	0.7470	0.7363	0.7360	0.7360	0.7493	0.7492	0.7489	0.7493	0.7485	0.7479	0.7440	0.6571	0.7489
0.7	0.0697	0.0861	0.7425	0.7394	0.7389	0.7387	0.7303	0.7305	0.7307	0.7416	0.7422	0.7416	0.7469	0.7469	0.7456	0.7369	0.6450	0.7379
0.8	0.0560	0.0708	0.7205	0.7208	0.7208	0.7205	0.7194	0.7185	0.7181	0.7282	0.7273	0.7276	0.7275	0.7267	0.7256	0.7174	0.6232	0.7204

Table 4c. Model 4, Size-Corrected Rejection Rates, rho = 0.6.

a2	LM	LM_dwh	t	rt1	rt2	rt3	rt1ggls	rt2ggls	rt3ggls	rt1sgls	rt2sgls	rt3sgls	rt1cgls	rt2cgls	rt3cgls	gmm2	dm	hhm
$n = 100$																		
0.0	0.4808	0.4968	0.8867	0.8764	0.8757	0.8751	0.8238	0.8238	0.8222	0.8547	0.8532	0.8514	0.8612	0.8606	0.8599	0.8458	0.8196	0.8729
0.1	0.4744	0.4927	0.8779	0.8668	0.8667	0.8663	0.8134	0.8130	0.8118	0.8431	0.8418	0.8427	0.8509	0.8499	0.8492	0.8367	0.8073	0.8632
0.2	0.4613	0.4761	0.8828	0.8681	0.8673	0.8670	0.8170	0.8163	0.8152	0.8400	0.8390	0.8375	0.8538	0.8532	0.8533	0.8427	0.8184	0.8651
0.3	0.4235	0.4430	0.8731	0.8633	0.8626	0.8622	0.8153	0.8147	0.8128	0.8432	0.8410	0.8389	0.8505	0.8498	0.8486	0.8353	0.7963	0.8591
0.4	0.3970	0.4137	0.8643	0.8564	0.8556	0.8548	0.8119	0.8112	0.8086	0.8367	0.8356	0.8337	0.8434	0.8432	0.8412	0.8304	0.8029	0.8526
0.5	0.3660	0.3798	0.8553	0.8506	0.8493	0.8492	0.7981	0.7961	0.7940	0.8307	0.8298	0.8298	0.8367	0.8359	0.8340	0.8176	0.7847	0.8467
0.6	0.3310	0.3490	0.8410	0.8344	0.8336	0.8317	0.7905	0.7901	0.7895	0.8188	0.8177	0.8163	0.8313	0.8295	0.8269	0.8006	0.7602	0.8307
0.7	0.3110	0.3258	0.8212	0.8164	0.8158	0.8151	0.7668	0.7671	0.7650	0.7938	0.7928	0.7907	0.8113	0.8094	0.8051	0.7811	0.7520	0.8087
0.8	0.2933	0.3049	0.7970	0.7980	0.7965	0.7948	0.7523	0.7522	0.7520	0.7771	0.7768	0.7743	0.7956	0.7918	0.7905	0.7652	0.7218	0.7934
$n = 200$																		
0.0	0.4831	0.4978	0.9966	0.9962	0.9962	0.9962	0.9915	0.9915	0.9914	0.9945	0.9945	0.9945	0.9953	0.9953	0.9953	0.9953	0.9899	0.9960
0.1	0.4654	0.4836	0.9960	0.9955	0.9955	0.9954	0.9913	0.9911	0.9909	0.9936	0.9937	0.9936	0.9944	0.9944	0.9944	0.9946	0.9890	0.9951
0.2	0.4304	0.4462	0.9958	0.9953	0.9953	0.9953	0.9904	0.9901	0.9898	0.9929	0.9928	0.9927	0.9942	0.9942	0.9941	0.9945	0.9881	0.9952
0.3	0.3718	0.3921	0.9944	0.9936	0.9936	0.9936	0.9895	0.9895	0.9892	0.9917	0.9916	0.9916	0.9920	0.9919	0.9918	0.9923	0.9859	0.9935
0.4	0.3217	0.3376	0.9936	0.9926	0.9926	0.9925	0.9884	0.9882	0.9879	0.9912	0.9910	0.9909	0.9915	0.9913	0.9909	0.9910	0.9832	0.9927
0.5	0.2669	0.2848	0.9926	0.9914	0.9914	0.9915	0.9859	0.9857	0.9857	0.9892	0.9890	0.9889	0.9902	0.9901	0.9898	0.9903	0.9818	0.9916
0.6	0.2248	0.2426	0.9903	0.9896	0.9896	0.9896	0.9841	0.9838	0.9832	0.9880	0.9879	0.9877	0.9883	0.9877	0.9877	0.9868	0.9784	0.9893
0.7	0.1937	0.2099	0.9863	0.9846	0.9847	0.9845	0.9802	0.9800	0.9796	0.9833	0.9831	0.9831	0.9851	0.9843	0.9831	0.9813	0.9720	0.9837
0.8	0.1742	0.1904	0.9818	0.9799	0.9796	0.9793	0.9762	0.9760	0.9752	0.9801	0.9796	0.9794	0.9817	0.9810	0.9798	0.9777	0.9620	0.9794

by data generation process. The tables have the same format in each case, with the heteroskedasticity control, **a2**, in the first column, followed by the p-values for the heteroskedasticity test statistics from the original model and the augmented model, **LM** and **LM_dwh**, respectively.

Model 1 Results

In Model 1, the heteroskedasticity is related to strong external IV, z_2. In this case, the "specific" and "correct" GLS estimators and tests are identical. Table 1a contains the test rejection rates using a nominal 5% level of significance when the null hypothesis of no endogeneity is true ($\rho = 0$). When there is no heteroskedasticity in the data generation process (**a2** = 0), the regression-based Hausman test **t** rejects at about the 5% rate, but as heteroskedasticity increases in strength the rejection rate steadily increases at all sample sizes with rates approaching 10% when **a2** = 0.8. When there is no heteroskedasticity in the data generation process (**a2** = 0), the regression-based Hausman test **rt1** rejects at more than a 5% rate in all sample sizes and all heteroskedasticity strengths. The robust t-tests **rt2** and **rt3** have less over-rejection. In particular, we find throughout, in all models, the robust t-test using $hccme = 3$, which is the "jackknife-like" correction from MacKinnon and White (1985), is generally the best robustification, especially if samples are small, and even if heteroskedasticity is not present.

Using a generalized approach to correcting for heteroskedasticity (modeling heteroskedasticity as a function of z_2, z_3, and x_3, which is an overspecification of the true DGP in which heteroskedasticity depends only on one of these at a time) in the augmented equation (**rt1ggls**, **rt2ggls**, and **rt3ggls**) results in rejection rates that are too high when **n** = 100, but the t-tests do not exhibit the same increasing rejection rate as the least squares test **t**. As the sample size increases, the over-rejection rate diminishes. In particular, **rt3ggls** is an improvement at all sample sizes.

Using the correct heteroskedasticity model (**rt1sgls**, **rt2sgls**, and **rt3sgls** are identical to **rt1cgls**, **rt2cgls**, and **rt3cgls** in this case) offers a small improvement relative to the more general model, but for low levels of heteroskedasticity, these tests tend to over-reject in smaller samples with **rt3sgls** having rejection rates closest to 5%. When **n** = 400, **rt3cgls** rejects at about the correct rate.

The test using the two-step GMM estimator (**gmm2**) under-rejects, but its size improves in larger samples. The test based on the difference between the least squares and GMM estimators (**dm**) over-rejects, but its performance improves as the sample size increases. The size of Hahn, Ham, and Moon's test (**hhm**) is nearly correct for all sample sizes and across varying strengths of heteroskedasticity. When **n** = 100, only **rt3** is somewhat better.

Tables 1b–1c contain size-corrected rejection rates for data generation processes with moderate ($\rho = 0.3$) and strong ($\rho = 0.6$) endogeneity. The size correction was achieved by sorting the values of each test statistic computed when there is no endogeneity ($\rho = 0$) and locating the 95th percentile. Rejection rates were then computed using this critical value for each test statistic. We anticipated that one of the GLS estimators may have an advantage when heteroskedasticity is modeled roughly correctly, especially when the sample size is small. This seems to be the case. For example, in Table 1b, when **n** = 200 and **a2** ≥ 0.4 (LM tests for heteroskedasticity are significant at 5% level), the more general GLS test (**rt1ggls–rt3ggls**) has higher power than **hhm**, which has size-corrected power that decreases with the strength of heteroskedasticity. If heteroskedasticity is strong (**a2** ≥ 0.5), the GLS-based test is noticeably more powerful than **hhm**. If the correct model for heteroskedasticity is chosen, the improvement occurs when **a2** ≥ 0.3 and increases as heteroskedasticity increases. When $\rho = 0.3$, the dramatic improvement with strong heteroskedasticity continues for sample sizes of **n** = 300 and **n** = 400. When $\rho = 0.6$, the improvement remains in small samples, with the power of the test based on the more general GLS model (**rt1ggls–rt3ggls**) improving on **hhm** when **a2** ≥ 0.5 and the correct GLS model providing an improvement on **hhm** when **a2** ≥ 0.4. When **n** > 200, all the tests for endogeneity have size-corrected power approaching 1.0.

Model 2 Results

In Model 2, the heteroskedasticity is related to the weaker external IV, z_3. Table 2a contains the tests rejection rates using a nominal 5% level of significance when the null hypothesis of no endogeneity is true ($\rho = 0$). In this case, heteroskedasticity in the DGP is not translated as directly into the augmented DWH regression, as noted by comparing **LM** and **LM_dwh**. Consequently, the standard **t** test in the DWH regression does not suffer as much size distortion as in Model 1. Correcting generally, specifically, or correctly for heteroskedasticity leads to slight over-rejection in smaller samples, though using **rt3ggls**, **rt3sgls**, or **rt3cgls** again makes significant improvements. The GMM test **GMM2** under-rejects for all sample sizes and the GMM/OLS contrast **dm** over-rejects. The Hahn, Ham, and Moon test

hhm rejects at close to the nominal 5% rate in all sample sizes and at all levels of heteroskedasticity. When $\rho = 0.3$, any improvement relative to **t**, or **hhm**, is offered by the more general GLS estimator only in larger samples and when heteroskedasticity is severe. For example, see Table 2b[13] for **n** = 300 and **a2** ≥ 0.7 (LM_dwh < 0.10). For $n \geq 300$, the GLS estimators based on the incorrect culprit z_2 and on the correct culprit z_3 yield improvements at a2 ≥ 0.5, when **LM_dwh** is significant or close to it, at the 10% level. When $\rho = 0.6$, the **LM_dwh** shows little evidence of heteroskedasticity for **n** = 100 or **n** = 200. In larger sample sizes, all tests reject close to 100% of the time.

Model 3 Results

In Model 3, the heteroskedasticity is related to the internal IV, x_3. Table 3a contains the test rejection rates using a nominal 5% level of significance when the null hypothesis of no endogeneity is true ($\rho = 0$). Unlike Model 2, the heteroskedasticity in the DGP is revealed in the DWH regression. Nevertheless, even when heteroskedasticity is severe, the usual DWH **t** test has size that is close to correct. This result holds in all sample sizes. The more general GLS-based tests tend to over-reject in small samples, with **rt3ggls** being better than the rest. Using the specific or correct model of heteroskedasticity introduces less over-rejection, with **rt3sgls** and **rt3cgls** being better than the other robust adjustments. The GMM-related tests have the same flaws as in earlier models, and Hahn, Ham, and Moon's test **hhm** has close to the correct size in all cases. When $\rho = 0.3$ or $\rho = 0.6$, the usual DWH **t** test and its robust versions perform as well or better than **hhm** or the GLS estimators.

Model 4 Results

In Model 4, the heteroskedasticity is related to the exogenous variable z_4 that is not related directly to the DGP, but is weakly correlated (0.3) with the other exogenous variables. Table 4a contains the test rejection rates using a nominal 5% level of significance when the null hypothesis of no endogeneity is true ($\rho = 0$). With **LM_dwh**, there is no evidence of heteroskedasticity until the sample size **n** = 400. The usual DWH **t** test and its robust version **rt** have size that is approximately correct even in small samples, while in small samples, **rt2** and **rt3** over-reject and under-reject, respectfully. The general GLS-based tests over-reject in smaller samples, although as usual **rt3ggls** is better than the rest. The specific and correct GLS estimator tests have less of a problem, and as is now usual the *hccme* = 3 versions are an improvement over the other robust tests. The **gmm2** test under-rejects and **dm** over-rejects, as in previous cases. The Hahn, Ham, and Moon test **hhm** has good size across all sample sizes and heteroskedasticity strengths. When $\rho = 0.3$ in smaller samples, the GLS tests are no improvement over the usual DWH **t** tests, or **hhm**. Indeed the usual DWH **t** tests are best. When **n** = 400, the GLS tests offer slight improvement when **a2** is large, and the **LM_dwh** test average *p*-value is significant at the 10% level.

CONCLUSIONS

We have performed experiments in the context of four models. In none of these experiments, did the GMM-related test have good size or power. In the first case, the heteroskedasticity is driven by a strong external IV. Here the GLS estimators, with robust covariance using *hccme* = 3, have good size, especially in larger samples, and power that is superior to the usual DWH regression-based test. Also, while the intent of this paper was not to propose or endorse any pretesting scheme, it is true that when the usual LM $= nR^2$ heteroskedasticity test is significant at 10% or better (approximately) in the DWH regression, then the GLS-based tests provide power superior to the test proposed by Hahn, Ham, and Moon. In the second set of experiments, the heteroskedasticity was driven by a weak external IV. The benefits of the GLS procedures were greatly diminished in this case, but still appeared in larger samples in which the LM test detected heteroskedasticity in the DWH regression. In the third experiment, the heteroskedasticity driver was an included exogenous variable, and in the fourth model, it was driven by an unrelated exogenous variable. In these cases, the usual DWH regression **t** test is superior in almost all cases to the more elegant alternatives. The test of Hahn, Ham, and Moon has some positives. In all experimental designs, it does well with the nominal rejection rate 5%. We did not explore 1%, 10%, or 20% nominal rates. This is of some importance, as the usual advice for declaring a variable endogenous and using IV/GMM estimation rather than OLS/GLS is some type of weak significance with the Hausman test. For example, Wooldridge (2010, p. 132) counsels in an example that with a DWH *t* significance at the 10% level, using "2SLS is probably a good idea...." The opposite advice may follow from Chmelarova and Hill (2010, p. 98) who find the risk of the pretest estimator improved when the level of significance of the Hausman test is lowered to a small value. With respect to size-corrected power, HHM does not come out as most powerful in any of the scenarios, but the combination of good size and power make it a generally useful tool. With respect to the estimators we have considered, we did not make any adjustments to the size of the residuals in the OLS versus GMM contrast test statistic in Eq. (10), or in the HHM test. For all the reasons stated above, these might be good things to consider.

Thus, it seems to be the case that the source of heteroskedasticity has an effect on the success of testing for endogeneity. While we did not examine pretesting strategies, this would suggest that we test for heteroskedasticity in the DWH regression (25), and if it is related to a strong instrument, then use the GLS estimator-based tests for endogeneity, probably using $hccme = 3$. If heteroskedasticity is related to an included exogenous variable, or some omitted exogenous factor, then the usual DWH t-test, perhaps robustified, is fine. This is clearly important ground to cover. Guggenberger (2010) examines the consequences of the Hausman pretest on subsequent hypothesis tests and concludes that the pretest should be skipped and the 2SLS t-statistic used. Chmelarova and Hill (2010) focus on quadratic estimation loss. Kiviet and Pleus (2012) have given careful thought to Monte Carlo design factors that may be considered when studying pretest estimator performance.

NOTES

1. See, in particular, Davidson and MacKinnon (1990, p. 225) and MacKinnon (1992, p. 125).
2. Greene (2012, p. 33).
3. Dividing W_{DWH} by K_1 produces the F-statistic version.
4. Wooldridge (2010, p. 132).
5. Of course, take care when using statistical software. The default is D_0 in SAS 9.2 and LIMDEP 9.0, and D_1 in Stata 12.0 and EViews 7.0. SAS and Stata offer *hccme* methods = 2 and 3.
6. See Eq. (5) in Harvey (1976), and Judge, Hill, Griffiths, Lütkepohl, and Lee (1988, pp. 370–371, 538–541). Versions of this procedure are available in Stata (REGH) and SAS, PROC AUTOREG with HETERO statement.
7. See MacKinnon (1992, pp. 125–126).
8. An alternative test would be to focus on the coefficients of the potentially endogenous regressors X_1. Another alternative, considered in the Monte Carlo simulation, would be to compare the GMM objective function at the unrestricted estimates and the restricted estimates, imposing $\beta_1 = \beta_2 = \bar{\beta}$. These tests were not better than the other alternatives and we do not report their results.

9. Cameron and Trivedi (2005, p. 378) note that a bootstrap estimate of the covariance matrix is feasible. In earlier investigations, the authors found this approach no better than less computationally demanding approaches and we do not pursue it here.

10. This was presented by Lingling Han (2006). See http://analytics.ncsu.edu/sesug/2006/CC15_06.PDF.

11. We used the general LM tests rather than tests based on the specific model of multiplicative heteroskedasticity.

12. The full set of results, along with computer code to implement the tests, are available at http://www.learneconometrics.com/pdf/AIE29/index.html

13. See http://www.learneconometrics.com/pdf/AIE29/index.html for complete tables.

REFERENCES

Baum, C. F., Schaffer, M. E., & Stillman, S. (2003). Instrumental variables and GMM: Estimation and testing. *The Stata Journal, 3*, 1–31.

Cameron, A. C., & Trivedi, P. K. (2005). *Microeconometrics: Methods and applications*. New York, NY: Cambridge University Press.

Chmelarova, V., & Hill, R. C. (2010). The Hausman pretest estimator. *Economics Letters, 108*(1), 96–99.

Creel, M. (2004). Modified Hausman tests for inefficient estimators. *Applied Economics, 36*, 2373–2376.

Davidson, R., & MacKinnon, J. G. (1990). Specification tests based on artificial regression. *Journal of the American Statistical Association, 85*, 220–227.

Davidson, R., & MacKinnon, J. G. (1993). *Estimation and inference in econometrics*. New York, NY: Oxford University Press.

Durbin, J. (1954). Errors in variables. *Review of the International Statistical Institute, 22*, 23–32.

Greene, W. H. (2012). *Econometric analysis* (7th ed.). Upper Saddle River, NJ: Pearson Education, Inc.

Guggenberger, P. (2010). The impact of a Hausman pretest on the asymptotic size of a hypothesis test. *Econometric Theory, 26*, 369–382.

Hahn, J., Ham, J. C., & Moon, H. R. (2011). The Hausman test and weak instruments. *Journal of Econometrics, 160*, 289–299.

Han, L. (2006). *Generating multivariate normal data using PROC IML, SESUG 2006*. The Proceedings of the South East SAS Users Group, Atlanta, GA, 2006.

Harvey, A. C. (1976). Estimating regression models with multiplicative heteroskedasticity. *Econometrica, 44*, 461–465.

Hausman, J. (1978). Specification tests in econometrics. *Econometrica, 46*, 1251–1271.

Judge, G. G., Hill, R. C., Griffiths, W. E., Lütkepohl, H., & Lee, T. C. (1988). *Introduction to the theory and practice of econometrics* (2nd ed.). New York, NY: Wiley.

Kiviet, J. F., & Pleus, M. (2012). *The performance of tests on endogeneity of subsets of explanatory variables scanned by simulation*. University of Amsterdam Discussion Paper 2011/13.

MacKinnon, J. G. (1992). Model specification tests and artificial regressions. *Journal of Economic Literature, 30*, 102–146.

MacKinnon, J. G., & White, H. L. (1985). Some heteroskedasticity consistent covariance matrix estimators with improved finite sample properties. *Journal of Econometrics*, *21*, 53–70.

Wooldridge, J. M. (2010). *Econometric analysis of cross section and panel data* (2nd ed.). Cambridge, MA: MIT.

Wu, D. (1973). Alternative tests of independence between stochastic regressors and disturbances. *Econometrica*, *41*, 733–750.

A HAUSMAN TEST FOR SPATIAL REGRESSION MODEL

Monalisa Sen, Anil K. Bera and Yu-Hsien Kao

ABSTRACT

In this chapter we investigate the finite sample properties of a Hausman test for the spatial error model (SEM) proposed by Pace and LeSage (2008). In particular, we demonstrate that the power of their test could be very low against a natural alternative like the spatial autoregressive (SAR) model.

Keywords: Hausman test; spatial autoregression model; spatial error model; specification test; Monte Carlo study.

JEL Classifications: C01; C12; C31

INTRODUCTION

In his monumental foundation paper on mathematical statistics, Fisher (1922) identified these fundamental problems: (i) problems of specification, (ii) problems of estimation and (iii) problems of distribution. Ninety years after that, model specification still remains an intriguing problem, and that is more so in the field of econometrics. The initial stages of development in

Essays in Honor of Jerry Hausman
Advances in Econometrics, Volume 29, 547–559

ISSN: 0731-9053/doi:10.1108/S0731-9053(2012)0000029023

econometrics were characterized by an emphasis on estimation. Routine testing of estimated econometrics models came much later, and the 1970s and 1980s can be regarded as the golden age of econometric model specification testing with contribution like Durbin (1970), Hausman (1978), Breusch and Pagan (1980), Bera and Jarque (1982), White (1982), Newey (1985) and Tauchen (1985), just to name a few. Among these the Hausman test has a very distinct characteristic; in contrast to the classical type tests (within the likelihood principle framework) that require parametric forms of the null and alternative hypotheses, Hausman (1978) proposed a general class of specification tests without that requirement.

In spatial data analysis, model specification issues have become an integral part of spatial econometric modelling. Starting with Anselin (1988), there are many papers that developed tests specifically geared to spatial regression models, see Anselin and Bera (1998) and Anselin (2010) for literature surveys. Pace and LeSage (2008) were the first to suggest a Hausman test in spatial econometrics context, specifically for the spatial error model (SEM).

The purpose of this chapter is first to provide a brief review of the Hausman test, through some unconventional examples, and then to explore the finite sample performance, in terms of both size and power, of the test proposed in Pace and LeSage (2008). The rest of the chapter is organized as follows. In the next section, we lay out a framework for the Hausman test and discuss its far reaching implications. The third section sets out the SEM and summarize the results of Pace and LeSage (2008). In the fourth section, we discuss an empirical illustration using the familiar Columbus crime data of Anselin (1988). Simulation results on the size and power of the Pace and LeSage (PL) test are presented in the fifth section. The last section concludes the chapter.

A HELICOPTER TOUR OF HAUSMAN TEST

Hausman (1978) argued that the failure of a model can be detected through the failure of an orthogonality condition, for example, in the standard regression model

$$Y = X\beta + u \tag{1}$$

a useful specification test can be derived by checking on the basic assumption

$$\text{plim}_{n\to\infty} \frac{X'u}{n} = 0 \tag{2}$$

where n is the sample size.

The test he originally proposed is based on comparing two estimators: One of these is asymptotically efficient under the correct specification of the model (the null hypothesis) but is inconsistent under misspecification (the alternative hypothesis); the other estimator is consistent under the null as well as the alternative. Hausman derived the asymptotic distribution of the 'difference of these two estimators' whose asymptotic variance simply boils down to the difference of the variances. And this property greatly simplified the implementation of the Hausman test in practice.

To express the Hausman statistic (HS) algebraically, let us consider an econometric model which depends on a vector of parameters θ with p elements. The model considered by Hausman is more general and need not be completely specified by θ. Assume that under the null hypothesis of no misspecification, the consistent, asymptotically normal and efficient estimator of θ is $\tilde{\theta}$ which, under misspecification, is inconsistent. Suppose there is another estimator, $\hat{\theta}$, which is consistent under the null as well as the alternative. Then the test for the null hypothesis of no misspecification can be conducted by examining the quantity $\hat{\delta} = \sqrt{n}(\hat{\theta}-\tilde{\theta})$ which under no-misspecification and certain regularity condition is asymptotically distributed as normal with mean zero and variance $\Omega = Var(\sqrt{n}\hat{\theta}) - Var(\sqrt{n}\tilde{\theta})$. Thus, the HS can be expressed as

$$HS = \hat{\delta}'\hat{\Omega}^{-1}\hat{\delta} \tag{3}$$

where $\hat{\Omega}$ is a consistent estimator of Ω. The model under test is rejected if HS exceeds the critical value based on the χ_p^2 distribution.

Example 1. (Stat 101: Spirit of the Hausman test)

Let $y_1, y_2, \ldots, y_n$ be a random sample from the population $N(\mu, \sigma^2)$ and consider the null hypothesis $H_0 : \mu = \mu_0$ against the alternative $H_a : \mu \neq \mu_0$. We set $\theta = \sigma^2$ and consider two estimators: $\hat{\sigma}^2 = \sum_{i=1}^n (y_i - \bar{y})^2/(n-1)$ and $\tilde{\sigma}^2 = \sum_{i=1}^n (y_i - \mu_0)^2/(n-1)$, where $\bar{y} = \sum_{i=1}^n y_i/n$. A test can be based on the difference

$$\tilde{\sigma}^2 - \hat{\sigma}^2 = n(\bar{y} - \mu_0)^2/(n-1) \tag{4}$$

From the generalized Neyman–Pearson lemma, the locally most powerful unbiased test is based on

$$F=\frac{(n-1)(\bar{y}-\mu_0)^2}{\hat{\sigma}^2}=\frac{(n-1)^2}{n}\frac{\tilde{\sigma}^2-\hat{\sigma}^2}{\hat{\sigma}^2} \tag{5}$$

which under $H_0 : \mu = \mu_0$ has exact distribution $F(1, n-1)$. F is not exactly a Hausman test; the spirit is, however, the same. That is, diagnosis of a model (or testing *one parameter*) can be based on comparing two estimators of a *different parameter*.

Example 2. (A Hausman test for normality?)

Let $H_0 : Y \sim N(\mu, \sigma^2)$, where μ and σ^2 are unknown. The estimator $\hat{\sigma}^2 = \frac{1}{(n-1)}\sum_{i=1}^{n}(y_i-\bar{y})^2$ is 'always' consistent. Consider another estimator

$$\tilde{\sigma}^2=\frac{1}{(n-1)}\left(\sum_{i=1}^{n}a_i y_i\right)^2 \tag{6}$$

where $a=(a_1,a_2,\ldots,a_n)'=(m'V^{-1})/(m'V^{-1}V^{-1}m)^{\frac{1}{2}}$, with $E(y_{(i)})=m_i$, and $cov(y_{(i)},y_{(j)})=v_{ij}$ for $i,j=1,2,\ldots,n$, and $y_{(i)}$ is the ith order statistic from $N(0,1)$. Note that $\tilde{\sigma}$ is not consistent under non-normality, but it is the best linear unbiased estimator of σ under normality.

One can run a generalized least squares (GLS) regression

$$y_{(i)}=\sigma m_i+\varepsilon_i$$

with $E(\varepsilon_i)=0$ and $Cov(\varepsilon_i,\varepsilon_j)=v_{ij}$, $i \neq j$ and obtain $\tilde{\sigma}^2$ in Eq. (6). A Hausman test for normality can be based on $\hat{\sigma}^2-\tilde{\sigma}^2$. Indeed one of the most popular and widely used test for normality in the statistics literature is that of Shapiro and Wilk (1965) which compares $\hat{\sigma}^2$ and $\tilde{\sigma}^2$.

Example 3. (White's information matrix and moment tests)

Assume that a random variable Y has a density $f(y;\psi)$ where $\psi \in \Theta$ is a $q \times 1$ vector of parameters. Suppose there is a $r \times 1$ vector of functions $m(y;\psi)$ that satisfies

$$E_f[m(y;\psi)]=\int m(y;\psi)f(y;\psi)dy=0 \tag{7}$$

then $m(y;\psi)$ is called moment criteria. If $f(y;\psi)$ is indeed the data generating process (DGP) and $\hat{\psi}$ is a consistent estimator of ψ, the sample moments

$$\overline{m}(\hat{\psi}) = \sum_{i=1}^{n} m(y_i; \hat{\psi})/n \tag{8}$$

will be expected to be close to zero. Hence, a test for $f(y; \psi)$ being the correct specification of the DGP can be tested using $m(\hat{\psi})$ after suitably accounting for the sampling error. White (1982) information matrix test can be put into this framework of moment tests of Newey (1985) and Tauchen (1985) by taking

$$m(y; \psi) = vech\left(\frac{\partial^2 lnf(y; \psi)}{\partial\psi\partial\psi'} + \frac{\partial lnf(y; \psi)}{\partial\psi} \cdot \frac{\partial lnf(y; \psi)}{\partial\psi'}\right) \tag{9}$$

where *vech* denotes column operator of stacking distinct elements of a asymmetric matrix. Thus $m(y; \psi)$ is a vector with $r = q(q+1)/2$ elements. Information matrix equality dictates that under correct specification $E[m(y; \psi)] = 0$, and the sample counterpart of this expectation is $\overline{m}(\hat{\psi})$ in Eq. (8). If we dissect $\overline{m}(\hat{\theta})$, we find that it is nothing but the difference of two *estimates* of the standard information matrix, namely the difference of

$$-\frac{1}{n}\sum_{i=1}^{n} \frac{\partial^2 \ln f(y_i, \hat{\psi})}{\partial\psi\partial\psi'} \tag{10}$$

and

$$\frac{1}{n}\sum_{i=1}^{n}\left[\frac{\partial lnf(y_i, \hat{\psi})}{\partial\psi} \cdot \frac{\partial lnf(y_i, \hat{\psi})}{\partial\psi'}\right] \tag{11}$$

known as, respectively, the Hessian and outer product of gradients (OPG) version of the information matrix.

Thus, many of the standard testing procedures can be put into the framework of the Hausman specification test.

PACE AND LESAGE TEST

One of the most popular models in spatial regression is the SEM:

$$\begin{aligned} y &= X\beta + u \\ u &= \rho W u + \varepsilon \end{aligned} \tag{12}$$

where y is an $n \times 1$ vector of observations on the dependent variable, X is an $n \times k$ matrix of observations on the explanatory (exogenous) variables, u is an $n \times 1$ vector of error terms, ρ is the spatial autocorrelation coefficient, W is $n \times n$ observable weight matrix and ε is an uncorrelated and homoscedastic error term, assumed to follow $N(0, I\sigma^2)$. In the PL framework, the model under test is SEM, which can be expressed as

$$y = X\beta + (I - \rho W)^{-1}\varepsilon \tag{13}$$

assuming $(I - \rho W)$ is nonsingular for all $|\rho| < 1$. Thus, we can write the variance-covariance matrix of u as

$$Var(u) = \sigma^2[(I - \rho W)(I - \rho W)']^{-1} = \Omega(say) \tag{14}$$

For the spatial Hausman test, Pace and LeSage (2008) considered the following two estimators:

1. The OLS estimator

$$\hat{\beta} = (X'X)^{-1}X'y$$

2. The maximum likelihood (ML) estimator obtained from the SEM model. Let $(\tilde{\beta}', \tilde{\rho})$ be the ML estimator of (β', ρ). We can express $\tilde{\beta}$ as

$$\tilde{\beta} = [X'(I - \tilde{\rho}W)'(I - \tilde{\rho}W)X]^{-1}X'(I - \tilde{\rho}W)'(I - \tilde{\rho}W)y \tag{15}$$

which is a GLS estimator given $\rho = \tilde{\rho}$, as it follows from Eq. (14).

When the DGP is SEM, $\tilde{\beta}$ is consistent and efficient by ML properties. Writing $\hat{\beta}$ as

$$\begin{aligned}\hat{\beta} &= (X'X)^{-1}X'[X\beta + (I - \rho W)^{-1}\varepsilon] = \beta + (X'X)^{-1}X'(I - \rho W)^{-1}\varepsilon \\ &= \beta + (X'X)^{-1}Z'\varepsilon\end{aligned}$$

where $Z = (I - \rho W')^{-1}X$, it is easy to see that $\text{plim}_{n\to\infty}\hat{\beta} = \beta$, since

$$n^{-1/2}Z'\varepsilon \xrightarrow{D} N(0, \sigma^2 Q)$$

with $Q = \lim_{n\to\infty} X'\Omega X$. Thus, under SEM, $\text{plim}_{n\to\infty}(\hat{\beta} - \tilde{\beta}) = 0$ and the asymptotic correct size of the PL test is guaranteed [also see, Pace and LeSage (2009), pp. 61–63]. This is quite evident from their Monte Carlo results reproduced in Table 1.

Given the simplicity of the procedure and ease of implementation, this test is widely used in practice. For instance, Bivand (2010) applied the PL test to both US 1980 election turnout data and the housing data of Lucas

Table 1. Monte Carlo Result: Empirical Versus Theoretical Sizes with $n = 3{,}000$.

ρ	Size				
	0.01	0.05	0.10	0.25	0.50
0.30	0.0093	0.0499	0.0984	0.2472	0.5023
0.60	0.0098	0.0521	0.0964	0.2498	0.5067
0.90	0.0130	0.0533	0.1049	0.2576	0.5038

Source: Table 1 of Pace and LeSage (2008).

County in Ohio and found that the null hypothesis of SEM model is rejected, consistent with the conclusion that favours the spatial Durbin model (SDM) based on AIC model selection criterion. Cox and Ross (2011) used the PL test as a diagnostic check for their model of the irrigation system in New Mexico, and could not reject their SEM. Gerkman (2012) tested a Hedonic model for the house prices in Helsinki, and the SEM was rejected in favour of the SDM. Other papers that used the PL test include Osland and Pryce (2010), Ross, Farmer and Lipscomb (2011), and Duncan et al. (2012).

AN EMPIRICAL ILLUSTRATION: CRIME IN COLUMBUS

To illustrate the usefulness of the PL test, we consider a simple spatial relationship between crime and housing value and income in 1980 for 49 neighborhoods in Columbus, OH [Anselin (1988)]:

$$CRIME = \beta_0 + \beta_1 INC + \beta_2 HOUSE + u$$

This model has been used in a number of papers to benchmark different estimates and specification tests; for instance, see McMillen (1992), Getis (1995), Anselin, Bera, Florax and Yoon (1996), and LeSage (1997). For this case it appears as if we know the 'true' model. In addition to the SEM model in Eq. (12), we consider

1. Standard regression specification

$$y = X\beta + u \tag{16}$$

which we will call the OLS model.

Table 2. Parameter Estimates for the Crime in Columbus Data.

Parameters	OLS	SEM	SAR	SAC
β_0	68.6 (4.73)	59.89 (11.16)	45.51(7.20)	45.62 (4.7)
β_1	−1.59 (4.78)	−0.94 (2.84)	−1.04 (3.38)	−1.03 (−3.17)
β_2	−0.27 (2.65)	−0.30 (−3.34)	−0.26 (−3.003)	−0.26 (−3.0)
τ	N/A	N/A	0.42(3.66)	0.42 (2.39)
ρ	N/A	0.56 (4.19)	N/A	0.019 (0.06)
Log-Likelihood	−170.395	−166.39	−165.57	−165.50

(t-statistics are given in parentheses).

2. Spatial autoregressive (SAR)

$$y = \tau Wy + X\beta + u \tag{17}$$

and

3. A combination of Eqs. (12) and (17):

$$\begin{aligned} y &= \tau Wy + X\beta + u \\ u &= \rho Wu + \varepsilon \end{aligned} \tag{18}$$

which we will term spatially autocorrelated combined (SAC) model.

In Table 2 we present the estimation results for the four models.

From the t-statistics result it is clear that SAR model is most appropriate. Anselin et al. (1996) performed extensive specification tests on this model and found the robust Rao's score test statistic for testing $H_0 : \tau = 0$ allowing for the presence of ρ, and obtained $RS^*_{\tau|\rho} = 3.72$, while $RS^*_{\rho|\tau} = 0.08$. Thus, collecting together the enormous empirical evidence, we can say that spatial dependence is clearly present, and SAR not SEM should be the model of choice. However, when we apply PL test comparing OLS and SEM estimates (of β_0, β_1, and β_2) we found PL = 5.58, when compared to a χ^2_3 critical value, we cannot reject the SEM model. This prompts us to study the finite sample properties of PL test when the data is generated from the SAR model, which is addressed in the next section.

MONTE CARLO RESULTS

Pace and LeSage (2008) reported the empirical size of their test for $n = 3{,}000$ and size = 0.01, 0.05, 0.1, 0.25 and 0.50. However, many of the empirical applications of spatial regression are with much smaller sample sizes. Our Monte Carlo experiments are conducted for $n = 50,100,150,200$ and 250. We generated data under the model (12) with $k = 5$, set the values of the parameters as $\beta' = (\beta_0, \beta_1, \beta_2, \beta_3, \beta_4) = (1.5, 3.0, 5.0, 7.0, 9.0)$, $\sigma^2 = 0.2$, $\rho =$ 0.6 and 0.9, and the weight matrix W is set according to the rook criterion [see Anselin and Bera (1998, p. 245)]. Empirical sizes of the test based on 10,000 replications and using χ_5^2 critical value are reported in Tables 3 and 4 for $\rho = 0.6$ and 0.9, respectively. It is clear that the empirical sizes indeed are quite close to their nominal values (in many cases, lower) as also noted in Pace and LeSage (2008) for $n = 3,000$.

To make sure that the results are not specific to the rook W matrix, we also repeat the experiment when W is the first-order contiguity matrix [see Anselin and Bera (1998, p. 243)], and in Table 5, the empirical sizes are given for $\rho = 0.6$. It appears the results are quite robust to the specification of W.

For analysis of power of the test, we generated the data under SAR model in Eq. (17), but with the same parameter values of β, σ^2, and set $\tau = 0.6$ and 0.9. Tables 6 and 7 confirm that the power of the PL test is very low under the alternative of SAR process. Even under different weighting schemes, the results are very similar, as confirmed by the results in Table 8.

Table 3. Size of the Test for $\rho = 0.6$, When W Is Rook Design.

n	Size		
	0.01	0.05	0.10
50	*0.009*	*0.031*	*0.089*
100	*0.008*	*0.011*	*0.096*
150	*0.003*	*0.029*	*0.074*
200	*0.017*	*0.048*	*0.096*
250	*0.007*	*0.059*	*0.122*

Table 4. Size of the Test for $\rho = 0.9$, when W Is Rook Design.

n	Size		
	0.01	0.05	0.10
50	*0.007*	*0.036*	*0.081*
100	*0.006*	*0.039*	*0.075*
150	*0.001*	*0.079*	*0.084*
200	*0.009*	*0.048*	*0.099*
250	*0.012*	*0.049*	*0.170*

Table 5. Size of the Test for $\rho = 0.6$, when W Is First-Order Contiguity Matrix.

n	Size		
	0.01	0.05	0.10
50	*0.008*	*0.011*	*0.069*
100	*0.009*	*0.017*	*0.091*
150	*0.001*	*0.024*	*0.087*
200	*0.016*	*0.058*	*0.076*
250	*0.003*	*0.059*	*0.112*

Table 6. Power of the Test for $\tau = 0.6$, when W Is Rook Design.

n	Size		
	0.01	0.05	0.10
50	*0.006*	*0.005*	*0.014*
100	*0.002*	*0.012*	*0.026*
150	*0.003*	*0.019*	*0.036*
200	*0.003*	*0.016*	*0.031*
250	*0.002*	*0.010*	*0.020*

Table 7. Power of the Test for $\tau = 0.9$, When W Is Rook Design.

n	Size		
	0.01	0.05	0.10
50	*0.006*	*0.005*	*0.014*
100	*0.010*	*0.047*	*0.086*
150	*0.004*	*0.197*	*0.032*
200	*0.007*	*0.024*	*0.048*
250	*0.018*	*0.051*	*0.099*

In Tables 9 and 10, we also reported the average values of OLS and ML estimates (assuming SEM is the correct specification) of β with 10,000 replications, when the data was generated under the model with $\beta' = (\beta_0, \beta_1, \beta_2, \beta_3, \beta_4) = (1.5, 3.0, 5.0, 7.0, 9.0)$ as before. The results are quite

Table 8. Power of the Test for $\tau = 0.6$, When W Is First-Order Contiguity Matrix.

n	Size		
	0.01	0.05	0.10
50	*0.004*	*0.008*	*0.019*
100	*0.001*	*0.017*	*0.096*
150	*0.002*	*0.019*	*0.073*
200	*0.004*	*0.019*	*0.091*
250	*0.002*	*0.090*	*0.080*

Table 9. DGP Is SAR; Average of Values of OLS Estimators $\hat{\beta}$ with True Values of $\beta' = (\beta_0, \beta_1, \beta_2, \beta_3, \beta_4) = (1.5, 3.0, 5.0, 7.0, 9.0)$.

n	Parameters				
	$\hat{\beta}_0$	$\hat{\beta}_1$	$\hat{\beta}_2$	$\hat{\beta}_3$	$\hat{\beta}_4$
50	*22.185*	*2.8604*	*5.0077*	*7.1185*	*8.7780*
100	*21.590*	*3.0571*	*5.1296*	*7.1384*	*8.9227*
150	*22.171*	*2.9772*	*5.1967*	*6.7707*	*9.0857*
200	*21.862*	*2.9935*	*4.9947*	*6.9395*	*8.9265*
250	*21.734*	*3.1005*	*5.0133*	*7.0770*	*9.0165*

Table 10. DGP Is SAR; Average of Values of MLE (Under SEM) $\tilde{\beta}$ with True Values of $\beta' = (\beta_0, \beta_1, \beta_2, \beta_3, \beta_4) = (1.5, 3.0, 5.0, 7.0, 9.0)$.

n	Parameters				
	$\tilde{\beta}_0$	$\tilde{\beta}_1$	$\tilde{\beta}_2$	$\tilde{\beta}_3$	$\tilde{\beta}_4$
50	*22.216*	*2.8197*	*5.0129*	*7.1031*	*9.0085*
100	*21.622*	*3.0449*	*4.9942*	*7.1238*	*8.9275*
150	*22.175*	*2.9735*	*5.1981*	*6.7638*	*9.0827*
200	*21.868*	*2.9855*	*5.1224*	*6.9281*	*8.9034*
250	*21.743*	*3.0957*	*4.9913*	*7.0713*	*8.7926*

intriguing. From Table 9, we observe that except for the intercept coefficient, all the OLS estimates appear to be consistent even when the true model is SAR. The similar phenomenon happen in Table 10 for the (wrong) ML estimator. The estimators of the intercept term is inconsistent but both $\hat{\beta}_0$

and $\tilde{\beta}_0$ seem to have the *same* probability limit. Possibly, these explain the almost zero power of the PL test for the SEM against the SAR model.

CONCLUSION

It is quite possible that PL test has power against certain alternative models. However, since in spatial regression analysis, SEM and SAR are the two most widely used competing models, having reasonable power against the SAR model should be a minimum requirement. What we need is to look for two other different estimates that have *same* limit under the tested model, but *different* ones under misspecification. We leave this agenda for future research.

ACKNOWLEDGMENT

A preliminary version of the chapter was presented at the 11th Advances in Econometrics Conference in honor of Jerry Hausman, 17–19 February 2012. Louisiana State University, Baton Rouge, LA. We would like to thank the participants in the conference, especially Badi Baltagi, Jerry Hausman, R. Carter Hill and R. Kelley Pace for helpful comments and discussion. We are also grateful to two anonymous referees for giving a thorough reading and offering suggestions that improved the exposition of the chapter. The remaining shortcomings are solely ours.

REFERENCES

Anselin, L. (1988). *Spatial econometrics: Methods and models*. Dorddrecht: Kluwer Academic.

Anselin, L. (2010). Thirty years of spatial econometrics. *Papers in Regional Science*, *89*, 3–25.

Anselin, L., & Bera, A. K. (1998). Spatial dependence in linear regression models with an introduction to spatial econometrics. In A. Ullah & D. E. A. Giles (Eds.), *Handbook of applied economic statistics* (pp. 237–289). New York, NY: Marcel Dekker.

Anselin, L., Bera, A. K., Florax, R., & Yoon, M. J. (1996). Simple diagnostic tests for spatial dependence. *Regional Science and Urban Economics*, *26*, 77–104.

Bera, A., & Jarque, C. (1982). Model specification tests: A simultaneous approach. *Journal of Econometrics*, *20*, 59–82.

Bivand, R. (2010). *Comparing estimation methods for spatial econometrics techniques using R. Norwegian School of Economics*, Department of Economics Research Paper Series 26.

Breusch, T. S., & Pagan, A. R. (1980). The Lagrange multiplier test and its applications to model specification in econometrics. *Review of Economic Studies*, *47*, 239–254.

Cox, M., & Ross, J. M. (2011). Robustness and vulnerability of community irrigation systems: The case of the Taos Valley Acequias. *Journal of Environmental Economics and Management*, *61*, 254–266.

Duncan, D. T., Castro, M. C., Gortmaker, S. L., Aldstadt, J., Melly, S. J., & Bennett, G. G. (2012). Racial differences in the built environment-body mass index relationship? A geospatial analysis of adolescents in urban neighborhoods. *International Journal of Health Geographics*, *11*, 1–21.

Durbin, J. (1970). Testing for serial correlation in least-squares regression when some of the regressors are lagged dependent variables. *Econometrica*, *38*, 410–421.

Fisher, R. A. (1922). On the mathematical foundations of theoretical statistics. *Philosophical Transactions of the Royal Society A*, *222*, 309–368.

Gerkman, L. (2012). Empirical spatial econometric modelling of small scale neighbourhood. *Journal of Geographical Systems*, *14*, 283–298.

Getis, A. (1995). Spatial filtering in a regression framework: Experiments on regional inequality, government expenditures, and urban crime. In L. Anselin & R. Florax (Eds.), *New directions in spatial econometrics* (pp. 172–185). New York, NY: Springer.

Hausman, J. A. (1978). Specification tests in econometrics. *Econometrica*, *46*, 1251–1271.

LeSage, J. P. (1997). Bayesian estimation of spatial autoregressive models. *International Regional Science Review*, *20*, 113–129.

McMillen, D. P. (1992). Probit with spatial autocorrelation. *Journal of Regional Science*, *32*, 335–348.

Newey, W. (1985). Generalized method of moments specification testing. *Journal of Econometrics*, *29*, 229–256.

Osland, L. & Pryce, G. (2012). Housing prices and multiple employment nodes: Is the relationship nonmonotonic? *Housing Studies*. (Forthcoming).

Pace, R. K., & LeSage, J. P. (2008). A spatial Hausman test. *Economics Letters*, *101*, 282–284.

Pace, R. K., & LeSage, J. P. (2009). *An introduction to spatial econometrics, statistics: A series of textbooks and monographs series*. Boca Raton, FL: Chapman & Hall/CRC.

Ross, J. M., Farmer, M. C., & Lipscomb, C. A. (2011). Inconsistency in welfare inferences from distance variables in hedonic regressions. *The Journal of Real Estate Finance and Economics*, *43*, 385–400.

Shapiro, S. S., & Wilk, M. B. (1965). An analysis of variance for normality (complete samples). *Biometrika*, *52*, 591–611.

Tauchen, G. (1985). Diagnostic testing and evaluation of maximum likelihood model. *Journal of Econometrics*, *30*, 415–443.

White, H. (1982). Maximum likelihood estimation of misspecified models. *Econometrica*, *50*, 1–25.